The FRUIT & NUT BOOK

HELENA RADECKA

A
PHOEBE PHILLIPS
EDITIONS
BOOK

The FRUIT & NUT BOOK

HELENA RADECKA

MCGRAW-HILL BOOK COMPANY
New York   St. Louis   San Francisco   Mexico

Copyright © 1984 by Phoebe Phillips Editions.
All rights reserved. Printed in Spain. Except
as permitted under the Copyright Act of 1976, no
part of this publication may be reproduced or
distributed in any form or by any means or stored
in a data base or retrieval system, without the
prior written permission of the publisher.

1 2 3 4 5 6 7 8 9   8 7 6 5 4

Library of Congress Cataloging in Publication Data

Radecka, Helena.
  The fruit and nut book.

  Bibliography: p. 9
  Includes index.
    1. Cookery (Fruit)   2. Cookery (Nuts)   3. Fruit-
culture.   4. Nuts.   1. Title.
TX811.R33   1984   641.6'4   84-753

ISBN 0-07-051092-X   (H.C.)
ISBN 0-07-051093-8   (PBK)

In memory of my mother, who taught and encouraged me
all her life

CONTENTS

FOREWORD   8

INTRODUCTION   9

FAVORITE FRUITS AND NUTS   10

Almond – Apple – Apricot – Avocado   Banana – Blackberry – Black Currant – Blueberry – Brazil Nut   Cashew Nut – Cherry – Chestnut (sweet) – Coconut – Cranberry   Date   Fig   Gooseberry – Grape – Grapefruit   Hazelnut   Kiwi Fruit – Kumquat   Lemon – Lime – Litchi   Mango – Melon (and Watermelon)   Nectarine   Olive – Orange   Papaya – Passion Fruit – Peach – Peanut – Pear – Pecan – Persimmon – Pineapple – Pine Nut – Pistachio – Plum – Pomegranate Quince   Raspberry – Red Currant, White Currant – Rhubarb Strawberry   Tangerine   Walnut

LESS COMMON FRUITS AND NUTS   186

Akebia – Akee (Ackee) – Atemoya – Barbados Cherry – Berries (Barberry; Bearberry; Boysenberry; Cloudberry; Dewberry; Honeyberry; Huckleberry; Juneberry; Loganberry; Wineberry; Worcesterberry; Youngberry) – Breadfruit – Butternut – Calamondin Orange/Panama Orange – Cape Gooseberry/ Ground Cherry – Carob – Cashew Apple – Citron – Cornelian Cherry – Crab Apple – Custard Fruits (Custard Apple, Custard Banana) – Elderberry – Feijoya – Golden Naranjilla – Guava – Hickory Nut – Jackfruit – Jujube – Loquat – Macadamia – Mangosteen – Medlar – Mulberry – Natal Plum – Prickly or Cactus Pear – Rambutan – Rosella – Rose Hip – Rowan – Sapodilla – Sapote – Sloe – Tamarind – Tree Tomato/Tomarillo

PRESERVING   198

Jams, Marmalades and Jellies – Fruit Cheeses and Butters – Pickles and Chutneys – Canning – Fruit Vinegars and Syrups – Drying – Freezing

BASIC RECIPES   203

Pastry – Desserts – Garnishes – Sauces – Wines and Liqueurs

MEASUREMENTS   207

NUTRITION   207

Rapid-action Diets – High-fiber Fruit Diet – Vegetarian Diets – Low Blood Sugar Diet – Fruit in Children's Diets – Buying and Preparing Fruit – Vitamin and Mineral Chart

HOW TO GROW FRUITS AND NUTS   213

Bush Fruit (Black Currants; Red and White Currants; Gooseberries; Worcester-berries; Blueberries and Cranberries) – Cane Fruit (Raspberries; Blackberries; Other Brambles – Vines (Grapes; Melons; Kiwi Fruit/Chinese Gooseberry; Passion Fruit) – Perennials (Temperate Climate Fruits: Strawberries, Rhubarb – Warm Climate Fruits: Bananas, Papayas, Pineapples) – Stone Fruit (Apricots; Cherries; Peaches, Nectarines and Almonds; Plums) – Citrus Fruit – Other Tree Fruits (Temperate Climate Fruits: Apples and Pears, Medlars, Mulberries – Warm Climate Fruits: Avocado/Alligator Pears, Dates, Figs, Loquats, Litchis, Mangoes, Olives, Persimmons, Pomegranates, Quinces) – Nut Trees (Temperate Climate Nuts: Walnuts, Chestnuts, Hazelnuts/Filberts – Warm Climate Nuts: Brazil Nuts, Cashew Nuts, Coconuts, Peanuts, Pine Nuts, Pistachios) – Greenhouse Cultivation – Indoor Cultivation

MENU PLANNER   248

BIBLIOGRAPHY   250

INDEX   251

FOREWORD

Every day we are bombarded with publicity celebrating a revolutionary future of electronic technology and modernized industry. Yet, almost unheralded, there has already been a revolution which is transforming our daily lives – the multi-colored revolution in supermarkets and produce markets.

Only a decade ago a winter table setting was brightened with just a few yellows and greens from apples and pears, with the occasional orange or grapefruit and maybe a bowl of walnuts.

Today there is a riot of color throughout the year, even during the gloomy months of late fall and winter: ripe mangoes, glowing persimmons, new citrus hybrids, fresh figs bursting with purple flesh, sharp kumquats and crimson cranberries, nuts of every kind, fresh dates – even strawberries from California for Christmas dinner.

In summer the abundance becomes almost overwhelming: all the old favorites are available, plus loganberries and blueberries, rough and smooth avocados, pink-flushed guavas, exotic mangosteens, juicy limes and rich pomegranates... the list is endless and it continues to grow every year.

For once, the marketing chiefs have brought us the perfect package: natural portion control, filled to the brim with vitamins, minerals and fiber – plus a delicious flavor.

There is no moment of the day when we cannot enjoy a piece of fruit, happy in the knowledge that we are satisfying our bodies as well as our appetites.

As if all this were not enough, there are hundreds of other ways to use fruits and nuts – cooked with meats or in vegetarian dishes, blended into superb drinks with or without alcohol, puréed and pounded for sauces, steeped for wines and liqueurs, distilled for remedies, and sliced and chopped to soothe our skins....

This happy revolution, which seems to have brought only pleasure and better health to us all, was reason enough for me to write this book – and is, I hope, reason enough for you to enjoy it.

Such a compendium as this would not have been started without the inspiration of my publisher, Phoebe Phillips Editions, and the encouragement of cooks and food writers from all over the world. Many are listed, as they should be, in the bibliography; others are friends and colleagues who have given their time and advice without stint.

There must be a special mention for two researchers who worked tirelessly to gather in the harvest of material: Ursula White and Cecile Landau. My thanks, too, to Hilary Evans who drew the illustrations which decorate the pages, and to Caroline Reeves who designed the book. Tessa Clark has been editor, adviser and arbiter – a burden which she has carried with unfailing good temper and helpfulness.

HELENA RADECKA

INTRODUCTION

The first part of the book is an alphabetical listing of fifty of the more popular fruits and nuts – from almond and apple to tangerine and walnut – that are normally available from most fruiterers and supermarkets.

Each starts with a brief description of the fruit or nut, with information about where it grows, advice on buying, storage and freezing, and hints on preparing it for cooking. This introduction also highlights some of the best-known ways in which it can be combined with other ingredients.

Recipes include health drinks, soups and appetizers, main course dishes, salads, cakes and breads, desserts, pies and puddings – plus preserves and wines and liqueurs as well as non-alchoholic drinks. Suggestions for cosmetics and remedies are also given, often using leaves or blossoms of a particular fruit or nut.

This section is followed by a selection of over thirty unusual fruits and nuts. Many are from the tropics or subtropics and are becoming increasingly available far from their native habitats. There is a short description for identification, followed by information on how the fruit or nut is best used. Some individual recipes are included and, wherever relevant, you are referred to recipes for similar fruits, or to general recipes.

Preserving and Basic Recipes follow, with detailed instructions for jams and jellies, fruit cheeses, pickles and chutneys, etc which can be adapted for different fruits and nuts. There are also the various kinds of pastry, sauces, etc required for some recipes in the main part of the book.

The next section, Nutrition, includes a selection of special diets for people with particular problems as well as weight-watchers, and a vitamin and mineral chart.

For enthusiastic gardeners there is How to Grow Fruits and Nuts with instructions for cultivating tree, bush and stone fruits, vines and cane fruit, perennials, citrus fruit and nuts. Greenhouse and indoor gardening are also included.

Finally, the Menu Planner gives instant suggestions for lunch or dinner parties. The appropriate recipes for each course are listed with their page numbers.

A bibliography and index complete the reference section.

ALMOND

Where would we be in springtime without our glimpse of pink blossom on the delicate branches of almond trees in our gardens and parks? But the juicy nuts we eat are likely to have come from much farther afield. Italy, France and Spain have long been producers and even in the Middle Ages, Spain was doing a roaring trade in these popular sweet nuts – a favorite dessert among the rich.

The tree itself is related to the cherry, plum and peach, and basically – though there are many varieties – there are two kinds; the bitter almond and the sweet. The former yields tiny quantities of prussic acid (refined away before it reaches us) and an oil which is used in cosmetics and to flavor liqueurs. It is the sweet almond which is so familiar in cakes, desserts and pastries. The tree is thought to have originated in the Near East, but is now happily cultivated all around the Mediterranean, in North Africa and the Canary Isles, South Africa, Australia and California.

Almonds can be bought in the shell and keep very well in this state. They can also be bought shelled, whole, slivered, flaked, ground or crushed. They are usually ready-blanched, but you can do this easily yourself by putting the shelled whole nuts in a bowl and pouring over boiling water. Leave them to steep for about 15 minutes as the water cools, and the brown skins should rub away easily.

To toast them, spread peeled nuts evenly on a baking sheet and bake in a preheated 350° oven for 8–10 minutes. Take care the nuts do not char.

An easy alternative is to buy almond extract, though when you do, make sure you have the *true* extract of almonds, and not the almond-flavored substitute which may never have seen a real nut.

Almonds freeze well plain or toasted; don't salt them, but wrap them tightly in foil. They should last for four months if toasted, and up to a year if plain.

Whole shelled nuts can be salted and served with cocktails, whole or flaked ones can be scattered over salads. They can be combined with fish, such as trout and used to make a delicious soup.

Almonds are probably best in dessert specialties. Think of crisp little macaroons, and rich-tasting praline.

Almonds can be added to flour when making pastry cases for tarts and pies, though beware of over-handling the mixture. The nuts contain up to fifty per cent oil and the pastry will be heavy if too much of the oil is "worked out." Marzipan or almond paste is an essential ingredient of Christmas, wedding and other cakes. It can be bought in handy slabs, and – with a few drops of almond extract added to improve the flavor if you wish – molded into fruit and novelties to serve as *petits fours*.

More unusually, almonds have long been thought to prevent drunkenness. Plutarch recommended eating them before imbibing, and Gerard says that "five or six, being taken fasting, do keepe a man from being drunke."

COSMETICS

Oil of sweet almonds, one of the most important ingredients in cosmetics, is soothing, healing, whitening and nourishing. It can be used on its own as a cleanser or as a softening treatment for rough, red hands, and is especially good for strengthening broken nails and for softening cuticles.

NOURISHING LOTION

An egg beaten with a tablespoon of almond oil makes an excellent nourishing lotion for very dry skin. So does a mixture of almond oil or ground almonds with milk or honey.

Mix well, pat into your face or hands, and leave for 15–20 minutes before rinsing off with tepid water. If you have made a very runny mixture, add it to your bath, and use any extra as a body rub.

FACE MASK

Ground almonds are ideal for adding to a runny ingredient, such as honey or fruit juice, to make a face mask.

For a cleansing paste, mix ground almonds with a little rose, orange-blossom or elder-flower water. Alternatively, combine them with milk or buttermilk to make a soothing and nourishing paste, good for rough or reddened skin.

CHRISTMAS ALMOND SOUP

1 heaping cup whole or 1½ cups
   ground almonds
5 cups creamy milk
One 2 inch cinnamon stick
Sugar
1–2 drops real almond extract
   (optional)
2–3 tablespoons raisins
6 tablespoons boiled rice (cooked
   measure)

It is best to blanch, peel and pulverize whole almonds just before they are needed. If you are using ground almonds, put them in a bowl.

In a heavy pan, very slowly bring milk to a rolling boil with the cinnamon stick. Stir in 2 or 3 tablespoons sugar and pour boiling hot over almonds, stirring until smoothly blended. Pour milk mixture back into saucepan. Taste, add a little more sugar and intensify flavor with a drop or two of almond extract if liked. Stir in raisins and cooked rice. Slowly bring to boiling point once more. Discard cinnamon stick and serve soup in a heated tureen.

Serves 4–6.

TROUT WITH ALMONDS

*⅔ cup almonds, blanched and
  slivered*
Butter
Juice of 1 small lemon
4 medium-size trout, cleaned
Seasoned flour
1 tablespoon oil
*Parsleyed lemon wedges for serving
  (see method)*

Start by preparing the almonds. In a small pan, sauté the almonds in 3–4 tablespoons butter until crisp and a deep golden color. Stir in lemon juice and keep hot.

Rinse trout and wipe them dry with paper towels. Coat them on all sides in seasoned flour.

In a skillet large enough to take all the trout side by side in one layer, fry the trout until cooked through and golden brown, about 5 minutes on each side, using 1 tablespoon oil and 2–3 tablespoons butter.

Transfer trout to a heated serving platter. Reheat the pan of almonds if necessary. Pour them over the trout, together with their buttery sauce. Garnish with lemon wedges coated on their cut sides with finely chopped parsley. Serve very hot.

Serves 4.

NOODLES WITH ALMONDS

1 small mild onion, finely chopped
½ cup butter
*1 heaping cup almonds, peeled and
  slivered*
Salt and freshly ground black pepper
Freshly grated nutmeg
Lemon juice
*1 pound flat noodles (tagliatelle),
  cooked and drained*

In a large, deep skillet or wide saucepan, simmer onion in butter until transparent and golden but not brown. Stir in almonds and fry gently, stirring frequently, until they turn a deep golden color. Season to taste with salt, freshly ground pepper, a grating of nutmeg and a squeeze (about 1 teaspoon) of lemon juice.

Place the hot, cooked noodles in a deep, heated serving bowl. Pour over the sautéed almonds and their buttery juices. Toss well and serve.

Serves 4–6.

FLOUNDER WITH ALMOND SAUCE

*¾ cup blanched almonds,
  slivered*
3 tablespoons butter
3 tablespoons flour
1¼ cups milk
Salt and freshly ground black pepper
1 tablespoon lemon juice
1 lb flounder fillets
*Lemon wedges and parsley for
  garnish*

Brown the almonds in 2 table-spoons butter. Add flour and cook gently, stirring, for 1–2 minutes. Add milk gradually to this roux, stirring constantly until the sauce is boiling. Simmer for about 5 minutes. Add salt, pepper and lemon juice. Set aside and keep warm.

Melt the remaining butter. Lay flounder fillets on a greased broiler pan, brush with butter, and broil gently without turning until the fish begins to flake.

Put on a warm plate, cover with the almond sauce, and garnish with lemon wedges and parsley.

Serve immediately.

Serves 4.

BUTTERED CELERY AMANDINE

Almonds make the perfect garnish for all kinds of vegetables. This dish goes well with lamb, poultry and lightly cooked fish.

12 crisp stalks celery
Butter
Salt and freshly ground black pepper
*2–3 scallions, white bulbs only, thinly
  sliced*
*¾ cup almonds, peeled and
  slivered*
¼ cup dry or medium sherry wine

Trim celery stalks and slice them into ½ inch pieces. In a heavy pan, melt ¼ cup butter until foaming. Stir in celery. Sprinkle with salt and fresh-ly ground black pepper, and sauté gently until celery is golden and each piece is coated with butter, about 5 minutes. Then cover pan and simmer for a few minutes longer until celery is soft but still rather crunchy. Stir in sliced scallions and cook, un-covered, for 2–3 minutes longer.

In a small skillet, sauté slivered almonds in 2 tablespoons butter until a rich golden color, taking great care that they do not burn. (Add a little more butter if it is absorbed too quickly.)

Sprinkle the almonds with sherry and cook, stirring, for about 2 or 3 minutes longer.

To serve, pour celery and its juices into a heated serving dish. Spoon the browned almonds over the top of the celery, together with their buttery sauce.

Serves 6–8.

CHOCOLATE ALMOND CAKE

A beautifully moist cake, full of flavor, that is equally good served as a dinner dessert or with tea or coffee.

8 ounces semisweet chocolate
2 tablespoons strong black coffee or milk
6 eggs, separated
6 tablespoons sugar
1 cup ground almonds
Butter and flour for cake pan
Granulated sugar or sifted confectioners' sugar or lightly sweetened whipped cream for serving

In the top of a double boiler, combine the chocolate, broken up into small pieces, with the coffee or milk, and melt over simmering water. Beat until smooth.

Beat the egg yolks and sugar together lightly. Then gradually beat in the melted chocolate and the ground almonds.

In a large bowl that is spotlessly clean and dry, beat the egg whites until they form stiff peaks. With a large metal spoon, carefully fold them into the chocolate almond mixture.

Have ready a deep, loose-bottomed cake pan about 8 inches in diameter, which you have buttered and dusted lightly with flour. Spoon the cake batter into the pan. Bake in a preheated 375° oven for 45 minutes, or until the cake is well risen and feels firm and dry to the touch.

Allow the cake to cool and settle before unmolding it.

It may be served either dusted with granulated sugar or a sifting of confectioners' sugar, or covered with a layer of *very* lightly sweetened whipped cream.

ST MARTIN'S ALMOND CROISSANTS

If fresh yeast, which you can sometimes buy from a bakery or in a healthfood shop, is unobtainable, use 2 packages active dry yeast for the croissant dough, reconstituted according to the directions on the can or package.

In Poznań, in Western Poland, these almond croissants are traditionally baked on St Martin's Day — November 11.

4 cups flour
3 eggs
1 tablespoon sugar
1 cup milk
2 (0.6 oz) cakes compressed yeast (see above)
¼ cup butter, melted and cooled
Beaten egg, to glaze

Almond paste
1 cup ground almonds
½ cup sugar
About 3 tablespoons cream

Sift the flour into a bowl and put it aside to warm gently until needed. In another large bowl, beat the eggs with the sugar until fluffy. Stir about 6 tablespoons hot water into the milk to raise its temperature to lukewarm. Crumble the yeast over the top and stir until completely dissolved.

Beat the milk mixture into the eggs, followed by the melted butter.

With a large wooden spoon, beat in about half of the flour. Then, using your hand, knead in as much as possible of the remaining flour to make a soft yet manageable dough. Continue to knead until dough is smooth and springy, and leaves the sides of the bowl and your fingers quite clean. (This operation can be done quickly and efficiently in an electric mixer fitted with a dough hook.) Roll the dough into a ball. Cover the bowl with a cloth or put it in a large plastic bag and seal opening. Leave to rise in a warm, draft-free place until dough has doubled in bulk, about 2 hours.

Meanwhile, prepare the almond filling. Mix the ground almonds and sugar together, and gradually work in enough cream to make a soft paste. Divide it into 16 pieces.

When dough has doubled its bulk, deflate it with the palm of your hand and knead briefly until smooth again. Divide it in half and work with one piece of dough at a time.

On a lightly floured board, using a lightly floured rolling pin, roll out the dough into a rectangle measuring 12 × 6 inches.

With a large, sharp knife, cut the rectangle in half lengthwise, then cut each strip across in 4, to make 8 3-inch squares.

Lay a square with one of its points facing toward you. Roll a piece of almond paste into a rope about 3½ inches long. Lay it on the square of dough slightly up from the point. Fold the point of dough up over it, then roll the square up to the point opposite. Bring the ends around to form a crescent, twisting them once or twice to seal in the roll of almond paste.

Transfer the crescent to a baking sheet.

Repeat with the remaining dough and almond paste, making 16 crescents in all.

Leave to rise again until crescents are puffy, about 30 minutes. Then gently brush with lightly beaten egg. Bake for 7 minutes in a preheated 400° oven, then lower temperature to 375° and continue baking for a further 7 minutes, or until crescents are a rich golden color.

Cool on wire racks.

ALMOND CRESCENTS

Rice paper for baking sheets
1 cup ground almonds
½ cup sugar
2 tablespoons ground rice
¼ teaspoon real almond extract
2 large egg yolks
About ¼ cup finely chopped blanched almonds

Line 2 large baking sheets with rice paper.

In a bowl, combine ground almonds with sugar, ground rice and almond extract. Beat egg yolks lightly with a fork. Pour them over the almond mixture and, using a large wooden spoon or your fingers, work to a paste.

Roll into a thin rope. Cut into 4 inch lengths and roll each length in chopped almonds. Bend lengths into U-shapes and arrange on lined baking sheets.

Bake crescents in a preheated 325° oven for 20 minutes, or until they are firm and almonds are tinged with gold. Cool cookies and trim off excess rice paper.

ALMOND MACAROONS

Tasteless oil and rice paper for baking
  sheets
2 egg whites
1 cup ground almonds
1 cup sugar
2 tablespoons ground rice
½ teaspoon vanilla
¼ teaspoon real almond extract
Blanched split or shredded almonds
  for decoration

Prepare 2 large baking sheets. Brush them very lightly with oil and line them with rice paper.

In a small bowl, stir egg whites with a fork just enough to break down their gelatinous threads. In another, larger bowl, stir the almonds, sugar and ground rice together. Gradually beat in the egg whites and flavoring extracts. Mixture should be of a medium-soft consistency. If necessary, add a few drops of cold water.

Using a pastry bag fitted with a plain, ½-inch nozzle, or dropping the mixture from a small spoon, make little rounds of mixture on the baking sheets, spacing them apart so they can spread. Press a split almond or a pinch of shredded almonds in the center of each macaroon.

Bake macaroons in a preheated 300° oven for about 25 minutes, or until they are lightly colored and feel dry to the touch.

Slip the sheets of rice paper onto a rack to cool.

When macaroons are cold and crisp, crumble off the excess rice paper around sides.

Store in an airtight container.

The macaroons can be used to decorate creamy desserts.

SWISS ALMOND COOKIES

When rolling and shaping these little cookies, keep extra flour down to a minimum.

1 cup flour
⅛ teaspoon baking powder
½ cup softened butter
½ cup sugar
1 cup ground almonds
Sieved raspberry jam or other
  smooth, sharp-flavored jelly to
  sandwich cookies
Sifted confectioners' sugar to dust
  cookies

Sift flour and baking powder into a bowl. Cut in butter. Stir in sugar and ground nuts and work by hand until dough holds together. Roll into a ball and chill lightly, covered, for 1 hour.

On a lightly floured board, using a rolling pin lightly dusted with flour, roll out dough thinly. Cut out 1 inch rounds with a plain cookie cutter. Arrange on baking sheets.

Bake cookies in a preheated 325° oven for about 7 minutes, or until lightly colored. Allow to cool slightly on baking sheets before transferring to wire racks.

When cold, sandwich cookies with jam or jelly. Dust them with sifted confectioners' sugar. Store in an airtight tin or jar until ready to serve.

MARZIPAN

Traditional Christmas cakes, wedding and christening cakes, as well as Simnel cakes for Easter, would be unthinkable without marzipan or almond paste, made with the purest ingredients — almonds, sugar, eggs and a little flavoring. Synthetic almond extract will ruin it and unless you can get the real thing, it is best left out altogether. Some prefer the marzipan to be slightly less sweet and the sugar may be scaled down to, say, three-quarters the quantity of each. Whole eggs, egg yolks or just egg whites may be used to moisten the marzipan, plus a little water, or orange-flower water for flavor, if necessary.

2 cups ground almonds
2 cups confectioners' sugar, sifted
1 cup sugar
2–3 teaspoons lemon juice
Few drops of real almond extract
2 eggs, lightly beaten (see above)
Orange-flower water (optional)

Mix ground almonds and sugars together in a bowl. Sprinkle with lemon juice and almond extract. Then, with your fingertips, gradually work in the beaten eggs until ingredients combine to form a firm but malleable paste. This will take some time to achieve so keep working the ingredients patiently until they lose their crumbliness and begin to stick together. Only if the eggs are not enough to bind the ingredients together, sprinkle with a little cold water and/or orange-flower water — no more than about a tablespoon should be enough.

Roll into a ball and wrap in wax paper or a plastic bag.

ALMOND PRALINE

Use praline in cake fillings, in creams and sweet sauces, or to scatter over ice creams and puddings.

The almonds are usually left unskinned, just wiped with a damp cloth to remove the powder on the surface. However, for a richer flavor they should be blanched, peeled and lightly toasted.

Take ⅔ cup sugar to each cup of nuts. In a heavy pan, carefully melt the sugar in a little water with a squeeze of lemon juice. (For ⅔ cup of sugar, you will need about 5 tablespoons cold water and 1 teaspoon lemon juice.) Heat the syrup, swirling the pan around gently and frequently, until it turns into a deep golden caramel (340° on a candy thermometer). If the nuts have not been peeled and toasted, they should be stirred into the syrup before it starts changing color. Otherwise, wait until the caramel is nearly at the right stage. Add the nuts all at once and mix well. Take great care not to let the caramel darken too much at this stage. Like all caramel syrups, it will carry on cooking from the heat of the pan for a minute or two after it has been removed from the heat.

Have ready a large, cold surface (marble is ideal but an ordinary metal baking sheet will do). Rub it all over with a wad of paper towel dipped in tasteless, odorless oil (ie, not olive oil).

Scrape the praline out onto the prepared surface and leave until quite cold and hard. With a spatula, prise the praline off the surface and crush it to a fine powder with a mortar and pestle or coarsely by breaking it down and rolling it with a heavy rolling pin.

If the praline is not to be used immediately, it should be broken up and stored in pieces in a dry jar which is absolutely airtight to prevent it turning damp and sticky. Then crush or pound it to the required degree of fineness just before use.

APPLE AND ALMOND PACK

This is good for rough skin (on elbows and knees, for instance), and can also be used as a face pack for dry skin.

Peel and grate a firm apple. Add about the same amount of ground almonds, and mix in milk (or cream) until you have a slightly gritty but spreadable paste. Spread the paste on your elbows, knees (or anywhere else with less than smooth skin) or face, and leave to dry. Rub off from arms and legs – preferably over a bath – or wash off from your face with warm water.

APPLE-BASED REMEDIES

A diet of grated apple, in moderation, will often clear up diarrhea in a couple of days. Use slightly unripe fruit, and peel them first.

Cider vinegar has been hailed as a cure for almost every ill under the sun. Most people are justifiably sceptical about this claim, but it is an excellent blood cleanser and helps to eliminate a vast variety of toxins. Up to two teaspoons in a tumbler of water, two or three times a day, will help digestion and promote energy.

APPLE

Of all the fruits that grow in the temperate world, the apple is the undoubted king. The moist, cool climate seems to bring out all of its sharp flavor in a crisp, juicy texture, and the farther south one goes, the softer and mealier the apples become and the blander their sweetness. In the tropics, apples give way to altogether more exotic fruits.

The apple is thought to have originated in the mountains of the Caucasus and its cultivation goes back to the Stone Age, even farther if the story of Adam, Eve and the Tree of Knowledge is to be taken literally. Some think that it was not an apple tree at all that was involved but another fruit, possibly an apricot or a fig, but the majority still come down in favor of the apple.

The Ancient Egyptians cultivated apple trees and the Greeks and Romans knew them well. By the end of the fourth century AD, there were thirty-seven varieties of apple on record. From then on, wherever western civilization went, apples went too – to the New World, to the Antipodes as well as throughout the Old World, to settle wherever the climate and growing conditions suited it. Today, there are well over a thousand varieties of apple in existence but the search for perfection continues unabated. Commercial growers have still to find the perfect apple, one that is a heavy cropper and resistant to disease, of equally good flavor and appearance, unaffected by packing and lengthy transportation.

The apple's versatility cannot be overemphasized. It can be enjoyed at any time of day, in any course of a meal. A fine French cuisine, that of Normandy, relies heavily on apples – fresh, cooked with all kinds of meat, poultry and game, or sliced into large open tarts. The French also have a magnificent apple brandy called Calvados. Americans have applejack and the British are famous for their cider. Last but not least, there is cider vinegar, which is infinitely preferable to some harsh, inferior potions that go by the name of wine vinegar.

As far as the cook is concerned, apples fall into three main categories: all-purpose apples, for cooking and eating out of hand; apples only to be used raw; and apples for cooking only.

When choosing apples in the store or market, select fresh, firm fruit with a smooth, shiny skin and good color. A pale, anemic color is usually a sign of immaturity and consequent lack of flavor, which is unlikely to improve, no matter how long you wait. A slightly shriveled skin could be caused by incorrect or overlong storage. An over-ripe apple, which also tends to be over-size, will be mealy and rather soft to finger pressure, and its flavor will be impaired.

Apples are best frozen as pie slices or purées or apple sauces. Blanch slices in acidulated water and dry or sugar freeze. They can also be dried.

Apples are not just for eating by themselves, for cooking with, or for making wine. They are also very good for you and "an apple a day keeps the doctor away" is an old saw which is based on scientific fact. Apples, particularly the peel, are rich in vitamins and contain at least six essential minerals, as well as malic acid which is a powerful aid to digestion. A raw apple is good for the teeth and gums and sweetens the breath; eaten last thing at night it will help you to sleep well. Apple seeds can be poisonous, but only in considerable quantities – a cupful has been known to be lethal.

BREAKFAST APPLE SHAKE

2 tart apples, peeled and cored
1¼ cups milk
Pinch ground cinnamon
1 tablespoon honey
Ice cubes (optional)

Chop the apples and put in the bowl of an electric blender with the milk, cinnamon and honey.

Blend until smooth and creamy, serve with ice cubes if desired.

Serves 2–3.

Note: Skimmed milk can be substituted for full fat milk to increase the nutritional value of this drink.

Hot Apple Soup

Serve this soup at an informal winter meal instead of the usual cup of hot tomato or vegetable. Use either sweet or tart apples, adjusting the sugar to taste. In fact, if you have an embarrassment of apples stored up for the winter, let your surplus guide your choice.

Potato flour gives the soup a particularly attractive, satiny texture, but if it is difficult to find in your area, cornstarch may be used instead.

1½ pounds apples
One 2 inch cinnamon stick
Twist of thinly peeled orange rind
3 tablespoons potato flour or
   cornstarch
About 1¼ cups orange juice
½–¾ cup sugar
Lemon juice
1¼ cups hot light cream
Ground cinnamon or cinnamon
   croûtons for serving (page 205)

Wash, quarter and core 1 pound apples. Put them in a pan with the cinnamon stick, orange rind and 2½ cups water. Bring to a boil and simmer, uncovered, until the apples have disintegrated. Rub the mixture through a sieve, discarding the cinnamon stick and rind. Pour the soup back into the rinsed-out pan.

Blend the potato flour or cornstarch smoothly with a few tablespoonfuls of orange juice. Reheat the soup and when it is halfway to a boil, stir in the flour or cornstarch paste, together with the remaining orange juice. Sweeten to taste with sugar, bring to a boil, stirring, and simmer gently for 3 or 4 minutes.

Peel and core the remaining apples. Grate them into long shreds on the coarsest side of a grater. If the soup is not to be served immediately, squeeze a little lemon juice over them and toss lightly with a fork.

Just before serving, bring the soup to simmering point. Stir in the grated apples and cream. Taste for sweetness and serve, each portion garnished with either a pinch of cinnamon or a few cinnamon croûtons.

Serves 4.

Polish Herring and Apple Appetizer Salad

A dish to start a couple of days ahead, unless your local delicatessen can offer you herrings that have already been desalted and filleted.

1 pound salted herrings
2 tablespoons finely chopped mild
   onion or shallots
6–8 tablespoons coarsely chopped,
   peeled apple
½ cup thick sour cream
2 tablespoons lemon juice
½ tablespoon sugar
1–2 tablespoons finely chopped
   parsley, chives or green scallion
   tops for garnish

Desalt the herrings for 48 hours as follows. Place them in a large bowl in the kitchen sink and let cold water trickle over them constantly until required; or, alternatively, cover them with cold water and leave them for 48 hours, changing water frequently – several times a day.

Drain the herrings thoroughly. Fillet them, discarding all skin and bones, and cut each fillet into bite-sized pieces. Arrange the pieces in a shallow serving dish.

In a small bowl, mix the onion or shallots and apple with the sour cream, and flavor to taste with lemon juice and sugar. Pour over the pieces of herring and mix lightly but thoroughly to coat them completely. Scatter the top with parsley, chives or scallion tops and put aside in a cool place for a couple of hours to develop flavors before serving.

Serves 6.

Waldorf Salad

This salad can be turned into a light main course luncheon dish by mixing in 1½–2 cups cubed cold roast chicken, pork or ham.

4 red-skinned apples
3–4 tablespoons lemon juice
4–6 stalks celery
⅔ cup raisins
½ cup coarsely chopped walnuts
¾ cup thick mayonnaise (page 205)

Quarter, core and cut the apples into small dice without peeling them. Toss them with lemon juice to prevent discoloration. Halve celery stalks lengthwise if they are thick and slice them thinly.

Rinse the raisins and drain them thoroughly.

In a large mixing bowl, combine the apples and their juices with the remaining ingredients. Add mayonnaise and toss lightly until well mixed. Pile into a bowl and serve.

Serves 4–6.

BAKED CHICKEN WITH APPLES

Chicken and apples form the perfect partnership and the addition of dry cider will do much to reinforce the refreshing, sharp flavor.

Serve this dish with a potato purée, rice or noodles, and follow with a fresh green salad.

1 roaster chicken, about 3½ pounds
¼ cup butter
3 slices Canadian bacon,
   diced
1½ pounds firm, aromatic apples
Salt and freshly ground black pepper
1¼ cups dry hard cider

Clean the chicken carefully and cut it into 8 or 9 neat pieces. Dry the pieces with paper towels and put them aside until needed.

In a large, heavy skillet, melt the butter until foaming but not colored. Add the diced bacon and fry gently until limp and golden but not crisp. With a slotted spoon, drain bacon bits and put aside on a plate until needed.

In the fat remaining in the skillet, sauté the chicken pieces over moderate heat until a rich golden color on all sides.

Quarter, core and slice the apples vertically. (I prefer not to peel them, as the skin helps the slices to keep their shape.)

In a heavy, ovenproof casserole with a tight-fitting lid, arrange a third of the apple slices. Lay half of the chicken pieces on top and scatter with half of the bacon pieces. Season lightly with salt and freshly ground black pepper. Repeat with another layer of apples, the remaining chicken pieces and bacon pieces, season lightly and top neatly with the remaining apple slices.

Pour the cider into the juices remaining in the skillet, and over a moderate heat, scrape the bottom and sides of the pan clean with a wooden spoon. Pour the simmering liquid all over the top layer of apples. Cover the casserole tightly and bake in a preheated 375° oven for 40–45 minutes, or until the chicken is tender. Serve straight from the casserole.

Serves 6.

DOLMEH SIB Persian Stuffed Apples

8–10 large, tart apples
Butter
Ground cinnamon (optional)

Stuffing
5–6 tablespoons yellow split peas
1 Bermuda onion, finely chopped
2 tablespoons butter or oil
1 pound lean ground beef
½ teaspoon ground cinnamon
Salt and freshly ground black pepper

Basting sauce
4–6 tablespoons cider vinegar
2–3 tablespoons sugar

Start by preparing the stuffing. Boil the split peas in unsalted water until they are very soft, about 30 minutes. Meanwhile sauté the onion in butter or oil until soft and lightly colored. With a slotted spoon, transfer onion to a plate and in the same fat sauté beef until it changes color. Return onion to the pan and mix well.

When split peas are soft and almost mushy, drain them thoroughly and mix them with the beef and onion. Sprinkle in the cinnamon and season to taste with salt and freshly ground black pepper. Leave to cool.

Meanwhile, prepare the apples. Wipe them clean with a damp cloth and core them from the stem end to within about ½ inch of the bottom. Core out some of the pulp as well, leaving thick shells firm and unbroken. Chop up the pulp.

Lightly butter a baking dish that will take all the apples in a single layer. Scatter the apple pulp evenly over the dish.

Sprinkle with a pinch of cinnamon, if liked, and moisten with a few tablespoons water.

Stuff the apples with a meat mixture and arrange them side by side on the chopped apple pulp. Dot each apple with a flake of butter. Bake in a preheated 350° oven for 30 minutes.

Prepare a sweet-sour basting sauce for the apples by combining the vinegar and sugar with ¾ cup water. Bring to boiling point, stirring until sugar has dissolved, and simmer for 1 minute.

Spoon a little boiling sauce into the cavity of each apple. (Any sauce left over may be poured over the chopped apples lining the baking dish.) Continue to bake apples for about 15 minutes longer until they are quite soft. Crush the apple pulp and pan juices together, and serve as a sauce for the apples. Serve hot.

Serves 4–5.

SALADE PARISIENNE
(Winter Fruit and Vegetable Salad)

A fresh winter salad to serve with poultry or cheese, or a plate of sliced ham. Prepare the salad shortly before serving.

2–3 large, crisp apples
2 large potatoes, boiled in their skins
3 heads Belgian endive
2 bananas
1 large stalk celery
3 carrots
½ cup coarsely chopped nuts
⅓ cup raisins

Dressing
3 tablespoons salad oil
1 tablespoon lemon juice
Pinch of paprika
Salt and freshly ground black pepper

Make the dressing for the salad first. Put the oil, lemon juice, paprika, salt and black pepper to taste in a screwtop jar. Close tightly and shake well to emulsify dressing.

Peel, core and dice the apples, and put them in a large bowl. Peel and dice the potatoes, and add them to the apples. Trim the endives. Slice them thinly, together with the bananas and celery, and add them to the bowl. Shred the carrots coarsely and add them. Finally, add the nuts and raisins.

Toss all the ingredients gently with a large kitchen fork until well mixed. Shake the dressing once more and mix it lightly but thoroughly into the salad. Correct seasoning and chill lightly until ready to serve.

Serves 6.

Note: If you find the salad is rather "dry," make up some more dressing in the same proportions and add it to the bowl (the exact amount needed will depend on the juiciness of the fruit and vegetables).

Fresh Apple Relish

Excellent served with roasts of meat and game, and curried meat dishes. Use well-flavored, crisp apples such as jonathan or mcintosh for this.

1 pound apples
1½–2 tablespoons sugar
1 tablespoon crumbled dried mint
Cider or white wine vinegar

Peel the apples and grate them coarsely into a bowl containing the sugar, mint and about 3 tablespoons vinegar.

Toss lightly but thoroughly until well mixed (this will prevent the apples discoloring).

Taste and add more sugar or mint if liked, and if necessary pour in a little more vinegar so that apples are thoroughly moistened.

Baked Apples

4 large baking apples
At least 2 tablespoons butter
⅔–1 cup firmly packed dark brown sugar
About 1 teaspoon ground cinnamon
4–6 tablespoons apple juice or hard cider
Whipped cream for serving

Quarter, peel and core the apples, and slice them thinly. Butter a baking dish that will hold them comfortably.

In a large bowl, toss the sliced apples with sugar and cinnamon to taste. Transfer them to the baking dish and moisten with apple juice or cider. Dot the top with small flakes of butter.

Bake apples in a preheated 375° oven for 30–40 minutes, or until they are a rich golden color on top and feel soft when pierced with a fork or skewer.

Serve hot or warm, with a bowl of chilled, lightly sweetened whipped cream.

Serves 4–6.

Bulgur Pilaf with Apples and Almonds

A very good side dish to serve with lamb, pork and poultry. If the meat dish is an oven roast, put the pilaf into the oven to cook with it in a tightly covered casserole after the initial frying. Otherwise, cook on top of the stove.

Bulgur (cracked wheat) is widely available in stores that sell Russian and Middle Eastern foods, as well as health food stores.

1 large Bermuda onion, finely chopped
¼ cup butter
1 cup bulgur (cracked wheat)
3 tart, crisp apples, peeled, cored and diced
¼ teaspoon crumbled dried thyme
¼ teaspoon celery seed
1 tablespoon finely chopped parsley
2 cups well-flavored chicken broth
Salt and freshly ground black pepper

Almond garnish
6–8 tablespoons slivered blanched almonds
¼ cup butter

In a large, heavy saucepan or flameproof casserole with a tight-fitting lid, sauté onion in butter until soft and golden. Stir in dry bulgur and sauté for a few minutes longer over moderate heat until lightly colored and aromatic. Add diced apples and continue frying, stirring, until each cube is coated with butter. Sprinkle with dried thyme, celery seed and parsley, and stir in chicken broth.

Bring to boiling point, cover pan tightly and either cook over the lowest possible heat for about 25 minutes until all the broth is absorbed, or bake in a preheated 350° oven for roughly the same length of time. When bulgur is cooked, fluff it up with a fork and correct seasoning with a little salt or pepper if necessary.

Have almonds already sautéed until golden in butter.

Serve the bulgur in a heated bowl with hot almonds and butter poured over the top.

Serves 4–6.

Italian Apple Cake

2 tablespoons flour
Pinch of salt
¾ cup milk
1 tablespoon sugar
½ teaspoon vanilla
2 tablespoons raisins
2 eggs
2 small apples
Butter for frying
Sifted confectioners' sugar for serving

First prepare a thin batter by blending the flour and salt smoothly with the milk. Stir in sugar and vanilla.

Rinse raisins and put them aside to drain in a strainer.

Beat eggs lightly in a large bowl and gradually beat in prepared batter. When smoothly blended, stir in drained raisins. Put aside while you quarter, peel, core and slice apples paper-thin. Stir apples into batter.

Select a thick skillet 7–8 inches in diameter and a flat plate that is slight-ly larger. Grease plate lightly all over with butter. In the skillet, melt a large pat (about 2 tablespoons) butter and when sizzling, tilt skillet around so that entire surface is coated.

Pour in batter, making sure apple slices and raisins are evenly distributed in the skillet. Cook over low heat until batter has set on top and pancake is a rich golden brown underneath.

Carefully turn pancake upside down onto the buttered plate. Melt a small pat of fresh butter in the skillet and slide the pancake back in to cook and brown the other side over low heat.

Invert pancake onto a heated serving dish.

Dredge with confectioners' sugar and serve immediately, cut in wedges like a cake.

Serves 2 as a snack, 4 as a dessert course.

Swiss Apple Tart

The Swiss like to fill these tarts, or *Wähen*, with all sorts of fresh fruit, but the most popular one is made with apples.

5–6 firm, tart apples
¼ cup butter
1 teaspoon vanilla
One 9 inch sweet pie pastry case, pre-baked (page 203)
3 small eggs
½ cup sugar
1¼ cups light cream
Sifted confectioners' sugar
  for serving

Peel, core and slice apples thickly. In a large, heavy skillet, simmer apple slices in foaming butter until they are golden and just tender but not mushy, turning them over gently once or twice with a large spatula. Sprinkle with vanilla and, using the spatula, carefully transfer the slices to the pre-baked pastry case in a neat, even layer.

Beat eggs with sugar until thick and lemon-colored. Add cream and mix well. Place tart pan back on baking sheet. Cover apples with egg mixture, pouring it in quite slowly over the back of a wooden spoon to avoid disturbing apples.

Return tart to the oven for 30 minutes, or until custard has set, no longer trembles when baking pan is pushed, and is lightly colored on top. Cool to lukewarm and dust with confectioners' sugar before serving.

Serves 6–8.

Apple Snow

A great childhood favorite that — unlike so many others — is equally popular with adults.

About 1½ pounds tart apples, peeled, cored and sliced
3 egg whites
¼ cup sugar
Whipped cream for serving

Make a simple, smooth apple purée with the apples and 1 tablespoon of water. When soft, rub them through a fine sieve to break down any lumps. (Taste, and sweeten with a little sugar and flavor with a little lemon juice if liked.)

Leave until cold, then measure about 1¼ cups purée.

In a large, clean bowl, beat egg whites until they stand in soft peaks.

Gradually beat in sugar and continue to beat egg whites to a stiff, glossy meringue. Gently fold in measured apple purée.

Spoon into tall glasses and top with swirls of whipped cream.

Serves 4–6.

Baked Rice and Apple Pudding

A favorite Polish winter dish.

1 cup short-grain rice
¼ cup butter
Salt
⅓ cup raisins
1–2 tablespoons chopped
  crystallized orange peel
2 pounds crisp, tart apples
White or dark brown sugar
1 teaspoon vanilla

Put the rice in a saucepan. Add 2½ cups of boiling water, 2 tablespoons of the butter and a generous pinch of salt; stir well and cook very gently with the lid half on the pan until the water has been absorbed and the rice is very soft.

Stir in the raisins and peel, cover tightly and put aside while you prepare apples.

Barbecued Apples

With well-flavored, firm apples all you need do is first to rinse and dry them thoroughly, and pluck out their stems. Then wrap each apple tightly in a square of heavy-duty foil or a double thickness of ordinary kitchen foil.

While the main course is being eaten, set foil-wrapped apples on the glowing coals. After about 10 minutes turn them over and cook for 10–15 minutes longer on the other side.

Serve hot with brown sugar or syrup and teaspoons for scooping out the pulp.

A more sophisticated way to deal with apples for a barbecue is to stuff them before cooking. First cut squares of foil for them as above and grease the inside of each square with butter. Rinse, dry and core apples, and stuff cavities with a mixture of 1 teaspoon each dark brown sugar, chopped raisins and chopped hazelnuts or walnuts, a generous pinch of finely grated lemon rind and a pinch of ground cinnamon. Pour a teaspoon of rum over each cavity and top with a flake of butter.

Wrap each stuffed apple in its buttered foil. Stand them on a grid over hot coals, and bake until soft, or bake in a preheated 400° oven for 30 minutes.

Peel, core and slice the apples very thinly into a bowl. Add sugar to taste, sprinkle with vanilla and toss well with a large fork.

Grease a large baking dish generously with some of the remaining butter, and cover bottom with a third of the rice mixture. Cover with half of the apples, followed by half of the remaining rice, then all the remaining apples (and their juices, if any) and the rest of the rice, spreading it out as evenly as possible with the back of your spoon.

Dot the top of the pudding all over with flakes of remaining butter and bake in a preheated 350° oven for 45–50 minutes, or until surface is crusty and golden brown.

Serve hot.

Serves 6.

SOUTHERN APPLE PIE

About 1 pound basic pie pastry for a 2-crust, 9 inch pie (page 203)
1½–2 pounds tart apples
Lemon juice (optional)
½–¾ cup white or ⅔–1 cup firmly packed dark brown sugar, or half and half
¼ teaspoon ground cinnamon
⅛ teaspoon grated nutmeg
2 tablespoons flour
Pinch of salt
⅓ cup raisins
1–2 tablespoons butter
Sugar for sprinkling

Start by lining a pie pan with pastry, overhanging the sides a little, and cutting out a lid to go on top. Put aside until needed.

Quarter, peel and core apples, and slice them thinly into a bowl. If they are not too sour, or are rather old and tasteless, toss them with a tablespoon of lemon juice. Blend sugar with spices, flour and salt, and sprinkle over apples. Add raisins and toss lightly until thoroughly mixed.

Pack apple mixture into pastry-lined pie pan. Dot surface all over with flakes of butter.

Lay pastry lid in position. Press all around sides to seal them, then flute rim attractively between forefinger and thumb. Cut slits in top crust.

Bake pie in a preheated 450° oven for 15 minutes, then reduce heat to 350°, and continue to bake for 35–40 minutes longer, or until top crust is a rich golden color and apples feel soft when prodded with a skewer through one of the slits. Sprinkle with sugar.

Serves 6–8.

APPLE CIDER SAUCE

2 tablespoons butter
3 tablespoons flour
2½ cups hard apple cider, warmed
¼ teaspoon ground cloves
¼ teaspoon ground ginger
Honey or brown sugar

Melt the butter in a saucepan over gentle heat. Mix in the flour and cook, stirring, for 1–2 minutes. Slowly stir in the apple cider and add cloves and ginger. Bring to a boil, still stirring, then remove from heat. Sweeten with honey or brown sugar.

SHERRIED APPLES WITH SPICED NUTS

6 large baking apples
Butter
¾ cup medium sherry wine
Whipped cream for serving

Nut stuffing
¼ cup butter
½ cup firmly packed dark brown sugar
1 teaspoon ground cinnamon
1 tablespoon medium sherry wine
½ cup chopped walnuts

Prepare apples in usual way, coring them and peeling away about a third of the skin, from the top.

Prepare nut stuffing by creaming butter and brown sugar together until light. Beat in cinnamon and sherry until thoroughly blended, then stir in chopped nuts.

Fill apples with stuffing. Arrange side by side in a buttered baking dish. Pour sherry evenly over the top.

Bake apples in a preheated 375° oven, basting frequently with pan juices, for 30–40 minutes, or until they feel soft when pierced lightly with a skewer.

Serve lukewarm or cold, with a bowl of whipped cream.

Serves 6.

HOT APPLE CHARLOTTE

Butter and bread crumbs for baking dish
12 slices bread
2 cups milk
2 eggs
1 tablespoon sugar
8 apples, peeled, cored and sliced
2 tablespoons chopped candied peel
2 tablespoons chopped raisins
3 tablespoons confectioners' sugar, sifted
1 teaspoon vanilla

Butter a deep baking dish (a soufflé dish is ideal) and coat it with bread crumbs. Toast the bread slices lightly on both sides until golden but not browned.

Dip each slice of toast on both sides in a mixture of milk beaten with eggs and sugar, and put them aside on a plate. Mix the apples with the candied peel, raisins, confectioners' sugar and vanilla.

Arrange four layers of toast and three layers of apples in the baking dish (ie, starting and ending with a layer of toast). Pour in any remaining milk mixture.

Bake the charlotte in a preheated 400° oven for 45 minutes, or until the top is crisp and golden.

Serve hot.

Serves 4–6.

APPLE SAUCES

When making an apple sauce, the first question to ask yourself is how it is to be served and the kind of dish it is intended to complement, whether it is a heavy meat such as roast pork, a light dish of poultry or veal, even a sweet pudding or cake. This will help you to decide the kind of flavor and texture the sauce is to have.

Its texture may be silky-smooth, made with apples that have been cooked in the very minimum of water, or none at all, then rubbed through a sieve, put through a vegetable mill or puréed in an electric blender or food processor.

Reheat the thick purée with sugar to taste and beat in a large pat of butter, which will make it even more satiny.

For a less smooth sauce, crush the cooked apples well with a fork, allowing some small pieces to retain their natural texture. And for the most substantial kind of sauce, first dice the peeled, raw apples and sauté them gently in butter until lightly colored on all sides. Then cover the pan and "sweat" the apples over very low heat until they are quite soft.

Sweeten if necessary, season lightly and if you have some heavy cream handy, stir in two or three tablespoonfuls to amalgamate with any pan juices.

For an apple sauce to serve four, you will need about 1 pound apples. Traditionally, a sauce is made with sour, green baking apples but often a far more interesting version will result from aromatic sweet apples that cook well such as newtown pippin or winesap. Compared with baking apples, these not only have a richer flavor, but will also retain more shape and texture. Instead of white sugar, sweeten the sauce with a little dark brown sugar, or even better, a tablespoon or two of apple jelly or orange marmalade.

There are many other flavorings with which you can experiment. A small quince cooked and puréed with the apples will transform the flavor of the sauce. Moisten it with a good splash of white wine or cider and let it boil down until it thickens again, or use a few tablespoons of dry white vermouth (a useful alternative when you do not have a bottle of wine already open). A squeeze of lemon juice will balance the sweetness of the sauce.

For a much stronger sauce, beat in a tablespoon or two of grated fresh horseradish or dried horseradish flakes.

Finally, at the other end of the flavor spectrum, a little finely chopped mild onion or shallot sautéed in the butter before adding the pieces of apple, will give the sauce a definite flavor. Crush the apples. Season with salt, freshly ground black pepper and a pinch of sugar if necessary, and serve hot.

OLD-FASHIONED APPLE BUTTER

This is a good way of using up a surplus of apples from the garden. Any kind is suitable, either one variety or a combination of two or three in equal amounts. Windfalls will do perfectly well and crab apples make an excellent butter. Experiment with different spices to flavor the butter. Cinnamon and cloves are the most popular, but grated nutmeg and ground allspice are also frequently added.

6 pounds apples
5 cups sweet hard cider
Sugar
1½ teaspoons ground cinnamon
½ teaspoon ground cloves

Rinse apples and chop them. There is no need to peel or core them.

Put them in a large kettle with cider and barely enough water to cover. Bring to boiling point and simmer the apples until soft and pulpy, stirring occasionally.

Rub contents of pan through a sieve, discarding peels, seeds and other debris.

Measure pulp and return it to rinsed-out pan. Measure ½ cup of sugar for every 1 cup of apple purée.

Bring purée to simmering point, stirring frequently. Add measured sugar and spices. Stir until sugar has dissolved, then simmer, stirring regularly at an ever-increasing rate as purée thickens to ensure that it does not stick to the bottom of the pan. The butter is ready when no surplus liquid can be seen collecting around the edges of a small mound of purée which you have spooned out onto a saucer.

Pack into canning jars and process in a boiling-water bath.

See also page 200.

APPLE CHUTNEY

4 pounds peeled, cored and quartered apples
1 pound (about 3 cups) raisins, chopped
1 pound dried dates, pitted and chopped
5⅓ cups firmly packed brown sugar
2½ quarts brown malt vinegar
⅓ cup mustard seed
½ cup ground ginger
1 tablespoon salt
1 tablespoon cayenne, or to taste
2 garlic cloves, peeled and very finely chopped

Combine all the ingredients in a large kettle and mix well. Stir constantly over low heat until sugar has dissolved.

Bring to boiling point and simmer for between 1½ and 2 hours, stirring at an increasing rate as chutney thickens to prevent it sticking to the bottom of the pan.

Pour into a bowl and leave until the following day before packing into canning jars and processing (page 200).

Fills about 7 jars.

APPLE AND PLUM CHUTNEY

3 pounds plums
1 pound Bermuda onions
4 pounds peeled, cored and sliced apples
5 cups brown malt vinegar
5⅓ cups firmly packed light or dark brown sugar
3 cups raisins
3 cups currants
1 teaspoon salt
1 teaspoon cayenne
1 teaspoon white pepper
1 teaspoon ground ginger

Pit the plums and cut them into chunks.

Peel and chop the onions.

In a large kettle, combine fruit and onions with all the remaining ingredients, and heat gently, stirring, until sugar has dissolved. Then boil, stirring very frequently, until chutney is thick, about 1 hour.

Cool and when quite cold, pack into canning jars and process as usual (page 200).

Fills about 8 jars.

APPLE AND GREEN TOMATO CHUTNEY

1 pound green tomatoes
1 pound apples, quartered and cored
1 pound onions
1⅓ cups raisins
1⅓ cups firmly packed brown sugar
2 tablespoons salt
2 tablespoons ground ginger
2 tablespoons cayenne
½ teaspoon ground cloves
2½ cups brown malt vinegar

Put tomatoes, apples, onions and raisins through a grinder, together with brown sugar, and put in a large kettle. Blend salt and spices smoothly with some of the vinegar. Mix with remaining vinegar, pour into kettle and mix well.

Place kettle over low heat and stir until sugar has dissolved and mixture comes to a boil. Then boil gently for about 1 hour, stirring more and more frequently as chutney thickens to prevent it sticking to the bottom of the pan. Cool.

Pack and process as usual (page 200).

Fills about 4 jars.

BOTTLED APPLES IN CIDER

Use windfalls which are too unripe (or badly bruised) to eat raw.

Apples (see above)
Brine made with 2 tablespoons salt to
    5 cups water

Cider syrup
1 cup sugar
2½ cups cider
Thinly peeled rind of
    1 lemon

Start by preparing syrup. Dissolve sugar in 5 cups water with cider and lemon rind (use a potato peeler or a small, sharp knife to peel off yellow part of rind as thinly as possible). Stir until sugar has dissolved and bring to boiling point.

Remove pan from heat, cover, and leave until quite cold.

Prepare apples. Quarter, peel and core apples, cutting out all bruised and discolored parts, and drop into brine to prevent discoloration.

Rinse apples thoroughly. Wipe them with a damp cloth or paper towels, and pack tightly into prepared jars. Cover with cold syrup and process as usual (page 201).

APPLE JELLIES

The color of an apple jelly depends very much on the apples used. The brighter and riper they are, the darker the jelly will be. Green apples and windfalls make a pale golden jelly that sets well, and windfalls as well as crab apples make good jelly with a sharp, tart flavor. Apart from the more conventional uses, a tablespoon or two of apple jelly may be added to apple sauces to sweeten and flavor them, or it can be eaten with cheese.

All kinds of herb jelly to serve with meat may be made with an apple jelly base — mint jelly to serve with lamb, sage jelly for pork, and jelly flavored with bay for ham. The jelly itself should be perfectly clear or, if liked, can be colored green with a few drops of food coloring. Just before jell point is reached, a little finely chopped fresh mint or a few sage or bay leaves may be stirred in.

6 pounds apples
1 lemon
2 cups sugar per 2½ cups of juice

Chop apples but do not peel or core them. Finely grate rind of the lemon, sprinkle it over the apples in a large kettle and cover with 3 quarts water. Bring to a boil and cook until apples are very soft and pulpy. Tip the contents of the pan into a jelly bag and allow to drip dry, or leave the apple pulp to drain in a hair sieve.

Measure juice and measure 2 cups of sugar per 2½ cups juice.

In the rinsed-out pan, combine the apple juice with the sugar and strain in the juice of the lemon. Bring to a boil slowly, stirring frequently, until sugar has dissolved. Then boil rapidly until jell point is reached, skimming scum from the surface as necessary.

Cool slightly, ladle into jelly glasses and seal.

See also page 199.

RUSSIAN SOURED APPLES

This is an unusual way of preserving apples for the winter, slightly reminiscent of the way sauerkraut would be made. Russians serve soured apples as an accompaniment for fried breaded scaloppine and chops of various kinds. The apples should be tart, crisp ones, all of the same medium size and without blemishes. For souring the apples, you will need a large, old-fashioned glazed pot or urn, a round wooden board to fit inside the top of it and a large, smooth stone, scrubbed clean, rinsed with boiling water and wrapped in cheesecloth, to place on top.

10–11 pounds apples
About 1 ounce fresh black currant
    leaves
1 cup rye flour
½ cup sugar or ⅓ cup honey
1 teaspoon salt

Wash and drain apples thoroughly. Scrub your pot or urn and line bottom with a layer of fresh black currant leaves.

On this place a layer of apples, fitting them tightly side by side. Cover with more black currant leaves. Continue in this manner until apples have all been packed into pot, ending with a layer of leaves.

Prepare preserving liquor. In a large bowl, work rye flour to a smooth paste with a little cold water. Stirring rapidly, pour in 4½ to 5 quarts of boiling water, making sure flour does not go lumpy. Stir in sugar or honey and salt, and put aside until cold.

Pour cold liquor over apples to cover them completely. Then place wooden board on top and weight it down with the cheesecloth-wrapped stone to prevent apples floating to the top. They must at all times remain submerged. Allow apples to marinate in a cool, dry place (such as a garage, outhouse or cellar) for at least 4 weeks before tasting them. They will keep for several months, at least until the following spring. Should mold form on the liquor and turn the stone slimy, skim the liquor, scrub the stone and the cheesecloth separately, and scald them with boiling water before replacing them.

APRICOT

Although the apricot is a temperate fruit, it is rare to find fresh apricots at their peak of ripeness in the cooler climates of the north. The main reason for this is that the trees blossom early and an unexpected frost would wipe out the crop. So unless you live in an apricot-growing area, you are unlikely to find them fresh and in an edibly ripe state.

Another problem with fresh apricots is that although they taste best when they have ripened on the tree, once they reach this stage they are extremely perishable, and lengthy transportation over long distances by conventional methods would be sure to spoil them. Consequently, many of the fresh apricots offered in markets were picked when they were still far too hard and immature. Such fruit will never ripen properly and develop its full apricot flavor. The apricots will even start to shrink and shrivel but remain hard and greenish to the end. Unless you can be sure of getting naturally ripened fresh apricots, you would be better advised to concentrate your attention on one of the excellent forms of preserved apricots available, which are many and plentiful – dried, canned or turned into jams, nectars and candies.

Apricots are thought to have come originally from China but early on they were introduced into the Near East, hence their botanical name, *Prunus armenica*. There their popularity has never waned and apricots appear in all kinds of dishes, from soups to desserts. Since those times, apricots have spread all over the world. They flourish in the warmth of southern Europe, Australia and California.

Dried apricots are produced in several grades of quality. Finest of all are the large, plump dessert apricots, carefully packed so that they are not squashed out of shape. At the other end of the range are the leathery orange-colored scraps which can only be used for cooking and chopping or puréeing.

Even if you make most of your own jams and preserves, you will probably have discovered that an apricot preserve is one of the few exceptions worth buying, with dozens of uses in the kitchen. Make sure it contains just apricots and sugar. Then it can either be eaten as it is or spread in layer cakes. You will also need apricot preserve to make an apricot glaze for brushing over open fruit tarts.

Apricots can be halved or sliced then frozen in a syrup made from 2 cups sugar to 5 cups water; add 2 ounces ascorbic acid for each 2½ cups syrup. Plunge the whole apricots into boiling water first for about thirty seconds, and peel, pit and halve or slice them.

Apricots can be made into wine and brandy.

They are one of the best natural sources of Vitamin A, especially when dried. Essential for healthy skin and mucous membranes. Vitamin A is also needed for good sight; insufficient amounts can cause night blindness, impair sight and increase susceptibility to colds and other illnesses. Although it is one of the few vitamins which can theoretically build up to toxic levels, this doesn't normally happen if it is taken naturally.

MOISTURIZING MASK

The Vitamin A content of apricots is especially beneficial to dry skins. Either fresh or dried fruit is suitable.

If using fresh apricots, simply remove the pits and mash the fruit; if using dried, soak for an hour or so in water before chopping finely and mashing. Mix the fruit pulp with enough oil (olive, safflower, peanut, avocado or almond) to make a spreadable paste.

Clean your face thoroughly, and pat the paste on, avoiding the area under the eyes. Leave on for about 20 minutes, then wash off gently with warm water.

APRICOT CHICKEN SOUP

¾–1 pound chicken pieces
Salt
1 chicken bouillon cube (optional)
½ cup short-grain rice, rinsed and drained
1 cup peeled and diced potato
1 cup plump dried apricots, rinsed and cut into strips
Freshly ground black pepper
Ground cinnamon
¾ cup light cream
¼ cup finely chopped fresh dill or parsley

Rinse chicken pieces and put them in a large pan. Sprinkle with salt and cover with 2 quarts cold water. Add a crumbled chicken bouillon cube if liked at this stage. Slowly bring to boiling point and simmer for 20 minutes.

Skim the surface clear of any scum and fat.

Stir in rice, diced potato, apricots, and a generous pinch each of freshly ground black pepper and cinnamon. Simmer until the ingredients are quite soft and chicken meat is falling off the bones.

With a slotted spoon, lift out chicken pieces. Bone them, sliver meat and return to the soup. Stir in cream. Correct seasoning if necessary. Bring to just below boiling point and serve, each portion sprinkled with chopped dill or parsley.

Serves 6–8.

PORK CHOPS IN APRICOT SAUCE

This is also a good way of preparing chicken pieces and is delicious served with brown rice or a fluffy potato purée.

½ pound dried apricots
1¼ cups dry white wine or cider
6 thick pork chops
Seasoned flour
1 onion, finely chopped
3 tablespoons oil
2 tablespoons dark brown sugar
2–3 tablespoons coarsely chopped blanched almonds or walnuts

Rinse the apricots thoroughly under cold water. Put them in a bowl, cover with wine or cider and leave to soak overnight.

The following day, trim pork chops of any excess fat and dust them all over with well-seasoned flour. Remove about a quarter of the apricots from the wine and blend the remainder together with the wine to a smooth purée in an electric blender or food processor. Chop the whole apricots coarsely and stir them into the purée.

In a large skillet, cook the onion in half the oil until soft and golden. Remove the onion with a slotted spoon and put aside until needed. Heat the remaining oil in the skillet and fry the chops, 2 or 3 at a time, until golden brown on both sides. Transfer them to an ovenproof casserole as they are done, making two layers in all and sprinkling each layer with some of the sautéed onion.

Deglaze the skillet with 6–8 tablespoons water, stirring and scraping the surface clean with a wooden spoon. Bring to a boil and pour over the chops. Cover with the apricot purée.

Put on the lid and bake in a preheated 350° oven until chops are quite tender, about 1 hour. For the last 15 minutes of baking time, remove the lid, sprinkle the surface with a mixture of sugar and nuts, and continue baking until sugar has dissolved and surface is bubbling. Serve from the casserole.

Serves 6.

LAMB AND APRICOT POLO

2 Bermuda onions, finely chopped
¼ cup butter
2 pounds lean boned lamb, cubed
Salt and freshly ground black pepper
½–1 teaspoon ground cinnamon
½ pound plump dried apricots, quartered
6–8 tablespoons raisins
About 2 cups light chicken broth
Juice of ½ lemon
1–2 tablespoons apricot preserve, to taste

In a heavy pan or flameproof casserole, sauté onions gently in butter until transparent and lightly colored. Transfer to a plate with a slotted spoon. In the remaining butter, brown the lamb cubes all over, a portion at a time. Return the onions and all the lamb to the pan. Season lightly with salt, pepper and cinnamon, and stir in the apricots and raisins. Sauté gently for a few minutes longer. Pour in hot chicken broth (or water) to cover. Bring slowly to simmering point, cover the pan and cook gently for about 2 hours until the lamb is tender and the apricots soft and pulpy, adding more broth if it evaporates too quickly.

Half an hour before the lamb is ready, flavor to taste with lemon juice and apricot preserve.

Just before serving, correct seasoning, and add a little more cinnamon if liked.

Serves 6.

APRICOT CREAM

½ pound dried apricots, soaked overnight
¾ cup sugar.
6–8 tablespoons Madeira wine
Lemon juice (optional)
2 egg whites
¾ cup whipping cream

Pour the apricots and their soaking water into a pan. Stir in half the sugar and 2 or 3 tablespoons more water if necessary so that fruit is barely covered. Bring to boiling point and simmer until apricots are very soft. Drain them thoroughly. Pour cooking juices back into the pan and boil until reduced to a few tablespoons of thick syrup. Stir into apricots and leave until cold.

Add Madeira to apricots and process to a smooth, thick purée in an electric blender or food processor. Taste, and blend in a little more sugar, Madeira or a squeeze of lemon juice if liked. The purée should be well flavored but must remain thick.

Beat the egg whites until they form soft, floppy peaks when beaters are lifted. Gradually beat in remaining sugar and continue to beat to a stiff, glossy meringue. Whip cream lightly.

Fold meringue into apricot purée, followed by whipped cream. Spoon into a glass serving bowl or into individual dishes and chill until ready to serve.

Serves 6.

APRICOT ICE CREAM

½ pound dried apricots, soaked
   overnight
2–3 tablespoons lemon juice
4 eggs, separated
1 cup vanilla-flavored sugar (page
   205)
1¼ cups whipping cream
Thin almond tuiles or lady fingers for
   serving

Rinse the apricots thoroughly before leaving them to soak overnight. The following day, simmer them for 10–15 minutes, or until very soft, with more water to cover if necessary. Drain apricots and reserve ¾ cup of the cooking liquid. Pour this into the goblet of an electric blender (or a food processor fitted with the steel blade), add the apricots and process to a thick, smooth purée. Flavor to taste with lemon juice and blend in the egg yolks, one at a time.

Pour the apricot purée into a heavy pan and cook over gentle heat, stirring constantly, until purée becomes very thick. Take care not to let it come to boiling point or the egg yolks will curdle. (If you feel apprehensive about this, heat the purée in a double boiler over simmering water, stirring constantly, until it thickens.) Pour thickened purée into a large bowl and leave until cold.

Beat egg whites until soft peaks form when beaters are lifted. Then gradually beat in sugar and continue to beat to a stiff, glossy meringue. Whip the cream lightly in a separate bowl until it thickens.

Fold the meringue into the apricot purée, followed by the whipped cream.

Taste and flavor with more lemon juice or sugar if necessary.

Freeze in an ice cream maker, following manufacturer's instructions. Or pour into ice trays or a large, shallow freezer container, cover and freeze.

Remove the container after about 1½ hours, or when the ice cream has frozen around the edges, and with a fork beat it thoroughly, turning the sides into the center.

Cover the container and freeze for 3–4 hours longer, or overnight. Transfer the container to the refrigerator about 1 hour before serving.

Serve the ice cream with crisp cookies.

Serves 6.

APRICOT ALMOND SWEETS

Use good-quality, plump dried apricots, not the leathery pieces which have often lost a great deal of their flavor. Instead of adding the ground almonds and almond flavoring, the sweetened apricot paste may be left as it is and the candies decorated with bright green, peeled pistachio nuts. If you do decide to use almonds, be sure to get real almond extract as the artificial one tastes unpleasantly synthetic.

½ pound plump dried apricots
Granulated or sifted confectioners'
   sugar
1 tablespoon ground almonds
   (optional)
1–2 drops almond extract (optional)
Slivered blanched almonds or peeled
   pistachio nuts, to decorate

Wash the apricots and dry them thoroughly. Put them through the fine blade of a meat grinder, or twice if necessary through the coarser blade, to reduce them to a rather coarse paste.

Sweeten to taste with sugar and mix in the ground almonds and almond extract if used. Work the paste with your fingertips until ingredients are smoothly blended.

Sprinkle a board lined with wax paper with an even layer of sugar. Roll the apricot paste into marble-sized balls, coat them with sugar and leave to dry and harden overnight.

The following day, decorate each sweet with a few almond slivers or a peeled pistachio nut. Place in little paper cases and serve with after-dinner coffee.

Note: If the apricot paste is too dry to roll into smooth balls, it can be moistened with a few drops of lemon juice or cold water.

APRICOT MERINGUE CAKE

At least ⅔ cup butter
6 egg whites
Pinch of salt
1½ cups sugar
1¼ cups flour
1 jar (about 1 pound) apricot jam
Lemon juice (optional)

Meringue
2 egg whites
½ cup sugar

Start by baking the cake base a day before it is to be served. Grease a deep 8 inch springform cake pan with butter. Line it with parchment paper and butter that lightly as well. In a small, heavy pan, melt ⅔ cup butter without letting it sizzle and put it aside to cool.

In a large, spotlessly clean and dry bowl, beat the 6 egg whites with a pinch of salt until soft peaks form. Gradually adding sugar, continue to beat to a stiff, glossy meringue. Sift flour and fold into meringue a little at a time alternately with melted butter. Spoon into prepared cake pan. Bake in a preheated 400° oven for 40 minutes, or until cake is well risen and springs back when pressed lightly with a fingertip. Remove cake from the oven, place on a cake rack and leave it to cool in its pan overnight.

The following day, loosen sides of cake by slipping a knife blade around them and carefully unmold cake. Peel off lining paper. With a serrated knife, cut cake into three layers.

Put apricot jam in a heavy pan. Taste it and if it is very sweet, sharpen flavor a little with lemon juice. Heat jam slightly so that it will spread more easily. It may also be thinned down with a tablespoon or two (no more) of boiling water.

Place bottom layer of cake on a large baking sheet which has been greased very lightly with butter. Then put layers together again, spreading apricot jam between them and over top and sides of cake as well.

Prepare meringue. Beat egg whites until soft peaks form. Then gradually beat in sugar and continue to beat until stiff and glossy.

Spread meringue all over top and sides of cake. Place cake in a preheated 220° oven. Bake for 3 minutes only then, without opening oven door, turn off heat and leave cake until cold.

Serves 6–8.

QUICK SAUCE

One 16 ounce can apricots in
* syrup*
About 1 tablespoon sugar
1 teaspoon arrowroot or potato flour
About 1 tablespoon lemon juice
1–2 teaspoons Kirsch, orange liqueur
* or brandy (optional)*
Confectioners' sugar (optional)

Drain apricots, reserving syrup. Put them in an electric blender or food processor. Sprinkle with sugar and process to a smooth purée. Pour into a small pan.

Blend arrowroot or potato flour smoothly with 3 or 4 tablespoons reserved syrup and stir into apricot purée, together with the lemon juice. Bring to boiling point and simmer, stirring, for 3 or 4 minutes until sauce has thickened and no longer tastes of raw starch.

If sauce is to be served hot, thin it down with a little more of the reserved syrup if too thick, then taste and add more sugar or lemon juice if liked. If it is to be a cold sauce, let it cool after it has been thickened, then stir in liqueur or brandy if used, and finally adjust sweetness with a little confectioners' sugar (which dissolves most easily) if necessary.

APRICOT WINE

The ingredients listed will produce a medium-dry white wine. For a sweeter wine, use 7 cups sugar and a liebfraumilch yeast.

4 pounds fresh apricots, or 1 pound
* dried apricots*
1½ cups chopped raisins
1 Campden tablet
1 teaspoon pectic enzyme
1 teacup cold strong tea
1 yeast nutrient tablet
Burgundy yeast
5 cups sugar

Wash the fruit. If you are using fresh apricots, discard the pits, but do not remove the skin. Chop the fruit into small pieces and place it in the prepared vessel, such as a plastic pail. Add the raisins, Campden tablet, pectic enzyme and 4½ quarts water. Cover the pail and then leave it for 24 hours.

Quickly uncover the pail and add the strong tea, the nutrient tablet and the activated yeast (see manufac-

APRICOT BRANDY

The apricots remaining after the liqueur is drained off are delicious on their own or added to cakes and pies.

2 pounds fresh apricots
4 cups sugar
1½ quarts brandy

Wash the fruit. Halve it and discard the pits. Take a large, wide-neck storage jar, with a screw top (a kilner jar is ideal). It should be thoroughly clean and sterilized (see general instructions for wine making). Arrange the fruit in layers in the jar, sprinkling sufficient sugar to cover over each layer. The fruit should be tightly packed. Screw the top on loosely and leave for 4 days.

Unscrew the lid and add the chopped apricot kernels, if you are using them. Pour sufficient brandy onto the fruit to cover it. Re-seal the jar and leave it for at least 6 months, at room temperature.

Strain off the liquid and siphon it into prepared bottles.

The liqueur may be drunk immediately, but is better if stored for at least 6 months.

Makes 1½ quarts.

turer's instructions for quantity and method of use). Replace the lid and leave for 7 days in a warm place (65–75°). During this period, stir once a day to ensure that all the fruit is kept moist. Do this quickly and always make sure the pail is firmly covered at all other times.

Using a fine sieve, strain off the liquid into a clean container. Put the remaining fruit pulp into a linen bag. Seal the bag tightly and squeeze out as much juice as possible into the same container. Stir in the sugar and quickly siphon into a prepared fermentation vessel, filling to within 1 inch of the cork. Leave to ferment under an air-lock in a warm place (65–75°). This will take approximately 3 weeks.

Rack, store for at least 6 months, and bottle in the usual way. It is advisable to keep this wine for at least a year before drinking.

See also page 205.

Makes 4½ quarts.

APRICOT JAM

Fruit that is too hard and unripe for eating fresh is perfect for jams.

3½ pounds slightly under-ripe fresh
* apricots*
Juice of 1 large lemon
1 teaspoon finely grated
* lemon rind*
6 cups sugar

Wash the apricots, pit them and put them through the coarse blade of a meat grinder. In a large kettle, combine the apricots with the lemon juice and rind, and stir in the sugar. Leave for an hour or two to allow sugar to draw out the apricot juices. (If there doesn't seem to be enough, you could add up to ¾ cup water.)

Place the pan over low heat and stir frequently until sugar has dissolved. Then raise heat, bring to boiling point and boil rapidly, stirring frequently, until jam has thickened and jell point is reached. Skim off any scum that forms on the surface.

Cool slightly, pack and process. See also page 198.

Fills about 5 jars.

APRICOT GLAZE

A few heaping tablespoons apricot
* preserve*
Lemon juice
Kirsch or brandy (optional)

Put the preserve into a small pan, taste, and if it seems too sweet, mix in some lemon juice. Add a little boiling water and heat gently, stirring, until runny. If you like, add some Kirsch or brandy to improve the flavor.

Rub the glaze through a sieve, and brush it on your tart while it is still warm and rather liquid.

AVOCADO

Until the Second World War, few Europeans had seen, let alone tasted, an avocado (also known as an alligator pear). Outside the tropics and subtropics, it was virtually unknown, although it has been cultivated for food since time immemorial. (In Mexico, traces of avocado have been found in excavations said to date back to at least 7,000 years BC.) However, in spite of its long history and culinary importance, cooks are still cautious about preparing it in any other than the most conventional, well-tried ways — with vinaigrette dressing or mayonnaise and seafood, meat or diced vegetables, as a creamy soup or a dip for *crudités* and salty crackers. Occasionally, they may venture into the world of Mexican cooking to try a *guacamole*, but few are aware how wonderful a really ripe avocado tastes when it is turned into a cream or ice cream.

An avocado may be small and oval or large and pear-shaped like its namesake. Its skin may be smooth and shiny or leathery and rough, varying from pale green to purple bordering on black. None of this affects its flavor. The flesh of a ripe avocado is always a pale golden green with a buttery texture and a rich, slightly nutty flavor. The skin should be unmarked (it spoils easily if bruised) and the avocado should feel heavy for its size. Once it has ripened, it will yield slightly to gentle pressure when cradled in the palms of your hands.

However, to facilitate transportation, avocados are usually harvested when still rock hard and arrive in the markets in this state. Once they soften they deteriorate rapidly, so it is far safer to buy them hard and ripen them at home. This will take a few days. Put them in a brown paper bag or a drawer or dark cupboard, and leave them at room temperature until they soften. They can then be held in this state for a few days at the bottom of the refrigerator.

There is only one real drawback to preparing avocados. Uncooked, they will soon turn an unappetizing shade of muddy brown if cut, peeled or puréed and left exposed to the air for any length of time. Discoloration will be slowed down by brushing the surface with lemon or lime juice as soon as it has been cut, but this will last for no more than a few hours. Alternatively, cover the cut surface tightly with plastic wrap and put it in the refrigerator. Treated in this way, an avocado half will keep reasonably well for several days.

A dish made with puréed avocado can also be stored tightly wrapped in the refrigerator. And some people maintain that a purée will stay pale and creamy indefinitely if it is stored with the avocado seed buried in it. But this is a far from reliable measure. The one sure solution to the problem of discoloration is to leave the preparation of an avocado to the very last moment.

Avocados have a high protein and vitamin content.

NOURISHING CREAM

Avocado oil, one of the most versatile beauty preparations, is obtainable from specialist shops. It can be used on its own as a hair conditioner, or as a cleanser or moisturizer; it blends well with fruit to make packs for dry skin, and revives dry, scaly skin when added to bathwater.

Thoroughly blend an egg yolk, a scant teaspoon of avocado oil, a few drops of glycerine and 1 teaspoon of runny honey. Add enough rosewater to make a creamy consistency. Store in the refrigerator.

MOISTURIZER

Because avocados contain so many vitamins, minerals and natural oils, they can be used to make a nourishing moisturizer for dry skins.

Thoroughly mash half an avocado with a little lemon juice and some gently heated almond oil. Apply to the face, and leave for about 20 minutes. Wash off with warm water.

AVOCADO HEALTH DRINK

This is almost a light meal in itself. The avocado is one of the most nutritious fruits, containing a large number of vitamins, minerals and natural oils. The use of an electric blender is essential.

Pulp of 1 large, ripe avocado
Juice and grated rind of 1 lemon
3 tablespoons honey
1 cup milk
2 tablespoons plain yogurt

Put all the ingredients into an electric blender and process until smooth. Taste. Add extra honey or salt, if necessary. If the consistency of the mixture is too thick, add extra milk. Serve chilled in a chilled glass.

Makes 1 large glass.

GUACAMOLE

Guacamole is one of the best-known Mexican contributions to gastronomy. Serve as a dip.

1 large, ripe avocado
1 ripe tomato
1 tablespoon finely chopped onion
1 tablespoon lemon juice
Salt

Peel avocado. Halve lengthwise, remove the seed and mash the pulp. Peel and seed the tomato, and mix with the avocado pulp. Add onion, lemon juice and salt and blend mixture in an electric blender.

Serves 4—6.

Note: The guacamole can be enriched with 1 tablespoon brewer's yeast and a dash of wheatgerm oil before blending.

Avocado Dip

1 large, ripe avocado
1 tablespoon lemon juice
1 teaspoon grated onion
½ small clove garlic, crushed
4–6 tablespoons sour cream or plain yogurt
1–2 tablespoons thick lemon mayonnaise (page 205)
Salt and white pepper

Peel and halve avocado, and remove seed. Cut avocado into chunks and place in the goblet of an electric blender. Immediately sprinkle with lemon juice, add remaining ingredients except for salt and pepper, and process to a smooth cream. Season to taste with salt and white pepper.

Pour into a serving bowl and serve. If dip has to wait for a short time, store the bowl, covered, in the refrigerator.

Serves 4–6, but any number of people if doubled in quantity, and served with other dips.

Avocado with Cream Cheese Dressing

2 large, ripe avocados
Lemon juice

Cream cheese dressing
4 ounces cream cheese
1–2 tablespoons light cream
1 tablespoon lemon juice or cider vinegar
1 teaspoon sugar
½ teaspoon celery salt

Prepare dressing first so there will be time to chill it lightly before use. Blend cheese smoothly with cream. Beat in remaining ingredients and adjust flavoring to taste. Chill lightly.

Shortly before serving, halve avocados lengthwise and remove seeds. Brush cut surfaces carefully all over with lemon juice to prevent discoloration.

Place avocado halves on individual serving dishes. Spoon some of the dressing into hollows and serve, with remaining dressing in a separate dish.

Serves 4.

Stuffed Avocados

6 large, ripe avocados
Lemon juice
Crisp lettuce leaves, for garnish
Lemon mayonnaise (page 205) for serving

Vegetable stuffing
6–8 tablespoons cooked corn
6–8 tablespoons cooked green peas
6–8 tablespoons diced cooked green beans
1 tablespoon finely chopped chives or green scallion tops
3–4 tablespoons thick lemon mayonnaise
Salt and freshly ground black pepper
2–3 drops hot pepper sauce

Peel avocados, cut them in half lengthwise and remove seeds. Brush them all over with lemon juice to prevent discoloration. Lay 2 avocado halves on each of 6 plates lined with crisp lettuce leaves.

Prepare vegetable stuffing. In a bowl, mix corn, peas and diced green beans together. Add chives or scallion tops, bind vegetables with mayonnaise and season to taste with salt, freshly ground black pepper and a few drops of hot pepper sauce.

Pile stuffing in cavities of avocados and top each half with a dollop of mayonnaise. Serve immediately.

Serves 6.

Creamed Avocado Soup

A rich, luxurious soup that will take only minutes to make in an electric blender or food processor.

2 large, ripe avocados
About 2 tablespoons lemon juice
1 quart chilled chicken broth
Salt and white pepper
Hot pepper sauce
¾ cup whipping cream, chilled
Finely chopped chives, chervil or green scallion tops for garnish

Halve the avocados lengthwise, remove seeds and peel them. Cut one half into thin slivers or neat cubes. Brush them carefully all over with about 1 tablespoon lemon juice to stop them discoloring and put aside.

Combine the remaining avocado halves, lemon juice and chicken broth in the goblet of an electric blender or food processor, and process to a smooth purée. Season to taste with salt, a pinch of white pepper and a few drops of pepper sauce. Blend in the chilled cream and pour into a chilled soup tureen. Stir in the reserved avocado slices or cubes and taste for seasoning.

Cover the tureen and chill the soup until ready to serve.

Serve in chilled soup bowls, each portion garnished with finely chopped fresh herbs.

Serves 4–6.

CHILLED AVOCADO SOUP

3 small, ripe avocados
Lemon juice
¾ cup sour cream or thick plain
  yogurt
1¼ cups jellied chicken or
  beef broth
4 ripe tomatoes
¼ cup finely chopped scallions
Salt
2–3 drops hot pepper sauce
Finely chopped chives or scallion
  tops for garnish

Halve avocados lengthwise and remove seeds. Peel avocados. Cut one of them into small, neat dice and immediately toss with 1 or 2 tablespoons lemon juice to prevent discoloration. Chop remaining avocados coarsely. In an electric blender or food processor, blend chopped avocados with sour cream or yogurt until smooth. Gradually blend in broth.

Peel and seed tomatoes. Cut one of them into small cubes and add it to the blended avocado. Chop remainder and blend into soup.

Pour soup into a large bowl. Stir in cubed avocado and tomato, together with their juices, and finely chopped scallions. Season to taste with salt, a few drops of pepper sauce and a little more lemon juice if liked. Chill well before serving.

This is a thick, rich soup. Serve small portions in chilled soup bowls, garnished with chopped chives or green scallion tops.

Serves 6.

Note: If you find the soup too thick for your taste, thin it down with a little tomato juice or more broth.

VEAL ROLLS WITH HAM AND AVOCADO

A perfect dish for spring, quite light in itself but also very suitable should the weather turn chilly. Serve with rice or a potato purée and a large, tossed green salad. The best mustard to use for this dish is a coarsely ground brown French mustard such as Moutarde de Meaux, but any spicy French mustard, coarse or smooth, will do very well.

8 small veal scaloppine (about 1½
  pounds)
8 small slices prosciutto (raw Parma
  ham) or thinly sliced lean cooked
  ham
Coarse French mustard
2–3 tablespoons butter
6–8 tablespoons chicken broth or dry
  white wine
1 large, ripe avocado
¾ cup thick cream
Salt and white pepper
Sieved hard-cooked egg yolk for
  garnish (optional)

Trim veal scaloppines and pound them as thinly as possible without tearing them. Trim prosciutto or ham slices to fit veal, leaving a narrow border all around. Spread each scaloppine with ½ to 1 teaspoon French mustard. Top with a slice of prosciutto or ham, roll up tightly and secure each roll with a couple of short wooden toothpicks.

In a deep, heavy skillet or flameproof casserole with a tight-fitting lid, brown veal rolls all over in butter over moderate heat. Add chicken broth or wine, stirring and scraping bottom of pan clean with a wooden spoon. Cover pan tightly and cook gently for 20–30 minutes until veal is quite tender. Give pan a shake now and again so that veal rolls do not stick.

While veal is cooking, peel and seed avocado, and slice it thinly. Remove veal rolls to a heated serving dish. Keep hot. Blend cream into pan juices. Carefully stir in avocado slices and continue to cook for a minute or two longer to heat them through. Taste sauce for seasoning, adding a pinch of salt or white pepper if needed.

Discard toothpicks from veal rolls. Surround them with avocado slices and pour cream sauce over the entire dish.

Decorate with sieved hard-cooked egg yolk if used and serve.

Serves 4.

EGGS WITH AVOCADO SAUCE

An unusual and very attractive supper dish that also makes a good appetizer.

2 large, ripe avocados
2 teaspoons cornstarch
¼ cup light cream or creamy milk
Salt and white pepper
Few drops of hot pepper sauce
8 eggs, hard-cooked
Fried croûtons (page 205)
  for garnish

Halve, seed and peel avocados, and either process them in an electric blender or food processor, or rub through a nylon sieve.

In a medium-sized pan, blend cornstarch smoothly with cream or milk. Beat in avocado purée. Bring to boiling point, stirring constantly, and simmer, stirring, for 4 or 5 minutes until sauce has thickened and no longer tastes starchy. Season to taste with salt, white pepper and a few drops of hot pepper sauce.

Shell eggs (hot), cut them in half lengthwise and arrange cut side up on a heated serving dish. Spoon avocado cream sauce over the top, garnish dish with the crisp fried croûtons and serve.

Serves 4 as a supper dish, up to 8 as an appetizer.

AVOCADO SALAD

¾ cup vinaigrette dressing made with
  a mild cider or white wine vinegar
Salt and freshly ground black pepper
2 large, ripe avocados
Lettuce leaves for garnish

Pour dressing ingredients into a bowl and season with salt and freshly ground black pepper, beating vigorously to make an emulsion.

Peel avocados, slice them in half lengthwise and remove seeds. Cut avocados into long, thin slices or large dice, dropping them into the bowl of vinaigrette as you do so. Mix lightly but thoroughly, making sure that pieces of avocado are coated on all sides with dressing.

Line a serving bowl with crisp green lettuce leaves and pour avocados and their dressing into the center. Serve immediately.

Serves 6.

Avocado Pilaf

Serve this unusual pilaf with broiled or roast lamb and poultry.

Rice
1 small onion, finely chopped
¼ cup butter
1½ cups long-grain rice
3–4 tablespoons dry vermouth
3½ cups hot, well-seasoned chicken
    broth

Avocado mushroom garnish
¼ pound button mushrooms
3 tablespoons butter
1 medium-size firm tomato
⅛ teaspoon dried oregano
Garlic salt
Freshly ground black pepper
1 large avocado
About 1 tablespoon
    lemon juice

In a heavy, flameproof casserole which has a tight-fitting lid, sauté the onion gently in butter until soft and transparent but not colored. Stir in the rice and continue to sauté, stirring, until each grain is shiny and individually coated with butter. Add the vermouth and broth, mix well and bring to boiling point. Cover.

Transfer the casserole to a pre-heated 400° oven and bake for about 20 minutes until the rice has absorbed all the liquid, leaving the grains moist but separate.

Meanwhile, prepare the garnish. Trim and slice the mushrooms, and sauté in 2 tablespoons butter for a few minutes until lightly colored but still firm. Peel, seed and dice the tomato. Add it to the pan, together with a sprinkling of oregano, garlic salt and black pepper to taste. Simmer for 4 or 5 minutes longer, making sure tomato does not disintegrate.

While vegetables are simmering, peel, halve, seed and dice the avocado neatly, and toss gently but thoroughly with lemon juice to prevent discoloration.

Stir avocado into simmering garnish, remove from heat and put aside, covered.

When ready to serve pilaf, add garnish, together with its juices, and the remaining butter, and toss gently with a large fork until thoroughly mixed.

Allow to stand for a minute or two before serving.

Serves 6.

Note: The temperature at which the rice cooks is not crucial.

If there are other dishes in the oven requiring a lower temperature, it may take a little longer for the rice to absorb the broth but it will certainly come to no harm.

Avocado Ice Cream

Provided the avocado used is very soft and ripe, this recipe will make an unusual ice cream with a subtle, light flavor and a beautiful, jade-green color.

1 large, very ripe avocado
¼ cup fresh lime juice
5 tablespoons sugar
¾ cup heavy cream

Peel and seed avocado, and cut it into chunks. Put them in an electric blender or food processor with lime juice and sugar, and process to a smooth purée. In a large bowl, whip cream until thick.

Gradually beat in avocado purée, and continue to beat until light and fluffy. Taste and beat in a little more lime juice or sugar if necessary, bearing in mind that freezing the mixture will modify flavors.

Pour mixture into ice cube trays or a shallow freezer container. Cover with foil or a lid and freeze until ice cream is solid around sides but still soft in the middle.

Scrape ice cream into bowl again and beat until it is uniformly smooth and creamy. Then pour it back into container(s) and freeze again until firm.

Transfer ice cream to refrigerator to soften slightly about 1 hour before serving.

Serve small portions with delicate shortbread cookies.

Serves 6.

Avocado Lime Cream

This is simple and quick to make, and quite sensationally good and pretty, but only when made with very ripe avocados and juicy fresh limes. Lemons would be too harshly acid. Serve in small portions (the cream is rich), accompanied by a dish of *langues de chat* or delicate shortbread cookies.

2 large, ripe avocados
6 tablespoons sugar
Juice of 2 limes

Peel avocados. Halve them lengthwise, remove seeds and cut avocados into chunks. Put these in an electric blender or food processor. Sprinkle with sugar and lime juice, and process to a creamy

Put purée in a bowl or plastic box and cover tightly. Chill thoroughly until ready to serve.

Serves 3–4.

Avocado Butter

Use this as you would ordinary butter – as a spread for bread or toast, or as a sauce for broiled or fried fish.

1 large, ripe avocado
Lemon juice (optional)
1 tablespoon oil
1 tablespoon ground cumin, or to
    taste
1 teaspoon salt
Pinch of cayenne

Halve, seed and peel avocado. Cut into chunks and sprinkle with lemon juice. Mash to a paste with a fork (or process in an electric blender or food processor) together with remaining ingredients. If you are not using it immediately, pack into a small dish, cover and store in refrigerator.

BANANA

Alexander the Great is known to have come across bananas on his travels to India and subsequently, thanks to conquerors and explorers, the banana plant spread throughout the tropical world, both Old and New. In Europe and temperate America, however, bananas were to remain virtually unknown until the 1890s, when the first refrigerated ships were developed to transport them safely over long distances. Today, it would be hard to imagine a fruit stall without a generous supply of bananas.

Of all the fruits from the tropics, bananas are one of only a few that should be harvested while they are still green and immature, then allowed to finish ripening *off* the plant. If they are left to ripen fully on the plant, they will develop a rather strong, unpleasant flavor. We, the customers, often make the mistake of using the fruit before it is fully ripe, not realizing that a skin lightly speckled with brown is a sign of ripeness and certainly does not mean that the banana is going bad. In fact, you will often find the best-flavored and most velvety textured banana inside a skin that is almost black. The best advice would be to buy bananas that are "unblemished" by all means but then to let them finish ripening and lose any green tints at room temperature (*not* in the refrigerator) before you eat them. The only exceptions are bananas which are going to be cooked (the cooking makes them easy to digest and brings out their flavor). In some areas, you will come across plantains. These look just like large, hard, green bananas but their sugar content is far lower than that of dessert bananas and they are used exclusively for cooking.

When using bananas, there are only a couple of points to bear in mind. Once it has been peeled and cut up, a banana soon starts turning brown, but this process can be slowed down by sprinkling it with lemon juice or some other acid fruit juice such as orange or grapefruit.

The other point to remember when making fruit salads is not to add the bananas too far in advance as prolonged soaking turns them unpleasantly slimy and spongy.

Bananas are not suitable for turning into preserves such as jams, nor are they good frozen, unless they have been made into ice cream. They are delicious made into drinks. Otherwise, the only preserved bananas you are likely to come across are dried ones, which make a rather sticky, sweet snack.

Bananas are exceptionally nutritious, high in proteins, vitamins and minerals. Easily digested, they are ideal for convalescents who are not allowed to eat rich foods, and babies can be given mashed bananas as an introduction to solid food.

HEALTH SHAKE

A standard milk shake recipe, in which you can use any other fruit. Bananas make a sweet, creamy shake.

1 cup milk
1 large banana (not too ripe), peeled
    and coarsely chopped
2 tablespoons plain yogurt
1 tablespoon honey
Pinch of grated nutmeg

Put all the ingredients into an electric blender and process until smooth. Add extra milk if the consistency is too thick to pour easily. Taste. If a slightly less sweet drink is preferred, stir in a teaspoon of lemon juice. Serve chilled in a chilled glass.

Makes 1 large glass.

FACE PACK

Because of their soft, vitamin-rich flesh, bananas make an excellent moisturizing and nourishing pack for dry skins.

Mash a fresh banana with enough oil (olive, safflower, peanut, avocado or almond) to make a spreadable paste. Clean your face thoroughly then pat the paste over your face and neck, avoiding the area under the eyes. Leave on for about 20 minutes, then wash off very gently with warm water.

BANANA CHIPS

There are several ways of making banana chips, coming from as far apart as Africa and South America, but they are all quite similar. Either plantains, or hard, unripe bananas with a greenish tinge, are used. Bowls of these are bound to create a sensation at a cocktail party.

Peel bananas (or plantains) and slice them into rounds about ½ inch thick. Drop them into a bowl of iced salted water and let them soak for about 30 minutes.

Drain slices and pat them dry with paper towels.

Heat a pan of vegetable oil to 375°. Fry banana slices until crisp and golden. They should be floating freely in the oil. Do not overcrowd the pan or they will clump together. Drain thoroughly on paper towels once more and serve very fresh, sprinkled with salt.

In a slightly more elaborate version, the bananas or plaintains are fried twice for extra crispness, rather like French fries. This time, slice them 1½ inches thick. Heat the oil to a slightly cooler temperature, at 325°. Deep-fry slices for 4 or 5 minutes until they are soft but still very pale. Drain thoroughly and dip in iced salted water as above.

Drain again and pat dry.

Lay slices in a single layer, well spaced apart, on a sheet of wax paper and cover with another sheet. With a rolling pin, gently but firmly roll the slices out to a thickness of about ¾ inch.

Now heat oil to 375° and fry flattened banana slices briefly until crisp and golden. They will be ready in about 1 minute. Drain thoroughly on crumpled paper towels. Sprinkle with salt and serve.

CHICKEN WITH BANANAS

Serve this Brazilian dish with fluffy white rice and follow with a crisp green salad.

1 roaster chicken, about 3 pounds
¼ cup lemon juice
Salt
¼ cup butter
1 medium-size onion, very finely chopped
2 large tomatoes, peeled, seeded and chopped
⅛ teaspoon sugar
1¼ cups dry white wine
6 firm, ripe bananas
¼ cup vegetable (corn) oil
1 cup grated Parmesan, or half Parmesan and half Swiss, or any other good melting cheese

Cut up chicken into 8 pieces, 2 from each breast and 2 from each leg.

On a large platter, rub the pieces with lemon juice and sprinkle them lightly with salt.

In a heavy, flameproof casserole, melt 3 tablespoons butter and add the onion, tomatoes and sugar. (With fresh tomatoes which may have little flavor, I also like to add a couple of teaspoons of tomato paste.) Simmer for a minute or two, then add chicken pieces and any lemon juice that might have drained off them, turning them over to coat them in sauce. Simmer, uncovered, for 5 minutes. Then pour in wine and slowly bring to simmering point again. Cover and cook gently until chicken is tender, about 35 minutes.

Meanwhile, peel bananas and halve them lengthwise. In a large, heavy skillet, brown bananas lightly on both sides in hot oil. Drain pieces well on paper towels.

When chicken is cooked through, arrange the pieces of banana on top, cut side down. Sprinkle with grated cheese. (I sometimes use a mixture of grated cheese and stale white bread crumbs.) Dot with remaining butter, flaked. Place in a preheated 400° oven and bake for 10 minutes, or until the topping is bubbling and golden.

Serves 4.

BANANA WALDORF

A variation of the popular Waldorf apple salad, to be served with main-course meat and poultry dishes.

6 medium-size tart, red-skinned apples
3 large, ripe bananas
2 large stalks celery
6–8 tablespoons chopped walnuts
About 1¼ cups lemon mayonnaise (page 205)
Lettuce leaves for garnish

Quarter, core and dice unpeeled apples into a large bowl. Peel bananas, slice them into thin rounds and add them to bowl. Finely chop celery stalks and add them to bowl, together with chopped walnuts. Toss lightly but thoroughly with a large fork.

Add mayonnaise and mix gently until pieces of fruit are individually coated (to protect them from discoloration). Chill lightly before serving. Serve in a bowl lined with crisp green lettuce leaves.

Serves 6.

BANANAS AND ONIONS

An unusual side dish to serve with pork, ham and veal dishes, especially roasts.

4 large, firm bananas
2 large sweet, mild onions
2 tablespoons butter
Salt
Lemon juice

Peel bananas and cut into thick rounds. Peel and slice onions thickly, and separate rings.

In a large skillet, sauté onions gently in the butter until about half-cooked, ie soft and transparent but not colored. Add sliced bananas and fry for about 10 minutes longer, turning contents of skillet over and over so that banana slices color on both sides.

Season lightly with salt. Sprinkle with lemon juice and serve hot.

Serves 4.

BROILED BANANAS

Butter
2 large, firm bananas
3 tablespoons orange juice
1 teaspoon lemon juice
2 tablespoons dark brown sugar
1–2 tablespoons blanched slivered
   almonds for decoration

Take a heatproof, shallow dish that can go to the table and grease lightly with butter. Peel bananas and halve them lengthwise. Arrange in baking dish. Mix orange and lemon juices together, and sprinkle over bananas, turning them to coat them thoroughly on all sides. Sprinkle with sugar and dot with flakes of butter. Broil bananas until sugar has melted and top is bubbling. Then scatter all over with slivered almonds and continue to broil until they are lightly toasted.

Serve hot.

Serves 4.

BANANES BRÛLÉES

Fold an equal volume of ripe mashed banana, sprinkled with a little lemon juice, into a bowl of whipped cream and flavor to taste with vanilla. The cream will probably need no sweetening if the puréed bananas were really ripe, bearing in mind that there is sugar to come for the topping.

Have the broiler preheated very hot. Spoon cream mixture into a flameproof dish, preferably one without a rim (eg a conventional soufflé dish). Sift a thick layer of dark brown sugar evenly over the top.

Broil the dish of banana cream until the sugar has melted into a glassy sheet.

Leave until cold and hard, and chill until ready to serve.

BANANA CREAM PIE

3 large, ripe bananas
Juice of 1 large lemon
One 8 or 9 inch rich pie pastry case,
   pre-baked (page 203)
¾ cup heavy cream
Angelica sprigs for decoration
   (optional)

Cream filling
2 tablespoons flour
2 tablespoons cornstarch
½ cup sugar
⅛ teaspoon salt
2 cups milk
3 large egg yolks
½–1 teaspoon vanilla
1 tablespoon butter

Start by preparing the cream filling. In a heavy pan, mix the first 4 ingredients together and blend in the milk. Stir over low heat until mixture comes to boiling point, then continue to simmer, stirring constantly, until it thickens and loses any floury taste.

In a bowl, beat egg yolks lightly. Blend in a few tablespoons of the hot milk mixture, then beat back into remaining mixture in pan and stir over low heat until it thickens. Do not let it boil again at this stage as egg yolks may curdle. Remove pan from heat and cool slightly before beating in vanilla and butter. Leave until cold, covered with a disk of parchment paper to prevent a skin forming on top.

Peel bananas. Cut them in slices about ¼ inch thick and toss them with lemon juice.

Assemble pie as follows. Spread half of the cream filling in the pre-baked pastry case. Cover surface with banana slices and top with remaining filling.

Whip cream and use it to decorate top of pie. Finish decoration by studding top with small sprigs of candied angelica, if available. Chill lightly for 30 minutes before serving.

Serves 6–8.

BANANAS WITH RASPBERRY SAUCE

4 firm, ripe bananas
3 tablespoons butter
1 tablespoon dark brown sugar
2 tablespoons orange liqueur

Raspberry sauce
¾ pound frozen raspberries
2 tablespoons orange liqueur
About 2 tablespoons confectioners'
   sugar

Start by preparing raspberry sauce. Leave raspberries at room temperature until partially thawed and softened. Process in an electric blender or food processor, then rub through a fine nylon sieve, and discard seeds. Beat in liqueur and sweeten to taste with confectioners' sugar. Pour sauce into a large pitcher.

Peel bananas and cut them in half lengthwise. In a skillet that will hold banana halves in one layer, melt butter. Add sugar and stir over gentle heat until it has melted. Lay bananas in buttery syrup flat side down and fry gently for about 3 minutes. Then turn them over and continue to fry for 3 minutes longer.

Pour raspberry sauce all over bananas and heat through gently. At the same time, warm remaining liqueur in a large metal serving spoon or ladle. When raspberry sauce is hot, put a match to the warmed liqueur and as soon as flames are well established, pour it over the pan. Serve immediately, before flames go out.

Serves 4.

BANANA CHEESE

2 large, ripe bananas
Lemon juice
1 cup cottage cheese
About 3 tablespoons sugar

Peel bananas and slice into thin rounds. Sprinkle with lemon juice to keep them from turning brown. In a bowl, beat cheese until fluffy, using an electric mixer if available.

Beat in sugar to taste, a tablespoon at a time.

Gently mix in bananas. Pile into a glass serving dish and chill lightly for about 1 hour before serving.

Serves 4.

BANANA ICE CREAM

Delicious with a sprinkling of chopped nuts, coarsely grated dark chocolate or macaroon crumbs.

3 large, very ripe bananas
½ cup sugar
⅛ teaspoon salt
¾–1 tablespoon fresh lime or lemon juice
1 teaspoon vanilla
1¼ cups heavy cream
¾ cup light cream

Peel bananas. Pull off and discard any stringy fibers, and cut bananas into chunks. Put them in an electric blender or food processor, together with sugar, salt, lime or lemon juice and vanilla, and process to a smooth purée. Taste and add more sugar, lime or lemon juice if necessary, bearing in mind that freezing will modify flavors.

In a large bowl, whip creams together until they thicken but not enough to make the mixture stiff enough to form peaks. Fold in banana purée. Pour mixture into ice cube trays or a shallow freezer container, cover tightly with a sheet of foil or lid, and freeze until ice cream is frozen hard around sides but still soft in the middle.

Scrape ice cream into a bowl and beat mixture vigorously until it is uniformly smooth and creamy again. Then pour it back into freezing container(s), cover and freeze until firm. Transfer ice cream to refrigerator to soften at least 1 hour before you are ready to serve.

Serve with crisp cookies.

Serves 4.

SPICED BANANA BREAD

6 tablespoons butter or soft margarine
½ cup sugar
1 pound ripe bananas
1 egg
2 cups flour
2 teaspoons baking powder
1 teaspoon ground cinnamon
½ teaspoon salt
About 3 tablespoons plain yogurt

Beat butter or margarine until creamy. Gradually beat in sugar and continue to beat until white and fluffy. Peel and mash bananas smoothly. Beat egg until fluffy. Gradually add banana pulp to creamed butter and sugar, followed by beaten egg, beating vigorously all the time.

Sift flour with baking powder, cinnamon and salt. Lightly mix flour into creamed ingredients alternately with yogurt to make a soft batter.

Pour batter into a well-greased, 9 × 5 inch loaf pan and bake in a preheated 350° oven for about 1 hour, or until loaf shrinks away slightly from sides of pan and is firm to the touch and lightly colored on top. Leave in the pan for about 10 minutes before unmolding onto a wire cooling rack. Slice when cold.

ORACABESSA

2 tablespoons crème de banane
1 tablespoon lemon juice
2 tablespoons dark rum
1 tablespoon crushed ice
½ banana, peeled and finely sliced
7-Up
Maraschino cherries for decoration

Put the liqueur, lemon juice, rum and ice into a cocktail shaker. Shake the ingredients together vigorously. Pour into a tall, chilled glass, place the sliced banana on top and add 7-Up to fill.

Decorate with maraschino cherries and serve.

Makes 1 large glass.

BANANA DAIQUIRI

¼ cup white rum
1 tablespoon crème de banane
1 tablespoon lime juice
½ banana, peeled and chopped
1 tablespoon crushed ice

Put all the ingredients into an electric blender and process until smooth and frothy. Serve in a tulip champagne glass.

Makes 1 glass.

BANANA WINE

Use black or spotted bananas for this sweet, spicy table wine.

3 pounds bananas (with skins)
7 cups sugar
1 teaspoon ground cloves
1 teaspoon ground ginger
½ ounce citric acid
1 Campden tablet
1 teaspoon pectic enzyme
1 quart strong tea
1 yeast nutrient tablet
Liebfraumilch yeast

Bring 3½ quarts water to boiling point in a large pan. Meanwhile prepare the bananas. Do not remove their skins, but slice them thinly and put into the prepared vessel (such as a plastic pail). Add the sugar, cloves, ginger and boiling water. Stir to dissolve the sugar. When the mixture is cool, add the citric acid, the Campden tablet and the pectic enzyme. Cover the vessel tightly and leave for 24 hours.

Uncover and quickly add the strong tea, followed by the nutrient tablet and activated yeast (see manufacturer's instructions for quantity and method of use). Re-cover the vessel and leave in a warm place (65–75°) for 10 days. Once a day, quickly remove the cover and push down any fruit that is floating on the surface.

Strain the mixture through a fine sieve into a clean container, extracting as much liquid as possible. It will be a rather cloudy liquid. Siphon this into a prepared fermentation vessel, filling to within 1 inch of the cork. Leave to ferment in a warm place (65–75°). This will take approximately 5–6 weeks. Leave until there is a good layer of sediment at the bottom, then rack. Store for 6 months before bottling. Keep for at least a year before drinking – the longer the better.

See also page 205.

Makes about 1 gallon.

BLACKBERRY

Blackberries have flourished wild for centuries. Blackberry seeds have even been found in the remains of a Neolithic man dug up in Essex, England. Possibly because of this, commercial growers have been reluctant to cultivate large fields of blackberry canes, preferring to rely on wild ones. They are late to ripen compared with other soft fruits, starting in late summer.

When you go picking wild blackberries, take a pair of thick gloves to protect your fingers against the thorns, which can be vicious. Some cultivated varieties have had the thorns bred out of them and cultivated berries also tend to be larger, with fewer seeds.

Blackberries should be washed only if necessary. You can eat them raw with plenty of sugar and cream, or instead of cream, flavor them with fresh orange juice. Alternatively, add a handful of shiny fresh berries to a mixed fruit salad, or bake them in a pie or open tart. Mixed with apples or pears, which start coming into season at the same time, they make an excellent baked pudding, topped with sponge and served with a custard sauce or cream. Or why not invent your own version of an English summer pudding, with blackberries and wedges of poached apple instead of the usual soft fruit, and call it autumn pudding? There is also a curious old English sweet called blackberry junket for which sweetened blackberry juice is allowed to stand in a warm atmosphere until it sets to the consistency of a light junket.

Above all, though, blackberries are for making preserves such as jams and jellies, either on their own or in conjunction with apples for their pectin. If you are making jam or jelly with blackberries only, use any standard raspberry recipe but be sure to include plenty of lemon juice for its setting properties.

Whole blackberries can be dry or sugar frozen; or the berries can be puréed and sweetened with sugar before freezing.

Medicinally, the valuable parts of the blackberry plant are the roots and leaves (infusions of which help cure dropsy and diarrhea), although the berries contain some folic acid and Vitamins C and E.

REMEDIES

An infusion of leaves helps to relieve diarrhea. Put torn or cut up blackberry leaves into a glass, ceramic or stainless steel container. Allow a cup of water to every tablespoon of leaves. Bring the water to a boil, pour it over the leaves, and leave to stand, covered, for 2½–3 hours. Strain. Drink up to a cup a day, a little at a time. (This infusion can also be added to bathwater to bring clearness and vitality to your skin.)

An infusion of the root has much the same properties as that of the leaf, and is also reputed to be good for dropsy. Allow a cup of water to each tablespoon of chopped root, and put in a stainless steel saucepan. Bring to a gentle boil, covered, and simmer for 1–3 hours. Strain and drink as above.

BREAKFAST CRUNCH

Ingredients in this recipe are measured in standard measuring cups, but you can use any size container provided the proportions remain the same. The quantities below make enough for about 20 servings — which can be stored in an airtight container.

2 cups wheat bran
2 cups rolled oats
1¼ cups sesame seeds
1¼ cups sunflower seeds
1 cup wholewheat flour
½ cup skimmed milk powder
¼ cup firmly packed brown sugar
½ cup nut oil
Blackberries
Milk (optional)

Mix together the wheat bran, oats, sesame and sunflower seeds, flour, skimmed milk powder, sugar and nut oil and store. Add blackberries, and milk if liked, just before serving.

BLACKBERRY SOUP

This soup can be served either hot or cold.

1 pound (3 pints) blackberries
3 slices stale bread
1 short cinnamon stick
3–4 whole cloves
About ½ cup sugar
¾ cup thick cream
Cinnamon croûtons for serving (page 205)

Rinse blackberries and put them in a pan with the sliced bread and whole spices. Pour over about 1 quart hot water and simmer until blackberries are very soft. Add a little more water if it evaporates too quickly. Rub contents of pan through a fine nylon sieve and discard seeds and spices. Sweeten to taste and stir in cream. Serve hot or lightly chilled, with cinnamon croûtons.

Serves 6.

BLACKBERRY ORANGE MOUSSE

1 pound (3 pints) blackberries
juice and grated rind of 1 orange
½ cup sugar
2 envelopes unflavored gelatin
1¼ cups heavy cream

Put blackberries in a dish. Add orange juice and rind. Sprinkle with sugar, mix well and put aside for a couple of hours to allow sugar to draw out juices. At the same time, soften gelatin by sprinkling it over 3 tablespoons cold water in a cup.

When ready to proceed, rub blackberries and their juices through a fine nylon sieve and discard seeds. Dissolve gelatin by standing cup in a bowl of very hot water and stirring until liquid is quite clear. Whip cream until it stands in soft peaks. Whisk dissolved gelatin into cold blackberry purée, wait until mixture turns syrupy, then fold into whipped cream. Spoon into a serving bowl and chill lightly until softly set.

Serves 4.

BLACKBERRY CUSTARD TART

One 9 inch pie pastry case, pre-baked
 (page 203)
1 pound (3 pints) blackberries
⅔ cup firmly packed light brown
 sugar
2 egg yolks
4 teaspoons cornstarch
1¼ cups light cream

Leave pre-baked pastry case to cool still in its pan (preferably one with a removable base).

Toss blackberries and sugar together lightly with a fork. Distribute fruit evenly in pastry case. Beat egg yolks and cornstarch together until well blended. Lightly beat in cream. Pour through a sieve over entire surface of tart. Bake tart in a preheated 325° oven for about 30 minutes, or until filling has set. This is best eaten lukewarm or cold.

Serves 6.

BLACKBERRY AND APPLE JAM

By the time fall comes around, there are not many fresh fruits left for the dedicated jam-maker. This is when blackberries come along, covering woody pathways and lanes.

4 pounds (12 pints) blackberries
1½ pounds apples
About 10 cups sugar

Pick over and if necessary rinse blackberries briefly. Put them in a pan with ¾ cup water and cook gently, stirring and mashing occasionally with a wooden spoon, until blackberries are very soft and pulpy. If you want to remove the blackberry seeds, rub cooked blackberries and their juices through a fine nylon sieve before mixing with the apples.

While blackberries are cooking, peel, core and thinly slice apples. Put them in a separate pan with ¾ cup water and simmer until apples have disintegrated to a pulp, mashing and stirring occasionally.

Combine pulped blackberries and apples, measure them and pour into a preserving kettle. Add the same quantity of sugar as there is of mixed fruit. Stir over low heat until sugar has melted. Then raise heat and boil briskly until jell point is reached. Skim off any scum that has collected on the surface toward the end of cooking time.

Cool slightly, pack and process.
See also page 198.

Fills about 8 jars.

BLACKBERRY WINE

6 pounds (18 pints) blackberries
1½ cups chopped raisins
1 Campden tablet
1 teaspoon pectic enzyme
1 yeast nutrient tablet
Burgundy wine yeast
5 cups sugar

Remove the stalks and wash the berries thoroughly in a colander under cold running water. Place in the prepared vessel (such as a plastic pail). Add the chopped raisins, the Campden tablet, pectic enzyme and 1 gallon cold water. Cover the pail and leave it in a warm place (65°) for 24 hours.

Uncover and quickly add the nutrient tablet and the activated yeast (see manufacturer's instructions for quantity and method of use). Recover and leave in a warm place (65–75°) for 7 days.

Using a fine sieve strain off the liquid into a clean container. Put the remaining fruit pulp into a linen bag. Seal the bag and press the pulp to extract as much juice as possible. Add this to the liquid. Stir in sugar.

Siphon the mixture into a prepared fermentation vessel, filling to within 1 inch of the cork. Ferment under an air-lock in a warm, dark place (65–75°).

Rack, store for at least 6 months in a dark place, then siphon into dark glass bottles. Mature for 2 years.
See also page 205.

Makes about 1 gallon.

BLACK CURRANT

It may come as a surprise that, botanically speaking, black currants are more closely related to gooseberries than to the red or white currants one usually associates with them. The history of black currants is a curious mixture of failure and success. Although they are actively discouraged in parts of the United States (on the grounds that black currant bushes are thought to carry a disease that affects pine trees), in the cooler, damper regions of Western Europe there will scarcely be a fruit garden that does not include a few black currant bushes.

The peak of their popularity was reached in the last century around Dijon in Burgundy, with the invention of *crème de cassis*, a rich, dark black currant liqueur which is either drunk on its own, added for color and flavor to fruit salads, creams and candies, or mixed with chilled white wine, preferably a white Burgundy, to make a refreshing summer drink called *Kir*.

Unless they are very ripe indeed, raw black currants are too astringently sour to eat as they are, but this rather bitter sourness disappears when the fruit is cooked, especially if a little spice is added. All kinds of pies can be made with black currants on their own or mixed with other fruit, such as apples. There are also other desserts that are well worth trying.

Black currants really come into their own for making preserves. Jams and jellies made with black currants are pectin-rich and set without difficulty. In fact, plenty of water must be added, otherwise the jam will set rock-hard before the fruit has had a chance to soften. Black currant juice is bursting with vitamins, especially Vitamin C, and often more suitable than orange juice for young children as it is more easily digested. If you make it yourself, you will be able to control the sweeteners and other additives that go into commercial preparations. Black currants have long been noted for their beneficial effect on sore throats, coughs, feverish colds and tonsillitis.

Black currants should be dry, bright and quite firm to the touch when they come off the bush. Even then, they should be used as quickly as possible. If a basket of ripe, juicy fruit is left overnight, chances are that mold will form and spread like wildfire so that by the following day the fruit will be unfit to use.

Keep fruit on the stalks until you are ready to use it. To remove the stalks, hold a bunch of fruit in one hand and use a fork to strip off the berries.

If at all possible, a surplus of black currants should be stored in the freezer; remove the stalks and pack in freezer bags or rigid cartons. If space is limited, some of your surplus crop may first be puréed by putting ripe fruit through a vegetable mill with a little water, or by blending briefly and rubbing through a sieve to trap seeds and pieces of skin. Then pack in small portions for the freezer. This purée is very strong and will probably need diluting with more water or fruit juice when you come to use it (orange juice goes very well with black currants).

Sweeten the purée with confectioners' sugar and use it as a sauce for desserts or a topping for a plain or chocolate ice cream.

BLACK CURRANT JUICE

This is a marvelously pure, healthy drink – rich in Vitamin C and free of any additives – to have in the winter pantry. Children are particularly keen on it. For winter coughs and colds, it makes a soothing bedtime drink, diluted with hot water and sweetened with more honey, and in summer all it needs is iced water or soda water or 7-Up and ice cubes, to make a refreshing thirst-quencher.

Rinse, drain and strip black currants. Put them in a large kettle, cover generously with water and bring slowly to boiling point. Simmer fruit until very soft, crushing and mashing it with a potato masher or a large fork. Alternatively, put the contents of the pan through the finest disk of a vege-table mill. Do not liquidize or blend it in any way that crushes the seeds and makes the juice bitter.

Strain the juice through fine cheesecloth or nylon, squeezing it well to extract as much of the liquid as possible. Sweeten lightly to taste with honey, fruit sugar or plain white sugar.

Have ready individual soda bottles with screw-top caps, thoroughly clean and sterilized in the same way as canning jars (page 201). Funnel the juice into them, filling the bottles right to the top if the juice is hot, but leaving about 1 inch head space for it to expand if it is cold. Screw on caps, not too tightly.

Fit a trivet into the pan in which bottles are to be sterilized or, failing a suitable trivet, line the bottom with thick cardboard, a folded cloth or several thicknesses of newspaper. Fit bottles side by side in the pan and pour in hot water to come at least three-quarters of the way up sides of bottles. Bring to simmering point and boil gently for 20–25 minutes.

Allow pan to cool slightly. Then, protecting your hands with a cloth, lift out the bottles one at a time and screw the caps down tightly. When cold, store in a dark cupboard.

Note: Raspberries and black cherries make good juice, but use much less water to boil the fruit so that the flavor of the juice will not be too diluted.

BLACK CURRANT PIE

Use rough puff pastry for a black currant (or any other currant) pie. To help avoid the base soaking up too much of the juices before the cornstarch has had the opportunity to thicken them, it is a good idea to stand the pie on a baking sheet that was put in the oven to heat up when you switched on.

1¼ pounds (2½ pints) black currants, washed, drained and stripped
1⅓ cups firmly packed brown sugar
3 tablespoons cornstarch
⅛ teaspoon ground cloves
Pinch of salt
About 1 pound rough puff pastry for 2-crust 9 inch pie (page 203 and above)
1 tablespoon softened butter
Sifted granulated or confectioners' sugar and chilled cream or ice cream to serve

Place black currants in a colander to allow any final moisture to drip away until you need them.

In a large bowl, mix the sugar, cornstarch, cloves and salt together thoroughly. Add the black currants and toss with a large-tined fork until well blended.

Roll out the pastry. Cut out a lid, leaving an overlapping edge all around of about ¾ inch and put aside until needed. With the remaining pastry line the pie pan, making a similar overlap around the edges. Fill the dish with the black currant mixture and dot with small flakes of softened butter. Moisten the pastry-lined edges of the pie pan with water and fit the pastry lid in position, pressing the edges together with your fingertips and fluting them decoratively. With the tip of a knife, make gashes all over the top.

Place the pie pan on the preheated baking sheet (see above) and bake in a preheated 400° oven for 45–50 minutes, or until the top of the pie is puffed, crisp and golden.

Cool the pie on a wire rack. Dust with granulated or confectioners' sugar and serve lukewarm with chilled pouring cream or with ice cream.

Serves 6–8.

SPICED BLACK CURRANT PUDDING

A substantial winter pudding with a topping of black currants from the freezer to remind you of summer. Other soft fruits may be used instead. Blueberries are especially good, or raspberries sweetened with sugar.

¼ pint frozen black currants, thawed
¼ cup firmly packed brown sugar
2–3 cloves
Butter or soft margarine

Pudding batter
1 cup flour
1 teaspoon baking powder
1 teaspoon apple pie spice
Pinch of salt
2 eggs
½ cup softened butter or soft margarine
6 tablespoons sugar
Finely grated rind of ½ large orange
2–3 tablespoons milk
⅓ cup currants

Mix the black currants, sugar and cloves together. Spread them over the bottom of a well-buttered pudding basin, crushing lightly with a fork to make an even layer.

To prepare the batter, sift the flour, baking powder, spice and salt together. Beat the eggs until light.

Beat the butter or margarine and sugar together with the orange rind until fluffy. Beat eggs and flour mixture alternately into butter and sugar mixture, a few tablespoons at a time, adding a little milk if necessary to soften batter. Beat in the currants.

Spoon the batter over the fruit in the pudding basin. Level the top and make a slight hollow in the middle with the back of the spoon. Cover the basin with foil or a double thickness of parchment paper, lightly buttered on the underside, and tie down with fine string. Lower the basin onto a trivet in a pan with boiling water to come halfway up the sides. Cover the pan tightly and steam the pudding gently for 1¼ hours, adding more *boiling* water if the water in the pan evaporates too quickly.

To serve, unmold the pudding onto a shallow dish and serve accompanied by lightly sweetened custard sauce or cream.

Serves 4–6.

Note: The pudding may also be cooked in a pressure cooker. Steam in 3 cups boiling water for 15 minutes without the pressure gauge, then pressure-cook at low (5 pounds) pressure for a further 25 minutes.

POLISH BLACK CURRANT KISIEL

Polish cooks would thicken this simple dessert with potato flour, whereas we would probably find cornstarch more easily available. As children, we used to love it thickened with arrowroot for the unusual glutinous quality that it gave.

A simple family Kisiel is best accompanied by a light vanilla custard sauce, but for grander occasions you could scoop it into individual meringue nests and top each portion with pouring cream and chopped nuts.

1½ pounds (3 pints) fresh or frozen black currants, stripped and rinsed
Sugar
¼ cup cornstarch
Juice of 1 large orange

Stew currants, ½ cup sugar and 2 cups water together for 10–15 minutes until juices run. Put half of the currants and their juices through an electric blender and return to the pan with the fruit.

Mix cornstarch, ¼ cup sugar and 3–4 tablespoons water to a smooth paste. Bring the black currants and their juices to simmering point. Stir in the cornstarch mixture; bring to a boil and simmer, stirring, for 3–4 minutes, until the mixture has thickened and lost its opaqueness. Cool slightly and add more sugar if necessary. Blend in the orange juice.

Pour into a decorative dish, cool and serve chilled.

Serves 6–8.

BLACK CURRANT YOGURT ICE CREAM

½ pound (1 pint) fresh or frozen black
 currants
Juice of 1 large orange
Finely grated rind of ½ large
 orange
⅔ cup firmly packed brown sugar
¾ cup heavy cream
¾ cup plain yogurt

Strip and rinse fresh black currants. Put fresh or frozen black currants in a pan with 2–3 tablespoons water and cook gently for 10 minutes. Rub fruit through a fine nylon sieve. Add orange juice and rind and sugar, and stir until dissolved.

In a large bowl, whip cream until very thick. Add yogurt and beat again until mixture is well blended and thick enough to hold impression of the beaters. Gently and thoroughly fold in black currant purée.

Pour mixture into ice cube trays or a plastic box with a lid. Cover with foil or the lid and freeze until ice cream is solid around the sides but still very soft and runny in the middle. Scrape it all into a bowl and beat until uniformly smooth and creamy again. Then pour the ice cream back into freezing container(s), cover and freeze until firm.

Place in refrigerator an hour before serving.

Serves 4–6.

WITCHES' FOAM

A lovely, easy, Scottish dessert. The jam must be of the finest quality.

4 egg whites
¼ cup syrupy black currant jam
 (below right)
Sweet wafer cookies or almond tuiles
 for serving

Combine egg whites and black currant jam in a bowl. Beat vigorously until meringue stands in firm peaks. Spoon into individual glass dishes and serve immediately with wafers or tuiles.

Serves 4.

BLACK CURRANT JAM I

A thick, rich jam for serving with bread or biscuits and butter at tea time. The butter in the jam not only clears away any remaining scum but also keeps the fruit itself soft, and the cloves give it a light touch of unusual flavor.

2½ pounds (5 pints) black currants
3 or 4 cloves
5 pounds (10 cups) sugar
Pat of butter

Rinse and strip the black currants, and put them in a preserving kettle with the cloves and 6 cups water. Bring to boiling point and boil for 20 minutes.

Add the sugar and stir over moderate heat until it has dissolved. Then raise heat and boil for a further 20 minutes, or until jell point is reached, skimming scum from the surface as necessary. Turn off the heat and stir in the butter.

Pack and process as usual.
See also page 198.

Fills about 7 jars.

BLACK CURRANT JAM II

A much lighter, syrupy preserve, delicious spooned over vanilla ice cream or a hot sponge pudding. Very ripe black currants and fruit which has been picked after a rainy spell will take several more minutes of hard boiling to reach jell point.

Alternatively, reduce water to 2 cups per pound of fruit.

Per pound (2 pints) of black currants:
1¾ cups sugar
2½ cups water

Rinse and strip the black currants, and place them in a preserving kettle with the sugar and water. Heat very gently until sugar has dissolved and bring to boiling point. Then raise heat and boil *hard* for 7 minutes, or until jell point is reached, skimming off scum as necessary.

Pack and process as usual.
See also page 198.

BLACK CURRANT JELLY

This is made in the same way as Red Currant Jelly, and may be used in similar fashion as an accompaniment for roast lamb and poultry.

Black currant juice (page 36)
Sugar

Measure the juice and for each 2½ cups allow 2 cups sugar. In a clean preserving kettle combine the two. Heat gently until sugar has dissolved. Then raise heat and boil until jell point is reached, skimming surface clear of scum with a large spoon.

Cool slightly, pack and cover.

See also page 199.

CRÈME DE CASSIS Black Currant Liqueur

For this a large glass flagon with a tight-fitting stopper, kept specially for this purpose, is brought out in our kitchen, but any large, wide-necked glass bottles or jars will do just as well. The brandy need not be of special quality—use the cheapest your market can offer. The black currants should be plump and juicy.

If they come from the garden, pick a handful of fresh young leaves at the same time and steep them with the fruit. They add a surprising amount of flavor.

Once a liqueur has matured, it has a hundred uses – in its own right, as a flavoring for ice creams, sherbets and desserts of all kinds, but above all for making the refreshing French summer drink called *Kir*. For this a splash of *cassis* is added to a glass of chilled dry white wine, enough to flavor it and turn it pink.

1¼–1½ pounds (2½–3pints) ripe black currants
2 cups sugar
One 2 inch cinnamon stick
2–3 cloves
Black currant leaves (optional)
1 bottle brandy (see above)

Pick over the black currants. Rinse them and shake them dry in a colander. Crush the black currants and sugar together with a fork until juices run, and pack them into a large glass flagon or jar. Add spices. (If black currant leaves are available, take about half-a-dozen, rinse them, bruise them lightly by crushing them in your hand and add them to the jar.) Fill with brandy. Close tightly.

Leave to mature for a month or so on a sunny windowsill or some similar warm place, giving the flagon a shake from time to time. After a month, strain liqueur through a sieve lined with a double thickness of cheesecloth, squeezing cheesecloth to extract as much liquid as possible.

Funnel the *cassis* into bottles (with tight stoppers) or a large decanter. The liqueur may now be drunk but it will keep indefinitely.

Note: Leftover brandy-steeped fruit can be added to fruit pies, spooned over ice cream or made into a sauce for a steamed pudding.

SOLBAERROM Danish Black Currant Rum

A sweet, homemade liqueur.

2 pounds (4 pints) black currants
6 blanched almonds
5 cups white rum
4 cups firmly packed light brown sugar

Wash the fruit, removing any damaged berries. Crush the fruit and blanched almonds and place in a large, wide-neck, screw-top jar (a Kilner jar is ideal). The jar must be clean and sterilized (see instructions for wine-making, page 205). Pour the rum onto the fruit and nuts. Seal the jar and leave in a cool place for a month, stirring daily.

Using a fine sieve, strain off the liquid into a clean container. Put the fruit and nuts into a linen bag. Seal the bag tightly and squeeze out as much juice as possible. Add the juice to the liquid in the container. Stir in the sugar, until dissolved. Bottle the liqueur in clean bottles. Cork tightly and leave to mature for at least 6 months, preferably a year.

Makes about 5 cups.

BLUEBERRY

Blueberries, blaeberries, bilberries – not forgetting huckleberries and whortleberries – are all varieties, either cultivated or wild, of the same family of berries, *Vaccinium*.

Throughout northern Europe, family expeditions into the woods in late summer in search of wild bilberries are almost as popular as mushrooming parties. Growing locations are jealously guarded and the berries are carried home in triumph, to be eaten with sugar and cream, and turned into compotes and other favorites. The berries leave purple stains on the teeth, around the mouth and on the fingers, so it is best to protect yourself by wearing rubber gloves when you pick them.

When the Pilgrim Fathers arrived in America, they found that the Indians were already gathering blueberries in the wild and using them in a variety of ways, both fresh and dried, sweet and savory. By the middle of the nineteenth century, blueberries were under large-scale cultivation in the woody swamplands of the northern states. Today blueberries are grown commercially in other parts of the world.

Cultivated blueberries are much larger than wild ones, the size of large, mature black currants. When ripe, they are a deep blue-black color with a noticeable, powdery white "bloom." If the berries are being gathered in batches, they can safely be stored in the refrigerator for a week or so until you have enough, provided they are not wet and sticky with juice, or shriveled. For longer-term storage, the freezer is the answer. Either freeze the berries in the containers in which they were bought, or spread them out in a single layer on a tray and freeze until rock-hard before storing in cartons or plastic bags. When they are thawed, the berries will be perfect, down to the bloom and ready for use.

Blueberries can be used in all sorts of ways, from creams to pies to pancakes. Or mix a cupful of blueberries into the apples you have sliced up for a pie or betty. Old American recipes have a delightful way of adding them to all sorts of biscuit and cake batters, an unusual alternative to the dried currants or raisins you might expect (but before adding the berries, remember to toss them with a little of the flour measured for the recipe so that they do not sink to the bottom).

Blueberries may also be turned most successfuly into a liqueur resembling the famous black currant *crème de cassis*, and can be made into decoctions which are good for coughs and head colds.

REMEDIES

This decoction of dried blueberries is good for coughs and head colds.

Use 1 ounce of dried berries to 2½ cups of water. Put the berries and water into an enameled saucepan, bring to a boil and simmer, covered, for 10–15 minutes. Strain into a glass or ceramic container and leave to cool. Drink in small quantities (a mouthful or so at a time) up to 2 or 3 cups a day.

A more palatable alternative is Culpeper's recommendation: "the juice of the berries made into a syrup, or the pulp made into a conserve with sugar."

Blueberries increase sugar tolerance; the following recipe, which combines them with green beans, is said to lower the blood sugar.

Mix dried pods of green beans (haricots verts) with twice their quantity of dried blueberry leaves. Pour boiling water over in the proportion of 2½ cups water to 2 tablespoons of the mixture. Steep for about 20 minutes, strain, and leave to cool. Drink half a cup, three times a day, with the permission of your doctor.

BLUEBERRY SOUP

This refreshing soup is served hot or cold in Scandinavian countries as a dessert. However, with less sugar and a swirl of plain yogurt on each portion, it makes a delicious summer appetizer. For a smoother textured soup purée the berries before adding the thickening.

1½ pounds (4½ pints) blueberries
Juice of ½ lemon
One 2 inch cinnamon stick
Pinch of salt
½ cup sugar
¼ cup cornstarch or arrowroot
¾ cup whipping cream
*Thin lemon slices for decoration (if
    serving hot)*

Rinse and drain the blueberries and pick them over to remove any little stems. Put them in a large pan with 2 quarts water, the lemon juice, cinnamon, salt and sugar and bring to a boil. Lower the heat and simmer the berries for about 5 minutes until the berries are just soft.

Remove the cinnamon stick. Mix the cornstarch or arrowroot to a smooth paste with a cup of cold water. Stir this into the soup in the pan, and continue stirring until the soup thickens slightly.

Remove the pan from the heat and leave to cool a little while you whip the cream. Pour into individual bowls for serving and decorate with whipped cream.

If serving the soup hot, thin lemon slices make a good extra garnish.

Serves 6.

STEAMED BLUEBERRY PUDDING

This light steamed pudding makes the most of the complementary flavors of lemon and blueberry. Be sure to serve it hot with custard sauce, cream, or lightly sour cream.

As a variation, try making it with wholewheat flour and wholewheat bread crumbs.

6 ounces (1 pint) blueberries
1 cup flour
2 teaspoons baking powder
Pinch of salt
4 cups soft white bread crumbs
½ cup butter or margarine
½ cup sugar
2 eggs
Finely grated rind and juice of 1 lemon
About ¾ cup milk

Pick over the berries, if necessary, to remove any stems, then rinse well and pat dry. Toss in a bag with a little of the flour until the berries are well coated, then set aside. Sift together the rest of the flour with the baking powder and salt, then add the bread crumbs and mix well. Stir in the blueberries.

In a separate bowl, beat together the butter or margarine and sugar until light and fluffy. Beat the eggs and add them a little at a time, beating well between each addition. Stir in the lemon rind and juice.

Gradually add the flour mixture to the bowl, adding just enough milk to give a soft consistency. Pour it into a greased 1-quart capacity pudding basin. Cover the top with a layer of well-greased foil or parchment paper, pleating it in the center to allow the pudding to rise. Tie securely with string and put in a steamer, or in a large pan with boiling water halfway up the sides, and steam or boil the pudding for 1–1½ hours.

Replenish with boiling water as necessary during cooking.

When cooked, unmold the pudding and serve.

Serves 6.

BLUEBERRY CUSTARD TART

Cultivated blueberries are usually mild and sweet, so they go well with a rich egg custard.

1½ pounds (4½ pints) blueberries
½ cup sugar
One 9 inch basic pie pastry case, pre-baked (page 203)
3 tablespoons lemon juice
¾ cup rich custard sauce, cooled (page 205)
Ground allspice
or cinnamon

Rinse the blueberries and pick them over to remove any stalks. Pat dry and mix the berries into the sugar.

Layer the sugared berries in the pastry case and sprinkle with lemon juice. Bake in a preheated 375° oven for about 10 minutes, until the blueberries are soft but not mushy. Cool.

Pour the custard over the lightly cooked blueberries in the tart. Chill well before serving and sprinkle the top of the tart with a little ground allspice or cinnamon.

Serves 6.

BLUEBERRY CINNAMON TOASTS

A quick-to-make and quite delicious family dessert.

2 slices white bread
1 tablespoon butter
¼ teaspoon ground cinnamon
2 tablespoons sugar
2 ounces (about ¾ cup) fresh or frozen blueberries, thawed
2–3 tablespoons heavy cream

Lightly toast the bread on both sides and butter while still hot. Mix the cinnamon with half the sugar and sprinkle over both toast slices. Put one slice into the bottom of an individual serving dish and cut the other one diagonally into quarters.

Crush half the blueberries with the rest of the sugar and layer over the toast in the dish. Sprinkle the whole berries on top, then arrange the triangles of cinnamon toast around the sides.

Pour over the cream and serve immediately.

Serves 1.

DEEP-DISH BLUEBERRY PIE

About 1 pound rich pie pastry
for a deep, 2-crust, 9 inch pie
(page 203).
1¼–1½ pounds (4–5 pints)
blueberries
1 cup + 2 tablespoons sugar
¼ cup flour
Juice of ½ large lemon
½ teaspoon finely grated
lemon rind
Lightly whipped cream for serving

Prepare the pastry and cut in half. Roll each piece into a ball, wrap in foil or plastic wrap and chill in the refrigerator for 30 minutes.

Roll out one ball of pastry to make a pastry lid for a deep, round pie dish about 9 inches in diameter, giving it a slight overhang. Put aside. Roll out the other ball of pastry more thinly and use it to line the pie dish with a slight overhang around sides.

In a bowl, combine blueberries with 1 cup sugar, the flour and lemon juice and grated rind, and toss lightly with a fork until well mixed. Pile up in lined pie dish.

Fit pastry lid in place and press around sides to seal them.

Trim off excess pastry and decorated edges by crimping or fluting them.

Cut a few holes or slits in the top to allow steam to escape.

Bake pie in a preheated 450° oven for 10 minutes. Then turn heat down to 350° and continue to bake for 35–40 minutes longer, or until pastry crust is crisp and well colored.

Serve warm, dusted with remaining sugar and accompanied by a bowl of unsweetened, lightly whipped cream.

Serves 8.

BLUEBERRY CREAM

This delicious old American recipe is suitable for wild or cultivated blueberries.

1¼ cups whipping cream
Sugar
5–6 ounces (1 pint) blueberries

Whip the cream lightly and add sugar to taste. Fold the blueberries into the cream, and serve with more sugar for people to help themselves.

Serves 2.

BLUEBERRY LOAF CAKE

Serve this for tea, or with your morning coffee – or try it as one of the dishes in a selection for brunch. Spread the slices with cream cheese.

¼ pound (1½ cups) fresh or frozen blueberries
½ cup butter
1 cup firmly packed brown sugar
2 eggs
½ teaspoon vanilla
2 cups flour
2 teaspoons baking powder
Pinch of salt
About 1 cup milk

Pick over fresh berries to remove any stems, then rinse and pat dry. Frozen berries do not need to be thawed.

Soften the butter, add the sugar and beat until the mixture is soft and fluffy. Beat the eggs and gradually add them to the mixture, beating well between each addition. Continue to beat until the mixture is well combined – about 2 minutes by hand but only seconds if using a food processor. Add the vanilla.

Toss the blueberries in a little of the flour and set aside. Sift the rest of the flour into a bowl with the baking powder and salt. Stir into the egg mixture alternately with the milk until the batter is smooth. Lastly, stir in the blueberries.

Lightly grease a loaf pan measuring about 9 × 5 × 3 inches and spoon the batter into the pan. Bake in a preheated 350° oven for about an hour, or until a skewer inserted into the center comes out clean.

Unmold the loaf on to a wire rack and leave to cool.

BLUEBERRY PANCAKES

6 ounces (1 pint) blueberries
1½ cups flour
1 tablespoon sugar
½ teaspoon baking powder
½ teaspoon baking soda
½ teaspoon cream of tartar
¼ teaspoon salt
About 1½ cups milk
1 egg
2 tablespoons butter, melted and cooled
1 teaspoon vanilla
Oil or fat for skillet
Warmed maple syrup and butter for serving

Rinse blueberries in a colander and shake off excess moisture.

Prepare pancake batter. Sift the next 6 ingredients together and put them in an electric blender or food processor. Pour in about half the milk and break in the egg. Switch on and blend until smooth. Gradually blend in enough of remaining milk to make a creamy batter that is thick enough to drop heavily from a spoon.

Finally, blend in melted butter and vanilla.

In a bowl, pour batter over blueberries and mix lightly but thoroughly.

Heat a heavy griddle or skillet and brush or rub with a wad of paper towel dipped in oil or smeared with margarine or shortening (not butter, which might burn).

Drop tablespoonfuls of blueberry batter onto hot pan, spacing them well apart so they can spread slightly. Cook over low heat until surface of pancakes is covered in bubbles and they are golden brown on the underside. Then loosen each pancake with a broad spatula, flip it over and cook until well risen and golden brown on the other side.

Serve hot with plenty of butter and maple syrup.

Serves 4.

BLUEBERRY BUCKLE

Native American cooking contains a variety of fruit dishes with delightful names such as grunts and humps and buckles. A buckle is traditionally made with blueberries, but when blueberries are scarce, try making one with another soft berry fruit such as raspberries. A buckle makes a lovely change for a late Sunday brunch with plenty of cream and a pot of coffee.

½ pound (1½ pints) blueberries or other soft fruit
2 cups flour
2½ teaspoons baking powder
¼ teaspoon salt
½ cup shortening
¾ cup sugar
1 egg, well beaten
About 1 cup milk

Cinnamon topping
½ cup flour
½ teaspoon ground cinnamon
½ cup sugar
¼ cup butter

Rinse blueberries and shake them dry in a large sieve or colander. Sift flour, baking powder and salt together. Beat shortening until creamy. Gradually add sugar and continue to beat until fluffy. Beat in egg, a tablespoon at a time. Add sifted flour alternately with milk to make a smooth, soft batter, but not too soft, otherwise topping will sink without trace. Pour batter into a greased, 9 inch square, deep baking pan.

Prepare topping. Sift flour and cinnamon into a bowl. Stir in sugar. Rub in butter to make a crumbly mixture. If you have a food processor, this can be done in seconds. Simply load all the ingredients into the bowl and blend until thoroughly mixed and crumbly.

Scatter blueberries evenly over batter and crumble topping over the surface.

Bake buckle in a preheated 350° oven for 45–50 minutes, until it is well risen, a rich golden color on top and firm to the touch.

Serve fresh and warm from the oven, with a pitcher of chilled cream.

Serves 6.

BLAEBERRY JAM

A traditional Scottish jam. Blueberries are called blaeberries in Scotland.

7 pounds (5 quarts) blaeberries
  (blueberries or bilberries)
1 pound thin red rhubarb stalks
5 pounds (10 cups) sugar
Pat of butter or margarine
  (optional)

Pick over the blaeberries, removing any stems or other debris, and if necessary rinse briefly with cold water.

Shake dry in a large sieve or colander. (It will probably be easiest to deal with the berries a batch at a time, draining them thoroughly and tipping them out into a wide, shallow dish or a large bowl.)

Wipe rhubarb stalks clean. Trim them and cut into 1 inch lengths.

Put rhubarb in a preserving kettle. Add a few tablespoons of cold water and the sugar, and stir over low heat until sugar has melted. Then raise heat, bring to boiling point and boil briskly for 10 minutes, stirring frequently.

Add blaeberries and continue to boil until jell point is reached, stirring and skimming off scum as it forms on the surface. Remove pan from heat and if liked, stir in a pat of butter or margarine to disperse any remaining scum.

Pack and process as usual.
See also page 198.

Fills about 8 jars.

BLUEBERRY LIQUEUR

This liqueur closely resembles *crème de cassis*.

The brandied fruit that remains should never be thrown away. It's delicious, and can be added to the fruit filling for mince pies, spooned over ice cream, or can be diluted, then thickened with a little cornstarch, to serve as a sauce for a steamed pudding or fruit pie.

1 pound (3 pints) blueberries
1 cup sugar
One 2 inch cinnamon stick
2–3 cloves, or small piece dried
  ginger root, bruised
Brandy

Crush the blueberries roughly with a fork, and mix in the sugar. Pack into a glass flagon (any bottle or jar with a wide neck will do), with the cinnamon and cloves or ginger. Fill the flagon with brandy and stopper it tightly.

Leave to mature on a sunny windowsill for at least a month, shaking frequently. After a month, strain the liqueur through a sieve lined with a double thickness of cheesecloth, squeezing the cheesecloth to extract as much liquid as possible. Funnel the liqueur into bottles (with tight stoppers) or a large decanter. The liqueur can be drunk immediately or can be kept indefinitely.

BLUEBERRY CHEESE

Fruit cheeses are sweetened fruit purées, cooked to remove the moisture content. When cool, they set solid. Slice or cut into fingers, but never spread.

2 pounds (6 pints) blueberries
1 quart water
Juice of 1 lemon
4 cups sugar

Wash the fruit in a colander under running, cold water. Remove any stalks and damaged berries, and put the fruit in a thick saucepan. Cover with water, bring to a boil quickly, lower the heat and simmer gently until the fruit is soft. Using a fine sieve, strain the contents of the pan. Discard the liquid.

Return the fruit pulp to the pan, add the lemon juice and simmer over a very low heat, until no liquid is noticeable. Remove from the heat.

Warm the sugar in another saucepan. Gradually add it to the fruit purée, stirring constantly to dissolve. Return the pan to the heat. Raise the heat slightly. Stirring constantly, continue to cook until the mixture is thick enough for a spoon to leave an impression when pressed into it. Pack and process as usual (page 200).

To use, unmold from the jar whole and slice. Serve with game, poultry or even bread and cheese.

BRAZIL NUT

Brazil nuts are in fact edible seeds. The tree on which they grow is – unsurprisingly – a native of Brazil, but is also found in Venezuela, Chile and parts of Africa, if not on the same scale.

Almost the entire Brazilian production is gathered from trees in the forests of the Amazon valley.

The broad-leaved evergreen trees grow to a great height. The fruits – each about the size of a man's head and weighing between 2 and 4 pounds – are produced on the upper branches, and the weight of the nuts causes them to fall as they ripen. Between twelve and twenty-two triangular nuts are tightly packed in each kernel, clustered like the segments of an orange. Their shells are extremely hard, and difficult to open without cracking the white kernel. It is often simpler and more economical to buy Brazils ready shelled – one pound of nuts in the shell will provide about 7 ounces of kernels. When buying in the shell, avoid nuts that rattle; this indicates age, and the nut will probably have shrunk and become dry, sharp and virtually uneatable.

The best season for the nuts is between November and February, which is why they are traditionally eaten at Christmas.

Brazils are delicious with poultry, add texture to salads, and can be dipped in rich plain chocolate to make chocolate Brazils. Like other nuts they are a good source of protein in vegetarian diets.

The Brazil has one of the highest fat contents of any nut – 66 per cent – and is 14 per cent protein. It is also a valuable source of several nutrients including calcium, iron and Vitamin B1.

WATERCRESS, BRAZIL NUT AND ORANGE SALAD

This light, tangy salad is a good accompaniment to fish or poultry.

2 bunches watercress
2 large oranges
¼ pound (1⅓ cups) shelled Brazil
  nuts

Dressing
1 tablespoon wine vinegar
1 tablespoon lemon juice
6 tablespoons olive oil
1 tablespoon plain yogurt
1 garlic clove, finely chopped
Pinch of ground cinnamon
Salt and freshly ground black pepper

Soak the watercress in a bowl of cold water for 1 hour, then wash thoroughly in a colander under cold, running water. Trim off any unwanted parts. Dry thoroughly in paper towels or in a salad spinner and place in a large serving bowl.

Peel the oranges. Make sure there are no traces of white pith left. Cut into thin slices and add to the serving bowl. Slice the nuts in half lengthwise. This is easier if you immerse them first in boiling water for a few minutes.

Add to the serving bowl, and leave in a cool place.

Put all the ingredients for the dressing into a small screw-top jar. Replace the lid tightly and shake vigorously. Taste, and adjust the seasoning if necessary. Leave dressing in the jar in a cool place. Just before serving, shake the dressing to mix thoroughly and pour it over the salad. Toss, and serve.

Serves 4.

BRAZIL NUT BAKE

Oil or butter
3 cups fine soft bread crumbs
2 cups shelled and finely chopped
  Brazil nuts
6 large tomatoes, peeled and coarsely
  chopped
3 tablespoons soy flour
3 tablespoons rolled oats
6 tablespoons tomato juice
1 teaspoon dried basil
1 teaspoon dried thyme
Salt and freshly ground black pepper

Grease a 5 × 3 × 2 inch loaf pan liberally with oil or butter. Coat the inside of the pan with 1 cup of the bread crumbs, pressing them down very firmly.

Put the chopped nuts into a large bowl. Add the tomatoes, the remaining bread crumbs, soy flour and oats. Mix well together with a wooden spoon. Add the tomato juice, herbs, and salt and pepper to taste. Blend in thoroughly with a wooden spoon.

Pour the mixture into the prepared pan.

Press well down and bake in a preheated 375° oven for 50 minutes, until firm to touch.

Allow to cool slightly before unmolding onto a warm plate.

Slice and serve hot or cold, with a spicy tomato sauce (home-made, if possible).

Serves 4–6.

DUCK WITH BRAZIL NUTS AND BANANAS IN ORANGE SAUCE

1 large duck, 5–6 pounds
1–1½ quarts fresh orange juice
2 teaspoons finely grated orange
  rind
Bouquet garni (2 sprigs parsley, 1
  sprig thyme, 1 bay leaf)
Salt and freshly ground black
  pepper
3–4 firm bananas
6–8 tablespoons flaked Brazil nuts
  (see method)
¼ cup orange liqueur or brandy
  (optional)
1 tablespoon cornstarch

Wash and dry duck both inside and out. In a flameproof casserole into which duck will fit comfortably, bring about 1 quart orange juice to boiling point with the grated orange rind, bouquet garni, ⅛ teaspoon salt and a grinding of pepper.

Lower duck into simmering juice and cook gently with the lid of the casserole half-on for 1 hour, turning duck several times.

Drain orange stock into a bowl. Place well-drained duck on a rack in a roasting pan.

Sprinkle bird with more salt and pepper, and place in a pre-heated 450° oven for 30 minutes to color and crisp its skin.

While duck is roasting, skim every scrap of fat from bowl of orange stock. Measure 2½ cups of stock, pour through a sieve and put it aside until needed.

Peel bananas and cut them into 2 inch chunks. Flake Brazil nuts by whittling them down individually with a small, sharp knife. (Twelve large nuts should be enough.)

Pour another 2 cups fresh orange juice into roasting pan, scraping up any crusty bits from bottom and sides of pan.

Add bananas, rolling them over so they are thoroughly coated, and stir in orange liqueur or brandy, if used. Baste duck thoroughly. Reduce oven to 350° and continue to roast duck for 30 minutes longer, or until it is quite tender, basting frequently.

Transfer duck and bananas to a heated serving platter, and keep hot. Skim any fat from pan juices. Pour in all but 3 or 4 tablespoons reserved orange stock and bring to boiling point, stirring and scraping bottom and sides of roasting pan clean with a wooden spoon. Pour contents of pan into a saucepan.

Blend remains of reserved orange stock smoothly with cornstarch. Stir into saucepan and simmer, stirring, until sauce has thickened.

Stir in flaked Brazil nuts, correct seasoning if necessary and simmer, stirring occasionally, for a few minutes longer.

Spoon some sauce over duck and serve remainder in a separate, heated sauce boat.

Serves 4.

NUTTY BUTTER COOKIES

Butter
½ pound (about 3 cups) shelled
  Brazil nuts
3 tablespoons granulated sugar or
  light brown sugar
1 cup flour
Pinch of salt
1 teaspoon vanilla
Sifted confectioners' sugar for
  decoration

Start by greasing 2 or 3 large baking sheets lightly with butter. Chop nuts finely by hand or blend them coarsely in an electric blender or food processor. Add sugar, flour and salt, and mix thoroughly.

Cream ⅔ cup butter until pale and fluffy, and beat in vanilla. Stir in nut mixture with a wooden spoon, working ingredients until thoroughly blended.

Between the palms of your hands, shape paste into balls the size of a marble. Arrange them on prepared baking sheets. Bake in a preheated 375° oven for 10 minutes, or until only lightly colored.

Dredge a sheet of wax paper or a large, flat plate with sifted confectioners' sugar.

Roll hot cookies in confectioners' sugar until coated on all sides and cool on a wire cake rack.

CHOCOLATE BRAZILS

1 pound semisweet cooking or candy-
  making chocolate
1 pound Brazil nuts, shelled

Put the nuts on a baking sheet and roast in a preheated 325° oven until the skins become flaky and parched. Remove from the oven, peel off the skins, wash the nuts and dry on paper towels. Put 1 inch of water into a thick saucepan and bring to a boil. Remove from the heat. Break the chocolate into small pieces and place these in a bowl that will sit securely over the hot water in the pan, without the water touching the bottom of the bowl. Put the bowl of chocolate over the steaming water, and melt. Use a candy thermometer to check the temperature of the chocolate. It should never exceed 120°. Cover the bowl to keep the heat in. Lift the lid off the bowl at intervals and stir the chocolate with a wooden spoon. When the chocolate has melted completely, remove the lid. Stir until the consistency is creamy and smooth.

Place the candy thermometer in the chocolate and leave until the temperature has fallen to 110°. At this temperature the chocolate should be of the right consistency for coating. To check this, pick up a small amount between the thumb and forefinger. The chocolate should set almost immediately. If it remains liquid, cool and test again.

Place the nuts on a tray by the side of the bowl of chocolate. Line another tray, placed on the other side of the bowl, with wax paper. Drop one nut at a time into the melted chocolate. Use a fork to submerge and turn the nut, so that it is completely covered. Lift out on the fork, tapping the fork on the side of the bowl to remove excess chocolate. Hold the fork over the tray lined with wax paper and angle the fork so that the chocolate Brazil nut slides off. Make sure the chocolate nuts are well spaced on the tray. Leave for about an hour, until the chocolate is completely hard, before eating.

CASHEW NUT

The cashew nut is the fruit of the cashew, cadju or acaju tree, and a relation of the mango. Early explorers in South America brought it back with them and were responsible for its arrival in Africa and Asia. Today it is extensively cultivated in India and East Africa – Mozambique and Tanzania are big exporters, especially to the United States.

One of nature's stranger growths, it consists of a large fleshy apple below which hangs the true fruit, a kidney-shaped, olive-colored single nut. The kernel, the part we eat, is encased in a dark rind containing an extremely acrid juice, and a smooth, gray, tough outer layer.

An edible oil produced from the cashew is said to equal olive oil for cooking.

In the tropics cashews are eaten raw, or roasted and added to sweet and sour vegetable dishes. Cashews are familiar in Indian and Chinese restaurant dishes in the West and are available in most vegetarian food shops as well as supermarkets.

At home cashews are easily blanched for cooking, or can be roasted and lightly salted and stored in an airtight tin or jar in a cool place.

They are an unusual addition to casseroles and fish dishes, and can also be used to make a delicious butter.

Cashews are rich in protein, Vitamin B and minerals, especially magnesium, with a high proportion of unsaturated fatty acid and almost no cholesterol. They contain an extremely caustic oil, cardol, which is driven off in roasting. It has been successfully applied to corns and warts, as well as to ringworms.

The cashew apple has a pleasant acid taste, and is used in the West Indies and Brazil to make an alcoholic beverage sometimes known as *kaju*. The Brazilians also use it for making vinegar and jam.

NUT AND SEED DRINK

¼ cup sunflower seed kernels
¾ cup cashew nuts
3 tablespoons honey
¾ teaspoon soy milk or skim milk powder
Salt to taste

Put the sunflower seed kernels, cashew nuts and 1 cup of cold water in the bowl of an electric blender. Leave to soak for about 15 minutes, then blend until smooth.

Add the remaining ingredients and 2 cups of cold water to the mixture and blend until smooth. Chill.

Serves 3.

BAKED FISH WITH CASHEW STUFFING

Use either one large fish, such as a sea bass or red snapper for four people, or one small fish – rainbow trout or whiting – per person. Start preparing the dish well in advance; the fish must marinate for several hours.

½ cup olive oil
Juice of 2 lemons
1 clove garlic, crushed
Salt and freshly ground black pepper
1 large or 4 small fish, cleaned and washed
Butter
1 large onion, chopped
1 large sweet green pepper, seeded and thinly sliced
¾ cup cashew nuts
2 tablespoons chopped parsley
Lemon slices for garnish

Make a marinade by blending together ¼ cup of the oil, the lemon juice, crushed garlic, salt and pepper in a dish large enough to take the fish. Add the fish, cover well with the marinade and leave for 4 hours. After 3½ hours, preheat the oven to 400°. Butter a baking dish large enough to take the fish in a single layer.

Heat the remaining oil in a skillet. Add the onion and fry gently until soft, then add the sliced pepper and cashew nuts. Cook, stirring continuously, until the pepper is soft. Remove the pan from the heat and add half the chopped parsley. Add salt and pepper to taste. Blend the contents of the pan together well, to form the stuffing.

Fill the center of each fish with an equal portion of the stuffing. Close up the opening. Put the fish into the prepared baking dish and cover with the marinade. Bake for 30 minutes, until the flesh parts easily from the bone. Baste with the marinade, if necessary, while cooking, to keep the fish moist. Transfer the cooked fish to a warm serving platter. Garnish with the lemon slices and the remaining parsley.

Serves 4.

CHICKEN WITH CASHEW NUTS IN HOISIN SAUCE

Most of the ingredients for this recipe are available in specialist Chinese grocery stores and gourmet shops.

2 large dried Chinese mushrooms
1 whole chicken breast
1 tablespoon dry sherry wine
1 teaspoon flour
2 tablespoons corn oil
½ cup bamboo shoots cut into 1 inch
  pieces
6 water chestnuts, diced
2 tablespoons Hoisin sauce
½ cup unsalted, raw cashew nuts

Soak the mushrooms in warm water for about 20 minutes. Meanwhile remove the skin and bones from the chicken and discard. Cut the meat into 1 inch cubes. In a medium bowl blend together the sherry and flour. Add the chicken, make sure it is well covered by the marinade, and leave for at least 10 minutes. When the mushrooms are soft, dry on paper towels and slice across into sections about ⅛ inch thick.

Heat the oil in a wok (or large, good quality skillet) over a high heat. When the oil starts to sizzle, add the cubed chicken and stir continuously for about 2 minutes or until the chicken is white. (When stir-frying, it is essential to stir throughout the cooking process, otherwise the food will burn.) Keep stirring and add the mushrooms, bamboo shoots and water chestnuts.

Cook for a further minute.

Sprinkle on the Hoisin sauce, mix in well and stir the mixture over the heat for another 3 minutes. Add the cashew nuts and stir well in. Serve immediately with fried rice or Chinese noodles.

Serves 2.

VEAL AND CASHEW NUT CASSEROLE

3 pounds veal for stew
Salt and freshly ground black pepper
¼ cup butter
2 tablespoons oil
1 large Bermuda onion, chopped
2 plump cloves garlic, crushed
1 large tomato, peeled, seeded and
  diced
1½ cups cashew nuts
1¼ cups tomato juice
1 teaspoon flour
2 teaspoons Worcestershire sauce

Remove any sinews, fat etc, and cut veal into bite-sized cubes. Season all over with salt and pepper.

In a large, heavy, flameproof casserole, melt butter in oil. Brown veal cubes all over in hot fat, a portion at a time, transferring them to a plate with a slotted spoon as you do so. In fat remaining in casserole, gently fry onion and garlic until limp and lightly colored. Stir in tomato and continue to fry, stirring, until mushy.

Add veal cubes and cashew nuts. Pour in tomato juice and mix well. Bring to simmering point, cover casserole and cook gently for 1 hour, or until veal is almost done. Occasionally stir veal and turn cubes over.

Blend flour smoothly with Worcestershire sauce. Stir it into sauce and simmer uncovered, stirring frequently, for 20–30 minutes longer, until veal is tender and sauce is thick and reduced. Correct seasoning and serve with plain boiled rice.

Serves 6–8.

CASHEW NUT BUTTER

Nut butters are usually very popular with children. Make a small quantity at a time and keep in the refrigerator in a sealed container. Cashew nuts need very little added oil.

Nut butters can be blended with chopped fruit or vegetables (celery, green pepper, raisins, grated carrot) to make a variety of delicious spreads.

1½ cups unsalted, raw cashew nuts
Sunflower oil
Salt

Put the nuts, a ½ cup at a time, into an electric grinder or food processor. Grind until they are the consistency of flour, then transfer to a medium bowl. Repeat until all the nuts are ground, then add the oil, drop by drop, and blend into the ground nuts with a wooden spoon. (This can be done more efficiently in an electric blender with a hole in the top.) Continue adding oil and blending until a thick paste forms. Taste the mixture and add salt if desired.

Pack the nut butter into a small, clean jar or other container.

Seal the container and store it in the refrigerator.

CHERRY

Cherries are native to Asia Minor, their very name deriving from Cerasus, the ancient city where Europeans first came across them. Since then, migratory birds have helped to spread cherries to most parts of the temperate world.

The arrival of the season's first cherries is a sure sign that summer has arrived. They are eaten fresh or cooked in all kinds of compotes, pies, cakes and puddings. A large proportion of the crop is used to make delectable jams and syrups, or canned. They are also preserved in brandy or *eau-de-vie* for special occasions and used to make spirits and to flavor all sorts of liqueurs based on brandy, gin, even whiskey. Maraschino liqueur is flavored with cherries, but Kirsch is probably the most famous of all, a clear, colorless spirit from Switzerland and the Black Forest, with a light, bitter almond flavor that goes superbly with all kinds of fruit from pineapple to strawberries.

The color of ripe cherries runs from golden streaked with red to deep, purple-black. There are also white royal ann cherries and a variety that stays a pale green color even when fully ripe and sweet. Basically, cherries can be divided into two categories – sweet cherries, which can be light- or dark-fleshed, and are either eaten raw or cooked, and sour or "tart" cherries such as the famous Morellos, which are used primarily for pies and preserves, and for making liqueurs. Dukes cherries are a cross between the two.

When the season ends, switch to canned cherries by all means but do check first if they have been pitted or not. Pitting cherries can be a tedious job, although a cherry-pitter is a time-saving gadget that can double up as an olive-pitter. Check, too, when buying dried cherries (available in some health food stores), whether they have been pitted. Reconstituted overnight in a bowl of water, then simmered in a light sugar syrup, they make a lovely compote or topping for ice cream, but they will be difficult to eat if they still have the irritating pits.

To prepare cherries for cooking, rinse them first if necessary, then take off the stems. Remove the pits over a large bowl to catch any juices that might escape, dropping the cherries into the bowl as you do so.

Whole cherries can be dry or sugar frozen; stem, wash and dry them first. Freeze pitted ones in a sugar syrup made from 2 cups sugar to 5 cups water. Allow ½ teaspoon ascorbic acid for every 2½ cups syrup.

REMEDIES

The bark of the wild black cherry tree is well known as a remedy for coughs and colds, and it is traditionally combined with coltsfoot to cure fever as well as coughs and bronchitis.

The bark should be dried in the shade, not in the sun as is usual with most plants.

Put 2 tablespoons dried wild or sour cherry bark and 2 tablespoons dried coltsfoot leaves or flowers in an enamel or stainless steel saucepan. Bring 2½ cups water to a boil, pour it over the mixture, and simmer very gently for 15–20 minutes. Strain. Sweeten to taste with honey and allow to cool. Take up to half a cup, 3 or 4 times per day. Children can take half that dosage.

Cherry trees also yield a gum which has soothing properties similar to those of gum arabic, and may be substituted for it in various recipes. Culpeper says this gum "dissolved in wine, is good for a cold, cough and hoarseness of the throat; mendeth the color in the face, sharpeneth the eye-sight, provoketh appetite, and helpeth to break and expel the stone."

CHERRY STALK TEA

This recipe was once well known as a diuretic. The stalks can be of wild cherry or of the sour varieties.

Pour 2½ cups boiling water over 1 tablespoon dried stalks and steep for 10–15 minutes, before straining and cooling. Drink lukewarm, a mouthful at a time, up to 3 or 4 cups per day.

ICED CHERRY SOUP

When fresh cherries are not in season, canned fruit may be used, provided they are pitted and packed either in water or a very light syrup.

1½ pounds sour black cherries (see above)
¾ cup sugar
One 3 inch cinnamon stick
1 tablespoon potato flour or cornstarch
¾ cup heavy cream
Lemon juice (optional)
4–6 tablespoons cherry brandy

Stem and pit fresh cherries.

In a large saucepan, dissolve the sugar in about 1 quart water. Add the cinnamon stick, bring to boiling point and boil gently for about 5 minutes. Then add the cherries and their juices, and continue to simmer until they have softened, about 30 minutes.

Blend the potato flour or cornstarch smoothly with 2 or 3 tablespoons cold water. Stir into the poached cherries and simmer, stirring, until soup is slightly thickened and has lost its opaque, floury look. Discard the cinnamon stick.

Take a large cupful of the cherries and their liquid, and process smoothly in a food processor or electric blender. Return purée to the soup and leave until cold. Blend in cream. Then taste and adjust flavors, adding more sugar and a few drops of lemon juice, if necessary. Chill until ready to serve.

Just before serving, stir in a few tablespoons of cherry brandy, to taste. Serve in chilled soup bowls.

Serves 6–8.

DUCK WITH CHERRIES

4 pound duck, cleaned,
   and giblets
Salt
3 carrots, peeled and sliced
1 small onion, chopped
1 garlic clove, crushed
1 teaspoon dried marjoram
1 teaspoon dried basil
1 wineglass red wine
Freshly ground black pepper
Sugar
½ pound sour cherries

Season the duck, by rubbing the skin and the inside of the carcass with salt. Put to one side, in a large casserole dish.

Arrange the carrots, onion and giblets around the duck. Sprinkle the garlic, marjoram and basil over it. Pour in the wine and about 1 cup water, and add salt, pepper and sugar to taste.

Cover the casserole and bake in a preheated 350° oven for 2 hours or until the duck is tender.

Remove the casserole from the oven. Uncover and pour off the liquid and vegetables into a large saucepan. Put the duck onto a plate and set aside to cool. Boil the contents of the saucepan over a high flame until reduced by half. Strain off the liquid into a small bowl and chill in the refrigerator for 1 hour. Discard the vegetables.

Meanwhile, stem and pit the cherries and put into a bowl.

Take the chilled liquid out of the refrigerator. The fat content should form a layer on the surface. Remove this. Reheat the remaining liquid until not quite boiling. Pour over the cherries and chill in the refrigerator until the sauce has turned to jelly. Remove from the refrigerator, unmold from the bowl and slice. Serve the duck cold, surrounded by slices of the jellied sauce in which the cherries are embedded.

Serves 4.

CHERRY COMPOTE

If you are feeling extravagant, stir a tablespoon or two of cherry brandy into the syrup at the very end. Serve the compote with chilled cream. A plate of almond macaroons is also nice but not really necessary.

2 pounds sweet black cherries
1½ cups sugar
One 3 inch cinnamon stick
3–4 cloves
Spirals of orange and lemon rind

Stem and pit the cherries.

Place remaining ingredients in a large, wide pan or flameproof casserole. Pour in 2½ cups of water and bring to boiling point over moderate heat, stirring until sugar has dissolved. Simmer for 5 minutes to make a syrup.

Drop cherries and their juices into simmering syrup and poach gently until they are just tender, about 10 minutes. With a slotted spoon, transfer cherries to a serving bowl.

Boil remaining syrup briskly for about 5 minutes to thicken it slightly. Strain over cherries. Cool and chill.

Serves 6.

CHERRY LAMB MAYONNAISE

¾ pound ripe, sweet cherries, red or
   black
1 pound lean, cold roast lamb, sliced
   ½ inch thick
3–4 stalks celery
6–8 tablespoons chopped, lightly
   toasted almonds
About ¾ cup thick lemon
   mayonnaise (page 205)
Salt and freshly ground black pepper
Crisp lettuce leaves
   for garnish

Stem and pit the cherries. Trim any visible fat from lamb. Cut it into ½ inch cubes and add to cherries. Trim celery stalks. Dice them and add to bowl, together with chopped almonds. Mix in enough mayonnaise to bind ingredients together, tossing lightly with a large fork, and season to taste with a little salt and freshly ground black pepper.

Line 4 individual plates with lettuce leaves and pile salad on top.

Serves 4.

CHERRY BREAD CRUMB PUDDING

¾ pound ripe cherries
2½ cups brown bread crumbs
Finely grated rind of 1 lemon
6 tablespoons sugar
1¼ cups light cream
4 eggs, separated
Butter, for pudding basin

Cherry sauce
¼ pound ripe cherries
¼ cup sugar
Juice of 1 lemon
Red food coloring
1–2 tablespoons cherry brandy or
   orange liqueur (optional)

To make pudding, first stem and pit the cherries. Add bread crumbs, grated lemon rind and sugar to the bowl with the cherries, and toss with a fork until thoroughly mixed.

Bring cream to just below boiling point and pour over bread crumb mixture. Mix lightly and cool to lukewarm.

Meanwhile, in separate bowls, first beat egg whites until they stand in peaks, then with the same beater, beat egg yolks until creamy. Stir egg yolks into bowl of bread crumb mixture and finally fold in egg whites.

Spoon mixture into a large, well-buttered pudding basin or steaming mold. Cover with a double thickness of parchment paper or foil buttered on the inside and tie down with string. Steam pudding for 1 hour, or until it has risen and is firm to the touch.

While pudding is steaming, prepare a simple cherry sauce. Pit cherries, working over a small pan and dropping them into it as you do so. Add sugar, lemon juice and about ¾ cup water. Bring to boiling point, stirring until sugar has dissolved, and simmer for 15–20 minutes, or until cherries are very soft. With a fork, crush them slightly to release juices. Intensify color with 1 or 2 drops of red food coloring and, if liked, flavor to taste with a little cherry brandy or orange liqueur.

When pudding is ready, unmold it onto a heated serving platter and pour cherry sauce over and around it.

Serves 6–8.

CHERRY PIE

For this, the best cherries to use will, naturally, be pie cherries, the kind that often grow in the garden and are just too astringent to eat raw. Use them for making pies such as this one, for jams and other preserves. Ice cream makes a lovely accompaniment for a cherry pie.

About 1 pound rough puff pastry
for a 2-crust, 8–9 inch
pie (page 203)
1¼ pounds pie cherries
4–5 drops almond extract
About 1¼ cups sugar, or to taste
5 tablespoons flour
1 tablespoon butter
Sugar for sprinkling

Roll out about half of the pastry to make a lid. Put aside. Roll out remaining pastry rather more thinly and use it to line bottom and sides of pan with a slight overhang.

Stem and pit the cherries, and put them in a bowl. Sprinkle with almond extract. Blend sugar and flour together, and toss with cherries. Pile cherries in pastry-lined pan and dot all over with tiny flakes of butter. Moisten pastry edges lightly with water, fit pastry lid in position and seal the two together, pressing lightly and fluting edge neatly. Cut a few gashes in pastry lid to allow steam to escape.

Bake pie in a preheated 450° oven for the first 15 minutes. Then lower heat to 350° and continue to bake for 30 minutes longer, or until pastry lid is crisp, puffed and golden.

Sprinkle pie with sugar and allow to cool until it is lukewarm before serving.

Serves 6–8.

Bigarreau.

CHERRY CHEESECAKE

This can be made with either cottage or cream cheese, but whichever one of these is used must first be well drained in a sieve or squeezed dry wrapped in cheesecloth, and cottage cheese must also be rubbed through a sieve to make it smooth. Make the cheesecake the day before you propose to serve it to give it time to "settle."

Crumb crust
1½ cups finely crushed graham
crackers
1 tablespoon sugar
2 tablespoons butter, melted

Cheese mixture
1 pound cream or cottage cheese (see
above)
¾ cup sugar
3 eggs
Finely grated rinds of 1 lemon and 1
orange
¼ cup heavy cream or sour cream
1½ tablespoons self-rising flour,
sifted

Cherry topping
Two 16 ounce cans pitted black
cherries in syrup
Lemon juice
1 teaspoon arrowroot, potato flour or
cornstarch

Prepare crumb crust. Mix crushed cracker crumbs, sugar and butter together. Press firmly and evenly over the bottom of a 7–8 inch springform cake pan.

To prepare cheese mixture, beat the well-drained cream or sieved cottage cheese with sugar until fluffy. Add eggs one at a time, beating well between each addition. Beat in grated orange and lemon rinds, and then cream. Beat until blended. Finally, lightly but thoroughly fold in flour.

Spoon cheese mixture into crumb crust, and bake in a preheated 400° oven for 10 minutes. Turn oven down to 300° and continue to bake for 1½ hours longer, or until cheese filling is risen and firmly set. Allow to cool. Then chill for several hours, preferably overnight.

The following day, prepare cherry topping. Drain cherries thoroughly and arrange them closely on top of cheesecake. Measure 5 tablespoons of their syrup into a small pan. Sharpen flavor to taste with a little lemon juice. Heat gently while you blend arrowroot smoothly with another tablespoon of cherry syrup. Stir into hot syrup. Bring to boiling point and simmer, stirring, until translucent and thickened. Cool. Spoon over cherries. Put back in refrigerator to set.

To serve, run a knife blade around sides of cheesecake and carefully unmold it onto a flat dish.

Serves 8.

CLAFOUTIS

The texture of a clafoutis should be a cross between a baked custard and a pancake, soft but firm enough to unmold when cold.

3 tablespoons flour
Pinch of salt
3 tablespoons vanilla-flavored sugar
(page 205)
2 eggs
1 egg yolk
1 tablespoon light vegetable oil
1¼ cups milk
1 pound ripe black
cherries
Butter
Sifted confectioners' sugar for
decoration

Sift flour, salt and sugar into a bowl, and make a well in the center. Add the eggs and egg yolk, and work them into the flour with a wooden spoon to make a smooth paste. Beat in the oil. Then gradually add the milk, beating vigorously to make a smooth, light batter. Put aside to rest while you prepare the fruit.

Generously butter a tart pan or ovenproof porcelain dish about 10 inches in diameter.

Stem and pit the cherries and spread evenly in the pan. Cover them with the batter, pouring it over the back of a spoon to avoid disturbing them. Dot the top with a few tiny flakes of butter.

Bake clafoutis in a preheated 350° oven for 40–45 minutes, or until a knife blade slipped through to the bottom comes out clean.

Serve warm from the dish, dusted with confectioners' sugar. Alternatively, the clafoutis may be unmolded and served lukewarm or cold, in wedges like a pie.

Serves 6–8.

EASY KIRSCH CAKE

¾ cup flour
3 tablespoons cornstarch
3 eggs
¾ cup sugar
1 tablespoon Kirsch
Butter, for baking pans
Grated dark chocolate
   for decoration

Cherry filling
One 16 ounce can black cherries in
   syrup, pitted
¼ cup sugar
2 tablespoons Kirsch

Kirsch cream
1 cup whipping cream
2 teaspoons sugar
2 tablespoons Kirsch

Butter two 8½ inch layer cake pans thoroughly. Line bottoms with buttered parchment paper. Sift flour and cornstarch together 3 times.

Have eggs at room temperature and break them into a large bowl. With mixer at moderate speed, beat eggs until thick and fluffy. Gradually beat in sugar and continue to beat vigorously until mixture leaves a momentary trail on the surface when beaters are lifted. Beat in Kirsch and finally fold in flour mixture. Distribute evenly between prepared cake pans. Bake in a preheated 350° oven for 20–25 minutes until layers are well risen and very lightly colored. Allow to cool on cake racks for 5 minutes before loosening sides and unmolding cakes from pans. Leave until cold.

To prepare the cherry filling, drain syrup from cherries into a small pan. Add sugar, stir over low heat until dissolved, then boil until reduced to 8 or 9 tablespoons. Cool to lukewarm, stir in Kirsch and leave until cold.

To prepare the Kirsch cream, whip cream until thick. Add sugar and Kirsch, and continue to whip until cream holds its shape.

To assemble cake, lay one cake layer on a large, flat serving dish and spoon more than half of the cherry syrup over it. Spread with half of the cream and scatter evenly with cherries, pressing them in lightly. Soak underside of other cake layer with remaining syrup and quickly lay it on top, saturated side down. Spread with remaining cream. Sprinkle evenly with grated chocolate and chill thoroughly before serving.

Makes 12 portions.

CHERRIES IN BRANDY

For this you will need plump, ripe sour cherries, brandy (one of the least expensive ones will do perfectly well), sugar and a great deal of patience to resist opening the jar and sampling the cherries while they are maturing. This will take a minimum of 8 weeks but the longer they are left, the better they will be.

Choose perfect cherries that still have their stalks attached. With a pair of scissors, trim the stalks down to about ¾ inch. Wipe the cherries clean by rolling them gently between the folds of a damp cloth. (Do not rinse them unless absolutely necessary.)

Pack the cherries into a tall, wide-mouthed glass jar that has a tight-fitting lid, tapping the jar gently on the table from time to time to "settle" the cherries so that you can fit in as many as possible.

Fill the jar with brandy, covering the cherries completely. Close the jar tightly and put it away for a minimum of 3 weeks, preferably longer, say 4.

Open the jar and spoon in enough sugar to come halfway up the sides. Then screw down the lid again and shake the jar gently until the sugar has dissolved.

Put the jar of cherries away in a cool, dark cupboard for a further 8 weeks (or longer if possible), frequently giving it a good shake.

The cherries are best served in small glasses, 5 or 6 to a glass, with some of the brandy poured over them.

CHERRY JAM

½ pound red currants
3 pounds ripe sour cherries
6 cups sugar

Rinse the red currants and strip off any stalks.

Place in a pan with a few tablespoons of water over low heat until juices run. Then continue to cook gently, mashing occasionally, until red currants are soft and pulpy.

Meanwhile, stem and pit the cherries over a bowl to catch any juices.

Rub the red currants through a fine nylon sieve and return purée to the rinsed-out pan. Add the pitted cherries and their juices, slowly bring to boiling point and simmer gently until cherries have softened.

Add sugar and continue to cook gently, stirring frequently, until sugar has dissolved. Then raise heat and boil rapidly until jell point is reached, skimming as necessary.

Cool slightly. Pack and process.

See also page 198.

Fills about 5 jars.

CHESTNUT (SWEET)

The sweet chestnut tree, which grows up to 115 feet high and bears creamy flower "candles" in spring, was originally from southern Europe. The nuts fall to the ground in green casings covered with prickly spines, and must not be confused with their inedible relative, the horse chestnut.

The sweet chestnut is cultivated in Spain, Italy and France, and is used in soups, stews, sauces and stuffings. Whole (shelled) chestnuts combine well with Brussels sprouts, while Mont Blanc is one of the world's classic desserts.

To peel chestnuts, make a small nick in the flat side of their shells, and roast them in a 375° oven for six to eight minutes; or put them on top of the stove in a pan of cold water just to cover, and bring the water to a boil. As soon as the water is bubbling briskly, take the pan from the heat and peel off the shells and inner skins. This is easier to do while they're hot, but remember to hold them in a cloth. Don't allow them to continue boiling, or they will turn floury and be impossible to peel.

It may be easier to buy dried nuts. Put these in a bowl and pour over boiling water, then leave them to soak for up to twenty-four hours. If you do not need whole nuts, use cans of purée. Be sure you know which you are buying – the sweetened or the unsweetened variety.

To freeze chestnuts, remove every scrap of skin. Blanch them, then plunge them into cold water before patting dry and freezing in plastic bags.

Sweet chestnuts contain more starch and less fat than most other nuts, which is why they are so easily ground into flour, and are rich in Vitamins B and C. Their leaves and bark are also useful medicinally.

CREAM OF CHESTNUT SOUP

½ pound chestnuts
2 tablespoons butter
1 tablespoon oil
2 carrots, thinly sliced
1 small parsnip, thinly sliced
1 small stalk celery, thinly sliced
1 large potato, peeled and sliced
2 cups well-flavored chicken
  broth
1¼ cups light cream
Salt
3–4 tablespoons dry sherry wine
Crisp croûtons for garnish

Peel and skin the chestnuts, and chop them into small pieces.

In a large pan, heat butter and oil together, and sauté carrots, parsnip and celery for 2–3 minutes. Cover pan and "sweat" vegetables for about 10 minutes longer until they soften slightly. Add the chestnuts and potato. Cover with chicken broth, bring to boiling point and simmer with the lid half on until chestnuts and vegetables are disintegrating, about 45 minutes. Add a splash of hot water if liquid in pan evaporates too quickly.

Process the contents of the pan in an electric blender or put them through a vegetable mill. Return purée to rinsed-out pan. Reheat gently, blending in the cream smoothly with a wire whisk. Do not allow soup to boil again at this stage.

Season with salt and flavor to taste with sherry. Serve immediately with a bowl of croûtons to scatter over the top.

Serves 4–6.

REMEDIES

Chestnut leaves are traditionally believed to be good for coughs.

Infuse 1 ounce fresh or dried leaves (picked in early summer) in 2½ cups boiling water. Allow to cool, and drink one cupful three times a day, or use as a gargle.

To cure diarrhea, boil 1 ounce crushed wood or bark in 2½ cups water for 2 minutes only; strain and take 2 or 3 cupfuls a day.

CHESTNUT STUFFING

2 pounds chestnuts, skinned and
  peeled
Broth
½ cup butter, melted
2 cups bread crumbs, white or
  wholewheat
1 pound bulk sausagemeat
1 tablespoon chopped parsley
Salt and freshly ground black pepper

Put the chestnuts in a saucepan with just enough broth to cover. Simmer gently over low heat until they are cooked through and almost dry.

Rub the chestnuts through a sieve into a bowl and mix well with the remaining ingredients.

Note: These quantities are enough for a 12–14 pound turkey.

CHICKEN WITH CHESTNUTS

Serve the casserole with floury, plain-boiled potatoes or a creamy potato purée.

2–3 slices bacon
1 Bermuda onion, finely chopped
1 large clove garlic, crushed
¼ pound button mushrooms, sliced
1 tablespoon light cooking oil
One 3–3¼ pound roaster chicken, cut up
Salt and freshly ground black pepper
1 teaspoon crushed dried rosemary
½ teaspoon dried thyme
¾ cup Marsala or medium sherry wine
6–8 tablespoons chicken broth
1 can peeled whole chestnuts, about 10 ounces drained weight
2 tablespoons butter

Cut bacon into small dice. In a heavy, flameproof casserole, fry bacon gently until fat runs. Stir in onion and sauté gently until soft and golden.

Stir in garlic and mushrooms, and sauté for 2–3 minutes longer, taking care garlic does not burn as this would make it bitter. Cover and put aside.

Heat the oil in a large, heavy skillet and fry chicken pieces, a few at a time, until golden brown on all sides. Transfer to the casserole, giving each piece of chicken a generous sprinkling of salt and freshly ground pepper as you do so. When all the chicken pieces have been dealt with, sprinkle them with rosemary and thyme, and mix well with the onion and mushrooms.

Pour over Marsala or sherry.

Deglaze skillet with chicken broth, stirring and scraping surface clean with a wooden spoon, and pour into casserole.

Bring to simmering point, cover and cook gently for 15 minutes.

Meanwhile, drain chestnuts thoroughly. In the same skillet, toss them lightly in butter, taking care butter does not brown too much.

Stir chestnuts and all their butter into casserole. Cover again and continue to cook gently for 15–20 minutes, or until chicken pieces are tender.

Correct seasoning if necessary and serve.

Serves 4.

CAUCASIAN LAMB

2 pounds lamb leg sirloin chops
3 tablespoons butter
2 Bermuda onions, finely chopped
Salt and freshly ground black pepper
About 2 cups chicken broth
1 pound chestnuts, peeled and skinned
Juice of 1 lemon
Finely chopped parsley for garnish

Trim off all fat and gristle from the lamb chops, and cut meat into about 12 pieces. With a meat pounder or rolling pin moistened with water, pound meat out thinly.

In a heavy, flameproof casserole with a tight-fitting lid, brown meat on both sides in butter, a portion at a

CHESTNUT SAUCE

A good sauce for chicken and turkey. Use stock in which you have boiled a fowl or skimmed juices from the roasting pan, supplemented with broth made with a bouillon cube.

2 tablespoons butter
2 tablespoons flour
1¼ cups cooking juices and chicken broth (see above)
½ pound chestnuts, peeled, skinned and chopped
Salt
½ teaspoon sugar
⅛ teaspoon ground cinnamon (optional)

In a heavy pan, melt the butter. Blend in the flour with a wooden spoon and cook gently, stirring, until mixture turns a rich golden color and has a nutty aroma. Gradually add cooking juices and broth, beating vigorously to prevent lumps forming. When sauce is smooth and simmering gently, stir in the chestnuts. Season lightly with salt. Add sugar and cinnamon if liked, and continue to cook gently for 15–20 minutes, stirring occasionally. Correct seasoning and serve hot.

time to avoid overcrowding the casserole. Stir in onions and season generously with salt and freshly ground black pepper. Add a few tablespoons of the broth, stirring and scraping bottom of casserole clean with a wooden spoon. Cover tightly and cook gently.

Add chestnuts to casserole, together with remaining broth. Mix well, cover and continue cooking gently until meat and chestnuts are quite tender.

Five minutes before the end of cooking time, stir lemon juice into stew.

Correct seasoning if necessary and transfer to a heated serving dish. Garnish with parsley, and serve.

Serves 4–6.

MONT BLANC

1 pound chestnuts
Salt
1 cup sugar
¾ cup whipping cream
2 tablespoons brandy or ½ teaspoon vanilla

Peel and skin the chestnuts. In a pan, cover them with water and add a pinch of salt. Bring to boiling point and simmer for 45–60 minutes until they are quite soft. Drain the chestnuts thoroughly. Using a potato masher, mash them to a purée together with the sugar and a pinch of salt. Press the purée through a potato ricer or food mill, allowing it to fall lightly onto a plate.

Whip the cream until it thickens and forms very soft peaks, flavoring it with brandy or vanilla, and a little more sugar to taste if liked.

Spoon the cream over the mound of chestnut purée. Serve immediately.

Serves 4.

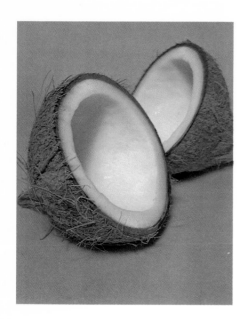

COCONUT

Man has to take the responsibility for moving many food crops around the world, but the coconut is one of the few which has taken an active part in its own propagation. Because of its buoyancy and the hardness of its protective shell, the coconut has from time immemorial drifted thousands of miles across both Indian and Pacific oceans, taking root where it was carried ashore – and where it felt happy to be. It still grows best near the sea, but it will also grow inland if it has the company of humans. A nineteenth-century traveler to Sri Lanka was heard to remark that "the natives have a superstition that the cocoa-nut will not grow out of the sound of a human voice, and will die if the village where it formerly thrived becomes deserted."

We are all familiar with pictures of the coconut palm, with its tall, slender, leaning trunk and its impudent crown of giant leaves – some up to 20 feet in length – sheltering the nuts the tree bears every year.

Experts tend to argue as to whether the coconut originated in India or Malaysia – but as far away as West Africa, it is one of life's staple foods. (The Ibo tribe fringing the Niger river have very special prayers for peace, prosperity, health and lots of coconuts.) But the coconut is far more than a food. Besides the refreshing coconut water, the sugary sap from the young flower branches is tapped and drunk fresh, or fermented into "toddy" – a wine with the alcoholic strength of beer. Toddy, in its turn, can be distilled into "arrack," a spirit at least as potent as brandy. Copra, from the dried flesh inside the nut, is used in cosmetics, and coconut oil can be used in cooking.

Coconut is perhaps most familiar to us as the fresh, whole nut, or in its dried shredded form. Shredded coconut, often lightly and deliciously toasted, is familiar as an ingredient of sweet desserts. Think of little coconut macaroons, familiar from childhood, crusty on the outside and moist and chewy in the middle, or steaming coconut puddings to cheer the family on a winter's day, and the perennially popular ambrosia made with coconut.

When buying a whole coconut, pick one that feels heavy for its size, hold it to your ear and give it a gentle shake. There should be plenty of water splashing about inside. To open it, pierce two of its brown eyes and pour out the water from inside. Put it, eyes down, on a hard surface and give it a blow with a hammer. Once it has split or broken into small pieces, the creamy white flesh inside can be scraped out and stored. Leftover coconut can be shredded or grated, moistened with a little coconut water and packed into small containers for freezing (up to 6 months).

Coconuts are very nutritious, especially if they are fresh when they contain appreciable amounts of minerals, particularly potassium, and vitamins. The oil is used in cosmetics and suntan lotions.

NECK CREAM

Coconut oil has many cosmetic uses. This recipe will prevent wrinkles, and is also a firming, nourishing neck cream.

Put 1 part beeswax, 2 parts lanolin and 6 parts coconut oil into a double boiler. Melt, beat well, and remove from the heat. Add 4 parts camomile infusion a little at a time, as if making mayonnaise.

SUNTAN LOTIONS

Coconut oil is very effective in promoting a rich, even tan. It can be used on its own, or mixed with olive or sesame oil (both of which are also good tanning agents) to give a better consistency – it solidifies unless the weather is very warm. A few drops of bergamot essence can also be added for an even deeper tan, as well as for its scent, but take care: it is very potent, and not suitable for sensitive skins.

A less sticky suntan lotion can be made in the same way as the neck cream, using 1 part lanolin to 1 or 2 parts coconut oil and 2 or 3 parts rosewater (or diluted cider vinegar).

COCONUT MILK

When recipes call for coconut milk or cream, they do not mean the watery liquid you hear slopping about inside when you shake a fresh coconut, but a milk which is made as follows.

In the goblet of an electric blender or food processor, place a cupful of finely chopped fresh coconut meat and pour over a cupful of boiling water. Blend or process until the two are reduced to a thick and rather rough purée. Alternatively, shred coconut meat on the coarse side of a cheese grater and put it in a bowl. Cover with an equal volume of boiling water and leave to soak for 30 minutes.

Strain through a fine sieve or a colander lined with cheesecloth, gathering up sides and wringing cheesecloth to extract all moisture.

The first "pressing" results in a thick, creamy liquid. For a thinner version put contents of cheesecloth bag in a small pan, cover with another portion of water, cold this time, and slowly bring to boiling point. Remove from heat and leave to soak for another 30 minutes before squeezing liquid out as above.

If fresh coconuts are not available, you can use dried shredded coconut instead. Or you can use creamed coconut which comes in slabs or packets from markets and grocery stores. About ¼ pound (about ½ cup) soaked in water will produce a thicker liquid, while about 1 ounce (2 tablespoons) soaked in water will produce a thinner one.

FISH AND COCONUT CURRY

This fairly mild curry is popular in South India and Sri Lanka. Use ghee (clarified butter), available at most Indian grocers, if possible. It is the best fat for Indian cooking, because it can be heated to a high temperature without burning.

1 cup coconut milk (see opposite page and method)
4 large cod steaks
1 teaspoon turmeric
Salt
¼ cup ghee or butter (see above)
2 small onions, sliced
2 green chili peppers, chopped
½ inch piece of ginger root, peeled and sliced
Juice of 1 lemon
2–3 tablespoons plain yogurt

Prepare coconut milk, following the method described on the opposite page, up to the "first pressing" stage.

Wash the fish steaks and dry them on paper towels. Mix the turmeric and 1 teaspoon salt together in a small dish. Rub the mixture all over the fish. In a thick skillet, heat the ghee (or butter). Add the fish and fry over a medium heat for a few minutes on each side. Take the fish out of the pan and set aside.

Add the onions, chilis and ginger to the skillet and cook until the onions are light brown. Stir in half the coconut milk and cook for a further minute.

Put the fish steaks back into the pan. Pour over the remaining coconut milk. Bring to a boil. Cover the pan and simmer gently over a low heat for 15 minutes or until the fish is cooked. Uncover the pan and stir in the lemon juice. Taste the sauce and season. Remove the pan from the heat and stir in the yogurt. Return to the heat for a few minutes, but do not allow the sauce to boil. Serve with boiled rice.

Serves 4.

CHICKEN IN SPICED COCONUT SAUCE

2 cups dried shredded coconut
2½ cups milk
One 3½ pound roaster chicken, cut up
Peanut oil
2 Bermuda onions, finely chopped
1 large clove garlic, crushed
¼ teaspoon each ground cinnamon, ginger and sharp (hot) paprika or cayenne
⅛ teaspoon ground cloves
2–3 teaspoons soy sauce
Salt and freshly ground black pepper
½–¾ cup chopped roasted peanuts

This coconut milk is richer than the one described on the opposite page. In a small pan, combine coconut with milk. Slowly bring to boiling point and simmer for 5 minutes. Then draw pan off heat and cool to lukewarm.

Strain contents of pan through a sieve lined with cheesecloth, wringing out as much of the milk as possible. Put aside.

In a large, flameproof casserole, brown chicken pieces on all sides in 2 or 3 tablespoons peanut oil, removing them to a plate as you prepare them. When they are all done, pour off all oil remaining in casserole, leaving behind any brown bits. Add 2 tablespoons fresh oil and sauté onions and garlic gently until transparent and golden but not charred. Sprinkle in spices and fry, stirring, for a minute or so longer. Mix in soy sauce and prepared coconut milk. Season lightly with salt and freshly ground black pepper.

Return chicken pieces to casserole, spooning sauce over them so they are submerged. Cover and cook very gently for about 30 minutes. Then stir in chopped peanuts, taste for seasoning and continue cooking for 15 minutes longer, or until chicken is quite tender.

Serve with a bowl of rice.

Serves 4.

Note: Do not waste coconut left behind after preparing milk. Spread it out on a baking sheet to dry for 2–3 hours in a preheated 250° oven, raking it over with your fingers from time to time. Use it to sprinkle over iced cakes and plain ice cream, or to decorate candies.

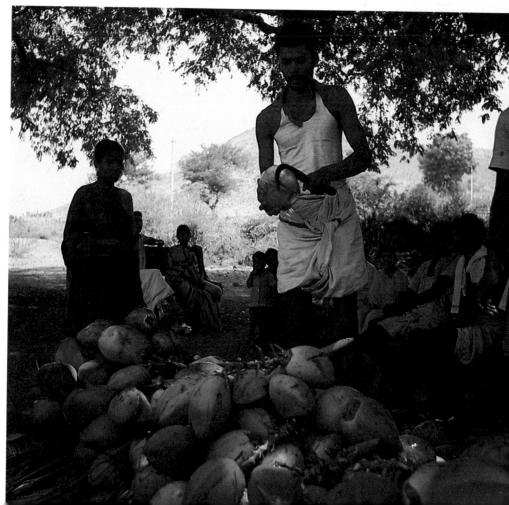

COCONUT RICE

A traditional accompaniment, delicious with European-style meat and especially poultry dishes, as well as the hot Indian curries which it was originally intended to accompany. Use basmati rice, a delicate, long-grained rice available in Indian stores and some gourmet shops. Failing that, ordinary long-grain rice will do perfectly well. It will not need pre-soaking like basmati rice, but can take more liquid, say ½ cup more.

1 cup basmati or long-grain rice
1 tablespoon oil
1 tablespoon butter
3 whole cloves
3 whole cardamom pods, lightly
    crushed
2–2½ cups coconut milk
    (see page 54)
1 teaspoon salt
3–4 tablespoons toasted shredded
    coconut for garnish

Wash the rice under the cold tap until the water runs clear. If using basmati rice, place it in a bowl with cold water to cover and leave it to soak for at least 30 minutes before draining it thoroughly.

In a heavy pan with a tight-fitting lid, heat the oil and butter together until foaming. Add the cloves and cardamom pods, and swirl the pan around over moderate heat until the aroma begins to rise and the spices seem to puff out, about 3 minutes.

Add the rice and stir over moderate heat until each grain is separate and golden, and shiny with melted fat. Draw the pan from the heat and cool slightly before pouring in the coconut milk – 2 cups if using basmati rice, 2½ cups for plain, long-grain rice. Add salt and stir well.

Bring to boiling point. Stir well with a fork once more. Reduce the heat to a bare simmer, cover pan tightly and cook gently for 15 minutes, undisturbed. Most of the liquid will have been absorbed, leaving the rice grains rather moist.

Switch off the heat. Gently fluff the rice grains up with a fork. Clamp on the lid again and leave to stand for 10–15 minutes longer.

To serve, pile the rice in a heated serving dish. Scatter toasted shredded coconut over the top.

Serves 3–4.

COCONUT CREAM PIE

A rich pie, best served in a pre-baked pastry shell made of pie pastry, or use a meringue case.

If making a meringue, use the 3 egg whites left over from the cream filling and 6 tablespoons sugar; to prepare the base and shape the case, follow the instructions given for Coconut Meringue Case, below.

1 pre-baked pie crust (page 203) or
    meringue case 8 or 9 inches in
    diameter
Whipped cream and shredded
    coconut for decoration

Coconut cream filling
¼ cup cornstarch
⅔ cup sugar
¼ teaspoon salt
2½ cups creamy milk
3 egg yolks
1 teaspoon vanilla
1 tablespoon butter
1⅓ cups dried shredded
    coconut

Prepare coconut cream filling first. In the top of a double boiler, blend cornstarch smoothly with sugar, salt and milk. Bring to boiling point over direct heat, stirring constantly, and simmer for 2 or 3 minutes until sauce is thick and smooth.

In a bowl, beat egg yolks lightly. Beat in a few tablespoons of the hot cornstarch sauce, then beat back into rest of sauce. Fit top of pan over simmering water and stir until sauce is smooth and has thickened again. Take care not to let sauce come to boiling point at this stage, or egg yolks may curdle. Lift off top part of pan. Beat in vanilla, butter and coconut. Pour into a bowl and leave until cold, stirring occasionally to prevent a skin forming on top.

Fill pie crust or meringue case with cream filling and chill lightly.

Serve decorated with cream and sprinkled with coconut.

Serves 6–8.

COCONUT MERINGUE CASE

Filled with whipped cream and decorated with fruit, this makes a delightful dessert that will serve 6 to 8 people. Or the same mixture may be shaped into individual meringues with 2 large spoons, dried out in the oven on prepared baking sheets and sandwiched with whipped cream.

Tasteless oil
1 cup fresh or dried shredded
    coconut
3 tablespoons sifted confectioners'
    sugar
3 egg whites
⅛ teaspoon salt
¼ teaspoon cream of tartar
¾ cup sugar
1 teaspoon vanilla

Start by preparing baking equipment. A meringue case is baked on a baking sheet lined with parchment paper that has been marked with an 8 or 9 inch circle with a pencil and brushed very lightly with oil. Or it may be baked in a pie pan similarly greased with oil (just enough to prevent meringue sticking).

In a small bowl, toss the coconut with confectioners' sugar until strands are individually coated. Put aside. In a large, spotlessly clean and dry bowl, beat egg whites with salt until foamy. Add cream of tartar and continue to beat until very soft peaks form. Then beat in sugar, a couple of tablespoons at a time, and continue to beat to a stiff, glossy meringue. Beat in vanilla.

Sprinkle sugared coconut over the top and gently but thoroughly fold it into the meringue, using a large metal spoon.

Shape meringue into a neat nest on baking sheet, following pencil guideline on parchment paper, or pile into pie pan and smooth out bottom and sides with the back of a spoon, shaping sides so they extend about an inch above the rim of the dish.

Bake meringue case in a preheated 300° oven for about 1 hour or until it is a light golden color and firm to the touch. Loosen meringue case while still lukewarm, then leave until quite cold on the baking sheet or in the pie pan before transferring to a flat serving dish.

Fill and decorate.

STEAMED COCONUT PUDDING

⅔ cup dried shredded coconut
1¼ cups milk
¼ cup butter
¼ cup sugar
2 eggs, separated
1 cup soft white bread crumbs
1 cup cake crumbs
½ teaspoon vanilla
Butter for pudding basin
Orange or lemon custard sauce for
*   serving (page 205)*

In a pan, cover coconut with milk. Bring to boiling point and simmer for 10–15 minutes. Cool.

Meanwhile, beat butter until creamy. Beat in sugar and continue to beat until light and fluffy. Beat in egg yolks, one at a time. With a wooden spoon, mix in the bread and cake crumbs, the coconut and milk mixture, and vanilla. Beat egg whites until stiff but not dry and fold them into pudding.

Pour mixture into a well-buttered pudding basin. Cover with a double thickness of parchment paper or foil buttered on the underside. Tie down securely with string. Stand basin on a trivet in a pan with boiling water to come halfway up sides, cover tightly and steam for at least 1 hour, or until pudding is well risen and firm to the touch.

Unmold onto a heated serving platter. Coat with a hot orange or lemon custard sauce and serve.

Serves 4–6.

COCONUT SAUCE

¼ cup unsalted butter
½ cup sugar
2 egg whites
3–4 tablespoons dried shredded
*   coconut*
Lemon juice
Vanilla

Beat butter until light and creamy. Add sugar gradually, beating vigorously until mixture is very pale and fluffy. Beat egg whites until they stand in stiff peaks. Fold them into the creamed mixture, together with coconut. Flavor with lemon juice and vanilla.

Spoon butter into a glass serving dish and chill until firm.

LEMON COCONUT CREAMS

These candies are quick, simple and foolproof to make, providing you use a candy thermometer to determine the temperature.

2 tablespoons butter
1½ cups sugar
6 tablespoons evaporated milk
Juice and grated rind of 1 lemon
2 cups dried shredded coconut

Line a large baking sheet with wax paper. In a thick-bottomed saucepan, melt the butter over a low heat. Stir in the sugar, 3 tablespoons cold water,

COCONUT ICE

A favorite British candy, made with dried shredded coconut.

Butter
¾ cup milk
4 cups sugar
2⅔–3⅓ cups dried shredded
*   coconut*
1 teaspoon vanilla
Red food coloring

Grease an 8 inch square baking tin with butter.

Put aside until needed.

In a heavy pan, mix milk with ¾ cup water. Add sugar and 2 tablespoons butter, and heat gently, stirring, until they have dissolved. Bring to boiling point. Cover pan and simmer for 2 minutes. Then remove lid and boil gently for 7–10 minutes longer, stirring frequently, until temperature of liquid reaches 240° on a candy thermometer (soft-ball stage).

Draw pan off heat. Add coconut and vanilla, and beat vigorously with a wooden spoon until mixture is thick and creamy. Pour half of the mixture into the buttered baking tin. Tint the remaining mixture pale pink with a few drops of red food coloring (for safety's sake, administer a drop at a time on a toothpick until the right shade is reached). Pour it out evenly over the white layer of coconut ice, if necessary leveling it out with the back of a spoon.

When ice is setting but not hard yet, mark it into about 60 1 inch squares with the point of a sharp knife.

Leave until quite cold before cutting along the marks to divide cubes completely.

the evaporated milk, and grated lemon rind. Bring to a boil slowly and continue to boil, stirring frequently, until the temperature is 240°. Remove the pan from the heat. Leave to cool.

When cold, add the lemon juice to the mixture, and beat until creamy. Shape the mixture into balls about ¾ inch in diameter. Put the coconut into a small bowl. Roll the balls in the coconut, and arrange on the prepared baking sheet.

Leave the candies in a cool place for several hours.

COCONUT MACAROONS

A cheaper alternative to pure almond macaroons. To pursue the deception, flavor the mixture with a few drops of real almond extract instead of vanilla.

1⅓ cups dried shredded coconut
½ cup sugar
2 teaspoons flour or cornstarch
2 egg whites
½ teaspoon vanilla
Rice paper for baking sheets

In a bowl, stir coconut, sugar and flour together until well mixed. Beat egg whites until they hold soft peaks and mix lightly with dry ingredients. Sprinkle in vanilla (or almond extract) while you are mixing.

Drop large teaspoonfuls of coconut mixture, well spaced apart, on baking sheets lined with rice paper. Bake in a preheated 325° oven for 20–30 minutes, until macaroons are lightly colored and firm to the touch.

Cool on a wire rack. When cold, crumble off excess rice paper around sides of each macaroon. Store in an airtight box or jar.

Makes 12–24, depending on size.

CRANBERRY

Although varieties of cranberry are to be found growing wild in cool, swampy areas all over Europe, Asia and North America, only the large, bright red berry native to North America, *Vaccinium macrocarpon*, has become an important culinary fruit. In America, it has been cultivated commercially on an ever-increasing scale for nearly 200 years.

When the first settlers arrived in America in the sixteenth century, they found that the local Indians had long been using the cranberries they gathered in the wild in a variety of ways. They added the berries to pemmican, a nutritious and long-lasting sausage of sun-dried chopped venison or bear meat and fat, which early North American explorers included in the provisions they carried on long journeys; and mixed them into succotash, a dish of fresh lima beans and corn, which is still a favorite today. Cranberries were used to treat arrow wounds and added to poultices, while cranberry juice was used as a dye with which to decorate their rugs and blankets. The Indians quickly introduced the settlers to this marvelously versatile fruit and showed them where and when to look for it. So it is quite possible that cranberries accompanied the first Thanksgiving turkey as they do to this day.

European cranberries are smaller and darker in color than the American variety, and are used to make sauces and relishes very similar to the American ones. The British often serve cranberries with the Christmas turkey, preferably cold on Boxing Day, whereas the Europeans use the sauce to accompany meat dishes of all kinds, especially game.

Cranberries are available fresh, frozen and preserved in the form of sauces, jellies and juice. The cranberries sold fresh in fall and winter are almost invariably in excellent condition, plump, bright and dry. They also freeze perfectly in their boxes or plastic bags.

Cranberries are far too sour and astringent to eat without sugar, but with generous sweetening they become deliciously tart. Chopped up raw, or cooked, they may be used on their own or matched with other flavors and textures such as oranges or apples and almonds or walnuts.

The color of cranberries is so brilliant, their flavor so sharp and penetrating, that just a small amount will go a long way. They can be used to make dips, sherbets and ice creams. Or try chopping up a handful of berries and add them to pancake batter, a biscuit dough, or the batter for a rich fruit cake in place of some of the dried fruit.

Cranberries contain a significant amount of Vitamin C.

CRANBERRY AND TURKEY PIE

2 tablespoons butter
3 tablespoons flour
¾ cup chicken broth
¾ cup milk
1½ cups turkey meat cut into small pieces
½ pound mushrooms, cleaned and sliced
2 stalks celery, cleaned and chopped into 1 inch lengths
½ pound (1½ pints) fresh cranberries
3 tablespoons medium sherry
½ cup light cream
Juice of 1 lemon
½ pound rough puff pastry (page 203)
1 egg, lightly beaten

Melt the butter in a large, thick saucepan, and stir in the flour to form a smooth paste. Gradually pour in the chicken broth and milk, stirring continuously to form a smooth sauce. Cook over a low heat until the sauce begins to thicken. Remove from the heat and add the turkey, mushroom slices, celery and cranberries. Pour the sherry, the cream and lemon juice into the saucepan. Stir the mixture and heat gently, without boiling. Leave over a low heat to keep warm, but do not allow to boil.

Grease a large deep pie dish. Roll out the pastry on a floured board until about ⅛ inch thick. Transfer the contents of the saucepan to the prepared pie dish. Cover with the pastry. Brush the pastry with the beaten egg. Bake in a preheated 425° oven for about 30 minutes or until the pastry has become brown.

Serve immediately.

Serves 4–6.

SKIN BLEACH

This mixture helps to bleach reddened skins, freckles and fading suntans.

Take a good handful of fresh cranberries, crush them, and mix with enough buttermilk to make a not too runny paste. Spread this on the affected part and leave for 15–20 minutes. You may need to cover it with a cloth to keep it in place. Wash off with lukewarm water.

As buttermilk has an astringent effect, you will probably need to apply a moisturizer if you have a dry skin.

CRANBERRY STUFFING

An unusual and delicious stuffing that will be enough for a 10 pound turkey, a goose, 2 large ducks or a crown roast of pork. You will need about ½ pound day-old bread that has been trimmed of crusts.

1 pound (3 pints) cranberries
½ cup butter
¾ cup sugar
About ½ pound (8 cups) trimmed day-old bread cubes (see above)
2 teaspoons crumbled dried marjoram
Salt and freshly ground black pepper
2 tablespoons finely chopped parsley
1¼ cups unsweetened orange or apple juice

Rinse cranberries. Shake them dry in a colander and put them through a meat grinder.

In a large, preferably wide pan, melt butter without letting it sizzle or color. Add minced cranberries. Cook gently for 5 minutes, stirring frequently. Stir in sugar and continue cooking over low heat for a few minutes longer, stirring until sugar has dissolved.

Stir in bread cubes, turning them over to coat them individually with cranberry sauce. Sprinkle with marjoram and season generously with about 2 teaspoons salt and a grinding of black pepper.

Finally, stir in parsley, sprinkle with fruit juice, and cook gently for 5 minutes, stirring frequently.

Allow to cool, then use the stuffing as required.

CRANBERRY FLUFF

1½ pounds (4½ pints) fresh or frozen cranberries, thawed
2 cups sugar

Pick over berries, if using fresh ones, and rinse well. Pat dry. Put them into a blender or food processor with the sugar and work to a fine-textured purée. With a blender, you may have to do this in batches. Turn the purée into a bowl and leave for 3–4 hours to set.

Serve with crisp wafer cookies.

Serves 6.

CRANBERRY DIP

For serving with fresh fruits.

3 ounces full-fat cream cheese
¾ cup plain yogurt
¼ cup cranberry sauce or cranberry orange sauce (page 61)

Beat the cream cheese until softened, then beat in the yogurt until smooth. Stir in cranberry sauce or cranberry orange sauce to taste.

Serves 4.

CRANBERRY ORANGE COMPOTE

This refreshing mixture may either be served with the main course or spooned over ice cream or cake and eaten for dessert.

2 pounds (6 pints) cranberries
2 large, thin-skinned oranges
Sugar
¼ cup orange liqueur or brandy

Rinse and drain cranberries. Scrub 1 orange under cold water but leave it unpeeled. Peel the other one, stripping off every scrap of white pith (discard peel and pith). Cut both oranges up. Pick out and discard all the seeds.

Put cranberries and oranges through a meat grinder. In a bowl, mix them together with sugar to taste and orange liqueur or brandy. Cover bowl and chill for several hours before serving.

CRANBERRY FROSTING

¼ cup butter, softened
1 egg yolk
2 tablespoons cranberry jelly
½ teaspoon vanilla
1 cup confectioners' sugar

In a small bowl, combine the softened butter with all the other ingredients. Beat until smooth and thick. Use the frosting for layer cakes or cup cakes.

CRANBERRY RELISH

½ pound (1½ pints) fresh cranberries
1 small, thin-skinned orange
½ small lemon
1 small, tart apple
1 cup sugar

Rinse cranberries and drain them thoroughly in a colander. Cut the orange into chunks, removing the seeds. Cut the end off the lemon half, removing any seeds. Quarter and core the apple.

Put all the ingredients through the coarse blade of a meat grinder. Mix them together in a bowl, spoon into a large, screw-top jar, and store in the refrigerator for at least 24 hours.

CRANBERRY TART

From *The Cook's Oracle* by Dr Kitchener (1823).

"Take Swedish, American, or Russian Cranberries, pick and wash them in several waters, put them into a dish, with the juice of half a Lemon, a quarter of a pound of moist (ie unrefined soft brown) or pounded Loaf (granulated) Sugar, to a quart of Cranberries. Cover it with Puff or Tart (rich pie) Paste, and bake it three quarters of an hour; if Tart Paste is used, draw it from the oven five minutes before it is done, and ice it,* return it to the oven, and send it to table cold."

*The following instructions are given by Dr Kitchener for icing fruit tarts, puffs or pastry:

"Beat up in a half pint mug the White of two Eggs to a solid froth; — lay some on the middle of the pie with a paste brush, — sift over plenty of pounded Sugar, and press it down with the hand, — wash out the brush, and splash by degrees with Water till the Sugar is dissolved, — and put it in the oven for ten minutes, and serve it up cold."

CRANBERRY SHERBET

This refreshing sherbet makes a change from the more usual flavors, but it is no coincidence that orange juice is added to complement the tart cranberry flavor. However, if you find the juicy purée too sweet, sharpen it with a little lemon juice before freezing.

*½ pound (1½ pints) fresh or frozen
   cranberries
1 cup sugar
One 3 inch cinnamon stick
¾ cup orange juice
1 teaspoon unflavored gelatin
1 large egg white
A little whipped cream for decoration
Thin orange slices for decoration*

Pick over the cranberries, if using fresh ones, then rinse well. Put in a saucepan with 1 cup water. If using frozen berries, use a little less water. Bring to a boil and simmer the cranberries until soft, then purée in a blender or food processor and return them to the pan.

Add the sugar, cinnamon and orange juice and bring to a boil. Boil without stirring for 5 minutes. Remove the cinnamon stick.

Dissolve the gelatin in 1½ tablespoons cold water, then stir it into the hot juice in the pan and continue stirring until the spongy gelatin dissolves completely. Take the pan off the heat and allow to cool, then chill.

Beat the egg white until stiff, then fold this into the chilled purée. Turn the mixture into a container and cover with foil. Freeze until slushy.

Remove and beat well to break up the ice crystals, then cover again and freeze until firm.

About 15 minutes before serving, transfer the sherbet to the refrigerator to soften. Decorate with whipped cream or with thin orange slices.

Serves 4.

CRANBERRY LAYER DESSERT

Another Scandinavian special. The rich taste of the dark rye bread contrasts well with the cranberries, and would also complement a mixture of raspberries and red currants.

*1 pound (3 pints) fresh or frozen
   cranberries, thawed
¼ cup lemon juice
½–⅔ cup sugar
¼ pound dark rye bread
1¼ cups whipping cream*

Pick over berries, if using fresh ones, then rinse well under cold running water. Dry well on paper towels. Make sure frozen ones are thoroughly thawed, if using these.

Put the berries in a pan with the lemon juice and cook over moderate heat for about 10 minutes. Stir in sugar to taste and allow the berries to cool completely.

Crumble the rye bread, or use a blender or food processor to make it into bread crumbs. Whip the cream until it holds soft peaks. In 4 individual glasses, arrange the cranberry sauce, crumbs and whipped cream in layers, sprinkling a few bread crumbs over the top.

Decorate with a swirl of whipped cream and chill well before serving.

Serves 4.

CRANBERRY PARFAIT

This luscious dessert is popular in Finland, where cranberries abound. You can also use raspberries or strawberries. If using frozen fruit, remember to thaw them first.

*2 egg yolks
1¼ cups confectioners' sugar
5 ounces (1 pint) cranberries
2 cups heavy cream
A little extra whipped cream for
   decoration (optional)*

In a bowl, beat together the egg yolks and sugar until the mixture is foamy. Purée the cranberries in a blender or food processor and whisk into the mixture. Adjust sweetness to taste.

Whip the cream until it holds soft peaks, then fold this into the cranberry mixture until colored an even pink.

Rinse out a 1-quart metal mold in cold water, then pour in the parfait mixture. Freeze for at least 8 hours, or overnight.

To unmold the parfait, dip the outside of the mold in hot water for about 20 seconds, then invert it onto a serving dish. Decorate with whipped cream, if liked.

Serves 4–6.

SIMPLE CRANBERRY SAUCE

Recipes for a basic cooked cranberry sauce are two a penny. This one is very simple, but if you substitute red wine or port for the water, the sauce will be superb.

*1 cup sugar
¾ cup water (see above)
1 pound (3 pints) fresh cranberries*

Dissolve the sugar in the water over low heat, and then add the cranberries. Simmer, stirring frequently and very gently, until the skins all pop (with a snap rather like the famous rice cereal when milk is poured over it) after about 7 minutes.

CRANBERRY ORANGE SAUCE

A Christmas preserve to make ahead of time and store in the refrigerator or freezer, ready to brighten up the cold turkey that almost inevitably appears on the table after Christmas. It will keep for up to a month in the refrigerator, several months if stored in the freezer.

1 cup sugar
1¼ cups fresh orange juice
¾ pound (about 2½ pints) fresh
  cranberries
1 teaspoon finely grated orange rind

In a heavy pan, dissolve the sugar in orange juice over low heat, stirring. Add the cranberries and grated orange rind, and bring to a boil, stirring. Simmer, covered, for a few minutes until the cranberries pop open and soften.

Pour into a jar (for the refrigerator). Or a carton (for the freezer). Cover tightly and store in the refrigerator (see above).

CRANBERRY ALMOND SAUCE

An interesting combination of textures and flavors. Store for, say, a month in the refrigerator.

1 pound (3 pints) cranberries
2 cups sugar
¾ cup fresh orange juice
6–8 tablespoons blanched slivered
  almonds
Finely grated rind of 1 small orange

Rinse cranberries in a colander and shake them dry. In a large, heavy saucepan (or a small preserving kettle), mix cranberries, sugar and orange juice, and sprinkle with 5 or 6 tablespoons water. Stir over low heat until sugar dissolves, then raise heat to moderate, bring to boiling point and boil, stirring frequently, for about 5 minutes until cranberries pop open. Skim surface clear of scum and stir in almonds and orange rind.

Allow to cool, stirring occasionally. Pack into jars, cover and store in the refrigerator or freezer.

CRANBERRY CANDY

You can use any soft fruit that you like in this Italian recipe.

1 pound (3 pints) fresh cranberries
2 ounces purple grapes
3 cups firmly packed light brown
  sugar

Line a pan about 15 inches square and 3 inches deep with parchment paper. Oil the surface of the paper lightly.

Wash the fruit in a colander under cold running water. Discard any stalks or damaged berries. Put the cranberries and grapes into a bowl, and crush with a wooden spoon. Press this pulp through a fine sieve to remove the seeds and skins. Put the remaining pulp in a thick saucepan, and cook over a medium heat for 30–40 minutes, stirring occasionally, until it has the consistency of thick jam. Leave on one side.

In another saucepan, dissolve the sugar in ¾ cup of water over a low heat. Bring to a boil, stirring frequently, and cook until the syrup reaches a temperature of 310° on a candy thermometer. Drop a little of the syrup into a bowl of iced water. Remove immediately. This sample should snap firmly into two when bent. If it does not, heat the syrup a few more degrees and test again, until the test sample snaps firmly into two.

Remove the syrup from the heat, stir in the fruit pulp, return the pan to the heat and cook the mixture gently, stirring constantly, until the surface appears to cloud over. Pour into the prepared pan and leave to set, in a cool place. When almost set, mark into squares.

When set, turn out of the pan and break into separate pieces.

APPLE CRANBERRY SAUCE

Delicious with any dish of roast poultry, and an economical way of making a few cranberries go a long way.

½ pound peeled, cored sour apples,
  thinly sliced (prepared weight)
½ pound (1½ pints) fresh or frozen
  cranberries
1 cup sugar

Combine all the ingredients in a heavy pan. Add about ¾ cup water and slowly bring to boiling point, stirring until the sugar has dissolved completely.

Cover pan and cook gently for 10–15 minutes longer until cranberry skins have burst and fruits have become pulpy.

Pour into a bowl. Cool slightly. Then whisk until well blended and fluffy.

Serve cold.

CRANBERRY PARTY PUNCH

A sparkling, non-alcoholic party punch.

1 cup sugar
1 quart cranberry juice
3 cups orange juice
¾ cup lemon juice
5 cups ginger ale
2 lemons
Ice cubes for serving

Make a sugar syrup by dissolving the sugar in ¾ cup water in a heavy-based pan. Stir from time to time until the sugar is dissolved, then set aside to cool.

Mix together the cranberry juice, orange juice and lemon juice and chill until ready to serve. Just before serving, pour in the ginger ale and sweeten to taste with the sugar syrup. Thinly slice the lemons and float the slices on top of the punch. Put in some ice cubes and serve.

Makes about 20 glasses.

DATE

One of the first foods eaten by man, dates are still a staple in the diet of desert nomads and play an important part in many Arab dishes.

Date palms may well have grown in the Garden of Eden. They have been found in the tombs of the pharaohs and the cultivation of date palms is depicted on Assyrian murals. To the Muslim, the date palm is "the tree of life" which was fashioned by God out of the dust left over after the creation of Adam.

Dates were introduced into California by the Spanish in the second half of the eighteenth century and have flourished there ever since.

Fresh ripe dates are delicious eaten on their own as a snack, just as they are, or with soft white cream cheese. Or try halving them lengthwise, pitting them and adding them to a fresh mixed fruit salad. However, remember that unless you are simply snacking on fresh dates, it is always a good idea to peel off their papery outer skins as these are hard and have an unpleasant, acrid taste.

Dried dates, with which most people are far more familiar, are produced in a variety of forms. The finest quality are large specimens, carefully packaged side by side in rectangular, rounded-end boxes with tiny white plastic forks to help extract them. Smooth and plump, they are barely distinguishable from fresh dates until you taste them. Although they have none of the cloying sweetness normally associated with dried dates, they are rather sweeter than the fresh fruit.

Next come the dates which have been pitted and dried whole but are less carefully packed in large cartons. These may be stuffed and eaten whole, sliced into winter vegetable and fruit salads, or chopped and mixed with other dried fruits in substantial puddings, breads and cakes. You will find that dates go well with most other fruits, particularly orchard and citrus fruits which need sweetening. These dried dates should not be confused with the dried olive-sized fruits known as red dates or jujubes which you will find in Oriental stores and which are used in Chinese cooking to flavor both savory and sweet dishes.

Finally, slab dates are cheapest of all. These are fine for cooking and baking but must always be carefully examined for stray pieces of broken pit.

Dates are rarely used in preserves or as a flavoring base for liquors. One strong date liqueur called *sirop* was described by someone who tasted it as "the strongest and most dreadful drink ever invented."

Especially when dried, dates are among the most nutritious of fruits, high in potassium and folic acid. They are also an excellent restorative and energy-giving food for anyone recovering from a debilitating illness.

The 1837 edition of the *London Encyclopedia* records that the male flowers, if eaten when still tender and sprinkled with a little lemon juice, are "provocative."

DATE AND WALNUT SPREAD

A delicious – and healthy – spread.

½ pound (about 1½ cups) pitted
   dates
2–3 teaspoons lemon juice
½ cup chopped walnuts

Chop the dates very finely, or work to a paste in a blender. Heat gently in a pan with the lemon juice and 2 cups water until thick. Cool a little, then add the walnuts. Store in a screw-top jar.

MOROCCAN DATE SALAD

A good buffet dish or appetizer. You can use a mild herb vinegar instead of orange-flower water.

1 crisp head lettuce
3 oranges
⅓ cup finely chopped pitted dates
½ cup finely chopped walnuts
½ teaspoon ground cinnamon

Dressing
2 tablespoons lemon juice
1–2 tablespoons sugar
2 tablespoons orange-flower water
   (see above)

Wash the lettuce, removing any bruised outer leaves. Shred the remainder and arrange in the bottom of a salad bowl. Peel the oranges and slice them thinly across the segments into circles. Arrange these over the shredded lettuce. Sprinkle the dates and walnuts over the top.

Whisk together the lemon juice, sugar and orange-flower water and pour over the salad. Sprinkle with cinnamon and serve.

Serves 6.

KOREAN RICE WITH DATES

Use fine Chinese or Indian basmati rice for this dish. It is also very good made with brown rice, although it will absorb more water (say 2 cups) and take longer to cook. This rice goes beautifully with poultry or lamb dishes.

1 cup rice (see above)
¼ cup plump dried dates
Salt

In a large sieve, rinse rice under cold water until water runs clear. Leave to drain for about 1 hour.

Cut each date lengthwise in four and remove pits.

In a heavy pan with a tight-fitting lid, combine rice, quartered dates, a generous sprinkling of salt and 1¼ cups water.

Leave to soak for 30 minutes.

Bring to boiling point, stir well, lower heat to a bare simmer and cover pan tightly. Cook for 15 minutes. Then, without touching lid, let pan stand for about 15 minutes longer before fluffing up rice with a fork and serving.

Serves 3–4.

DATES WITH CREAM

2 tablespoons tasteless vegetable oil
½ pound (about 1½ cups) pitted fresh (or very plump dried) dates
1 cup chilled heavy cream
2 tablespoons coarsely chopped pistachio nuts

In a large, heavy skillet, heat oil and add dates. Sprinkle with a tablespoon of water and fry, stirring, just long enough to heat dates through and evaporate water, 1 or 2 minutes.

Whip cream very lightly, just enough to thicken it without making it stiff enough to hold its shape. Stir in chopped pistachio nuts.

With a slotted spoon, place hot dates in a serving dish.

Pour cream and nuts over the dates and serve.

Serves 4–6.

STEAMED DATE PUDDING I

A perfect pudding for a chilly winter's day. Serve it with a sauce, vanilla custard, clear lemon or sherry sauce. A wedge of leftover pudding should be wrapped in foil and reheated in a preheated 350° oven for 20–30 minutes before serving with some more sauce.

½ pound (about 2 cups) plump dried dates
1½ cups flour
2 teaspoons baking powder
⅛ teaspoon salt
Butter
⅓ cup sugar
2 eggs, lightly beaten
Juice and finely grated rind of 1 small lemon
6–8 tablespoons milk

Pit dates and cut them into small pieces (about the size of large raisins). Sift flour, baking powder and salt together. Put aside until needed.

Cream ½ cup butter with the sugar until fluffy. Add eggs, a few tablespoons at a time, alternating them with a tablespoon or two of the flour to prevent mixture curdling. Beat well between each addition. Beat in lemon juice and grated lemon rind. Fold in flour mixture alternately with enough milk to make a batter that falls from spoon in blobs.

Finally, fold in dates.

Spoon batter into a large, well-buttered pudding basin. Level batter and make an indentation in the middle with the back of your spoon. Cover bowl with a double thickness of parchment paper or with foil, well buttered on the underside. Tie down with fine string. Place on a trivet or rack in a pan with boiling water to come about halfway up sides. Cover tightly and steam in simmering water for about 1½ hours, or until pudding is light-textured and well risen, replenishing with more *boiling* water as it evaporates.

Unmold pudding onto a heated serving platter and serve hot with the sauce of your choice.

Serves 6–8.

Note: If you wish to steam the pudding in a pressure cooker, follow manufacturer's instructions.

CHINESE DATE CRÊPES

10–12 crêpes about 9 inches in
diameter (page 92)
1¾ pounds plump dried dates
1 tablespoon sesame oil
About 1 cup sugar
Peanut or corn oil for frying

Make crêpes and keep them soft and warm under a large plate or wrapped in foil.

Rinse dates. Put them in a bowl and steam in a covered pan over simmering water for 15 minutes. Cool. Remove pits and take off as much of the hard outer skins as possible. Cut dates up and blend to a paste in an electric blender or food processor.

In a large skillet, heat sesame oil. Add date paste and sugar to taste, and cook over low heat, stirring constantly, for about 7 minutes.

Spread each crêpe with date paste. Fold in half and fry in a little oil until rich golden on both sides.

Cut crêpes in strips and serve immediately.

Serves 6.

DATE SQUARES

¾ cup walnuts
1¼ cups fine wholewheat cookie or
graham cracker crumbs
½ teaspoon baking powder
⅛ teaspoon salt
3 eggs
⅔ cup firmly packed dark brown
sugar
½ teaspoon vanilla
1 cup pitted and chopped dates
Butter for baking pan

In a food processor or electric blender, grind the walnuts finely. Tip them into a bowl and put them aside. Mix cookie or graham cracker crumbs well with baking powder and salt.

Beat eggs until fluffy and lemon-colored. Gradually add sugar, beating vigorously, and vanilla. Fold in crumb mixture, followed by ground walnuts and dates.

Pour mixture into a buttered large, square cake pan and bake in a preheated 350° oven for 30 minutes, or until the surface is lightly colored and feels firm to the touch.

Allow the slab to cool in its pan before cutting it in 4, and each quarter into 4 squares.

DATE BREAD

A good, basic loaf which freezes well. Add a handful of chopped walnuts to vary the texture, or half a teaspoon of apple pie spice.

¼ cup butter
1 cup firmly packed light brown sugar
1 egg
2 cups flour
½ teaspoon salt
1 teaspoon baking soda
½ cup pitted and chopped dates

In a pan over moderate heat, melt the butter and sugar in ¾ cup water. Stir, then take off the heat and allow to cool. Beat the egg and stir in the cooled butter and sugar mixture.

Sift the flour into a bowl with the salt and soda. Make a well in the center and pour in the liquid ingredients. Add the dates and mix well until the batter is smooth. Pour into a greased 9 × 5 × 3 inch loaf pan and bake in a preheated 350° oven for 50–60 minutes.

Test the center with a skewer – if it comes out clean, the date bread is ready to be unmolded onto a wire rack to cool.

CHOCOLATE DATE CAKE

For this cake you will ideally need a large tube pan that is about 9 inches in diameter.

However, if you do not have one of these, the cake may be baked in 2 large layer cake pans, then put together and covered with cream. If liked, the cake may also be decorated with a sprinkling of coarsely grated bittersweet chocolate or studded with whole pitted plump dried dates.

3 tablespoons flour
2 tablespoons unsweetened cocoa
powder
1 teaspoon baking powder
4 eggs, separated
1 cup sugar
1–2 tablespoons fresh orange
juice
1 cup chopped pitted
dried dates
1½ cups chopped walnuts
Pinch of salt
Butter for cake pan
1½ cups whipping cream

Sift flour with cocoa and baking powder. Beat egg yolks and sugar together until thick and fluffy. Beat in a tablespoon of orange juice. Sift flour and cocoa mixture again over the surface, and with a large metal spoon, lightly fold it in, together with a little more orange juice if necessary, to make a light, creamy batter. Fold in chopped dates and walnuts until thoroughly mixed.

Beat egg whites with a pinch of salt until stiff but not dry. Gently fold into cake batter. Immediately spoon batter into cake pan or pans that have been thoroughly greased with butter. Bake in a preheated 325° oven until cake is well risen, lightly colored on top and has shrunk away slightly from sides of pan.

Allow cake to "settle" for 15 minutes before unmolding onto a wire rack. Leave until quite cold before covering and/or putting layers together with lightly sweetened whipped cream and decorating it if liked (see above).

MARZIPAN DATES

Choose top-quality dried dessert dates, the kind that come neatly packed in pretty, oblong wooden boxes with rounded ends. Carefully slit each date down one side, remove pits and replace them with a piece of marzipan. Lightly press the dates back into shape. Finally, roll each date in sugar.

For chocolate dates, you will need a 3½ ounce bar of good-quality dark dessert or semisweet cooking chocolate. Break the chocolate into the top of a double boiler or a bowl fitted snugly *over* a pan of simmering water, and heat gently just long enough to melt the chocolate. Beat in a pat of butter.

When chocolate is smooth, using two forks, coat each stuffed date with chocolate, allowing excess to drip back into the pan. Leave to cool and harden on a rack over a baking sheet to catch any drips, or on a sheet of non-stick paper. When dry, arrange the dates in little paper cases.

MOROCCAN STUFFED DATES

A variation on the familiar theme of dates stuffed with marzipan. Afterwards, instead of being coated with sugar only, they are sometimes dipped in thick syrup, then rolled in sugar and allowed to dry before serving.

1 pound dried dessert dates
½ pound (about 2½ cups) almonds
About 4–5 tablespoons sugar
2–3 tablespoons orange-flower water
Sugar for decoration

Carefully slit dates down one side and remove pits. Blanch and peel almonds and toast them in the oven, spread out on a baking sheet, shaking sheet and stirring them frequently so that they brown evenly. Allow almonds to cool.

In an electric blender or food processor, grind almonds finely. Stir in sugar to taste and gradually add enough orange-flower water to make mixture hold together. (This may take some time, as when making an ordinary marzipan.)

Stuff pitted dates with small rolls of orange marzipan and lightly press them shut again. Roll dates in sugar and serve in little paper cases.

RUM DATES

Plump dried dessert dates
Rum
Blanched almonds or shelled walnuts
Sifted confectioners' sugar

Slit dates down one side and carefully remove pits.

Select a large, wide-necked bottle with a good lid. Pour in rum to come about a quarter of the way up. Then pack in pitted dates to fill bottle about three-quarters full. Close bottle tightly, lay it on its side and allow dates to macerate in the rum for about 3 months. Every day or so, roll the bottle around to keep the dates wet with rum.

Empty the bottle into a sieve set over a bowl to catch the remains of the rum. Pat dates lightly with paper towels to remove any excess rum. Stuff each date with an almond or a piece of walnut in place of the pit and lightly press shut again.

Roll dates in sifted confectioners' sugar and pack in a clean, dry glass jar or box. When serving the dates (they make a lovely *petit four* with after-dinner coffee), stick a wooden tooth pick in each one.

DATE SWEETENER

A liquid counterpart to date "sugar," from *Fruit and Vegetables in Particular* by Rita Greer, who, when faced with the daunting task of devising a diet for her husband that was not only sugar-free but restricted in almost every other way imaginable, produced not one but three books of delicious food.

1 pound package cooking dates (ie, slab dates)

Put the date slab on a cutting board and, using a large kitchen knife, cut into thin slices. Put into a medium saucepan with 2½ cups cold water and bring to a boil. Simmer for 10 minutes, stirring from time to time. Allow to cool. Beat with a wooden spoon until you have a smooth, thick sweetener. Spoon into screw-top jars and store in the refrigerator. Keep for up to a week and use as required.

Use in cake-making, for mixing with fruit juice, adding to soups, stews, casseroles and anything which doesn't need a dry sweetener. If you prefer to liquidize the sweetener it needs only a 5-second whizz.

Although cooking dates are supposed to be pitted, very often little fragments remain and sometimes even whole pits. The quickest way to locate these is to search the cooled mixture with clean fingers.

DATE "SUGAR"

Over the past few years, refined white cane and beet sugars have been subjected to a great deal of criticism as "empty calories" with no nutritional value. Brown sugar is only marginally better, provided it is not just white sugar that has been dyed brown. Date sugar, on the other hand, is pure dried fruit ground whole, an unrefined natural sweetener that behaves and looks very much like brown sugar.

Store it in an airtight and moisture-proof jar as it will quickly absorb any moisture in the air and turn unmanageably sticky and lumpy.

1 pound unpitted dried dates

Pit the dates, cutting each one in quarters, and arrange the pieces in one layer on a large, ungreased baking sheet. Dry out the dates in a preheated 250° oven until they are rock hard. This will take several hours, anything up to a whole day or night, depending on the quality of the dates. Turn the oven off, leave the door ajar and allow dates to cool to room temperature.

Drop the pieces of date, a few at a time, onto the whirling blades of an electric blender or food processor, and blend until they are reduced to a fine powder. Store as directed above.

Makes about 1¼ cups.

FIG

From the Mediterranean to the West Coast of America, figs flourish in warm regions. They will even grow reasonably well and produce fruit as far north as Scotland, albeit under glass, but their native home is probably the Middle East. Indeed, the botanical name of the variety *Ficus carica* comes directly from the ancient region of Caria in Asia Minor.

In the classical world, figs were cultivated with enthusiasm. They are known to have been a staple in the diet of the Spartans. Remains of dried figs have been found in Pompeii, and both the ancient Greeks and Romans respected their alleged aphrodisiac properties. The Romans fed figs to the geese they kept to warn them when invaders threatened their city. They introduced this custom to the Gauls, and in this are said to lie the origins of *foie gras*, the great French delicacy, made with the livers of force-fed geese.

Figs can be green, brown or purple-black when they are ripe, depending on the variety. But to be at their best, they must be very ripe indeed, which can be awkward as figs cannot be ripened off the tree and ripe figs do not travel well. A fig is ready to be picked when a drop of nectar collects in its "eye," opposite the stem end, and the fruit feels quite soft when gently pressed. If the figs are not to be eaten at once, store them in the bottom of the refrigerator.

Fresh figs may be eaten on their own or matched with other flavors as appetizers or desserts. The Italians traditionally accompany them with Pecorino, a hard ewe's milk cheese which is rather like Parmesan. Experiment with other cheeses such as a mixture of cream cheese and mild, soft Gorgonzola or Dolcelatte, moistened if necessary with a little thick cream. Beat this mixture together until light and smoothly blended, and spread it over the cut surfaces of fresh figs which have been halved lengthwise. You will need three or four large, juicy fig halves per person for an appetizer. Another excellent partnership is that of ripe figs and paper-thin slices of *prosciutto* (raw Parma ham). A less expensive dish for breakfast is fresh, ripe figs with crisp-cooked bacon and a good grinding of black pepper.

For those who cannot sample the fresh fruit, there are always plenty of preserved ones, in particular canned figs, which are quite close to fresh poached ones and can in many cases be used in their place, and dried figs. Drying figs alters them radically, toughening their skins and making the seeds inside hard and gritty. Both white and black figs are dried. The black are less easily available and somewhat less sweet than white ones, but are full of flavor. Like most other dried fruit, they are graded by quality. Cellophane packages of large, moist, dried figs pressed in neat rows and topped with a bay leaf come from Izmir (Smyrna) in Turkey. These are delicious to eat as a snack by themselves, but the moisture left in them means they easily start to ferment and turn inedible. It is far better to buy fully dried, whole figs from a health food shop. If you rinse off any white powder from the surface, snip off the hard stem ends and soak overnight in cold water, you'll find they can often be eaten just as they are. Or after soaking, simmer them in the water for 30–40 minutes until very soft and plump. Sweeten the water with sugar or honey as desired and cool before serving. Occasionally, too, you will find small boxes of figs preserved in honey, and crystallized Chinese figs, both of which are delicious.

Sweet, ripe figs, peeled or unpeeled, can be frozen whole with or without sugar; first remove the stems. Alternatively, crush and sugar freeze them. In either case, you will need to sprinkle the fruit with lemon juice.

FIG POULTICE

Long known for their laxative properties, figs were also used as "emollient cataplasms" or soothing poultices, for external application to boils, sores, carbuncles and the like.

Originally they were roasted, but today the simplest method would be to wrap fresh figs loosely in foil and bake in a preheated 375–425° oven for 15–20 minutes. Cut in half and cool. Apply to the part to be treated, holding it in place with a piece of cloth if necessary.

Alternatively, boil the figs in as little water as possible, then mash to make a paste. Cool, and apply as above.

FIG APPETIZER

12 fresh figs
½ pound (1 cup) cream cheese
¼ cup heavy cream
A little lemon juice
12 crisp lettuce leaves
Paprika or a little cayenne for
   sprinkling

Trim the stalks from the figs and cut each one into quarters almost through to the base. Beat the cream cheese with the cream and lemon juice and spoon or pipe into the center of the figs. Arrange each fig on a lettuce leaf and sprinkle with paprika or a little cayenne.

Serves 6.

ITALIAN FIGS WITH SALAMI

This is an appetizer which should be served only when the best, sweet, ripe figs (either white or black) are available.

Per person:
3 ripe figs
About 1 ounce Italian salami,
    sliced

Chill the figs in the refrigerator for several hours before serving. Or, if time is short, drop them into a bowl of ice water and chill until they are very cold indeed, then drain them and pat them dry.

Carefully skin salami slices.

Just before serving, peel the outer skin from each fig and slash a deep cross through the top (stem end) to expose the red flesh and seeds.

Arrange the figs and salami on separate platters so that each guest can help himself.

Note: If salami is not available, the figs are also delicious eaten with raw Parma ham (prosciutto) or raw Westphalian ham, sliced paper-thin.

KHOSHAF
Syrian Fruit Salad

This refreshing fruit salad can be made with any combination of dried fruits, including figs. Prepare two days in advance.

¼ pound (about 1 cup) dried figs
⅓ cup dried apricots
2 tablespoons raisins
2 tablespoons blanched almonds
2 tablespoons pine nuts (optional)
1 tablespoon honey

Wash all the dried fruit carefully in a colander under cold running water. Put into a large bowl, cover with cold water and place the bowl in the refrigerator to soak for 48 hours.

Remove the bowl from the refrigerator. Stir in the nuts and honey. When the honey has dissolved, taste the liquid and add further honey if desired. Serve chilled.

Serves 4.

FIG AND ORANGE COMPOTE

This makes a good winter dessert, when the variety of fresh fruit available is limited. Prepare well in advance.

½ pound (about 2 cups) dried figs
1 tablespoon honey
3 large oranges
1 tablespoon liqueur (Cointreau or
    Grand Marnier)
Unsweetened whipped cream

Wash the figs in a colander under cold, running water, then leave to soak in a pan of cold water for 3 hours. Put the pan over a low heat, add the honey and cook the figs gently in the soaking water until just soft. Do not overcook. Remove from the heat, lift out the figs using a slotted spoon and place in a bowl.

Return the pan to the heat and boil the liquid rapidly until it starts to thicken, forming a syrup. Pour this honey syrup over the figs and leave to cool.

Thirty minutes before serving, peel the oranges, removing all traces of pith. Cut into thin slices and arrange in a serving dish, with the figs and syrup. Pour in the liqueur. Serve slightly chilled, with the whipped cream.

Serves 4.

FIGGY PUDDING

This traditional pudding was eaten on Mothering Sunday in Britain, and in many parts of the country figs were always in demand on Palm Sunday. Serve this one with a sherry flavored white sauce.

6 ounces (about 1½ cups) dried figs
6 tablespoons butter
½ cup firmly packed brown sugar
Grated rind of 1 lemon
¾ cup flour
1 cup soft bread crumbs
¼ cup ground almonds
Pinch of apple pie spice
1 teaspoon baking powder
1 egg
3 tablespoons sherry wine
A little milk

Soak the figs overnight, if necessary, then drain and chop, removing any stalks.

Soften the butter, beat in the sugar and lemon rind until the mixture is light and fluffy, then fold in the flour, bread crumbs and almonds.

Add the spice and baking powder and stir to mix.

Beat the egg until foamy, then add to the mixture with the sherry and just enough milk to make a soft batter. Pour or spoon the batter into a well-greased 1-quart capacity pudding basin and cover with buttered foil or parchment paper, making a pleat in the center to allow the pudding to rise.

Tie securely with string.

Steam in a steamer, or in a large pan half-filled with boiling water, for 2–3 hours, replenishing with hot water during cooking.

Unmold and serve while hot.

Serves 4.

FIG AND APPLE CRISPY BAKE

½ pound (about 2 cups) dried figs
4 large tart apples, peeled, cored and
    thinly sliced
2 tablespoons wheat germ
¼ cup honey
¼ cup sunflower oil
¾ cup chopped mixed nuts
Yogurt

Wash the figs in a colander under cold, running water. Put about 1 inch of water in a medium saucepan. Bring to a boil. Add the figs. Cover the pan and cook over low heat for 5 minutes. Remove from the heat. Strain off the liquid and discard. Cut the steamed figs into small pieces.

Grease a baking dish. Arrange the apple slices and chopped figs in the prepared baking dish. Mix the wheat germ, honey, oil and nuts in a bowl, and sprinkle this mixture over the fruit. Bake in a preheated 350° oven for 30 minutes, and serve hot with yogurt.

Serves 4–6.

FIGS AND ICE CREAM

8 large, ripe, fresh figs
4–6 tablespoons light rum
4 scoops vanilla ice cream
Coarsely grated dark chocolate for
    serving

Carefully wash figs and pat them dry with paper towels. Snip off any remaining stems. Quarter each fig vertically and lay them cut side up in a deepish platter or wide bowl. Sprinkle with rum. Cover bowl and chill figs for at least 2 hours, gently turning them over a couple of times.

When ready to serve, put a scoop of ice cream in each of 4 individual glass dishes and surround with figs and their liquor. Sprinkle scoops of ice cream generously with chocolate. Serve immediately.

Serves 4.

FIGS AND PEACHES IN CREAM

A delightfully extravagant dessert that shows the fruits off to advantage.

4 large ripe peaches
¾ cup white wine
2 tablespoons sugar
1 vanilla bean, split lengthwise
4 large ripe figs (about ½ pound)
About 2 tablespoons lemon juice
¾ cup heavy cream
About 1 tablespoon vanilla-flavored
    sugar (page 205)
Flaked blanched pistachio nuts or
    toasted flaked almonds for
    decoration

Peel the peaches one at a time as follows. Drop a peach into boiling water for 60 seconds, or just long enough to loosen the skin. Then gently lift the peach out with a slotted spoon and holding it in the folds of a large dish towel to protect your fingers, carefully peel off the skin. Cut each peach in half vertically and remove the pit.

In a wide pan, combine the wine, sugar and vanilla bean. Bring to simmering point and cook gently for 5 minutes. Drop the peach halves into the simmering syrup and carefully turn them around once or twice to make sure they are thoroughly coated. Then remove the pan from the heat and leave the peaches to cool in the syrup.

Meanwhile, peel the figs, halve them vertically and brush them all over with lemon juice. Add them to the peaches in their syrup, tucking the figs under the peach halves if necessary to make sure they are totally submerged. Leave the fruit in the syrup until ready to serve.

Assemble each portion on a small flat dish as follows. Lay 2 peach halves on it, pitted side up, and cover with 2 fig halves, cut side up.

Whip the cream lightly and sweeten to taste with vanilla-flavored sugar. Top each portion with dollops of the whipped cream and decorate with pistachio nuts or almonds.

Eat with small dessert knives and forks.

Serves 4.

FIGS IN BRANDY

Fresh figs are not always readily available, but if you keep a can of figs in syrup in your pantry, you'll be able to rustle up this quick dessert when unexpected guests call. It's just as good (some say even better) if fresh figs are used and the brandy and sherry are replaced by orange juice.

3 tablespoons brandy
2 tablespoons sherry wine
1 tablespoon grated orange rind
¼ teaspoon ground cinnamon
One 2 pound can figs in syrup
¼ cup toasted flaked almonds

Heat the brandy and sherry in a pan with the orange rind and cinnamon, but do not allow it to boil.

Drain the figs, reserve the syrup and arrange the figs in a single layer in a serving dish. Pour over the hot brandy sauce, adding about 3 tablespoons of the reserved syrup. Set aside for at least an hour.

Just before serving, sprinkle with toasted almonds.

Serves 4.

FIG JAM

2 pounds green (unripe) figs
Sugar
1 teaspoon finely grated
    lemon rind
2–3 tablespoons
    lemon juice

Trim the stalks from the figs, then put the figs in a large bowl and pour over enough hot water to cover them. Leave the figs to soak for about 3 minutes.

Drain them and chop each one into small chunks. Weigh the fruit and put into a large, heavy-based pan with their equal weight in sugar. Add the lemon rind and the juice, then cook over low heat, stirring from time to time, until a clear syrup forms. Thin it down with a little water if the mixture becomes too thick.

Pack into sterilized canning jars and process in a boiling water bath as usual.

Store in a cool, dry place.
See also page 198.

Fills about 3 jars.

GRANDMOTHER'S FIG AND WALNUT PRESERVE

Although I never tasted the original myself, my mother has more than once described the wonderful fig preserve which Grandmother in Istanbul used to prepare especially for my father. If you have access to a supply of fresh figs, it is well worth using some of them up for this preserve. In Turkey, it would be eaten with a glass of water or a small cup of black Turkish coffee.

2 pounds fresh figs
Small shelled walnuts
3½ cups sugar
1 tablespoon lemon juice

Wash figs and pat each one dry individually. Cut off any remains of stem and with the point of a knife, dig a small hole quite deeply into the stem end. With the tip of your forefinger, push a shelled walnut quite deeply down inside the fig. Repeat with remaining figs, stuffing each one with a walnut.

In a large pan, preferably enameled, combine the sugar and lemon juice with 2 cups water, and bring to boiling point, stirring until sugar has dissolved. Simmer syrup for a few minutes, then add stuffed figs. Bring to boiling point slowly once more. Remove from heat, cover and leave overnight.

The following day, simmer figs in syrup until softened and swollen but not broken or burst. With a slotted spoon, lift figs out of syrup and pack them quite tightly in sterilized canning jars. Simmer syrup to thicken it if necessary and pour over figs, covering them completely.

Cover jars and process as you would jam (page 199).

Fills about 4 jars.

Note: In another version of this preserve from the same part of the world, the figs are pricked lightly all over with a fork and dipped in brandy before they are cooked in syrup, presumably to help keep them from turning moldy.

SPICED FIG PRESERVE

A useful, chutney-like preserve that can be made at any time of the year. Serve it with plain roast poultry, the "paler" meats such as lamb, and game dishes of all kinds.

1 pound dried figs
2 cups cider vinegar
2½ cups white or 3⅓ cups firmly
*   packed brown sugar*
2 tablespoons whole cloves
Twist of orange rind
1 cinnamon stick (2–3 inches long)

The day before you plan to make the preserve, rinse the figs thoroughly under the cold tap and cover them with lukewarm water.

Leave the figs to soak overnight in the water.

The following day, combine the remaining ingredients in a heavy, enameled pan. Stir in ¾ cup water and bring to boiling point over low heat, stirring with a wooden spoon until sugar has dissolved. Continue to simmer gently while you finish preparing figs.

Cut off and discard tough, knobbly stem ends from figs, then halve them or cut them in quarters if they are very large.

Add figs to the simmering syrup and continue to cook for about 1 hour longer, stirring more frequently as the mixture thickens in case it should stick to the bottom of the pan.

Discard orange rind and cinnamon stick. Pack in hot, clean jars and process as usual (page 200).

Fills about 2 jars.

DULCE DE HIGOS
Candied Figs

This will be particularly useful for anyone who has a tree with figs which have not had a chance to ripen – a common hazard in an uncertain temperate climate.

1½ pounds green (unripe) figs
1 tablespoon salt
3 cups sugar

Scrape figs with a pumice stone. Place them in a pot with 1 quart water and the salt. Bring to boiling point, remove from heat and allow to stand for about 30 seconds.

Repeat this procedure 4 times (5 times in all). Drain and wash figs thoroughly in 2 or 3 changes of warm water.

Remove stems from figs and make a little cross cut in the stem end of each fig.

In a large pan, dissolve sugar in 1¼ cups water and bring to boiling point over low heat. Add figs and simmer gently for 10 minutes. Let them stand in syrup for 24 hours. Repeat this procedure another 2 times (3 times in all), by which time figs should be transparent.

Store in boxes or jars.

FIG BONBONS

½ pound (about 2 cups) moist,
*   dried figs*
¾ cup finely chopped toasted
*   almonds*
½ cup sugar

Mince the figs, either in a grinder or, preferably, in a food processor, to form a thick paste. Put the minced figs and chopped almonds into a bowl and knead together by hand.

Line a tray with wax paper. Put the sugar in a bowl. Pinch off small pieces of the fig and almond mixture and form into balls about 1 inch in diameter. Roll the fig balls in the sugar to coat them and place on the prepared tray. Leave to stand for 15 minutes until the sugar is partly absorbed. Roll each bonbon once more in the sugar to coat and return to the tray. Leave for at least an hour before eating.

GOOSEBERRY

Like their botanical cousins, black currants, gooseberries grow best in a cool climate. In Europe, they have been cultivated since the early Middle Ages, and the British, who grow particularly fine gooseberries, have immortalized them in the form of pies and, above all, in English gooseberry fool.

The French liking for a sharp gooseberry sauce with fatty fish such as mackerel is shown by their name for the berries, *groseilles à maquereau.*

Gooseberries can be used for cooking when they are still far too hard and sour to eat raw. In England, the first gooseberry pie traditionally used to be served at Whitsun, which falls some time in May. This is intentional. Immature green gooseberries contain far smaller, and consequently less troublesome, seeds than ripe ones. Also, their pectin and acid content are at their peak at this time, so they make easy jams and jellies either on their own or in conjunction with other fruits which may not be as rich in natural pectin.

The berries will be ready by the time elderflowers come into bloom, and this has given rise to an exceptionally successful combination of flavors — that of gooseberries and the faint, aromatic flavor of elderflowers, reminiscent of muscat grapes. But take care not to overdo this flavoring. One or two heads of blossom wrapped in a square of cheesecloth, tied with fine string and suspended in a pan of jam or jelly while it cooks, are enough.

The gooseberry season lasts for many weeks from the time the first green berries appear on the bush ready for cooking. When it is over, you can switch to excellent preserved fruit in cans or bottles, or from the freezer. Whole gooseberries are best frozen dry, in bags; wash, dry, top and tail them first. Alternatively, the berries can be puréed and frozen.

GOOSEBERRY STUFFING

2 ounces (about ½ cup) green
  gooseberries
1 medium-size onion
2 tablespoons butter, melted
1½ cups soft white bread crumbs
1 tablespoon chopped fresh herbs —
  thyme, parsley or sage
Salt and freshly ground black pepper
2 tablespoons chicken broth

Top and tail the gooseberries and wipe them. Peel and finely chop the onion and sauté it in the melted butter until transparent. Chop and add the gooseberries. Cook until soft, then stir in the bread crumbs and herbs. Season with the salt and pepper and bind with broth.

Note: Use this to stuff pork — chops or roasts — as well as duck, turkey or chicken.

ELIZA ACTON'S GOOSEBERRY SAUCE

"Cut the stalks and tops from half to a whole pint of quite young gooseberries, wash them well, just cover them with cold water, and boil them very gently indeed, until they are tender; drain and mix them with a small quantity of melted butter, made with rather less flour than usual (ie a *beurre manié*). Some eaters prefer the mashed gooseberries without any addition; others like that of a little ginger. The best way of making this sauce is to turn the gooseberries into a hair-sieve to drain, then to press them through it with a wooden spoon and to stir them in a clean stewpan or saucepan over the fire with from half to a whole teaspoonful of sugar, just to soften their extreme acidity, and a bit of fresh butter about the size of a walnut. When the fruit is not passed through the sieve it is an improvement to seed it."

As usual, Miss Acton has come up with a perfect formula, this time for gooseberry sauce. Follow the second version starting "The best way of making this sauce." Well-drained, puréed gooseberries do not need thickening with flour.

Personally, I have never warmed to the idea of eating gooseberry sauce with broiled mackerel, classic though the combination may be. Instead, I sweeten it slightly more (exactly how much sugar you add will depend on the ripeness of the gooseberries, but keep them sharp), and serve it with roast poultry or a heavy meat such as pork.

GOOSEBERRY PIE

1–1¼ pounds (about 2 pints) slightly under-ripe gooseberries
About 1 pound rough puff or basic pie pastry for a 2-crust, 8 or 9 inch pie (page 203)
½–⅔ cup white or ⅔–1 cup firmly packed brown sugar
¼ cup flour
3–4 tablespoons butter
Creamy milk or egg glaze

Top, tail and rinse gooseberries, and drain them thoroughly. Allow them to drip dry in a colander while you roll out pastry. Cut a top for your pie pan, then line pan with remaining pastry.

In a bowl, toss gooseberries with sugar and flour, and pile them into the lined pie pan. Dot with flakes of butter. Moisten edges lightly with water. Place pastry lid in position and press sides down gently with your fingertips to seal them. Flute or crimp edges neatly and make a few gashes in top crust to allow steam to escape. Brush with creamy milk or egg glaze.

Bake pie in a preheated 450° oven for 10 or 15 minutes. Then lower heat to 350° and continue to bake for about 30 minutes longer, or until pastry crust is crisp and richly colored, and a gooseberry prodded with a skewer through one of the gashes in the pastry feels soft.

Serves 6–8.

Note: Egg glaze consists of an egg yolk lightly mixed with a couple of tablespoons of cream or milk.

GOOSEBERRY CHARLOTTE

1½ cups soft bread crumbs
¼ cup ground almonds
2 teaspoons grated lemon rind
¼ cup sugar
About 1 pound (2 pints) bottled or lightly poached gooseberries, drained
¼ cup butter

Mix together bread crumbs, almonds, rind and sugar. Arrange in layers in a buttered ovenproof dish, alternating with drained gooseberries and finishing with a layer of crumbs. Dot with butter and bake in a preheated 350° oven for about an hour. Serve with cream.

Serves 4.

ENGLISH GOOSEBERRY FOOL

Do you crush or purée the fruit for a gooseberry fool? Modern recipes usually advise you to rub the cooked berries through a sieve or purée them in an electric blender, but as Jane Grigson points out in her book *Good Things*, the word "fool" comes from the French *fouler*, to crush.

Frozen green gooseberries make an excellent fool.

1 pound (2 pints) hard green gooseberries
3–4 tablespoons butter
Sugar
1¼ cups whipping cream

Top and tail the gooseberries, and put them in a pan with the butter buried among them. Moisten with 2 tablespoons water. Cover pan tightly and cook gently, shaking pan occasionally, until gooseberries are soft and have turned a golden green color. Crush them lightly with a fork once or twice during cooking. Sweeten to taste and put aside.

In a large bowl, whip cream until it stands in soft, floppy peaks. With a large metal spoon, fold in the gooseberries and their juices. Pile in a large glass bowl and chill thoroughly before serving. Serve accompanied by a dish of delicate cookies such as almond tuiles, *langues de chat* or even wafers.

Serves 4–6.

GOOSEBERRY ORANGE FOOL

1 pound (2 pints) under-ripe gooseberries
About ⅓ cup sugar
Finely grated rind and juice of 1 orange
Pat of butter (optional)
1¼ cups thick custard sauce (page 205)
¾ cup heavy cream

Rinse gooseberries. Top and tail them, and put them in a pan with sugar, orange rind and juice, and butter if used. Cover tightly and stew gently until gooseberries are very soft. Then either purée gooseberries and their juices in an electric blender or food processor, or crush them to a pulp with a fork. Cool to lukewarm and beat into custard sauce, which has also been cooled. Taste and add a little more sugar if liked. Leave until quite cold.

Whip cream to soft peak stage and fold in gooseberry custard. Spoon into stemmed glasses and chill lightly before serving. Serve accompanied by a dish of ladyfingers.

Serves 4–6.

GOOSEBERRY SOUFFLÉ

1 pound (2 pints) green
   gooseberries
¾ cup sugar
4 eggs
1¼ cups heavy cream
1½ envelopes unflavored gelatin
Green food coloring (optional)

Wash and poach the gooseberries in ¾ cup water with ½ cup of the sugar to taste until tender. Purée in a blender or food processor, then rub through a sieve. You should have about 1¼ cups.

Butter a 6 inch diameter soufflé dish and tie a band of buttered foil or parchment paper to stand 3 inches above the rim.

Separate the eggs. Beat the yolks with the remaining sugar and purée until the mixture thickens. Lightly whip half the cream and fold it in.

Dissolve the gelatin in 5 tablespoons water over low heat, add the coloring, if using, and stir into the soufflé mixture. Lastly, beat the egg whites until stiff and fold into the soufflé. Leave to set.

Remove the paper collar and decorate with the rest of the cream, stiffly whipped, to serve.

Serves 4–6.

GOOSEBERRY COMPOTE WITH ICE CREAM

Make a simple gooseberry compote. First top and tail hard green gooseberries. Drop them into a syrup made of 1 cup sugar dissolved in 1¼ cups water, and simmer until tender but not broken or mushy. Allow berries to cool in the syrup. (When fresh gooseberries are not in season, you could, of course, poach some frozen ones or just use a can of gooseberries in syrup.)

Taste poached berries and sweeten them with a little more sugar if necessary.

Serve in tall sundae glasses. At the bottom put a few tablespoons of poached gooseberries. On them put a large scoop of plain vanilla ice cream. Decorate with a generous swirl of very lightly sweetened whipped cream and finally sprinkle with chopped nuts – either green pistachio nuts or lightly toasted blanched almonds.

GOOSEBERRY JAM I

Hard, immature green gooseberries have the advantage of containing much smaller seeds than mature, soft ones, but you will find it quicker to make jam with them if they are softened in water before the sugar is added. A rich, thick gooseberry jam makes a delicious spread for a plain, sponge layer cake or hot, buttered scones.

2 pounds (4 pints) hard, green
   gooseberries, rinsed, topped and
   tailed
4 cups sugar
Pat of butter or soft margarine
   (optional)

In a preserving kettle, simmer gooseberries in 1¼ cups water, mashing occasionally with a potato masher or a large wooden spoon, for 10–15 minutes, until the gooseberries are very soft and mushy. Remove from the heat.

Stir in the sugar until quite melted. Return the pan to the heat and boil briskly until jell point is reached, stirring occasionally and skimming scum from the surface as necessary. Stir in the small pat of butter or margarine at the last moment to clear away any remaining scum.

Pack and process as usual.
See also page 198.

Fills about 6 jars.

GOOSEBERRY JAM II

Ripe gooseberry jam is preferred by many people for its aromatic perfume, which can be improved upon even more if you use a strip of orange or tangerine peel. Those who find the seeds troublesome should rub the hot jam through a fine-meshed sieve before packing it.

2 pounds (4 pints) ripe gooseberries,
   rinsed, topped and tailed
4 cups sugar
Strip of dried orange or tangerine peel
   (optional)
Pat of butter or soft margarine
   (optional)

In a preserving kettle, combine the gooseberries with ¾ cup water, the sugar and strip of peel, if used. Cook over moderately low heat, stirring occasionally, until sugar has melted and gooseberries are soft. Then raise heat and boil briskly until jell point is reached, skimming foam from the surface. Remove peel and stir in the pat of butter if liked, to disperse any remaining scum. Strain through a sieve if desired (see above). Pack and process.

See also page 198.

Fills about 6 jars.

GOOSEBERRY RASPBERRY JAM

You do not need a large amount of raspberries but their presence is quite unmistakable. Unlike most gooseberry preserves, this one calls for fruit which is quite ripe and well colored.

3 pounds (6 pints) ripe gooseberries
½ pound (1½ pints) raspberries
4 cups sugar

Rinse, top and tail gooseberries, and put them in a preserving kettle. Stir in raspberries. Heat gently, stirring and mashing with a large wooden spoon or a potato masher, until juices run. Then raise heat and boil fruit until soft and pulpy, about 15 minutes, stirring occasionally.

Rub contents of pan through a fine sieve. Discard seeds etc, and return purée to the rinsed-out pan. Bring to boiling point and simmer purée until it thickens, about 30 minutes, stirring frequently.

Add sugar, stir over low heat until dissolved, then raise heat and boil briskly, stirring frequently, for 10–15 minutes, or until jell point is reached. Skim any scum from the surface if necessary.

Pack and process as usual.
See also page 198.

Fills about 6 jars.

POLISH GOOSEBERRY PRESERVE

If you thought all you could make with gooseberries are thick jams and jellies, this lovely preserve of translucent whole gooseberries suspended in a golden syrup will make you think again. It takes some time to make, but it is well worth putting by a batch for Christmas gifts.

2 pounds (4 pints) green (unripe)
gooseberries
4 cups sugar

Top and tail gooseberries. Rinse them in a colander and shake them dry.

In a preserving kettle or large saucepan, make a syrup with sugar and about 1¼ cups water, stirring over low heat until sugar has dissolved. Simmer for a few minutes. Remove from heat and stir in gooseberries. Leave for several hours. Then return pan to low heat and bring slowly to just below boiling point. Remove from heat and leave overnight in a cool place.

The following day, bring contents of pan to just below boiling point over low heat once again, only this time maintain this steady, low temperature for several hours until the gooseberries are soft and translucent but not in danger of losing their shape. During this time, on no account stir the gooseberries with a spoon for fear of crushing them. Instead, gently swirl the whole pan around from time to time to keep them on the move. Take care, too, that they never come to a pronounced boil. As the gooseberries soften, they become very fragile and either stirring or boiling could break them up. Toward the end of cooking time, skim the surface clear of any scum.

Pack and process as usual (see page 199).

Fills about 4 jars.

SPICED GOOSEBERRY ORANGE PRESERVE

4 pounds (8 pints) slightly under-ripe
gooseberries
2 oranges
¼ cup orange liqueur
6 cups sugar
½ teaspoon ground cinnamon
⅛ teaspoon each freshly grated
nutmeg and ground cloves
Fresh orange juice (see method)

Rinse the gooseberries thoroughly; top and tail them. With a potato peeler or a small, sharp knife, peel the oranges very thinly, avoiding any of the bitter white pith. Sliver the peel finely. Put it in a small pan, cover with cold water and bring slowly to boiling point. Boil for 1 minute, then drain the peel thoroughly and put it in a small bowl.

Stir in the orange liqueur and leave to macerate for 1 hour.

Meanwhile, put the gooseberries in a preserving kettle with about 1¼ cups water and boil for 15–20 minutes, just long enough to soften skins, mashing fruit lightly with a potato masher or a large wooden spoon or mallet.

Stir in the sugar and spices. Squeeze the peeled oranges and add enough fresh orange juice to make 2 cups. Stir juice into the gooseberries and cook over low heat, stirring, until sugar has dissolved. Then raise heat to moderate and continue to cook, stirring frequently, until the preserve is rather thick. Skim off any scum on the surface.

Finally, stir in the slivered orange peel and any remaining liqueur, bring back to boiling point and boil gently for 15 minutes. Stir frequently at this stage or the preserve may stick to the bottom of the pan.

Pack and process (page 199).

Fills about 8 jars.

GOOSEBERRY CHUTNEY

2 pounds (4 pints) green (unripe)
gooseberries
About 1 quart brown malt
vinegar
1 pound slab dates
1 pound (3 cups) raisins
1 Bermuda onion
2 ounces preserved (crystallized)
ginger
5⅓ cups firmly packed brown
sugar
3 tablespoons salt
1 teaspoon cayenne

Rinse, top and tail the gooseberries, and put them through a meat grinder. In a large, heavy, preferably enameled pan, cover gooseberries well with vinegar.

Bring to boiling point and simmer until soft.

Meanwhile, put the dates and raisins through the grinder, and finely chop the onion and ginger. Add sugar, salt and cayenne to the gooseberries, and stir until sugar has dissolved. Finally, add all the remaining ingredients and boil, stirring frequently, until chutney is very thick, about 45 minutes.

Pack and process as usual.
See also page 200.

Fills about 6 jars.

MRS MARSDEN'S GRAND RECIPE FOR GOOSEBERRY WINE (1843)

"4 quarts of berries to a gallon of pure soft water

"Crush the gentlemen, pour the water upon them cold. Let them reside in the tub 3 days. Poke them up and stir them very often with a long pole, then strain the liquor through a sieve, but do not squeeze the berries. Add 3½ lbs of lump sugar to each gallon of liquor. When well dissolved barrel it and allow it to work, which it will, I say months, until cleared. Add liquor to keep it full. Then (when clear) bung it up well and in 6 months bottle it with new fresh corks and seal them.

"*Note:* The berries must be all nicely picked, free from stalk or flower, cleaned and ripe..."

GRAPE

The grape was probably one of the first fruits seriously cultivated by man. The Bible tells how Noah planted a vineyard when he decided to settle down and become a "husbandman." He must also have devised a way of making wine and it was not long before he discovered the effects of over-indulgence in fermented grape juice (wine). Ever since then, men have enthusiastically been growing grapes and turning them into wine.

Grapes are thought to have originated somewhere near the Caspian Sea. Fossils of recognizable vine leaves show just how old the plant is. The ancient Egyptians certainly knew grapes and used them to make wine 6,000 years ago, followed by the Greeks and Romans, who developed viticulture to a high degree. Then, as they colonized Western Europe, the Romans planted vines wherever the conditions would support them, in France and as far north as the Rhineland, even in southern Britain. In the British Isles, viticulture was practiced on quite a large scale, first by the Roman colonizers and then by the monks until a change in the climate forced them to abandon it. As European culture spread, grapes spread with it and today there is hardly a corner of the globe that has not been colonized by the grape.

Both dessert and wine grapes can be eaten, black, red or white. Grapes are one of the few fruits which cannot be judged by sniffing them. Size and flavor do not always go hand in hand, and the only sure way of finding out is to taste one. Grapes should be plump and juicy when you bite into them, highly colored and firmly attached to the bunch. If you have the chance – and a good-tempered grocer – give the bunch a sharp shake. If it "shatters," shedding grapes all over the place, it is no longer fresh.

Store grapes on a plate in a cool room or at the bottom of the refrigerator. Like strawberries, they should be washed quickly just before serving and drained on a soft, dry cloth. If you do not want to damage the "bloom" on a handsome bunch of black hothouse grapes, serve them as they are and place a bowl of chilled water on the table so that each person can rinse his own.

A handsome bunch of chilled grapes makes a refreshing finale to an elaborate meal, either on its own or on top of a bowl of mixed fresh fruit. Provide a pair of grape scissors so that each person can snip off a small cluster. Small green or white seedless grapes are very good in savory dishes, and purple or green varieties, seedless or with the seeds removed, are excellent in all sorts of salads, and with poultry and fish dishes. Grapes make good preserves.

The best-known product associated with grapes is, of course, wine. This has always been recommended – in *reasonable* quantities – as a cordial: it will stimulate your appetite, revive and invigorate you, and also help you to relax, and sleep. Brandy is admitted to be medicinal even by those who dislike it. Wine mulled with spices (cinnamon, cloves, nutmeg) and sweetened with honey rather than sugar makes an excellent nightcap. Teetotallers may drink plain, unfermented grape juice to help insomnia; again, honey rather than sugar is best if sweetening is necessary.

A significant portion of the world's annual grape crop of roughly 50 million tons is dried to make raisins, golden raisins, and currants. As with most other dried fruit, you can choose between naturally sun-dried varieties and fruit treated with chemicals and preservatives such as mineral oil. The method used is clearly stated on the label.

Store raisins and currants in tightly stoppered jars. If they have dried out too much, plump them up in boiling water for an hour before use. They will also be delicious soaked overnight in brandy, sherry or orange liqueur, or just orange juice. Another way to restore moisture to very dry fruit is to steam it, covered, in a sieve over simmering water for 15 to 20 minutes.

Mixed with nuts these dried fruits make excellent snacks. They can be used in salads, with meats and in rice dishes, or added to breads, and rich fruit cakes – a fine way to bring summer into the winter kitchen.

Nutritionally, grapes are most valuable in their dried form. Besides being rich in energy, they contain significant amounts of copper, necessary for the assimilation of iron.

LOTION

This is an old recipe for removing freckles, tan and/or sunburn. It makes an acid face bleach, milder than lemon.

Moisten a bunch of unripe green grapes in water (ripe ones work less well). Sprinkle with a mixture of 1 tablespoon powdered alum and 1 teaspoon salt. Wrap grapes in brown paper, and bake in hot ashes or slow oven for 15 minutes. Squeeze juice of grapes and wash face with the liquid. Allow to dry for 15 minutes, then wash off with tepid water.

A similar extract of green grapes can be used as a tonic suitable for all types of skin.

For really oily skin, white wine is a marvelously astringent cleanser and toner.

ROAST PHEASANT WITH GRAPE STUFFING

*1 dressed young pheasant, about 3
    pounds or a little more*
6 tablespoons butter
8 juniper berries
¼ teaspoon crumbled dried thyme
Salt and freshly ground black pepper
1 pound seedless green grapes
*¼ pound mixed nuts, coarsely
    chopped*
*2 slices fat salt pork or fresh pork
    sides*

Wipe pheasant clean with a damp cloth both inside and out, and pluck out any stray pin feathers with a pair of tweezers. In a small pan, melt butter without letting it sizzle. Crush juniper berries with the flat side of a knife blade and stir them into the butter, together with thyme, a teaspoon of salt and a generous grinding of pepper. Brush bird with juniper butter both inside and out. Reserve remaining butter.

Prepare stuffing. Strip grapes from their stalks and rinse well in a colander. Place half of them in a bowl and crush to a pulp with a fork. Stir in remaining grapes and the nuts, and pour over remaining juniper butter. Toss until well mixed. Stuff tightly into pheasant (the stuffing will shrink in cooking as the grapes collapse). Skewer opening shut and truss bird. Lay slices of salt pork or fresh pork sides over breast of pheasant. Place in a roasting pan, on a roasting rack if you have one.

Roast pheasant in a preheated 425° oven for the first 15 minutes. Then baste with pan juices, lower heat to 350° and continue to roast for 35–40 minutes, or until pheasant is tender, basting regularly with pan juices.

Remove salt pork, trussing skewers and strings from pheasant and transfer it to a heated serving platter. Skim fat from pan juices and deglaze the pan out with a splash of water (or, even better, wine), stirring and scraping pan clean with a wooden spoon.

Serve in a separate heated sauceboat with the pheasant.

Serves 2–3.

DUCKLING VÉRONIQUE

After sole and chicken, duckling is an obvious candidate for preparing Véronique-style, with grapes.

1 dressed duckling, about 5 pounds
*½ teaspoon freshly ground black
    pepper*
½ teaspoon freshly grated nutmeg
1 tablespoon oil
1 tablespoon butter
1¼ cups port wine
2 tablespoons currant jelly
½ pound purple grapes

Quarter the duckling and cut away as much fat as possible. Wash and dry the pieces, and rub them with a mixture of salt, pepper and nutmeg.

In a heavy, flameproof casserole that has a tight-fitting lid, heat the oil and butter together until sizzling, and over a moderate heat fry the pieces of duckling until the fat runs and the duckling is a rich, golden brown color on all sides. Take the duckling out of the casserole.

Pour off all the fat from the casserole. Pour in the port, stirring and scraping the bottom clean with a wooden spoon. Stir in the currant jelly. Bring slowly to simmering point, and add the duckling pieces. Cover the casserole and cook gently for 1 hour, or until the duckling feels tender when pierced with a skewer.

Meanwhile, wash and drain the grapes. Halve them and remove seeds.

When the duckling is tender, transfer the pieces to a deep, heated serving dish. Keep hot. Skim the pan juices of all remaining fat and add the grapes. Simmer, uncovered, for 5–10 minutes longer, or until the juices are well reduced, stirring frequently. Taste for seasoning and adjust if necessary. Spoon over the pieces of duckling and serve.

Serves 4.

QUAIL WITH GRAPES

6 dressed quails
Salt and white pepper
¼ cup butter
Chicken broth
3–4 ounces seedless green grapes
¾ cup dry white wine

Wipe the quails with a damp cloth and season them both inside and out with salt and white pepper. In a heavy, flameproof casserole wide enough to take all the quails in one layer, brown the birds all over in hot butter.

Moisten with 2 or 3 tablespoons broth, cover the casserole tightly and cook gently for 15 minutes, turning quails once or twice.

Add grapes and wine, bring back to simmering point, cover and cook over low heat for 15 minutes longer, or until quails are tender. Serve from the casserole.

Serves 6.

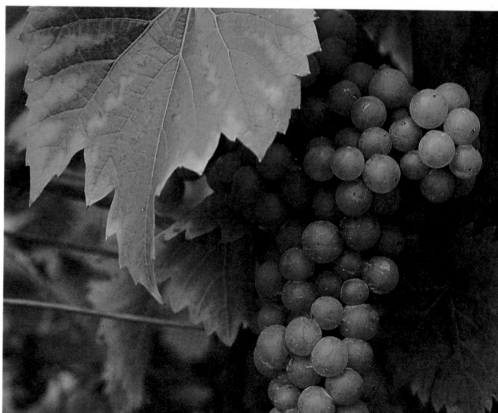

CHICKEN AND GRAPE SALAD

1½ pounds cooked chicken
¾ cup thick mayonnaise (see page 205)
¼ cup thin cream or half and half
2 tablespoons cider vinegar
1 shallot, finely chopped, or 1 tablespoon very finely chopped mild onion
½ sweet red pepper, cored, seeded and finely diced
2 stalks celery, diced
1 pound green grapes
Salt and white pepper
Pinch of sugar (optional)
Lettuce leaves for serving
Coarsely chopped blanched almonds for garnish

Skin the chicken and dice it.

In a large bowl, thin down the mayonnaise by beating in the cream and vinegar. Stir in the chicken, shallot or onion, red pepper and celery. If seedless grapes are used, rinse and drain them thoroughly, separate them and add them to the bowl whole. Otherwise, first rinse them, halve them and remove seeds. Mix all the ingredients lightly but thoroughly, and season to taste with salt, white pepper and a pinch of sugar if liked.

Serve on a bed of crisp lettuce leaves, garnished with coarsely chopped almonds.

Serves 6.

AUSTRIAN GRAPE TART

Both green and black dessert grapes may be used for this tart, or a combination of the two.

The latter can look most spectacular if you arrange them in concentric circles, alternating the colors. Or, mark the tart into six equal sections and cover them alternately with black and green grapes.

2¼ cups flour
Pinch of salt
¾ cup butter
⅓ cup sugar
Finely grated rind of ½ lemon
6 tablespoons ground almonds
1 egg yolk, lightly beaten
2 tablespoons lemon juice

Filling
1 egg white
⅓ cup apricot preserve
Maraschino liqueur or Kirsch (optional)
1 pound dessert grapes
Chopped toasted almonds for decoration

Make the rich pastry first. Sift the flour and salt into a bowl. Lightly rub in the butter until the mixture resembles fine bread crumbs. Stir in the sugar, lemon rind and ground almonds until well mixed. Knead lightly to a dough with the egg yolk and lemon juice, adding a tablespoon or two of iced water if necessary. Roll into a ball. Wrap in wax paper or plastic wrap and leave in the refrigerator to "rest and ripen" for 1 hour.

If dough is too hard to shape when it comes out of the refrigerator, let it soften at room temperature. Then roll it out thinly and use it to line a large tart pan with a removable base. With a fork, beat the egg white just enough to break down its gelatinous threads and brush it lightly all over the bottom of the unbaked pastry shell. Prick lightly all over with a fork (held upright to avoid gashing the pastry). Bake "blind" for 8–10 minutes in a preheated 400° oven, then lower heat to 350° and bake for a further 15 minutes, or until pastry is cooked but only very lightly colored.

Make an apricot glaze by thinning the preserve down with 1 or 2 tablespoons boiling water. Flavor to taste with a little Maraschino liqueur or Kirsch, if liked.

While the pastry shell is still quite warm, brush the bottom with a thin coating of apricot glaze. Cool the pastry shell, still in its pan.

Meanwhile, rinse the grapes, dry them and neatly remove the seeds. Green grapes should also be peeled. Arrange the grapes closely side by side in the tart shell. Reheat the remaining glaze if necessary until liquid again and brush it over the grapes. Finally, sprinkle the center of the tart with a few chopped almonds.

Serves 6.

SWEDISH GRAPE GELATIN

The quality of vanilla you use to flavor the cream mixture is very important.

Failing real vanilla extract, sweeten the cream with vanilla-flavored sugar (page 205).

2 envelopes unflavored gelatin
6 tablespoons sugar
1 bottle medium white wine
2–3 tablespoons Madeira or sweet sherry wine
¾ pound small black grapes, halved and seeded

Vanilla cream
4 egg yolks
¼ cup sugar
2 cups whipping cream
1 teaspoon vanilla (see above)

In a cup, sprinkle the gelatin over ¼ cup cold water, and leave to soak. Meanwhile, dissolve the sugar in 6–8 tablespoons water in a large pan, and bring to boiling point. Remove from the heat.

Next, place the cup containing the soaked gelatin in a pan of very hot water and stir until the gelatin has dissolved and the liquid is quite clear. Combine with the cooling sugar syrup and mix well. Cool.

Stir in wine and Madeira or sherry, and taste for sweetness, adding a little more sugar and Madeira or sherry if necessary — the liquid should be quite strongly flavored as it loses some of its sweetness on setting.

When the mixture is very syrupy and on the point of setting, layer it with the grapes in a large (about 8 cup) mold, and chill until firmly set.

Meanwhile, prepare the vanilla cream. Beat the egg yolks and sugar together until very thick and lemon-colored. In another large bowl, whip the cream lightly until soft, floppy peaks form. Fold the egg mixture into the whipped cream, together with the vanilla. Chill the cream lightly until ready to serve.

Unmold the grape gelatin onto a flat serving dish and serve with the vanilla cream in a separate bowl.

Serves 6–8.

GRAPES IN SOUR CREAM

Seedless green grapes
Dark brown sugar, sifted
Thick sour cream or plain yogurt

Small seedless green grapes are the best for this. Large ones which have seeds must first be cut in half and have the seeds removed. Rinse and drain grapes thoroughly before seeding them. Lay them in a glass serving bowl.

Sprinkle with a generous layer of brown sugar and spread thickly with sour cream or plain yogurt beaten until smooth.

According to another version, about 1½ pounds seedless grapes are mixed lightly but thoroughly with 1¼ cups sour cream and about ⅔ cup sifted brown sugar, or to taste.

Chill well before serving and serve accompanied by a dish of delicate cookies.

Serves 6.

GRAPES IN VINEGAR

A delicious and unusual accompaniment for cold poultry, ham or pork, from Georgia in the Soviet Union.

1¼ cups cider vinegar
⅔ cup firmly packed brown
* sugar*
6 cloves
One 2 inch cinnamon stick
⅛ teaspoon salt
1 pound small seedless green
* grapes*

In an enameled pan, combine the first 5 ingredients with 1¼ cups water. Bring to a steady, rolling boil and boil for 10 minutes.

Rinse the grapes. Strip them from their stalks and drop them into the marinade. Simmer for 10–15 minutes longer, depending on size.

Pack in a perfectly clean, screw-top jar and leave for at least a few days to allow flavors to mature before serving, the longer the better.

CITRUS GRAPE CONSERVE

For this conserve the citrus fruits must all be thin-skinned, otherwise the result could be rather bitter.

2 pounds seedless green
* grapes*
1 large orange
2 large lemons
2 small limes
4 cups sugar
2 tablespoons small raisins
4–6 tablespoons coarsely chopped
* walnuts (optional)*

Strip grapes from their stalks and rinse them in a colander. Scrub citrus fruits under cold water. Quarter them, pick out seeds with the point of a knife and chop the fruit into small pieces. Put chopped fruit in a large kettle with about 2 cups water. Bring to boiling point and simmer for 10–15 minutes.

Stir in grapes, sugar and raisins, and cook over low heat, stirring constantly, until sugar has dissolved. Then continue to simmer for a further 45 minutes, or until mixture is thick and has reached jell point, stirring occasionally and skimming off any scum on the surface.

Add walnuts, if used. Mix well with the conserve, pack and process as you would jam (page 199).

Fills about 5 jars.

RED GRAPE WINE

This is a dark, Burgundy-type wine, which improves considerably with age, and it is a good accompaniment to game or red meat.

Use only the best-quality black grapes. It is important to ferment and store in a dark place to preserve the rich red color.

10 pounds black grapes
1 Campden tablet, crushed
Burgundy yeast
3 cups sugar

Remove the stalks and any damaged or over-ripe fruit. Place in a colander and wash thoroughly under cold, running water. Put the grapes in a prepared vessel (such as a plastic pail). Add the crushed Campden tablet. Cover and leave for 24 hours.

Quickly remove the cover and add the activated yeast (see manufacturer's instructions for quantity and method of use). Replace the cover and leave the pail in a warm place (65–75°) for 7 days.

Using a fine sieve, strain off the liquid into a clean container. Put the fruit pulp into a linen bag. Seal the bag and press hard. It should be possible to obtain almost 4½ quarts of juice (a small press or an electric fruit juice extractor is useful). Add this juice to the strained liquid. Stir in the sugar and quickly siphon into a prepared fermentation vessel, filling to within 1 inch of the cork. Ferment under an air-lock, in a dark, warm place (65–75°).

Leave until a good layer of sediment has formed on the bottom of the fermentation vessel. Rack, store for a minimum of 6 months, and siphon into dark glass bottles. Keep for a minimum of 1 year, and for 2 years for a full-bodied wine.

See also page 205.

Makes about 4½ quarts.

GRAPE JUICE

If you do not feel like going into wine production, you can make your own grape juice instead.

Use ripe purple grapes for the best color and flavor. Rinse them, strip off their stalks and put them in a pan. Then lightly crush the fruit with a potato masher or just with the palm of your hand so that the skins burst to expose the pulp and seeds. Cover with cold water and boil gently until the pulp softens and the seeds begin to float loose. Pour the contents of the pan into a jelly bag, or a large sieve lined with a double thickness of cheesecloth, and allow the juice to drip out, squeezing the bag at the end to extract every last drop.

The juice will keep, bottled, for several weeks in the refrigerator, or you can freeze it, or sterilize it in bottles. Dilute with water.

See also syrups, page 202.

WHITE GRAPE WINE

This is a sweet, white dessert wine. Use only undamaged, good-quality fruit. There should be no need to add water; sufficient juice can be extracted from the crushed fruit pulp (an electric juice extractor is useful).

10 pounds small seedless
   grapes
1 Campden tablet, crushed
Juice of 2 lemons
2 cups sugar
Liebfraumilch yeast

Remove the stalks and place the fruit in a colander. Wash thoroughly under cold, running water, removing any damaged grapes. Transfer to the prepared vessel (such as a plastic pail). Add the crushed Campden tablet and the lemon juice. Cover the vessel and leave for 24 hours.

Using a fine sieve, strain off any liquid into a clean container. Put the fruit pulp in a linen bag. Seal the bag tightly and press out as much juice as possible from the pulp. It is possible, by pressing hard, to extract nearly 4½ quarts of juice. Stir in the sugar and the activated yeast (see manufacturer's instructions for quantity and method of use).

Quickly siphon into a prepared fermentation vessel, filling to within 1 inch of the cork.

Ferment under an air-lock in a warm place (65–75°).

Rack, store for at least 3 months and bottle. Keep for a minimum of 6 months before drinking.

See also page 205.

Makes about 4½ quarts.

Black Hamburgh.

Raisins and Currants
CAUCASIAN LAMB PILAU WITH RAISINS

This is similar to the pilaus of the Middle East.

1–1½ pounds lean boned
   lamb
1 Bermuda onion
2 medium-size carrots
2 cups long-grain rice
⅔ cup raisins
2 tablespoons butter
1 tablespoon oil
1 teaspoon grated cinnamon
Salt and freshly grated black pepper
3 cups hot chicken broth
   (or water)

Wipe lamb clean and cut it into small pieces. Coarsely chop the onion and cut the carrots into matchsticks. In a large sieve, wash rice under cold running water until water runs clear. Rinse raisins in warm water in another sieve. Put both aside to drain.

In a large, flameproof casserole with a tight-fitting lid, sauté lamb in a mixture of butter and oil until richly browned all over. Season generously with cinnamon, salt, and freshly ground black pepper. Add onion and carrots, and sauté for a few minutes longer, scraping bottom of casserole clean with a wooden spoon. Stir in half the rice, level the surface and scatter raisins evenly over the top. Cover with remaining rice, leveling it out with your spoon. Pour hot broth or water over the entire surface. Then, using the handle of your wooden spoon, bore deep holes all over rice so broth can run easily right to the bottom of casserole.

Slowly bring to simmering point, cover tightly and cook over the lowest possible heat for 30–40 minutes, or until liquid is all absorbed, meat is cooked and rice grains are tender and separate.

Shortly before serving, carefully mix all the ingredients together. Allow to stand, covered, for 10 minutes before serving.

Serves 6.

CHICKEN WITH RAISIN STUFFING

1 large roaster chicken, about 4
   pounds with giblets
Salt
3 carrots, cut into chunks
2 stalks celery, with tops, cut into
   chunks
1 medium-size onion, stuck with 2
   cloves
3 black peppercorns
2 allspice berries
Bouquet garni (2 sprigs parsley, 1
   sprig thyme, 1 bay leaf)
Butter
1⅓ cups raisins, washed and
   drained
3 tablespoons mild, clear honey
⅛ teaspoon ground cinnamon

Wash chicken thoroughly both inside and out. Wash all giblets. Put chicken and giblets except liver (which tends to make stock bitter) in a large pot. Sprinkle with a tablespoon of salt. Pack vegetables, spices and bouquet garni around bird. Cover with water and very slowly bring to boiling point. Skim any scum from surface and simmer for 30 minutes, or until chicken is half-cooked. Then lift it out onto a plate, draining back all stock from its cavity into pot. Place chicken in a roasting pan. Let stock with giblets carry on simmering for at least 30 minutes longer before switching off heat.

In a skillet, melt 3 tablespoons butter and fry raisins for a few minutes, turning them over so they are individually coated. Stir in honey, cinnamon and salt to taste, and moisten with 3 or 4 tablespoons chicken stock. Simmer, stirring frequently, until stock is absorbed.

Stuff cavity of chicken with raisin mixture and skewer opening shut. Truss bird and lay breast side up in roasting pan. Coat bird all over with about ⅓ cup melted butter and sprinkle with salt.

Roast chicken in a preheated 400° oven for 45 minutes, or until it is crisp and golden brown, and juices run clear when leg is pierced with a fork through the thickest part close to the body. Baste occasionally with pan juices and a little more stock if necessary while chicken is roasting.

Serve hot.

Serves 6.

MAZUREK CYGAŃSKI
Polish Fruit and Nut Pastry

A traditional Polish Easter pastry. The exact combination of fruit that goes into it depends on the family's preference and the cook's whim, but dried dates, figs and/or apricots, finely slivered or chopped, are often included as well. I remember as a child during the war in Scotland, when dried fruit was scarce and nuts rarely seen, my mother in desperation supplemented the fruit she had with a large bar of coarsely chopped fruit and nut milk chocolate. Everyone loved it and a bar of chopped chocolate has been included in the family version ever since.

The fruit mixture is sometimes baked on a sweet pie pastry base that has first been lightly baked "blind," but I prefer it on rice paper (which can be bought from any good kitchen supplies store).

½ cup golden raisins
½ cup raisins
½ cup currants
4 egg yolks
1 whole egg
1 cup sugar
½ cup diced candied mixed peel
1 cup chopped blanched almonds
1 cup flour, sifted
Rice paper, for baking sheet

Pick over and rinse dried fruit, and dry on a clean kitchen cloth. Beat egg yolks, egg and sugar together until pale and fluffy. Put dried fruits in a bowl. Add candied peel and chopped nuts, and toss with a fork until well mixed. Add a couple of tablespoons of sifted flour and toss lightly until pieces are individually coated.

Sift remaining flour once more over beaten eggs and sugar, and mix it in gently, followed by fruit and nuts. Pour out onto a large baking sheet which you have lined with rice paper, overlapping edges where they meet and bringing the paper slightly up at the sides.

Bake in a preheated 350° oven for 30 minutes, or until top feels firm to the touch. Cool to lukewarm before cutting into individual rectangles with a very sharp or serrated knife.

Allow to cool completely on the baking sheet.

GERTIE'S CHRISTMAS PUDDING

The longer a fruit pudding matures, the richer it becomes; a Christmas or plum pudding should be prepared at least three months ahead.

The following recipe makes one 2 pound pudding, ample for six or seven post-turkey-and-trimmings adults and two children. Or you can double the ingredients, make two puddings and put one by for the following Christmas or, as some people do, for Easter, by which time it will be well matured.

Butter, for pudding basin
1½ pounds (about 4 cups) mixed dried fruit
⅔ cup diced candied peel
1 small tart apple
1 small lemon
⅔ cup firmly packed dark brown sugar
⅔ cup shredded beef suet
¼ cup ground almonds
½ cup soft white bread crumbs
¾ cup flour
1 teaspoon apple pie spice
Pinch of salt
2 large eggs
3 tablespoons molasses
3 tablespoons dark beer
3 tablespoons brandy

Butter a 2 pound pudding basin or steaming mold.

Cut disks of parchment paper, one to fit the bottom of the basin and one for the top of the pudding. Butter those as well. Fit the bottom disk in position and put the other one aside.

Pick over and rinse dried fruit if necessary, and dry it on a kitchen cloth. Put fruit in a large mixing bowl with the candied peel. Peel, core and finely chop the apple, and add it to the bowl. Finely grate the lemon rind and add it together with the strained juice of the lemon. Stir in brown sugar, shredded suet, ground almonds and bread crumbs. Sift in flour, spice and salt, and mix well.

Beat eggs. Pour over contents of bowl. Add molasses, beer and brandy, and continue to mix batter to a soft, dropping consistency.

Spoon batter into prepared pudding basin. Level top and lay the second disk of parchment in position, buttered side down. Cover basin with parchment paper and foil, or a double thickness of either, tying them in position with thin string.

In a steamer, or standing on a trivet in a large, covered pan with boiling water to come halfway up sides of basin, steam pudding for 4–5 hours. Replenish pan with more *boiling* water as it evaporates.

Cool pudding in its basin and store well-wrapped in a cool, dry cupboard to mature (see above).

On Christmas Day, steam or boil pudding as above for another 4 hours.

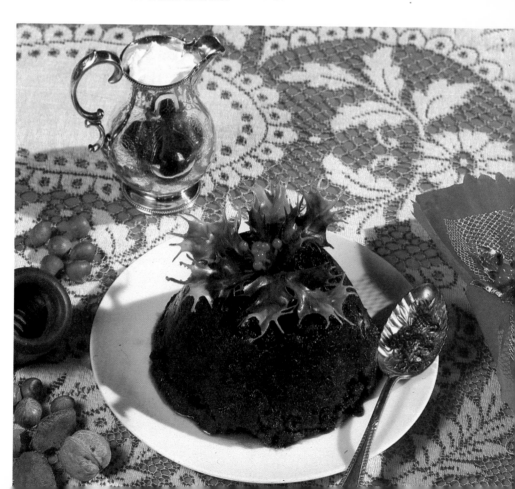

SELKIRK BANNOCK

3 packages active dry yeast
¼ cup sugar
4 cups white bread flour
2 teaspoons apple pie spice
Pinch of salt
¼ cup butter
¼ cup lard
¾ cup likewarm milk
  (optional)
1 cup golden raisins
⅔ cup raisins
⅓ cup currants
⅓ cup chopped mixed candied peel
Finely grated rind of ½ lemon
Butter, for baking sheets and to glaze
  bannocks

Reconstitute the yeast in ¾ cup water with 1 teaspoon of the measured sugar, following directions on the package.

Meanwhile, sift flour, spice and salt into a large bowl, and rub in fats until mixture resembles fine bread crumbs. Stir in remaining sugar. Make a well in the center, pour in frothy yeast mixture, together with another ¾ cup lukewarm water (or use milk if preferred) and knead to a soft, springy dough.

Add dried fruit, mixed peel and lemon rind, and continue to knead until they are well dispersed and dough is shiny and springy again. Roll into a ball, cover bowl and leave to rise in a warm place until dough has doubled in bulk; this will take about 2 hours.

Deflate dough. Knead lightly until smooth again and divide in half. Shape into 2 balls. Place each ball on a greased baking sheet and with the palm of your hand press it down lightly into a round. Cover and leave to rise until doubled in bulk again.

Bake bannocks in a preheated 375° oven until firm and a rich golden color, about 25 minutes.

As soon as the bannocks come out of the oven, rub them liberally all over with a butter paper or brush them with melted butter. Cool on a wire rack and store in an airtight tin.

The bannocks will actually improve in flavor as they mature over the next couple of days and will stay fresh for a long time, provided they are properly stored. If they become stale, they will be delicious eaten sliced and toasted and spread liberally with butter.

IRISH FRUIT CAKE

Butter, for cake pan
1⅔ cups raisins
1 cup golden raisins
⅔ cup currants
⅓ cup chopped mixed candied peel
Finely grated rind of 1 lemon
⅓ cup glacé cherries
½ cup blanched almonds
2½ cups flour
2 teaspoons apple pie spice
Pinch of salt
1 cup softened butter
1⅓ cups firmly packed dark brown
  sugar
3 large eggs
About ¾ cup dark beer

Start by preparing a deep, round and preferably springform cake pan 7 or 8 inches in diameter. Grease it lightly with butter, lining bottom and sides with greased parchment paper.

Rinse and drain the dried fruit thoroughly, and roll it over a clean cloth to dry. Then put fruit in a large bowl. Add the chopped peel and grated lemon rind. Quarter the cherries and add them as well. Finely chop the almonds, add them to the bowl, and toss with a fork until ingredients are well mixed.

Sift flour, spice and salt into another bowl. Toss a few tablespoons of this mixture with the mixed dried fruit — this will help to keep the fruit evenly suspended throughout the cake, preventing it sinking to the bottom.

Beat butter and sugar together until light and creamy. In another bowl, beat eggs until thick and lemon-colored. Beat a couple of heaping tablespoons of the flour mixture into creamed butter and sugar, followed by all the eggs, adding them gradually and beating well between each addition. With a large metal spoon, fold in remaining flour and all the fruit, together with about half of the beer, to make a soft batter.

Spoon batter into prepared cake pan. Level the top and make an indentation in the middle. Bake cake in a preheated 325° oven for 1 hour. Then lower heat to 300° and continue to bake for about 1½ hours longer until cake is firm to the touch in the middle and a thin skewer pushed right down through the middle to the bottom comes out feeling dry to the touch. Should top of cake brown too quickly, cover top of pan with brown paper or a double thickness of parchment.

Allow cake to cool in its pan for 10 minutes before unmolding it onto a wire cooling rack. Then, when it is barely lukewarm, turn cake over and peel off parchment paper from the bottom. Prick base all over with a sharp fork or skewer and soak it with about ¼ cup more dark beer, spooning it on gradually.

Leave until cold before wrapping and storing.

IRISH SPICED FRUIT LOAF

1⅓ cups golden raisins
1⅓ cups raisins
1 cup currants
1⅔ cups firmly packed light brown
  sugar
1¼ cups strong hot tea
Butter and flour, for loaf pans
2½ cups flour
2 teaspoons apple pie spice
2 teaspoons baking powder
2 large eggs

Rinse raisins and currants thoroughly, and shake or pat off all excess moisture. Put in a large bowl. Stir in sugar and cover with hot tea. Cover bowl and soak overnight.

The following day, start by greasing 2 small loaf pans with butter and dusting them with flour, tapping out excess. Sift flour, spice and baking powder together (any bran left in the sifter when sifting a wholewheat flour should be mixed in as well). Beat eggs until light and fluffy.

Beat flour mixture and eggs alternately into bowl of fruit, about one-third at a time. When thoroughly mixed, divide between prepared loaf pans, leveling tops.

Bake loaves in a preheated 325° oven for about 1½ hours, or until loaves are well risen and firm to the touch, and a thin skewer pushed right down to the bottom through the middle comes out clean and dry.

Cool loaves in their pans for 5 minutes before unmolding them onto wire cooling racks. When cold, slice and serve with fresh butter.

DUNDEE CAKE

This traditional Scottish fruit cake with its topping of whole almonds is an excellent standby to have on hand as it keeps so well. People who find the traditional English Christmas cake too rich and heavy will happily have a slice of this one instead.

Melted butter, for baking pan
2½ cups flour
½ teaspoon apple pie spice
Pinch of salt
1 cup butter
1 cup sugar
Finely grated rind of ½ orange and ½ lemon
½ teaspoon vanilla
5 eggs
1⅓ cups golden raisins
1 cup raisins
1 cup currants
⅔ cup chopped mixed candied peel
⅓ cup glacé cherries, quartered
½ cup ground almonds
½ cup finely chopped blanched almonds
1–2 tablespoons milk

Topping
1 egg white
½ cup whole blanched almonds

Brush a deep 8 inch cake pan with melted butter. Line the bottom and sides with parchment paper, and brush with melted butter as well.

Sift the flour, spice and salt together. Cream the butter, sugar, grated rinds and vanilla until light and fluffy. Add the eggs one at a time, together with a tablespoon of flour to prevent batter curdling, beating well after each addition. Fold in the remaining flour, followed by the dried fruit, mixed peel, glacé cherries, the ground and chopped almonds, and milk as necessary to help mix the batter.

Spoon batter into the prepared pan and smooth the top.

Prepare the topping. With a fork, beat the egg white lightly just enough to break down the gelatinous threads. Dip the whole almonds in egg white and arrange them on top of the cake in close, concentric circles, covering the surface completely.

Bake the cake in a preheated 350° oven for 30 minutes. Then reduce the temperature to 325° and continue to bake for about 2 hours longer, or until cake is richly colored on top and a skewer pushed right through the center down to the bottom comes out clean.

Remove cake from the oven and allow it to stand for 10–15 minutes before removing it from the pan and leaving it to cool completely on a wire rack.

FÜRSTENBROT Swiss Rusks

5 eggs
1 cup sugar
2 cups flour, sifted
1½ cups golden raisins
1½ cups unpeeled almonds, split or coarsely chopped
2 tablespoons ground cinnamon
Pinch of salt
Butter, for baking pan

Beat the eggs and sugar together until white and fluffy. Gradually beat in the flour, a little at a time. Stir in the raisins, almonds, cinnamon and salt until thoroughly mixed.

Pour the batter into a large, buttered loaf pan and bake in a preheated 375° oven for 45 minutes, or until well risen, golden and firm to the touch.

Allow the cake to remain in the pan for 24 hours, preferably standing on a wire rack and covered lightly with a cloth.

The following day, using a very sharp or serrated knife, cut the loaf into thin slices. Arrange them side by side on wire racks (or on the grids of a cooling oven) and let them dry out completely until they are crisp and golden.

Store in an air tight tin.

RAISIN WINE

This is a sweet, white wine. For a drier wine, use 2 pounds (about 5½ cups) each of currants and raisins, with only 5½ cups sugar. The rice gives the wine "body." Never ferment on the raisins and rice — only on the juice.

4 pounds (about 11 cups) raisins
Grated rind and juice of 1 orange
2¼ cups rice
6 cups sugar
Juice of 1 lemon
1 Campden tablet
1 teaspoon pectic enzyme
1 yeast nutrient tablet
Wine yeast

Put the raisins in a colander and wash under cold water. Pour 4½ quarts water into a large kettle and bring to a boil. Add the raisins and orange rind. Lower the heat and simmer for 20 minutes. Strain off the liquid, using a fine sieve and return it to the kettle. Heat until just boiling. Add the rice and simmer over a low heat for 5 minutes.

Put the sugar into the prepared vessel (such as a plastic pail). Strain the hot liquid onto the sugar and stir to dissolve it. Leave to cool, until the temperature falls to 65°. Add the orange and lemon juices, the Campden tablet and pectic enzyme. Stir, and cover the vessel. Leave in a warm place (65–75°) for 24 hours. Add the nutrient tablet and activated yeast (see manufacturer's instructions for quantity and method of use). Quickly siphon into a prepared fermentation vessel, filling to within 1 inch of the cork. Ferment under an air lock in a warm place (65–75°).

When fermentation is complete, rack, store and bottle in the usual way. Do not store the wine for less than 3 months. Keep in the bottle for a year, if possible, before drinking.

See also page 205.

Makes about 4½ quarts.

GRAPEFRUIT

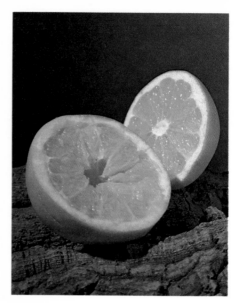

A native of the West Indies, the grapefruit is believed to be the only important citrus fruit to have originated outside Asia. It was identified as a distinct species in 1830 and commercial cultivation began in Florida fifty years later. But it was not until the twentieth century that it began to gain worldwide popularity, when it joined the orange as the most marketed citrus fruit. Today it is available throughout the year, exported from different countries at different times.

The grapefruit tree is said to be named from the clusters of young fruit that, with a little imagination, seem to resemble grapes. Today's big producers and exporters are in Florida and California (the United States currently produces seventy-five per cent of the world's crop), the West Indies, Central America and South Africa – the most prominent variety is Marsh's Seedless. There is also a Texan variety with pinkish pulp.

Buy large, firm fruit, with fine-grained skins, that are heavy for their size. Lighter ones will be pithy and less juicy. A big specimen can weigh as much as ¾ pound while small ones (not to be neglected) can be just 6 ounces.

Grapefruit can be served simply cut in half crosswise with the seeds removed, or broiled with sugar. It gives a special bitter-sweet sharpness to salads, combines well with oranges and lemons in marmalade, and gives a special tang to sherbets.

Half an average grapefruit provides an adult with his minimum daily Vitamin C requirement, and the fruit also contains most other nutrients except fat and Vitamin D. Segmented, canned fruit and juice both retain useful amounts of Vitamin C.

Grapefruits freeze well, either whole, segmented or as juice. The fruit should keep for about eight months; the juice for four months.

GRAPEFRUIT FLOWER WATER

Less well known than its orange-flower counterpart, grapefruit-flower water is equally kind to the skin, and can be used as a soothing and toning lotion.

You will need a large enamel saucepan with a slightly domed lid and a non-plastic handle (plastic will spoil the scent), a small heat-resistant bowl, a non-metallic rack or trivet, some small smooth pebbles, ice – and grapefruit flowers and leaves.

Put the pebbles on the bottom of the pan and cover them with grapefruit flowers and leaves. Now put the bowl on the rack in the center of the pan. Add a little water – enough to cover the flowers and leaves to stop them from burning, but not so much that it will dilute the scent.

Put the saucepan lid on and bring the water to a boil. When it boils, turn the lid over and fill it with ice. The steam will rise, meet the cold lid, condense, and run off into the bowl. Don't boil the water for more than 5 or 10 minutes or the distillate will be weakened.

The lotion can be used on its own, but won't keep long. To preserve it, and make a simple eau-de-toilette, add 20 per cent ethyl alcohol. For a face lotion, add 15 per cent glycerine to the mixture to counteract the astringent effect of the alcohol.

BROILED GRAPEFRUIT

An easy and invariably popular appetizer. Allow ½ grapefruit per portion, plus an extra one for every 4 fruit used. Slice them in half crosswise and scoop out sections, leaving behind pith and membranes, and working over a bowl to catch juices. Use a special serrated grapefruit knife for this or a sharp-edged teaspoon, and be careful not to puncture grapefruit shells. Gently squeeze remaining juice into bowl. With a pair of scissors, snip out all remaining pieces of membrane and fiber from shells.

Place a half-shell per person in broiler pan. Fill with grapefruit sections and some of the juices. Sprinkle thickly with dark brown sugar and dot with flakes of butter.

Set pan so tops of grapefruit are about 5 inches from source of heat and broil steadily until sugar has melted and is caramelized, and grapefruit underneath is heated through, 10–15 minutes. Serve hot.

GRAPEFRUIT AND CARROT SALAD

2 grapefruit
4 fresh young carrots
Crisp green lettuce leaves
6–8 tablespoons coarsely chopped toasted peanuts
2 tablespoons peanut oil
Salt and freshly ground black pepper
Pinch of sugar (optional)
1–2 tablespoons finely chopped parsley

Peel grapefruit and cut out segments, working over a dish to catch juices and picking out seeds with the point of your knife as you come across them. Squeeze out juice remaining in grapefruit piths into dish. Scrub or scrape carrots clean under cold running water and grate them coarsely.

Assemble salad in a large serving bowl (or in individual bowls) as follows. Line bowl with torn lettuce leaves. On this bed place grapefruit segments. Top with grated carrots and scatter with chopped peanuts.

In a cup or small bowl, beat the grapefruit juices you have saved with peanut oil. Season to taste with salt, freshly ground black pepper and a pinch of sugar, if liked. Pour dressing over salad and sprinkle with chopped parsley.

Chill briefly before serving.

Serves 6–8

MINTED GRAPEFRUIT SHERBET

1½ cups sugar
Thinly peeled rind of 1
  grapefruit and 1 lemon
2 cups pure grapefruit
  juice
¾ cup pure lemon juice
1 large egg white
Pinch of salt

To serve and decorate
Chilled fresh grapefruit segments
Confectioners' sugar (optional)
Chilled Crème de Menthe liqueur
Sprigs of fresh mint

In a large pan, stir sugar with 3¼ cups water over low heat until dissolved. Add grapefruit and lemon rinds (best peeled off with a potato peeler). Bring to boiling point and simmer for 5 minutes.

Remove from heat, cool and stir in grapefruit and lemon juices. Leave until cold.

Strain sweetened juice into ice cube trays or a large, shallow freezer container, cover with foil or a lid and freeze until solid around sides but still slushy, like wet snow, in the middle.

Scrape sherbet into a bowl and beat vigorously to break up any large ice crystals which may have formed.

When uniformly slushy, pour back into container(s), cover and freeze to the same state again. Beating and refreezing once more will ensure a smoother texture, but if time is short, this second stage may be omitted.

When ready to proceed, beat egg white with the pinch of salt until stiff but not dry. Then scrape sherbet into a bowl again and beat vigorously until slushy once more. Stir in beaten egg white until texture is uniform, and pour sherbet back into container(s). Cover and freeze until firm.

Transfer sherbet to refrigerator to soften slightly and develop flavors about 1 hour before it is served. To serve, scoop a ball of sherbet into each individual glass or bowl. Surround with 4 or 5 grapefruit segments, skinned, seeded and sweetened with a little confectioners' sugar if liked. Pour a tablespoonful of Crème de Menthe over the ball of sherbet and decorate with a small sprig of fresh mint. Serve immediately.

Serves 6.

CRANBERRY GRAPEFRUIT COMPOTE

Make this in late fall and winter, when fresh cranberries are in the markets, or use frozen cranberries.

1 cup sugar
½ pound cranberries
3 large grapefruit, peeled and
  segmented

In a saucepan, stir sugar with 1¼ cups water over low heat until sugar has dissolved. Then bring to boiling point and boil hard for 5 minutes. Add cranberries and simmer until their skins pop, 5–10 minutes. Cool and chill thoroughly.

Prepare grapefruit halves and divide between 6 glass bowls. Spoon cranberries and syrup over the top and serve.

Serves 6.

MIXED FRUIT MARMALADE

An easy preserve to make. Admittedly, its preparation is spread out over three days, but it will take only a few minutes of your time after the initial preparation of the fruit.

1 large grapefruit
1 large sweet orange
1–2 lemons
1 large sour apple
Sugar
Pat of butter or margarine (optional)

The first day. Cut the grapefruit, orange and lemon in half horizontally. Squeeze out their juice and pick out all the seeds. Cut the peels in pieces. Quarter, core and peel the apple. Put the citrus peels and apple through the coarse blade of a meat grinder. Stir in the fruit juices. Measure volume and add three times the volume in cold water. Cover.

The second day. Pour fruit and juices into a large kettle. Bring to boiling point and boil hard for 1 hour.

The third day. Measure the contents of the kettle. Heat gently while you measure out an equal volume of sugar. Add sugar to the pan and stir over moderate heat until sugar has dissolved. Boil for about 1 hour, or until jell point is reached, skimming off any scum as it rises to the surface. A small pat of butter or margarine stirred in at the last minute will clear any remaining cloudiness from the syrup.

Cool slightly. Pack and process.
See also page 198.

Fills about 3 jars.

HAZELNUT

Hazelnuts are part of the same family as the cobnut and filbert. In Scandinavian folklore, the tree was dedicated to the god Thor, and the king's symbolic staff was made from its wood. Forked hazel twigs are used, to this day, in water-divining.

Hazelnuts have been eaten since earliest times. There are records of their having been collected for food by Stone Age man, and references to them in the works of Theophrastus, the Greek philosopher, and Pliny, the Roman chronicler.

Today, they grow throughout Europe where the male catkins herald spring with their bright yellow anthers. In Britain they are particularly common in the county of Kent. However, this corner of England cannot satisfy the home demand and the nuts are imported from several sources including France, Italy, Spain, Turkey and Armenia.

Hazelnuts can usually replace walnuts and almonds in cakes and pastries, and can be served salted as snacks. They can be lightly roasted in a preheated 350° oven for 10–15 minutes depending on their size, until they are a golden brown. They can also be browned under the broiler. Their thin brown skins will rub off easily but, during roasting, they should be watched and stirred to avoid over-cooking and uneven coloring. Like all nuts, hazels quickly turn rancid. Once cooled after roasting, they should be stored in an airtight container in a cool place.

Ideally hazelnuts should be left in their shells for storing. They can also be frozen successfully. For recipes that call for ground hazelnuts, it is best to break them up in a small hand-rotary cheese mill to avoid extracting too much oil. Be careful, and handle them lightly during mixing to ensure that the oil does not separate, making the mixture too heavy. If you use an electric grinder, make sure you don't reduce the nuts to a powder. If they are to be added to flour and sugar, grind all three ingredients together in a blender or food processor to keep the nuts as dry as possible. But make sure this is done rapidly. They should not be worked too long. It obviously makes sense to grind only the amount of nuts necessary for a particular recipe.

Add ground hazelnuts to cookie and cake batters, decorate cakes with whole nuts, and caramelize them as an accompaniment to ice cream and after-dinner coffee.

Hazelnuts are high in protein and unsaturated fat, as well as in mineral salts and vitamins (especially calcium, Vitamin E and folic acid) and are recommended for heart complaints, and also anemia (which can be associated with lack of both folic acid and Vitamin E). Finally, an old recipe in Oxford's Ashmolean Museum gives hazel buds as an ingredient in an unguent which enables the user to see fairies!

HAZELNUT AND CHERRY SALAD

An unusual salad that combines two contrasting textures. It is good with cold poultry or game.

2½ pounds hazelnuts, shelled,
   roasted and skinned
2 pounds (6 pints) ripe sour cherries,
   pitted

Dressing
6 tablespoons sunflower oil
1 tablespoon wine vinegar
1 tablespoon orange juice
1 tablespoon plain yogurt
¼ teaspoon ground cinnamon
Salt and freshly ground black
   pepper

Place the nuts in a chilled salad bowl. Add all the cherries, except about six. Leave the bowl covered in the refrigerator.

Place all the ingredients for the dressing in a screw-top jar. Squeeze as much juice as possible from the remaining cherries, by crushing them with your fingers, into the jar. Screw the lid on tightly and shake the jar vigorously to mix. Chill the jar of dressing in the refrigerator for at least an hour. Just before serving, shake the dressing again before pouring over the cherries and nuts.

Serves 6.

COUGH REMEDY

For a persistent cough, pound hazelnuts with two or three times their weight of honey, and a little lemon juice, to make a perfectly smooth paste. Make this into pastilles, or dilute with hot water.

LOTION

For an astringent, stimulating yet soothing, lotion for greasy skin boil 1 ounce dried hazel leaves in 2½ cups water for 20–30 minutes. This lotion can also be used for raw, chapped hands.

HAZELNUT SOUFFLÉ

1 cup hazelnuts, shelled, roasted and
  skinned
¼ cup butter
6 tablespoons flour
1½ cups hot milk
4 tablespoons sugar
4 eggs, separated

Start by chopping hazelnuts. Put aside until needed.

Line a soufflé dish with parchment paper, so that the paper extends 3 inches above the top of the dish. Grease the paper well and coat lightly with some sugar.

Melt the butter in a thick-bottomed saucepan.

Remove from the heat, add the flour, and stir to form a paste. Gradually pour on the milk, stirring constantly, to form a smooth liquid. Return the pan to the heat and, stirring continuously, cook the sauce gently until it begins to thicken.

Remove the pan from the heat, stir in the sugar, then beat in the egg yolks, one by one. Add the chopped nuts to the mixture.

In a small, clean bowl beat the egg whites until very stiff. Fold this into the mixture in the pan, then turn into the prepared soufflé dish. Bake in a preheated 400° oven for 5 minutes, then lower the oven temperature to 375° and continue cooking for 20–25 minutes longer until the soufflé is brown and well risen. Serve immediately.

Serves 4.

NUSSTORTE

Make this rich cake for a special occasion.

6 eggs
¾ cup sugar
1½ cups flour, sifted
½ cup butter, melted
Few drops of vanilla

Filling
1 pound hazelnuts, shelled, roasted
  and skinned
2 pints heavy cream
¾ cup sugar

Icing
2 cups confectioners' sugar
3–4 tablespoons water

Line and grease a 10 inch round deep cake pan.

Put 1 inch of water into a small saucepan and bring it to a boil. Lower the heat. In a bowl that fits securely in the pan, over the hot water, beat the eggs and sugar together until thick and creamy. Remove the bowl from the heat. Carefully fold in the flour and melted butter. Add the vanilla. Stir well, then pour the batter into the prepared pan. Bake in a preheated 350° oven for 45 minutes, until firm and golden. A knife slipped into the center should come out clean.

Remove from the oven and cool until the cake has shrunk away from the side of the pan. Remove the cake from the pan and cool on a wire rack. When cold, slice across into 3 equal layers.

To make the filling, chop all but 6 of the roasted nuts finely (you may use an electric grinder for this but be careful that the nuts are not reduced to a powder). In a medium bowl, whip the cream until thick. Add two-thirds of the ground nuts and the sugar. Blend together well. Spread this between the cake layers, sandwiching them together.

Put the assembled cake carefully onto a serving plate.

In a small bowl, mix the confectioners' sugar and water until smooth. Spread this icing over the top and sides of the cake, with a spatula. While the icing is still wet, sprinkle the remaining ground nuts onto the sides of the cake. Decorate the top with the reserved whole nuts. Let the cake stand in a cool place for a few hours, before serving.

HAZELNUTS IN CARAMEL

Shell the hazelnuts, and roast and peel them if you want to bring out their nutty flavor.

Oil a large marble slab or a couple of baking sheets with tasteless oil. Arrange the nuts on the prepared surface in little heaps, each of which should be enough to make an individual mouthful.

For every pound of shelled nuts allow about 2 cups of sugar. In a heavy pan, melt the sugar with a few tablespoons of cold water and a generous squeeze of lemon juice. Over low heat, swirl the syrup around steadily until it turns a rich golden color. Immediately remove the pan from the heat and pour a spoonful or so of syrup over each heap of nuts so that they are completely coated and held together. Leave them to cool and harden.

Carefully prise each candy free from the slab or baking sheets with a round-bladed knife or a small spatula.

Store in an airtight jar.

HAZELNUT COOKIES

These cookies are quick and simple to prepare and store well in an airtight container.

1 pound hazelnuts, finely chopped
  (about 4 cups)
2 eggs
2 tablespoons honey
Pinch of salt
Few drops of vanilla

Line a baking sheet with parchment paper. Oil the paper well.

Put all the ingredients in a large bowl and blend into a paste with a wooden spoon.

Cover the bowl and chill in the refrigerator for 1 hour.

Remove and roll the paste into small balls, about ¾ inch in diameter. Place these on the prepared baking sheet, spacing well.

Bake in a preheated 325° oven for about 15 minutes until the cookies are golden brown. They should still be slightly soft to touch.

Leave the cookies to cool, before eating (or storing).

KIWI FRUIT

The kiwi fruit, or Chinese gooseberry, is native to the Yangtse valley in eastern China where it grows, like the grape, on a type of vine. The Chinese version is smaller and more prickly than the cultivated New Zealand variety.

Hairs on the greenish-brown skin should be rubbed off before the fruit is eaten; or take off the skin with a sharp knife or potato peeler. Leave the fruit in boiling water for 30 seconds if the peel is difficult to remove at first. A ripe specimen feels soft and gives slightly when lightly pressed. Under-ripe fruits continue to ripen off the vine – put them in a plastic bag with an apple or two, or a banana, both of which give off ethylene gas which helps to ripen the kiwis. They should be ready to eat – after an airing – in a few days, and keep well in the refrigerator once ripe.

You can cut the unpeeled fruit in half and scoop out the soft flesh with a teaspoon; or peel it, slice it very thinly across the core, and use it in salads, fritters, or as a garnish for meat dishes. Its taste and texture goes well with fruit-filled meringues and whipped cream to make that well-known antipodean specialty, Pavlova. Like many other exotic and tropical fruits, it makes delicious and refreshingly different ice creams.

Kiwi fruit contains an enzyme, actinidin, which prevents it from setting with gelatin, unless the fruit has been cooked first. The same enzyme makes the fruit an effective tenderizer for meat.

Kiwis can be frozen whole (rub the hairs off the skin first), as thick slices, in syrup made from 2 cups of sugar to 2½ cups of water, layered with sugar, or as purée.

They have a very high concentration of Vitamin C – higher than either black currants or citrus fruit – and are therefore excellent for invalids and convalescents. Peel them immediately before serving – exposure to the air causes vitamin loss.

KIWI CHICKEN SALAD

1 or 2 celery stalks
Small bunch of scallions
1 small head pale green crisp lettuce
1 pound cooked chicken meat
2 ounces button mushrooms
4 kiwi fruit
1–2 tablespoons flaked almonds
A sprinkling of bean sprouts

Dressing
5 tablespoons sour cream
5 tablespoons mayonnaise (page 205)
2 teaspoons lemon juice
Salt and freshly ground black pepper

Wipe, trim and chop the celery. Do the same with the scallions, chopping them finely. Wash and shred lettuce. Pile into a salad bowl.

Dice the chicken, removing any skin (there should be about 2 cups). Thinly slice the button mushrooms and add these to the salad with the chicken.

Peel and thinly slice the kiwi fruit and arrange over the salad with the almonds and bean sprouts.

Make the dressing by whisking the sour cream into the mayonnaise and sharpening it with lemon juice. Season well with salt and pepper and chill both salad and dressing before serving.

Serves 6.

AUCKLAND STEAK

Four ½-pound boneless sirloin steaks
1 ripe kiwi fruit, peeled and halved
2 ripe kiwi fruit, peeled and sliced for garnish
Oil

Preheat the broiler to high. Rub each piece of steak well with the halved kiwi fruit to impregnate it with the juice. Brush each steak lightly with oil. Grease the bars of the broiler rack.

When the broiler is red hot, place the prepared steak on the rack in the broiler pan, and cook for 1 minute on each side to brown. Then move further away from the heat and cook, turning the steaks every 2 minutes, to the desired degree of doneness.

Place the steaks on a warm serving platter and garnish with the sliced kiwi fruit.

Serve immediately.

Serves 4.

GRACE'S PAVLOVA

A classic foil for kiwi fruit, a Pavlova is also delicious served with any other fresh, acid fruit such as raspberries.

3 egg whites
1 cup + 2 tablespoons sugar
2 teaspoons white wine or cider vinegar
1 teaspoon vanilla
1 heaping teaspoon cornstarch
2 tablespoons boiling water
Whipped cream and peeled, sliced kiwi fruit for decoration

Mark a 9 inch circle on a sheet of parchment paper. Use it to line a lightly greased baking sheet and dampen it with cold water.

Place the first 6 ingredients in a bowl and beat until thick, white and fluffy. Meanwhile, preheat the oven to 300°.

Pile the meringue on the lined baking sheet and with the back of a large spoon, shape it into a "nest", hollowed out in the center. Bake for 10 minutes, then turn off the heat and leave it in the oven without opening the door for at least 1 hour, preferably overnight.

When ready to serve, transfer the meringue to a serving platter, fill it with whipped cream and decorate generously with fruit.

Serves 6–8.

KIWI ICE CREAM

6 kiwi fruit
⅔ cup sugar
3 eggs
1¼ cups heavy cream

Peel the kiwi fruit and mash well with half the sugar. Set aside for 15 minutes.

Separate the eggs and beat the yolks with the remaining sugar in the top of a double boiler, or in a heat-proof bowl over a pan of hot water, until thick and mousse-like. Allow this to cool.

Beat the egg whites until stiff and fold into the cooled egg mixture with the mashed fruit. Whip the cream until stiff and fold this into the mixture. Pour into a metal tray and freeze quickly until the edges of the mixture are frozen, then beat it well and freeze again until firm.

Serves 4–6.

KIWI FRITTERS

Most of the preparation for these can be done in advance. They then only take a few minutes to cook. The crisp, dry batter makes a nice contrast to the fleshy, tangy fruit center.

1 cup flour
1 teaspoon salt
1 egg
¾ cup milk
8 ripe kiwi fruit
Oil for deep frying
Sugar and lemon juice for garnish

Sift the flour and salt into a bowl and make a well in the center. Put the egg and half the milk in the well and, mixing from the center, work the mixture into a thick batter. Gradually stir in the remaining milk and beat until the batter is smooth. Put on one side. Wash, peel and slice the kiwi fruit in slices ⅓ inch thick.

Heat the oil in a deep pan until sizzling. Holding each slice of kiwi fruit on a fork, dip into the batter, coating the fruit well, then plunge into the hot fat. Fry a few slices at a time, until they are golden brown. Put the fritters, as they come out of the pan, onto a layer of paper towel to drain off surplus fat. Then transfer to a warm serving dish and keep warm in a low oven until all the fritters are cooked. Sprinkle with sugar and lemon juice before serving.

Serves 4.

KIWI FRUIT CHUTNEY

12 ripe kiwi fruit
3 medium-size onions, peeled and finely chopped
1 lemon, sliced
⅔ cup chopped raisins
2 cups cider vinegar
2 cups firmly packed light brown sugar
5 tablespoons coarsely chopped preserved ginger
1 teaspoon ground ginger
Salt
¼ teaspoon cayenne

Wash the kiwi fruit, then peel and put them in a preserving kettle. Add the rest of the ingredients. Stir well and bring to a boil. Turn down the heat to very low and simmer the contents of the kettle gently, stirring frequently, until a smooth pulp is obtained. This should take about 1½ hours.

Cool, pack and process (page 200).

Fills about 5 jars.

KUMQUAT

The name kumquat (or cumquat) comes from the Chinese word *chin chu,* which appropriately enough means "golden orange." These little natives of South West China have been cultivated there for over 1,000 years but were not seen in the western world until relatively recently. The small evergreen shrub from which they come has glossy, dark green leaves and flowers of the purest white, later succeeded by little miniature "golden oranges." At formal dinners in the Far East, guests are invited to pick fresh kumquats straight from dwarf trees which decorate the tables.

The kumquat is usually oval, and brilliantly colored. The thin, aromatic skin tastes sweet, though the segmented fruit inside tends to be more acid. Buy unbruised fruits with a slight sheen on the skin. Store them in a cool, dry place and eat within a week.

Kumquats can be peeled and eaten like oranges, or sliced and eaten whole, rind and all.

They are delicious simmered in a syrup, cooled, and served with a vanilla ice cream. Use them instead of oranges in a fruit salad, make them into a marmalade, or candy them.

Packed in foil or plastic bags after open-freezing, kumquats will keep in the freezer for up to two months; packed in rigid containers and covered with a cold sugar syrup (about 2 cups of sugar to 2½ cups water), they will freeze satisfactorily for up to twelve months. Thaw them overnight in the refrigerator, or for three hours at room temperature. And try canned kumquats if fresh ones are not available.

MELON AND KUMQUAT SALAD

An unusual blend of flavors and textures.

4 *small melons (such as cantaloupes)*
12 *candied or fresh kumquats*
8 *fresh or canned litchis, halved and seeded*
12 *glacé cherries, halved*
¼ *cup Kirsch or Cointreau*

Slice the tops from the melons and scoop out the flesh. Cut in small dice. Discard the seeds and scoop out the flesh with a melon baller, or dice it. Set aside.

Quarter the kumquats and mix in a bowl with the melon cubes, litchis and cherries and sprinkle with liqueur. Leave to macerate for 15 minutes, then pile the fruits into the melon cups. Chill for about an hour before serving.

Serves 4.

KUMQUAT BATH

Enclose a small handful of fresh or dried kumquat flowers, leaves and rind, in a bag made of muslin, cheesecloth or fine cotton. If the mixture is dried, make the bag big enough to allow for expansion. Either infuse the bag (like an outsize teabag) in boiling water and pour the result into the bath, or simply hang the bag under the hot tap. It can be used two or three times before being discarded.

KUMQUATS IN BRANDY

A tangy dessert to serve with ice cream. And there's no need to use the very best brandy...

2 *pounds fresh kumquats*
2 *cups sugar*
About 2 *cups brandy*

Wipe the fruit and remove any stalks. Make a small cross with a sharp knife in the base of each one.

Put the sugar in a heavy-based pan or a preserving kettle with 2½ cups water and stir over medium heat until the sugar has completely dissolved. Bring this syrup to a boil, add the kumquats and boil, uncovered, for about 15 minutes until the fruit is almost transparent.

Lift out the fruit with a slotted spoon and put into clean, dry, sterilized jars. Set aside.

Continue to boil the syrup in the pan until it is thick, and a temperature of 212° is registered on a candy thermometer. Take great care that the boiling syrup does not splash out of the pan.

Turn off the heat, let the syrup cool a little and then strain it. Stir in an equal amount of brandy.

Pour the brandy syrup into the jars to cover the fruit and leave until the syrup is completely cold. Cover, seal and label, and store for at least 4 months before using.

Add more brandy to the jars from time to time.

KUMQUAT MARMALADE

This has a sharper flavor than orange marmalade.

2 pounds kumquats
Sugar

Wash the kumquats thoroughly in a colander under cold running water. Do not peel, but slice finely. Put the sliced kumquats into an enamel saucepan, cover with about 1 quart water and leave overnight.

Put the pan on the heat and bring the contents to a boil. Lower the heat and simmer gently for 1 hour. Cover the pan and again leave overnight.

The next day, measure the quantity of kumquat pulp and liquid from the pan, then return to the pan and add 3 cups of sugar to each 2½ cups of liquid and pulp. Dissolve the sugar by stirring the mixture over a gentle heat. Increase the heat and boil rapidly, until jell point is reached. Pack and process as usual.

Keep for several months, at least, before using.

See also page 198.

Fills about 6 jars.

SPICED KUMQUATS

This recipe also works well with tangerines, or any of the small fruit of the orange family. (You'll need about 16 tangerines for this quantity of pickle.) Good with game and poultry, it should be ready after about three months.

2 pounds kumquats
½ teaspoon baking soda
One 3 inch cinnamon stick
½ inch piece fresh ginger root
12 allspice berries
12 cloves
1¼ cups white wine vinegar
3⅓ cups firmly packed light brown
*   sugar*

Wipe the fruit and remove any pieces of stalk. Pierce each fruit with the tines of a fork in several places so that the pickling liquid is able to penetrate.

Put the fruit in a large, heavy-based pan, or a preserving kettle with water

CANDIED KUMQUATS

These candies are delicious any time, but try them as a mid-afternoon treat, served with lemon or mint tea, or with coffee after dinner.

½ pound kumquats (about 2 dozen)
1¼ cups rosewater
1 cup sugar

Line a baking sheet with wax paper. Wash the kumquats thoroughly in a colander, under cold, running water. Do not peel or divide.

Put the rosewater and sugar into a thick saucepan and bring to a boil. Remove from the heat. Add the kumquats and stir. Return to the heat and heat to boiling point, then reduce the heat and simmer for 30 minutes. As soon as the sugar begins to caramelize (it will turn light brown), remove the pan from the heat. Lift out the kumquats on a spoon, allowing most of the syrup to drain off, and place, spacing well, on the prepared baking sheet.

Put the sheet of kumquats in the refrigerator for 15 minutes. Then peel the kumquats off the wax paper and store in an airtight container.

to cover. Add the baking soda and bring to a boil. Boil for about 5 minutes.

Put the cinnamon, ginger, allspice berries and cloves into a piece of cheesecloth and tie them firmly inside. Add this to the pan along with the vinegar, then cover and simmer for 10–12 minutes.

Remove the bag of spices and lower the heat under the pan. Add the sugar and stir over gentle heat until completely dissolved. Bring to a boil and simmer covered for another 15 minutes. Lift the fruit from the liquid with a slotted spoon and pack into clean, dry, sterilized jars.

Continue to simmer the liquid for another 10 minutes, then cool a little before pouring into the jars to cover the kumquats. Pack, process and store in a cool dry place.

See also page 200.

Fills about 3 jars.

KUMQUATS IN SYRUP

Kumquats are usually available in early summer, at the same time as mangos, papayas and other exotics. Although they are quite expensive, a few small jars of these pretty little fruits put by at this time will make unusual and attractive Christmas gifts.

2 pounds kumquats
2 tablespoons baking soda
4 cups sugar

Wash kumquats in warm water. Put them in a large bowl and pour on the baking soda dissolved in a few tablespoons of cold water. Then stir in 1 quart boiling water (or more, to cover) and leave until cold. Drain in a colander and rinse thoroughly. This preliminary step will help to soften the rinds of the fruit.

With a thin skewer or the tines of a sharp fork, prick each kumquat in 2 or 3 places to prevent it bursting. Place them in a preserving kettle and add just enough boiling water to cover. Simmer fruit until soft, about 15 minutes. Then lift them out of the pan with a slotted spoon and put them back in the (rinsed-out) bowl.

Add sugar to cooking water and stir over low heat until it dissolves. Then raise heat and boil syrup for 10–15 minutes to thicken it slightly. Carefully replace kumquats in pan and boil them until soft and translucent. Remove pan from heat and leave kumquats to soak in syrup overnight.

The following day, bring kumquats just to boiling point once more. Pack fruit in hot, sterilized glass jars, fill to the brim with syrup, cover and process as you would jam (page 199).

Fills about 3 jars.

LEMON

Lemons can be used in every kind of dish, from savory soups to desserts, as both flavoring and garnish. And slices of lemon may well have appeared before the start of the meal itself, floating in pre-dinner cocktails. Their usefulness does not end here. Lemon juice is used to acidulate water in which slices of food such as apples are soaked to prevent them turning brown when exposed to the air, or it can be brushed directly over cut surfaces that would otherwise discolor rapidly. On pale meats such as chicken or rabbit, lemon juice acts as a mild, harmless bleaching agent. It also makes a fine alternative to mild wine or cider vinegar, far preferable to the harsh malt variety for mayonnaises and salad dressings. Finally, always have a squeezed-out lemon half on a soap dish by the kitchen sink. Rub it on your hands to kill any odors left after handling foods like fish or garlic.

The original home of the lemon is thought to be southeast Asia. From there it gradually came west until in about AD 1000 the Arabs introduced it into the Mediterranean region. To begin with, it was only used medicinally, but gradually its culinary importance took precedence. Today, large quantities of lemons are grown all over the world.

Choosing lemons is easy once you know what to look for. Like all citrus fruit, a juicy specimen will feel heavy for its size. The deeper yellow its color, the less acid it is likely to be. Examine the skin, too. Thin-skinned fruit is usually finely textured. A thick skin often looks lumpy and is deeply pock-marked. Avoid hard-skinned lemons (which are probably old and may be rather dry inside) and any which have soft, spongy patches (they are probably already decaying inside and will soon turn moldy all over).

Lemon juice and grated rind are constantly used in the kitchen, often in very small amounts. When only a few drops of juice are called for, there is no need to cut a whole lemon in half. Simply use a thick needle or sharp skewer to puncture the skin at one end in several places, and squeeze the whole fruit until drops of juice run out. If you need to squeeze out a whole fresh lemon, its juice will run more freely if you first soften the fruit by rolling it over a hard surface under the palm of your hand.

Never waste the rind, even if it is not to be used immediately. Grate it off *before* halving and squeezing the fruit and store it in a tightly covered container in the freezer. Use it in its frozen state when you need a pinch for a recipe.

Invariably, however, there will be times when a lemon half, both rind and juice, is left over. It can be stored for two or three days in the door of the refrigerator, the cut surface tightly sealed with plastic wrap. (A whole lemon whose skin has been grated off should be kept in the same way.)

Finally, a good way of making the most of lemon chunks that might otherwise go to waste is to cut them in slices or wedges, arrange them in one layer on a baking sheet (so they are not touching) and freeze them hard. The pieces of lemon can then be tied up in a plastic bag ready to add, still frozen, to drinks, instead of fresh lemon and ice cubes.

Lemons are almost as valuable medicinally as they are in cooking, and are also used cosmetically in a number of ways.

COSMETICS

Lemon juice is a powerful natural bleach, and soothes the skin as well as whitening it. Instead of throwing out old lemon halves, rub them on roughened and discolored elbows. A lemon juice rinse is a very effective hair lightener, especially if you dry your hair in the sun. It also makes a good setting lotion.

LOTIONS

These lotions are easy to make and take advantage of the soothing and whitening properties of lemons.

For a toning and cleansing lotion, roughly chop one or two lemons, put them in an enamel or earthenware pan, press to extract the juice, cover with milk and bring very gently to a boil. Turn off the heat, allow to cool, strain, and add a little glycerine – just enough to give a pleasant consistency.

The following lotion will bleach dingy skin, sunburn and freckles, and will whiten and soften rough hands. Simply shake together roughly equal parts of lemon juice, glycerine and rosewater. Some people prefer less glycerine.

REMEDIES

For a sore throat, squeeze the juice of a lemon, or chop it roughly and simmer it in water for about 20 minutes to make a lemony liquid. In either case, when mixed with honey, hot water, and whiskey or vodka, it makes a soothing toddy that helps fight infection.

Lemon juice is a natural antibiotic, tonic, diuretic and restorative. A teaspoonful in a glass of warm water, taken first thing in the morning, promotes regularity; cleanses and generally tones up the system, and helps digestion. It is not usually recommended in cases of gout or rheumatism because of its acidity, but an infusion of the leaves can be substituted. This also helps to induce sleep, and has been used to bring down fevers in illnesses such as typhoid.

Lemon peel is also good for fevers as it helps induce sweating.

AVGOLEMONO
Greek Egg and Lemon Soup

In Greece, this classic soup is often based on other broths including meat, especially lamb, or fish.

6 tablespoons rice
1½ quarts well-flavored chicken broth
2 egg yolks
About 3 tablespoons lemon juice
Thin slices of lemon and finely
    chopped parsley for garnish

Rinse the rice in a sieve under cold water. Cover with cold water and leave to soak for 15 minutes.

Meanwhile, bring chicken broth to simmering point. Drain rice thoroughly, stir it into the broth and cook gently until tender, about 15 minutes. Remove pan from the heat.

In a bowl, beat egg yolks and lemon juice together thoroughly. Gradually beat in a ladleful of the hot broth and slowly pour the mixture back into the remaining soup, stirring constantly.

Reheat gently, stirring and taking great care that the soup does not come to a boil, or the egg yolks will curdle. Taste and flavor with more lemon juice, if liked. The soup should be very sharp and lemony.

Serve immediately, each portion garnished with a thin slice of lemon and a sprinkling of chopped parsley.

Serves 6.

VEAL IN LEMON PARSLEY SAUCE

A light summer dish that is quick and elegant.

6 thin veal scaloppine
Seasoned flour
1 tablespoon olive oil
¼ cup butter
Juice of 1 large lemon
2–3 tablespoons finely chopped
    parsley

Pound each scaloppine with a dampened meat pounder and cut it into small squares. Dust on both sides with seasoned flour.

In a large skillet, heat 1 tablespoon olive oil and 2 tablespoons butter, and brown veal quickly on both sides. Remove veal from the pan. Pour off fat and add remaining butter. When this has dissolved, stir in the lemon juice and parsley.

Stir the juices over low heat until well mixed.

Return veal to the skillet. Mix well until thoroughly hot and coated with buttery juices, and serve immediately.

Serves 6.

BAKED FISH WITH LEMON SOUR CREAM SAUCE

Serve the fish with rice, puréed potatoes or hot crusty bread and a tossed green salad.

Butter
1 thin-skinned lemon
1 mild, medium-size onion
1½ pounds small white fish fillets, cod
    or haddock
Salt and freshly ground black pepper
1 cup sour cream (see right)
¼ teaspoon sweet paprika
1 teaspoon coarse French-style
    mustard (eg Moûtarde de Meaux)

Grease a large, flat baking dish lightly with butter. Cut lemon horizontally into thin slices, discarding end pieces which are mostly rind and pith. Pick out seeds as you come across them and discard these as well. Cut onion into paper-thin slices. Arrange lemon and onion rings in baking dish in alternating, overlapping rows. Lay fish fillets on top in a single layer.

Sprinkle the fillets lightly all over with salt and freshly ground black pepper, and dot them with a few flakes of butter.

Cover dish with a sheet of foil and bake fish in a preheated 400° oven for 20 minutes, or until it can be flaked with a fork.

Blend sour cream with paprika, mustard and a pinch of salt.

Uncover fish. Pour sour cream mixture over the entire surface, spreading it out evenly. Immediately broil fish about 3 inches from source of heat until surface has become lightly colored.

Serve immediately.

Serves 4.

Note: Instead of sour cream, you might like to substitute half plain yogurt and half heavy cream, lightly beaten, or use yogurt on its own, beaten until smooth.

LEMON AND ARTICHOKE SALAD

An unusual way to use lemons, this luxury salad is perfect with broiled fish. Use canned artichoke hearts.

3 large juicy lemons
1 tablespoon salt
10–15 canned artichoke hearts
1 cup whole roasted almonds
1 teaspoon honey
2 tablespoons olive oil
Juice of 1 large lemon

Wash the lemons under cold running water, but do not peel or cut. Place them in a saucepan. Add the salt and enough water to cover, and bring to a boil over a medium heat. Continue to cook until the fruit starts to soften, then remove from the heat and drain.

Leave the lemons to cool.

When the lemons are cold, slice thinly and throw into a chilled salad bowl. Halve the artichoke hearts and add them to the lemons. Add the roasted almonds, the honey and the oil. Leave in a cold place until ready to serve (do not prepare more than 2 hours in advance). Just before serving, toss and sprinkle the lemon juice over the salad.

Serves 4.

LEMON HERB BUTTER

This makes a delicious stuffing for a whole baked fish, or it can be dotted liberally on freshly steamed vegetables, just before serving.

½ cup butter, softened
Juice and grated rind of 1 lemon
1 tablespoon finely chopped fresh parsley
1 teaspoon finely chopped fresh chives
½ teaspoon each finely chopped fresh basil and fresh chervil

Mash all the ingredients together in a bowl, or use an electric blender. Mix thoroughly. Use immediately or place in sealed container and store in the refrigerator until needed.

BAKED LEMON PUDDING

A deliciously tart pudding with which to round off a substantial family meal. As it bakes, it separates into two distinct layers – a light, spongy topping, with a rich, smooth sauce underneath that is reminiscent of lemon cheese.

3 eggs, separated
Finely grated rind and juice of 2 large lemons
1 cup sugar
Butter
¼ cup flour
1¼ cups milk
Pinch of salt

Beat egg yolks and lemon rind together until light. Gradually add sugar, beating vigorously. If mixture becomes too stiff to absorb all the sugar, thin it with some of the lemon juice, then beat in remaining sugar, followed by remaining lemon juice, and continue to beat until white and fluffy. Beat in a tablespoon of melted butter.

Sift the flour onto the lemon mixture, a tablespoon at a time, and gently stir it in. Gradually stir in the milk.

In a large bowl, beat the egg whites with a pinch of salt until they form stiff peaks.

Using a large metal spoon, lightly and gradually fold lemon mixture into the beaten egg whites.

Pour mixture into a large, buttered baking dish and bake in a preheated 350° oven for 35–40 minutes, or until pudding feels springy to the touch and is a rich golden color.

This is at its best warm but is also very good cold.

Serves 4–6.

LEMON CRÊPES

I have made these crêpes with unbleached white flour, which gave them the silkiest, most delicate texture I can remember. The final touch of frying the filled crêpes is not, strictly speaking, necessary but when some of the sugary lemon spills out over the hot pan, it caramelizes on the crêpes and makes them deliciously crisp.

1 cup flour (see above)
Pinch of salt
1 egg
¾ cup milk
1 tablespoon oil
Light brown sugar
Lemon juice
Butter

Start by preparing crêpe batter. Sift flour and salt into a bowl, and make a well in the center. Break in the egg. Dilute milk with ¾ cup water. Working with a large wooden spoon, break up the egg and gradually work it into the flour, slowly adding diluted milk as you do so. When batter is smooth and free of lumps, beat in oil.

Put aside to "rest" for 1 hour before frying crêpes.

When ready to fry crêpes, heat your crêpe (or omelette) pan (about 7 inches in diameter), and quickly brush surface with a butter paper or a wad of paper towel dipped in oil. Pour in just enough batter to coat bottom of pan, pouring back any excess left over after a thin layer has set on surface of pan. (Scrape off "trail" left on side of pan by crêpe batter when pouring excess out.)

When crêpe is lightly colored on the underside, loosen edges all around with a spatula and flip it over. Color on the other side, then turn out onto an upturned soup plate and cover with a folded dish towel to keep crêpe soft and moist. Stack crêpes on top of one another as you prepare them.

When time comes to serve crêpes, scatter each one with brown sugar and sprinkle with lemon juice, leaving a border of about 1 inch clear around sides.

Fold crêpes in four.

In a large, heavy skillet, melt a large pat of butter. When foaming, arrange a single layer of folded crêpes in pan and fry steadily until crisp and golden. Turn crêpes over and fry on other side, adding a little more butter as needed.

Serve hot, sprinkled with a little more sugar and lemon juice if liked.

Serves 4–6.

SUSSEX POND PUDDING

A traditional English steamed suet pudding with a buttery filling of lemon and brown sugar. The lemon rind does, however, sometimes remain tough even after prolonged steaming. To avoid this, first freeze the lemon hard, then allow it to thaw again before use.

2 cups flour
2 teaspoons baking powder
Pinch of salt
½ cup shredded suet
Milk and water, mixed
Butter, for pudding basin

Filling
½ cup butter
⅔ cup firmly packed dark brown
    sugar
1 large, thin-skinned lemon, frozen
    and thawed (see above)

To make pastry, sift flour, baking powder and salt into a bowl, and stir in suet with a fork until thoroughly mixed. Then add enough milk diluted half and half with water to make a softish dough.

Butter a medium-sized pudding basin or steaming mold. Take a quarter of the dough and roll it out on a lightly floured board to make a "lid" for the basin. Put aside. Roll out remaining dough and line the basin with it.

To make filling, slice the butter thickly and place half of it in the basin, together with half of the sugar. Prick the lemon all over with a sharp skewer, and place it on top. Cover with the remaining butter and sugar. Fit the pastry lid on top and press well to seal it to pastry on sides of basin.

Cover top of basin loosely with foil or a double thickness of parchment paper and tie firmly around sides with string. Place basin on a trivet in a large pan. Pour in boiling water to come halfway up sides of basin, cover tightly with a lid and boil gently for 3½–4 hours, replenishing pan with more boiling water as necessary.

To serve, unmold pudding onto a deepish serving dish to catch the buttery sweet sauce that flows out of it. Serve each portion with a piece of lemon.

Serves 6–8.

Note: The pudding will take an hour to cook in a pressure cooker at 15 pounds pressure.

LEMON CHEESECAKE

1 cup cottage cheese
3 eggs, separated
½ cup sugar
¾ cup sour cream
Juice and finely grated rind of 2 large
    lemons
½ teaspoon vanilla
3 tablespoons flour
3 tablespoons diced candied orange
    peel
3 tablespoons raisins

Beat the cheese until smooth and creamy. Beat in the egg yolks one at a time. Then, beating vigorously, gradually add the sugar, followed by the sour cream, lemon juice and vanilla. Sift flour over the surface of the mixture, folding it in gently, together with the lemon rind, candied orange peel and raisins.

In a large bowl, beat egg whites until stiff but not dry. Using a large metal spoon, carefully fold cheese mixture *into* the beaten egg whites. Spoon mixture into a well-buttered, 8 inch springform cake pan. (Failing a springform pan, use an ordinary deep cake pan, butter it, line the bottom with a disk · of parchment paper and butter this as well.)

Bake the cheesecake in a preheated 325° oven for 1 hour, or until it feels firm to the touch and is lightly colored on top. Switch off the oven and without opening the oven door, allow the cheesecake to stand for an hour. Then open the oven door and cool it for a further 30 minutes. Remove the cheesecake from the oven, let it stand until cold and chill it thoroughly before unmolding.

Makes 8 wedges.

LEMON MERINGUE PIE

One 8 or 9 inch basic pie
    pastry case, pre-baked
    (page 203)

Filling
5 tablespoons cornstarch
⅛ teaspoon salt
About ¾ cup sugar
6–8 tablespoons fresh lemon
    juice
3 egg yolks
Finely grated rind of 1 lemon
1 tablespoon butter

Meringue
3 egg whites
Pinch of salt
6 tablespoons sugar
1 teaspoon lemon juice or vanilla

Leave the baked pastry case in its baking pan (preferably one with a removable base).

In a heavy pan, stir cornstarch with salt and ½ cup sugar until well mixed. Gradually stir in 2 cups hot water and bring to a boil over high heat, stirring constantly. Lower heat and simmer for 3–4 minutes, stirring frequently, until mixture is thick and smooth, and no longer tastes floury. Remove pan from heat.

Beat egg yolks with remaining ¼ cup sugar. Slowly beat in several tablespoons of the hot cornstarch sauce, then pour the egg mixture into the pan of cornstarch sauce, beating or stirring vigorously with a wooden spoon. Place the pan over low heat and cook gently for a few minutes longer, stirring constantly, until sauce thickens again. Remove from the heat, beat in grated lemon rind and butter, and cool to lukewarm. Taste and add a little more lemon or sugar if you like.

Make a meringue. Beat the egg whites with a pinch of salt until they form very soft, floppy peaks. Add half of the sugar, a tablespoon at a time, beating vigorously until mixture is stiff and glossy. Finally, fold in the remaining sugar and the lemon juice or vanilla.

Pour the cooled lemon filling into the pastry case. Cover with meringue, spreading it right to the pastry rim so that the filling is sealed in (this will help prevent the meringue shrinking back while it is in the oven).

Flick up the surface of the meringue in rough peaks with the tip of a knife blade.

Bake the pie in a preheated 325° oven for 15–20 minutes, or until the surface of the meringue feels firm to the touch and the tips of the peaks are lightly colored.

Serve lukewarm.

Serves 6–8.

LEMON SOUFFLÉ

1 tablespoon unflavored
 gelatin
3 eggs, separated
¾ cup sugar
Finely grated rind and strained juice of
 3 large lemons
¾ cup heavy cream

Sprinkle gelatin over 3 or 4 table-spoons cold water in a cup and leave to soften for a few minutes. When mixture turns hard and stiff, stand cup in a small pan of very hot water and stir until gelatin has dissolved and liquid is quite clear. Allow to cool to room temperature.

In a heatproof bowl, mix egg yolks with sugar and beat in lemon rind and juice. Fit bowl snugly over a pan of simmering water, and beat over gentle heat until mixture is thick and fluffy. Remove bowl from pan and continue beating for a few minutes longer to cool it. Then slowly beat in dissolved gelatin.

Beat egg whites to a firm snow. In another bowl, carefully whip cream until thick and floppy but not stiff. Fold cream into lemon mixture, followed by egg whites.

Spoon into a serving bowl and chill until firm.

Serves 6.

FRESH LEMON GELATIN

A citrus-sharp finish to a heavy meal. Serve decorated with frosted grapes and accompanied by a bowl of lightly sweetened whipped cream.

Finely pared rind of 2 lemons
One 2 inch cinnamon stick
2–3 cloves
3 tablespoons unflavored
 gelatin
¾ cup sugar
1¼ cups fresh lemon juice

In a pan, cover the lemon rind, cinnamon stick and cloves with 1¼ cups cold water. Slowly bring to boiling point, remove from heat and leave to "infuse," covered, for 15 minutes.

Meanwhile, sprinkle gelatin over 6 tablespoons water taken from a measured pint. Leave to soften for 10 minutes, then place container in a bowl of hot water and stir until gelatin has dissolved and liquid is quite clear.

Stir into infused lemon liquid, which should still be warm.

Add sugar and stir until dissolved. Finally, stir in lemon juice and the rest of the measured pint of water. Strain into a large (6–7 cup) gelatin mold and when cold, chill in the refrigerator until firmly set.

Unmold and serve.

Serves 6.

SYLLABUB

A famous old English dessert, as served at the Sharrow Bay in Ullswater, in the Lake District, described as Britain's "most beautifully situated hotel."

1 orange
1 lemon
3 tablespoons sugar
¾ cup heavy cream
½ wineglass dry sherry wine
Peeled pistachio nuts for decoration

Finely grate the rinds and squeeze the juice of the orange and lemon into a large bowl. Add the sugar and stir until dissolved. Add the cream and sherry, and whisk slowly (preferably with a wire whisk) until syllabub is thick.

Pile in a glass serving bowl or in individual, tall, stemmed glasses (wine glasses, for example). Spike with pistachio nuts and serve accompanied by a dish of shortbread fingers.

Serves 4.

LEMON ICE CREAM

An easy recipe for a very special ice cream that makes a deliciously refreshing end to a meal.

Juice and finely grated rind of 1
 medium-size lemon
1 cup sugar
2 cups light cream

Blend lemon juice, grated lemon rind and sugar together until they are syrupy. Gradually blend or beat in cream. Taste and add a little more lemon juice or sugar if necessary, bearing in mind that freezing will weaken flavors.

Pour mixture into a freezer container, cover with a lid or a sheet of foil and freeze until mixture has solidified around sides and is thick and mushy in the middle.

Scrape into a bowl and beat thoroughly to break down any large ice crystals. When mixture is smooth and creamy, quickly pour back into freezing containers, cover and freeze until solid.

Transfer to refrigerator for about 1 hour to allow it to soften slightly before serving.

Serves 4.

MAZURCK CYTRYNOWY
Polish Easter
Lemon Bars

One 9 inch tart shell or large
  rectangular pastry base, pre-baked,
  made with basic pie pastry using 2
  cups flour (page 203)
4 large, thin-skinned lemons
8 cups sugar
4 cups ground almonds

Peel the lemons, scraping off white pith, and slice them horizontally, discarding seeds. In a deep, wide dish, sprinkle the slices with 1 cup sugar and put aside for at least 1 hour to allow sugar to dissolve.

In a heavy pan, mix together the almonds, remaining sugar, the syrup from the lemons and 3 tablespoons water. Stir over low heat until it becomes a smooth paste.

Arrange lemon slices neatly on the pastry base. Cover them evenly with the almond mixture and bake in a preheated 325° oven for 20 minutes, or until top feels dry to the touch.

Cool slightly before cutting into bars with a sharp knife.

Serves 8.

LEMONADE

This recipe makes a concentrate to serve diluted with an equal part of water and chilled with ice cubes.

2 cups sugar
3 oranges
6 large lemons

In a heavy pan, dissolve sugar in 2½ cups water over low heat. Bring to a boil, then remove from heat and leave to cool.

Meanwhile, grate enough rind from the oranges to make 2 tablespoons. Add it to the cooling syrup together with the squeezed juice of the oranges and lemons, and mix well. Leave for 1 hour to allow flavors to develop.

Strain through a cheesecloth-lined sieve. Pour into a stoppered bottle or pitcher and store in the refrigerator. It will keep for a few days.

Makes about 6 cups.

LEMON CURD

Use a double boiler for the curd, or improvise one by fitting a bowl snugly over the top of a pan of simmering water.

4 juicy, thin-skinned lemons
4 eggs
½ cup unsalted butter, softened
1½ cups sugar

Finely grate the lemon rinds, taking care to get rid of any bitter white pith. Squeeze lemon juice and put it through a strainer. Beat eggs until well mixed and foamy.

In the top of your double boiler, combine lemon rind and juice, softened butter and sugar, and stir occasionally over simmering water until butter has melted. Strain in the beaten eggs, stirring vigorously to blend all the ingredients thoroughly. Continue to stir over simmering water until the curd is smooth, thick and creamy, about 20 minutes. It will be very hot, but do not let it boil, or the eggs will curdle.

Pour the curd into small, hot, clean jars and allow to cool before covering as you would jam and storing in the refrigerator (page 199). It will keep for a maximum of 8 weeks.

Fills about 3 jars.

LEMON MARMALADE

This marmalade can be melted and poured over puddings.

12 juicy, thin-skinned lemons
4 cups sugar

With a potato peeler, peel the lemons very thinly so that you take only the colored zest. Cut it into thin, long slivers.

Squeeze the lemons. Collect all the seeds, tie them up in a cheesecloth bag and put them in a large kettle with 5 cups cold water. Leave to soak for at least 2 hours.

When ready to make the marmalade, add the lemon juice and shredded zest to the kettle with the soaking seeds, bring to a boil and boil briskly for 20 minutes. Stir in the sugar and cook gently, stirring, until it has dissolved.

Raise the heat again and boil until jell point is reached.

Remove the bag of seeds. Pour marmalade into hot, sterilized jars and process.

See also page 198.

Fills about 4 jars.

LIME

If the only lime you ever tasted was in the form of juice in a bottle, you would be forgiven for thinking that these fruits are grossly overrated. In fact, if you ever have the opportunity of tasting a fresh one, take it. Limes may look like small, mean-looking lemons with tough green skins and green-tinged pulp, but the taste of their juice is quite remarkable. The flavor is not unlike that of lemons, but more subtle and slightly sweeter.

Limes are thought to be native to southern Asia and to have been brought to the Middle East and the Mediterranean by the Arabs in the tenth century, but nowadays they are cultivated all over the subtropical world. The West Indies and Mexico are the world's principal suppliers.

It has been known for a long time that they are a particularly rich source of Vitamin C and contain about one-third more citric acid than lemons. They also keep well. For these reasons they were carried on long sea voyages by British seafarers in order to prevent scurvy, caused by a lack of Vitamin C in the diet. Hence the nickname "limeys" for British sailors.

Similar rules apply whether choosing lemons or limes, the only major difference being that the latter are always thin-skinned. Look for heavy fruits that are bright green in color. Once they start turning yellow, they lose much of the sharpness that people find so appealing. But do not be put off by brown scald marks on the skin. The pulp and juice inside are probably still fresh and edible.

In cooking of all kinds, from marinades for fish and poultry to desserts and preserves, limes play as diverse a role as lemons. Both the juice and rind are used. Try substituting them wherever you would normally use lemons to add a new accent to cooking.

Like lemons, limes can be cut in slices or wedges for freezing. Put them in one layer on a baking sheet so that they are not touching.

Cosmetically and medicinally, limes are as useful as lemons.

SEVICHE Mexican Fish Appetizer

All kinds of fish may be prepared in this manner.

1½ pounds fillets of sole, skinned (see method)
About ¾ cup fresh lime or lemon juice

Dressing
6 tablespoons olive oil
2 medium-size tomatoes, peeled, seeded and diced
2 canned hot green chili peppers, rinsed, seeded and chopped (but see method)
1 small mild onion, finely chopped
2 tablespoons finely chopped parsley
½ teaspoon chopped oregano
Salt and freshly ground black pepper

Ask your fish merchant to skin fish fillets for you or do it yourself as follows. Lay a fillet on its skin with the pointed (tail) end toward you. With a sharp knife cut fish from skin at the pointed end, going far enough to allow you to get a good grip on the skin. Then turn fillet over and pull skin sharply so it rips off in one piece, holding fish down with the other hand.

Cut skinned fillets into thin strips and lay them out evenly in a deep glass or porcelain dish. Pour over lime juice, adding some more if necessary to cover fish completely. Cover dish and leave to marinate in the bottom of the refrigerator for 3–4 hours, or until strips have lost their translucent, raw look and have turned opaque. Turn fish strips several times while they are marinating to ensure they are constantly coated in lime juice.

Prepare dressing. Assemble all the ingredients in a bowl and stir gently until thoroughly mixed. If you are not afraid of quite a fiery sauce, leave some of the seeds in the peppers. On the other hand, if hot green chilis are not available, a dash or two of hot pepper sauce may be substituted.

Shortly before serving, drain fish thoroughly. Mix gently with dressing and chill lightly until ready to serve.

Serves 6.

Note: A garnish of sweet, mild onion rings, slices of peeled and seeded avocado or whole green olives is sometimes used.

ASTRINGENT OR FRICTION

Limes are the most acid of all citrus fruits and this recipe uses an extract of the leaves and flowers in pure alcohol to make an effective astringent for greasy skin or a friction rub for the scalp.

Put about a cup of alcohol in a glass jar and add a generous amount of lime flowers and leaves. (Lime flowers in recipes generally refer to the linden, but the citrus lime is used in this recipe.) Steep for a week, strain, discard the flowers and leaves, and put a fresh batch in the strained alcohol. Repeat three or four times, or until the extract smells strongly of citrus. Dissolve half a teaspoon of simple tincture of benzoin in a quarter of a cup of witch-hazel, and add to the extract (these are both astringent, and the benzoin is also a preservative).

BROILED CHICKEN WITH LIME MARINADE

If you are worried that the bits of onion in the marinade could burn under the broiler and impart a bitter flavor, strain the marinade before use. Prepare it at least 24 hours before you need it; it will keep for several days in the refrigerator.

One 3 to 3¼ pound chicken,
  cut up

Marinade
6–8 tablespoons fresh lime juice
5 tablespoons peanut or corn oil
2 tablespoons finely chopped
  scallion, white part only
2 tablespoons dark brown sugar
1 teaspoon finely grated lime rind
1 large clove garlic, crushed
Salt and freshly ground black pepper

Start by preparing the marinade. Combine all the ingredients in a screw-top jar and shake well until sugar has dissolved. Place in the refrigerator until needed.

The following day, wipe the chicken pieces clean with a damp cloth or paper towels and prick them all over with a fork. Lay them in a single layer in a large dish and coat generously on all sides with marinade (strained if you prefer, see above). Cover the dish, place at the bottom of the re-frigerator and leave to absorb flavors for several hours, turning pieces oc-casionally.

When ready to cook the chicken, drain the pieces, brushing off any stray pieces of onion. Reserve the marinade for basting the chicken. Preheat the broiler.

Arrange chicken pieces on the rack of the broiler pan and broil for 30–40 minutes until cooked through and colored on all sides, turning frequent-ly and brushing with the reserved marinade.

The pieces should be juicy but the juices will run clear when the chicken is pierced with a fork.

Serve with a large green salad.

Serves 4.

LIME SHERBET

For ¾ cup lime juice you will need to squeeze 5 or 6 limes, depending on their size and how juicy they are. If you do not have enough of them, you can make it up with a *small* pro-portion of lemon juice.

¾ cup fresh lime juice (see
  above)
1½ cups sugar
A few drops of green food coloring
1 egg white

Squeeze lime juice, pour it into a pitcher and chill until ready to use it.

In a pan, dissolve sugar in 3 cups water and bring to boiling point. Simmer for 2 or 3 minutes. Remove from heat and allow to cool, stirring occasionally. Stir in chilled lime juice and tint syrup green with a few drops of food coloring. Pour into a shallow freezer container which has a lid or into ice cube trays, cover with the lid or with a sheet of foil and freeze until slushy, like wet snow.

When ready to proceed, first beat egg white to soft peak stage – it should not be too stiff. Turn the frozen lime syrup into a bowl and beat it thoroughly to break down any large ice crystals. Then beat in egg white, pour back into freezing con-tainers, and freeze until mushy again.

Sherbet can now be frozen until semi-firm and served, but if there is time, its texture will be even smoother if you turn it into a bowl and beat it vigorously once more before re-freezing it.

Serves 6.

CANDIED LIMES

12 juicy limes
1¼ cups sugar

Brush limes under cold running water, using a stiff brush (a wire one is best). Slash each one vertically from top to bottom in two or three places. Place limes in a large bowl of cold water to cover and leave to soak for 3 days. Change water every morn-ing and evening, gently squeezing out water from limes between the palms of your hands each time you do so.

On the fourth day, make a syrup with the sugar and ¾ cup water. Bring to boiling point, add well-drained limes and simmer for 15 minutes. Remove pan from heat and leave, covered, until the following day. Repeat boiling and cooling twice more, once a day over the next 2 days, by which time limes should be soft and translucent.

If not, carry on simmering a little longer on the third day.

Pack limes tightly into sterilized, canning jars (page 201), pour over syrup and cover. Store as you would jams or other preserves.

Fills about 2 jars.

LIME CURD

1 whole egg
2 egg yolks
5 tablespoons sugar
5 tablespoons fresh lime juice
6 tablespoons softened butter, diced

In a heatproof bowl, beat the whole egg and egg yolks lightly with the sugar and lime juice. Fit the bowl over a pan of simmering water, add the butter and stir over low heat until the butter has melted and the curd is smooth and thick, about 20 minutes. Make sure that the water does not touch the bottom of the bowl, and that the curd does not boil, or the eggs will scramble.

Pour into small, hot, clean jars. Cover as you would jam (page 199), allow to cool and store in the re-frigerator.

Fills about 1 jar.

LITCHI

Litchis – usually the canned variety – have long been familiar to lovers of Chinese food. Sweet, fragrant and juicy, with a refreshing, slightly acid after-taste, canned litchis are delicious, but the fresh fruit is infinitely more so.... No wonder a Chinese poet of long ago, when exiled to Canton in Southern China, wrote that "litchis could reconcile anyone to living in eternal banishment." His average daily consumption was recorded as being a mere 300; stouter stomachs were known to take up to 1,000, so popular was the litchi with the ancient Chinese court. The fruit has been cultivated in China for over 2,000 years and the Chinese have identified over fifty varieties.

The fresh fruits need to be peeled from their brittle brown skins and are pearly and translucent rather than opaque. The flesh is crisp, and they are so good in their natural state that it seems a pity to cook them. Their light, fragrant taste goes perfectly with traditional Chinese ingredients like chicken and almonds, and duck.

Fresh litchis keep well for up to three months in the refrigerator, and they can be frozen in a cold sugar syrup (1 cup sugar to 2½ cups water) for up to twelve months.

They are rich in Vitamin C, with a high sugar content.

LITCHI AND ALMOND CHICKEN

1 tablespoon vegetable oil
⅓ cup blanched almonds
2 large celery stalks, coarsely chopped
3 scallions, thinly sliced
1½ cups diced cooked chicken
½ teaspoon ground ginger
1 tablespoon soy sauce
½ pound litchis in syrup (see opposite; use at least 1¼ cups syrup)
½ tablespoon cornstarch

Heat the oil in a large skillet or wok until smoking slightly. Add the almonds, celery and scallions. Cook, stirring constantly, until the almonds begin to brown. Add the chicken and cook, still stirring, for a further 5 minutes.

Lower the heat, add the ginger and pour over the soy sauce and half the litchi syrup. Keep stirring the mixture, over a low heat, for 2 minutes. Remove from the heat.

In a small bowl blend the cornstarch and the remaining litchi syrup and pour this into the pan. Return the pan to the heat and cook, stirring constantly, until the sauce thickens.

Stir in the litchis and serve on plain boiled rice.

Serves 4.

LITCHI PORK

This Chinese dish originates in Fukien province, where litchis grow in abundance. Traditionally the surface of the pork is cut with a criss-cross pattern to resemble the skin of a ripe litchi.

10 ounces lean pork tenderloin
2 tablespoons cornstarch
1 teaspoon salt
1 pound fresh litchis
6 tablespoons vegetable oil
1 large onion, finely sliced
¾ cup chicken broth
1 tablespoon soy sauce
1 tablespoon sugar
2 teaspoons vinegar
2 teaspoons sesame oil
2 tablespoons medium sherry wine

Preheat the oven to its lowest setting. Slice the pork into small pieces about 1½ inches long by 1 inch wide and about ¼ inch thick. Using a sharp knife, mark one surface of the pork slices with a criss-cross pattern. On a plate, mix half the cornstarch and the salt. Coat each slice of pork lightly with this mixture and leave on one side.

Peel the litchis. Remove the seeds, wash under cold, running water and set on one side.

Heat the oil in a large skillet or wok until it smokes slightly. Add the pork and fry, stirring constantly, for 3–4 minutes. Then arrange the pork, criss-cross surface down in the pan, and allow to cook for a further 2 minutes. Remove the pork from the pan and keep warm.

Pour any excess oil out of the skillet. Add the chopped onion and fry stirring constantly for 2 minutes. Stir in the broth, soy sauce, sugar, vinegar, sesame oil and sherry. Remove the pan from the heat.

In a small bowl, blend the remaining cornstarch with 3 tablespoons water. Add this to the contents of the pan and return to the heat. Cook gently until the sauce thickens, then add the pork and litchis. Allow to boil and keep cooking, while stirring, for a further 2 minutes. Serve immediately on boiled rice or noodles.

Serves 4.

LITCHI AND PINEAPPLE PORK

Here's an "authentic" Chinese recipe all the way from San Francisco! I like to fry the pork first to make sure it is well cooked, then finish it in the sauce in the pan. The Chinese would add ½ teaspoon of monosodium glutamate to the sauce, but since this is now a controversial subject in the West, I leave this decision to you.

18 fresh litchis or a 16 ounce
    can litchis
One 16 ounce can pineapple
    slices
1 medium-size sweet green pepper
1 egg
1 pound pork tenderloin
About 1½ cups flour
Salt
Oil for frying
1 teaspoon soy sauce
½ cup sugar
3 tablespoons tomato paste
    or catsup
½ cup white vinegar
Freshly ground black pepper
2 tablespoons cornstarch

Peel the litchis if using fresh ones and remove the seeds; otherwise drain the can, discarding the juice. Drain the can of pineapple slices, reserve the juice and cut the pineapple slices into chunks. Remove core and seeds from the pepper and cut into ¾ inch squares. Beat the egg. Cut the pork into neat ½ inch cubes and dip these into the beaten egg until thoroughly coated on all sides.

Sift the flour into a bowl with about a teaspoon of salt. Add the pork and toss until well coated. Heat the oil in a deep-fat fryer and fry the pork cubes for 6–8 minutes, until browned, then drain well on paper towels.

In a wok or skillet, mix the soy sauce with the sugar, tomato paste or catsup, vinegar and ¼ cup of the reserved pineapple syrup. Bring to a boil and season with salt and pepper.

Stir the cornstarch into 3 tablespoons water to make a smooth paste, then gradually stir this into the mixture in the wok or skillet. Cook, stirring, until the sauce thickens, then add the pork, litchis, pineapple pieces and green pepper.

Stir-fry over a high heat until all the ingredients are very hot and well mixed together.

Serve at once with plain boiled rice.

Serves 4.

TROPICAL FRUIT SALAD

This can be an expensive dessert, but worth it for a special occasion. It is foolproof to make, but always impressive.

1 fresh mango
1 large banana
1 small pineapple
1 pound fresh ripe litchis
½ cup sugar
2½ cups Kirsch

Peel and slice the mango. Arrange the slices in a medium serving bowl. Peel and slice the banana into thick, ¼ inch chunks. Add these to the bowl. Remove the outer skin and core of the pineapple and cut across into ¼ inch slices. Add these to the fruit in the bowl. Peel the litchis, remove the seeds and wash under cold, running water.

Arrange the litchis on top of the other fruit.

In a small saucepan, mix the sugar and ¾ cup water. Place the pan over low heat and stir until the sugar dissolves. Continue cooking until the syrup boils, then lower the heat and simmer for 10 minutes. Remove the pan from the heat, allow the syrup to cool, then stir in the Kirsch. Pour this mixture over the fruit.

Place the bowl in the refrigerator, and leave to chill for at least 1 hour before serving.

Serves 4–6.

LITCHIS IN SYRUP

Fresh litchis appear infrequently in Western fruit shops and do not keep long. So when available, set some aside for preserving in syrup.

½ cup sugar
1½ pounds fresh litchis

Place the sugar and 1¼ cups water in a medium saucepan and gently bring to a boil, stirring until the sugar has dissolved. Leave to boil for 15–20 minutes until the syrup starts to thicken slightly. Remove the pan from the heat.

Peel each litchi, but do not remove the seed. Wash under cold running water and add to the sugar syrup. Pack and process as usual.

See also page 201.

Fills about 3 jars.

MANGO

The mango is one of the best and most popular of tropical fruits. The tree on which it grows flourishes in the hot, humid climate of India, its native home, but it has been introduced into countries including Brazil, Kenya and, most recently, Israel. Many cultivars have been developed, of which one of the most famous is the Indian Alphonso. The fruits vary in shape, size and color, from rather flat, yellowish-green specimens weighing about ½ pound to large, round, rosy-red ones that weigh well over a pound. Mangoes travel well and, like bananas, are often picked before they are fully ripe and allowed to ripen in cold storage while being shipped.

When choosing a mango, look for one that yields slightly to finger pressure. If the fruit is hard and unyielding, leave it to soften at room temperature for a few days then store in the refrigerator until ready to serve.

All mangoes are dealt with in the same way, whatever their shape and size. First, peel the skin off thinly with a sharp knife. Alternatively, mark the whole skin in segments like an orange and carefully peel them back with your fingers. Then cut away the large, flat seed from the flesh. To do this, slice down one side with the knife blade as close to the seed as possible, then repeat on the other side. Finally trim off any remaining flesh.

The flavor of a ripe mango has been described as a cross between a peach and a melon with gingery undertones. It is sweet and powerfully aromatic, and needs no accompaniment apart from a sprinkling of lime or lemon juice. Cubes of diced mango make an unusual addition to a fresh fruit salad, or the fruit can be turned into a variety of delightful mousses, creams, ice creams and other desserts.

Canned fruit in syrup and mango purée can be substituted when fresh mangoes are out of season. You may also be able to find dried fruit, imported from the Far East. And no curry dinner would be complete without a dish of mango chutney.

Mangoes are very high in Vitamin A – less so than carrots, but more so than apricots.

MANGO AND PORK SALAD

Serve this Thai dish with rice as part of a main course, or as an appetizer. The dried salted shrimp and fish sauce may be bought from a Chinese food store or gourmet shop.

2 large, unripe green mangoes,
  peeled and seeded
1 teaspoon salt
2 tablespoons lard
1 tablespoon finely chopped shallot
2 cloves garlic, finely crushed
6 ounces lean pork, finely chopped
1 tablespoon dried salted shrimp,
  pounded
1 tablespoon roasted peanuts, partly
  pounded
1 tablespoon fish sauce
1 teaspoon sugar
Salt and freshly ground black pepper
1 red chili pepper, finely shredded

Shred the mangoes into long, even strips, place in a bowl and sprinkle with the salt. Leave for 15 minutes, then wash the mango thoroughly in a colander, under cold running water, to remove all traces of the salt. Put the washed fruit into a large salad bowl.

In a skillet, heat the lard until smoking. Add the shallot and garlic and cook until lightly browned. Add the pork to the skillet and fry until crisp on the outside.

Using a slotted spoon, remove the shallots, garlic and pork from the skillet, dry on paper towels and set on one side to cool.

Add the shrimp, peanuts, fish sauce and sugar to the hot fat and stir well. Cook for 5 minutes, then remove from the heat and set aside for the contents to cool.

Just before serving, add the fried ingredients to the mango in the large bowl, mix well and season to taste. Sprinkle the shredded chili on top.

Serves 4—6.

REMEDIES

In parts of India and Bangladesh, dried mangoes, with milk, are often given to invalids and convalescents. They are also preserved in mustard oil and served during a meal as an aid to digestion.

Small, very unripe mangoes stewed in water to a soup-like consistency are reputed to be calming and strengthening to the nerves and stimulating to the appetite.

HAM AND MANGO MAYONNAISE

¼ pound thinly sliced prosciutto (raw
Parma ham) or 6 ounces thickly
sliced cooked ham
1 medium-size ripe mango
3–4 slices pineapple, fresh or canned
½ pound seedless green grapes
1 crisp, tart apple
1 large, ripe banana
4–5 tablespoons thick cream
4–5 tablespoons lemon mayonnaise
(page 205)
Milk (optional)
Salt
Crisp green lettuce leaves for garnish

If using *prosciutto*, shred it into ribbons and gently separate them. Cooked ham slices should have all excess fat trimmed off and then be cut into thin strips about 1½ inches long.

Prepare fruit shortly before assembling and serving the salad. Peel mango and slice flesh off the seed. Cut it into thin strips. Cut pineapple slices into small wedges, and strip grapes from their stalks. Peel, core and dice apple. Peel and slice banana thinly crosswise.

In a large mixing bowl, whip cream until it thickens and begins to hold its shape. If mayonnaise is very thick, dilute with a few drops of milk before folding it into whipped cream. Gently fold in *prosciutto* or ham and all the prepared fruit, tossing lightly with a fork until each piece of fruit is individually coated.

Taste and season with a sprinkling of salt if necessary. (Ham and mayonnaise may have already made salad salty enough.)

Pile salad into a bowl lined with lettuce leaves.

Serve immediately.

Serves 4.

Note: You can substitute ½ pound — or more — skinned and slivered cold roast chicken for the ham. You may also need a little more dressing and seasoning.

MANGO AND GINGER ICE CREAM TART

A dinner-party special that should not be assembled until the last moment to avoid the danger of the pastry going soggy.

Prepare the pastry and bake the tart shell well in advance on the day it is to be served, so that it is quite cold when you fill it.

3 large, ripe mangoes
4–5 tablespoons finely chopped
preserved ginger in syrup
3 tablespoons ginger syrup
1 deep 8 inch rich pie pastry case, pre-
baked (page 203)
1–1½ quarts vanilla ice cream
4–6 tablespoons finely chopped
toasted blanched almonds

Peel mangoes, slice flesh off the seed in lengthwise slices, and place in a dish. Scatter with chopped ginger, moisten with syrup and mix gently to coat slices all over. Cover dish and allow mangoes to macerate for several hours until needed.

Do not assemble tart until just before serving. If pastry case is still in its pan, unmold it onto a flat serving dish. With a large serving spoon, scoop up large curls of ice cream and arrange them in pastry shell. Arrange slices of mango neatly on top. Cover with syrup and juices which have run from the fruit, and sprinkle with chopped almonds. Serve immediately.

Serves 8.

MANGO SHERBET

⅔ cup sugar
¾ pound (about 1½ cups) mango
purée, fresh or canned
1–2 tablespoons lime or lemon juice

In a heavy pan, dissolve sugar in ¾ cup water over low heat. Bring to boiling point and boil hard for 6–8 minutes. Cool.

Combine the syrup with the mango purée and sharpen flavor with lime or lemon juice, bearing in mind that flavors tend to be modified by freezing. Pour into ice cube trays or a

MANGO MOUSSE

Cans of mango purée are usually stocked by Indian food stores but if fresh mangoes are available, use them instead. You will need 2 or 3 large ones which are very ripe and soft. Peel them, cut them off their seeds and blend the pulp to a purée with the ginger, lime or lemon juice and sugar to taste. Individual portions of mousse may be decorated with swirls of more whipped cream, or slices of mango.

One 16 ounce can mango purée (see
above)
1 teaspoon ground ginger
About ½ cup sugar
1–2 tablespoons lime or lemon juice
1 tablespoon unflavored gelatin
1¼ cups heavy cream

Pour mango purée into a bowl and blend in ginger, followed by sugar and lime or lemon juice to taste. Purée should be strongly flavored. If using a purée of fresh mangoes that has turned out rather fibrous, rub it through a fine nylon sieve.

Sprinkle gelatin over 2 or 3 tablespoons cold water in a cup and let it soak for 10 minutes. Then stand cup in a pan of hot water and stir until gelatin has dissolved and liquid is quite clear. Cool, then beat into mango purée. Leave until syrupy.

In a large bowl, whip cream until it thickens and forms very soft peaks. With the same beaters, beat the mango purée once more until smooth and light. Fold it lightly but thoroughly into cream. Divide between individual glasses and chill until set. Serve plain or decorated with more cream and fruit (see above).

Serves 6.

plastic box, cover with foil and freeze.

When the sherbet has solidified around the sides, scrape it out into a bowl and beat well to break down any large ice crystals. Pour back into the container and return to the refrigerator. Repeat once more, then freeze until solid.

About 30 minutes before you are ready to serve the sherbet, transfer the container to the refrigerator to allow it to soften slightly.

Serves 4–6.

MANGO CREAM

A rich, quickly made dessert from Central America.

2 ripe mangoes, peeled, seeded and chopped
1 orange, peeled and sectioned
6 tablespoons confectioners' sugar, sifted
¾ cup heavy cream, stiffly whipped
1 cup shelled, roasted and coarsely chopped pecans

Combine the mangoes, orange sections and sugar in a large bowl. Mix the fruits to a pulp using a potato masher or, preferably, an electric blender. Fold in the whipped cream and pecans. Chill the dessert and serve in tall glasses.

Serves 6.

MANGOES IN SYRUP

2 cups sugar
6 large ripe mangoes
1 teaspoon vanilla

In a large, wide pan, dissolve sugar in 2 cups water and simmer for about 30 minutes until reduced to a thick syrup.

If any scum forms on the surface, skim it off with a slotted spoon.

With a sharp, thin-bladed knife, peel mangoes and cut flesh from seeds in

MANGO FOOL CRÉOLE

2 ripe mangoes
3 tablespoons lime juice
2 tablespoons clear honey
¾ cup whipping cream

Peel the mangoes, discard the seeds and chop the flesh of one mango into neat dice. Sprinkle with half the lime juice and set aside.

Put the flesh of the second mango in a blender with the rest of the lime juice and the honey and blend to a smooth purée. Whip the cream until stiff, then fold into the mango purée with a metal spoon, leaving it streaky.

Stir the diced mango into the purée and put in a serving dish. Chill for about 1 hour before serving.

Serves 6.

lengthwise strips.

Stir vanilla into syrup. Drop in mango slices and cook over the lowest possible heat until mango is practically transparent but not disintegrating and syrup is very thick and reduced to about a quarter of its original volume.

Cool mangoes in syrup and chill thoroughly before serving.

Serves 6–8.

MANGO SAUCE

This sweet sauce, from the Caribbean island of St Kitts, is delicious with cold cuts or served as a dessert with ladyfingers and whipped cream.

3 almost ripe mangoes, peeled, seeded and chopped
⅔ cup firmly packed brown sugar
½ teaspoon ground ginger
½ teaspoon ground cinnamon
Pinch of salt

Place the mangoes and 1¼ cups water in a saucepan, and bring to a boil over a medium heat. Cover and simmer gently until the fruit is soft. Stir in the remaining ingredients, then cook uncovered, stirring occasionally, for 10 minutes, until the sauce is thick.

Serve hot or cold.

MANGO RELISH

1½ pounds green mangoes, peeled, seeded and coarsely chopped
1 quart vinegar
⅓ cup firmly packed brown sugar
6 tablespoons salt
4 teaspoons mustard powder
10 large garlic cloves, crushed
4 ounces ginger root, peeled and finely chopped
Pinch of cayenne
⅔ cup raisins
1 tablespoon turmeric

Put the mangoes and ¾ cup water into a saucepan. Bring to a boil, then simmer gently until the fruit is reduced to a pulp. Add the vinegar, sugar and salt, stir and continue to simmer for a further 5 minutes, until sugar is completely dissolved. Remove from the heat. Stir in the rest of the ingredients, and mix well.

Return the pan to the heat and bring to a boil, stirring continuously. Turn the heat down very low and allow the mixture to simmer, stirring occasionally, for about 2½ hours, until well reduced. Remove from the heat. Allow to cool slightly, pack and process as usual. Keep for a week in a warm place, then store in a cool, dry place for at least 1 month before serving.

See also page 200.

Fills about 3 jars.

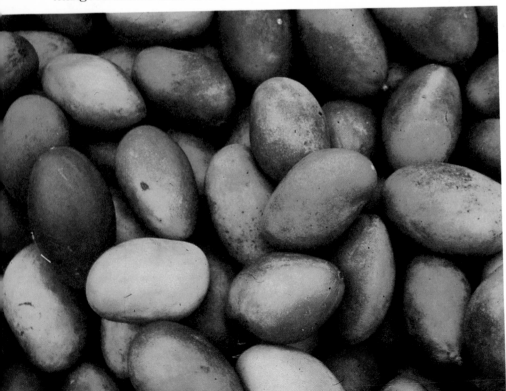

DRIED MANGO CHUTNEY

This is a spicy chutney rather than a pungent one, and is made with dried mangoes.

½ pound dried mangoes
¼ pound (about ¾ cup) pitted dates
1 pound small onions or shallots
Grated rind and juice of 2 lemons
About 1 inch fresh ginger root
1 teaspoon salt
2½ cups white vinegar
½ teaspoon chili powder
1 inch cinnamon stick
3 cups firmly packed brown sugar

Slice the mango pieces and put them in a bowl with water to cover. Leave to soak overnight.

Drain them and place in a large saucepan. Chop the dates, and peel and chop the onions or shallots. Put them into the pan with the mango, add the lemon rind and juice and grate the ginger over. Add the rest of the ingredients except the sugar and bring to a boil, stirring from time to time. Lower the heat under the pan and simmer for about 30 minutes, stirring occasionally to prevent it sticking to the pan.

Now stir in the sugar and continue stirring until it dissolves completely. Bring the chutney back to a boil and boil until it has thickened.

Remove the cinnamon stick and pour the chutney into clean, dry, sterilized jars. Process as usual. Store in a cool dry place for up to 3 months. Leave it to mature for 3 weeks before opening.

See also page 200.

Fills about 3 jars.

MANGOADE

This cooling drink from Jamaica makes an unusual non-alcoholic beverage for a summer garden party.

2 ripe mangoes, peeled, seeded and
*   coarsely chopped*
¼ cup sugar
Grated rind of 1 orange
2 cups orange juice
¾ cup lime juice

Purée the mangoes by rubbing through a fine sieve into a large bowl. Place the sugar, 2 cups water and orange rind in a small saucepan. Stir over a low heat until the sugar has dissolved, then remove from the heat and leave on one side to cool.

Slowly add the orange juice, the lime juice and the sugar syrup to the mango purée in the bowl, stirring constantly to blend. Alternatively blend the mango and the liquid together in an electric blender. Pour into a tall pitcher and refrigerate for several hours before serving, with ice, in tall chilled glasses.

Serves 6.

FRESH MANGO CHUTNEY 1

2 green mangoes
1 medium-size onion
1 green chili pepper
Small bunch of fresh coriander
Salt

Peel the mangoes and coarsely chop the flesh. Peel and chop the onion and chop the chili pepper. Strip the leaves from the coriander and wash and chop these.

Put all in a blender with salt and 2 tablespoons water and blend.

Serves 4.

FRESH MANGO CHUTNEY 2

2 green mangoes
1 green chili pepper
1 teaspoon salt
2 tablespoons chopped fresh mint
1½ teaspoons sugar

Peel the mangoes and coarsely chop the flesh. Chop the chili pepper. Put into a blender with the remaining ingredients and blend.

Serves 4.

MANGO TEA

1 fresh, ripe mango, peeled, seeded
*   and coarsely chopped*
1 tablespoon sugar
Juice of 1 lemon

Rub the chopped mango through a fine sieve or put into a blender to purée. Place the purée in a tall, heat-proof pitcher, add the sugar and lemon juice, and stir well.

Heat 1¼ cups water to boiling point in a small saucepan or kettle and pour onto the ingredients in the pitcher. Stir and cover.

If you want a hot drink, leave to stand for 5 minutes, stir well, then strain and sieve. Alternatively, leave until cool, then place in the refrigerator to chill. When ice-cold, strain into tall chilled glasses.

Serves 2.

MELON

Melons are gourds, the sweetest and most succulent members of the family which embraces cucumbers, summer and winter squash, and watermelons. Wherever they originated – the experts toss up between Asia and Africa – it is certain that they have been eaten and enjoyed by man for over 4,000 years. They are clearly shown in ancient Egyptian wall paintings of the time of the Pharaohs, and the Roman emperor Tiberius decreed that they should be served to him every day. The Arabs take the credit for introducing them to southern Spain, while the French king Charles VIII brought them from Naples to France in the Middle Ages.

The familiar honeydew, oval-shaped and with dark green or yellow ridged flesh, varies in sweetness and is often a good bet for serving as an appetizer with sugar, and ground ginger to add a little tang of spice. The honeyball, similar to the honeydew, is small and round, with a slight netting over the skin. The cantaloupe (a group of melons rather than one specific type) takes its name from the Cantalupo region not far from Rome. What we call cantaloupe is, in fact, the netted muskmelon; it is smaller and rounder than the honeydew, with pinky-orange flesh and smooth, creamy yellow skin covered with a thick, coarse netting. Serve these halved (if large-ish), or with the tops sawn off like a cap, and the seeds hollowed out. Casabas are pumpkin-shaped, with shallow ridges running from stem to blossom end on a light green to yellow skin. Cranshaws, or crenshaws, are large melons, slightly pointed at stem end, with shallow furrowing on a smooth, deep gold skin; the flesh is pale orange when ripe.

One of the tests for ripeness, whatever the type, is to lift the melon to your nose and *sniff* for fragrance. A ripe melon smells sweet, feels heavy for its size and – the time-honored double-check – the skin should give if pressed lightly at the stalk end; too soft, and it's over-ripe.

Melons make splendid baskets when scooped out and filled with other fruits for serving. Cut smaller ones with a serrated edge and fill with melon water ice or raspberries, with which the melon has a delicate affinity. Melons can make a welcome appearance in salads too. They will freeze for up to a year if the flesh is cut in cubes or scooped in balls, and layered with sugar, but the texture is somewhat woolly when thawed.

If serving fresh, melons are best when lightly chilled; too cold, and their full flavor is lost. Always wrap cut melons in foil or plastic wrap, otherwise their aroma will permeate everything else in the refrigerator.

Melons, especially cantaloupes, are rich in minerals and vitamins.

REMEDIES

Melon juice, often mixed with rose-water and a little sugar, is used as a remedy for fevers in the East.

The seeds have been used for dropsy, congestion of the liver, and strangury (painful retention of urine) and other urinary tract conditions.

COSMETICS

For a skin-brightening face mask, pound equal parts of melon, cucumber, pumpkin and gourd seeds, and mix with water to make an emulsion.

Melon juice will cleanse, soothe and nourish dry skin; that of cantaloupes, in particular, is an excellent moisturizer.

It can be used on its own or mixed with a little honey. To loosen dead, flaky skin combine a little almond oil with juice and rub into your face.

CHILLED MELON SOUP

I have tried several recipes for melon soup, but this one, which came from Jane Grigson's column in the magazine of the British newspaper *The Observer*, is my favorite.

2/3 cup sugar
1½ pounds (about 4½ cups) melon pulp (see method)
1 cup dry white wine
Juice of ½ lemon
¾ cup sour cream
Confectioners' sugar (optional)

Start by dissolving sugar in 2½ cups water. Bring to boiling point, stirring until sugar has dissolved, and simmer for 4 minutes. Cool.

Halve melon and scrape out seeds and fibrous pulp. Take off melon rind and cut flesh into chunks. To obtain 1½ pounds melon pulp, you will have to start with a melon which weighs about 2¼ pounds.

In a blender or food processor purée melon pulp, gradually adding the wine and sugar syrup to taste. If the melon is very sweet, use less syrup and add extra water. Finally, blend in lemon juice and sour cream. Taste and adjust flavors with a little more lemon juice, sugar syrup (or confectioners' sugar). Serve chilled.

Serves 6.

Note: When I can, I use fresh limes, instead of lemons.

KANG KUNG

This is a hot, spicy soup from Cambodia. The dried shrimp, fish sauce and mushrooms are available from specialist Chinese foodstores.

4 ounces dried shrimp
6 dried Chinese mushrooms
1 large, ripe honeydew melon
2 quarts chicken broth
2 tablespoons fish sauce
6 thin slices of fresh ginger root
1 teaspoon cayenne
2 tablespoons dry sherry wine

Put the dried shrimp in a small bowl. Cover with water that has just boiled and leave the shrimp to soak overnight, then drain.

The next day, put the dried mushrooms in another small bowl. Cover with boiling water and leave for 40 minutes. Drain the mushrooms, discarding the liquid. Slice thinly. Cut the melon into quarters. Remove the seeds and cut off the rind. Chop the flesh into small pieces.

Put the broth, fish sauce, ginger, cayenne, mushrooms and shrimp in a large saucepan. Heat quickly to boiling point, then lower the heat and simmer for 30 minutes. Lift out the ginger, using a slotted spoon, and discard. Add the melon and simmer for a further 5 minutes. Remove the pan from the heat and stir in the sherry. Return the pan to the heat and cook until almost boiling (do not boil). Serve hot.

Serves 6.

MELON AND CUCUMBER SALAD

This refreshing salad goes well with broiled lamb or pork.

1 medium-size cucumber
Juice of 1 large lemon
2 teaspoons salt
1 small, ripe honeydew melon

Dressing
10 tablespoons olive oil
5 tablespoons white wine vinegar
Juice of 1 small lemon
½ teaspoon salt
½ teaspoon freshly ground black
*   pepper*
1 tablespoon clear honey

Peel the cucumber, slice thinly and spread the slices out on a plate. Pour over the lemon juice, sprinkle with salt, and leave for 30 minutes.

Cut the melon in half, and scoop out the seeds. Cut off the rind and chop the flesh into small chunks. Place in a chilled salad bowl.

Drain any liquid off the cucumber slices, and add the cucumber to the melon. Leave in the refrigerator while preparing the dressing.

Put all the ingredients for the dressing in a large screw-top jar. Shake vigorously and place in the refrigerator to chill. Just before serving, shake the jar of dressing to mix the contents well, and pour over the cucumber and melon. Toss and serve.

Serves 4–6.

AVOCADO AND MELON COCKTAIL

An unusual, refreshing start to a rich meal.

1 large, ripe honeydew melon
2 large, ripe avocados
Juice of 1 large lemon
Sprigs of fresh mint for garnish

Cut the melon in half and remove the seeds. Then quarter the melon, remove the rind and cut the flesh into approximately ½ inch chunks. Place these in a salad bowl, together with any juice.

Cut the avocados in half, remove the seeds, then peel and cut the flesh into thin slices.

Put these on a plate and pour the lemon juice over them. Leave for 2 minutes, then add to the melon in the salad bowl.

Toss all the ingredients together, and place in the refrigerator to chill for at least 30 minutes. Serve in individual glasses, garnished with sprigs of fresh mint.

Serves 4.

PROSCIUTTO WITH MELON

An inspired partnership of fruit and meat, Italian style, this dish is child's play to put together – but its success depends entirely on the quality of the ingredients used. The *prosciutto* (raw air-dried ham from Parma) should be moist and ruby-red, cut in paper-thin slices. Admittedly, it is expensive, in the smoked salmon class, but only a very small amount is needed per portion.

Failing authentic, fresh *prosciutto*, try serving the melon with Westphalian ham, which is easier to find in good gourmet stores, and rather less expensive.

The melons, too, should be selected with care. Use 2 slices of juicy, ripe cantaloupe (¼ melon) per portion. When fresh ripe figs are in season, substitute them for the melon, allowing 3 average-sized ones per serving.

Per portion:
2 slices cantaloupe melon (see
*   method)*
2–3 large, paper-thin slices (about 2
*   ounces) prosciutto*
Lettuce leaves for garnish (optional)
Freshly ground black pepper

Several hours before the dish is to be prepared, put the whole melons in the refrigerator so they will come to the table well chilled.

Shortly before serving, assemble the dish. Slice the melon vertically in eight. Scrape out seeds and fibers, then with a sharp, pliable knife, carefully cut away the flesh in one piece, close to the rind. Lay 2 wedges, still on their rinds, on each individual plate. Alternatively, slice melon in half horizontally. Scrape out seeds and fibers. Then, using a melon baller or a small spoon with a round bowl (eg a measuring teaspoon), scoop out neat balls of melon and return them to their half-shells.

Arrange slices of *prosciutto* on a separate plate lined with a few lettuce leaves to prevent the ham sticking to it, or crumple 2 or 3 slices attractively over the top of each piece of melon.

Have the peppermill on hand for those who like to eat the melon sprinkled lightly with pepper. Serve well chilled.

BAKED SPICED MELON

Even the most experienced shopper can buy a melon that is never going to ripen sweetly enough to serve raw. The only solution is to cut your losses and treat it as a vegetable. This produces a surprisingly fine accompaniment for poultry, pork, and even the more strongly flavored game dishes and curries.

Melon
Salt
Ground cinnamon or
  allspice
Freshly grated nutmeg
Lemon juice
Brown sugar
Butter

Halve melon, scrape out seeds and peel off skin. Cut melon flesh into large (about 1 inch) cubes. Season lightly with salt, a sprinkling of cinnamon or allspice and a grating of nutmeg. Squeeze a little lemon juice over the melon, sweeten to taste with brown sugar and toss lightly with a fork until well mixed. Spread melon cubes out evenly in a shallow, buttered baking dish and dot with flakes of butter.

Bake in a preheated 350° oven for 20–30 minutes, or until melon is soft and juicy.

Serve hot.

MELON STUFFED WITH FRUITS

All kinds of fruit may be served in a melon shell. This recipe, and the three that follow, are variations on the theme.

1 large, ripe melon
¾ pound (3 pints) strawberries,
  hulled, or raspberries
½ pound (1 pint) red currants
½ pound (1½ pints) ripe red or black
  cherries, pitted
3–4 large, ripe peaches, peeled and
  cubed
Granulated sugar or sifted
  confectioners' sugar

Shave a thin slice from one end of the melon to give it a secure base. Take a thick slice from the other end (cutting about one-quarter of the way down) to expose the seeds inside. Scrape out all the seeds and fibers. Using a melon baller or a teaspoon with a round bowl, scoop out as much flesh as possible into a bowl. Add the strawberries, red currants, cherries and peaches.

Sweeten to taste, mixing gently to avoid crushing the fruit.

Pile the fruit into the melon shell. Replace the melon "lid" and seal the melon in foil or plastic wrap. Chill well before serving on a shallow dish.

Serves 4–6.

MELON WITH RASPBERRIES

Melon and raspberries go well together. Serve this simple but spectacular presentation as either an appetizer or dessert.

1 pound (3 pints) fresh or frozen
  raspberries, thawed
Sugar
Lemon juice
2 teaspoons unflavored gelatin
1 ripe honeydew melon

Put aside about a quarter of the best raspberries and rub remainder through a fine nylon sieve, discarding seeds. Measure 1¼ cups raspberry purée into a pan. Sweeten and flavor to taste with lemon juice — the exact amount of sugar and lemon juice you need will depend on the flavor of the raspberries in the first place. The purée should be sweet and sharp, as melon is quite bland.

In a cup, sprinkle gelatin over 4 or 5 teaspoons water and leave for 10 minutes to soften. Then dissolve gelatin by standing cup in a pan or bowl of hot water and stirring until it has melted and liquid is quite clear. Warm the pan of raspberry purée to more or less the same temperature as that of the dissolved gelatin — this is important, because if the gelatin is much warmer than the purée when the two are combined, the gelatin may set too fast and be unpleasantly "ropey." Blend the two thoroughly. Cool and chill until syrupy and on the point of setting.

Meanwhile, cut the melon in half lengthwise and scrape out seeds, fibers and a little of the pulp to make room for raspberries and gelatin. Stir reserved raspberries into purée, and divide between melon halves. Chill until gelatin is firmly set.

To serve, heat the blade of a large knife thoroughly by dipping it in boiling water. Wipe it dry and carefully slice each melon half in three lengthwise. Then take another large, sharp knife and cut the melon flesh free of its rind. Serve each wedge of melon sitting on its rind, accompanied by a small knife and fork.

Serves 6.

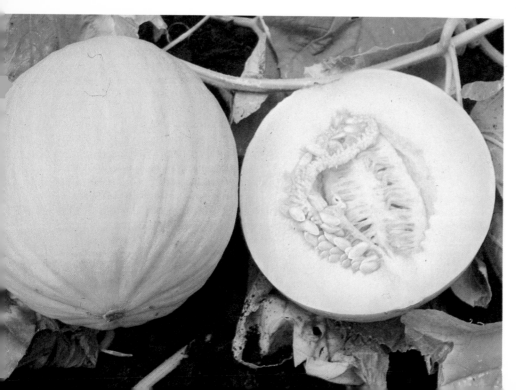

MELON À LA SCHEHEREZADE

This extravagant melon "basket" was created by Alice B. Toklas's mother.

1 ripe cantaloupe melon
1 ripe, but firm, peach
Two ½ inch thick slices of fresh
    pineapple
1 banana
2 ounces (1 cup) fresh strawberries
2 ounces (1 pint) fresh raspberries
1 tablespoon sugar
¾ cup dry champagne
1 tablespoon Kirsch
1 tablespoon Maraschino
1 tablespoon Crème de Menthe
1 tablespoon grenadine syrup

Wash the outside of the melon, then slice off the stem end. Scoop out as much of the flesh as possible, leaving the outer casing intact. Pour out any juice into a large bowl, and put this on one side.

Cut the melon flesh into small chunks. Peel and slice the peach thinly. Remove the core from the pineapple and chop into chunks, about the same size as those of the melon. Peel and slice the banana across thinly. Put all this fruit into a bowl.

Remove the stalks from the strawberries and raspberries and wash gently. Add to the rest of the fruit. Sprinkle the fruit with sugar and leave until it has dissolved, then pack the fruit into the melon case.

Add the champagne, Kirsch, Maraschino, Crème de Menthe and grenadine syrup to the bowl of melon juice. Mix well and pour onto the fruit inside the melon. Place in the refrigerator overnight.

Serve the fruit direct from the melon casing.

Serves 2.

MELON WITH PORT WINE

Allow a thick slice cut from a large, ripe, sweet melon or half a small one, eg a canteloupe, per person.

Clean out seeds and fibers, and either pierce flesh deeply all over with a fork or gash it at intervals with a spoon to allow port wine to seep right in. Lay on individual dishes or in small bowls and spoon 2 or 3 tablespoons port wine over each portion.

Allow to macerate for an hour before serving.

MELON WITH BLACK CURRANTS

Both fruits are available in early fall and complement each other well.

2 small, ripe cantaloupe melons
½ pound (1 pint) black currants
3 tablespoons sugar
1 tablespoon vodka
Fresh mint leaves for decoration

Place the melons in the refrigerator to chill. Wash the black currants in a colander under cold running water, removing any stalks and damaged fruit. Place in a small pan, with the sugar and just enough water to cover.

Cook over moderate heat until boiling, then lower the heat and simmer for 4 minutes. Remove the pan from the heat and allow to cool. Taste and add more sugar if desired. Purée the black currants by rubbing through a fine sieve. (Using an electric blender will not remove the seeds and the purée will still have to be sieved to remove them.)

Stir in the vodka.

Take the melons out of the refrigerator and cut across in half. Scoop out the seeds and fill the cavity with the black currant purée. Garnish with mint leaves and serve.

Serves 4.

MELON WATER ICE

½ cup sugar
1 small, ripe honeydew melon
Juice of 1 large lemon
1 egg white

Put the sugar and 1¼ cups water into a small saucepan. Place over a moderate heat and stir until the sugar dissolves. Bring to a boil and boil for 10 minutes.

Remove from the heat and set this syrup on one side to cool.

Cut the melon in half. Remove the seeds and scoop out the flesh, reserving any juice. Purée this (with the juice) by pushing through a fine sieve or, preferably, using an electric blender. Stir the melon purée into the cooked syrup.

Add the lemon juice to the purée and mix well.

Place this mixture in a freezing tray and place in the freezer. Leave for 1 hour. Then beat the egg white until stiff. Empty the half-frozen melon mixture into a bowl and beat it well until slushy. Fold in the stiffly beaten egg white.

Pour this mixture back into the freezing tray and return to the freezer. Freeze the water ice until solid (about 2–3 hours).

Serves 4.

BAKED MELON ALASKA

This dish is easy to make but does need a little careful pre-planning. Have ready a wooden baking board covered with foil (both are poor conductors of heat). Preheat the oven well in advance and have the melon ready and thoroughly chilled before you embark on the final stages.

If you want to make the Alaska even more spectacular, press half an empty egg shell deep into the top of the meringue just before it goes into the oven. Then, as you are going to serve it, fill the shell with brandy, rum or Kirsch, allowing just a little to trickle down the sides. Put a match to the alcohol and serve the Alaska as soon as flames are well established.

1 large, ripe honeydew melon
Lemon or lime juice
4 egg whites
¼ teaspoon cream of tartar
⅛ teaspoon salt
½ cup sugar
Mixed fruit-flavored and vanilla ice creams to fill melon
Sifted confectioners' sugar

Carefully peel off rind of melon. Lay melon on one side and cut off a thin slice so melon will lie steady. Then turn melon over and, from the side opposite to the slice, cut another slice, deep enough to expose seeds. Carefully scoop out seeds and fibers. Sprinkle cavity with lemon or lime juice. Put the "lid" back on, wrap melon tightly in foil or plastic wrap and chill thoroughly in refrigerator.

Preheat oven to 450°. Beat egg whites with cream of tartar and salt until soft peaks form when beaters are lifted. Gradually beat in sugar and continue to beat to a stiff, glossy meringue.

Lay melon on prepared board. Lift off and discard "lid" (for the purposes of this dish). Fill melon to the brim and over with scoops of ice cream of different flavors and colors. Cover entirely with meringue, working quickly and flicking up surface all over with a broad knife blade. Dust whole melon thickly with sifted confectioners' sugar.

Bake Alaska for about 5 minutes until meringue tips are tinged with brown and surface of meringue feels dry to the touch. Serve immediately, cut across in thick slices or wedges.

Serves 6.

WATERMELON

No one who has ever seen them, stacked in piles in the market or by the roadside, their dark green skins contrasting so vividly with the crisp, bright reddish pink of their glistening flesh, can fail to have been impressed by watermelons. Whether or not it is this association with sun and heat, the watermelon is somehow a happy fruit, one huge slice resembling the grin of a joyful child – perhaps the joyful child who is doing his best to sell them to you …

Redolent of sun and heat they may be but, amazingly in so much dryness, they manage to come up ninety-two per cent water – a natural refresher just where they are most needed, especially if you can negotiate the seeds. In Hungary and the USA, growers have managed to produce seedless varieties, but they wouldn't be appreciated in Greece, where the seeds are dried and sold on the streets, nor in southern China, where dried and toasted watermelon seeds are eaten by the handful and considered a great delicacy.

Rumor has it that in West Africa the fruits are gathered and thrown in heaps until they ferment, thus making the seeds easier to get at for grinding into meal and making into bread. A special, large-seeded variety has been cultivated, for as well as water, the huge fruits yield valuable minerals and the seeds cooking oil.

The watermelon is prized wherever it is found for its immensely refreshing qualities. In the southern states of the US, they have grown monsters of 40 pounds; luckily, the ones we see in the markets are more manageable. If choosing one, try and give the candidate a surreptitious thump – if it's ripe and ready, it should sound dull, flat and somehow heavy. This means its juice and flavor are at their peak. We don't often see the ones with the mottled gray skins, or those with whitish yellow flesh, and they certainly would not make the attractive table centerpiece that can be contrived from a ripe, green-skinned watermelon if it is carved out into a basket shape, complete with handle, and the flesh cubed, chilled and put back with a selection of fresh soft fruits such as strawberries, kiwi fruits, canteloupe scooped into balls, orange segments, slices of nectarine or peach and perhaps a litchi or two. If the fruit has been prepared first and macerated in a little white wine with a generous splash of brandy or orange liqueur, the dessert moves into the millionaire class. And for an extra touch of elegance (which costs almost nothing) serve the melon basket on a bed of crushed ice.

Like other melons, watermelons freeze well if they are layered in sugar but, also like other melons, the flavor can be disappointing.

Medicinally, the watermelon shares many of the qualities of the other melons. Its juice is also given as a remedy for fevers; its seeds too are nutritious and medicinal and have been used against worms. If used for a facial treatment, watermelon is more suitable for normal skins than for very dry or very greasy ones.

It is often recommended as an ideal ingredient in a diet, since it is exceptionally low in calories but comparatively high in vitamins and minerals, especially potassium.

CHILLED WATERMELON SOUP

4 pounds ripe watermelon
2½ cups sweet white wine
About 3 tablespoons sugar
1 teaspoon ground allspice
Finely grated rind of 1 large lemon
   (about 4 teaspoons)
1¼ cups chilled sour cream or thick
   plain yogurt

Quarter and peel watermelon, and cut it into small chunks, picking out and discarding as many of the large, black seeds as you can find.

Put watermelon chunks and any of their juices that have escaped in a pan.

Pour over wine, stir in sugar, allspice and grated lemon rind, and simmer until watermelon is very soft and pulpy, about 20 minutes, stirring and mashing occasionally with a wooden spoon.

Rub soup through a fine nylon sieve into a large bowl and discard fibers and any seeds left behind in sieve. Taste purée and add a little more sugar if necessary. Conversely, if flavor is very strong, purée may be diluted with a little water. Cool and chill thoroughly.

Shortly before serving, beat sour cream with a few tablespoons of chilled watermelon purée until smooth and liquid. Blend smoothly with remaining purée and return to refrigerator until ready to serve.

Serve small portions in chilled soup bowls.

Serves 6.

AMARGOSO SALAD

This dish from the Philippines makes a good appetizer for a Western-style meal, or a satisfying light lunch, served with thin buttered slices of wholewheat bread.

½ pound watermelon flesh, seeded
   and thinly sliced
½ pound shrimp, cooked, peeled and
   deveined
2 large firm red tomatoes, peeled and
   sliced
2 hard-cooked eggs, finely chopped

Dressing
3 tablespoons wine vinegar
½ teaspoon salt
2 teaspoons sugar
¼ teaspoon freshly ground black
   pepper

Boil about ¾ cup water in a medium saucepan. Drop in the melon slices, return to a boil and cook for a minute. Remove the pan from the heat, drain off the water, and place the melon in a serving bowl. Add the shrimp, tomatoes and chopped egg. Leave the bowl in the refrigerator to chill.

Put all the ingredients for the dressing in a large screw-top jar. Seal the jar, shake vigorously and place in the refrigerator to chill.

Just before serving, shake the jar of dressing again, pour over the salad, and toss.

Serves 4 as an appetizer. Serves 2 as a complete lunch.

GUYANAN WATERMELON

This tangy, refreshing Caribbean dessert is a good finale to a heavy dinner.

1 small watermelon, weighing about
   3 pounds
3 tablespoons sugar
¾ cup white rum
3 large, juicy oranges

Lay the melon on its side and cut a large slice off the top. Scoop out the flesh keeping the melon skin intact, and reserving any juice. Cut the flesh into small chunks, discarding the seeds. Keep the melon case.

Put the melon chunks and juice into a large bowl. Sprinkle over the sugar and pour on the rum. Peel the oranges, removing all the pith and divide into segments. Add to the melon mixture. Pile the fruit mix into the melon case. Place in the refrigerator and chill for at least 1 hour before serving.

Serves 6.

WATERMELON PICKLE

About 3 pounds watermelon rind
Brine (see method)

Syrup
2 cups cider vinegar
3 cups sugar
1 long (3–4 inch) cinnamon stick, in 2
   or 3 pieces
1 teaspoon whole cloves
1 teaspoon allspice berries
½ orange, thinly sliced
1 small lemon, thinly sliced

Cut away green skin from one side of watermelon rind and red flesh from the other. Cut rind that remains into 1 inch squares. Put them in a large bowl and cover with brine, made by dissolving ¼ cup salt in 1 quart water. Leave to soak overnight.

The following day, drain rinds and rinse thoroughly with cold water. Place in a large pan, cover with fresh water and bring to boiling point. Simmer, covered, for 20–30 minutes until rind is barely tender and turning translucent.

While rind is simmering, prepare syrup. In a large, stainless steel or enameled pan, combine vinegar with sugar and 2 cups water. Stir over low heat until sugar has dissolved. Tie up spices loosely in a square of cheesecloth and add them to the pan, together with slices of orange and lemon. Bring to boiling point and simmer gently, uncovered, for 20 minutes.

Drain watermelon rind and add it to the syrup. Bring to boiling point and cook gently, uncovered, until rind is soft and clear, about 30 minutes.

With a slotted spoon, lift squares of rind out of syrup and pack them into hot, sterilized canning jars. Strain boiling hot syrup over them to cover, leaving ⅛ inch head space. Seal jars and process. Cool and label them, and store in a cool, dry cupboard for several weeks.

See also page 200.

Fills about 3 jars.

Nectarine

The nectarine is a smooth-skinned variety of peach with a distinctive flavor that has been described as something like a cross between a peach and a plum. Its devotees could argue that its sweet and rich juice must indeed be nectar – the drink of the gods. Like the apricot, it tastes best when, heavy with juice, it is ready to fall off the tree at the lightest touch.

Known to man for 2,000 years, this natural mutation from the peach family is said to have originated in China, coming westwards via Persia and the old spice routes and reaching Europe in the sixteenth century. Occasionally, to prove its parentage, a smooth-skinned nectarine appears on a peach tree and vice versa.

Nectarines are at their best when fully ripe and freshly picked; unfortunately, they rarely reach the markets in that condition. But do not be deterred – choose soft, full, unblemished fruits that feel heavy for their size. Though they do not ripen satisfactorily once off the tree, they will soften nicely if left in a warm room for a few days.

Nectarines can be used instead of peaches in any recipes that use the latter – in casseroles with chicken, flambéed in brandy, or baked. Their great advantage is that they do not need peeling and the flesh holds its shape better when lightly cooked. If made into a purée and frozen – use about ½ cup sugar to every pound of fruit – you can have a taste of summer out of season. Thaw the purée, swirl it into stiffly whipped Chantilly cream, and top with freshly toasted almonds. The purée will keep in the freezer for up to 12 months. Nectarines can also be sliced (remove the pit), sprinkled with sugar, and frozen for the same length of time.

Sun-dried nectarines may be found in health food stores (the fruit is low in calories and a good source of Vitamins A and C and natural fiber), and can be chopped and added to cakes with other dried fruit such as apricots.

Chicken with Nectarines

A light and delicate summer main course that is quickly made and needs only a bowl of plain cooked rice as an accompaniment. Substitute small, firm peaches for nectarines if the latter are not available.

1 small roaster chicken, 2½–3
    pounds, cut up
2 tablespoons butter
1 tablespoon olive oil
Salt and freshly ground black pepper
⅛ teaspoon each crushed dried
    rosemary and thyme
¾ cup medium dry white wine
¾ cup strong chicken broth
1 tablespoon cornstarch
3–4 nectarines, peeled and sliced (see
    above)
6–8 tablespoons coarsely chopped
    cashew nuts
Pinch of sugar (optional)
Lemon juice (optional)

Wipe chicken pieces dry. In a wide, flameproof casserole, melt butter in oil and fry chicken pieces until golden brown on all sides. Sprinkle them all over with salt, freshly ground black pepper, rosemary and thyme. Try and pack all the chicken pieces in a single layer in the casserole, skin side up, or arrange them so that legs are on the bottom and breasts on top. Moisten with wine and chicken broth. Bring to simmering point. Cover and cook gently for about 30 minutes, until chicken is tender, turning pieces once or twice.

Remove chicken from casserole with a slotted spoon and keep hot. Blend cornstarch with 2 or 3 tablespoons cold water, stir into pan juices and simmer gently until thickened and no longer floury. Gently stir in sliced nectarines and nuts. Correct seasoning with more salt or pepper, a pinch of sugar and a squeeze of lemon juice if liked.

Return chicken pieces to casserole and spoon sauce, nectarine slices and cashew nuts over them. Reheat gently for 2–3 minutes longer and serve immediately.

Serves 4.

Note: You can transform this dish and give it an oriental accent by leaving out the lemon juice and flavoring the sauce with a good dash of soy sauce instead.

Sugared Nectarines

A lovely accompaniment for poultry, pork, ham and bacon. Use firm nectarines that are not quite ripe or juicy enough to eat as they are.

4 firm nectarines
3 tablespoons butter
3 tablespoons dark brown sugar
1–2 tablespoons lemon juice

Cut nectarines in two lengthwise and remove pits. Then, without peeling them, slice each half lengthwise as you would peaches.

In a heavy skillet, melt butter. Stir in sugar and continue to cook, stirring, until it melts and turns syrupy. Add nectarine slices, turning them over to coat them in syrup, and cook gently until heated through and lightly glazed. Finally, sprinkle with lemon juice. Serve immediately.

Serves 4.

BAKED NECTARINES

8 ripe nectarines
Lemon juice
1½ cups sugar
Long strip of orange rind
Long strip of lemon rind
8 whole cloves

Peel nectarines as you would tomatoes, first dropping them in boiling water for a minute to loosen skins. When peeled, place in a bowl of water acidulated with lemon juice.

Make a syrup by dissolving sugar in 1¼ cups water. Add strips of orange and lemon rind (peeled off with a potato peeler), bring to boiling point and simmer for 10 minutes.

Drain nectarines. Pat dry with paper towels and stick a clove in the stem end of each one. Arrange them side by side on their stem ends in a deep baking dish. Pour over boiling syrup. Bake in a preheated 350° oven, basting frequently with syrup, until nectarines are soft when pierced with a skewer but not mushy, 20–30 minutes.

Remove baking dish from oven. Allow nectarines to cool in their syrup, occasionally spooning syrup over them. Chill before serving. Serve in some syrup, accompanied by a pitcher of thick pouring cream.

Serves 4.

NECTARINE LIQUEUR

2½ pounds nectarines
4 cups sugar
1½ quarts vodka

Wash the fruit. Halve and discard the pits. In a large wide-neck canning jar with a screw top (cleaned and sterilized, page 201), pack the nectarines tightly in layers, sprinkling sufficient sugar to cover over each layer. Replace the top, but do not screw on tightly, and leave for 4 days.

Drain off the resultant syrup and store in the refrigerator in a tightly covered bowl. Pour the vodka over the nectarines in the jar, to cover the fruit. Re-seal the jar and leave it for 2 weeks at room temperature.

Strain off the liqueur, stir in the nectarine syrup and pour into clean, sterilized bottles. Keep for 3 months.

Makes 1½ quarts.

FLAMBÉED NECTARINES

Easy culinary pyrotechnics can be demonstrated with all kinds of fruits such as bananas, peaches or cored pears as well as nectarines. If you want to carry out the operation at the dining table, you will need a chafing dish.

4–6 large, ripe nectarines
½ cup butter
1 cup firmly packed light brown
  sugar
2 tablespoons lemon juice
5 tablespoons brandy

Peel nectarines but keep them whole.

In a chafing dish (or a flameproof casserole if working on the kitchen range), melt butter until foaming but not colored. Stir in sugar and lemon juice, and cook over moderate heat, stirring, until sugar has dissolved. Add nectarines and cook gently, uncovered, for a few minutes, turning them with a spoon and rolling them over to coat them in buttery syrup.

In a large kitchen ladle or small pan, heat brandy gently. Set a match to it and when flames are burning strongly, pour all over pan of nectarines. Allow flames to die down and serve.

Serves 4–6.

NECTARINE MARMALADE

If you are lucky enough to have a surplus of nectarines (they should not be too ripe and need not be of the best table quality), this is a lovely, subtly flavored preserve.

2 pounds nectarines
2 thin-skinned oranges
Juice of 1 lemon
About 3 cups sugar

Peel, halve and pit nectarines. Scrub oranges under cold running water. Dry them and cut off, and discard, the peel of one of them. Chop up nectarines and both oranges, discarding any seeds.

Put fruit through the coarse blade of a food processor.

Measure minced fruit into a large kettle and add the same volume of sugar. Add lemon juice and slowly bring to boiling point, stirring constantly with a large wooden spoon until sugar has dissolved.

Then raise heat and boil briskly, stirring occasionally, until jell point is reached. Toward the end of cooking time, skim surface clear of scum. Pack and process the preserve as usual.

See also page 198.

Fills about 6 jars.

OLIVE

Both green (young) and ripe (black) olives were widely enjoyed by the Greeks and Romans. Their remains have been found in Egyptian tombs, and the Cretans built up a thriving olive trade around 3,500 BC. The gnarled trees with their small, silvery leaves grow all around the Mediterranean area, where they are extensively cultivated – not least for their oil. The trees grow slowly – they are not considered fully productive and at their best until they are between fifty and seventy-five years old – and can survive for centuries.

As with humans, the older the olive, the more wrinkled the skin. The flesh of the ripe olive is naturally softer, which is why the green varieties lend themselves better to stuffing. They can now be bought, stuffed with all kinds of exciting things, in packages, cans or jars, or loose in brine from gourmet shops. You can stuff them yourself if you first remove the pit by slitting them down one side. (If you don't intend to stuff them, pit the olives by making a smaller cross-cut across the top.)

Three main types of olive are cultivated – two for the table (the larger queens and the smaller manzanillas) and a bitter little green variety for its highly flavored oil. The green-tinged *huile vièrge*, or first pressing, should be kept for use in mayonnaise and salad dressings. Cook with it only if you must. You can cheat (and economize) by adding four or five well-drained olives to a jar of bland salad oil, and adding more oil and/or olives as necessary until you get the flavor you prefer.

Alone or with other ingredients, olives make excellent appetizers to serve with cocktails. They add piquancy to salads; and a distinctive taste to casseroles and stews. Add them toward the end of the cooking time, or taste and texture will vanish leaving only their bitterness. Tapénade, an olive spread from Provence, is often called the caviar of vegetables. Anything labeled *niçoise* on a menu should have a touch of the olive, traditionally and authentically the small, ripe ones.

Olives can be frozen out of their brine for up to six months, but last very well in the refrigerator. If an opened jar develops a white mold on top, the brine is oxidizing; the olives are perfectly edible if rinsed.

Olive oil is valued medicinally for its soothing, healing and nourishing properties.

OLIVE CHEESE BALLS

An unusual tidbit to have with cocktails.

To make the olives easy to handle, spear each one with a wooden toothpick or cocktail stick.

3 ounces cream cheese
¼ cup grated Cheddar cheese
About 3 tablespoons heavy cream
A few drops of Worcestershire or hot pepper sauce
18–24 pimiento-stuffed green olives
1 cup blanched and finely chopped almonds

In a bowl, work first 4 ingredients to a smooth, thick paste (use an electric blender or food processor if you have one). Coat each olive completely with cheese paste and roll it in finely chopped almonds. Impale each olive on a cocktail stick and chill until firm before serving.

Note: Instead of chopped almonds, try rolling the coated olives in ground almonds which have first been toasted to a light golden color, or in sesame seeds.

OLIVE OIL HAIR TREATMENT

Olive oil is wonderfully nourishing for dry hair, and can also be used to counteract dandruff and to treat hair damaged by sun and salt water.

Warm a little oil to about blood heat. Massage it very thoroughly into your scalp. Cover your hair with a warm towel or bath cap and leave as long as possible before washing out.

GARLIC OLIVES

1 large can large imported ripe or green olives in brine
6 tablespoons olive oil
3–4 fresh, plump cloves garlic, finely chopped or crushed
½ teaspoon dried oregano

Empty the can of olives into a large, screw-top jar, draining off brine and reserving ¾ cup of it in a pitcher or bowl. With a fork, beat remaining ingredients into brine. Pour over olives. Screw down lid and shake gently until well mixed. Olives should be submerged in marinade.

Leave in the refrigerator for at least 24 hours to absorb flavors before serving, drained, with cocktails.

OLIVE CHEESE PASTRIES

1¼ cups flour
½ teaspoon salt
½ teaspoon baking powder
½ cup butter, diced
1 egg yolk
6–8 tablespoons milk
1 cup grated mild Cheddar cheese
24–36 green or ripe olives or a
    mixture of the two, pitted and
    halved

Start by preparing the pastry. Sift flour, salt and baking powder into a bowl. Cut in butter until mixture resembles fine bread crumbs. Beat egg yolk lightly and sprinkle it over bowl, together with enough milk to make a dough.

Roll dough into a ball, wrap it in plastic or foil and chill for 1 hour.

On a lightly floured board with a rolling pin dusted with flour, roll out dough into a rectangle ¼ inch thick.

(Let it soften at room temperature for a little while if it comes out of the refrigerator too hard to handle.) Sprinkle rectangle with grated cheese, fold in two and roll out into a ¼ inch thick rectangle once more. Repeat folding and rolling yet again. This time, roll out pastry more thinly.

With a plain 2 inch cookie cutter, cut out 24 circles of dough. On each circle place 2 or 3 pitted olive halves and fold circle in half over olive filling. Seal edges thoroughly. Arrange pastries on baking sheets and bake in a preheated 425° oven for 12–15 minutes, or until pastries are golden. Cool for a few minutes and serve hot.

Note: If you have any hot pepper sauce, shake a tiny drop over the olive filling before folding each pastry in half.

CHEESE AND OLIVE PÂTÉ

A very simple pâté with a rich taste, delicious with hot toast. If the olives are very salty and you have no time to soak them first, use fewer — and add 2 tablespoons chopped parsley instead.

½ cup butter
½ pound (about 1 cup) ricotta, or full-
    fat cream cheese
¼ pound mild blue cheese
1 garlic clove, crushed
1 cup green olives (see above)
Freshly ground black pepper

Soften the butter and beat into the ricotta or cream cheese, then beat in the blue cheese, and blend in the garlic.

Finely chop the olives – discarding the pits. Beat the finely chopped olives into the pâté and season with pepper.

Chill for about an hour before serving with hot toast.

Serves 8.

OLIVE AND SALAMI SALAD

Quick and simple to prepare, this is a good beginning for an Italian-style dinner. It also makes a delicious snack at any time.

¼ pound salami, thinly sliced
1 cup ripe olives, pitted
1 small onion, finely chopped
2 tablespoons olive oil
2 teaspoons wine vinegar
1 teaspoon coriander seeds,
    crushed
1 teaspoon finely chopped basil

Arrange the slices of salami around the edge of a serving plate. Put the olives in a small bowl with onion, olive oil, vinegar and coriander. Toss well and spread across the center of the serving plate.

Place the plate in the refrigerator for 30 minutes to chill.

Just before serving, sprinkle with chopped basil.

Serves 4.

PROVENÇAL TAPÉNADE

Although this savory paste takes its name from *tapéno*, the Provençal word for the capers it contains, olives predominate. Use a food processor or an electric blender to reduce the ingredients to a smooth purée in seconds. Failing one of these invaluable gadgets, you will have to make the *tapénade* in the time-honored way, first pounding the ingredients together in a mortar, then rubbing the paste through a sieve.

The paste can be stored for a couple of weeks in the refrigerator, poured into a screw-top jar and covered with a thin film of oil (beat this in before using the paste). It makes a fine spread for fresh country bread, washed down with rough red wine. Or you can dress hot pasta with it, or beat it into hard-cooked egg yolks and stuff them back into the egg whites to eat as an appetizer.

½ cup pitted ripe olives
2 tablespoons drained canned
    anchovy fillets, coarsely chopped
2 tablespoons drained canned tuna,
    flaked
3 tablespoons drained bottled capers
1 small, ripe tomato, peeled, seeded
    and coarsely chopped
1 teaspoon coarse French mustard
Olive oil
Freshly ground black pepper or hot
    pepper sauce

Assemble the first 6 ingredients in a food processor or electric blender and whirl to a smooth, homogenous paste (see left). Gradually blend in about 6 tablespoons olive oil. Taste and season generously with freshly ground black pepper or a few drops of hot pepper sauce. Purée will already be salty enough.

Store in the refrigerator.

ITALIAN PEPPER AND OLIVE APPETIZER

Prepare this salad at least 4 hours in advance to give it a chance to develop flavors, and serve it as part of an Italian antipasto platter. In a screw-top jar, the ingredients covered with olive oil to prevent them drying out, this salad will keep in the refrigerator for a couple of weeks.

For a really dramatic color effect, use bright red or yellow peppers, or a mixture of the two.

About 1 cup ripe olives, pitted
4 large sweet red or yellow peppers
About 6 tablespoons olive oil
2 large plump cloves garlic, finely
*   chopped or crushed*
Salt

If olives have been packed in brine, rinse them in cold running water *before* pitting them.

Peel peppers as follows. Put them under a hot broiler and turn them over regularly until their skins blister, burst and blacken. Then rub and peel off skins under running water. (If preferred, you can spear each pepper on a fork and turn it over an open gas flame to blister the skin.) Cut peppers in half. Remove cores and rinse out seeds. Slice into long, narrow ribbons.

In a serving dish, gently mix olives with peppers. Make a dressing by shaking olive oil in a screw-top jar with garlic and a pinch of salt. Pour over peppers and olives. Allow to marinate for a minimum of 4 hours before serving, gently turning ingredients over from time to time.

BEEF AND OLIVE STEW

1½ pounds beef for stew
2–3 tablespoons olive oil
2 medium-size onions, chopped
4 tomatoes, quartered
½ cup ripe or green olives, pitted
2 carrots, diced
1 eggplant (optional)
½ teaspoon dried thyme
Salt and freshly ground
*   black pepper*
2 cloves garlic, chopped
2 cups red wine

Cut the beef into neat cubes and fry in the hot oil until browned. Add the onions and fry until golden, then stir in the tomatoes, olives and carrot pieces.

Slice and add the eggplant, if using, and continue frying for a few minutes, stirring to prevent the vegetables sticking to the pan.

Add the thyme, salt and pepper and garlic, then pour in the wine. Turn down the heat to very low, press a piece of parchment paper on the surface of the stew, cover the pan with a lid and stew very, very gently for about 3 hours until the beef is tender.

Serves 4.

BRAISED DUCK WITH OLIVES

2 tablespoons butter
4 pound duckling
1 medium-size onion, finely chopped
1 glass port wine
1 teaspoon paprika
1¼ cups chicken broth
Bouquet garni
Salt and freshly ground black pepper
2 large tomatoes
12 large green olives
1 tablespoon flour

Melt the butter in a flameproof casserole and brown the duck all over.

Tip away any excess fat, add the onion and cover. Cook until the onion is transparent. Pour in the port wine and cook until reduced by half, then add the paprika and cook for about 2 minutes.

Pour in the broth and add the bouquet garni and salt and pepper. Cover the casserole and cook over low heat for about 45 minutes, or until the bird is cooked through.

If cooking in the oven, it should be preheated to 350°.

Peel, slice and seed the tomatoes.

OLIVE AND RABBIT STEW NIÇOISE

This dish is a specialty of the region around Nice in France.

3 tablespoons olive oil
2 large onions, finely chopped
2 garlic cloves, crushed
4 large or 8 small pieces of rabbit
¼ cup butter
¼ cup flour
2½ cups chicken broth
1¼ cups white wine
1 tablespoon tomato paste
1 teaspoon dried tarragon
1 teaspoon dried rosemary
1 cup green olives, pitted
¼ cup Madeira wine
Sprigs of parsley

Heat the olive oil in a large skillet. Lower the heat, add the onions and garlic, and fry for 5 minutes. Then add the rabbit pieces and cook, turning, until the meat is well browned. Remove the pan from the heat and set on one side.

Melt the butter in a large, heavy casserole, over a low heat, and stir in the flour to form a thick paste. Remove from the heat, and stir in the broth, wine, tomato paste and herbs. Mix well to make a smooth sauce. Add the rabbit, onions, garlic and oil from the skillet. Stir and return the casserole to the heat.

Cover and cook slowly, stirring occasionally, for 30 minutes. Then add the olives. Stir and cook for a further 30 minutes, until the rabbit is tender.

Just before serving, stir in the Madeira. Garnish with the parsley, and serve hot, with boiled potatoes and a green salad.

Serves 4.

Pit the olives and cut them into shreds. Blanch in boiling water for about 5 minutes, then drain and leave covered with cold water.

Take the duck out of the pot and remove the bouquet garni. Skim off excess fat and stir in the flour. Bring to a boil, still stirring, then add the tomatoes and drained olives, and return to a boil. Adjust the seasoning. Divide the duck into 4 portions and serve with the sauce.

Serves 4.

NOODLES WITH TOMATOES, CHEESE AND OLIVES

This is a superb side dish to accompany simple meat dishes such as fried veal cutlets or chicken.

1 pound flat noodles (tagliatelle)
Salt
2–4 tablespoons butter, coarsely cut up
6–8 ounces fresh Mozzarella cheese, cubed
¼ cup grated Parmesan cheese
½ cup plump ripe olives, pitted and sliced

Tomato sauce
1 medium-size onion, finely chopped
2 tablespoons butter
2 tablespoons olive oil
2 tablespoons tomato paste
1 large (16 ounce) can Italian peeled tomatoes
1 teaspoon crushed dried oregano
Salt and freshly ground black pepper
Pinch of sugar

Start by boiling noodles in salted water and draining them thoroughly. While noodles are cooking, prepare a simple tomato sauce as follows. In a pan, sauté onion in butter and oil until soft and golden. Stir in tomato paste and fry gently for 2 or 3 minutes longer, stirring. Pour in the whole can of tomatoes with its juices and about one-third of a can of water, and bring to boiling point, stirring and mashing tomatoes to a pulp with your spoon. Add oregano and season lightly with salt, a grinding of black pepper and a pinch of sugar. Continue to simmer sauce for about 15 minutes longer until reduced and slightly thickened. Correct seasoning if necessary, bearing in mind saltiness of olives and cheese that are to come.

To serve, pile hot drained noodles in a large, heated serving bowl. Add bits of butter, the cubed Mozzarella and 2 tablespoons grated Parmesan. Toss until thoroughly mixed. Pour simmering tomato sauce over the top and sprinkle with sliced olives and remaining Parmesan.

Give the noodles a final toss and serve very hot.

Serves 4–6.

TUNA OLIVE MAYONNAISE

Two 7 ounce cans tuna in oil
½ cup pitted ripe or stuffed green olives, chopped
2 boiled potatoes, peeled and diced
1 small mild onion, finely chopped
2 tablespoons finely chopped parsley
About ¾ cup mayonnaise (page 205)
Salt and freshly ground black pepper
Crisp green lettuce leaves for garnish

Drain cans of tuna, empty fish into a bowl and flake it with a fork. Add the next 4 ingredients and toss lightly but thoroughly. Fold in mayonnaise, adding a little more if necessary to bind ingredients creamily. Taste and season with a pinch of salt if necessary and a good grinding of black pepper. Chill lightly.

Serves 4.

OLIVE AND FENNEL SALAD

A Mediterranean salad that is a complete meal in itself.

2 large potatoes
Salt
1 large bulb fennel
1 small can anchovies
1 large sweet green pepper
1 head Belgian endive
1 small can artichoke hearts
24 ripe olives
3 hard-cooked eggs

Dressing
10 tablespoons olive oil
5 tablespoons wine vinegar
Juice of 1 small lemon
½ teaspoon salt
½ teaspoon freshly ground black pepper
½ teaspoon dry mustard
½ teaspoon sugar

Put all the ingredients for the dressing in a screw-top jar and shake.

Peel the potatoes and cut into small pieces. Boil in salted water until just tender. (They must not be too soft.) Cut the potato pieces into approximately ¼ inch cubes. Place in a salad bowl. Shake the jar of dressing and pour over the potatoes.

Cut the leafy top off the fennel. Divide the bulb. Slice and wash in a colander under cold running water and dry on paper towels. Drain the oil from the anchovy fillets. Cut open the pepper, seed and core it, and slice finely. Wash, divide and chop up the endive. Drain the artichoke hearts. Add the fennel, anchovy fillets, pepper, endive and artichoke hearts to the contents of the salad bowl.

Pit the olives and quarter the hard-cooked eggs. Toss the salad and garnish with the olives and eggs.

Serves 2–4.

ORANGE

The evergreen orange tree, with its dark, glossy leaves and scented blossom, is probably the best known of all the citrus family. China is thought to be the home of the sweet orange and India the home of the bitter variety. The species has a number of synonyms, but all oranges share the name *hespiridium*, from the Roman goddess Hesperides, who was thought to have brought the orange across the seas to Italy.

Goddess- or sailor-borne, the first arrival was the bitter orange, an ornamental shrub with sour, inedible fruit. The flowers and leaves are very aromatic, with a heady, lasting scent which can carry for miles. A mature tree can yield up to 60 pounds of blossom in a season. The white flowers are traditionally used in wedding bouquets and pot pourri mixtures, and orange-flower water – much beloved of French and English pastrycooks as a flavoring for cakes and dessert pastries – is used in cosmetics as well. The rind of the bitter orange is also valuable, providing *neroli*, or orange oil, and is used in many orange-flavored liqueurs, such as Curaçao and Grand Marnier.

The sour Seville orange was traditionally brought to Spain by the Moors, who forbade any unbeliever to taste one until he was converted to Islam. The juice was thought to be an aid to digestion, and today the Spanish groves are a picturesque but highly commercialized industry. Seville oranges, small and sharply flavored, are favorites for the traditional English marmalade. They can be combined with their cousins in the citrus family – grapefruit or tangerines – to produce delicious variations on the marmalade theme (see page 83). The bergamot orange is a separate cultivar; its special contribution is the oil that is processed from the rind and used in cosmetics and perfumes.

The sweet orange found its way across Europe first with the Romans and then with the Portuguese East Indian traders in the fifteenth and sixteenth centuries. Spanish ships on their way to colonies in the New World were required to carry orange seeds and young trees for the new plantations. Today, there are huge orange groves in North Africa, Israel, Florida and California. In the tropics, the fruit stays green.

Although there are many individual varieties, sweet oranges fall mainly into three categories: blondes or normal oranges, the most common; smaller blood oranges, their darker flesh flecked with reddish spots which may indeed tint the entire fruit; and navel oranges, with a prominent growth at the stem end – often an entire, miniature, undeveloped orange in itself. The navel has become the most popular orange for eating raw as it peels easily and can be divided into segments with the fingers.

The rind or zest contains enough oil to intensify any orange flavor in a dish. Rub the rind with a cube of sugar to absorb the oil, and add the crushed cube to the other ingredients. The peel can be candied for use in cakes, and any of the sweet or bitter oranges can be stuck with cloves and powdered with orris root to make sweet-smelling pomanders.

Orange segments (with all the pith removed) can be sugar frozen; use 1 cup sugar for every pound of fruit. Freeze Seville oranges whole in plastic bags. Grated rind can also be frozen.

As everyone knows, oranges are full of Vitamin C – one sweet orange supplies the average adult with enough of this important vitamin for one day. They also have valuable cosmetic properties. Orange-flower water soothes the skin, and orange oil is an important constituent in many creams and perfumes.

REMEDIES

Long before the importance of Vitamin C was understood, oranges, especially the bitter variety, were used for various medicinal purposes.

True orange-flower water, made from essence of orange flowers, is an excellent sedative. An infusion of dried orange flowers, though not so potent, is still effective, as are infusions and decoctions of the leaves.

The distilled oil of orange blossom is said to have a hypnotic effect when inhaled.

SKIN LOTION

Orange-flower water is a soothing skin lotion, and not as astringent as lemon. Make a distillation (see page 82), or add a few drops of essential oil of orange flowers (also called oil of neroli) to some distilled water. This will improve after a week or two, but will not keep indefinitely. Mix with glycerine – about 1 part glycerine to 3 or 4 of orange-flower water – to make a gentle toning lotion.

ORANGE-FLOWER BATH OIL

It is easy to make your own orange-flower bath oil, given a reasonable supply of sunlight.

Put the flowers (the leaves can be added too) into a glass jar and pour enough oil to cover them. Any unscented oil is suitable; olive oil is often recommended and almond oil, though expensive, is superb. A little wine or cider vinegar – a tablespoon to 1¼ cups – will help preserve it. Seal the jar and stand it in a sunny place for 2–3 weeks, shaking it twice a day. Strain the oil and repeat with fresh flowers. The process may need repeating 2 or 3 times before the oil is strongly enough scented.

POMANDER

Exotic-smelling pomanders perfume clothes and keep away moths.

Mark an orange into quarters, and use a knitting needle to make holes all over the skin, leaving enough space at the quarter marks to tie a ribbon around the orange. Press cloves firmly into the holes.

Now put the pomander in a paper bag with powdered orris root, which will "fix" the spicy fragrance, and shake it until well covered. Then store it in a warm, dry, dark place, still in its bag, for 2 weeks or so to dry out. Tie a pretty ribbon around it and make a loop for hanging it up.

DUCKLING WITH ORANGE

In France, this dish is called *à la bigarade* after the small, bitter Seville oranges which are used in its preparation – their flavor being uniquely suitable for a fatty bird like duck. But the Seville orange season, which comes in the middle of winter, is a very short one. So if you would like to prepare this dish at other times of the year, it's a good idea to stock up with a supply of Seville oranges in the freezer.

1 duckling, about 5 pounds
¼ cup butter
Salt and freshly ground black pepper
3 Seville oranges
2 lemons
¾ cup dry white vermouth
2 large, sweet oranges
1 tablespoon sugar
1 tablespoon wine vinegar
½ tablespoon cornstarch
2 tablespoons orange liqueur
   (optional, see method)
2 tablespoons currant jelly
1 tablespoon orange marmalade,
   preferably Seville
Thin slices of sweet orange and
   watercress sprigs for garnish

In a flameproof roasting pan, brown duckling all over in foaming butter, taking care butter does not burn. When bird is uniformly crisp and brown all over, sprinkle it with salt and freshly ground black pepper.

Roast duckling in a preheated 350° oven for 45–60 minutes, or until juices run clear when a skewer is pushed into the thickest part of the leg, closest to the breast. Baste regularly with pan juices and take care not to overcook duck as this will make it dry and tasteless.

While duck is roasting, peel Seville oranges with a potato peeler, taking only the colored rind (*no* pith). Cut rind into fine, hair-thin strips. Put them in a pan with plenty of water to cover, bring slowly to boiling point, drain thoroughly and put aside until

needed. Then cut oranges in half, squeeze out all their juice and strain into a large, wide-necked pitcher. Squeeze juice from lemons and strain into pitcher. Stir in dry vermouth.

Peel sweet oranges and, working over pitcher to catch juices, cut out segments. Remove seeds with the point of your knife. Squeeze all remaining juices from orange piths into pitcher.

When duckling is done, transfer it to a heated serving dish. Return it to the switched-off oven with the door left slightly ajar to keep hot while you finish garnish and sauce.

In a small, heavy pan, swirl sugar and vinegar together over moderate heat until sugar melts and turns into a rich golden caramel. Immediately pour in contents of pitcher, stirring until caramel has dissolved. Then add prepared orange segments and poach gently for 5 minutes. With a slotted spoon, lift orange segments out and arrange them carefully around duckling.

Pour off all but 1 or 2 tablespoons of fat from roasting pan. Pour in citrus syrup and slowly bring to boiling point, stirring and scraping bottom and sides of pan clean with a wooden spoon.

Process cornstarch smoothly with orange liqueur (or use water if you have no liqueur available). Stir into roasting pan and simmer for 2 or 3 minutes, stirring, until sauce is slightly thickened and no longer cloudy. Stir in blanched orange rind, currant jelly and orange marmalade, simmering until melted. Season generously with salt and freshly ground black pepper.

Spoon some of the sauce over duckling and pour remainder into a heated sauceboat. Decorate dish with paper-thin slices of fresh sweet orange and sprigs of watercress. Serve with sauce.

Serves 4.

MOROCCAN SPICED LAMB WITH ORANGE

A richly flavored dish which needs only a bowl of plain boiled or steamed rice as an accompaniment.

3–3½ pounds lean or boned lamb,
   cubed
1 teaspoon ground cinnamon
½ teaspoon ground cloves
Salt
¼ cup peanut or corn oil
2 Bermuda onions, finely chopped
1 clove garlic, finely chopped
A 2 inch piece of fresh ginger root,
   peeled and finely chopped
2–3 sprigs parsley
1 sprig thyme
¾ cup dry white wine
Finely grated rind and juice of 2–3
   oranges
Freshly ground black pepper
1 teaspoon flour
1 teaspoon Dijon-style mustard

Sprinkle cubes of lamb with a mixture of cinnamon, cloves and 2 teaspoons salt, turning them around to coat them on all sides. In a heavy, flameproof casserole over moderate heat, fry spiced lamb cubes, a portion at a time, in about half the oil until golden brown on all sides, transferring them to a plate with a slotted spoon as they are done.

In the remaining oil, sauté finely chopped onions with garlic and ginger until soft and golden. Return lamb to casserole. Add parsley and thyme sprigs tied together in a bouquet, and mix well. Moisten with wine and orange juice, and stir in grated orange rind. Finally, stir in about 1¼ cups water and season generously with freshly ground black pepper. Slowly bring to simmering point. Stir once more, cover and cook very gently until lamb is tender, about 45–60 minutes.

Blend flour and mustard smoothly with 2 or 3 tablespoons water. Stir into casserole. Mix well with sauce and bring to simmering point once more. Cook gently, stirring frequently, until sauce has thickened.

Discard herb bouquet. Correct seasoning with more salt or freshly ground black pepper if necessary and serve.

Serves 6–8.

ORANGE ONION SALAD

Delicious with roast or broiled lamb and pork, either hot or cold. Use a very sharp knife or one with a serrated blade for slicing the oranges.

4 juicy, sweet oranges
1 large, mild (Bermuda or red)
  onion
Salt and coarsely ground black
  pepper
Olive oil
Lemon juice or white wine or cider
  vinegar (optional)

Peel oranges, removing every scrap of white pith, and slice them thinly crosswise, working on a board to catch any juices. Pick out seeds with the tip of your knife and place the orange slices and their juices in a large, shallow dish.

Slice onion thinly. Separate it into rings and place them in a colander. Slowly pour over them a kettleful of boiling water (this is for the benefit of those who find raw onion troublesome). Shake off excess moisture and leave onion until cold.

Gently mix onion and orange slices together. Sprinkle to taste with salt and coarsely ground black pepper, and moisten with a few tablespoons of olive oil. Taste the salad and if it is too sweet, sharpen its flavour with a squeeze of lemon juice or a few drops of wine or cider vinegar.

Serves 4.

ORANGE AND CARROT SALAD

The orange-flower water, which gives this salad rather an Arab accent, can be bought in Greek, Middle Eastern and Indian stores, and is often stocked by druggists.

5–6 fresh young carrots
Juice of 1 lemon
1 tablespoon orange-flower water
2–3 teaspoons sugar, or to taste
Salt
2 oranges

Scrub or scrape carrots clean, and grate them coarsely. In a serving bowl, combine lemon juice with orange-flower water, sugar and a pinch of salt, stirring until sugar has dissolved. Peel oranges. Working over bowl to catch any juices, cut out orange segments. Pick out orange seeds as you come across them, and halve segments crosswise if they are large. Add them to bowl. Squeeze out any remaining juice from orange pith into bowl.

Add grated carrots to bowl, and toss lightly but thoroughly with a fork. Correct seasoning with a little more sugar or salt if necessary. Chill lightly before serving.

Serves 6.

THAI ORANGE AND PORK SALAD

A light, main-course salad for lunch.

4 large, sweet oranges
1 crisp head lettuce
4–6 ounces lean boned pork,
  trimmed
1 plump clove garlic, crushed
2 tablespoons peanut or other
  cooking oil
1 tablespoon finely chopped peanuts
1 teaspoon sugar
2 tablespoons dark soy sauce
Pinch of MSG
Pinch of paprika
Salt and freshly ground black pepper
Finely chopped parsley, chives or
  scallion tops for garnish

Peel and segment oranges, working over a plate to catch any juices and discarding seeds as you come across them. Take lettuce apart. Wash and pat leaves dry individually. Lay them, torn up if they are large, on a serving platter. Arrange orange sections on top and sprinkle with any juices you have saved. Put aside while you prepare dressing.

Cut pork into small, thin strips, discarding any fat or gristle as you come across it.

In a large skillet, sauté garlic in oil until golden but not burned (this could make it bitter). Add pork strips and stir-fry until lightly colored all over. Stir in chopped peanuts and continue to stir-fry for a minute or two longer. Sprinkle with sugar, soy sauce and 2 tablespoons water. Mix well. Season with MSG and paprika, and a little salt and/or freshly ground black pepper to taste if liked. Continue to stir-fry for a few minutes longer until pork is thoroughly cooked and sauce reduced.

Pour hot contents of pan over oranges and lettuce. Sprinkle with chopped parsley, chives or scallion tops.

Serve cold.

Serves 4.

ORANGE AND DATE SALAD

Serve this salad with the heavier kinds of meats such as pork and roast duckling.

¼ pound dried dates
3 tablespoons salad oil
1 tablespoon lemon juice
Salt
2 juicy oranges
Lettuce leaves and finely chopped
    walnuts for garnish

Cover dates with boiling water and leave to soften and plump up for about 10 minutes. Then drain dates thoroughly, pit them and cut into small pieces. In a bowl, beat oil and lemon juice together with a pinch of salt. Add dates and toss with a fork until well mixed.

Peel oranges, removing every scrap of white pith. Cut them horizontally into thin slices, picking out and discarding seeds as you come across them.

Line a serving platter or bowl with lettuce leaves. Arrange orange slices on them and spoon dates and dressing over the top. Sprinkle with a few chopped walnuts and serve.

Serves 4–6.

MEXICAN ORANGE SALAD

4–6 sweet oranges
1 large, green apple
Salt
Cayenne
Lettuce leaves for garnish

Peel oranges. Strip off every scrap of white pith, and segment the oranges, working over a bowl to catch juices. Cut each section in two or three, removing and discarding seeds as you come across them. Place in the bowl together with all the juices.

Peel, core and dice the apple, and add it to the bowl. Mix gently but thoroughly and season to taste with salt and cayenne.

Serve on a bed of crisp green lettuce.

Serves 4–6.

BEETS IN ORANGE SAUCE

Beets and orange are natural partners, and this dish makes a fine accompaniment for heavier meats such as pork, and game – especially in winter, when the choice of green vegetables can be limited.

1½ pounds beets, trimmed and
    peeled
¾ cup orange juice (juice of 2 small
    oranges)
Juice of ½ small lemon
2–3 tablespoons softened
    butter
1 teaspoon dark brown sugar
Salt
1 tablespoon cornstarch
2 tablespoons dry sherry wine

Shred the beets on the coarsest side of a grater and put them in a pan together with the orange and lemon juices, butter, sugar and a sprinkling of salt. Mix well. Push a sheet of parchment paper down onto the surface and cook gently until beets are soft, about 15 minutes.

In a small bowl, dissolve cornstarch in a mixture of sherry and 1 tablespoon water.

Pour into the pan of beets, stirring, and continue to cook, stirring constantly, until sauce has thickened and cleared.

Correct seasoning and serve.

Serves 4–6.

GLAZED CABBAGE À L'ORANGE

This is an unusual vegetable dish, especially good with pork.

1 large, juicy orange
1 small head white cabbage
1 Bermuda onion, finely chopped
¼ cup butter
6–8 tablespoons chicken broth
Salt and freshly ground black pepper
2–3 tablespoons currants (optional)
1–2 tablespoons dark brown sugar

Grate orange rind finely. Then peel orange and cut out segments. Discard any seeds and cut each segment in 2 or 3. Work over a dish to catch all the juice which may drip out and add orange segments to dish. Quarter, core and shred cabbage finely. Put it in a colander and slowly pour a kettle of boiling water over it. Shake off as much water as possible and put aside until needed.

In a heavy, flameproof casserole or saucepan, sauté onion gently in butter until soft and golden. Stir in shredded cabbage and continue to sauté for a minute or two longer until shreds are coated with butter. Mix in grated orange rind. Moisten with chicken broth and any juice that has drained from orange segments. Season to taste with salt, grind in some pepper, cover and cook gently until cabbage has softened, about 20 minutes. Then mix in pieces of orange and currants, if used, and sprinkle with sugar. Correct seasoning with a little more salt or freshly ground black pepper. Continue to cook gently, stirring frequently, until sugar has melted and is beginning to look slightly caramelized.

Keep hot, covered, until ready to serve.

Serves 4–6.

ORANGE RICE WITH ALMONDS

Pages have been written about the cooking of rice, each nation seemingly devoted to its own method of boiling, steaming or baking. My own favorite method is the way in which Turkish pilaus are made: the raw grains are first fried until thoroughly coated with fat and very lightly colored. Then *twice the volume* of boiling or very hot liquid is poured in (carefully, because it will spatter and sizzle alarmingly). When the bubbling has subsided, give the rice a good stir, clamp on the lid and leave the pot undisturbed over the lowest possible heat for 15–20 minutes, until all the liquid has been absorbed, leaving the surface dotted with tiny craters. And that's it.

Orange rice goes especially well with poultry dishes and ham.

1 teaspoon whole coriander seeds
1 medium-size onion, finely chopped
3–4 stalks celery, diagonally sliced
½ cup butter
1 tablespoon finely grated orange rind
2 cups long-grain rice
2 cups each well-flavored chicken broth and fresh orange juice
Salt
Sautéed slivered almonds for garnish

In a mortar, crush coriander seeds finely with a pestle. Put aside until needed.

Choose a large, flameproof casserole with a tight-fitting lid. In it, fry the onion and celery gently in half the butter until quite soft but only lightly colored. Add the crushed coriander seeds, orange rind and the remaining butter, and when this has melted, stir in the rice. Cook gently, stirring, until each grain is coated with butter. Then add chicken broth, orange juice and salt, to taste. Bring to boiling point, stirring, then lower heat to a bare simmer, cover tightly and cook for 20 minutes, or until rice grains are tender and all the liquid has been absorbed.

Heap rice into a heated dish.

Sprinkle sautéed almonds over the top and serve.

Serves 6–8.

GINGERED ORANGE RICE

A most unusual and subtly flavored dish of rice that makes a fine accompaniment for roast poultry, ham and pork or lamb chops.

3 tablespoons butter
1 medium-size onion, finely chopped
1 cup long-grain rice
Finely grated rind of 1 orange
½ teaspoon ground ginger
½ cup fresh orange juice
1½ cups well-flavored chicken broth
Finely chopped parsley for garnish

In a heavy pan, melt butter and fry onion gently until soft and golden. Stir in rice and continue to fry, stirring, until each grain is shiny with butter and lightly colored. Stir in orange rind and ginger, mix well and fry for a minute or two longer. Remove pan from heat and cool slightly.

Stir in orange juice and chicken broth. Bring to boiling point, stir once and lower heat to a bare simmer. Cover pan tightly and cook gently for 15–20 minutes (without lifting the lid once) until all the liquid is absorbed and rice grains are fluffy and separate. Garnish with parsley.

Serves 4.

ORANGE SOUFFLÉ PUDDING

A dish of ·thin, delicate almond cookies makes a delicious accompaniment for this dessert.

1 tablespoon unflavored gelatin
4 eggs, separated
¾ cup sugar
Finely grated rinds of 1 orange and 1 lemon
Juice of 3–4 oranges
Juice of 1 lemon

Sprinkle gelatin over 3 or 4 tablespoons cold water in a small cup. Then, when the gelatin has absorbed the water and set, stand the cup in a pan of hot water, stirring until the liquid is clear. Allow to cool to room temperature.

In a large bowl, beat the egg yolks, sugar and grated rinds together until thick and fluffy. Stir the gelatin into the orange and lemon juices, then gradually beat into the egg yolk mixture. Leave until syrupy.

Beat the egg whites until stiff but not dry. Fold them gently into the mixture. Spoon it into a serving bowl and chill until set.

Serves 6.

BOODLE'S ORANGE FOOL

There are many versions of this famous dessert, which was created by Boodle's, a London club founded in 1763.

4 rectangular slices stale pound cake
Finely grated rind and juice of 2 oranges and 1 lemon
3 tablespoons sugar, to taste
1¼ cups heavy cream
Crystallized orange segments and unsweetened whipped cream

Cut the pound cake into long, thin strips and arrange them over the bottom of a glass serving bowl.

In a small bowl, mix the grated rind and juice of the oranges and lemon with the sugar, and stir until it has dissolved. Whip the cream until thickened but not stiff, and gradually beat in the sweetened fruit juice. Pour over the strips of pound cake. Chill for several hours in the refrigerator.

Serve decorated with unsweetened whipped cream and crystallized orange segments.

Serves 4–6.

PETITS POTS DE CHOCOLAT À L'ORANGE

Oranges have a remarkable affinity for chocolate and their flavor will add magic to any chocolate confection. This dish comes from Robert Carrier's restaurant in London – a dessert that has become justly famous.

In the original version, the rind of an orange is first grated, then blended with the juice, which has been squeezed separately. However, provided the orange has a very thin skin and thus little white pith, which would make the dessert bitter, you can save time and trouble by blending the whole orange, minus any seeds, to a smooth pulp.

The recipe below makes ample for four. For six portions, simply increase the number of eggs to three.

4 ounces good-quality dark,
   bittersweet chocolate
2 tablespoons unsalted butter
2 thin-skinned oranges
Grand Marnier, Curaçao or
   brandy
2 eggs, separated

Break up the chocolate into the top of a double boiler, and add the butter. Cut 1 orange into chunks, saving juice; remove seeds and blend orange finely; add its juice and blend the two together thoroughly. Add to the chocolate. Stir over hot water until chocolate has melted and mixture is smooth. Remove top of pan, cool slightly and stir in 1 tablespoon orange liqueur or brandy.

In a bowl, beat egg yolks until fluffy. Strain in the chocolate mixture, beating constantly. Beat egg whites until stiff but not dry and fold into the chocolate mixture. Pour into individual little pots, custard cups or soufflé dishes; allow to become cold and chill until ready to serve.

Just before serving, cut 2 large, thin slices from the center of the second orange. Quarter them by making two crosswise cuts through each slice and lay two quarters point to point on top of each portion to make a bow-tie shape. Finally, pour a little more liqueur over the surface of each pot, just enough to make it look glossy.

Serves 4.

ORANGES IN MARSALA

7 sweet, juicy, thin-skinned
   oranges
¾ cup Marsala wine
2 tablespoons lemon juice
1 cup sugar

With a potato peeler, peel off the colored rind of 4 of the oranges as thinly as you can. With a small, sharp knife, shave off any white pith which may have come off as well. Slice rind into matchstick strips.

Drop strips into a small pan of cold water, bring to boiling point and drain thoroughly.

In a measuring cup, combine Marsala with lemon juice. Strain in the juice of 1 orange and add water to make 1¼ cups. Pour into a heavy pan, add sugar and bring to boiling point, stirring until sugar has dissolved. Stir in blanched strips of rind and· simmer, stirring occasionally, until strips are translucent and syrup has thickened and is reduced by about one-third. Add a little more boiling water if it appears to be reducing too quickly. Pour into a wide-necked pitcher. Cool and chill until ready to serve.

Peel remaining 6 oranges, slicing away every scrap of bitter white pith and the tough membrane beneath it. Then, working on a board or plate to catch any juices, lay each orange on its side and with a sharp knife, slice it horizontally. Pick out any seeds and reassemble each orange, sticking a couple of long toothpicks right down from top to bottom to hold slices in position.

Arrange re-formed oranges side by side in a glass bowl. Stir juices that escaped when you were cutting them into the syrup.

Pour syrup over oranges and top each one with a little bundle of caramelized orange rind.

Return to refrigerator until ready to serve.

Serves 6.

CRÊPES SUZETTE

These crêpes in orange liqueur sauce were named by Edward VII after his pretty young dinner companion, when a pan of *crêpes au liqueur* with which they were being served accidentally burst into flames.

For the crêpes use the batter given for Lemon crêpes on page 92, making them no more than 5 or 6 inches in diameter.

12–16 small, thin crêpes
½ cup unsalted butter
6 tablespoons sugar
Finely grated rind of 1 large orange
6 tablespoons fresh orange juice
1 teaspoon lemon juice
5 tablespoons Curaçao or Cointreau
2 tablespoons brandy

Prepare crêpes in advance and stack them on an upturned soup plate under a cloth to keep them soft and pliable. The orange butter may also be made in advance and stored in the refrigerator until needed.

Cream butter and gradually add 5 tablespoons sugar, beating vigorously until mixture is white and fluffy. Beat in grated orange rind, then slowly beat in orange and lemon juices, followed by 2 tablespoons of the orange liqueur. Do not worry if butter looks curdled at this stage. Scrape it into a bowl and chill until you are ready to use it.

Fry crêpes in orange butter either in a large, heavy skillet, preferably one with rounded sides so crêpes will slip out easily, or in a chafing dish at the table. First place the remaining orange liqueur and the brandy in a small pan, ready to heat up and set alight when needed. Next, melt orange butter in skillet. Place the first crêpe flat in the bubbling hot butter, submerging it totally, then fold it in four and push it to one side. Repeat with remaining crêpes. Distribute them evenly over bottom of skillet and allow to bubble gently while you proceed to the final stage.

Sprinkle crêpes with remaining tablespoon of sugar. Gently heat pan of brandy and liqueur, and when fumes start rising, carefully put a match to it. As soon as flames are well established, pour all over crêpes Take skillet from the heat and keep shaking it gently and spooning syrup over crêpes until flames die out. Serve immediately.

Serves 4–6.

ORANGE CHEESE BREAD

The flavor of this delicious tea bread improves tremendously if it is left to mellow for about 24 hours.

3 cups wholewheat flour
1/3 cup firmly packed dark brown sugar
1 teaspoon ground cinnamon
1/2 teaspoon salt
1/4 teaspoon baking soda
1 cup cottage cheese
Finely grated rind of 1 orange
1 teaspoon vanilla
1 egg
2 (0.6 oz) cakes compressed yeast or 2 packages active dry yeast
6 tablespoons orange juice
1/2 cup raisins
Margarine, for loaf pan

Stir the flour, sugar, cinnamon, salt and soda together until well mixed. Rub the cottage cheese through a sieve into another bowl and beat in the orange rind and vanilla. Beat the egg until foamy.

Dissolve compressed yeast in orange juice (if using dried yeast, follow package directions).

Make a well in the center of the flour mixture. Add all the remaining ingredients except the raisins and margarine, and knead vigorously until the dough starts to leave the sides of the bowl clean (it will still be very sticky). Work in the raisins so they are well distributed throughout the dough. Cover the bowl with a cloth and leave the dough to rise until doubled in bulk.

Grease a 9 × 5 inch loaf pan with margarine. Deflate the dough, knead lightly and transfer it to the loaf pan, which it will half-fill. Cover the pan with a cloth and leave the dough until doubled in bulk again. Then bake bread in a preheated 375° oven for 35 minutes, or until it is well risen and a thin skewer pushed through the center feels dry to the touch.

Let the loaf cool in its baking pan, lying on its side on a wire rack. Then remove the pan and let the loaf cool completely, still on its side, before storing (till the following day if at all possible).

ORANGE WALNUT CAKE

1 cup chopped walnuts
3 tablespoons flour
1 teaspoon baking powder
1/8 teaspoon salt
1 medium-size orange
4 eggs, separated
2/3 cup sugar
3 tablespoons melted butter
Walnut halves for decoration

Chocolate frosting
4 ounces bittersweet chocolate
2 tablespoons melted butter

Grind the walnuts finely in a blender or food processor. (Do not use a meat grinder, which tends to make the nuts too oily.) Mix the ground nuts thoroughly with the flour, baking powder and salt. Grate the rind of the orange finely and mix into the flour mixture.

Beat egg yolks until thick and lemon-colored, then gradually beat in 6 tablespoons of the sugar. Fold in the walnut mixture, followed by the juice of 1/2 the orange.

In another bowl, beat the egg whites until they form soft, floppy peaks. Gradually add the remaining sugar, beating constantly to make a stiff meringue. With a large metal spoon, fold meringue into yolk mixture.

Spoon cake batter gently into a well-buttered, deep 8 inch cake pan. Bake in a preheated 350° oven for 40 minutes, or until the cake is a rich golden color, feels firm when pressed lightly and has shrunk away slightly from the sides of the pan. Allow the cake to cool in its pan on a rack for 10 minutes before unmolding onto the rack and leaving it until cold.

To make chocolate frosting, break the chocolate into small pieces. Put it in a heatproof bowl, stand the bowl in simmering water and leave until chocolate has melted, stirring frequently. Beat in the butter and continue to beat until smooth.

Spread frosting over top and sides of cake with a broad-bladed knife. Decorate with walnut halves.

Leave until frosting has become dry to the touch.

ORANGE AND ALMOND CAKE

This cake, with its pure orange flavor, comes from Claudia Roden's *Book of Middle Eastern Food*. As Mrs Roden points out, the texture of the cake will depend on how long it stays in the oven. For a cake with a moist, pudding-like texture (which I like to serve as a dessert with lightly whipped cream), give it less time. If you want it to turn out firmer and drier, increase the baking time. In any case, have a look at it after 30 minutes. The cake will not go any flatter if the oven door is opened while it is baking.

Butter and flour, for cake pan
2 large oranges
6 eggs
1 cup sugar
2 cups ground almonds
1 teaspoon baking powder

Start by buttering and flouring a deep cake pan about 8 inches in diameter, preferably one with a removable base.

Rinse oranges and boil them in water to cover for about 2 hours until very soft. If you have a pressure cooker, this will take only 30 minutes at 15 pounds pressure. Lift oranges out of pan, cool them and cut them into large pieces, picking out and discarding seeds. Then pulp oranges, skins and all, in an electric blender or food processor, or by putting them through a sieve.

In a large bowl beat eggs until fluffy. Beating constantly, gradually add sugar. Gently stir and fold in ground almonds, baking powder and orange pulp. When thoroughly blended, pour into prepared cake pan.

Bake cake in a preheated 400° oven for about 45 minutes (see above).

Allow cake to cool in its pan before unmolding.

ORANGE SHORTBREAD

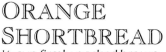

⅓ cup firmly packed brown
  sugar
7 tablespoons soft margarine
Finely grated rind of 1 large
  orange
1¼ cups flour
3 tablespoons cornstarch
1 teaspoon baking powder

If you have a food processor, put all the ingredients in it together, switch on, and your ball of dough will be ready in a couple of minutes.

Otherwise, cream the sugar with the margarine and the finely grated orange rind. Sift the flour, cornstarch and baking powder together, and combine with the sugar mixture to make a firm dough. Roll into a ball, wrap in plastic and chill for 1 hour.

Dust a board and your rolling pin *very* lightly with flour and roll the dough out about ⅛ inch thick. Cut out cookies with a 2 inch cutter and carefully, with a spatula, transfer them to lightly greased baking sheets. Prick each cookie two or three times with the tines of a fork.

Bake the cookies in a preheated 350° oven for 25 minutes, or until a rich golden color. Allow them to cool a little on the baking sheets before transferring to wire racks.

When quite cold, store in an airtight tin or jar.

ORANGE SWEETMEATS

2 large thin-skinned oranges
1 cup sugar
1 center slice lemon
2 tablespoons Grand Marnier,
  Curaçao or brandy (optional)

Wash the oranges and dry them thoroughly. Carefully strip off the peel from each orange in eight sections. If the white pith is thick, shave it down with a sharp knife. Roll the peels up tightly and thread them side by side to make a "necklace," using a large needle and a length of strong thread. Tie the ends of thread together.

In an enameled pan, cover the necklace of rinds with cold water and bring to a rapid boil. Drain and repeat twice more. The third time, continue to boil gently until the peels are quite soft, 10–15 minutes. Drain thoroughly and pat dry with paper towels.

Rinse the pan and in it dissolve the sugar in 1¼ cups water, together with the lemon slice. Stir in the liqueur or brandy, if used. Skim off scum if necessary. Add the rinds and simmer gently until they are very soft and the syrup is thick, 20–30 minutes. Cool in the pan, covered.

Remove the lemon slice, unthread the orange rolls and pack them into a glass jar. Pour over the syrup, cover the jar and store in a cool, dark cupboard.

CANDIED PEEL

There is a great difference – in flavor, texture *and* price – between orange peels candied at home and those that have been prepared commercially for the supermarket.

Home-candied peels are well worth having all year around but are particularly useful made in the fall, in time for Christmas baking.

Use either strips of orange peel, taken off lengthwise in quarters or sixths, or squeezed-out halves, cut into large pieces. If the peels have a thick layer of white pith attached, this should be left, but squeezed-out halves must first be parboiled for several minutes, then drained and scraped clean of the remains of pulp and other debris with a small, sharp spoon.

Put the peels in a pan, cover with water and simmer until quite tender, which will take about 1½ hours. Top up with more water as it evaporates.

Drain peels thoroughly, reserving water. Measure water, pour it back into the pan, and for every 1¼ cups add 1 cup sugar. If there is not enough syrup to cover the peels comfortably, more may be made with fresh water and sugar in the same proportions. Stir over low heat until sugar is dissolved. Then raise heat, bring syrup to boiling point and add peels. Make sure they are all thoroughly coated with syrup and put aside till the following day.

The second day, bring syrup to boiling point again and simmer for 5 minutes.

The third day, simmer peels until they are translucent, the syrup is very thick and nearly all of it has been absorbed. Lift out pieces of peel onto a wire rack lined with wax paper. Cover lightly with another sheet of wax paper and leave to dry in a warm, airy place. Take advantage of a cooling oven whenever it is available (a temperature of about 100° will be suitable) to help speed up the drying process.

Store candied peels in an airtight box or screw-top jar. Should they dry out too much and become impossibly tough to chop up for use, they can be softened again by soaking them for a short time in boiling water.

TRADITIONAL MARMALADE

In *The Feill Cookery Book*, published in 1907 by Messrs McNaught & Sinclair of Glasgow, the following recipe for marmalade was contributed by Messrs M. Campbell & Son, Preserve Makers, of 15 Hartington Place, Edinburgh. Although the recipe is over 70 years old, nothing seems to have changed in marmalade making.

7 bitter (Seville) oranges
5 quarts water
14 cups sugar

Wash the oranges in warm water and scrape off black specks, if any. Then with a very sharp knife cut the oranges across in thin slices right through skin and pulp. The seeds will fall out and they should be placed in a bowl. Then re-cut the slices so that the pieces of peel are not too long; these should then be placed in a bowl. Add the 5 quarts of cold water; place the seeds in a cheesecloth bag and let them soak in the water with the peel for 24 hours. Then place all together in a large kettle and boil for 1½ hours without the sugar (when it has boiled for about 1 hour take out the bag of seeds). Now add the sugar and boil for another ½ hour, fill up the pots and cover when cold.

ORANGE MARMALADE

It is almost worth borrowing, or even investing in, a pressure cooker for this recipe alone. It not only cuts the preparation time dramatically but also makes the best orange marmalade I know. Three pounds fruit is the maximum I would use at any one time in a large pressure cooker.

If you cannot find the time to make marmalade during the few weeks that Seville oranges are on the market, but do have a freezer, freeze a supply of oranges, tied up in a plastic bag, until you are ready. They will keep perfectly for up to a year (I once used oranges that were 2 years old most successfully).

Thaw them completely before use (overnight, at room temperature, is best), then use them in the same way as fresh fruit.

2 pounds Seville oranges
2 lemons
8 cups sugar
Small pat of butter or margarine
(optional)

Scrub the oranges and lemons thoroughly under cold water. Pack them in a pressure cooker with 2½ cups water, bring to 15 pounds pressure and cook for 15 minutes if oranges are very large, only 10 minutes if smaller. Reduce pressure.

Open the cooker and lift out the fruit with a slotted spoon. When they are cool enough to handle, cut them in half and with a sharp-edged teaspoon scrape all the pulp, pith and seeds out of the rinds into a bowl. Stir this back into the water remaining in the cooker and boil hard for 10 minutes.

Meanwhile, slice the rinds in half again lengthwise and cut them into matchstick strips.

Strain the boiled liquid through a fine sieve. For a crystal-clear jelly, line the sieve with double-thick cheesecloth and allow as much liquid as possible to drip through without squeezing or pressing through any pulp. However, if this is not important, press the pulp lightly against the sides of the sieve with the back of a wooden spoon to extract as much liquid as possible. Pour it back into the cooker.

Add sugar and stir with a wooden spoon over low heat until dissolved. Stir in shredded peel and boil briskly until setting point is reached. A small pat of butter or margarine stirred in at the last moment will take care of any scum.

Cool for 5 minutes and pour hot into hot, dry jars. Cover immediately and process as usual.

See also page 198.

Fills about 7 jars.

SAUCE MALTAISE

This orange-flavored Hollandaise sauce is a classic accompaniment for hot poached asparagus. Originally, it was made with blood oranges but ordinary ones will do very well. The amount yielded by the recipe below will be enough to dress about 1½ pounds asparagus and serve 4–6 people.

3 egg yolks
1–2 tablespoons lemon juice
Salt and white pepper
¾ cup unsalted butter
Finely grated rind of ½ orange
Juice of 1 small orange

In the top of a double boiler, or a bowl that fits snugly over (*not* in) a pan of simmering water, beat egg yolks with a tablespoon each of lemon juice and water, a good pinch of salt and a generous dash of white pepper.

Divide butter into 10 or 12 cubes and leave on a plate to soften slightly without turning oily.

Fit top of double boiler or bowl over simmering water. Drop in the first piece of butter and beat lightly by hand with a wire whisk until it is incorporated into egg yolks. Beat in one or two more pieces of butter in the same way, taking great care that sauce does not overheat, or it will curdle. If it looks in any danger of separating, immediately lift the top container off and quickly beat in a tablespoon of cold water to lower the temperature of the sauce slightly, beating vigorously until it is quite smooth again.

With the pan off the heat, continue to beat in butter, a piece at a time. Then flavor sauce with grated orange rind and thin it down slightly with orange juice.

Finally, taste and adjust flavor of sauce with more salt, white pepper or orange juice as desired.

Keep sauce hot until ready to serve by standing it over hot (*not* boiling) water. Give it an occasional stir, paying particular attention to the bottom and corners of the pan.

Serve sauce in a heated sauceboat.

Serves 4–6.

BISHOP

This is a form of mulled wine. When red wine is used instead of port it is called "Cardinal." When champagne is used, it is known as "Pope."

1 large orange
1 tablespoon whole cloves
½ teaspoon ground cinnamon
½ teaspoon ground cloves
½ teaspoon allspice
1 blade mace
½ ounce ginger root, peeled and finely chopped
5 cups non-vintage port wine
⅓ cup sugar
Juice of 1 lemon
Nutmeg

Preheat the oven to 250°. Stud the orange all over with the whole cloves. Place on a baking sheet and cook in the oven for about 1 hour.

Then, put all the spices and 1¼ cups water in a medium-size saucepan. Bring to a boil and simmer until the water is reduced by half. In a separate large saucepan, heat the port wine until almost boiling.

Remove from the heat. Strain the spiced water through a fine sieve onto the port. Add the baked orange. Return the pan to the heat and cook slowly for 10 minutes, but do not allow to boil.

When ready to serve, put the sugar and lemon juice in a punch bowl. Pour over the hot, spiced port. Stir and grate some nutmeg over the surface.

Serve hot, by ladling the wine into warm glasses.

Serves 6.

ORANGEADE

Make large quantities of this cooling drink to store in the refrigerator, ready to be served chilled with ice on hot summer days.

1 cup sugar
Grated rind and juice of 2 large oranges
Juice of 1 lemon
Soda water
Orange slices for decoration

Place the sugar and 1 quart water in

ORANGE WINE

The combination of Seville and sweet oranges gives this sweet, dessert wine a tangy "bite."

6 Seville oranges
6 sweet oranges
3 cups chopped golden raisins
1 teaspoon pectic enzyme
1 yeast nutrient tablet
Sherry wine yeast
6 cups sugar

Heat 4½ quarts water to boiling point. Meanwhile peel the oranges, keeping the peel thin and avoiding the pith. Chop the peel finely, and place in the prepared vessel (such as a plastic pail). Add the raisins, then pour on the boiling water. Stir, then cover and leave to cool to a temperature of 65–75°.

Squeeze the juice from the oranges into the vessel, add the pectic enzyme, nutrient tablet and activated yeast (see manufacturer's instructions for quantity and method of use). Cover the vessel tightly and leave in a warm place (65–75°) for 6 days.

Uncover the vessel and strain off the liquid through a fine sieve into a sterilized container. Stir in the sugar and siphon into a fermentation vessel.

Ferment under an air-lock. When a good layer of sediment has formed on the bottom of the vessel, rack, then store for at least a year before bottling.

Keep the wine for a further year before drinking.

See also page 205.

Makes about 4½ quarts.

a pan. Heat gently, stirring, until the sugar dissolves, but do not boil. Pour into a pitcher.

Add the rind and juices to the pitcher, stir, cover and leave to stand in a cool place for 3 hours.

Strain off the rind and chill in the refrigerator until wanted.

To serve, two-thirds fill a tall chilled glass then top up with soda water and ice.

Decorate each serving with a thin slice of orange.

ORANGE GIN

Use Seville oranges for this recipe – the sweet variety make rather a flat, sickly liqueur. Select fruit with an unblemished skin – only the peel is used.

2 cups sugar
4 Seville oranges
2 lemons
1 quart gin

Make a syrup by dissolving the sugar in 1 cup water and boiling for 15 minutes. Leave to cool. Meanwhile peel the fruit thinly, making sure that no pith is taken off with the peel. Chop the peel and place in a large wide-neck storage jar with a screw top. Pour on the sugar syrup and gin. Screw the lid firmly onto the jar.

Shake gently and leave for 2 weeks at room temperature.

Unscrew the lid, strain off the liqueur and bottle it. Keep for at least 6 months, preferably longer, before drinking.

Makes about 1½ quarts.

BUCK'S FIZZ

A perfect celebratory drink.

2 parts champagne
1 part fresh orange juice

Chill the champagne and the orange juice by placing in the refrigerator for at least 2 hours before you wish to use them. Just before serving, pour the ingredients into a chilled pitcher. Stir well and serve in tulip shaped champagne glasses.

PAPAYA

The papaya, also called a tree melon or paw paw, grows throughout the tropics of both the Old and New Worlds, from India to South America. It is known to have been cultivated by the Aztecs and Mayas, perhaps the first people to do so.

Even though you may never have seen, let alone tasted, a fresh papaya, the chances are you have eaten meat tenderized with the proteolitic enzyme *papain* which is extracted from the fruit.

Papayas do not look particularly inviting – a cross between small, oval melons and large dumpy pears of a faded green color. This changes dramatically once the fruit is cut open to reveal its brilliant coral or golden flesh and hundreds of shiny black seeds. These should all be scraped out with a teaspoon as they can taste quite peppery.

A ripe papaya yields slightly to pressure when squeezed gently between the palms of the hands and its skin feels soft. But unripe papayas are also edible. In the West Indies, they are treated as a vegetable and served cooked. If the fruit you have is ripe but still too hard to eat, leave it for a day or two in a warm cupboard, or wrapped in a brown paper bag in the kitchen, to soften.

CLEANSER AND TONERS

Papaya is used to "tenderize" the skin, in cosmetic face masks and lotions. It also makes a very effective occasional treatment for removing dead skin and freshening and bleaching the complexion. Pat on a little juice very gently: don't leave on more than 5 minutes before removing with lukewarm water.

FRIED PAPAYA

An unusual accompaniment that is delicious served with ham. Use firm, slightly under-ripe fruit that will not go mushy in the skillet.

1 large papaya
2 tablespoons butter
1 tablespoon lemon juice

Peel papaya and cut it horizontally into slices about ½ inch thick. Scrape out black seeds.

In a large, heavy skillet, melt butter. When it is foaming, lay papaya rings in it in one layer and fry until heated through and lightly colored, about 1 minute on each side.

Sprinkle with lemon juice and serve immediately.

Serves 4.

PAPAYA STRAWBERRY APPETIZER

2 large, ripe papayas, chilled
Fresh lime or lemon juice
1½ pints medium-size strawberries
Confectioners' sugar

Halve papayas lengthwise and clear out all the black seeds with a sharp teaspoon. Brush cut surfaces all over with lime or lemon juice. Lay halves on 4 individual glass dishes.

Clean or quickly rinse strawberries and hull them. They should all be of the same size; if there are large ones among them, halve or quarter them. Pile strawberries into papaya cups and sift sugar over the top.

Serves 4.

DULCE DE PAPAYA VERDE

Candied Green Papaya

This interesting recipe comes from *Good Food From Mexico* by Ruth Watt Mulvey and Luisa Maria Alvarez. As the authors say in their introduction to the recipe, this is "one of the most elaborate and one of the best ways" of preparing a dessert of green (unripe) papaya.

¼ cup slaked lime (food pure)
½ medium-size green papaya
About 2 cups sugar
2–3 fig leaves

Soak lime in about 2 quarts water for 1 hour. Allow it to settle, then strain it out through cheesecloth. Pour water back into bowl. Peel papaya, cut it into 2 inch squares, drop it into the lime water overnight.

The following day, remove papaya, wash and simmer lightly in fresh water to cover for about 10 minutes. Cool. Press the pieces of papaya gently between thumb and forefinger to remove all excess moisture.

Boil together sugar and 2 cups water, stirring, until sugar is dissolved and syrup forms a thread. Add papaya and fig leaves. Simmer gently over very low heat for about 20 minutes. Remove papaya pieces to a serving dish. Chill thoroughly. Although it has a somewhat candy-like quality, this sweet is served as a dessert, to be eaten with a fork.

Serves 6.

PAPAYA MILKSHAKE

1 small, ripe papaya
6 tablespoons coconut milk
  (page 54)
Juice of 2 large limes
Grated rind of 1 large lime
¼ cup sugar
¼ cup crushed ice
Lime slices for decoration

Peel the papaya, then cut it in half and remove the seeds. Chop the flesh coarsely and place in an electric blender. Add all the remaining ingredients except the lime slices, and blend until smooth and creamy. Pour into tall, chilled glasses and serve, decorated with a slice of lime.

Makes 3 large glasses.

PASSION FRUIT

Varieties of passionflower vine (*Passiflora*) flourish in South America, the West Indies, South Africa, Australia and along the shores of the Mediterranean. The best-known variety also called grenadilla (or granadilla), is purplish-black and wrinkled when ripe, with small edible seeds surrounded by an aromatic yellow pulp. Other fruits have orange or yellow skins.

It is generally eaten raw — just cut the fruit in half and scoop out the flesh with a teaspoon. Or the flesh can be added to cocktails, fruit punches, or other fruit juices. Beat it into whipped cream or ice cream for a refreshing and subtly different fruit fool or sundae, or use it in fruit salads.

The fruit keeps well in a freezer, but should be eaten before the skin becomes too thin and wrinkled or the flavor will not be at its best. The flesh alone will freeze for up to a year: before freezing, add half its weight in sugar then leave to stand, stirring occasionally, until the sugar is dissolved.

The passionflower plant has a long and respectable history as a sedative.

PASSION WHIP

1 small papaya
1¼ cups heavy cream
4 small passion fruit
½ teaspoon vanilla
1 teaspoon ground mace

Halve the papaya and discard the seeds. Scoop out the flesh, place in large bowl, and beat into a foamy purée.

In another bowl, whip the cream until stiff then gently fold this into the papaya purée. Mix together well and set on one side.

Cut the passion fruit in half and scoop out the flesh. Push through a fine sieve and fold into the cream and papaya mixture. Stir in the vanilla and mace, then turn the mixture into a serving dish.

Chill in the refrigerator for at least 1 hour before serving.

Serves 4.

ORANGE PASSION PIE

One 8 or 9 inch sweet pie
    pastry case, pre-baked
    (page 203)
10 large passion fruit
2 teaspoons unflavored gelatin
Juice of 1 lemon
2 eggs, separated
1 tablespoon brandy
2 large oranges
Unsweetened whipped cream
    for serving

Halve the passion fruit. Scoop out the flesh and pass through a fine sieve. Set aside.

Put the gelatin in about 5 tablespoons warm water and stir until the gelatin dissolves.

Whisk the lemon juice and egg yolks together well in another bowl that will fit into a small saucepan to make a double boiler. Boil about 1 inch of water in the saucepan, then lower the heat and place the bowl (not touching) over the simmering water. Stir the mixture constantly until it begins to thicken. Remove the bowl from the heat and stir the gelatin into the thickened egg and lemon mixture. Add the brandy and the passion fruit, blending well.

Leave this mixture to cool.

Beat the egg whites until stiff and gently fold them into the cold passion fruit mixture. Peel the oranges, removing any pith, and divide into segments. Fold these into the passion fruit mixture and spoon into the cooked pastry case. Place the pie in the refrigerator to chill for at least 1 hour, then serve with unsweetened whipped cream.

Serves 4–6.

PASSION CURD

6 small passion fruit
½ cup butter
1 cup sugar
3 eggs, beaten

Halve passion fruit and scoop out flesh. Sieve to remove seeds.

In a large, thick-bottomed saucepan, melt the butter over a low heat. Remove from the heat and stir in the sugar. Return the pan to the heat and stir continuously until the sugar dissolves. Then stir in the passion fruit and the beaten eggs, mixing thoroughly. Allow the mixture to simmer gently until it starts to thicken, stirring occasionally. Remove from the heat and cool slightly.

Pack and seal (page 199).

Fills about 3 jars.

PEACH

For hundreds of years, the succulence of ripe peaches has been a source of inspiration for artists, ranging from decorators of Chinese porcelain to great European still-life painters. Peaches are thought to be native to China, where they were cultivated 4,000 years ago, but early in their history they were introduced into Europe via Persia. The Romans called them Persian plums. Peaches were brought to the New World by Spanish conquerors in the sixteenth century. Over the next 300 years, they were taken all over the world, flourishing wherever they found a suitable climate, and today the cultivation of peaches is second in popularity only to that of apples.

There are two main types, "clingstone" and "freestone," with a few in-between varieties known as "semi-clingstone" and "semi-freestone." Most peaches have yellow flesh. White-fleshed ones are far rarer and considered to have the finest flavor. Because they are so prone to decay, peaches are usually picked when they are still in a hard-mature state. Such fruit will take several days to ripen at home. However, if they have been picked too soon, they will shrivel up without ripening, and have rubbery, tasteless flesh. Soft peaches must be used as quickly as possible as decay spreads very fast. Fine, ripe fruits are best eaten just as they are. If they are hard, you may prefer to poach them in a light sugar syrup.

To peel peaches, pour boiling water over a few fruits at a time, and leave for 1 or 2 minutes to loosen their skin. Then, hold each peach in a soft kitchen cloth and strip off its skin. If this is done with care, faint markings of color will remain on the surface of the peeled fruit. Halve the peaches lengthwise and remove pits.

Once the season starts, fresh peaches are cheap and plentiful throughout the summer months. This is the time to indulge in exciting soups, desserts and ice creams. Use them to garnish baked ham and roast duckling, instead of other fruits such as pineapple, oranges or cherries. For a low-calorie summer salad serve peeled and pitted peach halves stuffed with cottage cheese on a bed of crisp lettuce.

Canned peaches, either halves or slices, make a very good substitute for fresh fruit. Or use dried peaches, preferably sun-dried fruit that has not been treated with chemicals, for winter puddings and fruit salads.

Peel and pit peaches before freezing. Brush halves or slices with lemon juice and use a syrup made from 2 cups sugar to every 2½ cups water.

Peach juice is soothing and diuretic — and also an excellent moisturizer for the skin.

PEACH DRINK

Pack the goblet of an electric blender with chopped ripe peaches, and blend to a purée. Blend in a carton of plain yogurt, and dilute to taste with crushed ice.

COSMETICS

Peach juice is an excellent moisturizer, and peach kernel oil, like its close relatives almond oil and apricot kernel oil, is much used in cosmetics as it has a wonderful moisturizing, nourishing and healing effect on the skin. It is also excellent for massage. As it is unscented, it mixes well with perfumed essential oils, for use in aromatherapy or simply as a fragrance.

For a very quick, unfussy, pick-me-up for tired or rough skin, put a few drops of peach kernel oil into an eggcup and add a very little witch-hazel. Mix together with your fingers and pat gently on your face, stroking until it is absorbed. It leaves the skin feeling smooth and silky, and is particularly good for the neck.

CHILLED SUMMER PEACH SOUP

For this soup, the fruit must be sweet and aromatic, bordering on the over-ripe. Serve with a dollop of sour cream or lightly whipped sweet cream, if desired.

2–2½ pounds sweet ripe peaches
½ cup sugar
Finely grated rind of ½ lemon
1¼ cups white wine (medium), or
 hard cider
Confectioners' sugar and lemon juice
 (optional)

Peel peaches. Cut them in half lengthwise and remove pits. Slice peaches thinly. Crack open 6 peach pits, take out kernels and chop them finely.

In a large pan, make a light syrup with the sugar, lemon rind, chopped peach kernels and 1 quart water. Simmer for 5 minutes, then add about half of the sliced peaches and simmer until very soft but not mushy. Meanwhile, put remaining peaches in a glass serving bowl. Pour over wine or cider.

When poached peaches are tender, allow slices to cool in their syrup. Then pour peaches and syrup into the bowl and mix lightly but thoroughly with uncooked peaches and wine. Taste and sweeten with a little sifted confectioners' sugar or flavor with a squeeze of lemon juice if liked. Serve very cold.

Serves 4–6.

Note: To decorate the soup and make it more colorful, dot the bowl with some ripe red strawberries or raspberries, or float a glossy green leaf on the surface of the soup.

PEACH DUMPLINGS

An old American favorite from the Deep South to serve warm with pouring cream for Sunday supper.

6 ripe peaches
1 cup sugar
One 2 inch cinnamon stick
Twist of orange rind
1½ cups flour
1½ teaspoons baking powder
⅛ teaspoon salt
2 tablespoons lard, butter or
    shortening
Milk
Chilled pouring cream for serving

Peel peaches. Halve them lengthwise and remove pits.

In a wide, heavy pan with a tight-fitting lid, dissolve sugar in 1¼ cups water, adding cinnamon stick and orange rind (use only the colored part). Stir over low heat until sugar dissolves, and bring syrup to simmering point.

Lower peach halves into simmering syrup. Push a sheet of parchment paper down over them to prevent syrup evaporating too much and simmer until they are almost tender but still very firm. If peaches are ready before they are needed, leave them to cool in the syrup and bring to simmering point again just before adding dumplings.

Sift flour, baking powder and salt into a bowl, and rub in fat until mixture resembles fine bread crumbs. Stir in enough milk to make a dough that is soft but still holds its shape. Stop mixing as soon as this stage is reached as overhandling will make dumplings tough.

Shape dumplings as follows. Dip a metal tablespoon into simmering syrup. Shake it free of excess syrup, take a rounded spoonful of dough at a time and drop it on top of simmering peaches. Repeat with remaining dough, dipping spoon in syrup each time so dough will not stick to it. Cover pan tightly and simmer undisturbed for about 15 minutes until dumplings are light and airy, and they are no longer sticky and moist to the touch.

Cool to lukewarm, uncovered, and serve peaches, dumplings and syrup together in soup bowls, accompanied by a pitcher of pouring cream.

Serves 6.

PEACH MERINGUE PIE

For those with a sweet tooth, this is sheer self-indulgence. It is based on a great American favorite, the Angel Pie.

Meringue
4 egg whites
¼ teaspoon cream of tartar
1 cup sugar

Peaches and cream filling
4 egg yolks
½ cup sugar
Pinch of salt
Finely grated rind and juice of 1 large
    lemon
1½ cups heavy cream or ¾ cup
    each heavy and light cream,
    mixed
4–5 ripe peaches

Prepare the meringue shell well in advance. The preceding day will probably be the most convenient. First, line a baking sheet with silicone paper or a sheet of parchment paper lightly brushed with a wad of paper towel dipped in tasteless oil. On the lining paper, mark a circle 9 inches in diameter as a guide for the shell.

In a large bowl that is spotlessly clean and dry, beat egg whites until just frothy. Sprinkle with cream of tartar and beat to soft peak stage. Then gradually beat in sugar and continue to beat to a stiff, glossy meringue.

Shape meringue into a 9 inch nest, either using a pastry bag fitted with a large, plain tube, or in a far simpler (and less messy) way as follows. With a tablespoon, scoop up balls of meringue and place them around sides of circle. Then fill the center of the circle with more meringue and with the back of your spoon, smooth it out to form a nest. Finally, if you like, rough up the surface (neatly and regularly) with a skewer or the tines of a large kitchen fork.

Let the meringue shell dry out in a preheated 275° oven for at least 1 hour, or until it is hard and brittle, and very lightly tinged with gold. Then turn off the oven, leaving the meringue in it for several hours or overnight to cool completely.

Prepare cream filling. In the top of a double boiler, beat egg yolks just enough to mix them and make them foamy. Lightly beat in sugar, salt and the grated lemon rind and juice. Fit top of pan over simmering water and stir constantly until mixture is very thick and creamy. Take care not to let it boil or egg yolks will curdle. Cool, giving it an occasional stir to prevent a skin forming on top.

Whip cream until it stands in light, floppy peaks. Put aside about 4 heaping tablespoonfuls in a small bowl or cup for decoration. Gently but thoroughly fold remainder into cream filling. Chill lightly.

Peel and pit peaches, and slice them lengthwise. Pick out about 8 of the best slices for decoration.

Assemble the meringue pie as follows. Peel off lining paper and lay meringue case on a large, flat serving plate. Spread evenly with a thin layer of cream filling. Cover closely with slices of peach. Then spread remaining filling over the top. Decorate with reserved peach slices and dollops of whipped cream. Chill lightly until ready to serve but serve as soon as possible.

Serves 8.

PEACH SALAD

This makes a simple and good dessert on its own, but can also be served with creamy vanilla ice cream or simply chilled pouring cream.

4 large ripe peaches
Juice of 1 large lemon
¼ cup sugar
1–2 tablespoons coarsely chopped,
    skinned and toasted hazelnuts, or
    toasted flaked almonds

Peel peaches. Cut them in half lengthwise and remove pits. Crack pits open, remove kernels and chop them finely. In a small bowl, stir lemon juice and sugar together until sugar has dissolved. Stir in chopped peach kernels.

Slice peaches into a glass serving bowl. Pour sweetened lemon juice over slices and turn them gently until coated on all sides. Sprinkle with nuts and chill before serving.

Serves 4.

PEACH PARFAIT

A quickly prepared summer dessert, which can be made in advance. The parfait can be stored in the freezer before use.

4 large ripe peaches
½ cup sugar
Pinch of salt
3 egg yolks, beaten well
¾ cup whipping cream

Peel peaches. Remove the pits and chop the fruit into small pieces, then push these through a fine sieve (or use an electric blender) to make a purée.

Place ¾ cup water, the sugar and salt in the top of a double boiler or in a bowl over a pan of boiling water. Cook, stirring constantly, until the sugar dissolves. Then add the beaten egg yolks. Continue beating the mixture as it cooks over the hot water, until it thickens (do not allow to boil). Then beat in the peach purée and cook for a further 2 minutes, stirring constantly.

Remove the pan from the heat and stand the bowl containing the mixture in a bowl of cold water. Beat for a few minutes as it cools.

In another bowl, whip the cream until it is light and airy, but not stiff, then fold this carefully into the peach mixture.

Pour into a freezing tray and freeze. This should take about 3 hours, and the parfait does not need stirring during this time.

Serves 4–6.

PEACH AND ALMOND TART

This tart is made with fresh peaches but a large can of peach halves or slices, well drained of syrup, may be used instead.

One 8 or 9 inch basic pie pastry
*   case, pre-baked (page 203 and*
*   method)*
1 pound fresh, ripe peaches
*   (see above)*
3 eggs
1 cup ground almonds
1 cup confectioners' sugar,
*   sifted*
Flaked almonds for decoration
*   (optional)*

Bake the case very lightly, just long enough to set the pastry without coloring it.

Leave the pastry case in its pan or flan ring on a baking sheet.

Peel peaches. Cut them in half lengthwise, remove pits and either leave them in halves or cut each half into 6 or 8 slices, depending on size. Arrange peaches neatly in case.

Beat eggs until fluffy. Gently fold in ground almonds and confectioners' sugar until thoroughly mixed. Pour evenly over peaches and sprinkle with a few flaked almonds if they are available.

Bake tart in a preheated 375° oven until filling is set and a rich golden color, about 30 minutes.

Serve lukewarm or cold.

Serves 6.

ITALIAN STUFFED PEACHES

There are many versions of this classic. This one is simple and good.

4 large firm, ripe peaches
2 ounces amaretti cookies or
*   macaroons*
¼ cup blanched almonds
¼ cup sugar
1 tablespoon unsweetened cocoa
*   powder*
4–6 tablespoons white wine
Butter, for baking dish
Chilled pouring cream for serving
*   (optional)*

Cut peaches in half lengthwise and remove pits. Break pits open, remove kernels and chop them finely. Place in a bowl. Hollow out peach cavities slightly to make room for filling. Chop up scooped-out pulp and add to bowl. Crumble amaretti or macaroons and stir them into bowl.

Split 4 of the almonds in half and reserve for decoration. Chop remainder finely and add to bowl. Stir in 3 tablespoons sugar and the cocoa powder. Moisten with 2 or 3 tablespoons wine and work to a paste.

Stuff each peach cavity with some of the paste, rounding it up and smoothing it over with a knife blade. Arrange peach halves side by side in a lightly buttered baking dish.

Sprinkle them with remaining sugar and top each half-peach with an almond flake. Moisten with remaining wine.

Bake peaches in a preheated 375° oven for 25–30 minutes, until peaches have softened and mounds of stuffing are crisp and crusty on top.

Serve 2 peach halves per person while they are still very warm, accompanied by chilled, unsweetened pouring cream if liked.

Serves 4.

BROILED PEACHES

A good way to use peaches that are too hard to eat raw.

Halve and pit peaches. Lay the halves on a baking sheet, cut side up; sprinkle with brown sugar, dot with flecks of butter, and broil for 5–7 minutes until the butter and sugar have caramelized into a bubbling brown topping.

Serve hot with chilled cream.

PEACHES IN BRANDY

This preserve may be something of a luxury, but a few jars prepared and stored away at the height of the season when peaches are at their cheapest and best will make very acceptable gifts when Christmas comes around.

The peaches may either be sliced, as in the recipe below, or left in halves. In the latter case, however, it is a wise precaution to check that the necks of the jars you plan to use are wide enough for the peaches to slip through without bruising.

Any leftover poaching syrup is very good used (diluted with white wine or water, if necessary) for poaching other fresh fruit such as apples.

2 pounds ripe, unblemished
  peaches
1 cup sugar
About ¾ cup brandy

Peel the peaches, halve them verti-

cally and remove pits. Cut each peach half into 6 or 8 thin slices.

In a wide, shallow pan, dissolve sugar in 2½ cups water to make a light syrup. Drop the peach slices into the simmering syrup and poach gently until just cooked and still very firm. With a slotted spoon, transfer slices to hot, clean jars.

Boil syrup briskly until thickened and reduced to about one-third of the original amount. Strain it through a fine sieve.

Measure out about ¾ cup and stir in an equal amount of brandy.

Drain off any syrup that has accumulated in the jars of peaches. Then slowly pour in brandied syrup, wait a few minutes for it to "settle," and add more syrup, covering the peaches completely.

Cover jars as usual (see page 201) and store in a cool, dry cupboard. Leave for several weeks before tasting to allow flavors to develop.

PEACH AND STRAWBERRY WINE CUP

The type of fruit used with the peaches can be varied according to availability. This combination gives a cool, refreshing summer drink, ideal for a barbecue or outdoor party.

2 ripe peaches
1 pint strawberries
1¼ cups brandy
1 quart red wine
Soda water
Peach slices for decoration

Peel, halve and pit the peaches. Cut the halves into thin slices and place in a medium-sized bowl. Hull and wipe the strawberries, removing any damaged fruit. Cut in half and add to the peaches. Pour the brandy over the fruit and leave for 3 hours, stirring occasionally.

Pour the brandied fruit into a punch bowl or large glass pitcher. Add the wine and some ice. Leave in a cool place, until just before serving. Dilute to taste with soda water and decorate with peach slices.

Serves 10.

PICKLED PEACHES

1 pound dried peaches
2 Bermuda onions
1⅓ cups raisins
1 cup sugar
1 tablespoon salt
2 teaspoons ground ginger
1 teaspoon powdered mustard
2½ cups white malt vinegar

Rinse peaches thoroughly and put them in a bowl. Cover with 2½ cups boiling water and leave to soak overnight.

The following day, pour contents of bowl into a large, enameled, stainless steel or aluminum pan.

Parboil onions for 2 minutes. Drain thoroughly, chop finely and add to peaches, together with raisins and sugar. In a cup, blend salt, ginger and mustard powder smoothly with some of the vinegar. Pour into pan, together with remaining vinegar, and mix well. Bring to boiling point over low heat, stirring until sugar has dissolved. Then simmer for about 1 hour, stirring frequently to prevent mixture sticking to bottom of pan as it thickens. Take care not to mash peaches as you stir them. They should become very soft but stay intact.

Pour into clean canning jars.
See also page 200.

Fills about 4 jars.

PEANUT

The peanut, also known as the groundnut or goober, is thought to be native to South America and to have been taken to West Africa by Portuguese traders in the sixteenth century. It subsequently spread to the Dutch East Indies, India and China. There are many different varieties and sizes, but the peanut we know is grown in most hot countries.

Roasted and salted peanuts are popular snacks in the west, while in Africa the nuts are used in soups and stews. In Malaysia and Indonesia, peanuts are used in the rich sauce for a *satay* (or *saté*) dish – pieces of meat or chicken marinated in a soy sauce mixture, then threaded on skewers, broiled and served with a luscious peanut sauce. Then there is that American favorite, peanut butter, invented by a doctor from St Louis. Spread on slices of crusty fresh bread, it combines the moist consistency of ordinary butter with the nutrition and bulk of a meat or fish paste.

Peanuts are sold unroasted in their shells, shelled and unroasted, roasted without salt, and roasted and salted. Freeze-drying and salting, a more recent development, makes the nuts less sticky to handle. Roughly chopped, roasted and unsalted nuts can be sprinkled on fruit salads and ices. They can also be added to fudge.

Peanut oil is used for deep-frying and general cooking, in a bland-tasting salad dressing and, commercially, for making margarine. It keeps well if stored in cool conditions.

The high protein content of peanuts makes them a more than adequate meat substitute in vegetarian diets. One ounce of shelled, roasted peanuts contains slightly more protein than one egg or one ounce of cheese – and compares favorably in price.

Peanuts also have a high fat content, some carbohydrate, calcium and iron, and are a good source of Vitamin B.

PEANUT SOUP

This thick, spicy soup may be served either hot or chilled.

½ cup shelled, roasted, unsalted
   peanuts
5 cups chicken broth
Salt and freshly ground black pepper
Few drops of hot pepper or chili
   sauce
¾ cup heavy cream
1 tablespoon bitters
¼ cup dry sherry wine
Croûtons (page 205) or chopped fresh
   chives for garnish

Place the peanuts and 2 tablespoons of the chicken broth in an electric blender, or use a pestle and mortar to make into a thick paste. Put paste into a large saucepan. Gradually add the rest of the broth, stirring to avoid lumps. Season with salt and pepper to taste, add the pepper or chili sauce and stir well.

Place the pan over a moderate heat and bring the contents to a boil, stirring occasionally. Lower the heat and allow to simmer gently for 15 minutes. Remove the pan from the heat and stir in the cream. Return the pan to the heat and cook soup, stirring constantly, but do not allow to boil. Just before serving, stir in the bitters and sherry. If serving hot, garnish each portion with croûtons. Otherwise, chill thoroughly and sprinkle some finely chopped chives over each serving.

Serves 6.

PEANUT OIL HAND CREAMS

Mix a little peanut oil with an equal quantity of kaolin or fuller's earth, and a beaten egg yolk. Rub into your hands.

For a protective and nourishing barrier cream, combine equal quantities of beeswax, cocoa butter and peanut oil in the top of a double boiler. Heat until the wax and cocoa butter have melted. Beat well to amalgamate and allow to cool, beating frequently to prevent the mixture from separating.

PEANUT PORK

2 pounds lean pork shoulder
3 tablespoons peanut oil
1 cup very finely chopped or ground
   roasted peanuts
4–6 tablespoons soy sauce
⅛ teaspoon hot chili powder or
   cayenne

Cut pork up into bite-sized cubes. In a flameproof casserole, brown pork cubes all over in oil, a portion at a time if necessary to avoid overcrowding casserole. Stir in peanuts, soy sauce and chili powder. Cover casserole tightly and cook gently until pork is quite tender, about 1 hour, stirring frequently and adding a little water if casserole is very dry. Taste for seasoning and serve with plain boiled rice.

Serves 6–8.

GHANAIAN CHICKEN IN PEANUT SAUCE

This flavorsome stew is locally known as "Chop." Serve it like a curry with plain boiled rice, mango chutney and sliced bananas or plantains as accompaniments.

One 3½ pound roaster chicken
¾ cup shelled peanuts
1¼ cups coconut milk (page 54)
2 tablespoons peanut oil
1 medium-size onion, finely
   chopped
3 large tomatoes, skinned, seeded
   and chopped
1 garlic clove, crushed
Salt and freshly ground black pepper
½ teaspoon paprika (optional)
¼ teaspoon grated nutmeg
4 hard-cooked eggs, shelled

Cut up the chicken into pieces and set aside. Purée the peanuts in a blender or food processor with 2 cups boiling water. Transfer the purée to a saucepan and simmer gently for about 5 minutes, until the sauce is thick but still liquid. Stir in the coconut milk and set aside.

Heat the oil in a large skillet and fry the chicken pieces until golden brown on all sides. Remove them from the skillet with a slotted spoon and set aside.

Fry the onion until golden brown, then add the tomatoes and garlic and cook for 2–3 minutes until pulpy, stirring from time to time to prevent the tomato from sticking. Stir in the peanut sauce and season with salt, pepper and the spices.

Bring the sauce to a boil, return the chicken pieces to the skillet and simmer, uncovered, for 30–40 minutes, until they are very tender. Stir from time to time.

Five minutes before the end of cooking time, add the hard-cooked eggs and spoon over enough sauce to cover them. Serve when the eggs are heated through.

Serves 4–6.

GADO-GADO

2 medium-size potatoes, peeled,
   boiled and thinly sliced
6 ounces white cabbage, finely
   shredded (about 2 cups)
2 large carrots, peeled, sliced into
   julienne strips, and blanched
½ pound green beans, blanched
½ pound (4 cups) bean sprouts,
   washed
1 cucumber, peeled and diced
6 ounces spinach, washed, boiled
   and coarsely chopped (about 1 cup)
2 large onions, thinly sliced and fried
   until crisp and golden-brown
2 hard-cooked eggs, sliced

Sauce
1 cup shelled, roasted, unsalted
   peanuts
2 tablespoons peanut oil
1 small onion, finely chopped
2 cloves garlic, crushed
3 large green chili peppers, seeded
   and chopped
1 teaspoon brown sugar
Juice of 2 lemons
1¼ cups coconut milk (page 54)
1 teaspoon salt

Prepare the sauce first. Grind the peanuts with a little water to a thick paste in an electric blender or with a pestle and mortar. Leave to one side. Heat the oil in a skillet until sizzling, then add the onion, garlic and chilis, and cook until slightly browned. Stir in the peanut paste, sugar and lemon juice, and cook for a further minute, stirring constantly. Add the coconut milk, ¾ cup water and the salt. Mix well and allow the mixture to boil. Lower heat and let the sauce simmer, stirring occasionally, until thick and smooth, but still of pouring consistency. Taste, and adjust seasoning with more sugar and salt if necessary. Pour into a small serving bowl or sauceboat and leave to cool.

Just before serving, arrange the prepared vegetables on a large serving platter with the fried onions sprinkled on top. Garnish with slices of hard-cooked egg.

Serves 4. Each person takes a portion of the vegetables, and tops them with a spoonful of the sauce.

CHINESE EGGPLANT IN PEANUT SAUCE

To give this dish an authentic Chinese flavor you will need fresh ginger root and Oriental sesame oil, which is a dark golden brown color and has a rich, nutty flavor.

It is sold in bottles in Chinese groceries and should be used in small amounts mainly as a flavoring, and not a frying, medium.

One 1–1½ pound eggplant
2 cloves garlic, finely chopped
1 slice fresh ginger root, finely
   chopped
2–3 tablespoons peanut or
   corn oil
2 tablespoons crunchy peanut butter
Salt
½ teaspoon Oriental sesame oil (see
   above)

Peel the eggplant and cut it into large cubes.

In a wok or a large, heavy skillet with a lid, stir-fry the garlic and ginger in oil for ½ minute, taking care that the garlic does not burn, or it will taste bitter. Add the eggplant cubes and stir-fry for about ½ minute longer.

Blend peanut butter and ½ teaspoon salt with ¾ cup cold water. Stir into eggplant, bring to boiling point, cover and simmer for 6–8 minutes, or until eggplant is tender but not mushy. Correct seasoning with a little more salt if necessary.

Sprinkle with sesame oil, mix well and serve.

Serves 4.

PEANUT BRITTLE

Toast the shelled peanuts lightly and rub off their skins.

Prepare an oiled surface as for a praline (page 13). Then make a rich golden caramel. Stir in the nuts and mix well to distribute them evenly throughout the caramel.

Scrape out onto the oiled surface and if necessary lightly press flat with the back of your spoon.

Leave the slab of brittle to cool and harden before breaking it into pieces.

PEANUT MACAROONS

Peanut oil (optional)
¾ cup shelled peanuts, roasted
¼ teaspoon salt
1 large egg white
½ cup firmly packed brown sugar, sifted
½ teaspoon vanilla

Line 2 or 3 baking sheets with rice paper or use parchment paper and grease lightly all over with peanut oil.

Chop the roasted peanuts to a coarse meal by hand, in an electric blender or in a food processor fitted with a very coarse blade. Sprinkle them with salt and put aside.

In a large bowl, beat the egg white until it forms soft peaks. Gradually beat in the sifted brown sugar, followed by vanilla. Fold in the prepared peanuts.

Arrange heaped teaspoonfuls of the mixture about 1 inch apart on the prepared baking sheets. Bake in a preheated 325° oven for 15–20 minutes, or until macaroons are firm to the touch, slightly puffed and lightly colored.

Crumble off excess rice paper surrounding macaroons and place on a wire cooling rack. Or use a broad palette knife to lift macaroons from parchment paper and transfer them to the cooling rack.

INDIAN PEANUT CHUTNEY

This is an unusual chutney to serve with Indian dishes.

½ cup shelled roasted peanuts
1 tablespoon finely chopped fresh ginger root
¾ cup plain yogurt
1 teaspoon sugar
1 teaspoon ground coriander
Salt and cayenne

Put the peanuts, fresh ginger root, yogurt, sugar and coriander in the goblet of an electric blender or in a food processor. Season with about ½ teaspoon each salt and cayenne. Blend ingredients to a paste. Taste cautiously — chutney will be hot — and add a little more sugar, salt or cayenne if liked.

Spoon into a screw-top jar and store in the refrigerator until ready to serve with an Indian-style meal. The chutney will keep for several days in the refrigerator.

Note: Failing a blender or food processor for grinding the nuts to a paste, a very good chutney can be made with natural coarse-ground peanut butter from a health food store. This contains no additives apart from a little sea salt, so cut the salt by about half to begin with.

PEANUT SKILLET BISCUIT

A last-minute inspiration for a snack on a Sunday afternoon. You will need a deep, heavy skillet with a lid.

1½ cups wholewheat flour
2 teaspoons baking powder
Pinch of salt
2 tablespoons smooth peanut butter
1 teaspoon brown sugar
Milk or plain yogurt for mixing
Peanut or corn oil

Sift flour, baking powder and salt into a bowl — add bran to the flour mixture if it has stayed behind in the sifter. Rub in peanut butter as you would ordinary butter or margarine. Stir in the sugar. With a large, rounded knife blade, stir in enough milk or plain yogurt (or a mixture of the two, diluted if necessary with a little water) to make a soft dough.

Brush a large skillet very lightly with a wad of paper towel dipped in oil and put it on to heat gently, standing it on a heat diffuser for extra protection if it is not very thick.

Turn the dough onto a lightly floured board. Knead it very briefly until smooth, and pat it into a circle that fits the pan — use the lid as a rough guide if necessary.

Drop the round of dough into the skillet. Pat it out evenly with the palm of your hand if necessary and with the blade of a knife or spatula dipped in flour, mark it into 8 or 10 wedges. Heat the lid until very hot. Fit it on the skillet and cook over very low heat for about 20 minutes, or until the biscuit is lightly browned and crisp underneath, and feels dry to the touch on top.

Gently turn the biscuit onto a large, lightly oiled plate and slip it back upside-down into the skillet. Continue to cook uncovered until underside of biscuit is crisp and well-colored, about 15 minutes longer.

Cool on a wire rack. Serve warm with butter and syrup or jam.

PEAR

The first pears were the small, hard and green fruits of the wild pear tree, which can still be found growing all over Europe and as far east as the Himalayas, and are the ancestors of all the varieties developed since. By Roman times Pliny, that tireless compiler of informaton, could list thirty-eight varieties of pear and today there are over 3,000, of which only a few, admittedly, are widely cultivated.

Pears, apples and quinces all belong to the same family and can be used together or substituted for each other most successfully.

Like apples, pears can be divided into cooking and eating varieties, and perry (cider) pears. Different varieties mature at different times of the year. One of the best known is the tender, juicy Bartlett, known as the William pear in Europe. This develops from pale green to golden yellow when ripe. It can either be eaten as it is or poached in syrup or wine and served warm or cold with thick, chilled cream. Then there is the Bosc pear, elongated, thin, and russeted yellow, which keeps and cooks well. Finest of all for eating is the Comice pear, which is sweet, aromatic, buttery and tender.

A ripe eating pear yields slightly to finger pressure at the stem end. But pears are best bought before they are completely ripe and left to ripen at home at room temperature. A good trick is to leave them in a brown paper bag together with a ripe apple, which seems to trigger off the ripening process. Cooking pears have a smoother texture if they are picked before they are ripe as their texture tends to coarsen if they ripen on the tree.

A juicy, ripe dessert pear needs no accompaniment or cooking. However, pears that seem unpleasantly hard will be far better if they are first poached briefly in a light sugar syrup with a vanilla bean and a twist of lemon rind or a cinnamon stick.

Pears must be brushed with lemon juice or dropped into a bowl of acidulated water as soon as they have been peeled, as cut surfaces discolor rapidly. A firm cooking pear should be quartered and cored just like an apple, but if it is very soft and ripe all you need do is cut it in half, scoop out the nest of seeds with a pointed teaspoon, then pick out the fibers that run up toward the stem.

The simplest way to preserve pears is to can them in light syrup. They are also delicious canned in spiced vinegar, and turned into preserves. They can be peeled, cored and quartered or sliced, and frozen in a light sugar syrup made from 1 cup sugar to 2½ cups water, but they tend to discolor badly when thawed, so quite a lot of lemon juice must be added. Dried pears can be bought in healthfood stores for adding to dried fruit compotes and occasionally whole crystallized pears are included in a box of crystallized fruits.

Medicinally, pears are diuretic and mildly laxative, and infusions of their leaves and flowers help restore bruised or infected tissue.

HAND OR FOOT BATH

Boil 2 quarts water and leave until lukewarm. Add 4 handfuls of fresh pear leaves and/or flowers, cover to protect from dust, and leave to infuse for 4–5 hours. Just before bathing your feet or hands, boil another 2 quarts water, let it stand for 5 minutes, add the original preparation to it and reheat. Do not boil. Use for not more than 8 minutes.

PEAR SOUP

6 soft, ripe, dessert pears
Lemon juice
2 cups dry white wine
½ cup sugar, or to taste
¾ cup heavy cream
¾ cup light cream

Peel, halve and core the pears, and scoop out about 18 balls with a melon baller. Sprinkle them with lemon juice and toss lightly to prevent discoloration. Put them aside.

Cut the remaining pears into chunks and put them in a blender with the remaining ingredients. Blend until smooth.

Check for sweetness and chill the soup thoroughly.

Serve with pear balls.

Serves 6.

PEAR AND CHEESE SALAD

This is delicious on its own as a light main course or served as an accompaniment to cold roast poultry or ham.

1¼ cups thick homemade
    mayonnaise (page 205)
Light cream or creamy milk
    (optional)
1 pound Emmenthal or Swiss cheese,
    diced
3 large, ripe, dessert pears, cored and
    diced
6 ounces small seedless
    grapes
2 stalks celery, chopped or thinly
    sliced
1 cup coarsely chopped walnuts
Salt
Crisp lettuce leaves for garnish

Put mayonnaise in a large mixing bowl and if necessary thin it down to easy mixing consistency with a tablespoon or two of cream or creamy milk. Add the cheese, pears, grapes, celery and walnuts, and mix or toss gently until they are all coated with mayonnaise. Correct seasoning with a little salt if necessary.

Serve the salad in a bowl lined with lettuce leaves.

Serves 6.

PEARS, BEANS AND BACON

A traditional German dish from Holstein. The unexpected combination of ingredients works surprisingly well.

I like to serve it as a late-summer supper dish, made with fresh fruit and vegetables from the garden.

1 pound small, ripe pears
2 pounds green beans
About ¾ pound slab bacon
Salt and freshly ground black pepper
Finely chopped parsley for
    garnish

Wash pears. Remove stalks but leave fruit whole and unpeeled. Wash beans. Trim off ends and break beans into halves or thirds, depending on size. Cut slab of bacon into large (roughly ¾ inch) cubes.

In a large, flameproof casserole with a tight-fitting lid, sauté bacon cubes gently until they are colored on all sides and their own fat is running. Stir in beans and pour over about 2 cups boiling water. Sprinkle with salt and freshly ground black pepper. Lay pears on top.

Bring casserole to simmering point. Cover tightly and cook gently, undisturbed, for about 1 hour until beans and pears are quite tender but not mushy.

Top up with a little more water if it evaporates too quickly.

Serve sprinkled with finely chopped parsley.

Serves 4.

CHEESE BROILED PEARS

An unusual accompaniment for a hot meat dish such as pork, ham or broiled chicken.

4 slices bacon
4 ripe, round dessert pears
½ sweet green pepper
¼ cup butter
¼ cup fine stale bread crumbs
¼ cup freshly grated Parmesan
    cheese

Broil or fry bacon slices until they are crisp.

Halve the pears lengthwise and core them. Pat the cut surfaces dry and immediately brush them with the drippings from the bacon.

Seed the pepper, remove every scrap of white pith, and dice the flesh finely. In a skillet, melt the butter. Stir in the diced pepper, bread crumbs, Parmesan and crumbled bacon, and fry gently over a moderate heat for 2 or 3 minutes.

When ready to serve, arrange the pear halves cut side up in the broiler pan. Broil them under moderate heat for 10 minutes, or until they yield slightly to pressure. Spread the cheese mixture evenly over each cut surface, filling the cored cavities as you do so. Continue to broil for 3 or 4 minutes longer until the coating is bubbling and crisp on top.

Serves 6–8.

CURRIED PEARS

A tasty accompaniment for all kinds of poultry and meat dishes, especially ham.

4 firm, ripe pears
Butter
¼ cup firmly packed brown sugar
4 teaspoons curry powder
¼ cup chopped nuts

Wipe pears clean. Halve them lengthwise and scoop out cores, seeds and fibers with a sharp teaspoon, leaving them unpeeled. Butter a large, shallow baking dish and arrange pear halves in it, cored side up.

Prepare filling. Blend sugar with curry powder and moisten with ¼ cup melted butter. Mix in chopped nuts. Divide evenly between pear halves, pressing filling firmly into hollows.

Bake pears in a preheated 350° oven for 30 minutes, or until they feel tender when prodded with a skewer. Serve lukewarm.

Serves 4 or 8, depending on their size and your taste.

PEARS IN CREAM

8 firm pears
6–8 tablespoons brown sugar
½ cup butter
1¼ cups heavy cream
3–4 tablespoons milk
3 tablespoons Kirsch
Toasted flaked almonds for
    decoration

Peel the pears, quarter them and cut out cores. In a wide, shallow pan or deep skillet, arrange the pieces in a single layer. Sprinkle with sugar and cover with pieces of butter. Place pan over moderate heat and cook, shaking gently at frequent intervals, until sugar has melted and turned into a syrupy caramel.

Add the cream mixed with the milk and Kirsch, and bring to a gentle boil. Let it simmer for a few minutes, shaking the pan frequently, until the sauce thickens.

Pour into a serving dish. Sprinkle with toasted flaked almonds and serve lukewarm.

Serves 6.

SPICED PEAR PIE

A truly old-fashioned family pie. All sorts of spices may be used as a flavoring instead of the nutmeg and cinnamon mixture. Ginger is a great favorite, added in the form of ½ teaspoon ground ginger or finely grated fresh ginger root, but if you use it, leave out the orange.

About 1 pound rough puff pastry for a 2-crust 8 or 9 inch pie (page 203)
1½ pounds pears
Juice of 1 small lemon
¾ cup white or 1 cup firmly packed brown sugar
¼ cup flour
¼ teaspoon freshly grated nutmeg
¼ teaspoon ground cinnamon
⅛ teaspoon salt
Finely grated rind of ½ orange
2 tablespoons orange juice
1–2 tablespoons butter
Sugar for sprinkling

Roll out about half of the pastry and cut out lid for pie, allowing an extra ½ inch all around the border. Put aside. Roll out remaining pastry and use it to line a pie pan, again with an overlap.

Quarter pears lengthwise. Peel and core them, and slice them about ½ inch thick into a bowl. Sprinkle pears with lemon juice, turning them over so they are coated all over to stop them turning brown. In another bowl, blend sugar with flour, spices, salt and grated orange rind. Sprinkle pears with orange juice, followed by the spiced sugar mixture, and mix gently until pieces of pear are evenly coated.

Pile pears in pastry-lined pie pan and dot surface with flakes of butter. Moisten rim of pastry lightly with cold water and fit lid in position. Press lightly to seal edges, then flute or crimp edges neatly all around. Make a few slits or gashes in lid.

Bake pie in a preheated 450° oven for the first 10–15 minutes. Then lower temperature to 350° and continue to bake pie for about 30 minutes longer, or until it is puffed and golden brown on top, and a piece of pear prodded with a skewer through one of the slits in the lid feels soft.

Remove pie from the oven. Sprinkle generously with sugar and cool to lukewarm. Serve with a custard sauce or pouring cream.

Serves 6.

PEARS IN BUTTERSCOTCH SAUCE

Delicious but definitely not for the calorie-conscious.

Juice of 1 lemon
½ cup sugar
One 2 inch cinnamon stick
4 firm, round pears
4 scoops vanilla ice cream

Butterscotch sauce
½ cup butter
1⅓ cups firmly packed brown sugar
¾ cup light cream
1¼ cups heavy cream

Start by preparing a light syrup with 2½ cups water, the lemon juice, sugar and cinnamon stick. Bring to boiling point, stirring until sugar has dissolved, and allow to simmer while you prepare pears.

Peel pears. Halve them lengthwise and scoop out fibers, cores and seeds with a small, sharp spoon. Immediately slip pear halves into simmering syrup. Push a sheet of parchment paper down over the top and poach pears gently until they feel quite tender when pierced with a skewer. Allow pears to cool in their syrup and chill lightly in syrup until ready to proceed.

To make butterscotch sauce, melt butter, without letting it sizzle or color, in a heavy pan. Stir in sugar and, when it has melted, gradually beat in light cream, followed by heavy cream. Simmer, stirring, for a few minutes until sauce is thick and smooth. Keep hot. If sauce should thicken too much while it is waiting, thin it down again by beating in some of the pear syrup or some more cream if available.

To serve, put a scoop of vanilla ice cream in each of 4 individual glass dishes. Lay 2 poached pear halves on each ball of ice cream and pour some hot butterscotch sauce over the top. Serve remaining sauce in a separate sauceboat.

Serve immediately.

Serves 4.

Note: Some people like to indulge themselves even further by topping each portion with a swirl of unsweetened whipped cream and a pinch of chopped nuts.

PEARS IN CHOCOLATE SAUCE

Also known by the grander name of Poires Belle Hélène. Ideally, soft and juicy ripe pears should be used, in which case they will not need preliminary poaching. If pears are rather hard and woody, first poach them in sugar syrup flavored with a thin strip of lemon peel and either a piece of vanilla bean or a little vanilla extract, then chill them thoroughly before assembling portions.

6 ripe, round pears (see above)
Lemon juice
6 scoops vanilla ice cream

Chocolate sauce
6 ounces semisweet chocolate
3 tablespoons butter, softened
¾ cup whipping cream, or half heavy and half light cream
Vanilla to taste, or 1 tablespoon brandy or rum

Do not start this dish too far ahead of time unless the pears have to be poached and chilled first (see above). If not, peel, halve them lengthwise and core them, dropping them into a bowl of cold water acidulated with lemon juice as you do so to prevent them turning brown while they wait.

Prepare chocolate sauce next. Break chocolate into the top of a double boiler. Add butter and stir over simmering water until chocolate has melted and is smoothly blended with butter. Beat in cream a little at a time. When sauce is smooth, place top part of pan over direct heat, bring sauce to boiling point, stirring constantly, and simmer, stirring, for about 2 or 3 minutes.

Remove the sauce from the heat and flavor to taste with a few drops of vanilla, or with a tablespoon of brandy or rum.

Assemble individual portions as follows. Drain pear halves and lightly pat them dry with paper towels. Put a large ball of ice cream in each of 6 glass dishes. Press half a pear on opposite sides of each ball of ice cream, pointed ends up, and mask with warm chocolate sauce. Serve immediately.

Serves 6.

PEARS IN RED WINE

Use firm, hard pears for this. Comice or Bosc pears which are ripe but still hard are probably the best. Instead of using red food coloring for the syrup, you can tint it most attractively and at the same time enrich its flavor by adding a few tablespoons of *creme de cassis* (black currant liqueur) or red currant jelly. If you are afraid that the pears are not too flavorsome in themselves, dig a whole clove into the rounded (blossom) end of each one. Instead of red wine, port or sherry may be used for poaching the pears, but you will have to adjust sugar, depending on the sweetness of the wine.

This is an ideal dish to leave overnight in the slow oven of a solid-fuel stove, or to cook on low in an electric crock pot, in which the pears will take about 6 hours to become soft.

6 hard pears
Lemon juice
1 cup sugar
One 2 inch cinnamon stick
2 cloves
2 thin strips orange peel
2 thin strips lemon peel
2 cups red wine
Red food coloring (optional, see above)
Unsweetened whipped cream for serving

Peel the pears, keeping them whole and leaving their stalks intact. As you prepare them, drop them into a large bowl of cold water acidulated with lemon juice to prevent them turning brown.

In a heavy pan, preferably enameled, dissolve sugar in ¾ cup water. Add cinnamon stick, cloves and strips of orange and lemon peel. Stir in wine, bring to boiling point and simmer for 10 minutes.

Choose a deep, flameproof casserole or pan that will hold the pears upright in a single layer without letting them topple over. Pour over the boiling wine syrup. Cover tightly and either cook over the lowest possible heat or transfer to a preheated 325° oven. Cook pears until they feel soft when pierced with a skewer, basting tops occasionally with syrup if necessary. They will take anything from 30 minutes to well over 1 hour, depending on variety and ripeness.

With a slotted spoon, transfer pears to a wide, shallow dish. Boil syrup down rapidly to a medium-light coating consistency. When cooled slightly and spooned down the side of a pear, it should give it an attractive reddish gleam. If the color of the syrup does not seem bright enough, intensify it with 2 or 3 drops of red food coloring.

Spoon the hot syrup over the pears and continue to baste them several times until they are quite cold. Then chill until ready to serve, with unsweetened, lightly whipped cream.

Serves 6.

BAKED PEARS WITH ORANGE

4 cooking pears
½ cup sugar
Long strip of orange peel
Strained juice of 1 orange
4–6 tablespoons Curaçao or other orange liqueur
Whipped cream or pouring cream

Peel and quarter pears lengthwise, and cut out cores. Lay pears in a wide, shallow, ovenproof casserole with a lid.

In a small pan, dissolve sugar in ¾ cup water over low heat. Add the strip of orange peel, bring to simmering point and pour over pears. Cover casserole and bake in a preheated 350° oven until pears feel tender when pierced with a skewer, about 30 minutes. Stir in orange juice and allow to cool.

When pears are quite cold, transfer them to a serving bowl with a slotted spoon. Discard the strip of orange peel. Flavor the syrup remaining in the casserole with orange liqueur to taste and pour over pears.

Serve chilled with unsweetened whipped cream or chilled pouring cream.

Serves 4.

PEAR MARMALADE

5 pounds pears
About 4 pounds (8 cups) sugar
1 vanilla bean, split

Peel and core the pears. Cut them in chunks and put them in a preserving kettle. Cover generously with boiling water and boil until pears are soft. Then drain, reserving cooking water. Weigh cooked pears and allow 2 cups sugar to every pound (about 2 cups) of fruit pulp.

Put sugar in a preserving kettle with about ¾ cup pear water for every 2 cups of sugar, and slowly bring to a boil, stirring frequently until sugar has dissolved and skimming off scum from the surface. Add cooked pears and vanilla bean, and boil until jell point is reached, skimming toward the end if necessary.

Remove vanilla bean. Pack and process as usual.

See also page 198.

Fills about 5 jars.

PEAR AND APPLE PRESERVE

An unusual, lightly spiced jam that is not only delicious eaten with hot buttered toast or biscuits but also very good for flavoring and sweetening desserts, especially good spread over baked bread pudding. Apart from that, the jam is an excellent way of using up windfalls and surplus fruit from the garden.

2 pounds pears
2 pounds tart apples
Juice and finely grated rind of 2
*   lemons*
½ ounce whole cinnamon sticks
3–4 whole cloves
4 pounds (8 cups) sugar
Pat of butter (optional)

Quarter, peel and core the pears and apples, cut them into chunks and sprinkle them with lemon juice to prevent them turning brown.

In a small pan, boil the cinnamon sticks and cloves in 2½ cups water for 30 minutes. Strain the water into a preserving kettle. Stir in the sugar and heat gently, stirring, until sugar has dissolved.

Add the prepared fruit and all its juices, and the finely grated lemon rind, and bring to a boil. Cook rapidly, skimming off any scum as it forms on the surface, until jell point is reached.

Finally, stir in a pat of butter if necessary to clear the jam completely.

Pack and process as usual.
See also page 198.

Fills about 4 jars.

BOTTLED PEARS IN CIDER

Hard, ripe pears such as Seckel or Comice pears are canned in cider syrup in the same way as apples (see page 21). The only difference is that pears look best if they are left whole, with a short length of stem intact. They are then packed tightly into jars. You will manage to fit in the largest number of pears per jar if you stand the bottom row tightly side by side, stems up, followed by a row with stems pointing downward, and so on until jar is full. Cover with syrup and process as usual (page 201).

PRESERVED PEARS

Hard dessert pears are the best for this simple preserve, which makes a good accompaniment for all kinds of meat, poultry and game.

4 cups sugar
2 cups white malt vinegar
6 pounds hard pears

In a preserving kettle, or a large, preferably enameled, saucepan, dissolve the sugar in the vinegar over a low heat.

Peel pears but leave them whole. Place them in vinegar syrup. Cover with a sheet of parchment paper and simmer very gently until pears feel soft when pierced with a fine skewer or toothpick. If they are not submerged in syrup, baste frequently and carefully turn them over.

When pears are done, draw pan to the side of the stove, cover and allow to stand for 15 minutes (this is to preserve the color of the fruit). Then pack pears in jars, pour in syrup to within ⅛ inch of the brim and process as usual (page 201).

Fills about 10 jars.

PEARS IN BRANDY

These jars of preserved pears should be prepared at the beginning of October, when pears are in their best condition. They have to be left macerating in syrup and brandy for about three months, which means they will be ready for sampling at Christmas and New Year. Eat them as a dessert with their syrup and chilled, thick, unsweetened cream.

Choose the best, unblemished, ripe pears you can find for this. Bartletts and Comice pears are both very good, although very different in texture. Quarter pears lengthwise. Peel and core them, and pack them into sterilized jars with screw-top lids.

Make a sugar syrup, allowing 1 cup sugar to every 1¼ cups water, and simmer for 5 minutes. Cool slightly, then pour over pears to come about one-third of the way up jars. Fill jars with brandy (the cheapest stocked by your market). Screw on lids, then gently invert jars a few times to mix brandy with sugar syrup.

Store jars in a cool, dark cupboard for at least 3 months before you taste them. The sugared brandy in which they have been preserved can be drunk as a sweet liqueur or used to add flavor to light desserts and fruit salads.

You may also like to experiment with other kinds of alcohol, such as Kirsch, instead of brandy.

PECAN

The pecan is a native of the United States and a relatively late addition to the pantries of cooks in other parts of the world. The Indians, who were the first to discover its virtues, used to take supplies of roasted nuts on hunting expeditions and grind them and add them to stews. Its name comes from the Creek and Algonquin word *paccan*, meaning "nut having hard shell to crack"; in fact, the shells vary considerably in thickness. The thinner-shelled varieties are naturally the most popular.

Two American presidents have gone on record as enthusiasts — some of the trees planted by George Washington in his lovely garden at Mount Vernon more than 150 years ago are still flourishing, and Thomas Jefferson arranged to send many hundreds of pecans to his gardening friends in France. Pecans are now also cultivated in Australia, Israel and South Africa.

The nuts are sold shelled, either salted or roasted and should be stored in a sealed jar so that they don't turn rancid. Pecans are particularly oily. When fried, they should be taken off the heat before they turn too brown, or they will continue cooking in their own internal fat.

Pecans are mostly used in cakes and pastries — pecan pie is a famous traditional recipe in the American South — and can be substituted for walnuts, their close relative.

The nuts contain useful amounts of protein and Vitamin A — and less useful amounts of calories (125 to 1 ounce).

MEAT LOAF WITH PECAN STUFFING

An unusual variation on the traditional ground beef loaf. Serve with a spicy tomato sauce.

1 pound ground beef
½ cup seeded and finely chopped green pepper
2 small onions, finely chopped
1 teaspoon salt
1 tablespoon Worcestershire sauce
4 cups soft wholewheat bread crumbs
1¼ cups milk
2 eggs
¼ cup butter
2 large stalks celery, coarsely chopped
Freshly ground black pepper
1¼ cups beef broth
1 cup coarsely chopped shelled pecans

Grease a 9 × 5 × 3 inch loaf pan.

In a large mixing bowl, blend the ground beef, green pepper, onions, salt, Worcestershire sauce, half the bread crumbs, milk and one of the eggs. Mix thoroughly. Place *half* this mixture in the bottom of the prepared loaf pan.

In another bowl, mix together the remaining egg, the butter, the rest of the bread crumbs, the celery, pepper, broth and chopped pecans. Spread this pecan stuffing on top of the meat mixture in the loaf pan.

Put the remaining meat mixture on the top of the pecan stuffing, and smooth over the top with a knife. Bake in a preheated 350° oven for 1 hour, until firm and well browned. Allow to cool slightly before unmolding from the pan, then slice and serve with a hot, spicy, tomato sauce, and vegetables.

Serves 6.

OLD-FASHIONED AMERICAN PECAN PIE

About ½ pound pie pastry for a 9 inch pastry case (page 203)

Filling
About 1½ cups shelled pecans
3 cups firmly packed light brown sugar
3 tablespoons flour
¼ teaspoon salt
¾ cup milk
1½ teaspoons vanilla, or 2–3 tablespoons rum
3 eggs
6 tablespoons butter, melted

Line a 9 inch pie pan or deep tart pan with pie pastry and crimp rim attractively.

Cover unbaked pastry with pecans, arranged in concentric circles.

In a bowl or large pitcher, blend sugar with flour and salt. Heat milk to boiling point and with a wooden spoon or balloon whisk, beat it into sugar mixture.

Beat in vanilla or rum.

Beat eggs lightly. Gradually beat them into filling mixture, followed by the cooled, melted butter. Pour sugar filling gently over pecans, taking care not to disturb them.

Bake pie in a preheated 450° oven for the first 15 minutes, then turn heat down to 325° and continue to bake for about 45 minutes longer, or until filling is set and crusty on top, and pastry rim looks crisp and a rich golden color. Cool to lukewarm before serving.

Serves 8.

PECAN CHERRY CAKE

¾ cup shelled pecans
½ cup glacé cherries
3 eggs, beaten
¾ cup butter
¾ cup sugar
2 cups self-rising flour
Pinch of salt
1–2 tablespoons milk or whiskey

Roughly chop the pecans; rinse and dry the cherries and then halve them.

Beat together the butter and sugar until light and fluffy, then whisk in the beaten eggs a little at a time, beating well between each addition.

Sift together the flour and salt and toss the pecans and cherries in 2 tablespoons of this, then fold in the rest of the flour a third at a time. Lastly, add the pecans, cherries and milk or whiskey and stir lightly.

Pour the batter into a greased, lined cake pan, 7 inches in diameter, and bake in a preheated 350° oven for 1–1¼ hours, or until a skewer inserted into the center of the cake comes out clean.

PECAN COOKIES

¼ cup clear honey
¼ cup sunflower oil
2 eggs, beaten
2 tablespoons milk
½ teaspoon salt
½ teaspoon dried fennel seeds, crushed
4 cups wholewheat flour
1½ cups shelled pecans, coarsely ground
1 cup raisins, chopped

Grease a large baking sheet.

In a large mixing bowl, blend the honey, oil and eggs thoroughly. Gradually stir in the milk, then add the salt and crushed fennel seeds. Mix together the flour, nuts and raisins in another bowl. Then fold this bowlful carefully into the wet ingredients, to form a stiff dough. If the dough is too thick add a little more milk and if too sticky add a bit more flour.

Turn the dough onto a floured board, and roll out until about ¼ inch thick. Using a floured cookie cutter, cut out disks about 2 inches in diameter, and arrange these on the prepared baking sheet. Bake in a preheated 350° oven for 15 minutes or until golden-brown.

They will be slightly soft to touch, hardening as they cool.

PECAN BALLS

Serve these small balls with ice cream – they're particularly good with either vanilla or chocolate flavors.

½ cup butter
2 tablespoons sugar
1 teaspoon vanilla
1 cup shelled pecans
1 cup flour
½ cup confectioners' sugar

Beat together the butter, sugar and vanilla until light and fluffy. Grind the pecans as finely as you like, or finely chop them. Stir the chopped nuts into the butter mixture. Sift the flour into the mixture and work to a stiff paste.

Roll into about 30 small balls and place them on greased baking sheets.

Bake in a preheated 350° oven for about 12 minutes, then sift the confectioners' sugar over and continue baking for about 5 minutes just to glaze.

Cool on a wire rack and store in an airtight container.

CREAMY PECAN NOUGAT

3 egg whites
3 cups sugar
½ pound glucose
1½ pounds shelled pecans, chopped
A few drops of vanilla

Prepare a large baking pan, about 15 inches square and about 1 inch deep, by lining with rice paper. In a large bowl beat the egg whites until stiff.

Place ¾ cup of the sugar and ¾ cup water in a small saucepan. Put the pan over a moderate heat and stir until the sugar dissolves. Bring to a boil and allow to cook until the temperature reaches 250°. (Use a candy thermometer to determine this, or drop a small sample of the syrup into a saucer of cold water. It should harden immediately and be very brittle.) Remove the pan from the heat.

Pour the hot syrup onto the egg whites, beating all the time. Leave on one side.

Put the remaining sugar, another ¾ cup water and the glucose in a saucepan, over a moderate heat. Stir until the sugar and glucose dissolve, then allow to boil until the temperature reaches 260°. Remove the pan from the heat. Pour the hot glucose and sugar syrup onto the egg white mixture, stirring constantly. Then fold in the pecans and vanilla. Allow to cool.

Turn the mixture into the prepared baking pan. Press down well and smooth over the surface with a knife. Put another piece of rice paper on top then a wooden board on top to weigh the nougat down. Leave overnight. The next day, remove the board, unmold the nougat and cut into squares.

Store nougat in an airtight container ready for use.

SAVORY PECAN ROLLS

Serve these with creamy soups.

Slice a close-textured brown or wholewheat loaf (a few minutes in the freezer will make this easier). Butter generously and trim away crusts. Sprinkle with chopped pecans and grind over a little coarse salt. Roll up from the short end, stopping and cutting halfway. You should get 2 or 4 from each bread slice – depending on size.

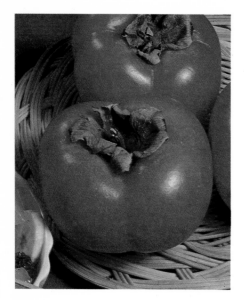

PERSIMMON

Just when you think you have had the best of summer's offerings, a mysterious fruit, looking like a rather squashed yellow tomato, begins to come on to the market. This is the persimmon, also known by the more romantic names of Sharon fruit or fruit of Sharon.

Persimmons were originally cultivated widely in China and Japan. Nowadays they are grown all over the temperate world, in the United States and especially throughout the southern Mediterranean. Several different species of different shapes and sizes are grown, some smooth and round, some pendulous and faintly ribbed, seeded or seedless.

The actual fruit is a berry, which matures and ripens in late fall, often after the first frosts, when most of the leaves have withered and fallen off the tree. In some places it is thought that a touch of frost actually helps the fruit to ripen, but this varies according to species. But persimmons must be completely ripe before they can be eaten. Until then, their high tannic content, which gradually disappears as they ripen, literally sets the teeth on edge. Once the fruit is fully ripe, however, it becomes sweet and aromatic, with a delightful, jelly-like texture.

This state of edible ripeness lasts for only a short time, and is followed rapidly by deterioration. Because of this, persimmons are usually sold before they are ripe enough to eat. Left at home at room temperature, it will be several days before they are ready. Admittedly, they will seem less attractive on the surface and look decidedly squashy and discolored, but this is as they should be.

Ripe persimmons are very good to serve raw on their own at breakfast. Slit the skin and ease it back to expose the pulp, which can be scooped out with a small spoon. The puréed pulp also makes an interesting alternative to apple sauce with meat and poultry. Persimmons freeze very well, either as whole fruits or a purée; just put them in the freezer.

Finally, persimmons are also excellent sliced and eaten with other fruit such as pineapple or added to mixed seasonal fruit salads. If you want to spark them up with a little alcohol, rum and Kirsch are particularly good.

The persimmon's medicinal properties are appreciated by both the Chinese and the American Indians. The former dry the calyx and use it as a remedy for fevers, etc, and a tea rich in Vitamin C can be made from the leaves.

PERSIMMON FLUFF

3 ripe persimmons
1 tablespoon unflavored
  gelatin
½ cup sugar
3 tablespoons lemon juice
1 teaspoon vanilla
2 egg whites
Pinch of salt
¾ cup whipping cream

REMEDIES

As might be expected, both the Chinese and the American Indians have long appreciated the medicinal qualities of the persimmon.

The Chinese use the dried calyx as a remedy for fevers, coughs, colds, catarrh and asthma: infused with crushed, dried ginger and a few cloves, it will help cure hiccups.

The American Indians make a tea from the leaves (dried are better than fresh) which is pleasant tasting and high in Vitamin C.

Stem and cut persimmons in halves or quarters. Scoop out pulp and rub it through a fine nylon sieve to trap seeds. Measure purée. There should be 1 cup or a little more – up to, say, 1¼ cups.

In a cup, sprinkle gelatin over ¼ cup cold water and leave to soften. At the same time, in a heavy pan, stir sugar with another ¼ cup water over low heat until dissolved. Place cup of softened gelatin in a pan of very hot water and stir until quite clear and liquid. Blend dissolved gelatin with hot syrup and add lemon juice. Cool slightly and mix thoroughly with persimmon purée and vanilla. Mixture should be strongly flavored. Add more lemon juice or sugar (preferably confectioners' sugar) if necessary. Leave until cold, then chill until syrupy and on the point of setting.

Beat egg whites with a pinch of salt until stiff but not dry. Whip cream separately until it thickens and stands in floppy peaks.

Finally, beat persimmon purée until light and frothy.

Fold cream into persimmon purée, followed by stiffly beaten egg whites. Pile into a glass serving bowl and chill until set.

Serve the fluff with delicate sweet cookies.

Serves 6–8.

PERSIMMON ICE CREAM

For this recipe use large, sweet persimmons that are so ripe they are like jelly.

3 large, ripe persimmons (see above)
About 6 tablespoons sugar
2 tablespoons lemon juice
1¼ cups heavy cream
¾ cup light cream

Stem and cut persimmons in half. Scoop out pulp and rub it through a nylon sieve, eliminating seeds. Sweeten pulp and flavor with lemon juice. Remember that freezing weakens flavors and a large amount of cream still has to be added, so flavor of pulp should be quite pronounced. Add sugar or lemon juice if necessary.

Mix creams together and whip just enough to thicken them. Mix lightly with persimmon pulp. Pour into ice-cube trays or a wide, shallow container. Cover tightly with foil or a lid, and freeze ice cream until it is solid around sides but still soft in the middle.

Scrape ice cream into a bowl and beat vigorously until mixture is quite smooth and creamy again. Pour back into container(s), cover and freeze until firm.

Transfer to refrigerator to soften slightly and allow flavors to develop about 1 hour before serving.

Serves 4–6.

PERSIMMON WATER ICE

Persimmons have a very high water content, yet freeze very well. This must be the easiest, quickest water ice in the world.

Take ripe persimmons and put them in the freezer, just as they are or in the form of a pulp. Freeze them hard, then thaw very slightly before serving.

The freezing process breaks down any remaining traces of tannic acid, leaving the iced fruit perfectly sweet and mellow.

PERSIMMON PIE

Persimmons can be used to make a deliciously different pie filling. Be sure though to select fruit that is ripe and juicy.

One 9 inch basic pie pastry case, pre-baked (page 203)
3 ripe persimmons
¾ cup sugar
Juice and ground rind of 1 lemon
½ teaspoon ground cinnamon
Unsweetened whipped cream

Wash the persimmons, remove the stems, quarter and scoop out the pulp. Rub the pulp through a fine sieve (or place in a blender) to form a purée. Meanwhile, prepare a syrup by dissolving the sugar in ¾ cup water and boiling this mixture for about 15 minutes.

Add the sugar syrup, lemon rind and juice and cinnamon to the persimmon purée, and blend them thoroughly.

Fill the pastry case with the fruit mixture and top with whipped cream.

Chill before serving.

Serves 6.

TRADER VIC'S PERSIMMONS WITH RUM

4 large, ripe persimmons
6 tablespoons rum (medium or dark)
⅓ cup firmly packed light brown sugar
¼ cup sour cream

Pull off persimmon stems and cut each persimmon in half lengthwise. Arrange 2 halves, cut side up, on each of 4 individual plates. Sprinkle them with rum and sugar, and spoon sour cream over the top. Serve with small spoons.

Serves 4.

Note: If sour cream is not available, top the persimmon halves with a little fresh plain yogurt, beaten with a fork until smooth.

REMEDY

Bromeline, the enzyme that makes pineapple good to eat after a rich meal, is also useful in other ways. To remove warts, either rub them with the juice, or put a piece of fruit over the wart and hold in place with a bandage or piece of cloth.

CUTICLE SOFTENER

Pineapple's "digestive" or softening action is utilized in this cuticle lotion.

Combine 2 tablespoons fresh pineapple juice with 2 tablespoons egg yolk and ½ teaspoon cider vinegar. Soak nails for half an hour.

PINEAPPLE AND BANANA DRINK

A welcome change from the usual breakfast glass of orange or grapefruit juice.

2 cups unsweetened pineapple juice
1 large ripe banana
Grated nutmeg

Chill the pineapple juice thoroughly. Peel the banana and slice it into chunks. In an electric blender, whirl the two together until smooth.

Divide between 6 small glasses. Sprinkle each glass with a tiny pinch of nutmeg and serve immediately.

Serves 6.

PINEAPPLE

Of all the fruits that came to us from the tropics of the New World, pineapples are undoubtedly among the finest. Christopher Columbus is thought to have found them on the island of Guadeloupe in the early 1490s. In an attempt to give people in Europe some idea of the flavor of this magnificent new fruit, one of his crew described its taste as a combination of melon, wild strawberries, raspberries and apples.

For centuries pineapples were a symbol of great luxury. Their exotic form appears sculpted in the stonework of grand houses, but only kings and the cream of the aristocracy could hope to taste the fruit itself. In Europe, the first home-grown pineapple was offered to Charles II of England by the Duchess of Cleveland in 1672. Not to be outdone, the gardeners of Louis XIV succeeded in growing pineapples in the hothouses at Versailles. This situation remained unchanged until the end of the nineteenth century, when canning techniques were perfected. Indeed, the canning of pineapples has been one of the great success stories of this process, so much so that, faced with a choice between the unripe fresh fruit and the canned version, even growers actually preferred the latter. Today, canned pineapple is available in a variety of forms: sliced and cored, cubed, cut in sticks or crushed, packed in a light syrup or its own natural juice. We have had crystallized or candied pineapple pieces for a long time and cartons of pure pineapple juice are almost as popular as the ubiquitous orange and grapefruit. It is excellent drunk on its own, lightly chilled, or as a fruit cocktail mixed with other juices. Fresh pineapples are also widely available.

A ripe, fresh pineapple will be very fragrant and heavy with juice, with a crown of spiky green leaves that are fresh and unwithered, and offer little resistance when you tug at them with your fingers. Under its tough, horny skin, a ripe fruit yields slightly to finger pressure. Turn it over and examine its underside closely for brown spots; this is where decay usually starts.

When the pineapple is cut open, its golden flesh has a hard, woody core running lengthwise through the center. This becomes tough and quite inedible as the fruit ripens, and must be cut out of halved or quartered fruit, or stamped out of slices with a small, plain, round cutter.

A fresh pineapple can be served on the half- or quarter-shell, or peeled and cut in pieces. For the former, first rinse and dry the fruit, together with its crown of leaves. With a sharp, pointed knife cut it in half from middle to base. Then turn the pineapple around and finish halving it, cutting through the crown of leaves. Finally, cut the flesh from the shell, leaving the latter just about ½ inch thick.

To peel a pineapple, first tug out the tuft of leaves at the top, holding them together tightly (this tuft makes an attractive house plant if you trim any stray pineapple flesh from the bottom and root it in a flowerpot of potting mixture or even ordinary garden soil). With a serrated knife take a thin slice from the top and bottom of the pineapple so that it will stand steady. Then, holding it firmly on its base, cut off the skin as far as the middle in thick, downward slices. Turn it upside down and peel off the rest of the skin in the same way. With the point of your knife, gouge out all the little brown "pines" that remain. Then halve, quarter or slice the pineapple and core it as usual.

Pineapples are best frozen dry; peel them and cut into slices or chunks.

Fresh ripe pineapple is delicious eaten as it is with a sprinkling of sugar and a few drops of Kirsch. Fresh uncooked pineapple contains an enzyme (*bromeline*) which has a digestive effect similar to that of the better known *papain* in papayas, though not so strong. This makes it an excellent fruit to eat raw at the end of a rich meal – cooking will destroy the enzyme. But pineapple can be served at any stage of a meal. Serve pineapple chunks on cocktail sticks with cheese with cocktails, thread them onto skewers with pieces of chicken and squares of green pepper to make colorful kabobs, and add them, fresh, candied or canned, to cakes and desserts of all kinds. Don't forget, though, that the *bromeline* will prevent any food recipes containing gelatin from setting (you will have to cook the pineapple first).

CHICKEN WITH PINEAPPLE CHINESE STYLE

This may not be an authentically Chinese dish but it is quite delicious nevertheless, and should be served with plain boiled rice.

1 chicken, about 2½ pounds
5 tablespoons soy sauce
1 tablespoon dry sherry wine
About 2½ cups peanut or corn oil
1 can (16 ounces) pineapple rings in natural juice
1 large onion
2 tablespoons raisins
½ tablespoon sesame oil
1 tablespoon cornstarch

Wash the chicken and pat it dry both inside and out. Lay it in a deep dish. Rub it all over with a mixture of soy sauce and sherry, and pour the remainder over the top.

Leave the chicken to marinate in this mixture for about 1 hour, turning it occasionally.

In a heavy casserole that will hold the chicken comfortably, heat 1 inch oil. While the oil is heating, drain the chicken thoroughly, reserving the marinade. When the oil is hot enough to sizzle when a few drops of water are shaken into it, lay the chicken in the hot oil, lower the heat and fry until golden brown all over. Meanwhile, drain the pineapple rings, reserving the juice, and cut each ring into 10 chunks. Chop the onion into slightly smaller chunks.

When the chicken is well colored, transfer it to a plate. Pour off all but 3 tablespoons oil and fry the onion chunks for 30 seconds, stirring and scraping the bottom and sides of the casserole with a wooden spoon.

Stir in the reserved marinade and pineapple juice. Turn the chicken over in this mixture, cover the casserole and simmer for 30 minutes, or until the chicken is very tender, turning it occasionally.

Remove chicken from casserole and cut the meat into chunks. Keep warm. Add pineapple and raisins to casserole, and simmer for 5 minutes. Stir in the sesame oil and cornstarch blended with 1 tablespoon cold water, and simmer, stirring, for 2 or 3 minutes until sauce has thickened and is no longer cloudy.

Return the chicken to the casserole. Reheat gently and serve.

Serves 4.

ROAST PINEAPPLE

A delicious and unusual way of presenting a fresh pineapple hot. The recipe is said to originate with the American Indian.

1 fresh pineapple
2 tablespoons liquid (clear) honey

Shorten pineapple leaves if necessary. Slice it in half lengthwise from top to bottom and with the point of a knife score the flesh deeply criss-cross fashion. Lay the pineapple halves in a baking dish and spoon a tablespoon of honey over each half.

Roast the pineapple in a preheated 400° oven for 20–30 minutes until bubbling on top. Cut each pineapple half in 2 or 3 lengthwise, depending on size, and serve hot.

Serves 4–6.

Note: Another good topping for the pineapple is a sprinkling of brown sugar and a few flakes of butter. Roast until bubbling.

PINE AND APPLE SALAD

3 slices fresh pineapple
4 crisp apples
2 tablespoons lemon juice
4 tablespoons dry or medium sherry wine
3–4 tablespoons sugar
2 tablespoons flaked or slivered toasted almonds for decoration

Slice off skin from pineapple slices. Cut out central cores if woody, and cut pineapple into individual bite-sized chunks. Place in a bowl. Quarter, core and peel apples, dice them and add them to bowl. Sprinkle with lemon juice and toss until apples are thoroughly coated to prevent discoloration. Sprinkle with sherry and sugar to taste. Toss again and allow to stand for a little while before serving sprinkled with toasted almonds.

Serves 6.

FRUIT IN A BLANKET

One of Robert Carrier's brilliantly simple recipes, created by accident when he forgot to broil a dish of *crème brûlée* which was waiting in the refrigerator, ready for a dinner party.

3 large, thin-skinned oranges
3 slices fresh pineapple
Orange juice and Kirsch
2½ cups heavy cream
1⅓ cups firmly packed brown sugar

Carefully peel the oranges, stripping off all the white pith, and slice them thinly crosswise, discarding any seeds. Quarter the pineapple slices. Arrange the fruit in overlapping slices in a deep, wide serving dish. Sprinkle with orange juice and Kirsch, to taste.

Whip the cream until soft peaks form. Pile it on the fruit and smooth it out evenly with a spatula. Sprinkle evenly with a layer of sugar about ⅛ inch thick. Chill until ready to serve.

Serves 6.

PINEAPPLE CREAM

An unusual recipe to find in a Victorian cookbook, making use of even the peelings of what was a precious fruit. From Mrs Bowman's *New Cookery Book* (1867).

"Boil the rind of a pine-apple, cut in pieces, in a quarter of a pint of milk for half an hour (add more milk if it all evaporates too quickly); then strain it, and add a pint of thick cream, three ounces of sugar, and a teaspoonful of lemon-juice (or a little more, to taste); thicken for ten minutes over the fire, and when cool, whisk into froth, and fill glasses."

Pineapple Ambrosia

1 cup dried shredded coconut
Sugar
1 ripe pineapple, about
    2 pounds
4 sweet, juicy oranges

In a bowl, moisten coconut shreds with ¾ cup hot water and put aside to soak for 30 minutes. Then drain off excess moisture in a sieve, squeezing shreds as dry as possible. Toss with 3 or 4 tablespoons sugar.

Cut off leafy crown of pineapple. With a razor-sharp, pointed knife, peel pineapple and cut out the brown pines. Working on a board or plate to catch any juices, lay pineapple on its side and slice it thinly. Cut out core.

Peel oranges and cut away the tough membrane under the skin and the white pith. Again working on a board or plate, lay each orange on its side and slice thinly. Discard any seeds.

Arrange a layer of pineapple slices in a large glass bowl. Sprinkle with sugared coconut. Follow with a layer of orange slices and more sugared coconut. Continue until all the fruits have been used up, ending with the remaining coconut.

Sprinkle with the pineapple and orange juices.

Cover the bowl and chill lightly for a couple of hours before serving.

To serve, place the pineapple crown on top.

Serves 4–6.

Pineapple Gelatin

Another recipe from Mrs Bowman's *New Cookery Book*. Obviously the author had discovered that raw pineapple contained an enzyme (if that is how she would describe it) that prevents setting unless it is first boiled. Use ordinary powdered gelatin instead of the isinglass, following the usual procedure of first softening it in a few tablespoons of cold water. Taste the juice and dilute it with less water if its flavor is too weak.

"Cut a fresh pine in slices; cover them with powdered sugar, and leave them a few hours; then pour off, and strain to obtain a pint of the syrup (the juice will flow more readily if the pineapple is first crushed in an electric blender or food processor – or you could start with a can or carton of unsweetened pineapple juice, sweetened to taste). Dissolve an ounce of isinglass in a pint of water and clarify it; pour it over the syrup and simmer five minutes over the fire; add a glass of Curaçao, and pour into a mould shaped like a pineapple. It will require to be very carefully turned out, and will then be very elegant."

Pineapple Upside-Down Cake

A spectacular cake, simple to make once you know how.

Butter
½ cup firmly packed light brown
    sugar
1 large can (16 ounces) pineapple
    rings, or about 8 slices fresh
    pineapple, cored
6–8 tablespoons dried shredded
    coconut or 8 glacé cherries (see
    method)

Cake batter
¾ cup butter
¾ cup sugar
1½ cups flour
1½ teaspoons baking powder
Pinch of salt
3 eggs
½–¾ teaspoon real almond extract
Milk (optional)

Start by preparing a baking pan. Grease a deep 8 or 9 inch square pan all over with butter. Line bottom with a square of baking parchment paper and grease that as well. In a small, heavy pan, melt ½ cup butter without letting it sizzle. Add brown sugar and stir vigorously with a wooden spoon. Butter and sugar may to some extent remain separate. Pour this mixture into the prepared baking pan and spread it out evenly with the back of your spoon.

Cut each slice of pineapple in four. Arrange wedges in rows on sugar topping in pan. Sprinkle thickly with shredded coconut and any remaining pineapple juice (if using canned pineapple, sprinkle coconut with a couple of tablespoons syrup from the can). Alternatively, arrange whole pineapple rings over bottom of baking pan and plug the cored-out middle of each ring with a glacé cherry.

To make cake, cream butter and sugar together until fluffy. Sift flour with baking powder and salt. Beat eggs until light and lemon-colored. Beat a good tablespoon of flour mixture into the butter and sugar, then gradually add beaten eggs, beating well between each addition. Beat in almond extract. Fold in remaining flour to make a soft batter. If it is very stiff, you can thin it down a little with 2 or 3 tablespoons milk. Spoon batter into cake pan and level off top with your spoon.

Bake cake in a preheated 350° oven for about 45 minutes, or until a skewer pushed down through middle of cake feels dry to the touch. Leave to cool for 5 minutes. Then slip a knife blade around sides of cake to loosen them if necessary, place a large, flat serving platter on top and invert cake pan on to it. Carefully remove pan and peel off lining paper if still attached.

Serve lukewarm, with a bowl of very lightly sweetened whipped cream if desired.

Serves 8.

PINE-APRICOT JAM

An unusual jam specially for city-dwellers, who may not have access to large quantities of conventional soft fruits but are more likely to find good-quality fresh pineapples going cheap in the local street market or supermarket. The apricots, which you will find unsulphured in health food stores, need not be high-quality plump ones.

1 medium-size, ripe pineapple
1 pound dried apricots
Juice of 3 lemons
1 tablespoon finely grated lemon rind
4 pounds (8 cups) sugar

Working on a board or over a plate to catch all the juices, carefully peel pineapple. Quarter it lengthwise, cut out woody core and chop pineapple into small pieces. Drain off all the juices into a measuring cup.

Cut dried apricots in pieces and wash them thoroughly in cold water. Put in a bowl.

Pour in pineapple juice made up to 2½ cups with water, plus another 5 cups water, and soak overnight.

The following day, pour contents of bowl into a preserving kettle. Stir in lemon juice and rind, bring to boiling point and simmer until apricots are quite soft. If pieces of pineapple are on the large side, shred them with a sharp knife or by whizzing briefly in an electric blender or food processor. Stir into the apricots, followed by the sugar, and continue to stir over low heat until sugar has dissolved. Then raise heat, bring to boiling point and boil briskly until jell point is reached. Toward the end of cooking time, skim surface clear of scum.

Pack and process as usual.
See also page 198.

Fills about 6 jars.

CRYSTALLIZED PINEAPPLE CHUNKS

1 large, ripe, firm pineapple
3½ cups sugar

Peel the pineapple and cut across into slices about ½ inch thick. Cut each slice in half, remove the core and then divide the remaining fruit into approximately ½ inch cubes. Place the cubes in a medium saucepan, and pour boiling water over to cover them.

Place the pan over a moderate heat and cook gently until the pineapple is just tender. Remove the fruit, using a slotted spoon, and place it in a large bowl.

Drain off 1¼ cups of the cooking water into another pan (discard the remainder). Stir in ¾ cup of the sugar and bring this mixture to a boil, stirring frequently. Remove from the heat and pour the syrup over the pineapple. Cover the bowl with a cloth and leave for 24 hours.

After 24 hours, drain off all the syrup into a small saucepan. Add ¼ cup sugar, stir to dissolve, bring the mixture to a boil and pour back over the pineapple in the bowl. Re-cover

the bowl and leave for a further 24 hours. Repeat this last process 5 times more. Then repeat once using 6 tablespoons sugar, and leave the fruit to soak in the syrup for 48 hours. Finally, dissolve 6 tablespoons sugar in the drained syrup, bring the mixture to a boil, and pour over the pineapple. Leave the fruit to soak for 4 days. Uncover the bowl and discard any liquid.

Line a baking sheet with wax paper. Arrange the crystallized pineapple chunks on the sheet. Turn the oven to its lowest setting. Place the sheet of crystallized fruit in the oven for 2–3 hours, until the chunks are dry, turning the fruit several times.

When the fruit is dry, put the remaining ½ cup sugar in a small bowl. Bring about 2½ cups water to a boil in a saucepan. Plunge each chunk on the end of a fork into the boiling water. Remove immediately, shake off excess water and dip in the sugar to coat. Return the fruit chunks to the lined baking sheet. Leave for several hours, before eating or storing in a sealed glass jar.

PINA COLADA

A popular and refreshing drink from Puerto Rico.

Per person:
½ pound fresh pineapple
2 ounces light rum
¼ cup thick coconut milk (page 54)
1 tablespoon crushed ice
1 Maraschino cherry for decoration

Crush the pineapple to extract the juice, preferably in an electric juice extractor (or use an electric blender), then strain off the juice from the pulp. Place the juice, rum, coconut milk and ice in an electric blender and blend thoroughly. Pour into a tall, chilled glass, decorate with cherry, and serve.

PINE NUT

Although the seeds of several pines are edible, the pine nuts sold in gourmet and specialist shops come mainly from the stone pine, a familiar and picturesque constituent of the Mediterranean coastal landscape with its dark green umbrella-shaped crown, cracked scaly bark and huge glossy brown cones. Since Roman times it has been widely planted along the Mediterranean coast from Spain to the Lebanon.

Pine nuts (also known as pine kernels and Indian nuts) have been used in Italy for centuries — at least since the first century AD. Called *pignoli, pinoli* or *pinocchio*, depending on the region, the nuts are traditionally used in soups, stews and ragoûts, and as a basic ingredient in that fragrant basil and garlic sauce for pasta called *pesto*.

In Spain, particularly in the Balearics, they are minced, chopped, or ground to a paste to flavor sauces; and in France, where pine nuts are known as *pignons*, they are occasionally used in the cooking of Provence in the south, and the Landais.

Pine nuts are high in protein and fat, and comparatively low in carbohydrates. Because of their high fat content they soon turn rancid and should be used quickly. Store them in a cool place in an airtight jar.

PINE NUT SOUP

½ pound pine nuts
2 cups creamy milk
1¼ cups chicken broth
2 scallions, thinly sliced
1 sprig mint
Pinch of grated coriander
Salt and freshly ground black pepper
Finely chopped parsley and/or chives
   for garnish

In a large, heavy pan, combine pine nuts with milk, chicken broth, scallions and mint. Season with coriander and a pinch each of salt and freshly ground black pepper. Bring to boiling point and simmer with the lid half on, stirring occasionally, until nuts are very soft, 25–30 minutes. Discard mint sprig.

Rub contents of pan through a sieve or the medium disk of a food mill, or purée in an electric blender or food processor.

Return to pan and correct seasoning. (If flavor of soup is too strong, dilute with a little more milk.)

Either serve soup hot or allow it to cool, then chill thoroughly before serving, garnished with finely chopped fresh parsley and/or chives. Serve in small portions as soup is very rich.

Serves 4–5.

PINE ESSENCE

For a glorious-smelling addition to your bath, fill a muslin, fine cotton or cheesecloth bag with pine needles. Infuse the bag in boiling water and pour the liquid into the bath, or simply hang the bag under the hot tap.

This essence is good for the skin and heart, and generally stimulating to the system.

PINE AND HERB PILLOW

To make a fresh-smelling herb pillow, crush together two parts dried pine needles, one part each dried rosemary (or lavender) and dried lemon balm, and a pinch of powdered orris root. Enclose the mixture in a linen or cambric case.

LEBANESE RAGOUT WITH PINE NUTS

Pine nuts transform this stew. If they are not available, substitute coarsely chopped skinned hazelnuts or walnuts. In winter, when fresh tomatoes have little flavor, use a couple of 16 ounce cans of Italian peeled tomatoes instead.

About ½ teaspoon ground cinnamon, sprinkled over the fried meat before the pine nuts are added, is a typically Middle Eastern touch.

Serve with plain boiled rice.

1 pound lean boneless lamb
2–2½ pounds ripe tomatoes (see
   above)
1 large Bermuda onion, chopped
1 large plump clove garlic, crushed
¼ cup butter
¼ cup pine nuts
Salt and freshly ground black pepper
Pinch of sugar (optional)
Finely chopped parsley for garnish

Wipe meat clean and cut it into small, bite-sized cubes, trimming off any fat or gristle. Peel, seed and coarsely chop fresh tomatoes. If using canned tomatoes, you need only cut them up and with them use some of the juices from the can.

In a large, heavy pan or flameproof casserole, sauté onion and garlic in butter until soft and golden. Add lamb and sauté over moderate heat until lightly browned on all sides. Stir in pine nuts and continue to sauté for a minute or two longer.

Stir in tomatoes. Season to taste with salt, freshly ground black pepper and a pinch of sugar if you think tomatoes need it. Slowly bring to simmering point and cook gently until meat is tender and sauce is reduced. Sprinkle with parsley.

Serves 4.

MEXICAN CHICKEN WITH PINE NUTS

Serve this dish with noodles.

1 roaster chicken, 2½–3 pounds
Salt
½ cup pine nuts
½ cup butter
2 tablespoons flour
6 tablespoons dry sherry wine
1 tablespoon ground cinnamon
2 tablespoons sugar
¼ cup raisins
¼ cup blanched slivered almonds

Quarter chicken, carefully removing any lumps of fat from body cavity. Put chicken pieces in a pan with just enough salted water to cover and cook gently, covered, until chicken is tender. This will take 45 minutes or more, depending on the quality of the chicken.

Meanwhile, grind pine nuts finely in an electric blender or food processor. In a small pan, melt 6 tablespoons butter and sauté ground nuts until a rich golden color.

Drain chicken pieces, reserving cooking liquid, and return them to the pan. Cover and keep hot.

Melt remaining butter in a small pan. Stir in flour and cook, stirring constantly, to a golden brown, nutty *roux*. Gradually add 1¼ cups reserved chicken liquid, stirring vigorously to prevent lumps forming. Bring to simmering point, stirring. Add nuts and their butter, the sherry and cinnamon mixed with sugar. Mix well and bring to simmering point once more. Pour over chicken pieces and cook gently, covered, for 15–20 minutes longer.

Finally, stir in raisins and slivered almonds. Taste for seasoning, adding a little more salt if necessary. Simmer for 5 minutes and serve.

Serves 4.

PESTO ALLA GENOVESE
Italian Basil and Pine Nut Sauce

A magnificently flavored cold sauce. It can be used as a dressing for pasta and *gnocchi* (dumplings), but they must be really hot for the sauce to release its full fragrance. Italians often stir a tablespoon or two of *pesto* into a pot of minestrone shortly before ladling it out.

If you have some of this precious sauce left over, it will keep best in a screw-top jar, covered with a layer of oil, in the refrigerator.

4 plump cloves garlic, peeled
About ½ cup pine nuts
1 large bunch fresh basil (30–40 large
    leaves)
½ teaspoon coarse sea salt
1 heaping tablespoon each crumbled
    or coarsely grated Parmesan and
    Pecorino cheese, or 2 heaping
    tablespoons Parmesan
6–8 tablespoons olive oil

Coarsely chop garlic cloves and pine nuts, and put them in a large mortar. Pound with a pestle until well mixed and broken down into a coarse paste.

Strip basil leaves from their stalks and either tear them into shreds or snip them up with scissors. Add basil to mortar with a sprinkling of salt (to help preserve its color) and continue to pound until all the ingredients are reduced to a thick purée. Then add cheeses, pounding vigorously until smooth. The Pecorino makes the sauce more piquant; all Parmesan gives a more mellow flavor.

Next, replace the pestle with a wooden spoon and gradually beat in olive oil, a spoonful at a time, as though you were in the latter stages of making a mayonnaise. Sauce should be creamy, thick and smooth. Allow it to stand for a little while before use.

Note: An electric blender or food processor will save a great deal of time and effort. Have the ingredients ready, chopped up as above. Pour the oil into the goblet of the blender first, and with the machine turned to its lowest speed, add the remaining ingredients and blend to a smooth, creamy sauce.

ITALIAN SPINACH WITH PINE NUTS

2 pounds fresh bulk spinach
⅓ cup small raisins
¼ cup butter
2 tablespoons olive oil
1 clove garlic
½ cup pine nuts
Salt
Freshly grated nutmeg

Wash spinach leaves in several changes of cold water, ripping out any hard ribs or thick stems as you come across them. Pack leaves into a pan (the water left clinging to them after washing will be enough to moisten them). Cook, tightly covered, until mound has collapsed and spinach is soft. While spinach is cooking, cover raisins with hot water and allow to soak and swell until needed.

When spinach is ready, turn the leaves out into a sieve or colander and with the back of a wooden spoon, press out excess moisture. If spinach leaves are large, slice them into wide ribbons.

In a deep skillet or wide, flameproof casserole, melt butter in oil. Peel garlic clove, bruise it lightly and add it to the foaming butter. Fry over moderate heat until garlic clove is a rich golden color. Do not let it burn or it will impart a bitter flavor.

Discard garlic clove. Add spinach, drained raisins and pine nuts to butter, mix well and cook gently, stirring, for 5 minutes, or until thoroughly hot. Season to taste with salt and a grating of nutmeg, and serve.

Serves 4.

PISTACHIO

The mild-flavored, green pistachio kernel in its pinky-red skin wrapped in a smooth white shell, is reputed to have been a favorite of the Queen of Sheba. A member of the same family as the cashew, its original home was in the warmer parts of central Asia, where it flourished in rugged mountain terrain, accessible only to goats and agile human beings. Immensely valuable to man's survival during the bitter winters, it became the subject of blood feuds among the nomadic tribes of Northern Persia and Afghanistan.

The Roman chronicler Pliny tells us that pistachio trees were brought to Rome by Lucius Vitellus, the Governor of Syria, in the first century AD, and they are now found all over the Middle East and around the Mediterranean. More recently, they have been planted in California, Texas and Arizona.

Pistachios are sold roasted and salted in their shells, and also as unsalted kernels. The former are for nibbling with cocktails, the latter are intended for cooking. In general, the greener the kernel, the better the quality of the nuts and though they are expensive, they will keep for a long time in a tightly sealed jar. Pistachio essences and extracts can sometimes be used instead of the nuts.

To skin pistachio nuts, put them in boiling water and soak for a few minutes, then drain and add some cold water. The skins will come off when you rub each nut between your forefinger and thumb.

Pistachios appear time and time again in the incredibly rich and sweet pastries of the Middle East. They make an attractive decoration for our rather more puritan Anglo-Saxon cakes and desserts, and are firm favorites with French pastry-cooks. They are also used in one of the most delicious of all ice creams.

Like all nuts, pistachios pack a very concentrated amount of goodness into a small space. They are particularly rich in potassium.

PORK AND PISTACHIO PÂTÉ

1 pound fresh pork sides
¼ slab bacon
¾ pound pork or lamb liver
1 medium-size onion or 2 shallots, chopped
2 cloves garlic
Salt and freshly ground black pepper
3 tablespoons brandy
¾–1 cup shelled pistachio nuts
2 bay leaves for garnish

Remove any bone from the pork sides. Grind together the pork, bacon, liver and onion. Crush the garlic with a little salt and stir into the mixture, then season with salt and pepper and stir in the brandy.

Add the pistachio nuts and mix in well so they are as evenly distributed as possible. Transfer the mixture to a 9 × 5 × 3 inch loaf pan and smooth the top. Arrange the bay leaves on top and cover with a foil lid.

Put the loaf pan into a roasting pan and half-fill the roasting pan with boiling water. Cook in a preheated 375° oven for about 1½ hours.

Remove from the oven and loosen the lid, but do not remove it. Leave overnight with weights on top.

Serve as an appetizer, or with a mixed or green salad for lunch.

Serves 8.

PISTACHIO RICE SALAD

This refreshing side salad is the perfect foil for cold roast meat or poultry – especially chicken, turkey or pork.

1¼ cups long-grain rice
1 cup shelled pistachio nuts, halved if liked
½ cup currants

Dressing
6 tablespoons oil
2–3 tablespoons vinegar
Salt and freshly ground black pepper
½ teaspoon ground cinnamon

Cook the rice in 2½ cups of boiling salted water for 10–12 minutes, then drain and rinse with hot water. Leave it to drain, then spread the rice on a flat serving dish to cool.

To make the dressing, whisk together the oil and vinegar until the dressing is cloudy. Season with salt, pepper and cinnamon.

Mix the pistachios and currants into the cooled rice and add the dressing. Adjust seasoning and serve.

Serves 4–6.

BAKLAVA

The best baklava I ever tasted was baked by Mme Nelly Douek for the party to celebrate the Bar-mitzvah of her grandson Simon. It had been stuffed with pistachio nuts and was quite memorable. Fortunately, Mme Douek's recipe for baklava is given in *A Book of Middle Eastern Food*, written by her daughter, Claudia Roden. According to Claudia, the secret of a baklava with light, crisp pastry is to pour ice-cold syrup over it as soon as it comes out of the oven.

Filo pastry can be bought in boxes of ½ and 1 pound from Greek and Turkish food stores. Once the package has been opened, it must be used as soon as possible, especially on a warm day, as it quickly dries out and becomes brittle. For the same reason, it is a good precaution to keep any unused sheets of pastry rolled up in a damp cloth until you get to them.

1 cup unsalted butter
1 pound (about 24 sheets) filo pastry
   (see above)
2⅔ cups shelled pistachio nuts
2 tablespoons sugar

Syrup
1 cup sugar
1 tablespoon lemon juice
1 tablespoon orange-flower water

Start by preparing the syrup and have it chilling lightly in the refrigerator before you proceed with the pastry. Dissolve the sugar in ¾ cup water together with the lemon juice. Bring to boiling point and simmer until it thickens enough to coat the back of a spoon. Stir in orange-flower water and simmer for 2 minutes longer. Pour into a pitcher, leave until cold and chill until ready to use.

Melt the butter without letting it sizzle and leave to cool. With a pastry brush, coat the bottom and sides of a large, deep baking dish, round or square, with melted butter. I often use a deep, rectangular roasting pan, but it is really up to you.

Fit half of the pastry sheets into the baking dish one after the other, brushing each sheet with melted butter and folding over the sides neatly if necessary to make them fit the dish. Do not worry if some of the pastry sheets tear. Simply fit them together again and brush them with butter. Only the 2 or 3 sheets at the bottom and on top need be perfect.

Mix the nuts and sugar together, and spread evenly over the pastry-lined dish. Cover with the remaining sheets of pastry, brushing each one with melted butter as before. When you get to the final sheet of pastry, which should be perfectly whole, gently fold it *under* the pastry like a bed sheet. Brush the surface with melted butter. With a sharp-pointed knife, cut the pastry diagonally into individual lozenges.

Bake the baklava in a preheated 350° oven for 30 minutes. Then turn the heat up to 450° and continue to bake for 15 minutes longer, or until the pastry is crisp and puffed, and a light golden color.

As soon as you take the dish of baklava from the oven, pour all the chilled syrup over the entire surface. Leave to cool.

When quite cold, run your knife blade down along the original lines between the pastry lozenges to make sure they are separated and lift out as many as you need on to a serving platter. The remainder may be left in the baking dish, covered with plastic wrap or foil.

PISTACHIO ICE CREAM

1⅓ cups pistachio nuts, skinned
3 tablespoons almonds, blanched
1 quart milk
1½ cups sugar
8 egg yolks
1¼ cups light cream

Place the nuts and a little of the milk in an electric blender and blend to a thick paste. Put the paste in a large mixing bowl.

In a saucepan, bring the rest of the milk to a boil, over a high heat. Remove the pan from the heat and gradually pour the hot milk onto the nut paste, stirring to mix well. Cover and leave for 20 minutes.

Beat the sugar and egg yolks together until thick and creamy. Slowly mix in the milk and nut mixture, stirring until smooth. Put into a thick-bottomed saucepan, place over a low heat and cook, stirring constantly, until thick. The mixture should coat the back of a spoon thickly. Remove the pan from the heat, allow to cool, then stir in the cream.

Pour the mixture into a freezing tray and place in the freezer to freeze for 1 hour.

Then tip the contents of the freezing tray into a large mixing bowl and beat well. Pour back into the freezing tray and freeze until solid.

Serves 4–6.

PLUM

Plums, both wild and cultivated, are to be found in a great variety of shapes, sizes and colors throughout the temperate world on both sides of the Atlantic.

Every region has its favored varieties, depending on climate. In the British Isles, for example, the Victoria, which was discovered in a Sussex wood in the early 1840s, is considered to be the supreme dessert plum. Although its flavor is not the finest, this golden-fleshed fruit can always be depended on to crop heavily under orchard conditions in Britain. Greengages are considered to have the finest flavor. Most dessert plums with a greenish-golden skin can boast a gage in their ancestry.

All dessert varieties can be cooked, but not all cooking plums can be eaten raw as they are usually rather dry, with a sharp, uninteresting flavor. Cooking transforms this. Most European cooking plums are descended from the wild blackthorn or sloe and the myrobalan or cherry plum, a native of Western Asia, with bright, juicy but rather tasteless red or yellow fruit. One of the finest species cultivated for jam-making is the damson. This small, oval plum with a dark blue skin is far too astringent to eat raw but makes superb preserves. Another excellent plum for eating and baking is the *Zwetschen*, a small, purple fruit with bronze flesh, which is in season for only a few weeks in late summer. And if you can find Mirabelles, do try them. These cherry-sized, golden plums are very good to eat raw and also make delicious compotes and fruit tarts.

Like pears, plums are best bought slightly under-ripe and taken home to finish ripening at room temperature. Fruit for making jams should be used before it is quite ripe. Ripe dessert plums are soft, yield slightly to finger pressure and have a delicious, light scent.

Plums make delicious chutneys, and can also be preserved in the freezer. Use ripe, pitted and skinned fruit (the skins are liable to toughen in freezing) and freeze them covered in sugar syrup made from 2 cups sugar to 5 cups water to avoid discoloration as they thaw.

But by far the most popular way of preserving plums is in the form of prunes. Only the best plums are used, preferably "freestone" ones (like peaches, plums can be either "freestone" or "clingstone"). They are sold both pitted and unpitted.

There are dozens of ways to serve prunes. They range from hot cocktail tidbits, wrapped in strips of bacon, speared on metal skewers or cocktail sticks and broiled until the fat runs, to juicy little after-dinner sweets, the pits replaced with a roll of almond paste, either plain, or flavored with a little orange liqueur or Kirsch. Prunes can also be cooked with meats in casseroles, with vegetables, chopped into winter vegetable salads, or turned into desserts of all kinds.

Prunes are well known as an effective but gentle natural laxative. They also stimulate the appetite, are good for sluggish livers, and, eaten regularly, will help to clear the skin.

HEALTH DRINK

Per person:
½ cup prunes, soaked overnight
2 tablespoons skimmed milk powder

Drain the prunes and remove pits. Chop, and put in the bowl of an electric blender with 1 cup water and the skimmed milk powder.

Blend until smooth and creamy.

CHILLED PLUM SOUP

1½ pounds ripe plums
⅓ cup sugar, or to taste
One 4 inch cinnamon stick
1 small, juicy orange, thinly sliced
2 slices lemon
½ bottle dry red wine
1¼ cups light cream

Rinse the plums, remove any stalks and put them in a pan with the sugar, cinnamon stick, orange and lemon slices (from which you have picked out and discarded any seeds). Pour in the wine and 1¼ cups water. Bring to boiling point, then cover and simmer gently until the plums are very soft.

Discard cinnamon stick, orange and lemon slices, and rub the contents of the pan through a fine sieve into a bowl. If using an electric blender, pit the plums first, then pass the puréed plums through a fine sieve to trap any remaining pieces of skin. Allow to cool, then taste for flavor, adding a little more sugar or lemon juice if necessary. (If the purée is very thick at this stage, it may also be thinned down with a little fresh orange juice or water.) Chill very thoroughly. Just before serving, blend in the cream.

Serve in chilled soup bowls, garnished to taste (see below).

Serves 6.

Note: There are several ways of garnishing this soup – with a light sprinkling of finely grated orange rind or a pinch of ground cinnamon, a dollop of thick cream or, most luxurious of all, a swirl of very lightly sweetened whipped cream flavored with orange liqueur.

PLUMS IN CREAM

1 pound sweet plums
1–2 tablespoons butter
2–4 tablespoons granulated or
*   brown sugar, or to taste*
1/8 teaspoon ground cinnamon
Small pinch of ground cloves
1/4 cup thick cream

Rinse and dry plums, cut them in half lengthwise and remove pits. In a large, heavy skillet, melt 1 tablespoon butter (or enough to coat surface of pan). Lay plums in pan, cut side up, in a single layer.

Sprinkle plums with sugar and spices, to taste. Fry plums gently, shaking pan and carefully turning plums over from time to time with a spatula, until flesh is a deep golden color but plums are far from mushy and still retain their texture.

Add a little more butter to the pan if necessary.

Spoon cream over plums. Mix lightly to blend with pan juices. Serve hot or cold.

Serves 4.

FRESH PLUM COMPOTE

1/2–2/3 cup sugar
Twist of orange or lemon rinds, or
*   one 2 inch cinnamon stick*
Lemon juice
1 pound ripe plums

Make a syrup by dissolving sugar in 2½ cups water with the orange or lemon rind, or cinnamon stick. Simmer for 15 minutes. Cool to lukewarm and flavor with lemon juice.

Wash plums. Cut them in half and remove pits. Then cut each half in two or three, depending on size. Put them in a bowl.

Pour syrup over prepared plums and allow to stand for at least 30 minutes before serving.

Serves 4.

PLUM COMPOTE WITH RED WINE SYRUP

An extravagant compote, lovely served with thick, chilled cream.

1½ pounds firm plums
Juice of 1 large orange
1 cup firmly packed light brown
*   sugar*
1¼ cups red wine
Finely grated rind of ½ large orange

Rinse plums. Halve them lengthwise and remove pits. In a bowl, sprinkle plums with orange juice.

In a saucepan, preferably a wide, enameled one, slowly dissolve sugar in red wine. Add grated orange rind and simmer for 10 minutes. Then stir in plums and their juices, cover pan and cook gently until plums are soft but not disintegrating. Cool plums in their syrup, then chill until ready to serve.

Serves 4–6.

PĄCZKI Polish Doughnuts

If you do not have any homemade plum preserve, excellent ones from Eastern Europe can be bought quite inexpensively.

Two packages active dry yeast may be used instead of fresh yeast, reconstituted according to directions on the package.

4 cups flour
Pinch of salt
4 eggs
6 tablespoons sugar
Finely grated rind of 1 orange
2 (0.6 oz) cakes compressed yeast
*   (see above)*
About 1 cup lukewarm milk
1–2 tablespoons dark rum or 2
*   teaspoons vanilla*
6 tablespoons butter, melted and
*   cooled*
Thick plum preserve (page 154)
About 3 pounds pure lard, for deep-
*   frying*
Thick rum-flavored water icing

Sift flour and salt into a large bowl, or the bowl of your electric mixer, and put it in a warm place to heat gently until needed.

In another bowl, beat the eggs and sugar together until light and fluffy. Toward the end, beat in grated orange rind.

Dissolve yeast in ¾ cup lukewarm milk.

Make a well in the warmed flour. Pour in dissolved yeast, beaten eggs and sugar, and knead ingredients vigorously to make a smooth and soft, elastic dough that leaves the sides of the bowl and your fingers quite clean. Use a little more milk if necessary. Finally, add rum or vanilla and gradually incorporate melted butter.

Roll dough into a ball. Cover bowl or slip it into a plastic bag so dough will not dry out, and leave it in a warm place to double in bulk. This may take about 2 hours or longer as the dough is rather rich.

Meanwhile, spread 2 large trays with clean kitchen cloths and dust them with a little extra flour. In a large, wide pan in which doughnuts are to be fried, melt lard without letting it sizzle.

Put aside.

When doughnut dough has doubled its bulk, deflate it with the palm of your hand and knead until smooth.

To shape doughnuts, break off a piece of dough the size of a small apple, roll it into a ball, then flatten it out, not too thinly, on the palm of one hand. Place a rounded teaspoon of plum preserve in the middle and close the dough up over it. This must

be done very carefully as otherwise the doughnuts might burst open while frying. As an extra precaution, pinch off a small piece of dough from the join so that the surface is quite smooth. Lay doughnuts on floured cloth, spaced apart slightly to allow for their rising. Cover with another cloth and allow to double in bulk once more. This time it should take less than half the time. When doughnuts are rising and starting to look puffy, very carefully turn each one over on to the other side with floured fingertips.

Reheat lard until a cube of bread dropped into it turns crisp and golden brown within 60 seconds. Carefully float 3 or 4 doughnuts in lard and fry steadily until they have turned a rich golden color on the underside, 2 or 3 minutes. Then gently flip them over to fry and color the other side. The doughnuts will rise above the level of the oil when you turn them, forming a pale ring around the middle.

As soon as doughnuts are cooked, lift them out of lard with a slotted spoon and drain on paper towels. Then, while still hot, brush tops all over with icing· and place on prepared dish to cool.

These are best eaten very fresh, preferably still just warm.

RITA'S PLUM CAKE

This can be served with cream as a dessert or with coffee or tea.

2 pounds Zwetschen or damson
  plums
1 egg
1 egg yolk
¾ cup sugar
¼ teaspoon vanilla
⅔ cup softened butter or soft
  margarine
¼ cup sour cream
2 cups self-rising flour
Granulated sugar for sprinkling

Rinse the plums in a colander. Shake off excess moisture. Halve and pit them, and put aside.

In a large bowl, beat the egg, egg yolk and sugar until fluffy and lemon-colored. Add vanilla and butter or margarine, and continue to beat until smoothly blended. Beat in sour cream.

With a wooden spoon, beat in flour a little at a time to make a stiffish batter. Depending on the type of flour used, a little more or less may be needed.

Spread the batter evenly in a 10 × 12 inch baking pan or ovenproof dish. Arrange the plum halves closely together in rows on top.

Bake in a preheated 375° oven until the cake mixture has risen up between the plums and is a rich golden color, about 1 hour.

Remove from the oven. Sprinkle sugar generously over the surface and leave to cool completely before cutting into rectangles and removing from baking pan with a broad-bladed spatula.

POWIDŁA ZE ŚLIWEK

Polish Plum Preserve

2½ pounds plums, Zwetschens if
  possible
1 cup sugar

Rinse plums and pick off any stems. Slit them in half and remove pits, dropping plums into a heavy, flameproof casserole or kettle as you do so. If pits are difficult to remove, just leave them in and chop up the plums as they will in any case have to be rubbed through a sieve once they are cooked.

To cook plums, first either heat them gently with a few tablespoons of water, tightly covered, on top of the stove until juices begin to flow, or heat covered casserole in a slow oven (or on the floor of a hotter one) to start juices off. Then place casserole over a low heat and cook, stirring and mashing occasionally with a wooden spoon, until plums are very soft and mushy.

Rub plums and their juices through a sieve or put through a vegetable mill and return purée to the casserole. Stir in sugar over moderate heat. When it has dissolved, continue to simmer purée, stirring, until it is very thick and reduced, and begins to come away from the sides of the casserole.

Spoon or pour hot plum purée into sterilized canning jars. Process in a boiling water bath as for jam (page 199).

Fills about 5 jars.

PICKLED PLUMS

7 pounds plums
3 pounds (about 8 cups) firmly
  packed brown sugar
5 cups brown (malt) vinegar
½ ounce each mace, cloves,
  cinnamon sticks and ginger root

Rinse plums and prick all over with a darning needle or sharp-tined fork.

In a large kettle, combine sugar with vinegar and spices. Bring to boiling point, stirring until sugar has dissolved, and simmer for 10 minutes. Then drop in plums and allow to simmer for a further 15 minutes.

Lift plums out of spiced vinegar and pack into canning jars. Bring vinegar back to boil. Strain through a sieve into jars, covering plums and filling jars completely. Process as usual. Mature for at least a month.

See also page 200.

Fills about 7 jars.

PLUM CHUTNEY

Ripe Santa Rosa plums make very good chutney.

2½ pounds plums
1 pound (about 3 cups) raisins
1¼–2 cups brown malt vinegar
1½–2 cups firmly packed brown or
   1–1½ cups white sugar
3 whole cloves garlic, peeled
2 tablespoons salt
¼ cup in all of ground ginger,
   cinnamon and allspice
3 tablespoons mustard seeds,
   bruised

Rinse plums, pit them and cut them into chunks.

Rinse raisins in a colander and leave to drain.

In a large, heavy kettle (an enameled pan is best, but care must be taken as chutney tends to scorch as it thickens), combine vinegar with all remaining ingredients and bring to a boil, stirring until sugar has dissolved. Add plums and raisins, and simmer until tender, stirring frequently. If chutney is still rather thin, continue to cook, stirring constantly, until the desired consistency is reached.

Pack and process as usual.

See also page 200.

Fills about 4 jars.

PLUM BRANDY

2 pounds dark red plums
5⅓ cups firmly packed light brown
   sugar
About 6 cups brandy

Remove any stalks and leaves from the fruit. Wash in a colander under cold, running water, then halve, removing pits.

In a large, wide neck, screw-top storage jar (a large Kilner jar is ideal) arrange the plums in layers, covering each layer with a generous coating of sugar. Add sufficient brandy to cover the fruit. Seal the jar tightly and leave it for 6 months at room temperature.

The liqueur is now ready to strain off and bottle. Keep in the bottle for at least 6 months before drinking.

Makes about 6 cups.

Damsons and Greengages

PLUM CHEESE

The finest of all traditional fruit "cheeses" is made with damsons. It is served in thick slices with cold poultry or game, or as a dessert.

3 pounds damsons
6 cups sugar
Finely grated rind of 1 orange
   (optional)

Rinse damsons and pull off any stems. Put fruit in a preserving kettle with barely enough water to cover and simmer until very soft and pulpy. Alternatively, at this stage, damsons may be cooked in the oven. Place them in a casserole, cover and leave in a 250° oven for several hours until juices have run from the fruit and flesh is very soft.

Put damsons through a food mill or rub through a sieve. Return pulp to preserving kettle. Stir in sugar and grated orange rind, if used. Allow sugar to dissolve and mixture to come to boiling point, then continue to cook and stir until cheese is thick enough to hold the impression of the stirring spoon. Scrape the bottom of the pan regularly to make sure none of the mixture has stuck.

When very thick, pour into suitable jars and process.

See also page 200.

PICKLED DAMSONS

The following recipe comes from *The Dumfriesshire Cookery Book*, first published in Dumfries, Scotland, by the Courier Press in 1935.

3½ pounds damsons
1 quart brown malt vinegar
3 cups sugar
½ ounce cinnamon sticks (snapped
   in half, or thirds if they are very
   long)
6–8 cloves

Wipe damsons and prick all over with a fork. Place in a large bowl.

In an enameled or stainless steel pan, boil vinegar, sugar, cinnamon and cloves together, stirring until sugar has dissolved. Pour over damsons and leave for 24 hours.

The following day, pour off vinegar and spices, and again boil them up and pour over damsons. Allow to stand for another 24 hours.

On the third day, pour entire contents of bowl into pan and boil all together for 15–20 minutes. Pack damsons into canning jars, strain vinegary liquid over them to cover them completely and process as usual.

See also page 200.

Fills about 4 jars.

CANDIED GREENGAGES

A Victorian sweetmeat which is still great fun to prepare. Serve some candied greengages on a dish of after-dinner petits fours, or use them to decorate a fruit cake.

The greengages should be slightly under-ripe and rather firm, gathered on a dry day, according to the original recipe, with the stalks left on.

1 pound greengages
   (see above)
¼ teaspoon baking soda
3 cups sugar
Sugar, to finish

Rinse greengages. With a darning needle or a thin skewer, prick a few holes in each greengage near the stalk. In a pan, cover greengages with cold water and slowly bring to boiling point. Immediately remove pan from heat, cover and leave until the following day.

Return pan to heat. Add baking soda, but this time remove from the heat before water reaches boiling point. With a slotted spoon, transfer greengages to a large bowl of cold water. Then place them in a large sieve or colander and leave them to drip dry.

Dissolve sugar in ½ cup of water and allow to boil steadily for a few minutes. Drop in greengages, bring back to boiling point and simmer for 5 minutes. Pour contents of pan into a bowl and leave for 24 hours.

The following day, drain all the syrup back into the pan. Bring to boiling point once more. Place green-gages back in syrup and simmer 5 minutes.

Repeat on 4 successive days, making it 5 times in all that the greengages have been boiled in sugar syrup. After the final boiling, lift greengages out of syrup with a slotted spoon, place in one layer in a sieve or colander and leave to dry in a warm, airy place. Old cookbooks suggest leaving the greengages to dry in the sun or near the fire but a cool oven with the door left ajar is not only more convenient but also rather more reliable.

Roll greengages in sugar before putting in paper cases and packing in an airtight box.

Prunes
LEEK AND PRUNE APPETIZER

½ pound whites of leek
12 plump prunes, soaked
   overnight
2 tablespoons round-grain (pudding)
   rice
1½–2 tablespoons sunflower oil
⅛ teaspoon ground cinnamon
   (optional)
Salt and freshly ground black
   pepper
Lemon wedges for serving

Wash the leeks carefully. Trim off stem ends and slice leeks into 1 inch lengths. Place them in a wide, shallow, flameproof pan in a single layer if possible. Add the prunes. Sprinkle in the rice, oil and the cinnamon, if liked, and season with salt and a generous grinding of black pepper. Pour in 1¼ cups hot water. Bring to boiling point. Cover tightly and cook gently for about 20 minutes, or until all the ingredients are cooked through but the dish is still rather moist.

Pour into a shallow serving dish and allow to cool.

Serve lukewarm or cold, garnished with lemon wedges.

Serves 4.

PRUNE AND BACON SKEWERS

Excellent served hot on a tray of cocktail appetizers.

Tamari almonds (lightly toasted almonds seasoned with soy sauce), which can be found in some supermarkets, make a very good and original alternative to the plain salted almonds with which the prunes are stuffed in this recipe.

24 large plump prunes, soaked
   overnight
24 salted almonds (see above)
12 slices bacon

Drain prunes and pat them dry with paper towels. With a sharp knife, slit each prune carefully down one side, remove the pit and replace it with an almond. Pat back into shape.

Cut each slice of bacon in half crosswise. Wrap each prune in a piece of bacon and secure it with a short wooden cocktail stick.

In a large skillet, fry the prunes gently until the bacon fat has run and is transparent, and the prunes are hot through. Drain well on paper towels and serve hot.

CAUCASIAN CHICKEN WITH PRUNES

1 roaster chicken, 3–3¼ pounds,
   cut up
Salt and freshly ground black pepper
3 tablespoons oil
2 Bermuda onions, very thinly sliced
½ pound (about 1½ cups) plump
   prunes, soaked overnight
1 teaspoon whole coriander seeds
¼ teaspoon crumbled dried thyme
⅛ teaspoon paprika
3 tablespoons finely chopped dill
2 tablespoons finely chopped
   parsley

Wipe the chicken pieces dry with paper towels and season generously with salt and freshly ground black pepper. In a heavy, flameproof casserole, brown the chicken pieces all over in oil, a portion at a time. Then return them all to the casserole, mix in the sliced onions and add just enough boiling water to half-cover the contents of the casserole (¾ cup or perhaps a little more). Cover the casserole and simmer very gently for 30 minutes.

Meanwhile, drain the soaked prunes and remove pits. In a mortar, combine coriander seeds with thyme and paprika, and crush them finely with a pestle.

When chicken and onions have cooked for 30 minutes, add the prunes, the crushed coriander mixture, finely chopped dill and parsley. Mix well to distribute prunes and seasoning evenly. Cover the casserole again and continue to cook gently for a further 40 minutes, or until both the chicken and prunes are very tender, and the sauce is thick and reduced.

Correct seasoning with a little more salt or pepper if necessary. Serve from the casserole.

Serves 4–6.

Roast Pork with Prunes

2½–3 pounds lean loin of pork in one
   piece (6 chops)
16–20 plump prunes, pitted
1 teaspoon ground ginger
Salt and freshly ground black pepper
1 Bermuda onion, peeled
1 small, thin-skinned orange
1 tart green apple, quartered and
   cored
1 tablespoon cooking oil
Cider or apple juice (optional)
1 tablespoon cornstarch

Have bone cut out of pork roast.
Remove some (about half) of the fat.
With a large metal skewer or similar
instrument that is strong and not too
pliable (a knife-sharpening steel, for
example, is very good), make a hole
right through the middle of the lean,
round chop of the meat. If necessary,
enlarge the cavity with the steel or
the handle of a wooden spoon. Push
in prunes tightly one after the other to
make a row of them side by side. Tie
the roast tightly in shape with thin
string in 4 or 5 places along its length.
Rub it all over with ginger and season
generously with salt and freshly
ground black pepper.

Lay pork roast in a roasting pan, fat
side up. Cut onion, orange and apple
into large chunks, and toss them with
oil and a sprinkling of cider, apple
juice or water. Arrange chunks of
onion and fruit around pork.

Roast pork in a preheated 425°
oven for the first 20 minutes to brown
it, then lower heat to 400° and continue to roast until pork is thoroughly
done, about 1 hour longer. Baste
regularly with pan juices, more cider
or apple juice, or water.

When meat is ready, transfer it to a
heated serving platter and remove
strings.

Pour contents of roasting pan
through a sieve into a saucepan,
pressing with a spoon to extract as
much juice as possible. Deglaze pan
with a few tablespoons of water,
scraping any crusty bits loose with a
wooden spoon, and add them to
pan. Skim excess fat from the surface. Blend cornstarch smoothly with
a little water and use as much as you
need to thicken sauce. Correct
seasoning with more salt and freshly
ground black pepper.

Pour into a heated sauceboat and
serve with meat.

Serves 6.

Steamed Prune Pudding

10 large juicy prunes, soaked
   overnight
Butter or soft margarine for pudding
   basin
3 tablespoons brown sugar

Pudding batter
1 cup flour
1 teaspoon baking powder
½ cup soft margarine or softened
   butter
6 tablespoons sugar
2 eggs, lightly beaten
¼ teaspoon almond extract
1–2 tablespoons milk

With a sharp knife, cut the prunes in
half lengthwise and remove pits.
Grease a pudding basin, put in the
sugar and smooth it out evenly over
the bottom of the basin with the back
of a spoon. Arrange halved prunes
evenly on top.

Cut a double thickness of parchment paper to cover the top of the
basin with a generous overlap and
grease lightly on one side.

Put aside until needed.

To make the pudding batter, sift the
flour and baking powder into a bowl.
In another bowl, beat the margarine
or butter and sugar together until
white and fluffy. Beat in about half of
the eggs, followed by 2 or 3 tablespoons flour mixture, the remaining
eggs, flour and almond extract. Finally, beat in a little milk if necessary to
make a soft batter that drops easily
from the spoon.

Pour the batter into the prepared
basin. Level off the top and make a
slight hollow in the center. Cover with
the parchment paper, buttered side
down, and tie around the sides with
fine string.

Lower the basin into a pan with
boiling water to come halfway up its
sides, cover the pan tightly and
steam gently for 1¼ hours, adding a
little more *boiling* water if and when
necessary.

To serve, unmold pudding and
serve accompanied by lightly sweetened custard sauce or cream.

Serves 4–6.

Prune Sauce

½ pound (about 1½ cups) plump
   prunes, soaked overnight
2–3 plump cloves garlic
Salt and freshly ground black pepper
Sharp (hot) paprika
About ¾ cup broth or water
2 tablespoons finely chopped
   parsley
2 tablespoons finely chopped fresh
   dill

Drain soaked prunes, reserving
liquid, and pit them. In a small pan,
cover pitted prunes with soaking
water, adding a little fresh water if
necessary to make sure prunes are
covered, and simmer until they are
quite soft and water has almost all
evaporated.

Meanwhile, crush garlic to a paste
with ¼ teaspoon salt.

Pour prunes and their juices into
the container of an electric blender or
food processor. Add garlic, its salt, a
grinding of black pepper and a generous pinch of sharp paprika. Blend
smoothly, gradually adding enough
broth (poultry or beef depending on
the meat it is to be served with) or
water to make a thick, creamy sauce.

Pour sauce back into pan. Stir in
chopped parsley and dill, and correct
seasoning if necessary. Bring to boiling point, stirring.

Pour the sauce into a bowl and
serve cold.

Prune Liqueur

Macerate a handful of prunes in a
small carafe of vodka or gin, sweetened with 2 or 3 tablespoons sugar.
Leave for a few weeks, swirling the
carafe around occasionally.

Pour off the vodka or gin into liqueur glasses.

POMEGRANATE

With its leathery yellow skin and hundreds of seeds encased in juicy, ruby-red kernels (arils), the pomegranate is a curious fruit which you either love or dislike intensely. The shrub-like tree on which it grows originally came from tropical Asia, but for a long time it has been cultivated throughout the Mediterranean region and the Middle East. Today it also grows quite happily in suitably warm areas in other parts of the world.

For thousands of years, pomegranates have been a symbol of wealth, prosperity and fertility. They are mentioned in ancient myths as a fruit favored by the gods; the Romans nicknamed them "apples of Carthage," and according to Jewish tradition pomegranates were – and still are – served at the New Year as a symbol of prosperity. Christian cultures have adopted similar customs. At the New Year, Greek children hurl whole pomegranates at their friends' houses "for luck."

Pomegranates come into season in the fall, but will keep fresh in cold storage for several months and can be bought in perfect condition throughout the winter. Don't worry if the skin is hard as wood; the kernels inside will be fresh and juicy. The seeds inside the kernels and the pith are both extremely bitter. To enjoy fresh pomegranates, cut the fruit open with a knife (a serrated blade will go through the tough skin more easily), then break it into pieces and scoop out the kernels with a teaspoon. Or roll a pomegranate over a hard surface until the kernels are squashed, then cut a small plug out of the skin so that the juice can be sucked out.

Whole kernels make a pretty garnish for almost everything; hot and cold meats, fresh fruit salads, even a cheese board can be studded with balls of cream cheese rolled in the kernels.

POMEGRANATE JUICE

A refreshing pre-lunch or pre-dinner drink. Follow instructions below to extract juice for cooking, but don't add sugar, etc.

2 ripe pomegranates
Fresh lemon or lime juice
Confectioners' sugar

Cut the pomegranates in half, and squeeze the halves in a strainer-juicer as you would an orange. Alternatively, place the kernels in a fine-meshed nylon sieve and crush them firmly with the back of a wooden spoon.

Take care not to bruise the seeds themselves.

Pour juice into a pitcher. Sharpen flavor with lemon or lime juice and stir in sugar, to taste.

Put 2 or 3 tablespoons crushed ice in a glass. Top up with chilled pomegranate juice, stir once and serve.

LIVER IN POMEGRANATE SAUCE

1½ pounds calf's or lamb's liver
Flour
3–4 tablespoons oil
Generous pinch each of dried
 crumbled thyme and rosemary
Salt and freshly ground black pepper
3 tablespoons pomegranate juice (see
 above)
Finely chopped parsley,
 for garnish

Have the liver cut in thin slices on the slant. Alternatively, buy the liver in one piece. Remove any outer membrane and, with a very sharp knife, cut the liver diagonally into large, thin slices. Dust each slice lightly with flour on both sides.

In a large, heavy skillet with a lid, brown the slices of liver in hot oil, a portion at a time, keeping them hot as you do so. Return all the slices to the pan. Sprinkle them with thyme and rosemary, and season with salt and freshly ground black pepper. Moisten with pomegranate juice, cover the pan and cook gently for 1 or 2 minutes until the liver is done.

Transfer the liver to a heated serving platter. Pour over pan juices, sprinkle with finely chopped parsley and serve immediately. Plain steamed or boiled potatoes make the best accompaniment.

Serves 4–6.

REMEDIES

Infusions made from pomegranate flowers or rind can be used to make compresses to stop bleeding, douches for vaginal discharges, and gargles for canker sores and sore throats. The juice is cooling and refreshing in cases of fever.

COSMETICS

To darken hair, apply an infusion of pomegranate flowers or bark. The astringent juice is good for oily skin, but will stain if left on for too long.

CHICKEN AND POMEGRANATE SYRUP

Chicken and pomegranates are a favored combination in the Caucasus and the Near East.

Two 2 pound chickens
¾ cup plain yogurt or
*   sour cream*
Salt and freshly ground black pepper
2 Bermuda onions
Fresh lettuce leaves and parsley
*   sprigs for garnish*
Pomegranate syrup (see right)

Split chickens in half lengthwise and firmly press them as flat as possible with the heel of your hand. Wipe pieces clean with a damp cloth and prick skin all over with the tines of a fork or a sharp skewer. Mix yogurt or sour cream until smooth and season generously with salt and freshly ground black pepper. Brush all over chicken pieces. Lay them on a large, flat dish and allow them to marinate for an hour or so before cooking them. At the same time, peel onions, slice them and separate into rings. Sprinkle the rings with salt, rubbing it in gently.

When ready to cook chicken, lay pieces flat on a rack and grill over hot coals or under a preheated broiler, turning and brushing occasionally with remaining yogurt. In all, it will take about 20 minutes on each side before juices run clear.

Meanwhile, rinse onion rings and press them dry between sheets of paper towel or the folds of a cloth.

Lay chicken halves skin side up on a heated serving platter. Garnish with lettuce leaves and sprigs of parsley. Strew chicken with prepared onion rings. Serve with a bowl of pomegranate syrup for each person to spoon some over his portion.

Serves 4.

POMEGRANATE SYRUP

This syrup has many different uses — with charcoal-grilled meats, as a topping for plain vanilla ice cream or one of the lighter sponge puddings, or simply drunk well diluted with iced water, milk or 7-Up.

Juice of 6 large pomegranates (see
*   Pomegranate Juice opposite)*
6 tablespoons sugar

Strain the pomegranate juice into an enameled or stainless steel saucepan. Stir in sugar and bring to boiling point over low heat, stirring constantly until sugar dissolves. Then raise heat and boil briskly, stirring frequently, until syrup has thickened and is well reduced. Skim off any scum from surface with a slotted spoon as you would from jam. Cool slightly.

Funnel syrup into a hot, sterilized bottle (page 201) and screw down cap. Store in the door of the refrigerator or any similar cool, dark place.

POMEGRANATE WATER ICE

An unusual, refreshing ice, for which it is essential that you use only ripe fruit.

Juice of 4 large ripe pomegranates
*   (see Pomegranate Juice left)*
Juice of 1 lemon
½ cup sugar

Strain pomegranate juice through a fine sieve. This should give about 2 cups juice. Add lemon juice.

Put the sugar and 1¼ cups water in a small, thick bottomed pan, and bring to a boil over medium heat, stirring frequently. Simmer for 10 minutes, then remove from the heat and allow to cool. When the syrup is cold, stir it into the fruit juice. Mix well and taste. Adjust the sweetness if desired, remembering that it will taste less sweet when frozen. Pour the mixture into a shallow freezing tray and freeze for 1 hour. Remove from the freezer, tip into a bowl, and beat for 1 minute.

Return to the tray and freeze for 3–4 hours more until solid. Serve alone or with other fruit, topped with pouring cream.

Serves 4.

GRENADINE

When pomegranates are plentiful — usually in the fall — you can make your own grenadine.

Measure 6 cups each fresh pomegranate kernels and granulated sugar into a bowl. Mix well, cover and leave for 24 hours.

The following day, pour the mixture into a heavy saucepan and very slowly bring it to boiling point, stirring and mashing the kernels gently with a spoon or wooden kitchen fork. Take care not to bruise the seeds. Strain the syrup through a fine nylon sieve, pressing the kernels gently to extract as much juice as possible, and pour it into tightly stoppered sterilized bottles (page 201).

QUINCE

A dish of ripening quinces will fill a room with the most unbelievable fragrance. The cooked fruit is just as powerfully flavored. You will need only a few slices to transform the taste of a dish made with apples or pears.

The fruit is thought to have come from Western Asia and the Eastern Mediterranean, where it is still widely used for all kinds of dishes from meat stews to sweetmeats and preserves. Today, however, quinces also grow in warmer temperate regions. In the United States, commercial cultivation is almost entirely confined to New York State and California.

Quinces were familiar to the Greeks and Romans, who dedicated them to Venus as a symbol of love, happiness and fruitfulness, and used their blossoms as a symbolic decoration for the bridal chamber. But although they were widely known and the beauty of their blossoms was especially admired, the fruits themselves never achieved overwhelming popularity. One exception was in Portugal, where they were used to make a preserve or jam.

Quinces should be gathered in the fall before they are quite ripe and left to finish ripening indoors. Some people maintain that the flavor will be improved if the fruit is left on the tree until after the first frost. Freshly picked quinces are covered in a white down, just as if they had been packed in cotton. This should be rubbed off gently with a damp cloth.

A raw quince is quite inedible, but cooking softens the flesh and turns it a deep golden, rosy color with a firm, rather gritty texture. Some people claim that pear-shaped specimens keep best and apple-shaped ones cook even better, but there is little to choose between them. The flesh discolors rapidly as soon as it has been cut and exposed to the air, so unless they are to be used immediately, peeled or sliced quinces should be kept in a bowl of water acidulated with lemon juice to preserve their color. Another point to bear in mind when making preserves is that over-cooking will turn the pieces rock-hard. Should this happen, the simplest solution is to use the preserve to sweeten other fruit pies and sauces. This will soften them again.

Quinces can be frozen in a syrup made from 1 cup sugar to 2½ cups water; peel, core and quarter or slice them first.

The seeds and peels of quinces are very rich in pectin and make easy jams and jellies, either on their own, or mixed with other fruit such as apples and pears. Excellent preserves can also be made with the fruit of the japonica, a relative of the quince.

COSMETICS

Quinces are used in many different countries for care of the hair – to increase growth, to cure baldness, to give body and to revive. Women in ancient Greece used a mixture of quince juice and privet to dye their hair golden.

Quince seeds have the useful property of turning to jelly when mixed with boiling water. In this classic recipe for a deep-cleansing clay mask, they not only soften the skin but also make the mask easy to remove.

Mix a teaspoon of quince seeds, dissolved in a little boiling water, with ¼ cup fullers' earth, 1 tablespoon lanolin, and enough rosewater to make a paste. Apply to the face and leave for 20 minutes before rinsing off.

CHICKEN WITH QUINCE STUFFING

1 roaster chicken, 3–3½ pounds
Salt and freshly ground black pepper
Corn or sunflower seed oil
1 pound quinces
Lemon juice
⅔ cup raisins
2–3 tablespoons softened
  butter

Wash the chicken both inside and out, and wipe it dry with paper towels. Season generously both inside and out, brush all over with a tablespoon of oil and put aside for 30 minutes while you prepare the stuffing.

Peel, quarter and core the quinces, and cut them into small chunks, dropping them immediately into a bowl of water acidulated with lemon juice to prevent them turning brown. When they are prepared, drain and dry with paper towels.

Mix the quince chunks with the raisins and butter. Stuff the cavity of the chicken with this mixture and skewer or sew the opening up. Truss the chicken.

In a heavy, heatproof casserole that has a tight-fitting lid, brown the chicken all over in 3–4 tablespoons oil, ending up with the chicken on its back. Moisten with a few tablespoons of hot water, cover the casserole tightly and cook over very low heat for 1 hour, or until the chicken is tender, turning it over once or twice and adding a little more hot water from time to time if necessary.

Serve with fluffy boiled rice.

Serves 4–6.

CAUCASIAN STUFFED QUINCES

¼ pound (about ¾ cup) shelled,
*   skinned chestnuts*
1 pound lean lamb, ground
½ cup finely chopped fresh dill
Salt
8 medium-size quinces
¼ cup butter
Sugar to taste
About 2 cups beef broth

To make stuffing, boil chestnuts for 15 minutes until softened.

Drain them, chop them up and mix them with ground lamb, dill and salt to taste.

Cut a ½ inch slice from the stem end of each quince and reserve it for the "lid." With an apple corer, scoop out cores to within ½ inch of the bottom, then scoop out some of the pulp to leave a shell ⅓ to ½ inch thick. (If quinces have uneven bases which prevent them from standing upright, it is a good idea to shave a thin slice off the bottom before hollowing out the quinces so that they will stand steady.)

Stuff quince shells with meat mixture and cover with reserved lids. Butter the bottom of a large, flameproof casserole that will hold the quinces side by side with little room to spare. Fit them into casserole. Sprinkle with sugar and dot with remaining butter.

Pour in beef broth. Cover and simmer for 50–60 minutes, or until quinces are tender, adding a little more broth if it evaporates too quickly. Lift quinces out of casserole with a slotted spoon. Serve, moistened with some of the pan juices.

Serves 4.

QUINCE COMPOTE

This exquisite compote, golden tinged with red, is delicious served either with roast poultry and meats, especially pork and lamb. Or it is very good as a dessert with chilled whipped or clotted cream.

4 quinces
Lemon juice
1 cup sugar
Thinly peeled strips of orange and
*   lemon rind*

Quarter, peel and core quinces, and slice each piece in 3 lengthwise. Drop into a bowl of water acidulated with lemon juice to prevent them going brown before they are all prepared.

In a wide pan, combine sugar with 2 cups water, the orange and lemon rinds, and bring to boiling point, stirring until sugar has dissolved. With a slotted spoon, transfer slices of quince from bowl of water to syrup. Sprinkle with 2 or 3 teaspoons more lemon juice. Simmer until quince slices have turned a translucent, rosy pink and feel soft when poked with a thin skewer.

Allow to cool in syrup before serving.

Serves 4–6.

JAPONICA JAM

Many gardeners are unaware of the excellent jams and jellies that can be made with the fruit of the ornamental quince.

2 pounds japonica fruit
Sugar
1 teaspoon ground cloves

Wash the japonicas, cut them up and put them in a preserving kettle with about 2 quarts water.

Bring to boiling point and boil until fruit is very soft and pulpy.

Rub the fruit through a sieve or vegetable mill. Weigh it and return it to the rinsed-out pan with 1½ cups sugar to every pound (about 2 cups) of pulp, and the ground cloves. Stir over gentle heat until the sugar has dissolved, then boil hard until jell point is reached.

Pack and process as usual.
See also page 198.

Fills about 5 jars.

QUINCE JELLY

One of the most beautiful jellies of all, a clear golden pink in color, with a unique aroma and flavor, quince jelly goes particularly well with pork, veal and poultry.

Wash the quinces under the cold tap and chop them up into large chunks. Cut out the cores and seeds as you come across them, and tie them up in a cheesecloth bag. Put the quinces and bag of cores etc, in a large pan. Cover with water and boil until very soft and pulpy.

Tip the contents of the pan into a jelly bag and leave suspended above a bowl to drip dry. Measure juice and measure 2 cups of sugar per 2½ cups of juice. Pour them into a preserving kettle. Stir over low heat until sugar has dissolved, then raise heat and boil until jell point is reached, skimming surface until it is quite clear of scum.

Pack and process as usual.
See also page 199.

QUINCE RATAFIA

First, wipe your quinces clean with a damp cloth. Then grate them, peels, seeds and all, into a large bowl, cover tightly and leave for 3 days. They will go rather black, but this is normal. Then squeeze the grated quinces through cheesecloth or press through a fine sieve to extract as much juice as possible. With a cup, measure this liquid into a glass flagon and mix in an equal volume of brandy (or vodka). Then, for every cupful of mixed liquid add ¼ cup of sugar and a whole clove. Drop in a cinnamon stick snapped in two, cover the flagon, and shake it well to dissolve the sugar.

Leave the ratafia to mature and mellow for at least 6 weeks before tasting it, then strain it through cheesecloth once more and re-bottle it. Drink this precious liqueur on its own in small glasses, or use it to flavor other sweets and fruit salads.

RASPBERRY

If you have ever caught your clothes on the thorns of a wild raspberry, it will hardly surprise you to learn that raspberries belong to the rose family, or *Rosaceae*. They grow wild in rocky woodlands throughout Europe from the British Isles and Scandinavia right across to Greece and Anatolia. In the south, people are still content to gather berries in the wild, but as early as the end of the Middle Ages northern gardeners had begun cultivating raspberries in their kitchen gardens. The fruit thrives in a cool, damp climate. When European plants were introduced into America, it was found that they were not suitable for the dry, hot conditions that prevailed there, and an indigenous native species had to be used instead.

The fragile, thimble-shaped berries ripen to various shades of red, ranging from scarlet to purple, almost black. There are also clear golden varieties. Raspberries vary greatly in size. The smallest of all are wild ones, which are full of seeds; many people are prepared to tolerate this, claiming that their flavor is finer than that of any cultivated fruit.

The berries are ripe when they are brightly and evenly colored, and slip easily off their hulls. Ideally, they should be used as soon as they have been picked as they rapidly turn moldy. When buying them, take a look at the bottom and sides of the container if you can for signs of dampness, which indicate that the contents are over-ripe, leaking and stale.

Raspberries should never be washed unless absolutely necessary and then given only the lightest of sprays with water. If they are not to be used immediately, they may be stored in the bottom of the refrigerator before cleaning, but bring them out well in advance of serving.

Fine raspberries need no accompaniment apart from a sprinkling of sugar. You can also serve them with lightly whipped cream flavored with orange liqueur or Kirsch, or with vanilla ice cream.

For special occasions, toss them with sugar, finely grated orange rind and juice, pile them into hollowed-out orange cups and decorate with sprigs of fresh mint.

Raspberries go well with many other fruits, in particular strawberries, peaches, apricots, pineapple and melon. The combinations are endless. Mix whole raspberries with crushed or shredded pineapple and serve with almond macaroons. Marinate raspberries and cantaloupe melon balls in orange liqueur, pile them into hollowed-out melon shells and serve lightly chilled. Alternatively, sieve the raspberries to make a purée and serve with a bowl of strawberries or a dish of lightly chilled, peeled ripe figs. Raspberry purée is also a feature of Nouvelle Cuisine.

Raspberries are rich in Vitamin C. They are also rich in pectin and so make very good jam. They can be canned, turned into juice or vinegar. But by far the best way of preserving them is in a freezer. Whole berries will come out looking as fresh as the day they were picked. For best results, freeze them on a baking sheet in a single layer before packing them into cartons or bags; if space is limited, process them first. This gives you the opportunity to use any squashed or crumbled fruit. Sweeten the purée lightly before it goes into the freezer but be prepared to adjust the flavor with more sugar before using it.

REMEDIES

Raspberries are renowned for their beneficial effects on women in childbirth; raspberry leaf tea is said to help prevent miscarriage, ease labor pains, speed delivery and help the uterus to contract after labor. A juice made by steeping raspberries and sugar together in a lidded glass container is excellent for preventing colds.

RASPBERRY SHRUB

This traditional drink is refreshing and cooling if you have a fever. It is also said to be good for the heart.

Fill a bowl (not of metal or plastic) with fresh ripe raspberries and pour over enough wine or, preferably, cider vinegar to cover. Let it stand for 3 or 4 days, stirring from time to time. Strain into a saucepan and sweeten to taste – roughly 2 cups of sugar to each 2½ cups of liquid (or you may prefer to use honey). Bring to a boil and let it simmer for 20–30 minutes, skimming off any scum that rises. Allow to cool. The addition of a wine glass of brandy to each 2½ cups liquid will help preserve it. Pour into clean bottles and cork tightly. Dilute with water to taste.

BERRY SOUP

This is a refreshing appetizer on a hot summer's day.

1 pound (4 pints) mixed berries:
  raspberries, strawberries,
  blackberries etc, as available
2 cups light cream
3 cups milk
1¼ cups thick sour cream
About ¼ cup sugar
Lemon juice
Ice cubes and sugared croûtons
  (page 205) for serving

Rub the fruits through a fine sieve or food mill, or purée them in an electric blender and then sieve out the seeds.

Blend the cream, milk and sour cream together with the puréed fruit. Sweeten to taste, and if necessary intensify the flavor with just a little lemon juice.

Chill the soup until ready for serving. Serve in a large tureen with a few ice cubes floating in it to keep it chilled throughout the course, and accompanied by a bowl of sugared croûtons to sprinkle over each portion.

Serves 8.

SUMMER PUDDING

In putting together the medley for an English summer pudding, think in terms of about 3 pounds fruit or a little more to pack a 1-quart mold, half of them raspberries, or a mixture of raspberries and a small container of very ripe loganberries. The cherries are there for texture as well as flavor, but if there are none just use more berries and currants.

1½ pounds (4½ pints) raspberries or
  mixed berries (see above)
¾ pound (2 pints) ripe sweet cherries,
  stemmed and pitted
½ pound (1 pint) black currants,
  stalked
½ pound (1 pint) red currants,
  stalked
¾–1 cup sugar
White bread (see method)
Thick chilled cream for serving

Gently mix the fruit and sugar together in a bowl. If it is a warm day, let the bowl stand for an hour or two in a sunny spot to help the sugar draw out the juices from the fruit and soften them. But if time and weather are against you, you can achieve the same effect by warming the mixture very gently on top of the range or in a cool oven for 10–15 minutes.

Meanwhile, cut slices of bread a good ¼ inch thick and trim off their crusts. Cut a round to fit the bottom of the mold, then line the sides with fan-shaped pieces, butting them together as closely as possible.

Pile the fruit into the mold, pressing gently but firmly as you go, until it is level with the top after a final light pressing. Save all the excess juices to touch up any pale patches when the pudding is unmolded.

Cover the pudding with more slices of bread. Place a *flat* plate that just fits inside the rim of the mold on top, or use a thick cardboard template cut to measure and sealed in plastic wrap. Weight it down and chill until the following day.

Serve unmolded, the top decorated with a representative selection of whole fruits, accompanied by a pitcher of chilled cream.

Serves 6–8.

RASPBERRY ORANGE CREAM

¾ cup sugar
Long strip of orange rind
1½ pounds (4½ pints) fresh or
  thawed frozen raspberries
2 tablespoons Curaçao, Cointreau or
  Grand Marnier
Lemon or lime juice and sifted
  confectioners' sugar (optional, see
  method)
2 cups heavy cream
Toasted flaked almonds for
  decoration

Dissolve sugar in 1¼ cups water. Add strip of thinly peeled orange rind. Bring to boiling point and boil hard until syrup has thickened and is reduced by about half. Leave until cold, then discard orange rind.

Rub raspberries through a fine nylon sieve. Blend in orange syrup and orange liqueur. Taste purée. Flavor should be sharp and sweet. If necessary, it may be intensified with a squeeze of lemon or lime juice or sweetened further with a little sifted confectioners' sugar.

In a bowl, whip cream until it stands in very soft peaks. Gradually beat in raspberry purée. Spoon into individual stemmed glasses.

Sprinkle each glass with just a pinch of toasted flaked almonds and chill before serving.

Serves 6.

FROZEN RASPBERRY CREAM

A simple dessert, light and refreshing, to serve with delicate almond meringues or tuiles.

Use fresh or frozen raspberries for the purée. One pound of fresh berries makes about 2 cups purée. Sweeten it lightly to taste with confectioners' sugar.

1¼ cups lightly sweetened raspberry
  purée (see above)
3–4 tablespoons Framboise
  or Kirsch
2 large egg whites
Pinch of salt
About 3–4 tablespoons sugar
2 cups heavy cream

Flavor the raspberry purée with Framboise or Kirsch and put aside until needed.

In a large, clean, dry bowl, beat the egg whites with a pinch of salt until they form soft, floppy peaks when beaters are lifted. Gradually adding 3 tablespoons sugar, continue to beat to a stiff, glossy meringue. In a separate bowl, whip cream until it is thick but not buttery.

Fold egg whites into whipped cream, followed by raspberry purée. Taste and add a little more sugar if needed to sweeten.

Pour mixture into a freezer tray or plastic bowl. Cover with a lid or a sheet of foil. Freeze until firm.

Transfer the container to the refrigerator about 1 hour before serving to soften slightly.

Serve with meringues or tuiles.

Serves 6.

RASPBERRY YOGURT ICE CREAM

Simply delicious and rather less fattening than a conventional ice cream made with cream only or an egg and cream custard.

½ pound (1½ pints) fresh or frozen
    raspberries
Juice of 1 large orange
Finely grated rind of ½ large
    orange
⅔ cup firmly packed light brown
    sugar
¾ cup heavy cream
¾ cup plain yogurt

If using frozen raspberries, mix them with the orange juice and grated orange rind, and leave until quite thawed. Otherwise, mix fresh raspberries with orange juice and rind just before use.

Rub fruit through a fine nylon sieve to make a purée. Add sugar and stir until dissolved.

In a large bowl, whip cream until very thick. Add yogurt and beat again until mixture is well blended and thick enough to hold impression of the beaters.

Gently and thoroughly fold in raspberry purée. If small lumps of cream remain unblended, you can break them down most easily by stirring with a small wire whisk.

Pour mixture into ice cube trays or a plastic box with a lid. Cover with foil or the lid and freeze until ice cream is solid around the sides but still very soft and runny in the middle. Scrape it all out into a bowl and beat until uniformly smooth and creamy again. Then pour the ice cream back into freezing container(s), cover and freeze until firm.

Place in refrigerator an hour before you plan to serve ice cream so that it has time to soften very slightly and develop its full flavor.

Serves 4–6.

RASPBERRY MOUSSE

Either fresh or frozen raspberries may be used to make this mousse, but if using frozen fruit allow a few ounces more to make up for the weigh lost when the juice drains off during thawing.

1 pound (3 pints) fresh raspberries or
    1¼ pounds (3¾ pints) frozen
    raspberries
2 envelopes unflavored gelatin
1¼ cups heavy cream
¼ cup sugar
4 eggs, separated
¼ pound almond macaroons
Whipped cream and whole
    raspberries for decoration

If using frozen raspberries, thaw them in a sieve set over a bowl to allow any juices to drip away. Then, in a food processor or blender, purée fruit. Press purée through a fine nylon sieve and discard seeds. Put aside. Sprinkle gelatin over 2 or 3 tablespoons water (or the juice that drained from the thawing raspberries) in a cup and allow to soften, then solidify. Stand cup in a small pan of very hot water and stir until gelatin has dissolved and liquid is quite clear. Cool to lukewarm.

In the top of a double boiler, or a heatproof bowl that will fit snugly over a pan of simmering water, beat cream, sugar and egg yolks together until fluffy and well blended. Fit pan over simmering water and continue to beat until custard has thickened. Remove pan from lower container and continue beating lightly until custard has cooled to lukewarm. Then stir in dissolved gelatin and raspberry purée until thoroughly blended. Allow to cool until syrupy but not set, stirring occasionally to prevent a skin forming on top.

Beat egg whites until they form soft peaks and fold them into the cold raspberry custard. Crush macaroons to crumbs (in a plastic bag with a rolling pin is easiest) and fold them in as well.

Spoon mousse into a glass serving bowl and chill until quite set.

Serve decorated with swirls of whipped cream and a few whole raspberries.

Serves 6.

RASPBERRY ALMOND MERINGUE

This delicious dessert, with its unusual combination of flavors, uses frozen raspberries. Make sure they are unsweetened.

½ pound almonds
1 cup sugar
4 egg whites
Pinch of salt

Raspberry filling
¾ pound (2½ pints) frozen
    unsweetened raspberries
1–2 tablespoons sugar
1¼ cups whipping cream

Dampen a large baking sheet slightly and line it with a sheet of parchment paper marked with a circle 9 inches in diameter.

In an electric blender or food processor, grind the dry (unblanched) almonds finely. Mix thoroughly with the sugar. In a large, clean, dry bowl, beat the egg whites with a pinch of salt until stiff but not dry. Using a large metal spoon, gently but thoroughly fold in the ground almonds and sugar. Spread the meringue evenly over the circle marked on the parchment paper, building up the sides slightly.

Bake the meringue in a preheated 325° oven for 1 hour, or until it feels firm and dry when you touch it, and is lightly colored. Leave until cold, then peel off the paper and transfer the meringue case to a large, flat serving plate.

Take about a dozen of the best raspberries. Place them on a plate in a single layer and leave to thaw in the refrigerator. These will be used to decorate the meringue. Sprinkle remaining raspberries with sugar. Place them in a large sieve fitted over a bowl and leave to thaw in the refrigerator. Whip the cream until firm but not buttery.

Shortly before serving, assemble the meringue. Fill the case with thawed raspberries. Cover with whipped cream and decorate with remaining whole raspberries.

Serves 8–12.

RASPBERRY TART WITH CREAM

From Mrs Bowman's *New Cookery Book* (1867).

"Fill the tart-dish with fresh raspberries, and less than a quarter of the weight in fine sugar; cover with a thin paste; bake half or three quarters of an hour, according to size; take it out of the oven, raise the cover, beat up the yolks of two eggs well, and mix with half a pint of cream and a tablespoonful of sifted sugar; pour this over the fruit, restore the crust, and return it to the oven for five or six minutes. Strew sugar over the crust, and serve hot or cold."

RASPBERRY SAUCE

A simple, delicious sauce with a thousand uses. You can pour it over fresh strawberries, peaches and practically any other fruit, or serve it with ice cream.

1 pound (3 pints) fresh or thawed
frozen raspberries
Lemon juice
Confectioners' sugar

Rub raspberries through a fine nylon sieve and discard seeds. Beat in lemon juice and confectioners' sugar to taste (about 2 or 3 tablespoons of each) and chill lightly until ready to serve.

RASPBERRY JAM

Raspberries
Their weight in sugar

In a preserving kettle, over low heat, cook raspberries with sugar until sugar has dissolved and juices run, stirring and mashing frequently with a potato masher or a wooden mallet. Then raise heat and boil briskly until jell point is reached, skimming off scum until surface is clear.

Cool slightly. Pack into jars and process as usual.

See also page 198.

Note: To make a smooth jam free of seeds that is particularly useful for filling layer cakes, first heat the raspberries without sugar until the juices run and the berries are very mushy, then rub them through a fine sieve. Discard seeds, return purée to the pan and proceed as above.

RATAFIA DE FRAMBOISE
Raspberry Liqueur

Raspberries produce a rich, fruity, deep pink liqueur. Use firm, undamaged berries.

2 pounds (6 pints) ripe, fresh
raspberries
1½ quarts vodka
4 cups sugar

Pick over and wash the fruit, then crush the berries slightly. Pack into a large, wide necked, screw-top jar (a Kilner jar is ideal) and pour over the vodka. Seal the jar and leave to stand in a cool place for 1 month, shaking occasionally.

At the end of this time, make a syrup by dissolving the sugar in 2½ cups water and boiling for 15 minutes. Open the jar containing the fruit and alcohol and strain off the liquid through a fine sieve into a clean bowl, pressing the fruit to extract as much juice as possible. Stir the sugar syrup into the fruit liqueur. Bottle and leave for 6 months before drinking.

Makes about 3½ pints (2 litres).

RASPBERRY RED CURRANT JAM

The Victorian cookbook from which this recipe comes boasts that "the addition of the currant-juice is a very great improvement to this preserve".

To every pound (3 pints) of
raspberries:
2 cups sugar
¾ cup red currant juice (page 166)

In a preserving kettle, crush the raspberries to a pulp with a potato masher or a wooden spoon. Bring to boiling point slowly, raise heat and boil for 15 minutes. Stir in sugar and red currant juice, and when sugar has dissolved, continue to boil the jam for about 30 minutes longer, or until jell point is reached, skimming surface until it is free of scum.

Cool slightly, then pack into jars and process as usual.

See also page 198.

RASPBERRY ACID

The following recipe, written on a scrap of paper, was found acting as a bookmark in my copy of *The London Art of Cookery*, published in 1783. It can also be made with strawberries.

"Put 12 lbs of fruit into a pan. Pour over them 2 quarts of spring water previously acidulated with 5 oz of tartaric acid. Let them remain 24 hours then strain them taking care not to bruise the fruit. To each pint of clear liquor add 1 lb & a ½ of loaf sugar finely pounded, stir it frequently and when quite dissolved bottle the syrup. The whole process must be cold and the bottles kept uncorked for some days as the liquor generally ferments a little."

Exactly the same recipe, contributed by a Mrs Campbell of Inverneill, appears in *The Feill Cookery Book*, published in Glasgow in 1907. Mrs Campbell adds: "It is useful as a beverage mixed with water and also for flavoring creams and jellies."

RASPBERRY RHUBARB JAM

The recipe and method are exactly the same as for Raspberry Red Currant Jam, except that instead of red currants, 1½ pounds rhubarb stalks, trimmed and cut into 1 inch lengths, are used. The fruit need not be sieved or puréed unless the raspberry seeds are going to be very troublesome.

RED CURRANT, WHITE CURRANT

To all intents and culinary purposes, there is nothing to choose between red currants and white currants, except that the latter lack the red pigment and are possibly slightly sweeter. On the whole, however, both are too sour to eat raw on their own, rather like black currants, though they do not have the characteristic strong aroma of black currant fruit and leaves, which some people find unpalatable.

Red and white currants are native to the northern hemisphere. They have long been a cultivated garden fruit but will happily grow wild and produce fruit in woods and hedgerows, particularly near water. Unlike black currants, they do not need a rich soil.

Add red currants to fresh vegetable and fruit salads in small amounts – too many could make a dish too sharp. Sprays of glazed red currants, sparkling like precious stones, make an enchanting decoration for a bowl of fruit or a cake, a dessert or a fruit tart.

For many people, especially anyone who wears dentures, red currants have one great drawback. Their seeds are numerous, tiny and hard, and become even harder when the fruit is cooked. My mother tells the story of painstakingly seeding red currants one by one with a pin for many hours. At the end she had no more than a pot of preserves to show for her trouble – but they *were* unforgettable preserves. Even if you are not prepared to go to those lengths, it may still be worthwhile eliminating the seeds by rubbing the cooked fruit through a fine sieve. Failing that, console yourself with the thought that some people actually enjoy biting on the seeds!

Red currant jellies are traditional with roasts of lamb, poultry, and game birds. They also make an excellent glaze rather along the lines of an apricot glaze, for brushing over pastries, cakes and open fruit tarts.

Otherwise, you can dry or sugar-freeze red and white currants whole, juice them, or mix them with other fruit.

Red currants contain much less Vitamin C than black currants, but are also good for fevers.

RED CURRANT JUICE

Red currant juice diluted with water or soda water makes a delightfully refreshing drink, ideal for invalids and convalescents.

Rinse red currants, strip them from their stalks and put them in the top of a double boiler or in a heatproof jar or pitcher standing in a pan of simmering water.

Add enough water to show at the top of the currants. Heat steadily until juices have run from the fruit, mashing lightly once or twice with a fork. Then strain through a very fine sieve or a colander lined with cheesecloth, pressing lightly to extract as much juice as possible.

The juice can be used in water ices and for jellies. If you have made a large quantity, it is worthwhile bottling and sterilizing it (page 202) for storing.

RED CURRANT AND CARROT SALAD

A deliciously refreshing summer salad to serve with a plate of cold meat, or perhaps poultry. For the best effect, the fruit and vegetables should be garden-fresh.

¼ pound (½ pint) red currants,
stemmed and rinsed
4 large, crisp carrots, coarsely grated
2–3 teaspoons sugar
Juice of 1 lemon
Lettuce leaves for garnish

In a bowl, toss currants, carrots, sugar and lemon juice together until well mixed. Taste for flavoring.

Arrange in a bowl lined with crisp lettuce leaves and serve.

Serves 4–6.

Note: A few drops of light soy sauce may add a welcome accent, or some may prefer a little hot pepper sauce, to taste.

RED CURRANT AND HONEY FOOL

An unusual – but very successful – combination of flavors.

1 pound (2 pints) red currants,
stemmed and rinsed
⅓ cup honey
Sugar (optional)
1¼ cups heavy cream, whipped
Lemon juice

Put the red currants in a casserole with the honey and just enough water to moisten. Cook, covered, in a preheated 350° oven until red currants are tender.

Rub through a nylon sieve and add sugar if necessary.

Fold the purée into the whipped cream and flavor with lemon juice, to taste.

Spoon into individual glass dishes and chill well before serving.

Serves 4.

Austrian Red Currant Tart

One 8 or 9 inch rich pie pastry case, pre-baked (page 203).

Red currants
10–12 ounces (1½ pints) red currants, stemmed
¼ cup sugar

Meringue
2 egg whites
Pinch of salt
6–8 tablespoons sugar

Dissolve sugar in about ¾ cup water – or just enough to "take" red currants. Bring to boiling point, drop in red currants and simmer gently for a few minutes. Lift fruit out with a slotted spoon, draining thoroughly. Boil the syrup rapidly until it is well thickened.

Cool and pour over fruit.

When ready to assemble tart, make a meringue. Beat egg whites with salt until they form soft, floppy peaks when beaters are lifted. Gradually beat in half of the sugar and continue to beat until the meringue is stiff and glossy.

Fold in remaining sugar with a large metal spoon.

Spread the red currant mixture evenly over the tart shell and cover with meringue, spreading it right to the pastry rim to seal the filling in. Flick up the meringue decoratively all over with a knife blade.

Return tart to a preheated 325° oven and bake for 25–30 minutes, or until meringue is very lightly colored and feels crisp and firm. Serve lukewarm or cold.

Serves 4–6.

Red Currant Water Ice

2½ cups red currant juice (see opposite page and method)
1 cup sugar
Juice of ½ lemon
Confectioners' sugar (optional)
2 egg whites
Whipped cream and sweet wafer cookies for serving

Simmer at least 1 pound (2 pints) red currants, and strain juice as described in the recipe for Red Currant Juice on the opposite page.

Prepare sugar syrup by dissolving sugar in 2½ cups water. Bring to boiling point and simmer for 10–15 minutes, skimming off any scum that forms on the surface.

Stir in lemon juice and allow the syrup to cool.

Combine 2½ cups each red currant juice and sugar syrup, and adjust flavor with more sugar or lemon juice. Pour into ice cube trays or shallow plastic boxes, cover with foil or lids and place in the freezer.

Freeze until the water ice is solid around the edges. The time this takes will depend on the size of the containers and the depth of the ice mixture.

When ice is sufficiently frozen, beat egg whites until stiff but not dry. Scrape all the ice mixture (both frozen and liquid) into another bowl and beat vigorously with a whisk or fork to break down any large ice crystals and make the mixture smooth again. Fold into beaten egg whites.

Pour the mixture back into container(s), cover and freeze until firm, several hours; or leave overnight if preferred.

An hour before serving, transfer the container(s) to the refrigerator to allow the ice to soften just a little.

Serve the water ice with swirls of whipped cream (also frozen hard if liked) and/or accompanied by sweet wafer cookies.

Serves 8–10.

Rodgrod Med Flode Scandinavian Fruit Mold

A similar dish is prepared in Germany, where it is known as *Röte Grütze*. The Scandinavians serve it with cream, whereas the Germans prefer a cold custard sauce or simply milk. Any soft summer fruits may be used to make the pudding but the combination below is one of the best.

1½ pounds (3 pints) ripe red currants, stemmed
¾ pound (2½ pints) raspberries
About 1½ cups sugar
¾ cup cornstarch
1 teaspoon vanilla

In a large, enameled pan, cover the fruits with 2 cups cold water. Bring slowly to boiling point and simmer for about 10 minutes, or until fruits are very soft, stirring and mashing occasionally with a wooden spoon. Rub contents of pan through a fine nylon sieve.

Pour the purée back into the rinsed-out pan and sweeten to taste. Blend cornstarch smoothly with about 1 cup cold water. Stir it into the fruit purée and simmer, stirring, for 3–4 minutes until the pudding is thick and smooth, and has lost its cloudy appearance and its taste of raw starch. Cool slightly and flavor with vanilla.

Rinse a large (roughly 1½-quart) mold with cold water and shake away excess. Pour in the fruit mixture. Cool and chill until mold is firmly set, about 2 hours.

Loosen edges of mold with the tip of a knife. Invert onto a shallow serving dish and gently but firmly shake out the pudding. Serve accompanied by a pitcher of pouring cream, cold custard sauce or milk.

Serves 6.

Red Currant Jelly

Red currant jelly is a classic accompaniment for roast lamb and poultry, with a thousand-and-one other uses in the kitchen, for both savory and sweet dishes.

Prepare the red currant juice following the instructions on page 166. However, there is no need to stalk the fruit, and do not try to squeeze the juice through the jelly bag or cheese-cloth-lined sieve – simply leave it for as long as necessary.

Measure the juice and for each 2½ cups allow 2 cups of sugar. In a clean preserving kettle, combine the two. Heat gently until the sugar has dissolved. Then raise heat and boil until jell point is reached, skimming surface clear of scum with a large spoon.

Cool slightly, pack in small jars and cover.

See also page 199.

Eliza Acton's Red Currant Jelly

This recipe, which is entitled "Superlative Red Currant Jelly" in Eliza Acton's *Modern Cookery* of 1845, makes a fine, sharp jelly with the minimum of fuss and trouble. With the addition of lemon juice, it is a very easy way of making a few pots of jelly with red currants from the freezer (I have successfully used fruit that was over a year old). As Miss Acton claims, the jelly is "of the finest possible flavor," and it will set firmly provided the currants are not too ripe and the growing season has been a dry, sunny one. The timing is spot on for frozen as well as fresh fruit, but the latter does not need the help of lemon juice.

2 pounds (4 pints) frozen red currants
4 cups sugar
Juice of 1 large lemon

Put the frozen red currants in a bowl (after weighing them) and leave to thaw overnight. The following day, add sugar and with a potato masher or a large fork, mash lightly to burst the currants. Pour into a preserving kettle and bring to boiling point over a low heat, stirring and mashing constantly. Stir in lemon juice, raise heat and boil rapidly for exactly 8 minutes, by which time it will have reached jell point on a thermometer. Stir constantly and skim off any scum (there will be less with frozen fruit than with fresh).

Strain jelly through a fine nylon sieve, pressing seeds and skins against sides of sieve with the back of a large wooden spoon to extract as much jelly as possible. Pour hot into hot, sterilized jars and cover immediately. Leave until cold before storing. When it is cold, the jelly will be spoonable but not set rock hard.

See also page 199.

Cumberland Sauce

This is a spicy sauce for serving with poultry and game.

¼ pound (½ pint) red currants
¼ cup sugar
½ teaspoon finely chopped shallots
Juice and grated rind of ½ orange and ½ lemon
¾ cup port wine
½ teaspoon mustard powder
Pinch of cayenne
¼ teaspoon ground ginger

Wash the red currants thoroughly in a colander, under cold running water. Discard stalks and damaged berries. Put currants in a pan with ¾ cup water, and cook over a low heat to soften the fruit.

Strain off the liquid through a fine sieve into another pan. Put the fruit pulp in a linen bag. Seal the bag tightly and squeeze to extract as much juice as possible onto the liquid already in the pan. Stir in the sugar until dissolved. Cook over a low heat until syrupy.

Add the shallots, orange and lemon juices and rinds, the port, mustard, cayenne and ginger to the fruit syrup.

Mix together very thoroughly and serve hot or cold.

Red Currant and Mint Sauce

This is a variation of the traditional mint sauce for serving with cold roast lamb.

2 tablespoons red currant jelly
1 tablespoon finely chopped fresh mint
Juice and finely grated rind of ½ orange

Put the red currant jelly in a bowl and break it into small pieces with a wooden spoon. Add the chopped mint, orange juice and rind. Mix together thoroughly and chill before serving.

Glazed Red Currants

Egg white
Sprays of red currants
Sugar

Lightly mix the egg white with a fork, just enough to break down any gelatinous threads. Coat each spray. Allow excess egg white to drip off, then coat the wet sprays with sugar. Gently lay them on sheets of wax paper to dry for about 15 minutes before use.

Red Currant and Mustard Sauce

A German sauce to serve with ham and bacon.

2 tablespoons red currant jelly
½ teaspoon mustard powder
Red wine

Put the red currant jelly into a bowl and mash it with a wooden spoon until it has a smooth jam-like consistency. Stir in the mustard powder. Gradually add red wine until the sauce has the consistency of pouring cream. Serve hot.

RHUBARB

Rhubarb is a leaf stem or stalk botanically, but to the Western cook it is a fruit, and a grossly underrated one at that. In cool, damp climates, rhubarb will flourish like a weed – possibly one of the reasons why it has so often been treated with disdain. Not so in Asia Minor, one of the areas put forward as its original home (the other one is farther east, possibly in Tibet). Persian cooks have invented a variety of delicious *koreshtha* in which meats such as beef are partnered with rhubarb to make sharp, sour sauces for serving with rice.

Rhubarb is thought to have reached Europe in the fourteenth century. Europeans were interested in its medicinal properties but rather slow to exploit its culinary potential. They acknowledged its importance as the first fresh fruit of the year ("spring fruit" was one of the names by which it was known), but tended to think of it as a mere substitute for what was to come later. Rhubarb sauce was an excellent accompaniment to fatty fish such as mackerel, but abandoned for gooseberry sauce as soon as the berries came into season. The sweet rhubarb dishes that are so popular today – compotes, pies, betties and preserves – are comparatively late arrivals. Writing in the mid-Victorian period, Mrs Beeton describes rhubarb as a newcomer which was practically unknown twenty years earlier.

Look for stalks which are neither too thick, nor thin and spindly. They should be firm and full of juice, and snap crisply in two when you bend them. Another, more discreet way of testing is to puncture the stalk with your thumbnail. If it is fresh, the juice will run out. Avoid stalks that flop and are flabby – they are also stale – and any that are over-thick or split.

Rhubarb benefits from being partnered with other flavors, especially orange, and spices such as cinnamon and ginger. It goes well with most other garden fruit and can be used to bulk them out if necessary. Remember, though, that cooking quickly reduces it to a pulp and will have to be very brief indeed if you want pieces to retain their shape.

Unless the stalks are forced or very young, they are bound to have developed a few "strings," but these are easy to locate and strip away as you cut up a stalk. Do not risk leaving them as they can be unpleasantly pithy when cooked. To prepare rhubarb for most recipes, wash and trim the stalks, stripping off any strings or tough fibers. Chop the stalks into ½–1 inch lengths. However crisp and juicy the leaves may look, they must never be eaten as they contain poisonous oxalic acid.

To freeze rhubarb, wash, trim and chop the stalks and plunge into boiling water for a minute. It can be sugar frozen (and packed in plastic, not aluminum, bags) or frozen in a syrup made from equal quantities of sugar and water. Rhubarb purée can also be frozen.

Medicinally, rhubarb is still appreciated. Powdered rootstock in small doses will stimulate the appetite – rhubarb is an ingredient of several herb-based aperitifs popular in Europe – and larger doses are an effective laxative.

RHUBARB HAIR LIGHTENER

Simmer 3 tablespoons rhubarb root and 2½ cups water in a stainless steel pan for 30 minutes.

Leave to cool and steep for 6–8 hours, then strain.

Use as a rinse after shampooing, and leave the hair to dry naturally. You could use white wine instead of water which would be more expensive, but also good for the hair.

PERSIAN BEEF WITH RHUBARB SAUCE

An unusual combination of flavors.

¼ cup butter
1 Bermuda onion, finely chopped
1 pound boneless beef for stew, cubed
6–8 tablespoons chopped parsley, preferably flat-leaf
½–1 teaspoon grated cinnamon
⅛ teaspoon freshly grated nutmeg or ground mace
Salt and freshly ground black pepper
1 pound washed and trimmed rhubarb
1–2 tablespoons lemon juice
⅛ teaspoon sugar

Melt half the butter in a heavy casserole and sauté the onion gently until transparent and golden. With a slotted spoon, transfer onion to a plate. Brown the cubed meat on all sides in the same fat. Mix in the sautéed onion, parsley and spices, and season to taste with salt and freshly ground black pepper. Add barely enough hot water to cover. Bring to simmering point; cover and cook gently for 1½–2 hours, or until meat is very soft.

Meanwhile, cut rhubarb stalks into 2 inch lengths. In a skillet, sauté the rhubarb lightly in the remaining butter. Add lemon juice and sugar, and continue to sauté for 2 or 3 minutes longer.

When beef is tender, add the rhubarb mixture to the simmering casserole and simmer, covered, for 5–10 minutes longer until the rhubarb is very soft and on the point of disintegrating.

Serve with rice.

Serves 4–6.

Note: Either chicken or one of the "pale" meats such as pork or lamb can be substituted for the beef.

BAKED CHICKEN WITH RHUBARB SAUCE

Serve with a fluffy potato purée or a bowl of boiled or steamed Basmati rice. No other accompaniment is needed.

One 3 pound roaster chicken
2 tablespoons melted butter
Salt
½ teaspoon ground cinnamon
½ teaspoon ground mace

Rhubarb sauce
4 stalks rhubarb (about 10 ounces),
   washed and trimmed
5 tablespoons sugar, or to taste
⅛ teaspoon salt
1½ tablespoons cornstarch
1 tablespoon butter
Lemon juice

Cut up chicken. Wipe the pieces clean and fit them side by side, skin side up, in an ovenproof dish or roasting pan. Brush all over with melted butter and sprinkle with salt.

Roast in a preheated 375° oven for 30 minutes, turning pieces over twice during this time and basting them with pan juices.

Meanwhile, prepare rhubarb sauce. Chop rhubarb stalks, and put in a pan with sugar, salt and 1¼ cups water. Bring to boiling point, cover and simmer for a few minutes until rhubarb is disintegrating. Blend cornstarch smoothly with a little cold water. Stir into rhubarb and simmer, stirring, until sauce has thickened and is no longer cloudy, 2–3 minutes. Beat in butter and correct flavor of sauce with lemon juice and a little more sugar and salt if liked.

Spoon hot sauce over chicken pieces to cover them generously. (Any sauce left over may be served with the chicken in a separate sauceboat.) Sprinkle chicken with cinnamon and mace, and return dish to the oven for 20 minutes longer, or until chicken is quite tender, basting frequently with sauce.

Serve with rhubarb sauce and any buttery pan juices well mixed together and poured over the top.

Serves 4.

TRADITIONAL RHUBARB PIE

Maybe this is the reason why rhubarb used to be called the "pie plant" and rhubarb pie was often referred to as "pie plant pie."

It is delicious eaten lukewarm with fresh thick cream, ice cream or a vanilla-flavored custard sauce.

The exact amount of sugar the pie needs will depend on the time of the year — rhubarb generally tends to need less added sweetness as the season progresses.

1–1¼ pounds washed and trimmed
   rhubarb
About 1½ cups firmly packed light
   brown sugar (see above)
¼ cup flour
½–1 teaspoon finely grated orange
   rind
⅛ teaspoon salt
About 1 pound rough puff pastry
   for a 2-crust, 8–9 inch pie
   (page 203)
2 tablespoons butter
Sugar for decoration

Chop rhubarb stalks. In a large bowl, blend sugar thoroughly with the flour, grated orange rind and salt. Add rhubarb and toss until well mixed.

Roll out about half of the pastry and cut out a lid for your pie pan, leaving a slight overhang all around. Put aside. Roll out remaining pastry and use it to line the pie pan, again with an overhang of about ½ inch. Fill dish with prepared rhubarb and dot with flakes of butter. Moisten pastry rim with water. Place lid in position and press lightly all around edges with your fingertips to seal them.

Flute or crimp edges neatly and cut a few gashes in pastry lid to allow steam to escape.

Bake pie in a preheated 450° oven for 10–15 minutes. Then turn oven down to 350° and continue to bake pie for about 30 minutes longer, or until pastry lid is well puffed, crisp and richly colored. Cool to lukewarm with a dusting of sugar sprinkled over the top.

To serve, see above.

Serves 6–8.

CREAMY RHUBARB PIE

This is made in the same way as the Rhubarb Pie on the left, but instead of using ¼ cup flour, cut it to 2 tablespoons and blend in 2 large, well-beaten eggs. Mix with the sugar, grated orange rind and ⅛ teaspoon salt. Fill the pastry-lined pie pan with rhubarb, dot with butter and pour over the egg mixture.

Fit the pastry lid in position and continue as for Rhubarb Pie.

SPRING PUDDING

Adjust the amount of sugar to taste, depending on the acidity of the fruit and whether forced pink rhubarb or more mature stalks are used. This makes an excellent prelude to the summer pudding that will follow as soft fruits ripen.

1 pound washed and trimmed
rhubarb
About ½ cup sugar
Lemon juice (optional)
Stale white bread slices, about
¼ inch thick
Thick cream or custard sauce for
serving

Chop rhubarb stalks, and place in a pan with the sugar and 2 or 3 tablespoons water. Cover and stew gently until rhubarb is very soft but has not disintegrated completely. Cool slightly. Taste and add a little more sugar if necessary, or a squeeze of lemon juice if liked.

Meanwhile, trim crusts from bread slices. Cut a round to fit the bottom of the mold, then line the sides with fan-shaped pieces, butting them together as closely as possible. Spoon half of the rhubarb into the mold, followed by a layer of bread and the remaining rhubarb. Cover with another layer of bread. Cover with a flat plate that just fits inside the mold rim or with a thick cardboard template cut to measure and sealed in plastic wrap. Weight it down and chill for several hours or overnight if possible.

Unmold the pudding onto a shallow serving dish.

Serve with thick cream or a custard sauce.

Serves 6.

RHUBARB FOOL

A quick, simple dessert which allows the full flavor of rhubarb to come through, mellowed by cream. Young, pink rhubarb will need less sweetening and no stringing, whereas more mature stalks have a stronger flavor. Serve the fool accompanied by crisp, delicate cookies.

1½ pounds washed and trimmed
rhubarb
Twist of orange rind
About ½ cup sugar
Lemon juice
¾ cup heavy cream
¼ cup light cream or creamy
milk

Wash, prepare and chop rhubarb stalks, and put in a heavy pan with 2 tablespoons water and the twist of orange rind. Cover tightly and cook gently until rhubarb is pulpy and disintegrating, shaking pan occasionally. Remove the orange rind and either crush the rhubarb with a fork, purée it in an electric blender or rub it through a fine sieve. Sweeten to taste and sharpen flavor with a little lemon juice. The flavor should be quite pronounced as the cream is going to dilute it.

Leave until cold.

In a large bowl, whip the creams together lightly until thickened. Fold in the rhubarb and a little more sugar to taste if necessary. Chill well before serving.

Serves 4–6.

RHUBARB BETTY

Serve with cream, a custard sauce or plain yogurt sweetened with brown sugar.

1 pound washed and trimmed
rhubarb
⅔ cup firmly packed dark brown
sugar
1½ cups flour
1 teaspoon baking powder
6 tablespoons soft margarine or
butter

Chop rhubarb stalks, and put them in a large baking dish. Add half of the sugar and toss with a fork until well mixed.

Sift the flour and baking powder into a bowl. Rub in the margarine, not too finely, and stir in the remaining sugar. Stir 2 or 3 tablespoons of this crumb mixture into the rhubarb. Then spoon the remainder over the surface, distributing it evenly but without pressing it down.

Bake in a preheated 350° oven for 1 hour, or until the rhubarb feels soft when pierced with a skewer, and the topping is crisp and golden. This can be served hot, lukewarm or even cold.

Serves 4.

Note: For a slightly different flavor, topping mixture may be spiced with a teaspoon of ground cinnamon, sifted in with the baking powder.

RHUBARB WITH OAT CRUMBLE

Serve with a light custard sauce, chilled pouring cream or plain yogurt which you have sweetened lightly and into which you have folded a little whipped sweet cream, say a maximum of half and half.

1 pound washed and trimmed
   rhubarb
3 tablespoons dark brown sugar
3 tablespoons orange juice

Topping
1 cup rolled oats
1 teaspoon ground cinnamon
¼ cup soft margarine or butter
⅓ cup firmly packed dark brown
   sugar

Chop rhubarb and lay in a baking dish. Add sugar and orange juice, and mix with a fork until fruit is thoroughly coated.

Prepare topping. Mix oats with cinnamon. Work in margarine or butter (a large-tined fork will make this easy), then add sugar and continue to mash with the fork until all the ingredients are thoroughly mixed and crumbly.

Spoon the topping evenly over the fruit. Bake in a preheated 375° oven for 35–40 minutes, or until the topping is crisp and the fruit underneath feels soft when pierced with a fork or skewer. Cool slightly.

Serves 4.

RHUBARB COMPOTE

Easy, quick and cheap, but no less delicious for all that. Serve with cream or yogurt, or spooned over ice cream.

1 pound washed and trimmed
   rhubarb
⅔ cup firmly packed light brown
   sugar

Chop rhubarb.

Heat sugar in 1¼ cups water, stirring until sugar has dissolved, and bring to boiling point. Immediately add rhubarb, lower heat and bring to simmering point once more. Cook gently for a few minutes with the lid half-on, swirling pan around occasionally, until pieces of rhubarb feel soft when pierced with a fork or skewer but have not disintegrated too much or gone mushy. Draw off the heat, cover and cool.

Serves 4.

Note: You can change the flavor of the compote quite appreciably by boiling a piece of orange rind, either fresh or dried, with the sugar, or by spicing the syrup with a cinnamon stick and 2 or 3 cloves. Leave them in the compote until just before serving.

RHUBARB MERINGUE TART

One 8 inch rich pie pastry case, pre-baked (page 203)

Rhubarb filling
1 pound washed and trimmed
   rhubarb
Strip of lemon rind
Sugar
2 egg yolks, lightly beaten
2 tablespoons melted butter

Meringue topping
2 egg whites
Pinch of salt
½ teaspoon cream of tartar
¼ cup sugar

Leave the pastry case in its baking pan on a baking sheet.

Prepare rhubarb filling. Chop rhubarb stalks and put them in a pan with the strip of lemon rind and a few tablespoons of water – just enough to cover bottom of pan. Cover pan tightly and simmer until rhubarb is quite soft and disintegrating. Then remove lemon rind. Sweeten rhubarb to taste, beating vigorously with a spoon to reduce it to a purée.

Cool to lukewarm, then blend in lightly beaten egg yolks and melted butter.

Pour rhubarb filling into pastry case and bake in a preheated 350° oven until filling is set but not colored, about 20 minutes. Cool slightly.

Meanwhile, prepare meringue topping. Beat egg whites until white and foamy. Add salt and cream of tartar, and beat to soft peak stage. Then beat in sugar, a tablespoon at a time, and continue to beat to a stiff, glossy meringue.

Pile meringue on top of rhubarb filling, spreading it right to the pastry edge so that filling is completely sealed in. With a knife blade, flick up surface of meringue decoratively. Return tart to the oven for 15–18 minutes until meringue is set on the surface and tips of flicks are tinged with brown. Leave to cool and serve lukewarm.

Serves 6.

Note: If you like the meringue to be hard and crisp all the way through, put it in a much cooler oven (300°) to dry out for 45–60 minutes. In this case, you could beat another 2 tablespoons sugar into the meringue.

RHUBARB BURNT CREAM

1 pound washed and trimmed
   rhubarb
Finely grated rind and juice of 1
   orange
Dark brown sugar
¾ cup heavy cream
¾ cup plain yogurt

Chop rhubarb stalks, and put them in a pan with grated orange rind, orange juice and ⅓ cup dark brown sugar. Mix well, cover and cook gently until rhubarb is reduced to a pulp. Pour into a flameproof baking dish and allow to cool.

When ready to finish the dish, preheat broiler so that it will be thoroughly hot when you come to use it.

Whip cream just until it has thickened. In another bowl, beat yogurt until smooth. Beat yogurt lightly into whipped cream until mixture is thoroughly blended and very thick again. Pile cream mixture over cooled rhubarb, spreading it out evenly with the back of the spoon. Sift a thick, even layer of brown sugar over entire surface.

Place dish under broiler and broil steadily until sugar has melted to make a glassy coating for the cream. The broiler should be turned up high but watch that the sugar does not start to burn. Leave until quite cold and hard on top before serving.

Serves 4–6.

RHUBARB JAM

Green rhubarb stalks make a beautifully green jam, while the jam from red rhubarb is golden pink. In either case use thick, mature rhubarb, not thin, pink, forced stalks.

To every pound of washed and
    trimmed rhubarb:
    2 cups sugar
    Finely grated rind of ½ lemon

Chop rhubarb stalks, measure them and put them in a preserving kettle. Add sugar and grated lemon rind. The rhubarb may now be left overnight to allow sugar to draw out some of its juices. Or proceed immediately as follows. Place the pan over very low heat until sugar has dissolved, stirring frequently to prevent rhubarb or sugar scorching before the fruit has released some juice. Then boil over moderate heat until jell point is reached, skimming off scum and stirring frequently.

Cool slightly, pack and process as usual.

See also page 198.

RHUBARB PICKLE SAUCE

4 pounds washed and trimmed
    rhubarb
5 cups firmly packed dark brown
    sugar
1 teaspoon ground cinnamon
1 teaspoon ground cloves
1 teaspoon apple pie spice
½ teaspoon salt
½ teaspoon freshly ground black
    pepper
2½ cups white wine or cider vinegar

Wash, prepare and chop rhubarb stalks, and put in a pan (preferably enameled) with all the remaining ingredients. Mix well and heat gently until sugar has dissolved. Then simmer over moderate heat until rhubarb has disintegrated and sauce is thick, stirring frequently to keep sauce from burning.

Cool sauce and pour into clean, dry bottles or jars. Process as usual. See also page 200.

Fills about 5 jars.

RHUBARB AND GINGER PRESERVE

A good example of how inexpensive rhubarb makes an excellent foil for other more expensive ingredients such as ginger. Start the preserve the day before it is to be cooked so that the sugar has plenty of time to draw out juices from the rhubarb. It makes an unusual spread for warm, fresh scones and bread, as well as slices of buttered gingerbread.

2½ pounds washed and trimmed
    rhubarb
5 cups sugar
Juice and finely grated rind of 1 large
    lemon
A 1 ounce piece of fresh ginger root
3–4 ounces crystallized ginger

Chop rhubarb stalks. In a large bowl, layer rhubarb with sugar, lemon juice and rind. Cover bowl and leave overnight at room temperature.

The following day, tip contents of bowl into a preserving kettle. Bruise the piece of fresh ginger root thoroughly all over. Tie it up in a square of cheesecloth and drop it into pan. Over low heat, stir contents of pan frequently until sugar has dissolved and juices are running freely. Then raise heat and boil vigorously, stirring and mashing frequently with your spoon (or a potato masher) until rhubarb is very soft and pulpy, about 15 minutes.

Dice crystallized ginger finely. Remove bag of ginger root from pan, squeezing back as much of the juice from it as possible. Add the diced ginger to the pan. Stir well, bring to a vigorous boil once more and boil until jell point is reached, about 7–10 minutes longer. Toward the end of cooking time, skim surface clear of scum.

Cool slightly, pack and process as usual.

See also page 198.

Fills about 5 jars.

RHUBARB ORANGE JAM

If you grow your own rhubarb, this is a very good and economical way of using up mature stalks before they turn fibrous.

2 pounds washed and trimmed
    rhubarb
3 sweet oranges
Sugar

Chop rhubarb stalks, and weigh before putting them in a preserving kettle. Rinse and dry oranges, and finely grate off the rind, stopping short of the white pith, which can be unpleasantly bitter. Peel off and discard every scrap of skin and pith from oranges. Slice them thickly crosswise, carefully picking out seeds. Collect seeds in a small bowl. Chop up slices of orange, picking out any tough pieces of skin and adding them to the seeds. Cover seeds with ¾ cup boiling water and put aside for at least 30 minutes. Weigh orange pulp and juices.

Add grated orange rind, chopped pulp and juices to rhubarb, and mix well. Place pan over very low heat and cook slowly, stirring and mashing occasionally, until juices run and rhubarb is very soft and pulpy (contents will have reduced by about one-third).

Weigh out equivalent of rhubarb and oranges in sugar (original weight). Add to rhubarb. Strain in soaking water from seeds. Stir over low heat until sugar has dissolved, then raise heat and boil briskly until jell point is reached. Toward the end of cooking time, skim surface clear of scum.

Cool slightly. Pack and process as usual.

See also page 198.

Fills about 5 jars.

Note: Instead of using chopped orange pulp, you may find it simpler and quicker to squeeze the oranges after grating off their rind and cook the rhubarb with orange juice.

STRAWBERRY

The appearance of the first strawberries is a sure sign that summer has arrived. According to the writings of Ovid, Pliny and Virgil, they were already well known in the Roman world. Much later, it was recorded that Henry VIII of England had paid 10 shillings for a "pottle" of strawberries. But in spite of their obvious popularity, these fruits must have been rather miserable specimens compared with the cultivated ones we have today. Attempts were made to breed better strains, but the real breakthrough did not come about until the nineteenth century, when two species imported from the New World, *Fragaria chilensis* and *Fragaria virginiana*, met by accident in France. Since then, the strawberry has never looked back.

In addition to the usual garden varieties, there is also the alpine strawberry, a miniature plant that produces fruit throughout the summer. Although it has been cultivated for centuries, it has so far resisted all attempts to make it grow any bigger. Smallest of all are the wild strawberries which grow in grassy woods and fruit from the end of June to August; they have the sweetest and most highly flavored berries of all.

When buying strawberries, look for fresh, clean fruit with bright green hulls and stems. As with other soft fruits, avoid washing if possible. If necessary, clean them lightly as follows. Lay the berries in a single layer on a cloth wrung out in cold water, roll the cloth up loosely and shake gently. Any grit or dust is transferred to the damp cloth, leaving the fruit clean. As a last resort, wash strawberries by floating a single layer in a large bowl of cold water. Swish the water gently with your hand, leave it for a minute to allow any grit to sink to the bottom, then quickly transfer the fruit to a colander to drain. Strawberries should always be cleaned or washed before they are hulled.

The only accompaniments recognized by purists are thick, chilled pouring cream and a bowl of fine sugar. But instead of cream, try using some fruit juice such as orange, lemon or even lime. Alternatively, bathe the berries in a thick purée of fresh raspberries or macerate them in orange liqueur, a little port or sweet white wine. Champagne can be quite sensational.

Make the most of strawberries while they last. Apart from jams, which are a great favorite, they do not make particularly good preserves. Unless you like crunching the berries in a semi-frozen state, freezing can be disappointing as the fruit turns flabby and loses its brightness when thawed. To avoid this, use small to medium-sized berries and freeze them in a thick raspberry purée so that the juices which the strawberries release as they thaw automatically blend with the purée. Alternatively, crush the strawberries to a pulp before freezing them, ready to use in other recipes.

A final warning. Strawberries have little natural pectin so more will have to be added in the form of lemon or apple juice, or bottled pectin, if a jam is to set properly. This is especially important if frozen fruit is used.

Strawberries are both delicious and good for you. They are particularly high in Vitamin C and folic acid, and also have significant quantities of iron, calcium and phosphorus.

COSMETICS

Strawberries are universally recommended for the skin, especially the face. They have a mild astringent and bleaching effect, and are used in many masks and creams.

Masks made from strawberries cleanse and refresh the skin, reduce oiliness, and lighten freckles. Mash berries that are too over-ripe to serve, pat or smear them on your face, and leave on as long as possible.

Strawberry juice can also be used, on its own or with milk. Take a piece of linen or cotton roughly the size of your face, cut holes for eyes and mouth, soak it in the juice, wring out lightly and apply. As it dries, re-soak and re-apply.

FACE CREAM

This light, creamy but not greasy, cream softens and tones the skin.

Take 1 part lanolin, 3 parts oil (almond, avocado, peach or olive), and 2 parts strawberry juice. Melt the lanolin in the oil in the top half of a double boiler. Remove from the heat and add the strawberry juice gradually, beating all the time until cool.

To make a large quantity, substitute up to 10 per cent of the oil with wheatgerm oil, to preserve it. Add the contents of a Vitamin E capsule (200 I.U.) for extra nourishment.

REMEDIES

Fresh strawberries are excellent for invalids and have been recommended for sufferers from liver complaints, gout and rheumatism.

Strawberry leaves and roots are often used to make a tea: use 2 tablespoons to 2½ cups water. They can also be boiled in wine. This relieves diarrhea and dysentery, problems of the liver and of the urinary tract, and is recommended for heavy periods.

An infusion of strawberry leaves can be used as a mouthwash to strengthen gums and freshen the breath. It makes a good gargle for sore throats and canker sores (and can be used as a compress for sores anywhere).

The juice removes tartar from the teeth, and the leaves can be dried, powdered finely, sprinkled on a dry toothbrush and used, very effectively, as a toothpowder. The root may also be used; equal quantities of dried, powdered sage are a good addition. Brushing with this mixture stimulates and strengthens the gums.

WILD STRAWBERRY SOUP

These tiny "miniature" strawberries, which may either be cultivated or gathered in the wild, have so much sharp flavor of their own that they should be allowed to speak for themselves as much as possible. Serve this soup hot or cold.

1 pound (2 pints) wild strawberries
About ½ cup sugar
2 egg yolks
¾ cup thick cream
Lemon juice (optional)
Sugared croûtons (page 205) or
    puffed wheat cereal for garnish

Pick over and rinse strawberries if necessary. Mix them with the sugar and either purée in an electric blender or food processor, or crush to a purée with a fork.

Dilute with 1 quart cold water. Pour into a pan and heat gently, stirring to dissolve any remaining sugar.

Beat egg yolks lightly with cream. Beat in a few tablespoons of the hot, puréed soup. Pour back into pan of soup and stir constantly over low heat until it thickens. Take great care not to let it boil or egg yolks will curdle. Taste soup and add a little more sugar or a squeeze of lemon juice if liked. Soup may be served either hot or cold; if the latter, cool and chill it lightly first. Serve garnished with sugared croûtons or puffed wheat cereal.

Serves 6.

HONEYED STRAWBERRIES

For about 1½ pounds (6 pints) strawberries, which will serve 4–6, prepare the following syrup. In a wide saucepan, dissolve ¼ cup runny honey and 2 tablespoons sugar in ¾ cup water. (Use mild honey for this. A strong honey would get in the way of the flavor of the strawberries.) Add a strip of lemon rind and simmer for 5 minutes.

Add strawberries to the simmering syrup and cook gently for 5 minutes before switching off the heat. Allow to cool to lukewarm before serving.

STRAWBERRIES IN CREAM

1 pound (4 pints) ripe, even-sized
    strawberries, hulled
Finely grated rind and juice of 1 small
    sweet orange
4–6 tablespoons sugar
1 cup whipping cream
¾ cup plain yogurt

In a bowl, sprinkle strawberries with orange rind and juice, and a tablespoon of sugar, and mix lightly together.

Beat the cream until it is stiff but not buttery. In another bowl, beat yogurt lightly until smooth. Fold whipped cream into yogurt and sweeten with 3 tablespoons sugar.

Fold strawberries and their juices into cream mixture, making sure they are individually coated, and sweeten with a little more sugar to taste if necessary.

Spoon into a serving bowl and chill thoroughly before serving.

Serves 4–6.

STRAWBERRIES IN LIME CREAM SAUCE

1 pound (4 pints) strawberries
¼ cup fresh lime juice
About 2 tablespoons sifted
    confectioners' sugar

Lime cream sauce
3 egg yolks
½ cup sugar
1 cup light cream
Thinly peeled rind of ½ lime
½ cup heavy cream

Start by preparing the sauce. In the top of a double boiler (or a heatproof bowl that will fit snugly over a pan of simmering water), beat egg yolks and sugar together until fluffy. In a heavy pan, scald light cream with the lime rind, peeled off with a potato peeler. Off the heat, pour gradually into the egg yolks and sugar, stirring vigorously with a wooden spoon. Fit top of pan or bowl over simmering water and cook, stirring, until custard is thick enough to coat back of spoon. Take care not to let it boil, or egg yolks will curdle. Leave until quite cold, stirring occasionally to prevent a skin forming on top. Finally, remove and discard the strip(s) of lime rind. Shortly before serving, whip heavy cream until thick and fold in lime custard sauce. Chill lightly.

Clean strawberries on a damp cloth or rinse them briefly if necessary. Hull them and halve or quarter any large ones so that they are all of the same size. In a bowl, toss strawberries gently with lime juice and sifted confectioners' sugar, to taste. Cover bowl and chill lightly until ready to serve.

To serve, turn strawberries over in their juices once more and divide between 4 individual glass serving bowls. Spoon lime cream sauce over each bowl and serve immediately.

Serves 4.

STRAWBERRY MERINGUED CREAM

This is a glorious concoction of strawberries, cream and crushed meringues. For special occasions, flavor the cream with a little fruit liqueur – Grand Marnier, Kirsch or Framboise – or plain brandy. Alternatively, you can use just a little vanilla-flavored sugar.

2 pounds (8 pints) strawberries
About ½ cup confectioners' sugar
6 tablespoons fruit liqueur (optional, see above)
1¼ cups heavy cream, chilled
¾ cup light cream, chilled
6 meringues

Clean and hull strawberries. Pick out a dozen or so of the best specimens and put them aside for decoration. Chop remaining berries up roughly and put them in a bowl. Sift confectioners' sugar, to taste, over the top. Sprinkle with liqueur or brandy if used. Mix lightly, cover and chill for 1 hour.

In another bowl, combine creams and whip until they hold their shape in soft peaks. Gently but thoroughly fold in chopped strawberries and all their juices. In the palm of your hand, crush each meringue into large pieces, dropping them onto strawberry cream. Fold into cream. Taste and add more sugar if necessary.

Pile cream into a glass serving bowl, dot with reserved whole strawberries and serve.

Serves 6–8.

FRAGOLE DAMA BIANCA
Italian Strawberries with Meringued Cream

1½ pounds (6 pints) ripe, red strawberries
¼ cup orange liqueur
Sugar
2 egg whites
¾ cup heavy cream
½–1 teaspoon vanilla

Clean or wash strawberries. Drain off any excess moisture and hull them. In a serving bowl, mix strawberries lightly with liqueur and sweeten to taste with about 2 tablespoons sugar.

Cover bowl and chill thoroughly for about 3 hours.

About 30 minutes before serving, beat egg whites until they stand in soft peaks. Beat in 6 tablespoons of sugar, a little at a time, and continue to beat to a stiff, glossy meringue. In another bowl, using the same beaters, whip cream with vanilla until it is very thick and beginning to stand in soft peaks.

Fold meringue and cream together lightly until well blended.

Pile cream on strawberries and return bowl to refrigerator to chill lightly for 30 minutes.

Serves 6.

STRAWBERRIES JUBILEE

A strawberry spectacular to serve with luxury ice cream. It also works beautifully with frozen berries. Whichever you choose, the final stage is most effective when it is carried out at the table.

2 pounds (8 pints) strawberries, fresh or frozen
6–8 tablespoons sugar
¾ cup Kirsch or Maraschino liqueur
About 1 quart ice cream

If using fresh berries, clean and hull them, keeping them as dry as possible. Sweeten to taste with sugar and put aside for 30 minutes.

Frozen berries should be sweetened according to whether they were packed with sugar or not, and allowed to thaw only to the stage where they are still very chilly and remain firm to the touch.

When the ice cream has been unmolded, ready to serve, bring the liqueur to haze point in a wide, shallow pan. Have a long match ready. Keeping the heat under the pan high, tip in the strawberries and shake them around in the hot liqueur until the juices have evaporated sufficiently for the alcohol to ignite. Let the flames get a good hold.

Tip the flaming contents of the pan over the ice cream and serve the dessert at once.

Serves 6–8.

SOYER'S STRAWBERRY SALAD

From Alexis Soyer's *Shilling Cookery for the People* (1855).

"A large pottle (basket) of ripe strawberries, picked (ie hulled) and put into a basin with two tablespoonfuls of sugar, a pinch of powdered cinnamon, a gill of brandy (or a few tablespoons liqueur, wine or fruit juice); stir gently, and serve.

"Currants and raspberries the same."

STRAWBERRY AND CURRANT SALAD

From Mrs Bowman's *New Cookery Book* (1867).

"A pretty dessert dish may be made of mixed early fruits, strawberries, white or red currants, gooseberries and cherries, all carefully picked, placed in alternate layers strewed with sugar, and piled up with taste. Either simple cream, or wine or brandy cream, should be poured over the salad."

FRESH STRAWBERRY TART

A tart made with fresh strawberries is quick and easy to make and always delicious.

Make a tart shell with a rich pie pastry (page 203) and when it is cool fill it with strawberries. Pack them tightly together with the pointed ends up. Make a glaze by melting ⅓ cup smooth strawberry jam with a little water. Strain the liquid, allow it to cool slightly, then spoon it over the fruit.

FRENCH STRAWBERRY ICE CREAM

1 pound (4 pints) ripe, red
strawberries
Juice of 1 lemon
About 1 cup sugar
¾ cup heavy cream
Red food coloring (optional)
Whole strawberries or fresh puréed
raspberry sauce for serving

Clean and hull strawberries. In an electric blender or food processor, blend strawberries to a smooth purée.

Blend in lemon juice, followed by enough sugar to give purée a strong, sweet flavor. (Remember that freezing will modify flavors, so use more lemon juice or sugar if necessary.)

In a bowl, whip cream until it thickens and begins to hold its shape softly. Gradually beat in strawberry purée. Add the food coloring at this stage if necessary.

Pour into ice cube trays or a shallow plastic box. Cover with foil or a lid and freeze until ice cream has congealed around sides but is still soft and creamy in the middle.

Scrape mixture into a bowl and beat vigorously until uniformly smooth and creamy once more.

Pour back into container(s). Cover and freeze until firm.

Transfer to refrigerator for about 1 hour to soften very slightly before serving.

Serve the ice cream with fresh whole strawberries, lightly sugared if necessary, or masked with a purée of fresh raspberries.

Serves 4–6.

STRAWBERRY AND RASPBERRY ICE CREAM

Prepare as above, using ½ pound (2 pints) each strawberries and raspberries, and rubbing purée through a nylon sieve before sweetening it.

STRAWBERRY AND RED CURRANT ICE CREAM

Prepare as above, using ½ pound (2 pints) each strawberries and red currants, and rubbing purée through a nylon sieve before sweetening it.

HOT STRAWBERRY SAUCE

Use over-ripe fruit which is no longer quite suitable for serving fresh for this sauce which is delicious poured over fresh fruit, ice cream or a sponge pudding.

1 pound (4 pints) very ripe
strawberries
1½ cups sugar
3 tablespoons Kirsch

Clean and hull strawberries, and wash thoroughly in a colander under cold running water. Make a purée by mashing the fruit with a fork or potato masher (or, ideally, use an electric blender). Leave the purée on one side.

In a thick-bottomed saucepan, heat the sugar and 1¼ cups water, stirring frequently, until boiling. Lower the heat and simmer, stirring occasionally, for about 20 minutes until the syrup thickens slightly. Leave to cool for a few moments before stirring in the strawberry purée and mixing thoroughly.

Just before serving, heat the mixture to desired temperature (do not boil). Remove from the heat, and stir in the Kirsch.

COLONIAL STRAWBERRY SHORTCAKE

A biscuit filled with fresh strawberries and eaten warm with cream may not sound very exciting – more a way of spinning out the precious fruit – but this American favorite is remarkably good.

2 cups flour
1 tablespoon baking powder
⅛ teaspoon salt
2–3 tablespoons sugar
6 tablespoons butter or
shortening
¾ cup light cream or
creamy milk

To finish
Softened butter
1½–2 pounds (6–8 pints)
strawberries
Sugar
Lemon juice (optional)
Lightly whipped cream

To make shortcake, sift flour, baking powder, salt and sugar into a bowl. Using your fingertips or 2 knives, work in butter or shortening until mixture resembles fine bread crumbs. Then, stirring with a knife blade, gradually pour in enough cream or milk to make a very soft dough that holds together. Turn it out onto a floured board and knead very briefly (literally, a few times only). Pat dough out into an 8 inch circle and place it on a buttered baking sheet, or fit it into a well-buttered layer cake pan that is 8 inches in diameter. Dot or spread surface with a tablespoon of softened butter.

Bake shortcake in a preheated 450° oven for about 15 minutes until it is well risen and nicely browned on top.

While shortcake is baking, clean and hull strawberries. Halve or slice half of them thickly, depending on size. Crush the remainder lightly with a fork. Sweeten the two portions of fruit with a little sugar and if liked add a few drops of lemon juice.

When shortcake is ready, unmold it onto a cooling rack until it is just cool enough to handle. Then with a serrated knife, carefully split it in two horizontally. Spread cut surfaces generously with more softened butter.

Lay bottom half of shortcake, buttered side up, on a serving dish and cover with crushed strawberries and their juices. Cover with the other piece of shortcake, buttered side down.

Pile sliced or halved berries on shortcake and top with a generous dollop of lightly whipped cream. Serve while still fresh and warm.

Serves 4.

Frogmore late Pine.

Frogmore late Pine.

Sir Joseph Paxton.

Vicomtesse Hericart de Thury.

CHOCOLATE STRAWBERRY CANDIES

These take both time and patience, so make a large batch in mid-summer when the fruit is plentiful and cheap. Box some as a gift or serve with coffee after a special meal.

2 pounds (8 pints) fresh, ripe
  strawberries
3 cups sugar
1 pound semisweet cooking
  chocolate

Clean and hull the strawberries, and wash in cold water, discarding any damaged berries. Purée by mashing or in an electric blender. Place the purée in a thick-bottomed saucepan. Stir in the sugar. Cook over a low heat, stirring constantly with a wooden spoon until the mixture is thick enough for a clean line to be left on the bottom of the pan when a spoon is drawn across it. Remove the pan from the heat.

Grease a large baking sheet. Distribute the strawberry mixture in little mounds – about 1 heaping teaspoon of mixture in each – on the baking sheet. Leave to set.

When each strawberry sweet is firm to touch, prepare the chocolate coating. Break the chocolate into small pieces and place in a bowl that will fit securely over a pan with hot water in it, without the water touching the bottom of the bowl.

Cover the bowl, and let the chocolate melt, stirring occasionally with a wooden spoon. When the chocolate has melted completely, beat until it is smooth and creamy. Place a sugar thermometer in the chocolate and leave it until the temperature has fallen to 110°. At this temperature the chocolate should be of the right consistency for coating. A small amount picked up on a finger should set immediately.

Place the sheet of strawberry sweets next to the bowl of chocolate. Line another, similar size, baking sheet with wax paper and place this on the other side of the bowl of chocolate. Drop the sweets, one at a time, into the chocolate. Use a fork to submerge and turn them. When well coated, lift out on the fork, tapping it on the side of the bowl to remove excess chocolate. Hold the fork over the tray lined with wax paper and angle the fork so that the chocolate candy rolls off. Make sure the candies are well spaced. Leave for several hours until the chocolate is completely hard. Store between pieces of wax paper in an airtight container.

STRAWBERRY PRESERVE

If this preserve is properly made, the strawberries remain whole, suspended in a clear, rosy syrup. The secret lies in never, at any point, stirring the fruit with a spoon which could bruise or mash the berries. Instead, lift the whole preserving kettle by the handle, using both hands, and swirl the contents around gently. This will keep the jam well "stirred" as it cooks, and also make all the scum collect at one point, where it can easily be skimmed off. Use firm, slightly under-ripe strawberries. Medium-sized are best.

3 pounds (12 pints) strawberries
6 cups sugar
Juice of 1 large or 2 small lemons,
  strained

Clean the strawberries if necessary and hull them. Lay them in a large, shallow dish and cover them evenly with 4 cups of sugar. Leave until the following day to allow sugar to draw out as much juice as possible.

Next day, pour off strawberry juices into a preserving kettle, together with as much of the sugar as possible. Add the remaining 2 cups of sugar. Place pan over low heat until all the sugar has completely dissolved, stirring frequently.

Bring the syrup to a boil and slide in the strawberries all at once. Bring to boiling point again and boil until strawberries are nearly ready and turning translucent, swirling pan around frequently and skimming off the scum with a large spoon as necessary (see above).

Then add the lemon juice and boil the jam until jell point is reached, shaking the pan frequently. Pack into jars and process as usual.

See also page 198.

Fills about 5 jars.

Note: For a special luxury strawberry preserve, dip the hulled end of each strawberry into a saucerful of brandy as you prepare them. This is a favorite Middle Eastern trick.

STRAWBERRY VINEGAR

This is a delicious accompaniment to hot sponge puddings and an unusual syrup for fresh fruit salads.

1 pound (4 pints) strawberries
2½ cups white wine vinegar

Put the strawberries and vinegar in a glass or china bowl. Cover with a clean cloth and leave for about 4 days. Stir the mixture occasionally.

Strain through a sieve and measure the liquid. For each 2½ cups allow 1½ cups of sugar. Combine the two in an enamel or stainless steel pan. Bring to a boil, stirring until the sugar has dissolved, and continue boiling for 10 minutes longer.

Pour into hot bottles and process as usual.

See also page 202.

SHERRIED STRAWBERRIES

2 pounds (8 pints) fresh, ripe strawberries, cleaned and hulled
¾–1 cup sugar
Sherry wine

Put alternate layers of strawberries and sugar in a wide-necked jar, filling the jar right up to the top. Pour in the sherry until the fruit is covered. Do this very slowly so that no air bubbles are formed.

If any bubbles remain trapped in the jar, release them by slipping a flat knife blade down the side of the jar. Be careful, though, not to pierce the fruit while doing so.

Seal tightly and store.

STRAWBERRY WINE

Making this sweet fragrant wine is an excellent way of using up the excess of fruit after a good harvest.

3 pounds (12 pints) ripe strawberries
1 pound ripe bananas
3 cups raisins, chopped
½ ounce citric acid
1 teaspoon pectic enzyme
1 Campden tablet
Madeira wine yeast
8 cups firmly packed light brown sugar

Clean and hull the strawberries and wash thoroughly under cold running water. Peel the bananas and chop coarsely.

Heat 4 quarts water to boiling point in a preserving kettle. Put all the fruit including the raisins in a plastic pail and mash well together. Pour the hot water over the fruit, cover and allow to cool to 65°. Then quickly stir in the citric acid, pectic enzyme and Campden tablet. Cover the vessel. Leave for 24 hours.

Quickly stir in the activated yeast (see manufacturer's instructions for quantity and method of use). No nutrient tablet is necessary in this recipe. Re-cover the pail and leave in a warm place (65–75°) for 6 days.

During this time, stir the mixture once a day to make sure the fruit is kept moist.

Using a fine sieve, strain off the liquid into a clean, sterile container. Put the fruit pulp into a linen bag. Seal the bag and squeeze out as much juice as possible into the strained liquid. Stir in the sugar. Quickly siphon into a fermentation vessel, filling to within 1 inch of the cork. Ferment in a warm, dark place (65–75°) under an air-lock. This will take about 4 weeks. When a deep layer of sediment has formed on the bottom of the vessel, rack until clear.

Store the wine in a dark place for 6 months, then bottle. Leave for 2 years before drinking.

See also page 205.

Makes 4½ quarts.

CHAMPAGNE COCKTAIL

6 strawberries
1 orange, peeled and sliced
3 tablespoons sugar
3 tablespoons lemon juice
¾ cup Cognac
1 bottle Champagne, well chilled

Chop the strawberries and orange very finely.

Sprinkle with the sugar and pour the lemon juice and Cognac over the fruit.

Chill the mixture for a minimum of an hour.

Immediately before serving, divide the mixture between 6 chilled champagne glasses. Fill the glasses with Champagne and serve.

Serves 6.

TANGERINE

The tangerine takes its name from Tangiers, and is thought to have reached Southern Europe from there. Its other common name, the mandarin (from the French *mandarine*), gives a clue as to its original cultivation in China and the Far East, where its delicately perfumed flowers are still used in scent-making. Like its close relatives the Japanese-sounding satsuma and the smooth-skinned clementine, the tangerine has a characteristic and inimitable flavor, and a loose skin that is quickly and easily peeled away. It is deliciously juicy, easy to segment and in today's highly bred versions even the few large seeds it may have come as a surprise. Fresh tangerines should weigh well in the hand, have a sheen on the skin and a good, bright color. Any signs of shrunken skin or spots of brown mean they've been on their way to market longer than is good for them.

Tangerines are fit companions for any other fruit in a salad and, because of their relatively low acid content, can be enjoyed by people with delicate digestions or sensitive stomachs. Their one drawback – often shared by the smaller satsumas – is that the tough white pith and membrane can be difficult to strip away before eating. To deal with this, carefully dip the segments into a bowl of almost-boiling water to soften the membrane for a few seconds. It should then be easy to release the flesh without breaking up the delicate juicy portions. Tangerines or mandarins take well to canning, while satsumas, being seedless, are ideal dessert fruits.

Tangerine skins are aromatic and full of oil. Extract this in the usual way by rubbing the wiped skin with a couple of cubes of sugar, then crush these and add them to the syrup for a fruit salad or sherbet. The skins of the larger varieties make effective containers for ices or sherbets made from citrus fruits, and can also be cut into strips and candied for use in cakes.

Tangerines can be used in any recipe which calls for oranges and freeze well for up to a year in a cold sugar syrup made from 1 cup sugar to 2½ cups water; peel and segment them, and remove membrane.

SMOKED TANGERINE CHICKEN

This Chinese method of preparing chicken calls for a large steamer. Star anise, an essential ingredient, is the dried star-shaped fruit of an evergreen tree, native to China. It can be bought in specialist Chinese food stores.

3 pound roaster chicken
1 tablespoon soy sauce
1 teaspoon salt
1 teaspoon white sugar
1 tablespoon sherry wine
Peel of 1 tangerine, sliced and dried
1 whole star anise
3 tablespoons brown sugar
Fresh coriander leaves (optional)

Wash the chicken, inside and out. In a large bowl, big enough to hold the chicken, mix a marinade of the soy sauce, salt, the white sugar and sherry. Place the chicken in the bowl and rub the marinade all over its inside and outside. Leave for 20 minutes. Then heat some water in the bottom half of a large steamer. Put the chicken in the top part and steam for 15 minutes.

Using a pestle and mortar or an electric grinder, grind the tangerine peel and star anise together as finely as possible. Mix this powder with the brown sugar. Take a large heavy casserole or pan, with a tightly fitting lid, and line with foil. Sprinkle the tangerine, anise and sugar mixture over the foil. Then place a trivet or wire rack in the casserole or pan and put the steamed chicken on this. Cover tightly.

Place the casserole or pan on a medium heat. When smoke starts to escape from under the lid, turn the heat down very low and allow the chicken to smoke for 20 minutes, until tender. Remove the pan from the heat, and allow to cool with the lid on. Then uncover and remove the chicken. Serve cold, with chicken slices arranged on a serving platter. Garnish with coriander leaves.

Serves 4.

HAND CREAM

Put some Vaseline (or any unscented cream like cold cream) into the top half of a double boiler. Add twice its weight of tangerine flowers and simmer for an hour, making sure the flowers are pressed into the cream. Strain.

CITRUS AND SYRUP DESSERT

This is a charming and quite unusual dessert. You can substitute any other small, thin-skinned citrus fruits such as mandarin oranges or clementines for the satsumas, or even kumquats, which are related to them, but satsumas are best because you can rely on them being seedless.

The fruits, glistening in their syrup, make an enchantingly pretty decoration for many other desserts, ranging from simple, light creams and cold, molded rice puddings to yeast savarins and babas which have been saturated with some of the poaching syrup. Alternatively, pile them up in a pyramid in a glass dish, coat them with syrup, dust the pyramid with finely chopped green pistachio nuts, and serve the satsumas with plenty of unsweetened thick cream or portions of vanilla ice cream. Serve with dessert knives and forks as well as spoons.

1 pound satsumas (about 6)
1 cup sugar

Rinse the satsumas. In a heavy pan into which the satsumas fit comfortably in one layer, dissolve the sugar in 1¼ cups water and simmer for a few minutes to make a syrup. Lower satsumas into it and adjust heat so that the syrup is barely simmering. Cook satsumas very gently for an hour or so until their skins are very soft and easily pierced with a skewer. Keep turning the satsumas over to ensure that they cook evenly, and after the first 30 or 35 minutes, pierce each fruit deeply in several places with a fork so that it absorbs plenty of syrup.

Cool in the syrup and chill lightly before serving.

Serves 6.

TANGERINES IN RUM AND CARAMEL SAUCE

This excellent, light winter dessert is very simple to prepare.

1 cup sugar
10 large tangerines
⅓ cup dates, pitted
½ cup chopped walnuts
2 tablespoons dark rum
Unsweetened whipped cream

Place half the sugar in a thick-bottomed saucepan and heat gently until it melts, stirring occasionally to prevent burning. When it is deep brown and bubbling, gradually stir in 2½ cups water. Do not lean over the pan, as this mixture will spit and bubble when the water is first added. When the bubbling has ceased, stir in the remaining sugar. Allow to boil and then simmer over a moderate heat, stirring frequently, until the syrup thickens.

Remove pan from the heat and leave to cool.

Peel the tangerines, removing any pith, and divide into segments (discard any seeds). Arrange the tangerine segments in a shallow glass serving dish. Chop the dates into small pieces and scatter these and the chopped nuts over the tangerines.

When the caramel is cool, stir in the rum. Mix well and pour this sauce over the fruit and nuts in the glass dish. Chill in the refrigerator for 30 minutes before serving with unsweetened whipped cream.

Serves 4.

TANGERINE SALAD

This is a good alternative to mince pie at Christmas – rich but light, and refreshing.

4 large tangerines
2 large ripe pears
Juice of 1 large lemon
¾ cup heavy cream
¼ cup finely chopped preserved
*   ginger*

Peel the tangerines, and remove the pith. Divide into segments (removing the seeds) and arrange in the center of a flat serving dish.

Peel the pears and cut into thin slices, removing the core. Arrange the slices on top of the tangerines. Sprinkle with the lemon juice.

Whip the cream in a small bowl until stiff. Spoon or pipe all around the edge of the pile of fruit. Decorate with the chopped ginger, and chill in the refrigerator for at least 1 hour.

Serves 4.

TANGERINE PRESERVE

2 pounds tangerines
2 thin-skinned lemons
4 cups sugar
Pat of butter or margarine (optional)

Quarter the tangerines and lemons. Pick out all the seeds with the point of a knife. Tie seeds in cheesecloth and put them in a preserving kettle with about 2½ cups water.

On a plate or board to catch all the juices, shred the fruit finely with a sharp knife. Add them to the pan and simmer, together with the seeds, until the peels are tender.

Stir in the sugar and heat gently, stirring frequently, until sugar has dissolved. Then boil hard until jell point is reached. Skim scum from the surface as it accumulates and, if necessary, stir in a pat of butter at the end of cooking time to clear the preserve completely.

Pack and process as usual.
See also page 198.

Fills about 4 jars.

WALNUT

Walnuts – dark, rich and unmistakable in flavor – were reputed to have been the favorite nut of the gods of ancient mythology. The magnificent, spreading deciduous trees with their rippling leaves and silvery gray bark are grown for their looks alone in parks and gardens all over the world. Though apparently native to southwest Europe and central Asia, walnut trees are cultivated commercially in Italy, France, Germany and California. To the French, a walnut is simply *le noix*, the nut, but we have aptly added the prefix *wal-* meaning "foreign."

Walnuts, shelled or unshelled, broken in pieces or halved, are readily available all year around. Many are kiln-dried in their shells to improve their keeping qualities and this process, together with the brown outer husk around the kernel, can make them taste bitter. If you blanch the whole nuts, without their shells, in boiling water for a minute or two, the brown husk will easily peel off.

Walnuts are rich in oil and protein and in France, particularly in the sunny south, their oil is a characteristic flavoring in salad dressings. It is very strongly flavored and though far from cheap, very little is needed. (It will also remove white heat marks from the tops of polished tables, but try rubbing those with halved nuts and keep the oil for cooking.) Whole walnuts can be picked and pickled while still green, before the hard shells have had time to form. Serve pickled walnuts with cold roast meats and poultry; once again, a little goes a long way. Walnuts are a deliciously different ingredient in soups, and also combine well with fish and poultry. The Italians scatter them over pasta and toss them with garlic, oil and parsley, while the Poles glaze halved nuts in a rich sugar syrup.

Walnuts are highly nutritious, and rich in Vitamin C when green.

MEXICAN WALNUT SOUP

1 potato, peeled and diced
1 quart chicken broth
6–8 tablespoons finely chopped
*   walnuts*
¾ cup light cream
Salt and freshly ground black pepper

In a saucepan, simmer potato in broth until soft, about 20 minutes.

Stir in walnuts and continue to simmer for 10–15 minutes longer. Stir in cream and season as necessary with salt and freshly ground black pepper.

Reheat soup without allowing it to boil again and serve immediately.

Serves 6.

REMEDIES

Walnuts are recommended for a variety of complaints from gout to eczema, diabetes to loss of virility.

Traditionally, a paste made from crushed, stale walnuts was applied to wounds or sores to prevent infection and help healing.

·HAIR TREATMENTS

Walnut oil, rubbed into the hair, will help cure split ends and is also good for dandruff.

Decoctions or infusions made from unripe green shells, the leaves or bark will dye hair brown or black — and are good for scalp and hair.

BALKAN TARATOR SOUP

1 quart plain yogurt
1 medium-size cucumber
Salt
Finely chopped fresh dill or parsley
*   for garnish*

Walnut paste (tarator)
¼ pound (about 1½ cups shelled
*   walnuts*
2–3 plump, fresh cloves garlic
3 tablespoons olive oil

Start by preparing the walnut paste. Whirl walnuts to a purée in an electric blender or food processor, or pound them in a mortar. Crush in the garlic cloves and continue to purée until well blended.

Beat in the olive oil a little at a time to make a thick, creamy paste.

In a large bowl, beat the yogurt until smooth together with 6–8 tablespoons ice-cold water.

Dilute the walnut paste with a few tablespoons of the yogurt to start with, then blend the two together very thoroughly.

Peel the cucumber. Cut it in half lengthwise and if the seeds are large, scrape them out with the tip of a small spoon. Cut the cucumber into small cubes and stir them into the soup. Season to taste with salt. Cover the bowl and chill the soup thoroughly. Serve garnished with finely chopped dill or parsley.

Serves 6.

TROUT WITH WALNUT SAUCE

Just as the French have created trout with almonds, so the Georgian Russians are famous throughout the Middle East for cold poached trout with walnut sauce.

4 trout, about ½ pound each,
*   cleaned*
Salt
3 black peppercorns
2 allspice berries
1 small bay leaf
2–3 tablespoons wine vinegar
Sprigs of parsley and fronds of fresh
*   dill for garnish*
1 lemon, cut in wedges

Walnut sauce
¾ cup shelled walnuts
1 tablespoon wine vinegar
Reserved fish broth
1 tablespoon each finely chopped
*   fresh dill and parsley*
Salt and sharp (hot) paprika

Wash the fish thoroughly both inside and out. Pat off excess moisture with paper towels and gently rub fish all over with salt.

Half-fill a wide, shallow pan, preferably one which will take all the fish flat in at most two layers, with water. Bring it to boiling point with salt, peppercorns, allspice berries, and the bay leaf, and simmer for a few minutes. Stir in wine vinegar. Slip fish into simmering water, making sure they are just covered, and simmer for about 15 minutes, or until flesh can be prised away from backbone with a fork. Allow fish to cool to lukewarm before lifting them out of pan. Reserve fish broth.

Cool fish completely. Then carefully remove skins, leaving heads and tails intact. Arrange them side by side on a serving platter. Decorate with parsley and dill. Garnish with lemon wedges and serve with a bowl of walnut sauce.

To make sauce, pound walnuts to a creamy paste in a mortar, or whirl in an electric blender or food processor. Blend in vinegar and enough fish broth to give sauce a thick pouring consistency. Add finely chopped dill and parsley, a little more salt if necessary and a good pinch of hot red paprika, to taste. Chill lightly and serve in a separate bowl with cold trout.

Serves 4.

ÇERKEZ TAVUĞU
Circassian Chicken with Walnut Sauce

One of the finest dishes from the *haute cuisine* of the Ottoman Empire.

1 small roaster chicken, about 3
*   pounds*
1 large onion, quartered
1 large stalk celery, cut into chunks
1 medium-size carrot, cut into
*   chunks*
Salt
1 bay leaf
3–4 black peppercorns
2 allspice berries
2½ cups broken walnut kernels
3 slices day-old white bread
Sharp or sweet paprika
Finely chopped parsley
*   for garnish*

Wash chicken and fit it into a large kettle. Surround it with pieces of onion, celery and carrot. Sprinkle with a good teaspoon of salt, throw in the bay leaf, black peppercorns and allspice berries, and pour in water to cover chicken. Bring slowly to boiling point and simmer for 50 minutes, or until chicken is tender but not disintegrating.

Draw pan from heat. Skim surface clear of scum and leave chicken to cool in stock. When cold, remove chicken and strain stock through a sieve into a bowl. Allow stock to 'settle', then skim off fat and any remaining scum from surface once more.

Skin chicken and remove meat from bones. Dice meat and put aside in a covered bowl (to prevent it drying out) until needed.

Put walnuts twice through the fine blade of a meat grinder into a bowl. Each time, press the nut "meal" firmly with the back of a metal spoon to extract any oil, and pour it off into a cup. Reserve this walnut oil.

Trim bread slices of crusts, soak them in a little of the chicken stock and gently squeeze out excess. Shred bread into bowl of walnuts. Mix them together with a generous pinch of paprika and put the whole through the meat grinder once more to blend ingredients thoroughly. With a wooden spoon, gradually work in enough chicken stock to make a thick, creamy sauce. Correct seasoning with a little more salt or paprika, if liked.

Gently mix diced chicken into sauce. Arrange in a serving bowl. Garnish with chopped parsley and sprinkle with reserved walnut oil. Serve cold with a selection of salads and chunks of fresh bread.

Serves 4–6.

CHINESE WALNUTS AND PEPPERS

This dish is intended to be served as part of a Chinese meal, but is delicious with almost any plain roasted or broiled meat or poultry.

1/4 pound (about 1½ cups) shelled
    walnut halves
1 sweet green pepper
1 sweet red pepper
1 small mild onion
2 tablespoons cider vinegar
2 tablespoons sugar
2 tablespoons tomato catsup
1 tablespoon soy sauce
½ teaspoon salt
Peanut or corn oil for frying
1 teaspoon cornstarch

Blanch and peel the walnuts, using the tip of a sharp knife to pick any pieces of skin out of the crevices. Halve the peppers lengthwise. Seed and core them. Cut the peppers and onion into ½ inch dice. Combine the next 5 ingredients in a small bowl with 3 tablespoons cold water. Put aside until needed. All this can be done in advance and the dish completed shortly before serving.

To cook the dish use a wok or a large, deep skillet. In it heat 2 tablespoons oil and stir-fry the walnuts until golden on all sides. With a slotted spoon, transfer them to a dish and keep warm.

Add another 2 tablespoons oil to the skillet and stir-fry the peppers and onion for about 30 seconds, just long enough to wilt them slightly without destroying their crisp texture. Pour over the vinegar mixture and bring to boiling point over high heat, stirring. Stir in the fried walnuts.

Blend cornstarch smoothly with a tablespoon of cold water. Stir into the pan juices. Bring to boiling point again, stirring constantly, and simmer for a minute or two longer until sauce has thickened. Serve immediately.

Serves 4–6.

POTATO SALAD WITH WALNUTS

A delightfully different recipe from the Northern Caucasus. This salad goes well with cold meat and poultry dishes of all kinds, and is ideal for the cold buffet table. It is also very good with fried fish.

1 pound waxy potatoes
Salt
¾ cup shelled walnuts
2 cloves garlic
Pinch of sharp (hot) paprika
2–3 shallots or 1 small mild onion,
    finely chopped
2 tablespoons finely chopped fresh
    dill and/or parsley
Juice of 1 lemon
2–3 tablespoons olive oil
Pinch of sugar

Scrub potatoes clean under cold running water. Boil them in their skins in salted water until tender but not falling apart. As soon as they are cool enough to handle, peel and slice or cut potatoes into small (roughly ¾ inch) cubes.

While potatoes are cooking, prepare walnut dressing. Chop walnuts very finely, whirl them in an electric blender or food processor, or put them through the coarse blade of a meat grinder. Crush garlic to a purée with a teaspoon of salt, and mix into walnuts, together with paprika, chopped shallots and dill and/or parsley. Sprinkle with lemon juice and olive oil, adding a little more if necessary to bind ingredients into a creamy dressing. Add a pinch of sugar and taste for seasoning.

Pour dressing over potatoes, turning pieces to coat them. Give seasoning a final check and serve.

Serves 4–6.

Note: If dressing is thicker than you would like, it can be thinned down with a little cold water.

BEET AND WALNUT RELISH

A side dish from Georgia in the Caucasus, which is usually served cold with cold meats.

1 pound raw beets
⅓ cup shelled walnuts
2 cloves garlic
Salt
3–4 sprigs fresh coriander (cilantro),
    finely chopped
2–3 tablespoons wine or cider
    vinegar, or lemon juice
Pinch of sugar
Freshly ground black pepper
2–3 sprigs parsley, finely chopped

Scrub the beets clean under cold running water and boil them in their skins until tender. Use a pressure cooker for this if available. When beets are cool, peel them and either dice them very finely or shred them coarsely on a grater.

Finely chop walnuts or whirl them to a coarse paste in an electric blender or food processor. Crush garlic to a paste with about ½ teaspoon salt. Blend pulp into walnuts, together with coriander. Moisten with vinegar or lemon juice.

Blend walnut sauce with beets. Correct seasoning with more salt if necessary, a pinch of sugar and freshly ground black pepper. Spoon into a serving dish.

Scatter with parsley and serve.

Serves 4–6.

SAVORY WALNUT OMELETTE

6–8 eggs
Salt and freshly ground black pepper
¼ cup finely chopped walnuts
Butter
Pinch of ground cinnamon
Green salad for serving

Beat eggs very lightly, just enough to mix yolks into whites, adding a tablespoon of cold water and a good seasoning of salt and freshly ground black pepper. Stir in chopped walnuts.

In a large omelette pan, melt about 2 tablespoons butter and make an omelette in the usual way.

Fold omelette in half. Glaze it with a lump of butter speared onto the tip of a knife and sprinkle with cinnamon. Serve with a bowl of green salad.

Serves 2–3.

SWEET WALNUT AND APRICOT OMELETTE

This flat omelette is served in wedges like a cake. It makes a substantial snack or light supper dish. Serve it straight from the pan or turned out onto a lightly buttered plate.

1½ cups plump dried apricots
Lemon juice
Sugar
4 eggs
Salt
Pinch of ground cinnamon
¼ cup finely chopped walnuts
Butter

Rinse apricots. Cover with warm water and leave to soak and soften for a couple of hours before proceeding. Drain and cut apricots into small pieces. Put them in a pan with barely enough water to cover, a good squeeze of lemon juice and 3 table-spoons sugar. Simmer, stirring frequently, until apricots have absorbed water and are thick and mushy. Beat in a little more lemon juice or sugar if liked and allow to cool.

Beat eggs lightly with a tiny pinch of salt and a little cinnamon. Do not make them too frothy. In the pan in which you are going to fry omelette (preferably one with a lid), sauté walnuts in 2 tablespoons butter until crisp and golden brown. Stir in apricots and spread mixture evenly over bottom of pan. Pour eggs over surface, cover and cook gently until eggs have set.

Failing a lid, cook over low heat until omelette starts setting. Then dot it with a few flakes of butter and finish the omelette under a preheated hot broiler.

Serves 4.

WALNUT MERINGUE BARS

These cakes are very rich so it is advisable to make individual portions rather small. The edible rice paper used instead of a pastry base can be bought from specialist food stores.

Rice paper, for baking sheet
½ pound (about 3 cups) shelled walnuts
7 tablespoons softened butter
3 egg yolks
1 cup sugar
¾ cup + 2 tablespoons flour, sifted
1 teaspoon vanilla
Juice of 1 lemon

Meringue
2 egg whites
10 tablespoons sugar
½ teaspoon vanilla

Line a baking sheet with a single layer of rice paper, overlapping edges slightly where they meet.

Put aside a handful of the best walnut halves for decoration and grind the remainder.

Beat the butter until pale and fluffy. Beat in the egg yolks one at a time alternately with sugar, ground walnuts and sifted flour. Beat in vanilla and lemon juice. Taste mixture (it is quite delicious, even in its raw state) and sharpen flavor with a little more lemon juice if liked. Spread the walnut mixture evenly over the lined baking sheet.

To make meringue, beat the egg whites until they form soft, floppy peaks. Gradually beat in sugar and continue to beat to a stiff, glossy meringue, adding vanilla toward the end. Spread the meringue evenly over the walnut mixture and decorate the top with the reserved walnut halves.

Bake in a preheated 350° oven for 30 minutes, or until meringue feels firm to the touch.

Allow to cool slightly before cutting the slab into small rectangles or squares. For this operation use a serrated knife blade with a gently sawing motion to make sure that the meringue does not crumble.

TO PICKLE WALNUTS

The method of pickling walnuts has not changed over the years as the recipe below, which comes from Mrs Bowman's New Cookery Book of 1867, shows.

A drachm is an apothecary's measure weighing 60 grains or ⅛ ounce.

"The walnuts are in a proper state for pickling when a needle will easily pass through them. Lay them in a strong brine of boiled salt and water, poured over them cold for six days; then make a new brine, and leave them three days longer; leave them to dry; spread on a dish three days, when they will become black; then boil the vinegar (malt vinegar is best for this); to every quart add an ounce of ginger, an ounce of black peppercorns, two ounces of mustard seed, two ounces of eschalots (shallots), in which stick half a dozen cloves, a drachm of mace, a drachm of pimento, half an ounce of horseradish scraped (boil the vinegar and spices together for about 10 minutes before using it to release flavors); put the walnuts into the jars, filling them two-thirds; then pour over them the boiling vinegar and spices, and when quite cold, close the jars.

Leave for a month."

SUGARED WALNUTS

1 pound shelled walnut halves
2 cups sugar

Blanch and peel the walnuts.

Dissolve the sugar in 1¼ cups water and boil hard until syrup has thickened. Drop in the walnuts and stir carefully over low heat for a few minutes until each nut is individually coated with syrup.

Lift nuts out with a slotted spoon onto a wire rack and leave to dry.

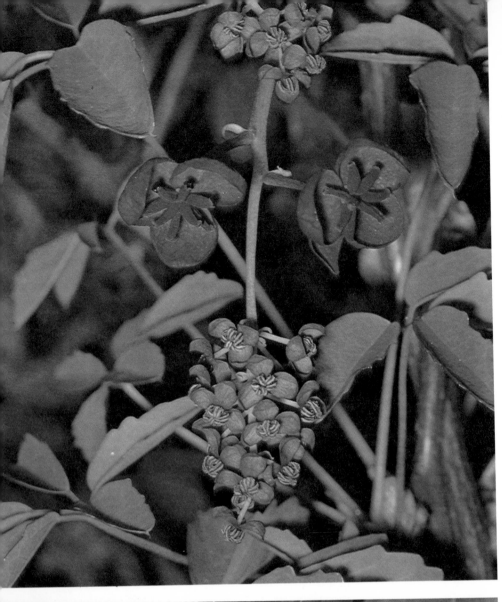

AKEBIA

A twining shrub, the akebia (left) is native to Japan, Korea and China, and although it will grow in temperate regions, sunlight and high temperatures are essential to ensure fruit with a good, pronounced flavor. Outside the Far East the akebia is grown mainly for decoration. The fruit is rarely exported.

Purple-gray, sausage-shaped akebia fruits are 2–5 inches long. As they ripen, the skin dries and becomes hard, finally splitting open to reveal soft, white flesh embedded with small, shiny, black seeds.

How to Use
The akebia's subtle flavor is best when it is eaten raw. Remove the seeds, sprinkle the flesh with a little lemon juice, and spoon straight from the fruit. For a quick, delicious dessert, blend the puréed flesh with an equal quantity of thick heavy cream, the juice of a small lemon, and 2 tablespoons Kirsch. Akebia pulp is suitable for any recipe that uses an uncooked fruit purée, but the delicate flavor can easily be masked by that of other ingredients.

AKEE (ACKEE)

The evergreen akee tree needs a subtropical or tropical climate to ensure healthy growth. A native of Guinea, West Africa, it was introduced to the West Indies by Captain Bligh of the *Bounty*, hence the plant's Latin name, *Blighia sapida*.

Especially popular in Jamaica, akee arils are there canned for export, and are now also naturalized in Florida.

The akee fruit (left), about the size of a small peach, has an outer casing which becomes hard as it ripens, changing in color from yellow to a rich scarlet. When fully ripe, the casing splits open to reveal three large, black seeds, surrounded by white, fleshy arils. Only these arils are edible. The seeds are poisonous (and even the arils are difficult to digest when under-ripe).

How to Use
Akee can be eaten raw, but is more commonly cooked. To prepare a simple and delicious salad, boil fresh akees in salted water for about 15 minutes until tender and golden yellow. Drain. When cold, serve with a vinaigrette dressing. Simply drain canned akees and toss them in the vinaigrette.

Salt Cod with Akee

This is perhaps the most traditional use of akee in Jamaica.

1 pound dried salt cod
24 fresh akees, or 18 ounce
*   can akees*
2 tablespoons groundnut oil
¼ pound salt pork, diced
2 medium-size onions, finely
*   chopped*
1 red chili pepper, seeded and finely
*   chopped*
4 scallions, in 1 inch lengths
½ teaspoon dried thyme
3 medium-size tomatoes, peeled and
*   coarsely chopped*
Freshly ground black pepper
Parsley sprigs and 1 large tomato for
*   garnish*

Place the fish in a bowl, cover with cold water, and leave overnight, until soft and fleshy. The next day, drain the fish, and wash well under cold, running water. Then pour about 2 inches of cold water into a fish steamer or casserole and place over a high heat. As soon as the water comes to a boil, lower the heat, add the fish, and allow to simmer gently until the fish is tender (about 30–45 minutes). If you are using fresh akees, add these to the casserole 15 minutes before the fish is done. If using canned akees, drain and set aside.

When the cod and akee are tender, remove the pan from the heat, drain off and discard the liquid. Remove the akees and set aside. Skin the fish, remove any bones, chop finely and leave with akees.

In a large skillet, heat the oil until sizzling. Add the diced salt pork and cook until crisp and brown. Remove the pork and set aside with the fish and akees.

Lower the heat slightly. Add the onions and green pepper and fry until tender and lightly browned. Then add the chili, scallions, thyme and 3 chopped tomatoes to the skillet. Stir well and cook for a further 5 minutes. Add the fish, akees and fried diced pork. Mix well together, then allow to heat through.

Stir and turn into a heated serving dish. Sprinkle over with freshly ground black pepper and garnish with the sprigs of fresh parsley and tomato wedges. Serve immediately, with hot jalapeño chilies.

Serves 4.

ATEMOYA

The atemoya is one of the custard apples (page 192), a hybrid between the cherimoya and the sweetsop.

This new plant will grow under a broader range of climatic conditions than either of its parents, and is one of several hybrids which have been bred to improve their commercial potential. Several cultivars are now grown in Israel, Australia, South Africa, Central and South America and in the southern and southwest regions of the United States.

An increasing number of the custard apples found in markets are varieties of atemoya; Israel has developed a large, high quality one with few seeds, that crops twice a year.

How to Use
Atemoyas are best eaten raw. See custard apple, page 192.

BARBADOS CHERRY

Despite its name, the Barbados cherry (below) is a native of Brazil. The small tree – maximum height 10 feet – was taken to Europe in 1757, principally for its decorative value, but in temperate regions it can only be grown under glass, or in an artificially heated environment. Plenty of sunshine is essential to produce good quality fruit.

The Barbados cherry is now found chiefly in Jamaica and Barbados, where several varieties have been developed; a popular garden fruit tree, it is exploited commercially. However, the fruit itself is rarely seen in markets or shops outside the West Indies.

The round, bright red, lobed berry or fruit is about the size of a cherry. The thin skin darkens as it ripens, sometimes becoming almost black. The Barbados cherry should be eaten only when the fruit is fully ripe, otherwise the normally sweet, juicy pink pulp can have a very slightly resinous taste.

The single seed is triangular and fluted.

How to Use
Barbados cherries are rich in Vitamin C, so are best eaten raw in order to obtain the full nutritional value as well as flavor.

However, they are also good in jams and pies; substitute for cherries in Cherry Jam (page 51) and Cherry Pie (page 50).

Barbados cherries can also be lightly stewed and served with whipped cream.

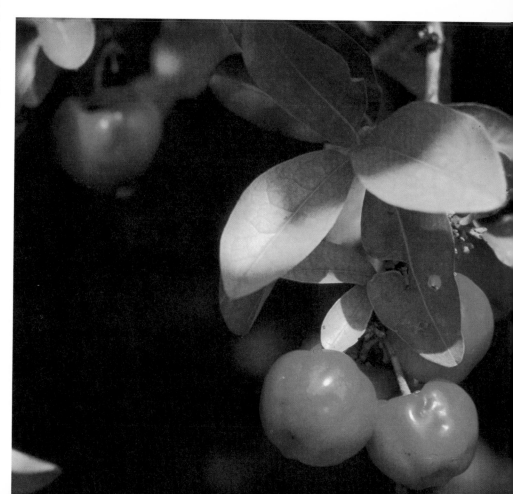

BERRIES

Although the following fruits are called berries, and can be treated in the same way, they are in fact berries, drupes or pomes.

A berry is a pulpy or fleshy fruit containing seeds but no true stone; barberries are an example.

Drupes are fruits in which the seeds are protected by a hard shell. Cherries are examples of one-seeded drupes but, confusingly, the fruits of some of the best-known "berries" such as raspberries are in fact collections of drupelets on a single receptacle. Dewberries and wineberries are examples.

Pomes are technically fruits in which the seeds are collected in a core; the "berries" of the juneberry are formed in this way.

Barberry

Once common, cultivated and wild, throughout Europe, the barberry bush has been eradicated from many farming areas, because it plays host to a common wheat parasite, black rust. However, with its bright yellow flowers and pendulous clusters of elongated, red or purple-blue berries, the barberry makes an attractive garden plant. The fruit is not sold commercially.

Most people find the flesh too acid to eat raw. However, barberries make good preserves.

Whole clusters were once candied, and the berries make an excellent jelly, traditionally eaten with mutton or venison (see Basic Jelly Recipe, page 199).

Bearberry

The name bearberry probably derives from the belief that bears feed on the bearberry shrub, an inhabitant of the colder regions of northern Europe.

Wild plants can be found in Canada, Ireland and in the extreme north of the British Isles, where the bearberry is sometimes confused with the cranberry.

It is usually cultivated for decorative reasons, though both the slimy, green leaves and the bright red berries can be harvested. (Arbutin, a drug used in the treatment of kidney disease is made from the leaves.)

Use bearberries instead of cranberries in Cranberry Tart (page 60), but remember to check the taste and add lemon juice or some other tart flavor if the berries are too sweet.

Boysenberry

The large, juicy, dark red boysenberry (below) is a hybrid (possibly of loganberry, raspberry and blackberry) created in California in the 1930s. It is mainly grown in the United States and only the canned variety is exported.

Similar in appearance to a giant loganberry, the success of this new fruit can be attributed to its ease of growth, few seeds and the lush, acidic but sweet, flesh.

The berries are delicious uncooked, sprinkled with a little sugar depending on taste, and topped with whipped cream. Use boysenberries like blackberries (page 34) or raspberries (page 162).

Boysenberry Summer Pudding

Summer pudding is traditionally made with early summer fruits — raspberries, red currants and, ideally, cherries. However, this version, for later in the season, is equally delicious.

1½ pounds (4½ pints)
   boysenberries
2 medium-size tart apples
¼ cup sugar
White bread (see method)
Thick chilled cream for serving

Wash and drain the berries and peel, core and slice the apples making sure you remove any bruised or damaged pieces.

Put the sugar in a saucepan with about 2 cups of water and bring to a boil. After about 5 minutes, add the prepared fruit and simmer, covered, until it is soft and pulpy. Strain, and set the juice aside until needed.

Press the fruit through a fine nylon sieve to remove the seeds, and add half the juice. Keep the remaining juice to touch up pale patches when the pudding is unmolded. Add more sugar if necessary.

Cut slices of bread ¼ inch thick, and trim off the crusts. Cut a round to fit the bottom of a bowl, and line the sides with fan-shaped pieces, fitting them closely together.

Put the purée in the bowl and cover with more slices of bread. Put a flat plate on top and weight it down.

Chill overnight.

Just before serving unmold onto a plate and patch up any pale pieces of bread with reserved juice.

Serve accompanied by chilled cream.

Serves 4–6.

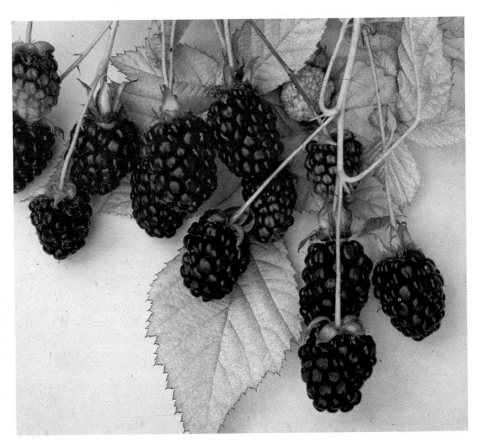

Cloudberry

The small, round, red or deep orange cloudberry grows in clusters on a creeping bramble which is native to the colder, northern regions of temperate zones.

Some cloudberries have even been found in the extreme arctic areas of Canada and Scandinavia. However, they are more abundant and accessible in the slightly milder, hilly areas of both countries, and also in similar parts of Wales and Scotland. Cloudberries are rarely cultivated.

The taste of these sweet, juicy berries has been likened to that of honey and sometimes baked apple. (In Canada, they are known as baked-apple berries.)

Cloudberries make an excellent pie filling; substitute for blackberries in Blackberry Tart (page 35).

Dewberry

The dewberry could easily be confused with the blackberry, and, indeed, in Europe it would be classified as such. In America the name is applied to blackberries that grow on trailing stems, rather than on upright bushes.

The trailing plants bear fewer berries, but mature earlier and the fruit is juicier than the bush-borne blackberry.

In America, several cultivars bearing especially large, lush fruit have been developed.

Use in the same way as blackberries (page 34).

Honeyberry

The honeyberry was originally native to most of tropical America, but wild and cultivated plants are now found mainly in the West Indies.

The oval, green berries grow in clusters, and grape-like bunches can be found on Caribbean market stalls. The thick, leathery skin is removed, revealing a large seed, surrounded by a thin band of yellow, juicy flesh that has a pleasant acid-sweet flavor when fully ripe. Unripe fruit can be extremely sour, which probably accounts for one of the honeyberry's common names – the Spanish lime.

The berries are rarely used in cooking. The seed can be cracked open, and the white kernel is roasted and then salted to be served as a snack with cocktails.

Huckleberry

The huckleberry is a native of America. The lesser known, red huckleberry is found along the north-west coast of the United States, while the popular blue huckleberry inhabits the eastern regions, spreading west and south where conditions are cool enough. It flourishes in shaded woodland.

The small bushes are extremely attractive and, outside America, are sometimes grown as ornamental plants in gardens.

The huckleberry has not been as fully exploited for its fruit as two of its close relations – the cranberry and blueberry. Blue huckleberries are so similar to blueberries that no distinction is made by many Americans. Others claim they are superior in flavor.

Use in the same way as blueberries (page 40).

Juneberry

The juneberry is the fruit of the *Amelanchier* group of shrubs and small trees. This easily cultivated plant has a wide variety of species, and amelanchiers can be found in regions as different in climate as southeast Asia, northern Britain and North America (which has the largest number of native species).

Ease of growth and attractive white blossoms make it a popular garden plant. However, the juneberry is not grown commercially.

The fruit is similar in appearance to the black currant, though the skin color can vary from deep purple to dark red, depending on species. The common British variety is easily confused with the black currant because of its blue-black skin.

Juneberries are especially popular in the United States, where they are still known by some of the early pioneer names: service berry, shad berry and swamp pear.

Use juneberries instead of apples in pies and puddings (pages 17–19). The berries are also good eaten raw.

Loganberry

A cross between a blackberry and a raspberry, the loganberry originated in California in 1881 – in the garden of Judge J. H. Logan.

The fruit looks like a large raspberry, and can be used instead of blackberries (page 34) and raspberries (page 162).

Wineberry

The wineberry is the fruit of an attractive garden shrub, native to Japan and north China. It can be grown in more temperate climates, but needs a light, well-drained soil, and plenty of water and sunlight while fruiting.

Wineberries are compound fruits, similar in appearance to blackberries (page 34) and raspberries (page 162). They can be used as an alternative to either. Whether you eat them raw or cooked, pick and use only when ripe.

Worcesterberry

The worcesterberry is an American hybrid of the gooseberry and the black currant. It has the same blue-black skin as the latter, but is about midway in size between its two "parents." It is uncommon even in the United States.

Use in the same way as black currants (page 37) and blueberries (page 40). The riper fruit is good eaten raw.

Youngberry

The youngberry is a hybrid of the dewberry and the loganberry, and looks like a large purple-black loganberry. Cultivation is still limited.

Eat raw or use as an alternative when a recipe calls for blackberries (page 34) or raspberries (page 162).

Youngberries and Bananas

1 pound (3 pints) ripe
*   youngberries*
2–3 ripe bananas
Sugar
¾ cup whipping cream
Flaked or chopped toasted almonds

Pick over youngberries. Peel and slice bananas. In the bottom of 4 individual glass serving dishes put a few slices of banana. Cover with a layer of youngberries, sprinkle with a teaspoon or two of sugar to taste, and press lightly with the back of a fork. Arrange remaining banana slices on youngberries. Top with the rest of the berries and a sprinkling of sugar. Chill before serving.

Serve decorated with lightly sweetened whipped cream and almonds.

Serves 4.

Note: Loganberries, boysenberries or wineberries can be used instead of youngberries.

BREADFRUIT

The breadfruit (below) is believed to be native to the Malay Archipelago, but for centuries has been widely cultivated in most tropical regions. Its main value stems from its high starch content, which makes it one of the great staple foods of the world. Captain Cook suggested its introduction to the West Indies as cheap nourishment for slaves.

Usually green skinned, but often tinged with yellow when fully ripe, this round fruit can be as large as 10 inches in diameter. The densely packed, seedless pulp is yellowish and sweet when ripe.

Baked slices taste very similar to freshly baked bread.

Fresh breadfruit is sometimes available in markets specializing in tropical produce, but it is usually canned for export.

How to Use

Breadfruit can be cooked in much the same way as potatoes: boiled and then mashed with butter and milk, sautéed, cooked, diced and mixed with mayonnaise to make a salad, and added to stews.

BUTTERNUT

A member of the same *genus* as the walnut, the butternut is found in the eastern half of North America. The nuts are gathered locally, but are not important commercially.

How to Use

Butternuts, with their soft, oily flesh, can be used in the same way as walnuts (page 182).

Breadfruit Pudding

1 pound fresh breadfruit pulp, or 1½ pound can breadfruit
⅔ cup firmly packed light brown sugar
¼ cup unsalted butter, melted
Grated rind of lemon or lime
2 tablespoons flour
½ teaspoon vanilla
2 cups milk
2 eggs, beaten
5 tablespoons dark rum
1¼ cups whipping cream

Grease a large ovenproof dish with a little additional butter.

If using canned breadfruit, drain. If using fresh breadfruit, place the pulp in a large saucepan, sprinkle lightly with salt, and add enough water to cover. Bring the water to a boil over a high heat, then lower the heat and allow the breadfruit to simmer for 20 minutes until tender. Drain.

Place the drained fruit in a large bowl and mash until smooth. Using a wooden spoon, blend in the sugar, followed by the warm melted butter, grated rind and flour. Mix well. Add the vanilla, milk, beaten eggs and 3 tablespoons of the rum.

Beat the mixture until smooth and creamy, then pour into the prepared dish and bake in a preheated 350° oven for about 45 minutes, until set. (A knife inserted in the pudding should come out clean.)

Leave to cool slightly, and meanwhile blend the remaining rum with the cream and whip until it begins to thicken. Serve warm with the flavored cream poured over.

Serves 4–6.

CALAMONDIN ORANGE, PANAMA ORANGE

The calamondin is known in Europe as an exotic houseplant and in the more tropical regions of the United States as an ornamental garden tree. Because it is grown largely for decoration, few people appreciate the culinary value of its fruit.

The calamondin orange (above) is similar in appearance to kumquats, though marginally larger.

How to Use

The flesh is sparse, but the peel makes excellent marmalade.

The sharp acid juice is a good alternative to lemon juice in recipes. Like kumquats, calamondins are an ideal size to preserve whole.

Calamondin Oranges in Syrup

1 pound calamondin oranges
4 cups sugar
3 tablespoons Kirsch

Wash the oranges thoroughly under cold running water, and pierce each fruit once with a fork.

Place the sugar and 2½ cups water in a large thick-bottomed saucepan, over a medium heat. Stir constantly until the sugar has dissolved, then allow to boil. Simmer the syrup gently for 10 minutes. Add the prepared fruit to the syrup and continue to simmer for 30 minutes, until the fruit begins to soften. Remove the pan from the heat.

Allow the contents of the pan to cool slightly. Stir in the Kirsch, then transfer the oranges and syrup to warm, clean jars. Seal. Keep for at least a week before using.

CAPE GOOSEBERRY, GROUND CHERRY

The Cape gooseberry (above) and ground cherry, members of the tomato family, are so closely related as to be almost indistinguishable.

Both plants are native to South and Central America, but the former owes its name to the fact that it is cultivated around the Cape of Good Hope in South Africa. Many varieties of ground cherry grow wild in Mexico and the southern parts of the United States. The most familiar species is cultivated in the eastern and central areas of North America where it is also known as the husk tomato.

The round cherry-shaped berries are usually about 3 inches in diameter. They hang from bushes, enclosed in enlarged, hardened, gray-brown calyxes commonly known as "Chinese lanterns." The decorative value of the "lanterns" makes the bushes popular garden plants.

Only ripe fruit should be eaten. The filled "lantern" often falls to the ground before the fruit is ready, but the ripening process continues. All fruit, ripe or unripe, should be kept in the hardened "lantern" until it is used.

Unripe berries are green, becoming increasingly golden-yellow as they mature. Some rarer varieties have a dark purple skin.

How to Use
The lightly seeded berries should be eaten whole. The distinctive sweet-sharp flavor is more pronounced if the fruit is gently stewed in syrup for about 10 minutes. The berries also make excellent jams and jellies (see Basic Recipes, pages 198, 199).

For a really superb finish to a meal, open the calyx and twist it without breaking. Using the calyx as a stem, dip the fully ripe berry into a vanilla fondant and dry.

CAROB

The tall, evergreen carob tree, a member of the pea family, is thought to be a native of the area once known as the Holy Land. Indeed, the carob fruit (below) is sometimes known as St John's bread, because it is believed the "locusts" John the Baptist ate in the wilderness were carob pods. Prized as much for the shade it provides as for its fruit, this tree now grows, wild and cultivated, in the drier parts of the Mediterranean.

The fruits are dark brown, flattened pods 4–8 inches long and about 1–2 inches wide. The sweet flesh inside contains 4–12 extremely hard brown seeds, or "beans."

The quality of the fruit varies from species to species, and cultivation has been largely aimed at producing fleshier fruit.

It can sometimes be difficult, however, to distinguish between wild and cultivated varieties; some of the fleshiest carob pods are found on wild, Sicilian species.

For centuries, the pods were harvested each September by shaking the branches of the tree with a long stick. They were then left to dry and used mainly as animal feed during the winter months. But the sweet chocolate-like flavor was also appreciated by humans and the dried pods were eaten as a confectionery. Because of their high sugar content, they were fermented to give a good yield of alcohol, and a medicinal syrup called "carob molasses" was also manufactured. (The modern pharmaceutical industry uses carob in cough syrups.)

How to Use
Fresh whole pods are rarely seen outside the growing region, although candy stores in Europe and the United States once sold the beans to chew. Now dried pods are often found in health food shops. Carob powder is a good substitute for cocoa, to which many people are allergic. Made by finely grinding the beans, it is used, exactly like cocoa, as a flavoring in drinks, puddings, ice cream and cakes. Many shops also stock carob "chocolate" bars and carob-coated cookies.

Carob Smoothie

This quickly made drink is rather thick and sweet, but should be a great favorite with children. (It is also highly nutritious.)

5 cups milk
3 tablespoons molasses
3 tablespoons carob powder
1 ripe banana
½ cup finely ground
*   peanuts*
3 tablespoons brewer's yeast

Put all the ingredients in an electric blender and process until smooth and creamy. Serve in tall, chilled glasses.

Serves 4.

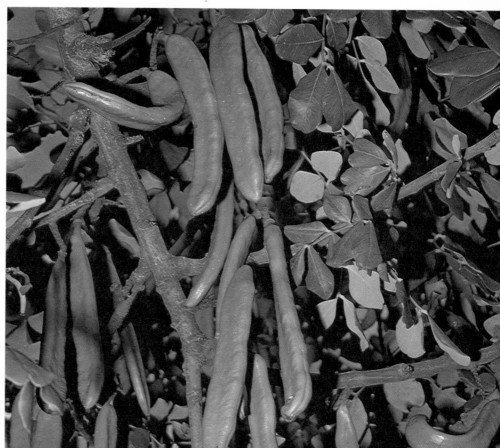

CASHEW APPLE

Botanically, the cashew apple is not a fruit. It is the name given to the swollen, pear-shaped stem that bears the true fruit of the *Anacardium occidentale* tree – the cashew nut.

The plant is believed to be a native of tropical Africa, but is now grown in many tropical and subtropical parts of the world, including Central and South America, the warmer areas of Europe, and, especially, India and the East.

The cashew plant belongs to the same family as poison ivy, and even the smoke from its burning leaves can cause a rash.

Although the nuts are exported, few people outside the growing areas will be acquainted with the "apple." This glossy, bright red or yellow fruit matures early and can be ready to pick (along with its nut) while the tree is still flowering. The soft, juicy flesh is refreshing, but acid. Unless the fruit is fully ripe it may be too tart for most palates.

How to Use
In some countries cashew apples are used for wines and liqueurs, and they are also interesting in preserves and pies. Basic recipes for these are on pages 198–207. They can also be eaten raw, or lightly stewed and served with whipped cream.

CORNELIAN CHERRY

The small cornelian cherry tree is a native of the temperate parts of Europe. Today, the attractive, yellow, tassel-like flowers, which can appear as early as February if the frost is not too severe, make it a popular garden plant in many other parts of the world.

Since Greek and Roman times, the tree has been cultivated for its fruit, which was pickled in brine, in a similar way to olives, or made into a sharp beautifully pink preserve or jelly. Today, you are unlikely to find the small, bright red, oval berries unless you grow the tree in your own garden.

How to Use
Cornelian cherries can be eaten raw, and also make good preserves – whole in syrup (substitute for calamondin oranges, page 190), and in jams and jellies (see Basic Recipes, pages 198, 199).

CITRON

The small, evergreen citron tree grows, wild and cultivated, throughout the drier parts of the Mediterranean region. The Latin species name *medica* means "coming from Medea." However, the plant is believed to have been introduced to that area in about 500 BC from its native Far East, where the skin was used for perfuming rooms in Japan and China. There are also several American cultivars.

The citron looks like an odd lemon, and is, in fact, a close relative. It is prized for its green-yellow skin, much rougher and bumpier than that of the lemon. The flesh tastes like, and can be used in the same way as, the lemon's. However, there is much less of it as the rind covers an extremely thick layer of white pith. The whole skin, rind and pith, is used in the commercial production of candied peel. Most of the citron trees cultivated in Greece, Sicily and Corsica are for this small but lucrative industry. Sometimes the rind alone is distilled to extract an essential oil used for liqueurs, perfumes and medicines.

How to Use
If you are lucky enough to find imported citrons for sale in your local market, you can prepare your own candied peel; substitute for oranges in Candied Peel, page 123. The rind can also be used instead of lemon rind. It is especially good in preserves.

CUSTARD FRUITS

"Custard" is the common name given to a variety of tree fruits that belong to the genus *Annona*.

Custard Apple

A number of hybrids especially cultivated for ease of growth, large size, and lack of, or few, seeds are available in the markets. These include the atemoya, described on page 187.

The true custard apple (*A. reticulata*), the cherimoya (*A. cherimolia*) and the sweetsop (*A. squamosa*) are pure species. They are native to the tropical parts of America, although the cherimoya does better in slightly cooler, subtropical regions like Peru, its original home.

All are borne on a small, attractive tree with a brownish down on its young branches and yellow-green flowers tinged with purple. It decorates gardens in Central America, India and most recently Australia. As early as 1690 custard apples were cultivated in the greenhouses of Europe. Now they are readily imported from the tropics.

Texture and skin color vary with type. The true custard apple has a smooth, yellow to reddish-brown skin marked with a net-like pattern. The green skin of the cherimoya is rough and covered with scale-like bumps, like a cone, and the sweetsop is similar though often smaller and more yellow.

All three fruits blacken as they become fully ripe.

Cherimoyas can weigh up to 14 pounds though the others are usually between a half and 1½ pounds.

Their shape has led to some colorful common names – in the West Indies the custard apple is known as "bullock's heart."

How to Use
The fruits are picked before they are ready for eating, and should be kept until the skin has completely blackened. Then cut the fruit in half and spoon out the soft, creamy white and very sweet flesh. As the name suggests, it has a custard-like flavor. The best quality cherimoyas have a mild taste of strawberries.

You cannot really improve upon the raw fruit, spooned out from the shell, but the pulp does make a delicious ice cream (substitute for avocado pulp in Avocado Ice Cream, page 29).

Custard Banana

A native of the southeast corner of the United States, the custard banana is rarely exported. Confusingly, it is sometimes called a pawpaw – a label more generally applied to the papaya fruit.

It is not in fact a banana, but a cylindrical berry 3–5 inches long. The thin, dark brown skin covers creamy, yellow flesh studded with small, black seeds.

How to Use
Like the custard apple, the banana must be allowed to ripen fully before it is eaten (the skin will be black), and, also like the apple, it is best eaten raw. The flesh tastes like a sweet blend of bananas and custard.

CRAB APPLE

More than twenty varieties of cultivated crab apple grow in Europe, Asia and North America, and large numbers of "domestic" apples have seeded themselves in the wild and reverted to their original form or crossed with true crabs.

The crab apple tree is similar in size, flower and foliage to the domestic apple, and is often grown as an ornamental tree. The apples themselves are small and oval or slightly pear shaped.

How to Use

Crab apples make the clearest and most brilliant of jellies, and can also be used very successfully to make fruit cheese (see Basic Recipes, pages 199, 200).

ELDERBERRY

The common elder and the dwarf elder are both members of the genus *Caprifoliaceae* and grow wild in northern temperate zones. Said to be the tree on which Judas hanged himself, the elder is popularly associated with evil spirits — it was long thought that burning its wood allowed evil to enter the house down the chimney (although there are also records of using its branches and leaves as charms against witches).

Its tiny berries grow in clusters, changing from spring green through shades of red to glistening black in autumn.

The berries are ready for picking when the weight of the clusters of fruit pulls the stem down. The raw fruit is best eaten within twenty-four hours of picking.

How to Use

Elderberry wine is one of the most delicious of homemade wines. Made by fermenting the juice of the ripened fruit, it is a dark, purplish brew that looks rather like port. In fact, fradulent use of it has been known when it was found to be mixed with port to make a deceptively cheaper "fortified wine." Information about wine-making is given on page 205.

The berries can also be used instead of blackberries (page 34), raspberries (page 162) and other soft fruits and the flowers add an aromatic flavor to gooseberry compotes and fools.

Remember to remove the stalks and sieve the flesh to get rid of the numerous, hard seeds.

FEIJOYA

The feijoya is native to Brazil, and was introduced into the warmer parts of Europe in 1890. Provided the climate is frost-free, the bushy, evergreen shrub will flourish and fruit abundantly in most soils. Because of this, it has become established in many subtropical areas of the world. It now grows wild in the South of France. Its appearance — the large flowers are milky purple with a red and yellow interior — make it a popular garden plant, especially in California, Australia, New Zealand, and on the Cornish Riviera in Britain.

The oval berry is about 2 inches long, with a tough but thin, waxy skin. It resembles a small passion fruit, but the juicy, yellow-green flesh, embedded with black seeds, tastes like a guava, with a slight strawberry and pineapple flavor — reason enough for its common name — "pineapple guava."

How to Use

The skin is easily peeled off and the flesh is delicious eaten raw, either alone or chopped into an exotic salad.

GOLDEN NARANJILLA

If you live in a temperate climate and wish to sample the golden naranjilla, you will need a greenhouse and a little patience. Under hothouse conditions, the plant — a tall, highly decorative shrub — is almost two years old before fruiting. Small, orange-like fruits will then appear every year.

The golden naranjilla is in fact a berry, but its resemblance to the orange probably accounts for one of its common names — the Quito orange.

How to Use

The best way to enjoy the sharp but delicious taste of the flesh is to eat it raw, though the abundance of tiny seeds can be annoying. The juice makes a refreshing drink.

GUAVA

The guava is a small deciduous tree, belonging to the myrtle family. In tropical America it can be seen growing both wild and cultivated. It was introduced to southern Europe by the Spanish.

The white or yellow-skinned guava, the most common and abundant species, has sweet but acidic flesh with a strong musky odor (present to some degree in any guava) that vanishes on cooking. There are several varieties; the guava pear is considered by the French to be the finest, although the Brazilians would contest this claim. Their "strawberry guava," with its deep purplish-red skin and juicy flesh, has a flavor similar to that of a strawberry.

New cultivars are tried out regularly with a view to improving the guava's quality and commercial status.

Canned fruits labeled "Guava Shells" have been seeded and cooked before canning.

How to Use

Guavas are rich in Vitamin C. There is a thriving juice industry, and the fruits can be used in a wide variety of dishes that require a soft, pulpy flesh that purées easily.

Ripe guavas can be eaten raw. They can also be cooked by simmering gently until just pulpy. A little sugar (or preferably honey) is usually added to the cooked fruit.

Bastida Goiaba

This cocktail is from Brazil, the leading producer of Cachaca, a liqueur distilled from fermented sugar cane, but light rum may be used instead.

3 small or 2 large "strawberry" guavas, peeled and seeded
2 teaspoons sugar
3 tablespoons Cachaca or light rum
1 tablespoon crushed ice

Put all the ingredients in an electric blender and mix thoroughly. Pour into a tall, chilled glass and serve.

Makes 1 glass.

HICKORY NUT

A member of the same *genus* as the walnut, the hickory is a close relative of the pecan. Native to North America, the nuts have a strong flavor.

How to Use

Hickory nuts can be used in the same way as pecans (page 140).

JACKFRUIT

The jackfruit tree, with its lush, dark green, leathery leaves, can grow up to 65 feet tall, and is therefore greatly appreciated for its decorative value. In its native India the prickly fruits grow to about the size of a large watermelon, weighing up to 50 pounds. The hard, prickly, light brown, outer rind of the jackfruit (above) encloses a surprisingly soft and juicy, yellow pulp, studded with large seeds. In Sri Lanka the seeds are more highly valued than the flesh; they are finely ground and sprinkled as a flavoring into many dishes. They can also be roasted and eaten like nuts.

Today, cultivation has spread to other parts of the world with a hot, humid climate – Africa, parts of America and, most recently, Australia. Once harvested, the jackfruit takes an extremely long time to ripen – six to eight months – and is therefore not commercially viable.

How to Use
Jackfruits are rarely found outside the tropics, and many people find the flesh unpalatable. The fruit is used raw or cooked: slices are lightly fried and served with curry, and it can be roasted or boiled and served as a vegetable.

JUJUBE

There are numerous varieties of the small, deciduous jujube tree in the Middle and Far East, along the Mediterranean, and in Australia and the United States. It is not readily available outside the countries where it is cultivated.

About the size and shape of a large olive, the fruit is initially green, changing to reddish-brown as the fruit ripens. The sweet, white flesh is rather slimy when the jujube is freshly picked, and the fruit is left to wither until the flesh is spongy, before being used or offered for sale.

How to Use
Rich in Vitamin C, jujubes soothe sore throats.

They are best either raw, or preserved: dried (when they taste like dates); and in jams and jellies (see Basic Recipes, pages 198, 199).

LOQUAT

The loquat, also known as the Japanese medlar or Japanese loquat, is a subtropical relative of the apple and pear. Originally from China, it is now grown in many warm parts of the world and will even fruit freely in milder regions.

The golden fruits are shaped like eggs; about 1½ inches long, they hang in clusters of up to ten. The flesh varies from pale yellow or even white to rich gold.

Some varieties have large seeds and comparatively little flesh.

How to Use
Ripe loquats are delicious when ripe, and best eaten raw. They can also be combined with other fruits in fruit salad or made into jelly (see Basic Jelly Recipe, page 199) but allow the fruit to stand in the water in which it was boiled for 24 hours before straining and measuring the juice.

MACADAMIA

Native to Australia, macadamias or Queensland nuts are also grown in Hawaii and to some extent in California. The evergreen tree on which the nuts are borne is similar to the orange but has long, prickly leaves.

How to Use
The nuts, which have a delectable, buttery taste, are roasted or can be eaten raw.

MANGOSTEEN

The mangosteen has only been successfully cultivated so far in its native Malaya and in the West Indies, although it is increasingly exported. Australian growers are working on its commercial potential, and closely related fruits are found in India and in the tropical regions of America and Africa.

The mangosteen is about the size and shape of a crab apple. A most attractive fruit, its thick, leathery rind is either dark red or purple on the outer surface and pale violet on the inside when the fruit is fully ripe. It contains five to seven snow-white arils, each surrounding a small seed.

How to Use
The fleshy arils, the edible part of the fruit, taste similar to a sweet ripe plum. They are best eaten raw.

MEDLAR

Of Central European origin, the medlar tree is often found wild in Britain and on the Continent.

Medlars (below) are about the size of a small plum, with tough, leathery skins that turn russet brown on ripening. They are best harvested in late fall when the fruit is still hard. The flesh turns soft and mealy as the fruit ripens, and when it appears half-rotten or "bletted" its pleasant, if rather acid, taste is quite palatable.

How to Use
The flesh of cooked medlars can be puréed and used in a fool (see Basic Fool Recipe, page 204) and the fruits also make good jams and jellies (see Basic Recipes, pages 198, 199) and cheeses (see Basic Cheese Recipe, page 200).

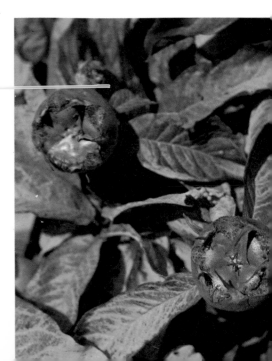

MULBERRY

There are about twelve species of mulberry tree, but the two most important are the black mulberry (*Morus nigra*) and the white mulberry (*Morus alba*). The fruits of the latter are not very well flavored and the tree is best cultivated for its pale green leaves, a food for silk worms.

In 1608, James I issued an edict to encourage silk production in England. Large numbers of mulberry trees were planted in gardens throughout the country, but confusion led to the black rather than the white being cultivated. The silk trade did not flourish, but the black mulberry trees with their delicious fruit did.

Today the black mulberry is exploited for its large, luscious fruit. Iran and Turkestan produce an abundance of high-quality, seedless varieties. However, production is not commercially viable — the fruit has to be fully ripe when picked, is best eaten immediately, and is easily squashed.

The berries look like inflated loganberries. Deep purple when fully ripe, the extremely juicy flesh has a sweet but acid flavor.

How to Use

Most people prefer to eat mulberries raw. Rinse the ripe berries gently, then sprinkle lightly with sugar, and serve with whipped cream. If you have a large crop, freeze some. Substitute them for blackberries (page 34) and raspberries (page 162).

Sopa de Amoras

This soup recipe comes from Brazil.

2 pounds (6–8 pints) ripe black mulberries
½ bottle (about 2 cups) white wine
1 teaspoon ground cinnamon
Sugar to taste

Wash the mulberries thoroughly in a colander under cold running water, and place in a large saucepan. Add the wine and enough water to cover. Bring the contents to a boil over a moderate heat, and simmer gently until mushy. Stir well. Remove the pan from the heat and stir in the cinnamon and sugar. Return the pan to the heat and heat through, but do not boil. Serve immediately with fingers of dry toast.

Serves 4–6.

NATAL PLUM

The white blossom that covers the shrub *Carissa grandiflora* for most of the year makes it an attractive and popular addition to subtropical gardens. Native to Africa, Australia and Asia, it was introduced into the southeastern part of the United States in the early twentieth century.

You are unlikely to encounter the scarlet, plum-like Natal plum outside its growing regions.

Although the plant is quite easy to grow, the fruit itself is not exploited commercially, perhaps because no matter how delicious, it is not especially distinctive.

How to Use

Use as you would plums (page 152). Only really ripe fruit should be eaten raw. Slightly under-ripe specimens are best for cooking and make a delicious jelly (see Basic Jelly Recipe, page 199).

PRICKLY OR CACTUS PEAR

Many cacti produce delicious fruit, but those of the *Opuntia* species — prickly pears (below) — are probably the most abundant and the best known.

The Spaniards introduced the plant to Europe from Mexico in the sixteenth century. It has since spread all around the Mediterranean, where it grows easily. After being introduced into Australia, it spread so rapidly that it became an agricultural pest, and its growth is now controlled by law, and banned altogether in some regions.

Deliberate cultivation of the fruit is widespread, but the harvest from wild and semi-wild varieties is abundant enough for the "pears" to be commonplace. Some are exported and are not too difficult to locate in specialist markets.

The so-called "pear" is in fact a large berry, covered in spines; size and color vary from species to species. They are shaped like an elongated apple (rather than a pear) and are all initially green, maturing to yellow or orange-red. Some are almost purple. Most are 1½–2 inches long, though one of the most commonly cultivated — also known as the Indian fig — can be up to 3 inches in length. Handle the pears with care — as their name suggests, the spine-covered skins are very prickly.

How to Use

Use the pulp in preserves or compotes if you wish, but remember to push it through a fine sieve to remove the numerous seeds. A few, less common cultivars are seedless. Most people prefer to eat the flesh raw. Carefully take a fully ripe "pear," slice it open lengthwise and dig out the juicy sweet flesh (white, yellow or orange, depending on species), avoiding the spines. The seeds are harmless if eaten, but are usually discarded. A more elegant method would be to peel off the spiny skin, slice the flesh, sprinkle with lemon juice, then serve topped with whipped cream.

RAMBUTAN

The tall rambutan tree is a native of the Malay Archipelago and is still most widely cultivated in Malaya. However, small plantations have been established in the Philippines, Australia and Central America. Despite the quality of the fruit, it is not exported in any significant quantity.

Ripe rambutans have a pinkish or orange-red outer casing, like that of a litchi, with soft spines or hair which give its nickname "hairy litchi."

How to Use
The soft, grape-like flesh is best eaten raw, either alone or in fruit salads. Rambutans may be used as an alternative to litchis (page 98).

ROSELLA

The rosella is not a true fruit, but consists of an inner seed pod enclosed by swollen, fleshy sepals.

A native of the tropics, the rosella is valued for its leaves, which are used as a herb, as well as for its fruit. However, it is usually cultivated for the fruit, and fair-size crops are grown in Australia, the West Indies, Hawaii and parts of the Far East. Whole rosellas are not exported. Outside the tropics, only the dried sepals and a syrup used for flavoring can be found in specialist food stores.

How to Use
Rosellas should always be cooked. If fresh, separate the red sepals from the seed pods, then stew them lightly. The slightly tart pulp is traditionally used in jams and jellies (see Basic Recipes, pages 198, 199). You can also cook the seed pods, but remember to sieve the pulp before using, to remove the seeds. Dried rosella sepals must first be soaked in hot water to soften them.

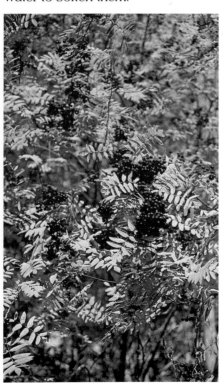

ROSE HIP

The rose family is large, and although all species are native to the northern hemisphere many grow throughout the world. Cultivar roses are mainly cultivated for their flowers although the bright red hips are decorative. All are edible, although some have a better flavor than others.

Rose hips from the wild single rose are usually bright red, round to oval in shape and about ½–1 inch long. The shriveled calyx from the flower is often still attached to the fruit. They can be easily gathered from hedgerows and in gardens.

How to Use
Only the fleshy, outer casing of the rose hip is used. Always cut the hip open, then remove and discard the hard, bristly seeds. The larger hips are good combined with other fruits — replace a proportion of the rhubarb with rose hips in Rhubarb Pie (page 170) and Rhubarb Fool (page 171). The best-known use, however, is to make rose hip syrup, a traditional source of Vitamin C (see Basic Syrup Recipe, page 202).

ROWAN

The rowan or mountain ash is a slender tree, native to all parts of Europe and western Asia. It is easily grown and widely cultivated for its ornamental value. In late spring and early summer it bears almond-scented white blossom, and in autumn large bunches of tiny, bright orange rowanberries (left). Ancient myth claims that those who shelter under its branches will be protected from witches and evil spirits.

How to Use
If you have a mountain ash in your garden or know where to find a wild one, be sure to catch the berries early, as the birds are also fond of them. They are bitter raw, but are rich in pectin and frequently used in jelly (see Basic Jelly Recipe, page 199).

SAPODILLA

In the West Indies, the fruits of the sapodilla tree are known as naseberries, and in Central America the tree is usually cultivated for the white sap that is tapped from its bark and used to make chewing gum. However, the fruit has always been prized and trees can now be found all over the tropics, including parts of America and Australia. Sadly, exports are limited.

The round to oval fruits are the size of large plums or small lemons. The green rind changes to a deep red-brown when ripe.

How to Use
Sapodillas should be eaten only when they are ripe, with sweet, juicy, fragrant flesh.

They are best eaten raw. Be careful, however: each fruit contains several black seeds which should never be swallowed as their rough surface will scratch your throat. You can scoop the flesh straight from the halved fruit or chop it into salads (sweet or savory). The pulp can also be puréed. Substitute for mango purée in Mango Mousse (page 101), leaving out the ground ginger; or use to make a fool (see Basic Fool Recipe, page 204).

SAPOTE

The name "sapote" describes a number of fruits. Only two of these – the true sapote and the green sapote – are members of the same botanical family (*Calocarpum*), though the flavor of all the fruits is similar. The true sapote tree is indigenous to Central America, while the green sapote can fruit well in cooler climates.

The fruit known as the true sapote resembles an untidy, misshapen brown ball. It is usually almost oval and 3–6 inches long, with thick rough, woody skin enclosing firm, reddish flesh and one large seed. The green sapote is about 5 inches in diameter and has thinner, pale green skin.

The flesh of the green sapote is invariably sweet and juicy, while that of the true sapote, at its best sweet and slightly spicy, can be rather insipid.

How to Use
Sapotes are usually cut up and eaten raw, though they lack acidity and many people find them too sweet to eat alone.

SLOE

A sprinkling of tiny, blue-black sloe berries (right) can be found growing wild in hedges in the fall every year. The small blackthorn tree which bears them is a member of the plum family and, botanically speaking, the sloe is a miniature plum. Growing wild in the temperate parts of Europe (not in the extreme north), the sloe's ancestry is obscure, though it appears to be native. Sloes are best picked after the first frost.

How to Use
The berries taste very bitter, but make a delicious jelly (see Basic Jelly Recipe, page 199).

Sloe Wine

Sloe gin is a traditional Christmas drink; this wine is less well known.

4 pounds sloes, stalks removed
3 cups raisins, chopped
1 Campden tablet
1 teaspoon pectic enzyme
Burgundy yeast
1 yeast nutrient tablet
3½ pounds (7 cups) sugar

Wash the sloes thoroughly in a colander under cold, running water. Place in a large, sterilized preserving kettle. Add 4½ quarts cold water, then place the pan on a moderate heat and bring the contents to a boil. Lower the heat, simmering gently, until the fruit just starts to become pulpy. Remove the pan from the heat and pour the contents into a prepared plastic pail. Stir in the chopped raisins. Cover the pail and leave the contents to cool to a temperature of between 65–75°. Uncover and stir in the Campden tablet and pectic enzyme. Re-cover and leave for 24 hours.

Stir in the activated yeast (see manufacturer's instructions for quan-

tity and method of use) and the nutrient tablet. Leave the covered plastic pail in a warm place (65–75°) for another 8 days. During this time, stir once a day to make sure the fruit is kept moist.

Using a fine sieve, strain off the liquid into a clean, sterile container. Place the fruit pulp in a linen bag. Seal the bag and squeeze it tightly over the bowl of strained liquid, to extract as much juice as possible. Stir the sugar into the bowl of liquid. Quickly siphon into a prepared secondary fermentor, filling to within 1 inch of the cork. Allow to ferment in a warm, dark place (65–75°) under an air-lock. Leave until a good layer of sediment has formed on the bottom of the vessel. This process will take about 4–5 weeks.

Rack until clear, store in a dark place for at least 6 months and finally pour into dark glass wine bottles and cork. Keep for at least a year, preferably longer, before drinking.

See also page 205.

Makes about 4½ quarts.

TREE TOMATO, TOMARILLO

Originally from Brazil, the tree tomato is a member of the tomato family and is cultivated in many tropical and subtropical parts of the world.

The plant grows quickly and easily, making it ideal for tropical fruit gardens. It can also be raised in a greenhouse, provided this is heated in winter. The oval fruits are about 2 inches long, with a tough yellow or red skin when ripe. Skin color varies with type – there are several – but the

yellow variety is said to have the sweetest taste.

How to Use
Peel off the skin before eating. The fleshy interior, like that of the tomato, is divided into cells, each full of small, dark, edible seeds. The taste is reminiscent of a rather sweet tomato. You can eat tree tomatoes raw; or use them to make a delicious jam (see Basic Jam Recipe, page 198).

TAMARIND

The tall tamarind tree is related to the pea and grows in nearly all the tropical areas of the world. A native of East Africa, its economic viability — the wood, bark, leaves and flowers, as well as the fruit, are useful — account for its widespread cultivation.

The fruit is a thick, curved, brown pod, 3–6 inches long, containing up to about 10 black seeds embedded in an acid pulp. When the fruit is fully ripe the pulp is rich brown and fairly sweet. Under-ripe tamarinds are extremely tart.

How to Use
The most common use is as a seasoning in savory dishes such as curries and chutneys.

Dried whole pods and seeds are exported, and should be easily obtainable in any good African or Asian specialty food store.

To make tamarind seasoning, steep 2 ounces dried tamarind pods in 1¼ cups of hot water (just boiled) for 1 hour. When the pods are soft, mash them in with the water then strain this mixture through a fine sieve and use the liquid as directed.

In countries where the tamarind is grown, the sweet, mature pulp is eaten raw, scooped directly from the pod. The pulp can also be used in any recipe demanding a soft fruit purée.

Tamarinade

This refreshing drink comes from Jamaica.

6 fresh or dried tamarinds
¼ cup sugar

Wash the tamarinds, then place in a bowl. Pour on 2 cups water and leave for 30 minutes.

If you are using dried tamarinds, boil the water first, then pour it over and leave until the fruit is soft and pulpy (about 1 hour).

Add the sugar and stir until it has dissolved. Then leave the liquid to stand for 5 minutes. Strain by pouring through a fine sieve. Serve chilled with ice, in tall, chilled glasses.

Serves 2.

PRESERVING

The word preserving probably conjures up visions of country kitchens, pantries with serried rows of luscious jams and jellies, and rows of apple slices drying in the attic. Nostalgic, perhaps, but very satisfying—and there is certainly no comparison between the flavor of a homemade preserve and its commercial counterpart.

On the next few pages you will find basic methods for the better-known processes, together with information on special equipment and ingredients.

JAMS, MARMALADES AND JELLIES

The basic principle is the same for all three preserves: fruit is cooked until soft, then combined with sugar and boiled until the mixture sets.

Jams and Marmalades

Marmalade normally describes a jam made from citrus fruit; shreds or chunks of peel are suspended in a clear jelly.

Equipment
Preserving kettle, or any very large saucepan with a solid base and wide top. If possible, it should be enamel-lined, or stainless steel.

Scraps of sterilized muslin or cheesecloth for holding seeds and pith.

Canning jars. Jars and/or glasses must be in prime condition, with lids, sealers or gaskets perfect too. All jars must be scrupulously clean; wash in warm, soapy water and rinse well with scalding water. Jars that will later be processed in a boiling-water bath are now ready for use, but others should be sterilized as follows: stand open jars upright in a kettle, fill with hot water until jars are submerged and boil for 15 minutes.

Keep jars in hot water off the heat, until filling.

The jars referred to in the recipes are 1 pint capacity.

Closures. Modern mason jars have 2-piece screwband metal lids (the lids should never be re-used because the sealing compound will never seal right the second time around). Old-style mason jars have one-piece caps for which new rubber rings are required each season. There are also old-style bailed jars with glass lids.

Jelly thermometer

Ingredients
Fruit. With the exception of apples (which should be fully ripe) and gooseberries (which should be half-ripe), it is best to use just-ripe or even slightly under-ripe fruit. This is because pectin, the mucilaginous substance which acts with sugar and acids to produce a set, is lowest in

ripe and over-ripe fruits. Sweet fruits like peaches require the addition of citric acid or the juice of more acid fruits to enable the pectin to work effectively.

Some fruits are naturally low in pectin; this can be counteracted by the addition of:

(1) *The seeds and pith of citrus fruits.* These contain pectin, and should be tied in a separate little muslin bag and cooked with the fruit. Use when making marmalade, but with other jams don't use too much or else the flavor of the jam will be affected.

(2) *Apple or lemon juice, or commercial pectin.* The usual ratio is ½–¾ cup apple juice or 2 tablespoons lemon juice to every 4 cups low-pectin fruit. Follow the manufacturer's instructions if you use commercial pectin.

Fruits especially suitable for jams are listed on the left.

Sugar. Dark sugars are not really suitable as they can change the color and flavor of the fruit.

Water. This is necessary to prevent dry fruit from scorching, and the amount used depends on the type of fruit.

As a rough guide, very juicy soft fruits need no water, moderately juicy ones like plums and apples need half their weight, and dry fruits like pears need an equal weight.

Basic Jam Recipe
Wash, drain and dry the fruit immediately before cooking, otherwise the jam may develop mold. Very soft fruits should be placed, in very small quantities, in a colander and immersed in a pan or bowl of cold water.

Slit the sides of stone fruit and put them into the pan—the pits will rise to the surface during cooking.

Add water to the fruit in the pan, if necessary.

Always start cooking on a low heat, bring to a boil and simmer gently until the fruit is reduced to a pulp. Do not stir. (If you are making marmalade,

Fruits for Jams and Jellies

Excellent jams and jellies can be made with apples (especially green tart ones), barberries, Cape gooseberries, cranberries, currants, damsons, grapes, gooseberries, jujubes, loganberries, medlars, quinces, rowans and sloes. Bearberries make good jams, while crab apples make a delicious jelly. All citrus fruits can be used to make marmalade.

Add additional pectin when making jams and jellies from the following: cherries, Natal plums, plums and rosellas. Jams made from apricots, figs, peaches, rhubarb, tree tomatoes, and all berries with the exception of those listed above will also need additional pectin, as will jellies made from guavas and rose hips.

Pectin Test
If you are in any doubt about the pectin content of the fruit you are cooking, apply the following simple test: Place 1 teaspoon of cooked fruit pulp in a cup and add 1 tablespoon of rubbing alcohol. After about a minute a clot will have formed; if this is firm the pectin content of the pulp is high, but if the clot easily breaks up into smaller ones, you should add more pectin to your jam or jelly.

citrus fruits will require at least 1½–2 hours at this stage, as the peel is very tough.)

Meanwhile, warm the sugar separately (without dissolving it) in a low oven; this speeds up the process, as cold sugar slows the boiling.

Add the pectin required to the fruit, and then add the sugar.

Stir the sugar gently with a wooden spoon as you add it, until it is completely dissolved.

Increase the heat, bring rapidly to boiling point, and keep at a vigorous rolling boil (less vigorous if making a whole fruit jam).

Do not stir, but occasionally draw a wooden spoon across the bottom of the pan to prevent the fruit from sticking.

Test the jam or marmalade for set when the mixture has begun to thicken, first lowering the heat. (Always test *before* you think jell point has been reached rather than *after*; once boiled too much, the preserve will become sticky and dark.)

To test for doneness. Use a jelly thermometer, making necessary adjustments for how far you live above sea level. Without a thermometer, use the refrigerator test: put a little jam on a cold saucer, chill and gently push your finger against the top. A surface skin will wrinkle when the jam is ready.

If jell point has not been reached, bring to a boil and try again in 2–3 minutes.

Finally, remove any scum with a slotted spoon.

Packing. Jams and marmalades are generally packed while very hot. Preserves should never be packed while just warm—mold may form—but any with whole fruit or peel can be allowed to cool very slightly, before being stirred to distribute pieces evenly throughout the jar.

Stand warm, clean, dry jars on several layers of newspaper and pour the jam or marmalade into them, using a ladle and funnel. Fill each jar to within ½ inch of the top.

Processing. Wipe off any preserve from the outside of the jars, and cap jam or marmalade immediately. Lift the jars into a deep kettle or canner half full of boiling water, and add more boiling water so that the jars are at least 2 inches below the water level. Return the water to a full boil and process for 10 minutes. Lift out the jars and complete the seals if necessary.

When completely cold, label and store in a cool, dry, dark place.

Jelly

Making jelly is simpler than making jam, although it is a more time-consuming process.

Unlike jams, which make use of whole fruits (or pieces of fruit), jellies are made from their juice.

A fruit, or combination of fruits, is cooked to extract as much juice as possible, which is then strained and combined with sugar.

A good fruit jelly is clear and bright and full of flavor. It should not be too firmly set.

Equipment
Preserving kettle, jars, thermometer and *sterilized muslin,* as for jam.

Jelly bag, or *colander* covered with 2 or 3 layers of thin muslin.

Ingredients
The same rules apply for fruit and sugar as with jams, but the minimum quantity of water is used. See opposite page for especially suitable fruits.

Basic Jelly Recipe
It is generally unnecessary to peel and core fruit, unless specifically instructed. Just wash and remove stems, and cut larger fruit into pieces.

Put the fruit into a pan with just enough water to cover it, add lemon juice if needed, and simmer gently until the fruit is soft. Soft fruits like berries and black or red currants are ready when the juice is running freely. You can help the process along by gently crushing with a potato masher or wooden fork. Hard fruits like apples and pears must be cut into pieces and cooked slowly until soft—about 30 minutes. Don't crush these—unlike soft, pulpy fruits they have tiny grains that will make the resulting jelly cloudy.

Prepare the jelly bag or colander lined with muslin and put a bowl underneath to catch the juice. Pour in the softened fruit and leave for several hours or overnight to allow the juice to drip through. Never try to force the juice through by pushing the pulp or squeezing the jelly bag as this will make the jelly cloudy.

Measure the juice, and then measure out the correct proportion of sugar—normally 2 cups for every 2½ cups of juice—warmed as for jam.

Place the juice in a clean preserving kettle, add the sugar, and bring gently to a boil, stirring constantly until the sugar is dissolved. Then boil the mixture rapidly until jell point is reached. Don't overboil—the jelly will never set.

To test for doneness. Use a jelly thermometer. Or take a small spoonful of jelly, allow it to cool, then turn the spoon on its side. If the jelly is done it will drop in large flakes instead of running off the spoon.

Take the jelly off the heat and skim off the scum.

Packing. Using a ladle and funnel pour the hot jelly into clean, warm, dry jars, pouring it down the side of the tilted jar to avoid air bubbles. Jelly may be covered with a ⅛ inch thick layer of melted paraffin wax, and does not require processing in a boiling-water bath.

Move the jelly as little as possible, and store in a cool, dry, dark place.

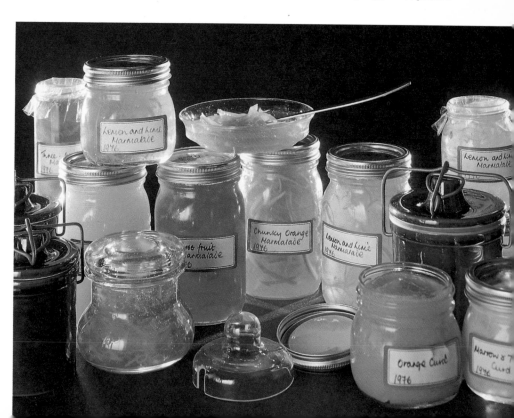

Fruit Cheeses and Butters

Fruit cheeses and butters are a traditional way of making use of windfalls and over-ripe fruit.

Fruit Cheeses

These can be served instead of cheese, or eaten as a dessert. They're also good with meat.

Equipment
Preserving kettle and *jars*, as for jam (page 198).

Jars. They must always be warm, clean and dry.

Ingredients
Fruit. Most fruits make good cheeses.

Sugar. Use refined white cane or beet sugar.

Method
Simmer the fruit in a kettle with just enough water to cover, until it is fine enough to pass through a sieve to remove pits and skins.

Measure the pulp and return it to the clean kettle. (If the pulp is runny, boil fast until it is thick.)

Warm an equal quantity of sugar in the oven, and add to the pulp.

Stir over a low heat until the sugar is dissolved, then simmer gently for about 1 hour, stirring constantly, until the mixture is so stiff and dry it will come away from the sides of the pan in a mass.

Packing. Press the mixture tightly into warm, clean, dry ½ pint or pint canning jars, leaving ½ inch headroom, and adjust the lids. Process for 10 minutes in a boiling-water bath as for jam (page 199).

Store for at least 2 months.

Fruit Butters

These can be served with bread and biscuits, or on layer cakes, and are also delicious with cold desserts and with meats.

Equipment and ingredients are the same as for cheeses; however, less sugar is used.

Method
Follow instructions for fruit cheese, but add only ½ cup warmed sugar for every 1 cup of pulp. Simmer until the water is absorbed and the mixture is thick and creamy.

Packing. Follow directions for fruit cheeses above.

Store for a few weeks and eat within days of opening.

Pickles and Chutneys

Pickles and chutneys are a simple yet delicious way to preserve fruits, without the problem of setting that complicates jam- or jelly-making.

The longer both these preserves are allowed to mature the better, so make them at least a month before you want to use them. If you can wait 3–4 months your patience will be rewarded.

A wide variety of fruit can be used for pickles and/or chutneys, including bananas, kiwi fruit, mangoes, papayas, tamarinds and watermelon, as well as all kinds of stone fruit like cherries and plums and tree fruit (apples, pears, etc).

Pickles

The aim of this method is to preserve one or more fruits in sweetened, spiced vinegar so that it keeps its shape and appearance.

Equipment
Preserving kettle, as used for making for jam (page 198).

Canning jars. Jars and lids must be scrupulously clean.

The jars referred to in the recipes are 1 pint capacity, unless otherwise stated.

Squares of cheesecloth when a recipe calls for whole spices.

Cheesecloth for straining vinegar if ground spices have been used.

Ingredients
Fruit. Always use unblemished, just-ripe fruit.

Vinegar. White or red wine and white distilled or cider vinegars can be used, depending on the color and flavor you want and the type of fruit used. The quantity varies in individual recipes.

Sugar. The type you use – white or brown, etc. – is up to you. Proportions of sugar to vinegar vary with individual fruits.

Other ingredients, depending on the recipe, include *whole* or *ground spices*, *herbs* and *lemon rind*.

Water may be added to less juicy fruits.

Method
Chop or cube fruits if necessary. If you are pickling whole fruits, like cherries or apricots, prick the skins to make sure they don't shrivel.

Keep pits in the fruit if you want the finished pickles to look as attractive as possible.

Put vinegar (and water if used) in a kettle together with the sugar and spices, if any. Tie whole spices in a cheesecloth square.

Bring to a boil, stirring until the sugar has dissolved. Add the fruit and cook gently, covered, until it is just tender. Put in clean, hot jars.

Return the vinegar to the pan and boil uncovered until it has become syrupy. Strain the vinegar through cheesecloth (twice if ground spices were used, to prevent the liquid from being cloudy).

Pour over the fruit, leaving about ½ inch headroom. Adjust lids; then process in a boiling-water bath for 10 minutes as for jam (page 199).

Keep for at least 1 month.

Chutneys and Relishes

As with pickles, fruit for chutneys and relishes is cooked in a basic mixture of vinegar and sugar (with other ingredients, depending on the recipe).

However, unlike pickles, the solid ingredients are finely cut up or minced and the flavor depends on long, slow cooking.

Equipment
Jars and preserving kettle, as for pickles.

Ingredients
Fruit. This need not be at its best. Remember, though, to make sure you remove all bad or blemished parts of the fruit.

Vinegar, sugar. The same rules apply as for pickles.

Other ingredients can include *strong-flavored vegetables* like onions, *herbs*, *spices*, *mustard*, *raisins* and other *fruit*, etc.

Method
Peel and finely chop or mince the fruit (and other solid ingredients if necessary). Put in a kettle with the rest of the ingredients including the vinegar and sugar, and bring to a boil, stirring until the sugar is dissolved. Then simmer gently, uncovered, for about 2 hours until the mixture is soft, individual ingredients are unrecognizable, and the chutney has thickened.

Packing. Pour the hot chutney into hot, clean jars, adjust lids and process in a boiling-water bath for 10 minutes (page 199).

Label, and keep in a cool, dark place for at least 2 months.

CANNING

Canning is a cheap, quick and reliable way of preserving fruit and the only way, apart from freezing, in which the fruit and its taste and texture remain virtually intact.

Basically, the canning process consists of packing fruit into sterile jars, covering it with syrup, and sterilizing it at a high temperature in a boiling-water bath.

The jars are sealed while they are still hot, to prevent contamination by bacteria.

Equipment

Jars. Use only canning jars, which must be in perfect condition. The glass must not be chipped, the metal must not be scratched or damaged, and rubber sealing-rings must not be flawed. Always use new rubber rings, and new metal lids if you are using screw-top jars.

Deep kettle or *canner* for processing. Usually made of heavy enameled ware, this has a rack to hold containers off the bottom of the kettle.

A pressure canner may also be used for processing.

Ingredients

Fruit. Must be fresh, just ripe, firm and clean.

A surprising number of fruits can be canned successfully. They include most berries and citrus fruits, apples, apricots, cherries, figs, grapes, guavas, litchis, Natal plums and plums, nectarines, peaches, dessert pears, pineapples and quinces.

Syrup. Generally made from 1 cup sugar to 2½ cups water, although very tart or tightly packed fruit may require more sugar. Put the water and sugar in a saucepan and bring to a boil, stirring until the sugar dissolves, and boil for 1 minute.

For luxurious preserves, add liqueur or brandy to the syrup.

Water can be used instead of syrup, but it is not as successful at preserving color and flavor.

Method

Sterilizing jars. Wash very thoroughly in hot soapy water, scrubbing inside with a brush and paying particular attention to the bottom corners and to the tops. Rinse them equally thoroughly in scalding water to remove all traces of detergent. Keep the jars covered or filled with hot water until used, to keep out all dust or airborne spoilers. Tops of jars

must also be sterilized.

The jars need not be dried, as the fruit slips more easily into wet jars.

Packing fruit into jars. Peel, core, pit, hull or husk the fruit as appropriate. Depending on type and size, it can be canned whole or it can be halved, sliced or cut into chunks; remember, though, that the pieces must be of uniform size.

Pack the fruit tightly into the prepared, still-wet jars, being careful not to bruise softer fruits. Tap or shake the jars to help the fruit settle.

Processing

Fruits may be packed in their containers raw or hot. For raw pack, uncooked fruit is packed firmly into jars and boiling syrup is added, leaving headroom to allow for the expansion of solids and bubbling-up of liquid during processing. With a hot pack, precooked fruit is packed in jars while still hot. Shake jars to settle the pieces of fruit, then insert a table knife down the side of the jars to release any air bubbles. Wipe the sealing edge of the jar to remove anything that could prevent a perfect seal, then cap the jar. For a modern mason jar, set the metal lid on the rim of the jar and screw down the band firmly tight. For jars with 3-piece glass closures, set a wet rubber ring on the rim of the jar, place the glass lid on the rubber and screw down the metal band; when the band is tight, give it a ¼ inch counter-turn to allow the jar to vent during processing. (After processing is completed, retighten the metal band.) For old-style mason jars, screw the porcelain-lined zinc cap down tight on the rubber-padded shoulder of the jar, then give a ¼ inch counter-turn to allow for venting. (Retighten after processing.) For bailed jars, set the rounded glass lid on the rubber ring and push the longer hoop up over the top of the lid to hold it firmly. (After processing, snap the lower bail down on the shoulder of the jar.)

Jars of raw-packed fruit must start their processing in hot—but never boiling—water; therefore, the total processing time is longer than for hot-packed foods, which start processing in boiling water.

Lift the jars into the kettle or canner that is half full of hot or boiling water, placing them on the rack so they do not touch each other or the sides of the bottle.

Add more hot or boiling water so

that the jars are at least 2 inches below the water level. Bring the water to a full boil, then begin timing the processing of the fruit.

The timing varies with individual fruits. For example, pint jars of hot-packed apricots, nectarines, peaches and plums require 20 minutes. If these same fruits are raw packed, in the same quantities, apricots, nectarines and peaches all require 25 minutes, while plums must be processed for 20 minutes. Sweet or tart cherries must be processed for 10 minutes if hot packed, 20 minutes if raw packed, while pint jars of hot packed or raw packed rhubarb require 10 minutes.

Hot packing is recommended for the following fruit—processing times are given in brackets: apples and pineapples (20 minutes); figs (90 minutes); gooseberries, loquats and papayas (15 minutes); guavas (16 minutes); firm berries like blueberries and currants (10 minutes).

Raw packing is recommended for mangoes and soft berries like raspberries and blackberries (15 minutes) and grapefruit (30 minutes).

When processing is completed, remove jars from kettle with a jarlifter and complete seals, if necessary. Set the jars on a rack or several layers of newspaper and allow to cool for at least 12 hours before testing the seals.

Storage. Test that the seal is complete before storing. On modern mason jars, the metal lids of 2-piece screw-band closures will have snapped down; any lids that are not concave should be tested by pressing—if it springs back the seal is gone. Old-style mason jars and bailed jars can be tested by tilting them so that fruit presses against the closure. If bubbles or moisture appear at the sealing point, the seal is poor.

For all jars, except old masons with a zinc cap, it is a good idea to apply the following, really tough test. Remove the screw-bands or bail with your fingertips, and hold each jar firmly by the lid only.

If the vacuum seal is complete, the lid will hold.

Label each jar carefully with the name of the fruit and the date, and store in a cool, dry, dark place.

Alternatively, you can wrap each bottle or jar in heavy brown paper; this protective wrapping will prevent the fruit losing its color.

FRUIT VINEGARS AND SYRUPS

Fruit Vinegars

Fruit-flavoured vinegars taste wonderful in salad dressings, and with fruit salads and hot puddings.

Equipment
Preserving kettle, as for jam (page 198).
Fine, sterilized muslin or cheesecloth.
Hot, dry canning jars.

Ingredients
Fruit. Soft fruits like berries and currants give wonderful results.
Vinegar. Use white wine vinegar, which won't overpower the flavor of the fruit.
White sugar.

Method
Put the fruit in a china or glass bowl, discarding any blemished or bad pieces. Bruise with a wooden spoon or kitchen fork and add 2½ cups vinegar for every 1 pound fruit. Put a cloth over the top of the bowl, and leave fo 3–5 days, stirring occasionally.

Strain the liquid through a fine cloth or nylon sieve, and measure. Put in pan, add sugar in the ratio of 1 cup to 2½ cups liquid.

Bring gently to a boil, stirring until the sugar is dissolved, and then boil for 10 minutes.

Pour the hot vinegar into hot, dry jars, to within ¾ inch of the top. Cap, then process in a hot-water bath – water just simmering – for 30 minutes. After processing, complete seals, if necessary, and allow to cool.

Syrups

Syrups can be diluted with water or soda to make a refreshing drink, and can also be used as a sauce for puddings and desserts.

Equipment
Preserving kettle and *hot, dry jars*, as for fruit vinegars.
Jelly bag or *colander* lined with 2 or 3 thicknesses of cheesecloth, as for jelly (page 199).

Ingredients
Fruit. Soft fruits are best. They must always be fresh, ripe and clean.
Sugar. As for jam (page 198).
Water. Very little is needed – just enough to start the juices flowing when the fruit is heated.

Method
Follow the instructions for making jelly (page 199), up to draining the juice through a jelly bag or colander. Unlike jellies, the fruit pulp can be pressed at the end of the process.

Measure the juice and put in a pan with sugar in the ratio of ½–¾ cup sugar for every 2½ cups juice, Stir over gentle heat until dissolved.

Strain again and pour into hot, dry jars, filling to within 1 inch of the top. Cap, then process in a hot-water bath – water just simmering – for 30 minutes. After processing, complete seals, if necessary, and allow to cool.

Label and store in a cool, dark place for up to 6 months.

Fruit juices can be sterilized in the same way.

DRYING

One of the oldest methods of preserving food, drying is a simple but somewhat lengthy process.

Outdoor Drying

Sun drying is the most desirable method – but only possible in a hot, sunny climate.

To be successful, you will need special trays – stretch cheesecloth across a wooden frame. Place the prepared fruit on the cheesecloth, cover with another piece of cheesecloth to protect the fruit from insects and dust, and put on a table in the sun until the fruit dries. This can take up to a week, so remember to bring the trays in at night.

Always bring the fruit indoors, too, if there is any moisture in the air during the day.

Indoor Drying

Fruit can be successfully dried indoors provided you bear in mind that the basic principle of the process – to remove all moisture from the fruit, thus inhibiting growth of the enzymes which cause deterioration – is based on having the correct temperature, and also on plenty of ventilation.

The warm air must circulate freely, so the fruit should be placed on a cake- or cooling-rack covered with cheesecloth.

Fruit can be dried in a very cool electric oven – the ideal temperature is 120°–150°. If your oven does not have a low enough temperature, use the residual heat left after cooking when the oven is turned off. An airing cupboard containing a hot-water boiler can also be used.

Leave the door ajar, whether you use an oven or cupboard.

Whatever method you use, it is vital that the temperature is correct, otherwise the fruit will "cook" and shrivel. Check the temperature with a thermometer.

Drying times vary according to the moisture content of the fruit – as little as 4–6 hours for apples and pears, as much as 2 days for whole apricots and peaches. The process can be interrupted, and the total drying time spread over as many days as necessary.

When finally dry, fruit must be allowed to cool completely for about 12 hours in a cool, dark place before being stored in scrupulously clean containers. Allow some ventilation into containers or the fruit may become moldy.

Individual Fruits

With the exception of citrus fruits and small soft fruits and berries (which become hard and shriveled), most fruits can be dried.

Common tree-growing fruits such as apples, pears and plums are especially suitable for drying, as are grapes and bananas.

Always use unblemished, just-ripe specimens.

Apples and pears should be cored and thinly peeled, then sliced in rings and dropped into lightly salted water to prevent their going brown. Dry on paper towels, then either thread the rings onto canes cut to fit the width of the oven for indoor drying, or else place them in a single layer on cheesecloth-covered racks.

Alternatively, pears can be quartered and dried on racks, with the cut sides uppermost.

Apricots, nectarines, peaches and plums can be dried whole but are better halved and pitted if large.

Dry cherries, dates, figs and grapes whole – also persimmons, but skin them first. To dry litchis, remove the shell-like skins, cut in half, remove the pit, and lay the halves cut side uppermost. Peel bananas and cut into slices.

FREEZING

Provided it is properly prepared, ̷̵ can be kept in a freezer for up t̷ year without loss of quality, flavor o̷ color.

Choose top-quality specimens that are in just-ripe condition. Wash, drain and dry thoroughly (but unless it is absolutely essential do not wash soft fruit).

Though pitted fruit can be frozen whole, it is economical of space to peel and pit or seed them and cut them into segments or rings, for close packing.

Containers
Use heavy-duty polyethylene bags sealed with paper-covered wire ties, or moisture-proof plastic, aluminum foil or waxed cardboard containers. Square or rectangular boxes use less space than round ones.

Always make sure containers are scrupulously clean – freezing does not destroy bacteria.

Label each container not only with a description of its contents, but also with the date of freezing.

Methods
There are basically three methods of freezing.

Dry pack. Place the prepared fruit on paper-covered trays in single layers and freeze overnight or until solidly frozen.

Pack the fruit into moisture-proof containers before returning to the freezer.

Wet pack with sugar. Pack the fruit straight into containers with a generous sprinkling of sugar between layers, in the proportion of ½ cup sugar to 1 pound prepared fruit.

This method is particularly suitable for soft fruit.

Wet pack with syrup. Pack the prepared fruit into containers with a syrup made by dissolving 1–2 cups sugar in 2½ cups water. The strength of the syrup varies with different fruits, but 1 cup sugar is generally used. Bring the syrup to a boil, and allow it to cool completely before pouring it over the fruit.

Leave a ½ inch space at the top of each container to allow for expansion during freezing.

Purées may be frozen, but they should not be kept in the freezer for longer than 8 months; fruit juices for up to 6 months.

Thaw fruit in the containers; this will take about 3 or 4 hours at room temperature.

̷̷ ̷̷d ̷̷ ̷̷ ̷̷ ̷kinds of pastry, mayonnaise and other sauces, garnishes, etc required

PASTRY

The quantities given for the following recipes are enough to line, or cover, one 8 or 9 inch pie pan.

If a greater quantity is needed, keep the same proportions between the ingredients.

Basic Pie Pastry

1 cup flour
Pinch of salt
2 tablespoons shortening
2 tablespoons butter or margarine

Sift flour and salt into a bowl. Cut shortening and butter or margarine into small pieces and add to flour, rubbing together with the tips of the fingers until the mixture looks like fine bread crumbs.

Add 1 or 2 tablespoons water and, using a round-bladed knife, mix to a stiff dough.

Leave in a cool place for about 30 minutes. Use as directed.

Rich Pie Pastry

1 cup flour
¼ cup butter or margarine
1 tablespoon sugar
1 egg yolk

Combine flour and butter or margarine as for Basic Pie Pastry (above).

Stir in sugar using a round-bladed knife. Beat the egg yolk together with a tablespoon of cold water and add to the mixture. Mix to a stiff dough.

Leave in a cool place for about 30 minutes. Use as directed.

Sweet Pie Pastry

1 cup flour
6 tablespoons butter or margarine
¼ cup sugar
2 egg yolks
2–3 drops vanilla

Combine flour, butter or margarine and sugar as for Rich Pie Pastry (above). Beat egg yolks with vanilla and add to the flour mixture. Mix to a stiff dough.

Leave for at least 30 minutes before rolling out. Use as directed.

for the recipes in this book. Basic methods for desserts are also included, as well as a section on wine- and liqueur-making.

Rough Puff Pastry

1 cup flour
3 tablespoons shortening
3 tablespoons butter or margarine
Lemon juice

Combine flour, shortening and butter or margarine as for Basic Pie Pastry (left). Add a squeeze of lemon juice to about 6 tablespoons water and mix with the flour mixture until it forms a soft dough.

Transfer to a floured board and roll to a rectangle of consistent thickness. Mark into thirds, then fold up the bottom third and fold down the top third to give 3 layers. Lightly seal the edges.

Turn the pastry through 90°, roll out into another rectangle and repeat the folding process.

Let the pastry rest in a cool place for 20 minutes, then repeat the rolling and folding process twice more. Allow it to rest a further 10 minutes.

Use as directed.

Pre-baked Pie Shell

Use basic pie, rich pie or sweet pie pastry made with 1 cup flour for an 8 or 9 inch pan.

Roll the pastry into a circle about ⅛ inch thick and about 2 inches wider than the pan.

Lift the pastry carefully on a rolling pin and transfer it to the pan. Don't stretch the pastry, but press it down gently onto the bottom and against the sides so that there are no gaps.

Trim the shell by rolling the rolling pin over the top of the pan to cut off any excess pastry.

Prick the pastry all over with a fork, and then line the bottom with a circle of foil.

Alternatively, cover the bottom with parchment paper weighed down with dried beans.

Bake basic pie and rich pie pastry in a preheated 400° oven for 15 minutes. Sweet pie pastry is baked for the same length of time, but in a preheated 350° oven.

After 15 minutes remove foil or parchment paper and beans, and bake for a further 5 or 10 minutes until lightly colored.

DESSERTS

Fruit Tart

Use basic pie, rich pie or sweet pie pastry for this recipe.

1 pound fruit
Sugar
One 8 or 9 inch pie shell, pre-baked (page 203)
Arrowroot

Cook fruit gently in a saucepan with sugar to taste until it is tender but still keeps its shape.

Drain fruit and arrange in the pie shell. Measure juice, add 1 tablespoon arrowroot for every 1¼ cups, juice and bring to a boil. Pour the juice over the fruit and leave to cool before serving.

Serves 6–8.

Note: Uncooked fruit may be arranged in the pastry case and covered with a glaze made from a suitably flavored jam, melted and mixed with water or lemon juice.

Basic Fruit Fool

A fool is essentially a mixture of fruit purée and whipped cream or rich custard. Some fruits like bananas and ripe guavas can be puréed raw, while others like red currants must be cooked first with sugar and just enough water to cover.

1¼ cups heavy cream, or ¾ cup
*   heavy cream and ¾ cup light*
*   cream, or 1¼ cups rich custard*
*   sauce (see opposite page)*
1¼ cups fruit purée
Sugar
Orange or lemon juice, vanilla
*   or other flavoring*

Whip the cream or creams and carefully fold in the fruit purée. If you are using custard, leave it to cool before adding the purée.

Add sugar and any other flavorings to taste.

Chill and serve in individual glass dishes.

Serves 6.

Basic Fruit Cream

A cream is essentially the same as a fool, except that it is never made with custard and the fruit may be cut into small pieces (or even left whole) instead of being puréed.

Double-crust Pie

Use basic pie or rich pie pastry for this recipe.

Pastry made with 2 cups flour
*   (see above)*
1–1½ pounds fruit
Sugar
Spices, lemon juice, etc. (optional)
1–2 tablespoons cornstarch or flour
*   (optional)*
Milk or beaten egg

Divide the pastry into 2 portions, one slightly larger than the other. Roll out one portion into a circle about ⅛ inch thick and about 2 inches wider than pie pan.

Transfer the circle to the pan, lifting it on a rolling pin, and pressing it down gently onto the bottom and against the sides. Trim any overhanging pastry level with the top of the pan.

Slice fruit if necessary, and toss with sugar to taste, spices or other flavorings such as lemon juice, and cornstarch or flour if necessary to thicken juices from the fruit.

The filling should be piled high in the center to allow for shrinkage as the fruit cooks.

Roll out the second portion of pastry into a circle about ⅛ inch thick and about 1 inch wider than the pan.

Moisten the edge of the pastry in the pan with water, then lift the second pastry circle and put it over the pan to form a lid.

Press the edges together to seal in the juices of the filling, and fold the overhang of the pastry lid under the pan's rim.

Cut a hole or slit in the center of the pie, to allow steam to escape. Brush top with milk or beaten egg and bake in a preheated 400° oven until the pastry is golden.

Serves 6–8.

Note: For a single-crust pie put fruit directly into pie pan, and cover with basic pie, rich pie or rough puff pastry made with 1 cup flour.

Basic Ice Cream

Ice cream can be made in a freezer or in the feezer compartment of a refrigerator.

1¼ cups fruit purée
½ cup sugar
1 teaspoon lemon juice
1¼ cups heavy cream, or ¾ cup
*   heavy cream and ¾ cup light*
*   cream*

Put the fruit purée, sugar and lemon juice in a bowl and mix well until smooth.

In another bowl whip the cream until thick but not so thick as to form peaks. Fold in the purée mixture, and transfer to an ice cube tray or shallow plastic box. Cover with foil and freeze until the ice cream is solid around the sides.

Scrape out into a bowl, beat until uniformly smooth, then return to the container. Freeze until firm. Transfer the ice cream container to the main compartment of the refrigerator about 30 minutes before serving.

Serves 6.

Note: The quantities of sugar and lemon juice will depend on the nature of the fruit, its sweetness or acidity.

For very rich fruits like avocados use proportionately less cream.

Basic Water Ice

The proportion of fruit juice or fruit purée to syrup can be varied, but they should combine to make about 1 quart.

½ cup sugar
2½ cups fruit juice, or 1¼–2 cups fruit
*   purée*
Juice of ½ lemon
2 egg whites

Put the sugar in a saucepan with 1½–2½ cups water, depending on the quantity of fruit juice or purée (see above). Bring to a boil, stirring frequently, then simmer for about 10 minutes. Leave to cool.

Add lemon juice and fruit juice or purée to the syrup. Taste and add more sugar or lemon juice if necessary.

Pour the mixture into a shallow tray, cover with foil, and put in the freezer.

When the water ice has a slushy consistency (after about an hour), turn it into a bowl and beat well to remove ice crystals. Beat egg whites and fold them into the water ice. Freeze again.

Transfer the water ice to the main compartment of the refrigerator about 30 minutes before serving.

Serves 6.

Basic Table Gelatin

2 cups fruit juice
1 envelope unflavored gelatin
Sugar

Put about 3 tablespoons fruit juice in a small bowl and sprinkle with gelatin. Leave gelatin to soften for about 10 minutes.

Meanwhile, put the remaining fruit juice in a saucepan and add enough sugar to sweeten it if necessary. Heat gently, stirring, until the sugar is dissolved and put aside to cool.

Place the bowl containing the softened gelatin over a pan of hot (not boiling) water until the gelatin dissolves. Add to the fruit juice, and stir gently.

Pour juice into a mold that has been rinsed with cold water, and chill until set.

To unmold the gelatin, hold the mold in a bowl of hot water for just a few seconds.

Serves 4–6.

Note: For a gelatin made with fruit purée instead of juice, sweeten the purée to taste with sugar and add enough water to make 2 cups. Dissolve gelatin with water and proceed as above.

VANILLA SUGAR

Put 2 cups of sugar in a jar with a vanilla bean. Close the jar tightly and store. The vanilla flavor will permeate the sugar.

GARNISHES

Croûtons

Cut slices of stale white bread into very small cubes. Fry in shallow or deep fat until golden brown. Drain well and salt lightly before serving.

Sugared Croûtons

Cut slices of sweet milk bread and spread them thinly on both sides with butter. Bake them in a preheated 400° oven for 15–20 minutes until they are crisp and golden.

Dice the baked bread and toss the cubes in sugar.

Cinnamon Croûtons

Follow instructions for sugared croûtons, but toss cubes in a mixture of ground cinnamon and sugar.

SAUCES

Thick Custard Sauce

Double the quantities given below for 2½ cups of custard sauce.

1¼ cups milk
½ vanilla bean
2 eggs
1 heaping tablespoon sugar

Heat the milk very gently in a saucepan with the vanilla bean. Do not allow to boil. Remove the pan from the heat, cover and stand in a warm place to infuse for 10 minutes.

Cream eggs and sugar together in a bowl. Remove the vanilla bean from the milk and gradually pour the milk onto the egg mixture, whisking all the time. Strain the mixture into a saucepan and heat very gently, over hot water or very low heat, until the custard is creamy, and stays separated if you run your finger through it on the back of a wooden spoon.

Rich Custard Sauce

Use 1¼ cups heavy or light cream instead of milk, and 3 egg yolks instead of 2 eggs.

Orange or Lemon Custard Sauce

Stir in 2 tablespoons orange juice or 1 tablespoon lemon juice when the custard thickens. Stir gently until the juice is blended with the custard.

Mayonnaise

1 egg yolk
½ teaspoon dry mustard
½ teaspoon salt
Freshly ground black pepper
¾ cup olive or salad oil
1 tablespoon white wine vinegar

Beat the egg yolk in a bowl until it is thick.

Add the mustard, salt and pepper, beating well.

Add the oil drop by drop to start with, whisking hard after every drop so that it is completely absorbed before the next drop is added. When the mixture is thick and shiny you can add the rest of the oil in a steady trickle, whisking all the time. Finally, add the vinegar and blend in well.

Makes ¾ cup.

Lemon Mayonnaise

Use 1 tablespoon lemon juice instead of white wine vinegar.

WINES AND LIQUEURS

The most important point to remember when making wine is to make sure that all the equipment is clean and rinsed in a sterilizing solution, usually 2 Campden tablets and ½ teaspoon of citric acid dissolved in 2½ cups cold water.

Wines also need a warm atmosphere (65–75°) for fermentation to take place successfully. Always store at about 55°.

Wines

Equipment
Specialized equipment is available from wine supply stores.

Primary fermentor. This is a large container in which the fruit is prepared for fermentation. It must have a close-fitting lid and be easy to keep scrupulously clean. A 10–20 gallon capacity plastic pail with plastic garbage bags as a lid are ideal. If you are going to make smaller quantities use a bucket-sized plastic pail, again with a close-fitting lid. Never use a metal primary fermentor (fermentation can only take place in an acidic solution which reacts with metals).

Secondary fermentor. The main fermentation occurs in this container, which should have a narrow neck and also be easy to keep scrupulously clean. A glass carboy satisfies these requirements and you will also be able to see the wine and check its progress. The standard 1 gallon glass jug is ideal for most recipes.

Fermentation lock (air-lock). This should be fitted into the narrow neck of the secondary fermentor.

Siphon. In its simplest form this is a length of tubing about 4 feet long. Plastic tubing is popular, although more sophisticated siphons can be bought.

Storage vessel. This can also be a corked glass carboy. If you are making a deep red wine, it is advisable to cover a clear glass vessel with a brown paper "jacket" to exclude light and preserve the rich coloring of the wine. A large glazed earthenware jar, which can be tightly sealed, also makes an excellent storage vessel.

Wine bottles. These must be thoroughly cleaned and sterilized before use.

Cylindrical corks or *screw caps.*

Corking gun. This is essential for inserting corks into bottles.

Linen bag. A large bag about 2 feet by 1 foot, which can be securely sealed, is useful for squeezing fruit pulp in order to extract the maximum juice.

With hard fruits, such as apples, a *small press* or even an *electric juice extractor* is a good investment, especially if you are sure you are going to make wine regularly.

Ingredients

Specialized ingredients are available from wine supply stores.

Fruit. Always use good quality, undamaged fruit. It should be washed thoroughly and pitted if necessary. There is no need to remove skin or peel.

Hard fruits like apples should be crushed before placing in the primary fermentor.

Water should be pure. Tap-water satisfies this requirement.

Sugar. White granulated sugar is suitable for most wine recipes. Brown sugar gives a slight caramel flavor to the wine. Sugar should always be added in the form of a syrup, made up of 4 cups sugar to 2½ cups water, unless it is added before the yeast.

Yeast. Use a proper wine yeast. It comes in several forms, usually as tablets or a liquid. Follow manufacturer's instructions for activation and use.

Yeast nutrient. Yeast, like any other living organism, needs nutrients if it is to grow and cause fermentation. Only grapes provide the natural food for wine yeast.

When using fruits other than grapes, nutrients must be added.

Acid blend. The yeast cannot ferment sugar, turning it into alcohol, unless it is in an acid solution. Although some fruits provide enough acid, it is sometimes necessary to add extra acid.

Grape tannin. This is necessary to give a wine "bite". As with citric acid, some fruits contain enough tannin. The cheapest way to provide extra is in the form of cold, strong tea.

Pectic enzyme. This is an artificial pectin-destroying enzyme. It is found in many fruits, and will cause haze in wine if not removed.

Campden tablets. A form of potassium metabisulfite, these are used for sterilizing.

Sterile conditions are necessary to prevent growth of unwanted molds and bacteria.

Raisins. Most recipes include raisins to give the wine true vinosity.

Basic wine recipe

All equipment must be thoroughly washed, dried and sterilized. Sterilization is essential to prevent the growth of molds and bacteria which will inhibit or even stop fermentation.

A standard sterilizing solution consists of 2 Campden tablets and ½ teaspoon citric acid dissolved in 2½ cups cold water.

Rinse your equipment – pails, bottles, corks, spoons, siphon – in this solution.

Preparing a must. The fruit mixture on which fermentation takes place is known as a must.

Put the prepared fruit in a clean, sterile primary fermentor. Add the chopped raisins, water, Campden tablet(s), pectic enzyme and acid blend (if required). Cover the pail and leave for at least 24 hours, in a warm place (65–75°).

Fermenting on the pulp. This preliminary fermentation improves the color and flavor of most fruit wines. However, not all recipes include this stage.

Quickly uncover the primary fermentor and stir in the yeast nutrient and activated yeast. Manufacturer's instructions should be followed for the amount of yeast to use and method of activation.

Replace the lid and leave for the time recommended in the recipe in a warm place (65–75°).

This fermentation gives off carbon dioxide which lifts the fruit up. It must be pushed down and stirred into the liquid, at least once a day, to keep it moist.

Do this quickly and be sure to keep the vessel closely covered at all other times.

Extracting the juice (young wine). Strain the fruit mixture through a fine sieve, taking out a jugful at a time, into a clean sterilized container.

Put the pulp into a linen bag or cloth. Close in the pulp tightly and squeeze out the rest of the juice into the sterilized container.

A small press or electric juice extractor is useful for large quantities of hard fruits.

Fermentation. Stir in the sugar syrup. (Some recipes ask for sugar to be added before the yeast.) Add tannin if necessary, in the form of grape tannin or cold strong tea – ½ teacup to 1 gallon wine.

Stir well, then siphon the young wine into a clean, sterilized secondary fermentor, filling to within 1 inch of the cork. Do all this quickly so that the young wine is not left uncovered for too long, to prevent bacteria entering and inhibiting fermentation.

Seal the secondary fermentor with a clean, sterile, tight-fitting air-lock.

When siphoning, place the secondary fermentor so that its top is below the level of the bottom of the container being emptied. Put one end of the siphon tube in the container of young wine and the other well into the secondary fermentor.

Leave the sealed secondary fermentor in a warm place (65–75°) until fermentation is complete and bubbling in the air-lock has ceased.

A layer of sediment (the lees) will appear on the bottom of the vessel as the wine clears from the top downward. Leave until there is a good layer of lees, then rack.

Racking. This helps to produce a clear, bright wine. It is usual to rack at least 3 times. All but the final racking should be into a clear vessel of similar type and size to the fermentation vessel – a glass carboy is ideal. Like all winemaking equipment it should be cleaned and sterilized in the Campden tablet solution. The final racking is into the storage vessel. It need not be clear, but should be of a size to be filled almost exactly with the quantity of wine produced.

Racking consists of siphoning off the clear wine, above the lees in the secondary fermentor, into a new vessel. Make sure the end of the siphon tube is above the lees when doing this. If necessary replenish with cold water to fill the vessel and keep air out of the wine. (The size of the receiving vessel should not be such that a large quantity of water needs to be added.)

Seal the vessel and leave in a cool, dark place (55°) until another layer of lees has formed (no longer than 10 weeks), then repeat the process until no lees form. Rack once more into a storage vessel keeping the end of the siphon tube just above the bottom of the vessel the wine is being racked from.

Seal the storage vessel tightly.

Storage. Leave the storage vessel in a cool dark place (55°) for 2 months. Then check for haze by pouring off some of the wine into a glass. This is unlikely to form, but if it has, rack the wine again and store for a further 2 months. Check again for haze. If the wine is not clear, add a teaspoon of pectic enzyme and continue to store. The total storage time must be at least the minimum time stated in the recipe.

Bottling. Prepare the corks by soaking them for 30 minutes in hot water, then rinsing in the Campden tablet solution to sterilize them.

Siphon the wine into clean, sterilized wine bottles to within 1¾ inches of the top. Cork using the corking gun. Fit a foil cap over the cork, to prevent bacteria entering the bottle. Label each bottle with the name of the wine and date of bottling.

Store the bottles on their sides (in a wine rack) in a cool, dark place (55°).

Keep at least 6 months before drinking.

Liqueurs

Fruit liqueurs are prepared by steeping the fruit in a commercially produced alcohol to extract the flavor, aroma and color.

No special equipment is needed, but all bottles, etc, must be scrupulously clean. If you want to make doubly sure the equipment is clean, rinse in the sterilizing solution given for wines.

Ingredients

Fruit Liqueurs can be made from most fruits, although those with a strongly distinctive flavor give the best results.

Alcohol. Choice of spirits is optional. Vodka is popular, and there are certain traditional combinations like cherries and brandy.

Sugar. White or brown sugar can be used, depending on the fruit and type of spirit.

Basic Liqueur Recipe

2 pounds fruit
4 cups sugar
1½ quarts spirits

Wash the fruit and remove pits if necessary. Pack fruit into a large wide-necked, screw-top glass jar, covering each layer of fruit with a generous layer of sugar. Berries should be crushed and mixed with the sugar before they are placed in the jar.

Fill the jar with spirits, tightly screw on the lid, and leave to mature for up to 6 months at room temperature.

Strain off the liqueur, and pour or syphon it into clean dry bottles.

Makes about 1½ quarts.

MEASUREMENTS

The list below gives metric measures for weight and liquid capacity, and their equivalents used in this book.

Weight

25 g	1 ounce
50 g	2 ounces
75 g	3 ounces
100–125 g	4 ounces
150 g	5 ounces
175 g	6 ounces
200 g	7 ounces
225 g	8 ounces
250 g	9 ounces
275 g	10 ounces
300 g	11 ounces
350 g	12 ounces
375 g	13 ounces
400 g	14 ounces
425 g	15 ounces
450 g	1 pound
500 g (½ kilo)	17½ ounces
1 kilo	2 pounds 3 ounces
1.5 kilos	3 pounds 5 ounces
2 kilos	4 pounds 6 ounces
2.5 kilos	5 pounds 8 ounces
3 kilos	6 pounds 10 ounces
3.5 kilos	7 pounds 11 ounces
4 kilos	8 pounds 13 ounces
4.5 kilos	9 pounds 14 ounces
5 kilos	11 pounds

Liquid Capacity

120 ml	½ cup
150 ml	⅔ cup
175 ml	¾ cup
250 ml	1 cup
300 ml	1¼ cups
325 ml	1⅓ cups
350 ml	1½ cups
375 ml	1⅔ cups
400 ml	1¾ cups
500 ml	2 cups
600 ml	2½ cups
750 ml	3 cups
800 ml	3½ cups
1 litre	4 cups (1 quart)
1.2 litres	5 cups
1.5 litres	6 cups (1½ quarts)
2 litres	8 cups (2 quarts)
2.5 litres	10 cups (2½ quarts)

Oven Temperatures

130°C	250°F
140°C	275°F
150°C	300°F
170°C	325°F
180°C	350°F
190°C	375°F
200°C	400°F
220°C	425°F
230°C	450°F

NUTRITION

Any normal diet (unless you are restricted for medical reasons) should include at least two servings of fruit a day. One of the easiest ways to manage this is to have fruit juice or sliced fruit at breakfast, and fresh fruit (instead of cake or pudding) as a lunchtime or dinner dessert.

RAPID-ACTION DIETS

Fruit is the basis of many "wonder diets" or "crash diets" – the sort that, typically, are taken up by the press and gain an international following until superseded by some even newer formula for rapid weight loss.

If you have the willpower to embark on one of these semi-starvation diets – and are prepared to cope with an essentially monotonous succession of mini-meals comprising only one or two ingredients – you will undoubtedly lose weight!

But it is certainly inadvisable to pursue such a diet for more than two or three days at a stretch without your doctor's approval.

This is because a "wonder diet" is unlikely to be a well-balanced diet, and therefore it cannot supply your body with all the essential nutrients in the right amounts and proportions. Some crash diets aim specifically to reduce the body's calorific intake; be very careful of these if the recommended intake falls below 1,000 calories a day and you take regular physical exercise.

Another thing to consider – and be prepared for – is that some all-fruit diets are inclined to have a laxative effect. Indeed, for some people on normal diets, a sudden switch to a fruit-only regimen may wreak havoc with the digestion; if the symptoms persist or cause any real pain, switch immediately to a more varied diet that includes fruit.

Older people are likely to find large quantities of rhubarb or stewed apples difficult to digest; they too should keep to milder forms of restricted fruit diet, including fruit juices.

Once you are down to your target weight you will still have to take care to prevent it from creeping up again. So when you have completed the crash diet change to a well-balanced maintenance one.

All in all, it is a good idea to talk to your doctor before embarking on any diet involving the loss of more than 5–10 pounds.

Single-fruit Diets

The theory about single-fruit – or any single-food – diets is simply that the appetite is diminished by boredom. An appetizer of sliced oranges or melon can be a delightful start to a meal; but when the main course is also sliced oranges or melon, and the dessert is sliced oranges or melon, it takes a determined food freak to continue eating huge quantities even if no limit is placed on the amount of fruit permitted.

This effect is important; if you in fact went on eating voraciously you would ingest an enormous number of calories.

As it is, a day a week on a restricted fruit diet can be added to your dieting program (unless your doctor advises otherwise).

Apples

A single good-sized apple, cored but unskinned, 4 times a day. It can be raw, puréed, baked or stewed, with spices but no sugar. To drink: water and pure unsweetened apple juice.

Bananas

2 medium-sized bananas and 1 glass of skimmed milk at breakfast, lunch and supper. To ring the changes you can liquidize the milk and bananas in a blender – adding a sprinkling of cinnamon, nutmeg or other spice – to make a creamy drink. Bananas are one of the high-calorie fruits, so don't add anything else to this diet.

Grapefruit

1 large grapefruit 3 times a day – with added spices sprinkled on, if you wish, but no sugar. If you really find grapefruit too sour on its own, add just a dab of honey. To drink: either grapefruit juice or else pure lemon juice diluted in hot water.

The theory that grapefruit is able to destroy fats in the system is without foundation but – like apricots, berries, lemons, melon, rhubarb and tangerines – it is low in calories.

A less spartan diet that includes grapefruit is as follows:

Breakfast: half a grapefruit, unsweetened; 2 eggs, cooked as you wish; 2 slices bacon; coffee or tea, without milk or sugar (but add an artificial sweetener if necessary).

Lunch: half a grapefruit; one small portion of meat or fish, with either a green-leaf vegetable like spinach, or a salad with lemon-juice dressing; coffee or tea, as at breakfast.

Dinner: the same as lunch.

Grapes

4 pounds fresh grapes, to be eaten at any time during the course of a day. Wash them well but don't skin them; in fact eat them whole.

To drink: a selection of herbal teas (sweetened if necessary with a dash of honey) and water.

Oranges

2 medium-sized oranges, 3 times a day. To drink: orange juice, up to 5 times a day – or water.

Once again, a sprinkling of spices like ground cloves – or a fragrant dried herb such as oregano – will ring the changes.

Pineapples

This fruit is the basis of the original "Beverly Hills Diet" created by ex-actress Judy Mazel. During an initial weight-loss period lasting 9 days, dieters are instructed to eat pineapples, papayas, grapes, kiwi fruit, bananas and watermelon in a given order prescribed by Miss Mazel.

After this period they then return gradually to a balanced diet or "normal" food.

Judy Mazel's book is available in hard cover and paperback.

Watermelon

As much watermelon as you like – but nothing else – each day. Watermelon is filling and satisfying, especially when it is absolutely ripe. Its calorie count is low.

Mixed fruit diet

Breakfast: either half a grapefruit or else a whole orange.

Lunch: a fresh fruit salad, unsweetened but spiced if you wish; or an assortment of whole fresh fruits such as apples, mangoes, melons, papayas, pineapples, various berries and cherries.

Dinner: as for lunch.

Nuts

You can relieve the monotony of an all-fruit diet with modest amounts of nuts (fresh, not roasted in oil).

Remember though that nuts are not only very high in protein but have a particularly high calorific content – higher, weight for weight, than fried bacon, cream cheese or fudge!

Brazil nuts, cashews and coconuts are especially high in calories, chestnuts comparatively low.

Orange Health Drink Diet

This is a good experiment for a long weekend, and will give your system a change from solid foods. If you keep to it for 2 to 3 days you will lose up to 5 pounds but don't stay on it for more than 4 days.

Make sure, too, that this is a relatively quiet, inactive period; you will need a reasonable amount of sleep and leisure.

1 quart skimmed milk
1 cup plain yogurt
2 eggs
Juice of 3 freshly squeezed oranges
1 tablespoon sunflower oil (or pure corn oil)
2 tablespoons honey
½ teaspoon vanilla

Mix all the above ingredients in a blender and chill. This will give you a day's requirement. Drink a glass at each mealtime, seasoning the drink with cinnamon, coriander or extra vanilla if you wish for the second day.

You can also drink water, mineral water and herbal teas as often as you like – but eat no solids at all.

If you find the diet a bit too spartan, make up an extra formula and drink up to an extra glassful each day.

HIGH-FIBER FRUIT DIET

When you are concentrating on adding bulk and roughage to your diet, fruit can be a useful addition to make bran and its derivatives more palatable.

Serve bran cereals with fresh fruit, sliced before the meal so that their juices can help to absorb and flavor the grains.

Add bran to cooked fruits – for example to apricot fluff puddings or hot apple sauce.

Berry dishes – those made with raspberries and blackberries in particular – are high in fiber. Make fruit betties with oat-flakes added to the crumbs.

When you roast chicken or turkey, add chestnuts and fresh cranberries to the stuffing along with some bran-or oat-flakes.

Beans of all kinds are extremely high in fiber. You can make marvelous salads with crisp apples, chopped nuts and cooked beans, all mixed with a vinaigrette dressing.

VEGETARIAN DIETS

Fruits and nuts feature prominently in all vegetarian diets, as they are the major source of many minerals and vitamins for vegetarians.

Recent medical research has come to the conclusion that we actually need far less protein than we used to think was necessary; nevertheless protein from nuts, cheese and eggs is very important to vegetarians. Mixed nuts are often used in vegetarian restaurants as a kind of ground meat.

Brazil nuts, hazelnuts, cashews and sunflower seeds ground up together can be stored in a refrigerator or freezer, and used whenever needed to make nut patties, meatless loaves, or crumbles for topping vegetables, stewed fruits, salads and puddings. This particular mixture is very high in methionine and lysine, and rich in unsaturated fatty acids.

Vegetarian diets usually have a high fruit content, as most people recognize that fruit is essential, but are sometimes too low in protein – so make use whenever possible of nuts as well.

LOW BLOOD SUGAR DIET

When the pancreas underproduces insulin, the sugar content in the blood rises and diabetes develops. But when the pancreas produces too much insulin the level of sugar in the blood is kept abnormally low – a condition that may cause a feeling of general physical weakness, depression and nervous irritability.

Confusingly, one of the reasons why the pancreas secretes insulin in excess is that it is over-stimulated when we eat too *much* sugar! So the cure for a low blood sugar condition is to cut back on sugar in your diet.

Among other things that means keeping away from the high-sugar fruits such as raisins, dates, figs, plums, bananas, grapes, pineapples, persimmons, avocados and olives. It is also necessary to avoid fruit canned in syrup.

However, you can eat grapefruit, oranges, lemons, tangerines, all kinds of berries, apples, pears, melons, kiwi fruit, mangoes, pomegranates, passion fruit, and also nuts. Natural unsweetened fruit juices are also permitted.

FRUIT IN CHILDREN'S DIETS

We have come a long way in the past decade from the theory that chubby children are automatically healthy and happy.

We now know that over-fed children are all too likely to grow into over-fed, and often unhealthy, adults, starting a battle with the bulge which may last all their lives.

So do your children a favor and be as sensible with them as you are with yourself. Of course children are growing fast and need extra nourishment and carbohydrates, but they don't need the "empty" calories that come with junk foods and excessive amounts of processed and fried snacks.

Bananas are among the easiest foods for young children to digest; learn to use them fresh. They are nice served mashed, but don't add sugar – a ripe banana has plenty of natural sugar, and filling carbohydrates as well.

Apples, plums and pears are all popular with older children as they can be held in the hand and munched after school or as dessert. Try to give children a wide variety of fresh fruit, so that there is something delicious for them to eat all through the year.

Children love working when the results of that work are obvious. Picking blackberries and gathering nuts – the fruits of the countryside – will provide enjoyable afternoons for all the family.

If you have a garden, see how many useful, versatile fruits you can grow. Don't forget crab apples, nor the many new thornless berries and vines with improved cropping for the table.

Make fruit dishes that you can pack into lunch-boxes, and add raisins, prunes and nuts for between-class nibbles.

Older children can explore cooking with fruit and nuts. Remember to be around, though, even if it's in the background, to guard against overheated ovens, overflowing saucepans, and sharp knives clumsily handled. If there is any caramel or boiling syrup involved, you can unobtrusively take over.

Some children have allergies – to, among other things, certain fruits – or other conditions which necessitate special attention to their diets, and it can be difficult for the active, sociable child to remember these limitations. It is best to explain what the diet is for, and what foods will make him or her ill; there is then less chance of the child accepting the wrong food because it is not polite to complain or make a fuss in someone else's house.

Few children are allergic to every kind of fruit; and any child on a restricted diet needs extra quantities of acceptable fruits and nuts to keep temptation at bay.

Have a talk with your doctor about this before exploring some of the new fruits now easily available from supermarkets.

An allergy to, say, strawberries is seldom transferred to loganberries or blackberries, or for that matter to litchis or kiwi fruits.

BUYING AND PREPARING FRUIT

For proper nutrition the emphasis is on *fresh* fruit; canned or preserved fruit is likely to have large quantities of sugar in the syrup, and in any case most of the vitamin and mineral content will have gone long before it is served.

A recent test showed the horrifying speed with which vitamins disappear even from freshly squeezed oranges: within half an hour, 25 per cent of the vitamin content had gone, within an hour another 20 per cent – and this without any cooking, which would reduce the vitamin level even further.

So make an effort to find a place to buy fruit at its best – newly picked where possible, or properly stored to conserve nutrients when it is ripened off the tree or bush.

Don't peel fruit before you have to, and eat the skins (washed first) when you can; they contain high proportions of essential nutrients.

Do remember, though, that some fruits are high in calories and carbohydrates. A large apple contains as many calories as a small piece of caramel or chocolate – but then, of course, it is full of many other good things that cooked sugars and chocolates lack.

Learn to include fruit in savory meals too. Remember how delicious cranberry sauce is with turkey, or prunes with pork.

Choose from among the recipes throughout this book to find new and exciting ways to serve fruit throughout a meal.

Vitamin and Mineral Chart

The chart below and on the pages that follow lists fruits and nuts that are relatively rich in nutrient minerals and one or more vitamins. It also indicates which has a relatively high fiber content, and gives a calorie count for each.

The calorie count refers to a quantity of 4 ounces of fruit but only 1 ounce of nuts. Most nuts – chestnuts are an exception – have a much higher calorific content than fresh fruits, weight for weight.

Vitamins

The full range of vitamins, in small but constant quantities, is necessary for a well-balanced diet. Fruit and nuts can supply many of these vitamins but not all of them; Vitamins B12 and D, for example, are not found at all in products of plant origin, but adequate quantities of them are contained in dairy products such as milk and butter, as well as in eggs.

Vitamin A
Vitamin A protects the body's epithelial tissue: the skin, and the mucous membranes lining internal organs including the stomach and intestines.

It is also necessary to ensure healthy eyes, hair and nails, and for resistance to infection.

Apricots, cherries, cantaloupe melons and rose hips are among fruits rich in Vitamin A.

Vitamin B
The B complex of vitamins embraces twelve different sub-groups. Among these are thiamin (Bl), needed for the metabolism of carbohydrates; riboflavin (B2), necessary for the metabolism of proteins; and folic acid, which is essential for the formation of the blood, and without which a form of anemia results. Peanuts are rich in folic acid.

Vitamin C
Vitamin C (ascorbic acid) is present in many fruits, and especially in black currants, rose hips, strawberries and citrus fruits. It is well known that scurvy is caused by Vitamin C deficiency.

This vitamin is also needed for the correct functioning of the adrenal glands. And extra amounts of it help to counteract the effects of the common cold and other debilitating infections.

Vitamin E
All sorts of extravagant claims have been made for Vitamin E, which is present in many kinds of nut. It is not, in fact, a cure for coronary heart disease, nor have its alleged rejuvenating properties been proved. However, Vitamin E does assist the normal development of the reproductive functions.

Minerals

In the same way as we need a balanced intake of vitamins we also require a regular diet of minerals, essential for the building of the body and for the metabolism of food. Some of these minerals – copper, zinc and selenium for example – are necessary in only very small quantities; these are known as the "trace elements."

Calcium and Phosphorus
Both calcium and phosphorus play a decisive part in the formation of bones and teeth. We need these minerals even when we are fully grown, because our bone tissue is constantly being renewed.

Magnesium
Magnesium also plays an important, if lesser, role in the formation of bones and teeth. It also assists in such essential functions as the regulation of the body's temperature and the healthy performance of the muscles and nerves.

Iron
A deficiency of iron, a constituent of hemoglobin, leads to loss of energy and anemia. Iron is essential in early childhood and puberty, as well as in pregnancy.

Nuts in particular are rich in iron, which is also present in certain fruits such as avocados and the more exotic tarmarind.

Sodium and Potassium
In a healthy body the two minerals sodium and potassium are present in balanced proportions; if they are not, the functions of muscles and nerves will be impaired and the body's powers of resistance and regeneration will be lowered.

Both sodium and potassium are contained in fruits and nuts, though the proportion of potassium is much higher.

Fruit	Quantity	Calories	Nutrients
ALMONDS, *shelled*	1 oz	140	Vitamins B, E; calcium, iron, magnesium, phosphorus, potassium, sodium; fiber
APPLE	1 small (4 oz)	35	Vitamin B; potassium
APRICOT,	4 medium-size (4 oz)	30	Vitamins A, B, C; phosphorus, potassium
dried	4 oz	200	+ calcium, magnesium; fiber
AVOCADO	½ medium-size (4 oz)	225	Vitamins A, B, C; iron, magnesium, phosphorus, potassium
BANANA	1 small (4 oz)	80	Vitamins B, C; magnesium, phosphorus, potassium

Fruit	Quantity	Calories	Nutrients
BLACKBERRY	4 oz	30	Vitamins C, E; calcium, magnesium, phosphorus, potassium
BLACK CURRANT	4 oz	30	Vitamin C; calcium, phosphorus; fiber
BLUEBERRY	4 oz	30	Vitamin C; fiber
BRAZIL NUTS, shelled	1 oz	155	Vitamins B, E; calcium, iron, magnesium, phosphorus, potassium; fiber
CASHEW NUTS	1 oz	160	Vitamins B, E; iron, magnesium, phosphorus, potassium; fiber
CHERRY	4 oz	45	Vitamins A, B, C; potassium; fiber
CHESTNUTS, shelled	1 oz	40	Vitamin B; calcium, magnesium, phosphorus, potassium
COCONUT, fresh dried shredded	1 oz 1 oz	90 150	Vitamin B; magnesium, phosphorus, potassium; fiber + sodium
CRANBERRY	4 oz	15	Vitamin C; potassium
DATE, pitted	4 oz	250	Vitamin B; calcium, magnesium, phosphorus, potassium
FIG, fresh dried	4 medium-size (4 oz) 4 oz	40 240	Vitamin B; calcium, magnesium, potassium + phosphorus, sodium; fiber
GOOSEBERRY, ripe	4 oz	40	Vitamin C; potassium
GRAPE, green purple dried (currants, raisins)	4 oz 4 oz 4 oz	65 60 250	Vitamin B; phosphorus, potassium; fiber Vitamin B; phosphorus, potassium; fiber + calcium, magnesium, sodium
GRAPEFRUIT	½ medium-size (4 oz)	20	Vitamins B, C; potassium; fiber
GUAVA	4 oz	60	Vitamins A, C; potassium
HAZELNUTS, shelled	1 oz	95	Vitamins B, E; calcium, magnesium, phosphorus, potassium, sodium; fiber
LEMON	1 medium-size (4 oz)	15	Vitamin C; calcium, phosphorus, potassium
LITCHI	4 oz	65	Vitamin C; potassium
LOGANBERRY	4 oz	20	Vitamin C; calcium, magnesium, phosphorus, potassium
MANGO	4 oz	60	Vitamins A, C; potassium; fiber
MEDLAR	4 oz	40	potassium
MELON, cantaloupe honeydew watermelon	small slice (4 oz) small slice (4 oz) small slice (4 oz)	25 20 20	Vitamins A, B, C; magnesium, phosphorus, potassium Vitamins B, C; potassium, sodium potassium

Fruit	Quantity	Calories	Nutrients
MULBERRY	4 oz	40	Vitamin C; calcium, phosphorus, potassium
NECTARINE	1 small (4 oz)	50	Vitamins A, B, C; phosphorus, potassium; fiber
OLIVE, *pitted green* *pitted ripe* *in brine*	1 oz 1 oz 1 oz	30 35 100	potassium; fiber + calcium, magnesium, sodium
ORANGE	1 small (4 oz)	25	Vitamin C; calcium, potassium
PAPAYA	4 oz	65	Vitamin C; potassium
PASSION FRUIT	1 large (4 oz)	15	Vitamin C; phosphorus, potassium
PEACH	1 medium-size (4 oz)	30	Vitamins A, B; potassium; fiber
PEANUTS, *fresh* *roasted & salted*	1 oz 1 oz	140 140	Vitamins B, E; calcium, iron, magnesium, phosphorus, potassium; fiber + chlorine, sodium
PEAR	1 small (4 oz)	30	Vitamin B; potassium; fiber
PECAN	1 oz	196	Vitamin A; magnesium, phosphorus, potassium; fiber
PERSIMMON	4 oz	88	Vitamins A, C; potassium; fiber
PINEAPPLE	4 oz	45	Vitamin C; potassium
PISTACHIO	4 oz	170	Vitamins B, E; iron, magnesium, phosphorus, potassium; fiber
PLUM, *dried (prune)*	2 medium-size (4 oz) 8 medium-size (4 oz)	40 150	Vitamin B; potassium; fiber + calcium, magnesium, phosphorus
POMEGRANATE	4 oz	90	Vitamin C; potassium
QUINCE	4 oz	25	potassium
RASPBERRY	4 oz	25	Vitamins B, C, E; calcium, magnesium, phosphorus, potassium; fiber
RED CURRANT	4 oz	20	Vitamin C; calcium, phosphorus, potassium
RHUBARB	4 oz	5	Vitamin C; calcium, phosphorus, potassium; fiber
SAPODILLA	4 oz	98	potassium
STRAWBERRY	4 oz	25	Vitamins B, C; calcium, phosphorus, potassium; fiber
TAMARIND	4 oz	230	Vitamin B; calcium, iron, phosphorus, potassium, sodium
TANGERINE	1 large (4 oz)	25	Vitamins B, C; calcium, potassium; fiber
WALNUTS, *shelled*	1 oz	130	Vitamin B; calcium, magnesium, phosphorus, potassium

HOW TO GROW FRUITS & NUTS

Even in a tiny garden it is worth reserving some space to grow your own fruit – a few raspberry canes, a black currant bush, even a grape vine. Not only will you ensure that you enjoy the freshest of fresh fruit; you can also have the enormous pleasure of growing a variety or type that is too unusual, or not commercial enough, to be sold in the stores.

Happily, many fruits and nuts have more than one appeal. Trees can provide delightful flowers and sometimes scent, bushes can be used to screen a rather mundane vegetable patch, and perennials provide color and ground cover for months at a time.

Some tropical and subtropical plants can be grown indoors if the outdoor climate is unsuitable, and will still bear fruit.

There are specialized and more technical books for the enthusiast, but we hope the brief paragraphs that follow will start you off in the right direction, making you aware how easy and rewarding it can be to harvest your own fruit.

BUSH FRUIT

The *Ribes* family of fruits – black currants, red and white currants, gooseberries and worcesterberries – does best in cooler climates – indeed, gooseberries positively like the cold and will grow up to the Arctic Circle.

All are native to the northern hemisphere, found wild from Scandinavia to the Himalayas. They are now cultivated in many other parts of the world. Because they are the host of a fungus which causes white pine blister rot currants and gooseberries may not be brought into Idaho, Maine, New Hampshire, New Jersey, Vermont and Washington. Other states discourage their introduction. Check with your County Agricultural Agent.

Currants and gooseberries make quite attractive, compact, even dense, deciduous bushes, up to 6 feet high and about the same across. They are not really ornamental enough to be grown as specimen bushes (flowering currants, with showy crimson, pink or scarlet blooms, are a different species, native to North America), but they are not difficult to grow and will crop very well in tubs. All *Ribes* are self-fertile, so a single bush is all you require. They can easily be propagated from cuttings.

Cultivation and Management

Spring frosts will damage the flowers and fruit buds, so protect the plants at blossom time. Netting may be used to protect bushes from birds.

Generally, cultivation is the same for all of the species. They have shallow root systems which dislike being disturbed. Once planted they will live and bear prolifically for up to thirty years, and in some cases even longer. This means that the ground must be very well prepared, not only thoroughly dug over and free of weeds, but given plenty of humus to retain moisture at the roots. Beds for black currants, which are greedy feeders, should be enriched with manure or compost. Once planted, the bushes will need regular fertilizing, mulching and watering. Potash is essential for red currants and gooseberries.

BLACK CURRANTS

Black currants like rich, damp, slightly acid soil; they will stand wet and shady conditions better than almost any other fruit, but set a much better crop if grown in full sun, as long as the position is not too hot and dry.

Cultivation

Black currant bushes have several shoots or stems growing from below ground level. Plants bought from a nursery are generally planted to a few inches extra depth to encourage the stems. After planting, cut down all shoots to just above ground level. This means no fruit in the first season, but the strong new shoots will require little or no pruning and can be left to bear fruit the following summer. The plants require generous feeding.

Pruning

As black currants bear fruit on wood formed the previous year, pruning is aimed at stimulating strong new growth. Cut back old wood (easily distinguished from young shoots by its much darker color) hard each year, by about a third. This is usually done immediately after cropping, but not later than early winter. You can combine pruning with harvesting by cutting out the older stems with their last crop of fruit.

Pests and Diseases

The most serious pest is black currant gall mite, which spreads reversion disease. Buy only stock certified free from the disease. If any bushes do become infected they must be dug up and burned.

Varieties

Not all varieties are suitable for all areas; ask the County Agricultural Agent in your area about suitable varieties.

Harvesting and Storage

Black currants ripen from midsummer onward, depending on the variety. Shiny and swollen currants should be picked before they begin to shrivel. If you are making juice or jelly it is not necessary to remove all the little stalks.

Red and White Currants

White currants are a blander variety of red currant.

Both types thrive in similar conditions to black currants, but are hardier, and more resistant to pests and diseases, in fact, less troubled by them than almost any fruit. They will also grow in much drier and poorer soil, although they do like plenty of humus and potash.

Cultivation

Red and white currants are usually grown as bushes on a short stem or leg, but they can also be grown as taller standards.

Pruning

They crop on old wood as well as on one-year-old shoots. In the first few years the aim is to build a strong permanent framework of branches, growing away from the center, which should be kept open. In early winter, prune back the leaders and any laterals required for the framework. Mature plants will not require so much winter pruning. Summer pruning is very beneficial; shortening back the laterals by about half will let light and air into the bush, encourage the wood and fruit to ripen, and lessen the chances of infection with mildew.

Red and white currants are quite often grown as cordons, and sometimes as fans, making the most of restricted space. They will crop on a sunless wall but not develop their best flavor. When grown as cordons, prune the leader back by about half each year and cut the laterals back hard. Summer-prune new growths to about four or five leaves.

Varieties

Both "New Perfection", a well-flavored red currant which does well on most soils, and the midseason "Red lake", which has huge fruits, are good, reliable varieties. The latter is also suitable for small gardens.

Harvesting and Storage

The fruit ripens in late summer, becoming clear, and almost translucent-looking. It is usually picked in whole bunches to avoid damage. All the fruit on a bush may not ripen at the same time.

Preserve by canning or freezing or as jelly.

Gooseberries

The gooseberry is much loved in England, where it is used in pies, preserves and even as a sauce with mackerel.

Gooseberries tolerate much cooler conditions than currants. They will do well in shade and can be grown on a sunless wall; some varieties will even survive heavy frosts. They are often grown with red currants and strawberries, both of which like the same balance of nitrogen and potash. They make dense bushes, often with a distinctive spreading habit; sharp thorns can make picking a painful task.

They can be grown as cordons – a method which can make it much easier to pick the fruit without getting impaled on the thorns. They do not, however, like too hot a wall; the heat will tend to scorch the fruit.

Cultivation

Gooseberries are cultivated in much the same way as red and white currants.

Pruning

Careful pruning will encourage more upright growth to make harvesting easier. They crop on older wood and on the previous year's growth.

Pests and Diseases

Watch out for sawfly and borer, blister rust and crown gall. The local Agricultural Experiment Station should be able to advise you about diseases affecting your area.

Varieties

Good varieties are: "Welcome," with pale, green-tinged fruit that turns pink as it ripens and "Pixwell." "White Imperial" is a reliable variety of white currant; ask the County Agent to recommend varieties for your area.

Depending on variety, berries can be hairy or smooth, and, when ripe, can be white, green, yellow, amber or even deep red. Size and color are not necessarily related to flavor, but on the whole red varieties are less sweet.

Harvesting and Storage

Depending on the variety, gooseberries ripen over a long period throughout summer. Fruit for cooking can be picked before the rest of the crop is ripe.

Gooseberries can be canned, frozen or made into jelly, jam or wines.

WORCESTERBERRIES

Worcesterberries have been considered hybrids, the result of a cross between the gooseberry and the black currant, but are now generally accepted as being a form of a North American species of the genus *Ribes*. They bear fruit which looks rather like a cross between a gooseberry and a black currant. It would not perhaps be the first choice where space is limited, but it makes delicious jam and is hardy and resistant to disease.

BLUEBERRIES AND CRANBERRIES

Various species of blueberry are grown in North America; the bilberry is found wild over much of northern Europe and Asia. The cranberries, too, of which the best known is the American cranberry, are all part of the genus *Vaccinium*.

The lowbush blueberry grows widely over much of the northeastern United States; it is not so much cultivated as managed by burning over the ground in rotation, which destroys unwanted weeds and stimulates new growth. Highbush blueberries are better for garden cultivation and are grown in many of the states along the Atlantic Coast. They vary in height from 4—20 feet.

Blueberries and cranberries are members of the heather family and need acid, damp soil as well as a particular fungus found only in such soils. Their natural habitat may be mountainous moorland, peat bog or the edge of coniferous woods where decaying pine needles provide ideal conditions.

Cultivation and Management

Land in which rhododendrons and heathers grow well should be ideal. They like plenty of sun and abundant water, but the drainage must be good. In swamps they are often found growing on tussocks. If your drainage is bad, make raised beds. Use moisture-conserving mulches, such as sawdust or peat. Tubs or pots are excellent settings, and blueberries are attractive shrubs. They should be protected from frost at blossom time.

Set out blueberry bushes in spring or fall, about 5 feet apart, with 6 feet or more between rows. They are shallow-rooting, so don't disturb the soil once the plants are in. Remove flowers in the first year to encourage formation of a healthy root system. For the first two years pruning is not necessary. After that, in early spring, cut out weak wood to encourage the growth of strong vigorous shoots. The object is to encourage plenty of new wood, because they fruit on the previous year's growth, on both new stems from the base of the bush, or on side growths from main branches. Birds are often a bother, but the berries are not much troubled by pests and diseases.

A single bush will produce berries, but you will get a better crop if you plant two.

Cranberries thrive in similar, but even damper conditions. They are planted 2 feet apart and immediately flooded ideally with rainwater, which is non-alkaline and keeps the soil acid. Another method is to dig a trench, line it with plastic sheeting, and fill it with peat. Cranberries need no pruning.

Good varieties are "Blueray," an early ripener and very hardy; "Coville," late season and excellent for canning, preserves or freezing, and "Herbert," which has the largest berries. Cranberry fruit-worm and blueberry maggot can sometimes be a nuisance. Spray two or three times after the petals fall.

Harvesting and Storage

Both blueberries and cranberries are best picked ripe, and are easy to freeze; do not wash beforehand and put straight into plastic bags.

CANE FRUIT

Raspberries, blackberries and other brambles are all part of the genus *Rubus*. Most species bear edible fruit, but a few are simply ornamental plants.

RASPBERRIES

Raspberries are perhaps the most delicious of all fruits, and among the earliest to come into bearing, after only eighteen months; only the strawberry fruits in less time.

Plant canes about 18–24 inches apart, with 5–6 feet between rows. The row should, if possible, run north to south so that no row shades, or is shaded by, another.

Red raspberries like plenty of moisture and do well in the cool, moist climates of the northeast and northwest states. Other forms to grow include the native black raspberry, called the Blackcap, as well as yellow- and purple-fruited varieties. Many of the varieties have a particularly fine flavor but all are much more untidy and rampant than varieties of red raspberry.

Cultivation and Management

Plant the young raspberry canes in late fall, with the roots just below the surface at a depth of not more than 2 or 3 inches. They like a rich, well-drained soil; if the soil is poor to start with, generous manuring and feeding will solve the problem. Good drainage is absolutely essential; if the soil is waterlogged the canes will die. Because raspberry canes have shallow roots, the ground must be thoroughly cleared beforehand.

Left to grow naturally, raspberry canes will trail on the ground under the weight of fruit, so they should always be supported, either by a single or double wire fence, individual stakes for each plant, or even a trellis.

In the spring of their first year cut the canes to the ground. This will encourage the growth of a strong, healthy system of young canes. As these develop they can be tied upright onto wires, about 4 inches apart.

The following spring, cut out the weakest canes leaving a few of the most vigorous on each stool. At this stage they can also be headed back – a few inches are removed from the end of the main shoots, to encourage fruit-bearing laterals to form; keep the leaders to a manageable length, and eliminate any end growth which may have suffered damage during the winter.

New canes (to bear the next year's crop) will now be growing up and should be tied in at intervals through the summer. Take care to avoid damaging these when the time comes to pick the ripe berries. As soon as fruiting is over, in late fall, cut down all the canes which have borne fruit to just above ground level, and thin the new ones, leaving about six of the strongest canes per plant (or stool).

Fall fruiting varieties fruit on the current year's growth, in the tips of the canes, and although the flavor is not always as good they do extend the season, and the canes may go on bearing until midwinter. Some will fruit twice, in summer and again later, but to encourage a good fall crop at the expense of the summer one, all these canes should be cut down to ground level in winter or early spring.

Propagation is easy; the stools are divided immediately after fruiting.

Pests and Diseases

Raspberries are susceptible to several diseases, and used to succumb quickly to air- or insect-borne viral or fungal infections. Nowadays, provided certified virus-free canes are planted, they will usually survive for about seven years before some disease inevitably creeps in and they have to be replaced.

One of the most common viral diseases is the Mosaic virus. There is no cure; infected plants must be dug up and burned; black and purple raspberries suffer most from viral diseases. Fungal diseases can be controlled with regular spraying with fungicides.

A tar oil spray in winter will kill aphid eggs. Spraying with malathion when the flowers open will kill insects, including the raspberry beetle. Birds will happily strip canes that are not protected by net.

Varieties

"Hilton" has large fruit; "Newburgh" is an early ripener and "Heritage" is one of the finest fall-bearing varieties. "Fall Gold" is a delicious yellow-fruited variety which fruits in early summer and again in the fall until frost. "Morrison" is a new heavy-cropping black raspberry; "Clyde" and "Sodus" are reliable purple varieties.

Harvesting and Storage
Leave hulls and stems on raspberries when picking – the fruit should drop easily off the cane if ripe. Raspberries are best eaten the day you pick them but can be frozen.

BLACKBERRIES

The straggling, thorny wild blackberry is a familiar sight but hybrids are the best choice for garden cultivation. Some varieties are ornamental, and thornless varieties have also been developed.

Cultivated plants yield fruit within two or three years, are much hardier than raspberries, flower later, will stand up to frost, and are not particularly fussy about soil.

Feed with plenty of manure or compost.

They dislike changeable, extreme climates with very cold winters and arid summers, and will not tolerate hot, dry winds. They thrive in partial shade.

Cultivation and Management
Blackberries fruit on laterals of the previous year's growth, and crop to some extent on old wood, which may sometimes be left in for more than one season. For the best crops cut out all old wood in early spring.

Blackberry canes are usually planted at least 8 feet apart, and twice that in the case of a vigorous variety such as "Darrow." Rows of canes should be 6 feet apart, or more. Unsupported canes will arch down and take root where the tip touches the ground, and soon become a dense untidy thicket, so young canes should be carefully woven or trained along wires or trelliswork. They are self-fertile.

Pests and Diseases
All blackberries are susceptible to the same diseases as raspberries. Some varieties succumb to orange rust; spray regularly for protection.

Varieties
One of the best known of the widely available varieties is "Bailey." It bears heavily, with fruits which have a real blackberry flavor, but is too vigorous to be suitable for a small garden, where "Oregon Thornless" is probably the best. This is mercifully free from spines, has a good flavor, and is both easy to contain and ornamental, with pretty, parsley-shaped leaves. One of the most delicious varieties, "Darrow", is resistant to orange rust.

Harvesting and Storage
Pick blackberries when they are well and truly ripe. They are best preserved in the form of superb jams and jellies.

OTHER BRAMBLES
Dewberries are very similar to blackberries, but fruit later and make low, trailing plants, more like vines than canes.

The loganberry has large, fine-flavored berries, with an upright habit, and is a little more tender than the blackberry. A thornless form is available. Loganberries are not self-fertile, so at least two plants must be grown.

Another related species is the wineberry, usually grown for its ornamental value; the canes are red-tinted in winter and the fruits develop from golden-yellow to rich red. The raw flavor is not outstanding.

The youngberry is unanimously regarded as being one of the finest flavored berries.

The boysenberry is also a cross with a special taste. Though very rampant, it will grow in dryish conditions, and there is a thornless variety.

VINES
GRAPES

For thousands of years the grape has been grown around the Mediterranean, where it gets the long, warm, dry summer and the cool winter it needs in order to flourish.

Grapevines will tolerate snow and frost in winter. But once new growth has started in spring they should not be exposed to frosts or strong winds, and all through the summer they should have as much sun as they can get.

The vines are very easy to grow. Given favorable conditions, even completely neglected specimens have been known to thrive and fruit quite prolifically.

Vines will grow on almost any soil as long as the drainage is good; this is essential, because waterlogged ground can cause root rot. Though poor soil is sometimes recommended, they do excellently in rich soil, which can encourage lush leaf growth and help to produce plump, sweet fruit.

Cultivation

Cuttings are planted in the dormant season. If you are going to support them on a trellis or post, erect the prop first; the roots are easily damaged and should not be disturbed. Gently spread out the roots in the planting hole, firm them in well, and give the soil a good mulch of manure or compost. Grapevines are very long-lived so it pays to do whatever is necessary to get them off to a good start. The ground must be kept clean and weed-free.

They can be trained to ramble over a trellis or pergola, or against a sunny wall — ideal if you have restricted space and do not wish to spend too much time on them. Because they respond well to having their roots restricted they will grow very happily in pots or tubs. They can be planted in rows in the open (usually as cordons) and kept to a manageable height by rigorous pruning and training; vines can be pruned more drastically than any other plant. They can be grown as espaliers and bushes as well as cordons and fans, and trained into almost any shape.

In cooler climates the extra protection of cloches is often necessary. This is easy when the vines are kept low, as in the Guyot system, or trained on a wall, and can mean the luxury of fresh grapes at Christmas.

Pruning

Although they will grow and bear fruit even if not given much attention, careful pruning is required for a very heavy crop of good quality fruit. They bear on two-year-old wood, so fruiting spurs on the previous year's wood must be encouraged, mostly by pinching off any non-productive shoots and superfluous leaves which compete for nourishment. At the same time at least one replacement shoot or cane must be grown on, which will bear the next year's fruit.

This principle applies whether you let a permanent trunk or rod grow, to produce spurs which in their turn produce fruiting wood, or whether you cut the canes right back after bearing.

If you want to make wine, grapes do not have to be thinned, but for the table, thinning is very important. Using special blunt-ended scissors, when the grapes are the size of small peas, remove all misshapen and overcrowded ones. Do not be afraid of over-thinning; to improve the quality, you can safely take out half to two-thirds of each bunch.

You may also need to reduce the actual number of bunches. Leave a foot between each spur.

Pests and Diseases

Grapevines are not often afflicted by any serious diseases; they may get mildew, which can be prevented by regular spraying. But beware of using hormone weed-killers, which can cause serious spray damage and distort the plants. The ripening fruit should be protected from birds with netting.

Varieties

Two varieties suitable for wine making have a good reputation for growing sturdily outdoors. "Niagara" is a light tawny grape which ripens in fall, and makes a pleasant, fruity wine. "New York Muscat" has a fine muscat-type flavor, and makes a sweet wine.

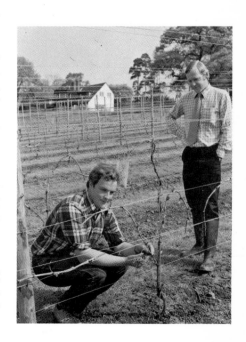

Harvesting and Storage

Fruit for eating should not be picked before it is fully ripe, and may even be left on the vine after the first frosts, when it will be extra sweet. Some grapes can be dried, but they do not freeze well; conserve by cooking or making them into juices or wines.

See Greenhouse Cultivation.

MELONS

Melon plants are annuals, with a life span of only four months from seed to fruit.

They thrive in warm, airy climates with night temperatures of at least 60–65°, but very hot and humid climates are actually not suitable since melons are particularly susceptible to fungal diseases. In cooler areas they grow very well under cloches, and should be started indoors three to four weeks before planting out; also, choose extra-early varieties.

Watermelons belong to a different genus, but are of the same family and require much the same basic cultivation.

Cultivation

Melons to be started indoors should be sown in peat fiber pots, so that growth is not checked by transplanting; where the climate is suitable, the seed can be sown outdoors in spring. Plant in clean, fertile ground and give them abundant water. They can be grown on the level, in pits, or on mounds, and sometimes in the curious combination of a depression (to collect water) circling a mound to keep the plant itself clear. They are very susceptible to stem rot so water must never be directed straight at the stem. For the same reason, when seedlings are set out, they are often planted with 1 inch of the soil ball above ground.

For the best growing conditions, all the melons should be pollinated on the same day so that they all develop equally. Otherwise, one fruit may grow at the expense of the others. The growing point is pinched out first to encourage production of laterals, the four strongest of which are then selected and trained out in the form of a cross. Remove any flowers that appear alone and prematurely. You will find it easiest to pollinate the flowers individually with a brush.

Another method of artificial pollination is to strip the petals from a male flower and push the exposed center into firm contact with a female flower. Female flowers can be identified by the embryo fruit at the base of the petals, which will swell soon after pollination. When the fruits are about the size of a large walnut, concentrate on the four best specimens (one on each lateral). Remove all other flowers and fruit, pinch out the tips of main shoots and any new growths, and stop the bearing shoots at two or three leaves beyond the chosen bud. Watermelons are an exception – the shoots are not pinched out, but left to trail.

Put a piece of wood or tile or an upturned flowerpot under each fruit, to keep it dry. Do not give the ripening fruits too much water or they will split.

Harvesting and Storage

Melons are ripe when the end nearest the stalk begins to show signs of circular cracking and parts easily from the stalk and/or when the end furthest from the stalk gives gently under thumb pressure. The flavor of a melon ripened on the plant is far superior to that of one picked unripe. Winter (casaba) melons may be picked before they are fully ripe, but even they are better if left on the vine. Melons are best when used fresh – they can be pared, cut up and frozen, but the flavor will be poor. They can also be used to make chutney and pickle – use the almost-ripe fruits before they are soft.

See Greenhouse Cultivation.

KIWI FRUIT (CHINESE GOOSEBERRY)

The kiwi fruit is a rampant perennial twining climber, with attractive heart-shaped leaves and fragrant creamy flowers. It will happily cover quite large spaces and is suitable for growing over pergolas or trellises.

Although the plant itself is hardy (it can even stand some frost) the fruit needs a long warm summer to ripen. A sunny wall gives it the extra warmth it needs in cooler climates.

Cultivation

Year-old grafted seedlings (or cuttings) of a known variety are best planted in the dormant season (not too deep, because the roots are shallow) in almost any well-drained soil. A deep sandy loam is ideal, well dug, with lots of organic matter and plenty of water. Put in any supports beforehand, and shelter the site from strong wind. Male and female plants are separate, so you will need at least two, about 10–15 feet apart; one male will pollinate up to seven females. The females can be identified by the embryo fruit at the base of the flower. Prune to 12 inches after planting.

Kiwis take some years to bear, but are long-lived.

Pruning

They crop on the current year's growth. Production of laterals is stimulated by cutting back growing tips; pinch back fruiting shoots to seven leaves beyond the last fruit and barren shoots to five leaves. They are very vigorous and will require regular pruning and removal of unwanted growth. The fruit may also require thinning.

Harvesting and Storage

Kiwis ripen in late fall and should be picked while still firm but not too hard. The fruit can be stored for six to eight weeks.

Kiwi fruit do very well in pots or tubs.

See Greenhouse Cultivation.

PASSION FRUIT

This tropical climber produces fragrant white flowers and delicious purple or yellow fruit; the yellow variety is much grown in Hawaii for its acid juice, but the purple variety is slightly easier to cultivate because pollination is simpler.

The passion fruit likes as much sun as possible and will not stand frost or cold wind. It will grow easily from seed, but does not always come true and may be self-sterile.

Cultivation

Seedlings or cuttings may be planted 2 feet apart in fertile, well-drained, not too heavy soil in early spring. The roots should be restricted or too much leaf growth will be made at the expense of the flowers.

Several shoots are usually sent up, but if there is only one, encourage it to branch by pinching out the tip. Laterals should appear after about 3 or 4 feet; if not, pinch out the growing tips. Train the shoots along supports; passion fruit climbs by means of its tendrils, and will rapidly cover a pergola or trellis. It may also be used as ground cover.

There will be very little fruit the first year.

Very little pruning is needed; cut out dead and unwanted growth, remove canes that have fruited (it bears on current wood) and generally keep the plant tidy. If necessary, prune while the plant is dormant by shortening back strong shoots by about one-third to encourage new growth. Leave a spur at the base of each cane for a replacement. It is an easy plant to grow and look after, though sometimes too much leaf growth results if it is too harshly pruned or overfed.

Harvesting and storage

The fruit is picked when fully ripe; it changes from translucent green to purple and parts easily from the vine. It stores well.

PERENNIALS
Temperate Climate Fruits
STRAWBERRIES

The strawberry, unlike most fruit, is a herbaceous perennial. There are three main types: summer-fruiting strawberries; perpetual or remontant varieties, sometimes known as everbearers; and pretty, small-fruited alpine strawberries. All are short lived.

Remontants and alpines are usually grown for no more than two years, since the crop deteriorates both in quality and quantity after the first year. Summer-fruiting varieties are usually left for slightly longer – three or at the most four years.

Strawberries like a medium or light moisture-retaining loam; they prefer it slightly acid, but will grow on most soils as long as the drainage is good. In damp soils, mound the earth into ridges about 3 inches high, and plant the strawberry crowns on top.

They should have plenty of sun, especially the perpetual varieties. Since they fruit best in their first year they are greedy for everything they can get; sun, water, food. Summer-fruiting varieties will tolerate a little shade and alpines actually prefer partial shade.

Cultivation and Management

The bed must be really well prepared; the plants have surface roots so that the ground around them cannot be dug over again during their life. The soil must be completely weed-free, with plenty of manure and compost dug in. The crowns should be at the right depth, with the earth halfway up the crown.

Summer-fruiting strawberries are usually planted in early or late summer to crop the next year; they are the quickest-bearing of all fruit. If they are not planted until the fall they will still bear a crop the next year, but pick off the blossom in order to build up healthy, well-established plants which will crop heavily the next year.

Perpetual varieties can be planted from spring until fall to bear the following year. They bear flowers and fruit continuously from spring until the frosts come. Some gardeners pick off the first flush of blossom. This eliminates the first crop of fruit, which would ripen at the same time as the summer-fruiting kinds, and encourages more prolific fall crops.

Strawberries are surprisingly easy and undemanding to grow. Protect the ripening berries from damp, dirt and pests with straw or plastic. Also protect against frost at blossom-time (late spring onwards) since frost-damaged flowers will set no fruit. Because they are so low growing, the plants are particularly susceptible, but in a small garden it is easy to cover them with straw or sacking at night, and remove it during the day.

Alpines, which carry their fruit on taller stalks, do not need protective layers of straw. They are worth growing for their ornamental value alone, quite apart from the delicate flavor of their berries, which is usually considered finer than that of their bigger cousins.

They are almost evergreen in mild climates, and make excellent ground-cover plants in borders, and edgings for herb beds.

While all strawberries are growing they need plenty of water, but must not be allowed to get damp as this encourages disease. When the berries begin to swell (but not before, as the flowers need the heat from the earth), place straw or plastic sheeting under the plants to keep the berries from getting dirty. Slug pellets will probably also be needed, and some form of protection against birds is essential. Many commercial growers grow the plants from seed through holes in black plastic sheeting. This prevents weeds, discourages pests, and keeps the fruit clean and warm. The plastic sheeting should slope away from the plants on both sides so that rain water does not collect around them.

The strawberry bed usually has three rows; one of new plants, one of two- and one of three-year-olds. Each year a row is dug in fresh soil, while the oldest row is taken out and the soil dug over and used for something completely different, often a vegetable; soil rotation is essential for strawberries.

Strawberry plants are usually planted 12–15 inches apart, depending on whether they will be left in for one year only or longer, and also on whether runners will be encouraged to root in the spaces between. Rows should be 30–36 inches apart.

Propagate from runners, except in the case of alpines, which are grown from seed sown in fall to fruit the following year. Some growers do not allow their plants to produce both fruit and runners, and remove all the runners from the fruiting plants while keeping a separate group of plants to propagate. Others prefer to take runners from plants that have proved themselves healthy croppers. The runners are pegged down and will quickly take root. If the runners are pegged directly into pots buried in the earth, when the new plants are large enough, in about four to six weeks, they are easily separated and transplanted. Some perpetuals do not produce runners and can only be divided, usually in early fall. Alpines can also be divided, but are less vigorous than when grown from seed.

Because they are ideal for a small space, pots and barrels have become increasingly popular in recent years. The fruit is easily protected against frost and birds, and there is no need for straw or plastic sheeting. Line the bottom of a large container, usually of clay or wood, with openings around the sides in which the plants are placed, and drainage holes in the bottom, with crocks or stones to help drainage. Then gradually fill the container with a suitable compost. As each opening is reached insert the plants from the outside. Plant the top of the container as well. Then simply keep them well watered and feed them occasionally with liquid manure.

Pests and Diseases

As soon as possible after cropping (so as not to damage the new shoots) all the old leaves are cut off and burned, together with the straw mulch. This removes a potential source of pests and disease, to which strawberries are unfortunately vulnerable. Birds and children are probably the worst pests, but slugs, snails and mice also love the berries.

Aphids can be very troublesome, disfiguring the plants as well as carrying virus diseases; insecticide should be sprayed on the plants at the first sight of insect pests. Only certified virus-free stock (available from specialist nurserymen) should be bought.

Varieties

"Catskill" is one of the oldest and still one of the best varieties of strawberry, suitable for all purposes, including container cultivation, and resistant to verticillium wilt. The summer-fruiting "Fairfax" and the everbearers "Ozark Beauty" and "Ogallala" are delicious.

Harvesting and Storage

Pick strawberries with their hulls and calyxes – and eat right away. Strawberries may be frozen but do not keep their shape.

See Greenhouse Cultivation.

RHUBARB

Rhubarb is, strictly speaking, not a fruit at all; it has however been valued as a winter substitute and is generally cooked and treated as a fruit. The edible part is the leaf stalk. Never eat the leaves – they contain a high level of poisonous oxalic acid.

Rhubarb does best in a cool climate, and will go dormant when it is too hot. It grows from divisions of roots or crowns; plants grown from seed are often feeble. Plant in good soil in an open, sunny position, and with plenty of feeding and watering.

Cultivation

Dig the ground deeply before planting, and work in about two buckets of compost per square yard, and a sprinkling of wood ash and bone meal. Otherwise the plants need almost no attention.

Plant crowns when dormant, in fall or spring, with the bud or eye 2 to 3 inches below soil level. Make sure that each root has at least one eye or bud. The ground should be moist but not wet. Space the plants 3 feet apart.

Cut off the flowerheads as soon as they appear, in order to concentrate strength in the leaves. Rhubarb crops from spring until summer, but not later. When finished, it is a good idea to mulch the crowns with manure. After four years the plants can be lifted and divided.

Varieties

Some reliable varieties are: "Giant Victoria," a large main-crop variety, and "Valentine Red"; in areas with mild winters "Giant Cherry" is a good choice.

Harvesting and Storage

The stalks are pulled out whole, never cut or broken off the first year, so the plant will have time to establish itself. In the second year, pull a few stems, as you need them; not too many, or the plant will give a poor crop next year. Always leave at least three or four strong stems on each crown. Do not pull any at all if you want to force them later on.

Rhubarb can be frozen, canned, or made into pickles, jams and wines.

Forcing

Rhubarb for forcing is usually grown from three-year-old roots, which can be lifted and divided in late fall or early spring. Add some more manure to the soil before replacing the plants.

Outdoors, cover each plant with an upturned container which excludes all light (a bucket is suitable), and cover it with straw and manure or compost for warmth. The stems will be ready in three weeks or so and will be a lovely brilliant pink. The plants will have lost most of their strength and are usually thrown away after all the stems have been gathered.

For indoor forcing, lift the plants in late fall or early winter and leave them on the ground until after the first frost; this makes them grow faster when brought indoors. Put them in a box, cover lightly with soil, water well and put in a warm, dark place; 60° is good. Water when necessary to keep the roots moist but not wet, and in five or six weeks the stalks will be ready.

Warm Climate Fruits

BANANAS

Though they look like trees, bananas are herbaceous perennials. What seems to be a trunk is technically a pseudostem, formed by the expanded leaf bases; the true stem is underground. What appear to be leaves are actually bracts.

There are hundreds of different varieties of banana, most of which have come a long way from the original seed-filled, unpalatable fruit — the result of years of intensive cultivation. Some are known as plantains. Bananas and plantains vary from small to large, short and stubby to long and slender, and yellow to green or reddish.

The flavor also varies, from sweet and fragrant fruit, usually eaten raw, to types used only for cooking, that are not necessarily very palatable even then. They are one of the most important of all tropical food crops, and grow up to 20 feet high.

Cultivation and Management

The only kind really suitable for the amateur to grow is the Cavendish banana. This is popular all over the world and will grow in subtropical conditions. It is disease-resistant and only grows to about 8 feet high. One variety, the Dwarf Cavendish, can be grown in a very small space. The size of the plants can be further controlled if only one sucker at a time is allowed to grow up and bear. The leaf sheaths which form the trunk unroll at the top into large, pale green leaves. The flowers appear above them and later curve downward. Since both male and female flowers are carried on the same plant only one plant is needed; the male flowers develop in the bell at the bottom (originally the top) of the flower stem, and the female flowers develop into the upward-pointing hands of fruit.

They are not difficult for an amateur to grow, as long as a humid climate with a minimum temperature of 65° can be provided. They will grow happily in hothouses and are suitable for growing in large pots. They like well-drained soil and as much sun as possible, with plenty of water during the growing season.

Harvesting and Storage

Bananas should be harvested while still green as they will ripen off the plant — or they will develop an unpleasantly strong flavor. The stem dies back after fruiting. Cut it out and allow a healthy shoot to take its place.

Well-known varieties of the Cavendish (or Chinese) banana are "Lady Finger," a comparatively tall plant with small and very sweet fruit, "Red Fig," and "Silk Fig."

See Greenhouse Cultivation.

PAPAYAS

Also known as tree melons or paw paws, papayas are herbaceous perennials, but are usually thought of as trees. The papaya "tree" is palm-like, with a soft, unbranched stem and a crown of large, deeply lobed leaves.

These tropical plants have spread to the subtropics and will even tolerate cooler conditions, which may however have an adverse effect on the taste of the fruit. They have a short life, about four years, but grow fast and bear fruit in twelve to eighteen months; they can reach 30 feet, but are kept lower in cultivation.

Papayas have a complicated sex life: plants can be male, female, or hermaphrodite (bisexual); they can be a mixture; they can even change sex during their short lifetime; and some males produce bisexual flowers and eventually fruit. In the tropics they tend to be hermaphrodite. In cooler climates the monosexual kinds do better. As one male will pollinate up to ten females, unwanted males are generally removed.

Papayas are known for their tenderizing qualities, which are also thought to help digestion.

Cultivation and Management

Papayas, like bananas, like deep, rich, well-drained soil, but they will tolerate much drier climates, especially in winter. While too much humidity may impair their flavor, they need plenty of water during hot dry summers. The temperature should not drop much below 60°.

The fruit looks like a large melon, often pear-shaped, and is carried in a cluster just below the leaf crown. As it ripens it turns from green to yellow or orange-yellow, sometimes reddish. The juicy, refreshing flesh is golden or pinkish, and it is best eaten raw, like a melon.

Harvesting and Storage

Papayas may be picked when unripe and left to ripen in warmth. If left on the tree until fully ripe the fruit becomes sweet, but its weight may tear it away from the stem and damage it. The fruit is usually cut, not pulled, off the tree. It can also be preserved, used for ice cream, candies, etc.

See Greenhouse Cultivation.

PINEAPPLE

One of the most delicious and popular of tropical fruits, the pineapple is grown commercially in many countries including Australia, Brazil (its original home), Malaysia, South Africa and, especially, Hawaii. It is, in fact, a multiple fruit — when individual flowers are fertilized they make small, succulent fruits which join together to form the flesh of the pineapple. The fruit is borne on a stem, 2–4 feet high, surrounded by long, sharp leaves. The spiky crown on top of the pineapple is a continuation of the stem, which also forms the hard core of the fruit.

Pineapples are divided into three main groups: the Spanish type (said to have been brought to Spain by Christopher Columbus), the Queen with small, juicy fruit, and the Cayenne or Kew Giant originally introduced for greenhouse cultivation in the mid-nineteenth century.

Cultivation and Management

Pineapples are easy to grow, given the right conditions: warmth, moisture and freedom from frost. Plant them in rich, well-drained soil in a sunny position and water freely during their growing period. Allow them to dry out between waterings. The plants bear fruit within about eighteen months.

Harvesting and Storage

Although pineapples taste best if picked when fully ripe, unripe fruit will ripen off the plant. Cut the pineapple from the stem — do not twist or break it off — and store in a cool, dark place.

See Indoor Cultivation.

STONE FRUIT

The genus *Prunus* includes a variety of delectable fruit: peaches and nectarines, almonds and plums, apricots and cherries. Most make attractive trees, and are often grown for the beauty of the flowers alone. The sight of almond orchards in blossom on Etna's southern slope is a spectacular feature of the early Sicilian spring. The Japanese have long found the contemplation of flowering cherries a rewarding occupation, and Chekhov's Madame Ranevskaya was deeply attached to her cherry orchard.

Prunus are all deciduous, hardy in temperate zones, and require much the same basic cultivation. Most grow up to 20 or 30 feet, but a dwarfing or semi-dwarfing rootstock (usually St. Julien A) will keep them much smaller, and make them suitable for cultivation in pots. The exception is the sweet cherry tree, which grows up to 60 feet, and for which no effective dwarfing rootstock is widely available.

Prunus trees grow best in moisture-retaining but well-drained, deep, neutral to slightly alkaline soil, and in a warm, sunny position with protection from frost and wind. Acid cherries will grow happily on a sunless wall, and some plums if well protected from frost will grow on east or west walls. Most need plenty of water, especially in the growing season, but hate being waterlogged. Nor do they take kindly to rapid changes from dust-dry to swamps. All the *Prunus* need a little more care than the hardier apple and pear trees.

CULTIVATION

In colder climates, although the tree itself is hardy, an early flowering period may mean frost-killed buds. Protect them by planting on a slope which will allow cold air to drain away, or by training as a fan or a bush near a sunny wall. Netting will add extra protection but should be removed as soon as the risk of frost is over to allow pollination to take place. Net the trees again later to protect ripening fruit from birds.

Too warm a climate eliminates the risk of frost, but all stone fruits need a cold dormant period to bear fruit. Plant at the beginning of the dormant season after harvesting and leaf fall, but before the real frosts begin.

Trees prefer growing in the open as bushes or standards, but, except for sweet cherries and almonds, will also thrive as fans or espaliers on a sunny wall.

PRUNING

Prune only in spring; in winter trees become susceptible to silverleaf disease, sometimes called fireblight or peach curl.

Apricots, cherries and plums do not need severe pruning. Peaches on the other hand fruit on the previous year's wood; after fruiting, the old wood must be cut out and new growth encouraged to replace it. Unwanted new wood should be cut back in spring, leaving some to grow on for the next year.

COMMON PESTS AND DISEASES

The most troublesome pests are plum curculio and aphids which can be controlled by spraying, usually with malathion. Brown rot affects the fruits of cherries, plums and nectarines; the diseased fruit must always be picked off and burned.

Anthracnose is a common fungoid disease for which Maneb is an effective treatment, as is Zineb; infected wood must be cut out and burned. Fireblight is a common bacterial disease; remove diseased areas and spray with Ag-rimycin.

Treat peach leaf curl by spraying with Ferbam during the dormant period; unfortunately, this may not always be entirely effective. If only a few leaves are affected the spread of the disease may be arrested by picking off and burning the diseased leaves. Watch out for peach tree borer, a serious pest, but easy to defeat by spraying with an appropriate preparation in late summer.

APRICOTS

Among the first fruit trees to bloom, their name means "the early one," an Arab-Greek mixture of *al* and *praecox* which survives in modern Portuguese as *albricoque.*

The fruit also ripens early, and, as there are often not enough insects around, may need to be hand-pollinated. Brush the flowers one after the other with a soft rabbit tail or thick, soft brush as they come into bloom.

Cultivation and Management
Apricots are self-fertile and do not need much pruning. They crop heavily on the short spurs of two- to three-year-old wood. They are hardy to zone 5, and in cooler regions they are nearly always grown as fans or cordons. They will grow up to about 8 feet (rootstock St. Julien A) and are suitable for growing in containers. Follow general instructions for stone fruit for cultivation, pruning, and pests and diseases. A good reliably hardy variety is "Goldcot," grown outside on a wall, or in a cool greenhouse.

Harvesting and Storage
Apricots are best harvested when they are fully ripe; the fruit will come off the spur easily, without tearing. They make good jams and other preserves.
  See Greenhouse Cultivation.

CHERRIES
There are sour or acid cherries, sometimes called Morellos, and sweet cherries, which include Dukes, an old-fashioned cross between sweet and acid cherries that is no longer very popular. The two types are very different in habit, but are cultivated similarly. Both kinds will grow as fans, standards or bushes, and will do well even in poor soil as long as they are given enough nitrogen and potash. In blossom, they are perhaps the most beautiful of all fruit trees; every inch of bare bark appears covered with white flowers.

Cultivation
Because sweet cherries normally grow to 60 feet or more, and no effective dwarfing rootstock has been found despite intensive research, they are definitely *not* suitable for the small garden. But sour cherries will grow happily on a sunless wall. The trees are hardy, but because the blossom is easily killed if warm spells are followed by a sharp drop in temperature, you will need to protect them with netting. They are self-fertile (and will pollinate sweet cherries) and are inherently dwarfing, even on vigorous stock, so they are most suitable for small gardens. They fruit mainly on the previous year's growth. It is normally about seven years before a tree bears a good crop.
  Follow general instructions for pruning, pests and diseases.
  The best-known variety of acid or sour cherries is "Montmorency" which has given its name to the type. "Emperor Francis" and "Merton Bigarreau" are good varieties of sweet cherry to grow.

Harvesting and Storage
Keep the stalks on the fruit when you pick them. Cherries can be frozen and canned and make excellent jams.
  See Greenhouse Cultivation.

PEACHES, NECTARINES & ALMONDS
Nectarines are simply smooth-skinned peaches, with a delicate flavor, but they are slightly less hardy, and their smooth skins make them more susceptible to brown rot. Be especially careful when spraying and protect the trees from birds – in cool zones grow in a greenhouse or conservatory.
  Almonds are closely related to peaches and are cultivated in the same way but often grown only for their blossom. There are flowering almonds which bear little or bitter fruit – make sure you buy the correct variety. Almonds are only partly self-fertile and may require pollinating like the apple.

Cultivation and Management
The soil should be well dug over and free of weeds. Some bone meal and fertilizer is useful in poor soil. A mulch of compost, peat or well-rotted manure will help retain moisture, essential while the fruits are growing, and also discourages weeds. Peaches and nectarines will crop in the fourth year, and will often survive for only another seven to ten years. The available dwarf peaches are even shorter lived. Peaches are eminently suitable for greenhouse cultivation, which yields luscious fruit.

Starting in late spring when peaches and nectarines are about the size of small cherries, and continuing gradually, thin the fruit to ensure a crop of good-sized fruit. Peaches should be about 12 inches apart (less for nectarines), on the upper, sunny, side of the branch if possible. Follow general instructions for pests and diseases.

Harvesting and Storage

Peaches and nectarines are ready to be picked when they come off the tree easily if lifted and very gently twisted. The fresh fruit does not store for long.

Almonds don't require thinning. They are harvested in the fall when they drop from the tree, and should be husked and left to dry in airy surroundings.

See Greenhouse Cultivation (peaches and nectarines).

PLUMS

Plums include the gages as well as the little golden Mirabelles and the myrobalan or cherry plums. Damsons, bullaces and Mirabelles are all small compact trees usually between 10 and 20 feet high. They are hardier than other stone fruit, and also used for making delicious preserves. Damsons, with their tart individual flavor, are especially popular for jams and pies. Strongly scented Mirabelles are excellent to eat, and are also used to flavor the world-famous white fruit brandies from the French Alsace region. Myrobalan plums are a different species often used as rootstocks for other plums. Very good jam can be made from their early ripening, cherry-like fruit.

Cultivation and Management

Plums are not difficult to grow; they do well as bushes or standards and also adapt easily to being trained as fans. A climate of cold winters and warm dry summers suits them, provided they are well protected from frost at blossom time. They need sun and warmth to bring out their full flavor.

Most plums will grow to 15–30 feet but can be kept to a much smaller size. The semi-dwarfing St. Julien A, compatible with all plums, peaches and nectarines, is a widely used rootstock. For even smaller plants there is the new rootstock Pixy for plums (but not peaches).

Many plums, including cherry plums and damsons, are self-fertile, but others need a pollinator, and will set heavier crops if a pollinator is available.

Prunes are simply dried plums; those dried in the sun have the best flavor. Varieties for drying are produced extensively in California and around the Mediterranean. Not all plums are suitable; some ferment before drying out.

Follow general instructions for pests and diseases.

Plums begin to bear about the fourth or fifth year. Pruning to keep the tree open must be done in summer, not winter, to avoid silverleaf disease.

Harvesting and Storage

The fruit ripens from late summer to early fall and should be picked fully ripe, and generally eaten or processed fairly quickly.

See Greenhouse Cultivation.

CITRUS FRUIT

Most citrus fruits are native to tropical or semi-tropical countries, but have taken well to cultivation. There are now vast groves in the Mediterranean region, Australia, California, South Africa, Latin America, Israel, the southern states and elsewhere. They are excellent container plants; most of them make pretty, ornamental trees and bushes, both small and large with glossy evergreen leaves, fragrant white flowers, and decorative fruit which can appear at the same time as the flowers, since the fruit may take as long as up to a year to mature. Indeed, grapefruit can take far longer and sometimes bears two crops simultaneously.

Citrus fruits are not particularly fussy about soil type, but it should be well-drained. Apart from warmth, they require sunshine, and a moist atmosphere in the growing season. Frost and drought are the worst enemies.

Cultivation

Citrus trees must never be allowed to dry out in hot weather. They are self-fertile and do not need pollinators, but they must be well nourished with nitrogen if the fruit is to ripen well. Apply general fertilizer in spring and a heavy mulch of organic matter in fall.

Oranges in particular are very susceptible to frost damage. Ironically, because frost comes so seldom in warmer climates it is all the more difficult to protect the trees. If you have a tree or tub in your garden, protect it with fine netting. (Commercial growers use smoke pots to prevent damage to the blossom.)

Pruning

Pruning is mostly straightforward; the plant is kept neat by removing shoots which are too low-growing or too vigorous. Very little pruning is needed once the trees mature.

Harvesting and Storage

The fruit is ripe when it feels heavy with juice. Most citrus fruits store well in a cool dark place.

Types of Citrus Fruit

Oranges are thought to derive originally from the Seville orange, now used for marmalade. The bergamot, a sub-species of the Seville, is a beautiful small tree with very fragrant flowers. Another sub-species is the blood-orange, thin-skinned with deliciously sweet rich crimson flesh. Other sweet oranges include the ever popular navel. Orange trees grow to 20 or 30 feet but can be kept much smaller.

Lemons and limes grow mainly in the Mediterranean basin, though they are now also cultivated in California, Florida, Australia, Israel, etc and are the tenderest of the citrus fruits. They have a more weeping habit than the orange, and grow to about 12 or 14 feet. Lemon trees can be quite thorny. The fruit varies in size. Limes make slightly bushier trees than lemons; the thin-skinned fruit may be green or yellow, but the acid flesh is always green.

Tangerines, also known as mandarins or mandarin oranges, are basically small, thin-skinned, very sweet, juicy, easily peeled oranges.

The name tangerine is sometimes kept for the more strongly colored varieties. Clementines are a variety of mandarin; so are satsumas, which have the advantage of being almost or completely seedless. They are the hardies of the citrus fruits, and will grow in slightly cooler conditions than oranges.

Grapefruits and pomelos are generally considered identical, although some authorities say the grapefruit is a hybrid between the pomelo and orange. Other names commonly used, sometimes as separate species, sometimes as synonyms for grapefruit are pummelo or shaddock. This does little to sort out the confusion, which was originally caused in part by a Captain Shaddock who introduced a fruit called pummelo to the West Indies.

However, taking grapefruit to cover all the related species, they are smallish trees of up to 18 feet, which bear large fruit in bunches, not unlike grape clusters. Some varieties have pink flesh; others are seedless. Grapefruit trees need even less pruning than orange or lemon trees, and are a little hardier than lemons.

Citrons, one of the earliest known species, are the sacred fruit used by the Jews in the Feast of Tabernacles. They have very thick skins and little flesh, and are used mainly for candied peel.

Kumquats are close relatives of the citrus species and will interbreed with them. They make excellent tub plants, very sweetly scented.

Kumquats are hardier than oranges and mandarins, and grow only to 6 or 8 feet. In a mild winter, they will need some protection from frost, and tubs should be moved indoors or under glass.

Hybrids

Intergeneric breeding is very easy, so it is not always possible to tell if a particular form is a species or a hybrid. Some hybrids, however, are well documented. Among them are the tangelo and the uglifruit, both tangerine/grapefruit crosses; the name of the latter speaks for itself. The calamondin is believed to be a lime/kumquat cross, although it has been classed as a separate species. It is much used as a rootstock for grafting, since it makes a small, disease-resistant tree. It is an attractive houseplant, suitable for cooler climates, and the fruit, though acid, is palatable. The peel is also edible.

See Greenhouse Cultivation.

OTHER TREE FRUITS
Temperate Climate Fruits
APPLES AND PEARS

Apples and pears require similar conditions, with a fair amount of sun, and a period of cold weather so that the fruiting buds mature in a dormant state. Apples always taste best when the winters are crisp and the summers are not too hot, but pears need more warmth.

Both apples and pears tolerate a wide range of soils as long as the drainage is good; but they grow and fruit best on a medium loam. Above all, the site should not be too exposed to spring frosts, which will damage the blossom and prevent fruit from setting. In temperate climates, a north slope helps drain away frosty air, and retards flowering until the worst of the winter weather is past. For flat land or warmer climates, simply choose from the later-flowering apple cultivars.

There are no late pears available; they all bloom about a month before the apple trees, so protect them if possible by planting them near a wall – this will also add reflected warmth later so the fruit ripens well. If you have long hot summers, pears are best grown in the open – otherwise the reflected heat will simply burn the leaves and the swelling fruit.

Young stock will need watering in dry conditions, and fruiting trees must get enough moisture to swell the young growth. Make sure there is water nearby, or at the end of a hose – each tree can absorb two or three gallons a day in drought conditions.

Cultivation

Except for cider and crab apples which are grown on their own roots and in their natural forms, dessert and cooking apples are grown in a variety of ways, from huge commercial orchards to back garden tubs. They are propagated on special rootstocks by grafting or budding, so the rootstock is very important; it determines the size (of the tree and fruit) and how soon the tree will bear.

A great deal of work has been done at the Royal Horticultural Society's research stations at East Malling and Malling Merton in Kent, England. Dwarfing apple rootstocks such as M (for Malling) 7, 9 and 26 and MM (for Malling Merton) 106 are known and used throughout the world for trees which are small and sturdy, yet bear abundant and tasty fruit.

The traditional orchard of standards is rarely planted today even by commercial farmers. Dwarfing stocks seem to have almost every possible advantage – they are easier to protect from wind and frost, easier to cultivate, prune and harvest, and come into bearing much earlier (often in the second or third year). There are a few disadvantages: some varieties require permanent staking, and if the tree is neglected, spurs from the roots may grow and gradually take over the entire tree.

An extremely dwarfing rootstock, M27, is now available, and produces trees only about 4 feet high, small enough to be grown in a tub or pot and ideal for a restricted space – even on a small balcony.

Remember, however, that apples are not self-fertile; at least two varieties must be grown for fruit, unless you can buy a tree with three or more varieties budded on one stock.

Pear trees are usually grafted on one of two quince stocks. Quince A will bear fruit after about four years and grows to between 10 and 15 feet, depending on the cultivar. Quince C is more dwarfing but unfortunately also more susceptible to virus infection.

Forms of Tree

Most trees can be trained into a variety of shapes. Forms grown in the open include: the old standard trees; spindle-bushes (also known as central leader trees) which are cone-shaped and crop heavily; dwarf bushes, grafted onto dwarfing stock, which fruit early and are easy to look after, but which require a fertile soil; and bush trees, which are rather taller, with a stem of between 2 and 3 feet.

Very restricted forms include the cordon, yielding about 10–12 pounds of fruit per tree, and the fan and the espalier, yielding 20–30 pounds; these are all very decorative against fences or walls.

For intensive cultivation cordons are grown in rows usually about 6 feet apart and with about 3 feet between each plant, though at East Malling experiments with the new M27 have had them in rows 4½ feet apart with 20 inches between plants.

Another restricted form is the dwarf pyramid; this grows to about 7 feet high and is, as the name implies, cone-shaped. It is a heavy cropper and forms a compact tree, but in a garden setting remember it requires staking, or supporting with wires, which can be unsightly.

Pruning

Prune the trees to obtain a high-quality crop of good appearance, size and flavor, on trees which are easy to look after. This means encouraging a framework of robust, well-spaced branches, generally in the shape of a vase or a pyramid so that light and air can circulate.

Neglected trees will still continue to bear fruit, but pests and diseases will flourish where too many branches are too close together, creating damp, humid conditions.

In its early years a tree is pruned in winter, to stimulate wood growth. Remove superfluous or weak branches and encourage robust ones growing in an appropriate direction.

Once mature (generally after about four years, or rather longer with pears) the tree is pruned only to encourage fruiting. With free-growing forms (standards and bushes) this is still done in the winter, but with restricted forms the main pruning is done in the summer to check vigor, encourage fruit formation, and keep the trees a manageable size.

Dwarf varieties, once established, often require little pruning, although some weak-growing varieties may need continued pruning to stimulate growth.

Some thinning is also often necessary to prevent a too-heavy crop – not all the blossom should be allowed to fruit. Keep about 6 inches between spurs, and the growing clusters may also be thinned by removing the central or king fruits as soon as they have formed. This will give more nourishment and vigor to the remaining fruits.

Pests and Diseases

A large number of pests affect apples and pears. Luckily many of them can be controlled by spraying with pesticides, some of which are compatible and may be applied together, such as malathion (for aphids, capsids, apple sawfly, red spider mite and pear sucker) and captan (for scab). Netting will provide some protection against birds.

The most troublesome pest with apples is codling moth. Spray with Sevin (which controls all caterpillars) or tie bands of sacking around the trunks soon after midsummer. The caterpillars will spin their cocoons and pupate in the sacking and both the sacking and cocoons can be burned together in late fall.

The most serious problem for pears is pear psylla, a highly destructive insect pest. Control by spraying regularly.

Shoots or fruit affected by mildew, canker, apple sawfly, scab or brown rot should always be cut out and burned.

A tar oil spray against aphids can be applied in winter, about every two or three years.

Varieties

Choosing which varieties to plant is mainly a matter of personal taste; some are very vigorous, even when grown on dwarfing stocks. At least two varieties must be planted; virtually all apples and pears need to be cross-pollinated. Even "self-fertile" trees will set a much better crop if pollinated by another variety. Two compatible varieties – which flower at the same time – can be planted; for example, "Yellow Transparent" and "Vista Bella", or the later-flowering "Golden Delicious" and "Crimson Winesap." Although most varieties have a normal number of chromosomes, some have little pollen and therefore are not good pollinators; others do not flower regularly, or will only pollinate certain other varieties. In such cases a third tree must be planted to ensure pollination.

You can avoid unsatisfactory pollinators altogether, but some are very desirable, such as the apple "Golden Delicious" or the pear "Kieffer." And, of course, the great advantage of growing your own trees is to have unusual varieties which are delicious but may be too difficult or too irregular for the commercial grower.

Warm Climate Fruits

AVOCADO (ALLIGATOR) PEARS

Many people have started to grow an avocado plant from its pit or seed, which will root very easily in a glass of water; planted out in a temperate climate it will be killed by the first cold spell. Given the right conditions, however, the avocado is an easy tree to grow and can fruit within seven years. Most species are natives of Central and South America but some come from Southeast Asia and the Canary and Azores islands. They are spreading, evergreen trees, usually about 30 feet high although they can grow to 60 feet. At least 55° is necessary in winter, more in summer although they will not tolerate too high a heat; about 80°–85° is ideal. Avocados need high humidity and plenty of water, especially in summer.

The trees grow successfully in many subtropical areas: the southern states, California and the Caribbean; parts of South Africa; Australia and Israel.

Cultivation and Management

They like a rich, acid soil and hate extremes of either waterlogged ground or drought. For growing in milder temperate zones, the Mexican variety is the hardiest and therefore the most suitable for the garden.

The fruit does not always set even in suitable conditions. This may be due, in part at least, to problems of pollination. Although each tree bears both male and female flowers, they do not open at the same time, so that at least two trees will be needed.

Pruning will keep them smaller and more manageable. To achieve a neat plant, pinch out the central shoot after three or four leaves have broken.

Harvesting and Storage

One reason for the fruit's popularity is that it ripens off the tree, and so can be picked while unripe. It can be transported long distances and still arrive in good condition. If you have your own tree, the fruit can be left until it is just ready to drop.

See Greenhouse Cultivation.

DATES

The date palm is one of the oldest cultivated plants, going back at least 5,000 years. It will grow to 100 feet or more and live for about eighty years. The palms are too big for all but colossal greenhouses, and to grow them outside you will need a dry subtropical climate, with water available. They are tolerant of wind and seaside conditions, and are often found along coast lines. They grow widely in North Africa and the Middle East, as well as Israel and the southwestern United States. Fruiting starts five to six years after planting, but maximum crops are produced after fifteen years.

The stem supports a spreading cluster of evergreen leaves with painfully sharp tips. The fruit hangs in clusters below the leaves, ripens from green to yellow, and then turns dark brown.

There are several different varieties, of which probably the best known is "Deglet Nour." The care and management of date palms is not difficult but they grow so tall that they are not recommended for the garden.

FIGS

The handsome glossy fig is related to the mulberry and has been domesticated since ancient times. Smyrna figs have been famous since 1000 BC. Although probably from Asia, the fig has naturalized over the warmer parts of the world, and is happiest in warm temperate climates.

The tree needs sun and warmth if it is to produce ripe, succulent fruit, and in cool areas it is best as a fan against a sunny wall, or in a cold greenhouse.

Varieties grown in the warmer areas, which include California, Texas, Mediterranean countries, South Africa and Australia, are, with one important exception, pollinated exclusively by means of an insect called the fig wasp which breeds only in the wild fig, or caprifig. So a few caprifigs are always interspersed with the others though their fruit is unpalatable. Happily, the common or Adriatic fig sets fruit without the wasp; it and its hybrids can be grown in colder climates, although most connoisseurs would say that the Smyrna fig (which also dries well) has the finest flavor.

Cultivation and Management

Figs grow well provided the soil is well drained and not too rich; the roots should not be allowed free rein, or the result will be a large elegant plant with luxuriant foliage but sparse fruit. It is best to restrict the root run with a special trench, about 3 feet deep and 3 by 6 feet. Pack the bottom with rubble or chalk, so that it blocks the main roots but is porous enough to allow good drainage. Pot cultivation in a large tub is ideal for restricting root growth.

The fig will produce two crops a year, on both one- and two-year-old wood. One crop starts developing at the end of the summer, overwinters as small, pea-sized embryos, and ripens the following summer, unless killed by winter cold. The next crop is produced on the current season's wood to ripen in the fall, with smaller and less juicy fruit. The second crop will not ripen in cool climates and should be removed.

In hot countries, the tree buds in early winter after a very brief dormant period, so three crops may be obtained: one in spring from the previous year's crop; one in summer; and another in fall on the current year's growth. This may, however, exhaust the tree and requires considerable management. Watering is always necessary during the growing season, especially for tub plants.

Pruning in the first three or four years is aimed simply at shaping the tree. Fan-trained trees are pruned in the same manner as peaches. Prune standards to make a strong framework of sturdy shoots with an uncrowded center.

Once the tree is mature, simply pinch out the tips of about half the young shoots, in order to encourage them to produce more strong young shoots which will carry a good crop of embryo figs.

In cool areas the embryo-bearing shoots must be protected right through the winter to avoid frost damage. Old bare branches may be shortened right back to encourage new growth.

Pests and diseases are rarely a problem.

Harvesting and Storage

Figs are ripe when they are soft, the skin is on the verge of splitting, and nectar collects in the "eye" of the fruit. Color is no guide either to ripeness or taste, as figs vary widely from palest yellow-green to dark green, and from reddish-brown to purple and almost black; the color of the flesh can be almost transparent, yellowish-green, pink, red or purple.

Figs are only at their best when tree-ripened so packaged figs seldom represent the peak of perfection. It is worth growing your own tree, even in a balcony tub, just for the experience of tasting a ripe fresh fig still warm from the sun.

Best eaten fresh, figs can be dried, canned, or preserved in jams or jellies.

The Indian fig is actually a large cactus, also called prickly pear. It probably came from South America, but it is naturalized throughout the Mediterranean countries.

See Greenhouse Cultivation.

LOQUATS

Sometimes known as Japanese medlar or Japanese plum, the loquat is from the apple-pear-quince family (the *Rosaceae*) and looks somewhat like a medlar. A native of central China, it has long been cultivated both there and in Japan, as well as in India. It is by nature a subtropical plant, but is now also grown in California, Australia, the West Indies and the Mediterranean countries, where it is very popular as an ornamental tree — it was first brought to Europe for the beauty of its foliage rather than for its fruits. It will not fruit in cooler climates, though the tree itself is hardy.

At full height it is a shady, evergreen tree of about 10 or 12 feet, but can be kept lower. The white flowers, carried throughout the winter, are intensely fragrant, and the pretty, golden-yellow fruits ripen early, in spring. Loquats make ideal pot plants, both in warm countries and in cooler areas where they are easily protected in the winter.

Loquats like most soils, but prefer a deep, light, not too alkaline loam, with plenty of water in the growing season. They can be grown from seed, but are generally grafted or budded, often onto quince stock for a dwarfing effect.

Cultivation and Management

The trees can bear so much one year that they have little or no fruit the next. Thin to prevent this biennial pattern from establishing itself. Cutting the flowers for indoor display may have the desired effect, although not all flowers will set fruit.

The trees need little pruning, but unfortunately the loquats themselves are vulnerable to fruit fly when ripe.

Harvesting and Storage

Pick loquats as soon as they mature, and never let them hang on the tree unless you want to keep it for ornamental purposes only. The fruit is sweet, juicy and refreshing, and although it is at its best eaten raw, can also be made into a delicious jelly.

LITCHIS

The litchi is another tropical plant which will grow in subtropical conditions: a hot, humid summer and a damp, cool but not too cold winter. A handsome, slow-growing tree, up to 40 feet, it has narrow, shiny leaves, often pinkish or coppery when young, and profuse whitish flowers in spring.

Litchis have always been highly thought of in China and India and their cultivation has now spread to Florida, Australia, parts of New Zealand, South Africa and Japan.

Cultivation and Management

The litchi will grow in many kinds of soil, but prefers a rich, deep, acid loam. It will tolerate damp soil quite happily, provided it is well drained, but not dried out.

The trees are particularly pretty when the fruit is ripening from pinkish to dark reddish brown. The brittle shell is covered with little bumps or tubercles and peels off easily.

Harvesting and Storage

The fruit will not ripen off the tree. Picking whole clusters or branches at a time removes old growth which will not fruit again and also helps to avoid damage to the fruit.

MANGOES

One of the longest-lived of all fruit trees, the mango has been cultivated in the tropics, especially India, for over 4,000 years. It probably originates in Malaya and the East Indies, and is now grown in tropical Asia, Africa, Central America and the Caribbean, as well as in many other parts of the tropics and subtropics, and in Israel.

Mangoes are attractive, shady, evergreen trees with lovely foliage and flowers – the Buddha is traditionally believed to have been given a mango grove for meditation.

The fruits hang on long, stiff stalks below the leaves. Depending on the variety, they ripen from dark green to soft orange, golden or reddish-gold and one color is often flushed with another.

Mango trees grow to 60 or 70 feet and are therefore generally only grown in the open where the climate is suitable. Although young plants require adequate water, they do not like too much rain, preferring a dry spring and summer. Mangoes grown in too humid a climate produce inferior fruit. Deep, rich, well-drained soil is ideal, but the plants are not fussy and will grow as long as there is room for the roots.

Cultivation and Management

Mangoes can be grown from seed, but it is usually more satisfactory to buy a grafted tree which will come into bearing after about three years. Flowers appearing earlier should be removed to prevent premature fruiting and ensure strong young growth.

The size of a mango tree can be controlled to some extent by pinching out the top of the central shoot when it is about 3 feet high, in order to encourage a lower, more spreading habit. Apart from this very little pruning is needed.

Harvesting and Storage

Pick the fruit when the color has turned, but before it becomes soft; the taste improves if the fruit is kept for a few days to ripen.

The sap or oil contained in the peel can be toxic or irritating to some people; be careful when picking the fruit.

See Greenhouse Cultivation.

OLIVES

Although few people would consider growing olives, it is in fact quite possible – olives can even be grown in pots. They have been cultivated for more than 5,000 years, often in the most unpromising ground. The tree does not usually grow very tall – about 30 feet on average – but with age (and it is extremely long-lived) it becomes thick and densely branched, often with the trunk split into three or more sections. The branches are covered with grayish, evergreen leaves. The flowers are white and usually inconspicuous, but about once every seven years they will put on a show.

Although the olive tree is hardy enough to withstand several degrees of frost, it needs Mediterranean climatic conditions to bear fruit: a cool, but not too cold, period in winter to encourage flower buds to form, and hot summers to set good-quality fruit.

Cultivation and Management

Though the tree survives in poor conditions and shallow soils, the best crops require a rich, well-drained soil with plenty of water in the growing season. Olive trees do not reach full productivity for fifty to seventy-five years.

To keep the trees a manageable size, remove over-vigorous shoots as necessary. Several varieties can be grafted onto one tree, which also eliminates the need for two trees to pollinate each other.

Harvesting and Storage

The main disadvantage of growing olives in your garden is that the crop is not edible right from the tree. Raw olives are bitter and must be soaked in a caustic soda solution before they can be eaten. Olives for pickling may be picked still green or when ripe and purplish-black, depending on the variety.

Olive oil is the most important product apart from the fruit. People who live in an olive-growing area arrange to take their crop (picked when ripe, or collected as the olives fall) to the local oil-press.

See Greenhouse Cultivation.

PERSIMMONS

Persimmons are natives of Asia and North America, and have become very popular in countries around the Mediterranean and in Australia.

Persimmon trees are comparatively hardy and will fruit as far north as the Great Lakes and Peking in China. Very ornamental, they are evergreen in some climates and deciduous in others (the leaves turn to glowing colors in the fall) with large, golden-orange or reddish fruit. They are not fussy about soil as long as it is alkaline and well watered. They will even grow in wet soils, though they prefer a medium loam.

Cultivation and Management

Persimmons can be budded or grafted onto a dwarfing rootstock to make a more manageable tree. Pruning is very simple: to keep the tree low and a good shape, cut back the central shoot when it is about 2 feet high, and encourage about four or five buds above 12 inches high to sprout and form a well-spaced framework of outward-facing branches; remove the other buds. The only pruning necessary once the tree is formed is to remove unwanted growth and keep the center uncrowded and open to light and air. Persimmons can be trained as fans or espaliers. Only one tree is necessary; the female flowers do not require pollination to set fruit.

The fruit is borne within two or three years, and must be fully ripe before eating or it will be astringent. It will ripen off the tree if kept in a warm place, so it can be picked while hard and unripe. Placing an apple nearby will hasten the ripening process because of the ethylene gas given off by the apple.

Harvesting and Storage

Persimmons are often left on the tree until the first frost. This is thought to improve their taste, which some people find unexciting at the best of times — others consider it delicious. Much depends on the climate. The best and sweetest fruit is found in the warmest and sunniest areas.

The fruit is best eaten raw, but it can be made into ice cream or fruit sauce; it will not bottle, dry or freeze well.

POMEGRANATES

Always pretty, the pomegranate tree is especially eyecatching when its brilliant red flowers are in bloom. It grows naturally around the Mediterranean and Middle East. The soft yellow or red fruit is also decorative. It is now also cultivated in the tropics, where it is evergreen, in many subtropical climates, and even in some cool temperate areas, where it becomes deciduous.

In hardiness the pomegranate is similar to the peach, and will flower in areas too cool for it to fruit unless protected under glass. It likes well-drained soil and hot, dry conditions. Apart from the water needed for the fruit to set, it should not be over-watered.

Cultivation and Management

The trees should be pruned to encourage low, spreading growth. Suckers and side-shoots should be removed or the tree will become bushy. They can be kept to below 15 feet, ideal for growing in pots.

Pomegranates begin to bear in about their fifth or sixth year and continue until they are about thirty years old.

Harvesting and Storage

The fruit ripens about six months after the blossom appears; it turns a dull yellowish-pinkish-brown, and will keep for several months; this actually improves the flavor and the seeds become more tender. The pith and seed kernels are always very bitter, and should never be eaten.

QUINCES

The quince is closely related to apples, pears and medlars. Although it will grow in cool temperate zones, it is happiest in Mediterranean climates. It is grown in parts of the United States, Portugal and Yugoslavia, as well as in Australia, Central America and southern Africa.

The quince tree grows in most soils and does particularly well in heavy, moisture-retaining ground, even in the wet conditions found beside streams. It has also been known to flourish in much drier conditions, but it must then be well watered during the growing season.

Cultivation and Management

Quinces do not take kindly to pruning and training, and although they can be grown against a sunny wall in the north they are more usually found free-standing. The attractive small trees have distinctive, crooked branches, and both flowers and fruit are ornamental. They are easy to grow, long-lived and require little pruning once mature (four to five years). The trees bear fruit in about five years.

The roots are shallow, so the ground should be kept weed-free to avoid undue competition for food and water.

Harvesting and Storage

It is not always easy to know when quinces are ready to be harvested. Their flavor develops on the tree, so they should not be picked too soon; some books recommend waiting until one fruit falls to the ground. They should be stored separately because of their very distinctive, powerful fragrance which will affect other fruit.

Quinces are sometimes confused with their near relatives, the ornamental or Japanese quinces, more commonly known as japonicas.

Japonicas are in fact grown for their showy flowers rather than their fruit, which, although edible, especially if cooked, has nothing like the fine flavor of the true quince.

NUT TREES
Temperate Climate Nuts

The temperate regions produce three well-known kinds of nut trees: the walnut family, chestnuts, and hazelnuts or filberts. All these trees have been cultivated for centuries; their nuts provide valuable food in winter and they have many other uses. Walnuts yield a uniquely flavored oil, once commonly used for cooking but now expensive and highly prized. Chestnuts can be made into the flour which is a traditional staple food in parts of France and Italy. Both are valuable timber trees as well.

WALNUTS

The most widely grown American walnut, the eastern black walnut (*Juglans nigra*), is one of the hardiest of nut trees. It is cultivated over many of the eastern and central United States for its excellent timber as well as for its nuts. The Old World walnut (*Juglans regia*) – also known as the English or Persian walnut, native to central Asia and southwest Europe – is smaller and not quite so hardy, because the flowers are easily killed by spring frosts. Although the nuts are generally considered finer, the timber is inferior. It is grown in several of the western states.

Walnuts require a deep, rich, well-drained soil to which some lime should be added if necessary. They are slow growers, and do not bear for the first six to ten years, but in time they will become magnificent trees of up to 70 feet or more so they are not suitable for small gardens.

Cultivation and Pruning

When walnuts are cultivated they are usually grown as bushes, half-standards or standards. They may be shaped to make a central-leader tree, but otherwise require very little pruning. Certainly they should not be severely pruned; there is a risk that the wood will die back and cause rotting. All wounds should be painted over. Avoid spring pruning; the trees are likely to bleed and become infected.

Pests and Diseases

Walnuts are susceptible to honey fungus, for which there is no cure. Infected plants must be dug up and burned, roots and all; the soil must then be sterilized to stop the disease from spreading.

Varieties

Walnuts carry both male and female flowers on the same tree, but not always at the same time, so check which variety you have and plant a complementary tree if necessary. The English or Old World walnut always needs a pollinator, but the American or black walnut does not.

Since the quality of the nuts varies with different varieties, buy a young tree of a known variety. Two of the best-flavored black walnuts, reliably hardy in northern zones, are "Snyder" and "Thomas"; Persian walnut varieties to look for are "Metcalfe" and "Hansen."

Harvesting and Storage

Walnuts are picked as soon as they begin to fall to the ground, though some authorities say they should be picked just before, as soon as the leaves start to fall. In any case they should not be left on the tree. As soon as they are picked, remove the husks, scrub them gently and let them dry in a well-ventilated place.

They will store, in containers between layers of sand or sprinkled with salt, for up to six months.

Other Members of the Walnut Family: Pecans, Hickory Nuts and Butternuts

Pecans are a species of hickory (*Carya illinoensis*), native to the South and Middle West and are now cultivated to a considerable extent in the southeastern states, from Texas to Georgia. They are now also grown in Australia, Israel and South Africa. The pecan is universally acknowledged to be one of the best flavored of all nuts, and makes a most delicious pie.

They can become huge trees of up to 160 feet high, but when grown in orchards they are often kept to 30 or 40 feet. One of the most widely grown varieties is "Success."

The hickory nut is native to northeastern states. The nuts have a very strong, aromatic flavor and are much used in cooking as well as eaten raw. The best nuts are considered to be those of the shagbark hickory. The trees grow best in a humid climate and are found wild on both upland slopes and in lower country near streams and other damp places. They are not widely cultivated; they do not transplant well, and are slow to come into bearing. The nuts will store for up to two years.

The butternut is a walnut species which comes into bearing relatively early (two to three years after planting) and produces delicious nuts not often found on the market. Its cultivation is similar to that of other members of the walnut family.

The hardiest walnut of all is the Carpathian walnut, grown in Canada and several of the northern states. It is a smaller tree, only 30 or 40 feet high, producing fine-flavored nuts.

Yet another type of walnut is the Japanese walnut or heartnut, with a flavor more like that of its cousin the butternut.

CHESTNUTS

The sweet or Spanish chestnut is one of the hardiest nut trees, native to southern Europe. Large wild chestnut forests can still be found in Corsica, France and Italy. The trees eventually grow to a huge size — up to 115 feet high. A single specimen in the landscape looks superb.

If you have lots of room and a sandy, acid, even dry soil with good drainage, you can grow a magnificent tree that will produce in late fall an abundant crop which should be picked up off the ground as soon as possible after the nuts drop from the tree.

In the United States the equivalent tree is the Chinese chestnut, which has replaced the native American chestnut killed by blight. It is a much smaller tree, only about 35 feet high, but a bad pollinator, so at least two trees should be planted. It is grown in eastern and central states.

Cultivation and Pruning

Little pruning is required. The trees will grow happily and only the over-crowded shoots, if any, should be cut out. They often make trees with two or more trunks, so if you want a central-leader standard (ie with one trunk only) cut back the lower laterals by half in spring, then, in late fall or early winter, prune them back level with the stem, until you have the desired length of stem. The roots can be lightly pruned to restrict growth.

Pests and Diseases

The trees are very seldom troubled by disease. Leaf spot sometimes occurs, but feeding the trees well can help prevent it.

Harvesting and Storage

Gather the nuts as soon as they fall. They may be stored between layers of sand for up to six months.

HAZELNUTS (FILBERTS)

Hazelnuts (or filberts) are native to both America and Europe. There are two species: *Corylus maxima*, which is narrow with the husk longer than the nut; and *Corylus avellana*, which is round, with the husk shorter than the nut. *Corylus maxima* is known as the giant filbert in America and filbert or hazelnut in England; *Corylus avellana* is called filbert in America and cobnut in England, though hazelnut and filbert are also used generally. Just to add to the confusion the Kentish cob is not a cob but a filbert — ie, long-husked.

Both species make small trees, up to about 15 feet high, and are often found wild. They will grow in most soils and under varying conditions, including shade and damp, but, like so many fruit and nut trees, they will produce a much better crop if they can have good drainage, plenty of sun, and clean, weed-free soil, preferably not too rich. They tolerate a fair amount of lime, and like protection from strong winds.

Each plant bears both female flowers and male catkins, so pollination is not usually a problem, except in some species which bear few or no catkins and therefore require another variety as pollinator. The flowers are small and red, usually borne on the weaker shoots; the decorative catkins vary from pale yellow to bright red.

Cultivation and Pruning
When cultivated, hazelnut trees can be grown as open-centered bushes and kept at a height of about 6 or 7 feet. Young trees (two or three year olds) are usually planted in winter, in ground which has been cleared of weeds and had lime added if necessary.

Before planting the tree, drive in a supporting stake. Space the trees about 15 feet apart.

In early spring, cut back the leaders by about half to an outward-facing bud to encourage the formation of an open-centered bush with half a dozen or so branches. To keep the tree at a manageable height, cut back any too-vigorous laterals, but not if they are bearing flowers which will turn into nuts. Any suckers, often found around the base, should be pulled out or twisted off. Follow the same process every spring and as the tree matures cut out at the same time any branches liable to cause disease or overcrowding.

In late summer, a type of pruning known as "brutting" is carried out. This consists of breaking off some of the stronger laterals, by hand, to about half their length. They are not broken right off, but left hanging on the tree. As with most summer pruning, this lets in light and air to ripen the fruit buds.

These "brutted" laterals are shortened back another inch or so in winter or early spring, usually at pollination time, in order to disturb the pollen and encourage fertilization. Help is often needed for pollination — shake the tree gently once a day.

Pests and Diseases
Diseases are not usually much of a problem with filberts. Nut weevil and winter moth caterpillar sometimes appear, but both can be quite easily controlled by spraying.

Varieties
Hybrids of European and American hazelnuts (*Corylus americana*) produce the best-quality nuts; look for "Potomac," "Bixby" and "Reed." Two varieties should be planted to ensure successful pollination.

Harvesting and Storage
Hazelnuts should be gathered when the shells are hard and brown and then left to dry before the husk is removed. They will store for up to six months if kept in layers of salt.

Warm Climate Nuts
BRAZIL NUTS
The equatorial forests along tributaries of the Amazon and the Rio Negro, and parts of Venezuela, Chile and Africa, are home to a handsome tree, whose trunk may reach 160 feet. It is not cultivated and the wild tree takes many years to bear its rather meager crop.

CASHEW NUTS
Although cashews originated in the tropics, they also enjoy subtropical conditions, and are found in Central and South America, the West Indies, India and East Africa.

The trees are even grown sometimes in the warmer parts of southern Europe and supposedly can withstand a very light frost.

Cashews grow in various soils, but thrive best in rich, well-drained ground. They require little attention and are attractive trees, especially when the fruit and flowers overlap; the flowers are small and sweet-smelling, and the cashew apples are bright red and yellow. These apples are actually the stems, swollen into a pear shape; the true fruit is the kidney-shaped nut underneath.

Though they taste a little tart, the apples are succulent when ripe.

The trees grow to between 15 and 30 feet sometimes to 40 feet; each one may yield from 67 to 133 pounds of nuts a year, and yields of 200 pounds have been known. Unhappily for gardeners there is one large snag: the cashew is a member of the poison ivy family; the shell of the nut contains a highly irritant oil which can blister the skin and painfully inflame the eyes.

COCONUTS

As a cultivated crop the coconut is often grown on small plantations, but the palms are also often seen in gardens in southern Florida. The trees thrive in sandy soil, near the sea but a little above high water, and like plenty of rain. The tall trunks (up to 80 feet high or more) are topped by a feathery crown. They take five or six years to fruit and another ten to come into full bearing, but continue until they are about fifty years old. A good yield is fifty fruit per tree, and some will produce up to a hundred a year. The fruits need a year to ripen, and a strong wind will bring down the harvest.

PEANUTS

Also known as groundnuts or monkey nuts, peanuts are not nuts at all, but beans, or legumes; the shell is in fact a dry, fibrous seed-pod. New pods form above the ground, then work through the soil and develop underground.

Peanuts probably originated in tropical Brazil, but are now widely grown throughout the tropics and subtropics as well as in the southern states and areas around the Mediterranean.

The plant requires a light soil, and will tolerate dry and sandy areas. It spreads like a vine, and produces a rewarding yield on good soil with a reasonable amount of water. It can be grown from seed. In spring, plant nuts 1 inch below the surface. In the fall the entire plant is harvested.

PINE NUTS

Also known as Indian nuts and pine kernels, pine nuts originally come from the stone pine, that lovely tree so characteristic of the Mediterranean coastline. In North America they can be obtained from the piñon or nut pine, as well as from various other species of pine, but the quality and flavor varies considerably.

The stone pine grows freely in a wild state all round the Mediterranean and requires little cultivation as such, although in parts of Spain and Italy specially planted belts of pines fringe the shoreline. The cones are collected during the winter and kept until early the following summer, when they are spread out in the sun until they open enough for the seeds to be removed. The pine nut itself is actually the kernel of the seed.

PISTACHIOS

A member of the cashew family, the green pistachio probably originated in Syria or Iran, and quickly spread throughout the Mediterranean region and the Middle East, where it has been cultivated for at least 3,000 years. It reached Italy during the reign of Tiberius. The tree takes well to fairly dry conditions and will grow in the same climate as almonds and olives. It is not difficult to manage and becomes an attractive small tree about 30 feet high, with spreading branches, bearing its flowers and fruit in clusters. Male and female trees are distinct, so at least one of each must be planted.

Today pistachios are also cultivated in India (which has become one of the leading exporters), Africa and parts of the United States.

Prune the tree only to keep an open shape and cut out broken or diseased branches. Keep watered and mulched in drought, and reasonably free of weeds. The nuts should be harvested when ripe; they can be salted and dried in the sun, when the shells will open naturally.

See Greenhouse Cultivation.

GREENHOUSE CULTIVATION

There are various reasons for growing fruit under glass. You can have fruit earlier than normal and the crops are better flavored and of higher quality than those cultivated outside. And of course there is the opportunity to grow fruit indigenous to warmer zones, which would not otherwise be possible.

Greenhouses and glasshouses or conservatories range from unheated glassed-in lean-tos to highly elaborate structures, but certain basic requirements are common to all. The site should be protected from cold winds and get as much sun as possible, even during winter when the sun is low and might be obstructed by buildings which present no problem in summer. Light as well as warmth is crucial to the proper development of fruit. If there is too much sun during the summer, the house can always be shaded: for example, by using blinds.

Even a simple, glassed-in shed or lean-to can provide ideal conditions for growing the most luscious peaches, nectarines, grapes, figs, passion fruit and citrus fruit.

However simple the house, adequate ventilation is extremely important. Aim for a "buoyant" atmosphere: freely moving air without draughts. The air in a greenhouse should never feel stuffy. Always open windows or ventilators gradually, to avoid those suddenly fluctuating conditions of temperature and atmosphere which most plants cannot tolerate. Automatic ventilators are now inexpensive and respond to temperatures both inside and outside the house. Many gardeners prefer convector heaters, which will keep the air moving gently even if they are not used to heat it. Proper ventilation also reduces the risk of grey mold and other mildews.

Humidity is another crucial ingredient. Although some plants need less than others, no fruit should ever be allowed to dry out entirely and all require abundant moisture while developing. Many fruits, especially the tropical varieties, require very generous watering and a high humidity. If you are serious about fruit growing you may want to divide the greenhouse in two, with cooler and less humid conditions in one half. Daily spraying in spring and summer not only benefits fruit but is good for the foliage; simply watering the soil may not create or maintain a moist enough atmosphere. It is of course also important to have efficient drainage; few plants like soggy soil.

The best way to manage and use a greenhouse properly is to visit it regularly. There is a constant interplay of heat, temperature and ventilation. Spray less if the day is overcast, and be careful not to overwater if a cold night is expected. Opening the ventilators on a windy day will bring the temperature down much more quickly than on a calm day. Thermostats and time-switches, automatic watering devices and the like, are all useful at vacation time and during working hours, but there is no substitute for keeping an eye on things personally.

Most gardeners who have grown fruit successfully would agree that it is also extremely rewarding.

Pests and diseases won't be a major problem, especially if you maintain the correct atmosphere. Good ventilation discourages mildew, and red spider mite will not flourish in a humid atmosphere. The greenhouse, including the woodwork, should be kept clean and free of any decaying matter. Keep the glass clean too; dirty glass will keep out an astonishing amount of light.

Indeed the most important aspect of fruit production is cleanliness — make sure your tools are clean and sterile so that the precious melons or avocado pears do not develop diseased spots or virus infections passed from one to another.

Good soil is very important. The usual soil is made up of three parts sifted compost to one part each of peatmoss and sand. If you can't be sure the soil you are using is adequate, ready-made composts are available.

If you decide you want to grow different fruits with differing soil requirements in the same house, this should not be a problem since so many fruit trees will grow happily in tubs.

While additional heat is not always necessary, it must be provided for some varieties and a little is useful if you want early crops. A cool greenhouse is one which can be kept at a minimum temperature of 45° to 50° in winter. With protection from wind and frost, this will suit many kinds of fruit, including some whose natural climate is ordinarily somewhat warmer. In the old days, the so-called "stove houses" for tropical plants were kept permanently heated to a minimum 65°. This is not usually considered necessary nowadays, since it has been found that a minimum of 55° is enough even for many of the tropical fruit.

Many different kinds of fruit can be grown successfully in an unheated greenhouse, and the quality of these is sometimes even better than that of outdoor crops.

Peaches, nectarines, apricots, grapes, cantaloupe and casaba melons, figs and strawberries all respond well, although a little extra heat may be necessary when they are first starting into growth.

Apples and *pears* can be potted in the fall and brought into a cold greenhouse in early spring, or when the buds are just beginning to swell. They will then crop earlier and the fruit will be of much better quality. Hand pollination will be necessary – remember to make sure that the varieties are compatible. (Poor pollinators often fruit better in greenhouse conditions.) Once the fruit has been harvested, move the trees outside again.

Alternate them with melons to make full use of the greenhouse all year round.

Apricots like similar conditions to peaches and nectarines (opposite) but be careful not to exceed a temperature of 45° at night during the early stages of growth, or the blossom may drop off. Choose a self-fertile variety for the greenhouse.

Avocado pears are notoriously difficult to grow as fruit under glass, but if you want to try, they require a minimum winter temperature of 55°, and up to 85°, with abundant watering in summer.

Bananas will grow in the same conditions as papayas (opposite), except that they must have adequate humidity at all times. The warmer the house the better, and the temperature should not be allowed to fluctuate too much.

Cherries require the same treatment as apples and pears.

Citrus fruits require a minimum winter temperature of 40°–50° and a summer minimum of 55°–65°. The most tender varieties are limes and lemons, and the hardiest are kumquats.

All kinds of citrus fruit must have plenty of ventilation, and can stand outdoors from June to September.

Figs will usually yield only one crop in an unheated greenhouse. In a heated house, with skilled management, they can give three crops, but the usual aim is for two, the first in summer and a second, generally better crop, in the fall.

When starting into growth they like a minimum temperature of 50° or more, and do not require ventilation until after the first crop has been harvested and the temperature reaches 80° or 90°. While the crops are ripening they should not be fertilized or over-watered. Stop feeding them when the second crop has been picked, but continue watering just enough to prevent the soil from drying out: remember that the embryos of next year's first crop are already there.

Figs should have about two months of cool dormancy, ideally above 40°. Outdoor figs in tubs may benefit from being brought in for the winter; if the weather is very cold, all ventilators should be closed.

Grapes grow extremely well indoors and this is an excellent way of producing delicious fruit in cooler climates. Hothouse cultivation is really only for specialists, but there are many varieties suited to cold greenhouses. The roots often grow outside the house so that only the fruiting wood gets protection from cold and wind. This usually gives very good results, and it means there is more room inside the greenhouse for other plants, as long as they also like a moist but well-ventilated atmosphere in summer and a cold winter.

The roots can be enclosed in beds or borders, restricted to start with but increased in size later on; for example, a 3 foot border the first year may be increased by a foot or two the next year, and so on to an eventual width of 8 or 10 feet. One advantage of having the roots outside is that they require less watering; vines, whether indoor or outdoor, are greedy for both food and water.

Indoor vines can grow to an impressive size and survive for centuries. In a restricted space they can of course be stopped at whatever length is appropriate. They may be grown vertically or horizontally, or trained into whatever shape is required.

A simple method of growing vines in a greenhouse is to train the plants along wires which have been strung the length of the house and attached to it by eye-bolts at 10 foot intervals. The wires should be at least 12 inches apart and set 6 inches in from the glass.

Correct ventilation is vital. There should be plenty of air movement but not a through draft. Good ventilation will help prevent mildew, and a suitably moist atmosphere discourages red spider mite. The important thing is to be consistent; don't suddenly increase or decrease ventilation or humidity. If you do heat the greenhouse it should be done gradually, and of course all heating must be turned off in winter. This is the time to prune the vine, and also give it another mulch.

Ask your county agent to recommend varieties that are suitable for greenhouse cultivation.

Ripe fruit should be cut off with scissors; bunches will keep for a little while if their stems are put in water.

Kiwi fruit are not usually grown under glass, but they can do exceptionally well in large containers. A heated house is not necessary. They will have to be hand-pollinated and fed regularly.

Mangoes are not a first choice for greenhouse cultivation, partly because of the size of the tree, but also because for best results they like rather special conditions: a comparatively dry period while in flower and fruit, but high humidity for about four months in between. Fairly constant high temperatures are necessary.

Melons grow well in greenhouses, especially the cantaloupe variety, which can be grown under cloches or in cold frames – the simplest method of growing under glass. Sow the seed in spring in a greenhouse heated to 65°. About four to six weeks later plant the seedlings out, one in the middle of each frame, and then keep the frames closed for a week to ten days and shaded if the sun is strong. Train the plants with one lateral to each corner of the frame. Increase the ventilation gradually and remove the shading. A dry atmosphere is necessary for pollination: if the weather is warm enough, remove the covers during the day, but replace them at night. Provide plenty of ventilation while the fruits are swelling, with shading if necessary in late summer.

Cantaloupe melons are also suitable for unheated houses, as are casaba or winter melons. The more delicately flavored musk melons need a heated house. Well-rooted seedlings can be set out, often on a "hot-bed" over a base of horse manure. Train the plants up wires and tie the laterals to horizontal wires or netting. Pollinate by hand when at least four female flowers on separate laterals are open; if all the fruits set, thin them out to three or four per plant.

The ripening fruit can be supported by special nets, like mini-hammocks, available from garden centers. The atmosphere should be humid but buoyant, with ventilation if the temperature goes over 70° – the ideal constant temperature.

Olives should have a minimum winter temperature of 40°, and must not be exposed to frost. If grown in containers, they can stand outside in summer and be brought in for the winter.

Pistachios like similar conditions.

Papayas like a warm house with a minimum winter temperature of 60°. They require little watering in winter, but they must have plenty during summer days.

Peaches and *nectarines* like a cool dormant period, during which they will withstand even below-freezing temperatures, so it is not necessary to heat the greenhouse at all unless you want very early crops. Too little heat is better than too much. Sun, good drainage and an area of up to 15 by 10 feet per tree are essential.

During the dormant period the house should have as much ventilation as possible. To encourage flowering and early good-quality fruit, close the ventilators when the buds begin to swell and heat the house to a minimum of 45°. Only open the ventilators if the temperature goes over 65°. Keep the atmosphere humid, preferably by daily spraying, with regular soakings in warm weather to stop the soil drying out. Regular fertilizing is also important.

Do not spray the trees while the fruit is actually ripening; keep the atmosphere humid and ventilate as much as possible – this will improve the flavor, as well as help to prevent mildew. After harvesting, leave the ventilators open to cool the house down for the dormant season – if the plants are in tubs they can be placed outside during the winter.

Although peaches and nectarines are self-fertile they will have to be hand-pollinated under glass, as few if any insects will be able to get into the house at blossom time when ventilation is minimal. Two recommended varieties that are for growing under glass are the peach "Reliance" and the nectarine "Arm King."

A great advantage of growing peaches under glass is that they seldom suffer from one of the most serious of peach diseases, peach leaf curl, although they are sometimes susceptible to mildew.

Strawberries respond well to greenhouse culture. New plants which have been potted on can be left outside in late autumn to go dormant, in a cold frame covered with straw or peat to protect them from frost. Don't cover them before late winter or early spring or they will make too much leaf growth. In midwinter, bring them into a cold greenhouse — the temperature should be just above freezing.

After about two or three weeks gradually raise the temperature to 45°. The earlier they are started, the earlier they will crop (in about three months' time), but it is easier to achieve successful crops if you leave them till early spring. When the flowers begin to appear (about a month later), gradually increase the temperature to 55° and ventilate at 75°. Hand-pollinate every day in order to ensure fruit.

When the fruit is swollen and begins to change color, stop the weekly feed or you will have soft insipid berries. Spraying can also be stopped, and the strawberries should have as much ventilation as possible. If you have been growing them with vines or peaches, the conditions so far will have suited both, but at this stage strawberries should ideally be moved somewhere drier and airier.

Ripe strawberries for Christmas can sometimes be achieved by bringing year-old plants into a warm house (55° minimum) in early winter.

"Ogallala" is a good, strong, everbearing variety; or ask your county agent to recommend varieties suitable for cultivating in a greenhouse.

In an unheated greenhouse the procedure is exactly the same, but bring the plants in during late winter or early spring. They will ripen ahead of outdoor plants.

INDOOR CULTIVATION

Although growing fruit indoors does not always produce the best quality, as conditions tend to vary too much, it is perfectly possible to do so, given plenty of light and water.

A humidifier is a great help, both for the fruit and for maintaining a healthy atmosphere in a centrally-heated house. Alternatively, stand the plant pots in a larger container with peat or some other substance which can be kept damp. Daily syringing is also helpful.

The following selection of plants will look attractive indoors, as well as producing fruit.

Akebia is an unusual trailing plant with fragrant purple flowers and interesting, sausage-shaped fruits, lavender or pale violet, which are a little insipid but much liked in their native China, where the plant is also valued for its medicinal properties.

Alpine strawberries will do very well indoors, grown in a strawberry pot or an ordinary 6 inch pot. If the young plants are potted in early winter and brought into the house about two months later, you can expect them to bear fruit by late spring.

Citrus fruits do well in pots indoors, provided they get enough light and water, and plenty of ventilation in hot weather, preferably by placing them outside.

One of the most suitable is the calamondin orange, a small, very ornamental tree that bears fruit when still young. One-year-old trees are sometimes available, but the plant can be grown from cuttings, or from seed, which usually takes up to a month to germinate.

Both flowers and fruit are usually prolific. It is disease-resistant and one of the hardiest of the citrus family.

The calamondin orange likes to feel a distinct contrast in the seasons and does not require too hot a room in winter. It should have a humid atmosphere, plenty of water, and some liquid manure during the summer. In winter it requires less watering, but the soil should never be allowed to dry out.

Pick the fruit by cutting it off cleanly. Pulling it off may tear the plant and leave a raw area in which fungoid diseases are all too likely to develop.

Some mandarin oranges are also suitable for growing indoors.

Feijoya is an unusual fruit which is also known as the pineapple guava—no relation to either of these, it has a taste reminiscent of both. Although it can grow into a tree it is easy to keep it pruned to the shape of a bushy shrub. The plant is very ornamental, with evergreen leaves, abundant, slightly fuchsia-like flowers, and attractive green fruit resembling passion fruit in appearance. The flower petals are also edible, either in salads or crystallized.

The feijoya will germinate in two or three weeks from seed sown in spring, or can be propagated from cuttings in summer—if possible over bottom heat, like pineapples. It will fruit when three or four years old. Hand-pollinate indoor plants to ensure fertilization.

The fruit falls when ripe, and should be eaten or cooked at once. It can also be picked while still a little unripe and allowed to mature off the tree; some people consider that this method improves the flavor. All the fruit is edible, except the thin outer skin.

Pineapples have been successfully grown indoors as pot plants. Although they need plenty of water while the fruit is developing, they can stand up to occasional periods of dry conditions better than most fruit. They need high temperatures and even in winter should be kept at 65°.

Choose a deep pot and weight the bottom well with plenty of stones, rubble or other heavy material which will allow good drainage; even a small pineapple can weigh as much as 3 pounds, and such a fruit growing at the top of a 3 or 4 foot plant will make the plant very top-heavy. Fill up the pot with a sandy loam.

If you cannot get a slip or sucker from an existing plant it is possible to grow pineapples by rooting the crown, or top. Cut it off cleanly and remove the lower leaves. To prevent the crown from rotting, let it dry for at least a day before planting it head down. Setting the plant over bottom heat will encourage rooting. A warm spot near a heating vent is ideal, but the soil *must* be kept moist. Once the plant has rooted, the soil should still be kept moist—not over-watered, but never allowed to dry out.

Pineapples like lots of light, so put it as near the window as you can, although preferably not at eye level; the sharp edges of the leaves are aggressive enough, but the tips can do serious damage.

The plant should fruit in about 18 months or so. Feed it with liquid manure while the fruits are developing. When they are full grown but still unripe the plants will not require so much water. The sweetest pineapples are those allowed to ripen fully on the plant. Pick them by cutting cleanly through the stalk an inch or two below the fruit. The same plant can produce two or more fruit in subsequent seasons on branches or suckers sprouting from the leaf axils. Alternatively these can be removed and used to form new plants. Another sort of shoot, called a slip, grows from the base of the fruit, and this too can be used for propagation.

Variegated pineapples are extremely decorative houseplants although their flavor, should the plant fruit, is not always as good as that of the ordinary pineapple.

MENU PLANNER

The recipes on these pages have been divided into various categories to help you make use of the widest possible variety of fruits and nuts when planning meals.

APPETIZERS AND SAVORIES

Polish Herring and Apple Appetizer Salad (page 15)
Avocado and Melon Cocktail (page 105)
Avocado Dip (page 27)
Avocado with Cream Cheese Dressing (page 27)
Stuffed Avocados (page 27)
Banana Chips (page 30)
Fig Appetizer (page 66)
Italian Figs with Salami (page 67)
Seviche (limes) (page 96)
Melon and Kumquat Salad (page 88)
Prosciutto with Melon (page 105)
Olive and Salami Salad (page 113)
Olive Cheese Balls (page 112)
Olive Cheese Pastries (page 113)
Cheese and Olive Pâté (page 113)
Garlic Olives (page 112)
Italian Pepper and Olive Appetizer (page 114)
Provençal Tapénade (olives) (page 113)
Papaya Strawberry Appetizer (page 126)
Savory Pecan Rolls (page 141)
Pork and Pistachio Pâté (page 150)
Prune and Bacon Skewers (page 156)
Leek and Prune Appetizer (page 156)

SOUPS

Christmas Almond Soup (page 10)
Hot Apple Soup (page 15)
Apricot Chicken Soup (page 22)
Chilled Avocado Soup (page 28)
Creamed Avocado Soup (page 27)
Blackberry Soup (page 34)
Blueberry Soup (page 40)
Iced Cherry Soup (page 48)
Cream of Chestnut Soup (page 52)
Avgolemono (lemon) (page 91)
Chilled Melon Soup (page 104)
Kang Kung (honeydew melon) (page 105)
Chilled Watermelon Soup (page 109)
Sopa de Amoras (mulberries) (page 195)
Chilled Summer Peach Soup (page 128)
Peanut Soup (page 132)
Pear Soup (page 135)
Pine Nut Soup (page 148)
Chilled Plum Soup (page 152)
Berry Soup (raspberries) (page 162)
Wild Strawberry Soup (page 175)

Balkan Tarator Soup (walnuts) (page 182)
Mexican Walnut Soup (page 182)

MAIN COURSES

Salt Cod with Akee (page 187)
Flounder with Almond Sauce (page 11)
Trout with Almonds (page 11)
Baked Chicken with Apples (page 16)
Dolmeh Sib (apples) (page 16)
Lamb and Apricot Polo (page 23)
Pork Chops in Apricot Sauce (page 23)
Eggs with Avocado Sauce (page 28)
Veal Rolls with Ham and Avocado (page 28)
Chicken with Bananas (page 31)
Brazil Nut Bake (page 44)
Duck with Brazil Nuts and Bananas in Orange Sauce (page 45)
Baked Fish with Cashew Stuffing (page 46)
Chicken with Cashew Nuts in Hoisin Sauce (page 47)
Veal and Cashew Nut Casserole (page 47)
Cherry Lamb Mayonnaise (page 49)
Duck with Cherries (page 49)
Caucasian Lamb (chestnuts) (page 53)
Chicken with Chestnuts (page 53)
Chicken in Spiced Coconut Sauce (page 55)
Fish and Coconut Curry (page 55)
Cranberry and Turkey Pie (page 58)
Chicken and Grape Salad (page 76)
Duckling Véronique (page 75)
Quail with Grapes (page 75)
Roast Pheasant with Grape Stuffing (page 75)
Caucasian Lamb Pilau with Raisins (page 78)
Chicken with Raisin Stuffing (page 78)
Auckland Steak (kiwi fruit) (page 86)
Kiwi Chicken Salad (page 86)
Baked Fish with Lemon Sour Cream Sauce (page 91)
Veal in Lemon Parsley Sauce (page 91)
Broiled Chicken with Lime Marinade (page 97)
Litchi Pork (page 98)
Litchi and Almond Chicken (page 98)
Litchi and Pineapple Pork (page 99)
Ham and Mango Mayonnaise (page 101)
Mango and Pork Salad (page 100)
Chicken with Nectarines (page 110)
Olive and Fennel Salad (page 115)
Olive and Rabbit Stew Niçoise (page 114)
Beef and Olive Stew (page 114)
Braised Duck with Olives (page 114)
Tuna Olive Mayonnaise (page 115)

Duckling with Orange (page 117)
Moroccan Spiced Lamb with Orange (page 117)
Thai Orange and Pork Salad (page 118)
Ghanaian Chicken in Peanut Sauce (page 133)
Peanut Pork (page 132)
Pear and Cheese Salad (page 136)
Pears, Beans and Bacon (page 136)
Meat Loaf with Pecan Stuffing (page 140)
Chicken with Pineapple Chinese Style (page 145)
Lebanese Ragoût with Pine Nuts (page 148)
Mexican Chicken with Pine Nuts (page 149)
Liver in Pomegranate Sauce (page 158)
Chicken and Pomegranate Syrup (page 159)
Caucasian Chicken with Prunes (page 156)
Roast Pork with Prunes (page 157)
Caucasian Stuffed Quinces (page 161)
Chicken with Quince Stuffing (page 160)
Baked Chicken with Rhubarb Sauce (page 170)
Persian Beef with Rhubarb Sauce (page 169)
Smoked Tangerine Chicken (page 180)
Circassian Chicken with Walnut Sauce (page 183)
Savory Walnut Omelette (page 184)
Sweet Walnut and Apricot Omelette (page 185)
Trout with Walnut Sauce (page 183)

SIDE DISHES

Avocado Pilaf (page 29)
Cheese Broiled Pears (page 136)
Gingered Orange Rice (page 120)
Orange Rice with Almonds (page 120)

VEGETARIAN DISHES

Some of these dishes can be used as main courses, others are more suitable as side dishes.

Hot

Buttered Celery Amandine (almonds) (page 11)
Bulgur Pilaf with Apples and Almonds (page 17)
Noodles with Almonds (page 11)
Bananas and Onions (page 31)
Coconut Rice (page 56)
Korean Rice with Dates (page 63)
Noodles with Tomatoes, Cheese and Olives (page 115)
Beets in Orange Sauce (page 119)
Glazed Cabbage à l'Orange (page 119)

Fried Papaya (page 126)
Chinese Eggplant in Peanut Sauce
    (page 133)
Gado Gado (peanuts) (page 133)
Curried Pears (page 136)
Italian Spinach with Pine Nuts
    (page 149)
Chinese Walnuts and Peppers
    (page 184)

Cold
Salade Parisienne (apples) (page 16)
Waldorf Salad (apples) (page 15)
Avocado Salad (page 28)
Banana Waldorf (page 31)
Watercress, Brazil Nut and Orange
    Salad (page 44)
Moroccan Date Salad (page 62)
Grapefruit and Carrot Salad (page 82)
Hazelnut and Cherry Salad (page 84)
Lemon and Artichoke Salad (page 92)
Melon and Cucumber Salad
    (page 105)
Amargoso Salad (watermelon)
    (page 109)
Orange Onion Salad (page 118)
Orange and Carrot Salad (page 118)
Orange and Date Salad (page 119)
Mexican Orange Salad (page 119)
Pistachio Rice Salad (page 150)
Red Currant and Carrot Salad
    (page 166)
Potato Salad with Walnuts (page 184)

DESSERTS

Apple Jellies (page 21)
Apple Snow (page 18)
Baked Apples (page 17)
Baked Rice and Apple Pudding
    (page 18)
Barbecued Apples (page 18)
Hot Apple Charlotte (page 19)
Italian Apple Cake (page 17)
Sherried Apples with Spiced Nuts
    (page 19)
Apricot Cream (page 23)
Apricot Ice Cream (page 24)
Avocado Ice Cream (page 29)
Avocado Lime Cream (page 29)
Banana Cheese (page 32)
Banana Ice Cream (page 33)
Bananas with Raspberry Sauce
    (page 32)
Bananes Brûlées (page 32)
Broiled Bananas (page 32)
Blackberry Orange Mousse (page 35)
Black Currant Yogurt Ice Cream
    (page 38)
Polish Black Currant Kisiel (page 37)
Spiced Black Currant Pudding
    (page 37)
Witches' Foam (black currants)
    (page 38)
Blueberry Buckle (page 42)
Blueberry Cinnamon Toasts (page 41)
Blueberry Cream (page 42)
Blueberry Custard Tart (page 41)

Steamed Blueberry Pudding
    (page 41)
Breadfruit Pudding (page 190)
Cherry Bread Crumb Pudding
    (page 49)
Cherry Compote (page 49)
Clafoutis (cherries) (page 50)
Coconut Pudding (page 57)
Cranberry Fluff (page 59)
Cranberry Layer Dessert (page 60)
Cranberry Orange Compote
    (page 59)
Cranberry Parfait (page 60)
Cranberry Sherbert (page 60)
Chinese Date Crêpes (page 64)
Dates with Cream (page 63)
Steamed Date Pudding (page 63)
Figgy Pudding (page 67)
Figs and Apple Crispy Bake (page 68)
Figs and Ice Cream (page 68)
Figs and Orange Compote
    (page 67)
Figs and Peaches in Cream (page 68)
Figs in Brandy (page 68)
Khoshaf (figs) (page 67)
English Gooseberry Fool (page 71)
Gooseberry Charlotte (page 71)
Gooseberry Compote with Ice Cream
    (page 72)
Gooseberry Orange Fool (page 71)
Gooseberry Soufflé (page 72)
Grapes in Sour Cream (page 77)
Swedish Grape Gelatin (page 76)
Gertie's Christmas Pudding (raisins)
    (page 79)
Cranberry Grapefruit Compote
    (page 83)
Minted Grapefruit Sherbert (page 83)
Hazelnut Soufflé (page 85)
Grace's Pavlova (kiwi fruit)
    (page 87)
Kiwi Fritters (page 87)
Kiwi Ice Cream (page 87)
Baked Lemon Pudding (page 92)
Fresh Lemon Gelatin (page 94)
Lemon Ice Cream (page 94)
Lemon Pancakes (page 92)
Lemon Soufflé (page 94)
Sussex Pond Pudding (lemons)
    (page 93)
Syllabub (lemons) (page 94)
Lime Sherbert (page 97)
Tropical Fruit Salad (litchis)
    (page 99)
Mango and Ginger Ice Cream Tart
    (page 101)
Mango Cream (page 102)
Mango Fool Créole (page 102)
Mango Mousse (page 101)
Mango Sherbert (page 101)
Mangoes in Syrup (page 102)
Baked Melon Alaska (page 108)
Baked Spiced Melon (page 106)
Melon à la Scheherezade (page 107)
Melon Stuffed with Fruits (page 106)
Melon Water Ice (page 107)
Melon with Black Currants (page 107)

Melon with Port (page 107)
Melon with Raspberries (page 106)
Guyanan Watermelon (page 109)
Baked Nectarines (page 111)
Flambéed Nectarines (page 111)
Boodle's Orange Fool (page 120)
Crêpes Suzette (oranges) (page 121)
Orange Soufflé Pudding (page 120)
Oranges in Marsala (page 121)
Petits Pots de Chocolat à l'Orange
    (page 191)
Dulce de Papaya Verde (page 126)
Passion Whip (page 127)
Broiled Peaches (page 130)
Italian Stuffed Peaches (page 130)
Peach Dumplings (page 129)
Peach Parfait (page 130)
Peach Salad (page 129)
Baked Pears with Orange (page 138)
Pears in Butterscotch Sauce
    (page 137)
Pears in Chocolate Sauce (page 137)
Pears in Cream (page 136)
Pears in Red Wine (page 138)
Persimmon Fluff (page 142)
Persimmon Ice Cream (page 143)
Persimmon Water Ice (page 143)
Trader Vic's Persimmons with Rum
    (page 143)
Fruit in a Blanket (pineapple)
    (page 145)
Pineapple Ambrosia (page 146)
Pineapple Cream (page 145)
Pineapple Gelatin (page 146)
Pine and Apple Salad (page 145)
Roast Pineapple (page 145)
Pistachio Ice Cream (page 151)
Fresh Plum Compote (page 153)
Plum Compote with Red Wine Syrup
    (page 153)
Plums in Cream (page 153)
Steamed Prune Pudding (page 157)
Pomegranate Water Ice (page 159)
Frozen Raspberry Cream
    (page 163)
Raspberry Almond Meringue
    (page 164)
Raspberry Mousse (page 164)
Raspberry Orange Cream (page 163)
Raspberry Yogurt Ice Cream
    (page 164)
Summer Pudding (raspberries)
    (page 163)
Red Currant and Honey Fool
    (page 166)
Red Currant Water Ice (page 167)
Rodgrod Med Flode (red currants)
    (page 167)
Rhubarb Burnt Cream (page 172)
Rhubarb Compote (page 172)
Rhubarb Crumble (page 171)
Rhubarb Fool (page 171)
Rhubarb with Oat Crumble
    (page 172)
Spring Pudding (rhubarb) (page 171)
Fragole Dama Bianca (strawberries)
    (page 176)

French Strawberry Ice Cream
(page 177)
Honeyed Strawberries (page 175)
Soyer's Strawberry Salad (page 176)
Strawberry Meringued Cream
(page 176)
Strawberry and Currant Salad
(page 176)
Strawberry and Raspberry Ice Cream
(page 177)
Strawberry and Red Currant Ice
Cream (page 177)
Strawberries in Cream (page 175)
Strawberries Jubilee (page 176)
Strawberries in Lime Cream Sauce
(page 175)
Satsumas in Syrup (page 181)

Tangerine Salad (page 181)
Tangerines in Rum and Caramel
Sauce (page 181)
Youngberries and Bananas
(page 189)

PIES AND TARTS

Southern Apple Pie (page 19)
Swiss Apple Tart (page 18)
Banana Cream Pie (page 32)
Blackberry Custard Tart (page 35)
Black Currant Pie (page 37)
Deep-dish Blueberry Pie (page 41)
Cherry Pie (page 50)
Coconut Cream Pie (page 56)

Cranberry Tart (page 60)
Gooseberry Pie (page 71)
Austrian Grape Tart (page 76)
Lemon Meringue Pie (page 93)
Orange Passion Pie (page 127)
Peach Meringue Pie (page 129)
Peach and Almond Tart (page 130)
Spiced Pear Pie (page 137)
Pecan Cherry Cake (page 141)
American Pecan Pie (page 140)
Persimmon Pie (page 143)
Raspberry Tart with Cream (page 165)
Austrian Red Currant Tart (page 167)
Creamy Rhubarb Pie (page 171)
Rhubarb Meringue Tart (page 172)
Rhubarb Pie (page 170)
Strawberry Tart (page 176)

BIBLIOGRAPHY

Berry, C. J. J., 130 NEW WINE MAKING RECIPES, Amateur Winemaker, Hampshire, 1967·

Bowen, Carol, A TO Z OF HEALTH FOODS, Hamlyn, Middlesex, 1979

Bon Viveur, 365 PUDDINGS, Daily Telegraph Publications, London, 1975

Boyd, Lizzie, BRITISH COOKERY, B.T.A., 1976

Chu, Grace Zia, THE PLEASURES OF CHINESE COOKING, Faber, London, 1974

Dinnage, Paul, THE BOOK OF FRUIT & FRUIT COOKERY, Sidgwick & Jackson, London, 1981

Dixon, Pamela, NEW WAYS WITH FRESH FRUIT & VEGETABLES, Faber, London, 1973

Farm Journal, FREEZING AND CANNING COOKBOOK, Doubleday & Co, New York, 1963

Fitzgibbon, Theodora, THE FOOD OF THE WESTERN WORLD, Hutchinson, London, 1976

Foster, Charles, HOME WINEMAKING, Ward Lock, London, 1969

Fredericks, Carlton, COOKBOOK FOR GOOD NUTRITION, Grosset & Dunlap, New York, 1960

Good Housekeeping's World Cookery, Ebury Press, London, 1962

Good Housekeeping Cookery Book, Ebury Press, London, 1976

Graham, Winifred, CHOCOLATES & CANDIES FOR PLEASURE & PROFIT, White Lion Publishers Ltd, London, 1977

Heath, Ambrose, THE PENGUIN BOOK OF SAUCES, Penguin, Middlesex, 1970

Hunter, Beatrice Trum, THE NATURAL FOODS COOKBOOK, Faber, London, 1975

Innes, Francesca, & Lincoln, Frances, THE COUNTRY KITCHEN, Weidenfeld & Nicholson, London, 1979

Johns, Leslie, & Stevenson, Violet, THE COMPLETE BOOK OF FRUIT, Angus & Robertson, London, 1979

Kaufman, William I., THE NUT COOKERY BOOK, Faber, London, 1966

Kimball, Yeffe, and Anderson, Jean, THE ART OF AMERICAN INDIAN COOKING, Doubleday & Co, New York, 1965

Lo, Kenneth, THE CHINESE COOKERY ENCYCLOPEDIA, William Collins, London, 1974

Mabey, David, & Mabey, Rose, JAMS, PICKLES & CHUTNEYS, Penguin, Middlesex, 1976

Maxwell Hudson, Claire, THE NATURAL BEAUTY BOOK, Macdonald & Jane, London, 1976

Maxwell Hudson, Claire, YOUR HEALTH & BEAUTY BOOK, Macdonald General Books, London, 1979

Nilson, Bee, PENGUIN COOKERY BOOK, Penguin, Middlesex, 1952

Olsen, Gloria Preston, CULINARY CLASSICS, Charter House Publishers, Tennessee, 1978

Orsini, Elizabeth, BOOK OF PIES, Pan, London, 1981

Ortiz, Elisabeth, CARIBBEAN COOKING, Penguin, Middlesex, 1977

Reekie, Jennie, NO NEED TO COOK, Pelham, London, 1977

Richardson, Rosamund, HEDGEROW COOKERY, Penguin, Middlesex, 1980

Sass, Lorna, TO THE QUEEN'S TASTE, John Murray, London, 1971

Singh, Dharamjit, INDIAN COOKERY, Penguin, Middlesex, 1970

Solomon, Charmaine, THE COMPLETE ASIAN COOKBOOK, Summit Books, Paul Hamlyn, Sydney, 1976

Tayleur, W. H. T., THE PENGUIN BOOK OF HOME BREWING & WINE MAKING, Penguin, Middlesex, 1973

The Complete Guide to the Art of Modern Cookery, translated by H. L. Cracknell & R. J. Kaufman, Heinemann, London, 1979

The Feill Cookery Book, MacNaughtan & Sinclair, Glasgow, 1907

The World Atlas of Food, Mitchell Beazley, London, 1974

Walker, Michael, CINZANO COCKTAIL BOOK, Queen Anne Press, London, 1980

Watt, Ruth Mulvey, & Alvarez, Luisa Maria, GOOD FOOD FROM MEXICO, Macmillan, New York, 1962

INDEX

ackee *see* akee
akebia, 186, 246
akee, 186–7
    salt cod with, 187
alligator pear, *see* avocado
almond, 10–13, 226
    almond essence, 10
    almond paste, 10, 13
    apricot almond sweets, 24
    bulgur pilaf with apples and, 17
    buttered celery amandine, 11
    chocolate cake, 12
    Christmas soup, 10
    cosmetics, 10
    cranberry almond sauce, 61
    crescents, 12
    cultivation, 227–8
    fig bonbons, 69
    flounder with almond sauce, 11
    Fürstenbrot, 81
    growing regions, 10
    lemon and artichoke salad, 92
    litchi and almond chicken, 98
    macaroons, 13
    Mazurck cytrynowy, 95
    Moroccan stuffed dates, 65
    noodles with, 11
    nutritional value, 210
    olive cheese balls, 112
    orange and almond cake, 123
    orange rice with, 120
    peach and almond tart, 130
    praline, 13
    preparation, 10
    prune and bacon skewers, 156
    raspberry almond meringue, 164
    St Martin's croissants, 12
    storage, 10
    Swiss cookies, 13
    trout with, 11
alpine strawberry, 174, 246
apple, 14–21
    apple and green tomato chutney, 21
    apple and plum chutney, 20
    apple cranberry sauce, 61
    apple snow, 18
    baked, 17
    baked chicken with, 16
    baked rice and apple pudding, 18
    banana Waldorf, 31
    barbecued, 18
    blackberry and apple jam, 35
    bottled in cider, 21
    bulgur pilaf with almonds and, 17
    canning, 201
    chutney, 20
    cosmetics, 14
    cultivation, 230–2, 244
    diet, 208
    Dolmeh sib (Persian stuffed), 16
    drying, 202
    fig and apple crispy bake, 68
    freezing, 14
    fresh apple relish, 17
    growing regions, 14
    hot apple Charlotte, 19
    hot soup, 15
    Italian cake, 17
    jam-making, 198
    jellies, 21, 199
    nutritional value, 210
    old-fashioned apple butter, 20
    pear and apple preserve, 139
    pine and apple salad, 145
    Polish herring and apple appetizer salad, 15
    remedies, 14
    Russian soured apples, 21
    salade Parisienne, 16
    sauces, 20
    sherried apples with spiced nuts, 19
    Southern apple pie, 19
    storage, 232
    Swiss apple tart, 18
    uses, 14
    Waldorf salad, 15
apricot, 22–5, 226–7
    apricot almond sweets, 24
    apricot brandy, 25
    apricot chicken soup, 22
    apricot cream, 23
    apricot meringue cake, 24
    canning, 201
    cosmetics, 22
    cultivation, 226–7, 244
    dried, 22, 202
    freezing, 22
    glaze, 25
    growing regions, 22
    ice cream, 24
    jam, 25, 200
    lamb and apricot polo, 23
    nutritional value, 210
    pickles, 200
    pine–apricot jam, 147
    pork chops in apricot sauce, 23
    preserve, 22
    quick sauce, 25
    storage, 227
    sweet walnut and apricot omelette, 185
    wine, 25
artichoke and lemon salad, 92
atemoya, 187
avocado, 26–9
    avocado and melon cocktail, 105
    avocado butter, 29
    avocado lime cream, 29
    chilled soup, 28
    cosmetics, 26
    with cream cheese dressing, 27
    creamed avocado soup, 27
    cultivation, 234, 243, 244
    dip, 27
    eggs with avocado sauce, 28
    growing regions, 26, 234
    guacamole, 26
    health drink, 26
    ice cream, 29, 204
    nutritional value, 210
    pilaf, 29
    preparation, 26
    salad, 28
    storage, 26
    stuffed, 27
    veal rolls with ham and, 28
azorole, 232

bacon: pears, beans and bacon, 136
    prune and bacon skewers, 156
banana, 30–3
    banana cheese, 32
    banana daiquiri, 33
    banana Waldorf, 31
    bananas and onions, 31
    bananes brûlées, 32
    broiled, 32
    canning, 201
    chicken with, 31
    chips, 30
    cosmetics, 30
    cream pie, 32
    cultivation, 224–5, 244
    diet, 208
    dried, 30, 202
    duck with Brazil nuts and bananas in orange sauce, 45
    growing regions, 30
    health shake, 30
    ice cream, 33
    melon à la Scheherezade, 107
    nutritional value, 211
    oracabessa, 33
    pickles and chutneys, 200
    pineapple and banana breakfast drink, 144
    preparation, 30
    with raspberry sauce, 32
    spiced banana bread, 33
    storage, 30
    wine, 33
    youngberries and bananas, 189
Barbados cherry, 187
barberry, 188
basil: pesto alla Genovese, 149
bay leaf jelly, 21
beans, French: pears, beans and bacon, 136
bearberry, 188
beef: Auckland steak, 86
    beef and olive stew, 114
    Dolmeh sib, 16
    meat loaf with pecan stuffing, 140
    Persian beef with rhubarb sauce, 169
beets: beet and walnut relish, 184
    in orange sauce, 119
berries: canning, 201
    fruit vinegars, 202
    unusual varieties, 188–9
    see also individual types of berry
bilberry, *see* blueberry
blackberry, 34–5
    berry soup, 162
    blackberry and apple jam, 35
    blackberry custard tart, 35
    blackberry orange mousse, 35
    breakfast crunch, 34
    cultivation, 218
    freezing, 34
    growing regions, 34, 218
    nutritional value, 211
    remedies, 34
    soup, 34
    storage, 218
    wine, 35
black currant, 36–9, 189
    black currant buckle, 42
    black currant yogurt ice cream, 38
    crème de cassis, 36, 39
    cultivation, 214
    freezing, 36
    growing regions, 36, 214
    jams and jellies, 36, 38, 39, 199
    juice, 36
    melon with, 107
    nutritional value, 211
    pie, 37
    Polish kisiel, 37
    remedies, 36
    solbaerrom (liqueur), 39
    spiced pudding, 37
    storage, 36, 214
    summer pudding, 163
    witches' foam, 38
blaeberry, *see* blueberry
blueberry, 40–3, 189
    blaeberry jam, 43
    blueberry buckle, 42
    blueberry cheese, 43
    blueberry cinnamon toasts, 41
    blueberry cream, 42
    blueberry custard tart, 41
    blueberry loaf cake, 42
    blueberry pancakes, 42
    cultivation, 216
    deep-dish pie, 41
    freezing, 40
    growing regions, 40, 216
    liqueur, 43
    nutritional value, 211
    remedies, 40
    soup, 40
    spiced pudding, 37
    steamed pudding, 41
    storage, 40, 216
boysenberry, 188, 218
    boysenberry summer pudding, 188
bran: breakfast crunch, 34
brandy: apricot, 25
    cherries in, 51
    figs in, 68
    kumquats in, 88
    peaches in, 131
    pears in, 139
    plum, 155
Brazil nut, 44–5, 241
    Brazil nut bake, 44
    chocolate Brazils, 45
    duck with Brazil nuts and bananas in orange sauce, 45
    growing regions, 44, 241
    nutritional value, 211
    nutty butter cookies, 45
    watercress and orange salad with, 44
breadfruit, 190
    pudding, 190
bulgur pilaf with apples and almonds, 17
bullock's heart, *see* custard apple
bush fruits, cultivation, 214–16
butter: avocado, 29
    cashew nut, 47
    lemon herb, 92
butternut, 190, 239, 240

cabbage: glazed à l'orange, 119
calamondin orange, 190, 229, 246–7
    in syrup, 190
cane fruit, cultivation, 217–18
canning, 201
cantaloup melon, 104
Cape gooseberry, 191
caramel: hazelnuts in, 85
    tangerines in rum and caramel sauce, 181
carob, 191

carob smoothie, 191
carrot: grapefruit and carrot
  salad, 82
  orange and carrot salad, 118
  red currant and carrot salad,
  166
cashew apple, 192, 241
cashew nut, 46–7, 192
  baked fish stuffed with, 46
  cashew nut butter, 47
  chicken in hoisin sauce
  with, 47
  cultivation, 241–2
  growing regions, 46, 241
  nut and seed drink, 46
  nutritional value, 211
  uses, 46
  veal casserole with, 47
celery: banana Waldorf, 31
  buttered celery amandine, 11
  Waldorf salad, 15
champagne: Buck's fizz, 125
  champagne cocktail, 179
charentais melon, 104
cheese: cheese and olive
  pâté, 113
  cheese broiled pears, 136
  noodles with tomatoes,
  olives and, 115
  olive cheese pastries, 113
  pear and cheese salad, 136
  see also cream cheese
cherimoya, 187, 192
cherry, 48–51, 226
  canning, 201
  cheesecake, 50
  cherries in brandy, 51
  cherry bread crumb
  pudding, 49
  cherry lamb mayonnaise, 49
  cherry stalk tea, 48
  clafoutis, 50
  compote, 49
  cultivation, 227, 244
  dried, 48, 202
  duck with, 49
  easy Kirsch cake, 51
  freezing, 48
  growing regions, 48
  hazelnut and cherry salad,
  84
  iced soup, 48
  jam, 51, 198
  juice, 36
  melon stuffed with fruits,
  106
  nutritional value, 211
  pecan cherry cake, 141
  pickles, 200
  pie, 50
  preparation, 48
  remedies, 48
  storage, 227
  summer pudding, 163
  uses, 48
chestnut, 52–3
  Caucasian lamb, 53
  chicken with, 53
  cream of chestnut soup, 52
  cultivation, 239, 240
  freezing, 52
  growing regions, 52, 240
  nutritional value, 211
  preparation, 52
  remedies, 52
  sauce, 53
  storage, 240
  uses, 52
chicken: apricot chicken
  soup, 22
  in apricot sauce, 23

baked with apples, 16
baked with rhubarb sauce,
  170
with bananas, 31
with cashew nuts in hoisin
  sauce, 47
Caucasian chicken with
  prunes, 156
Çerkez tavuğu, 183
with chestnuts, 53
chicken and grape salad, 76
chicken and mango
  mayonnaise, 101
Ghanaian chicken in peanut
  sauce, 133
broiled with lime marinade, 97
kiwi chicken salad, 86
litchi and almond chicken,
  98
Mexican chicken with pine
  nuts, 149
with nectarines, 110
with pineapple Chinese
  style, 145
with pomegranate syrup, 159
with quince stuffing, 160
with raisin stuffing, 78
with rhubarb sauce, 169
smoked tangerine chicken,
  180
in spiced coconut sauce, 55
salade Parisienne, 16
Chinese gooseberry, see kiwi
  fruit
chocolate: chocolate almond
  cake, 12
  chocolate Brazils, 45
  chocolate date cake, 64
  chocolate dates, 64
  chocolate strawberry
  candies, 178
  orange walnut cake, 122
  pears in chocolate sauce, 137
  petits pots de chocolat à
  l'orange, 121
chutney: basic recipe, 200
  see also individual fruits
cider: bottled apples in, 21
  bottled pears in, 139
  vinegar, 14
cinnamon: blueberry buckle, 42
  blueberry cinnamon toasts,
  41
  croûtons, 205
citron, 192, 229
citrus fruit: canning, 201
  cultivation, 228–9, 243,
  244, 246–7
  citrus grape conserve, 77
clementine, 180, 229
cloudberry, 188
cobnut, see hazelnut
coconut, 54–7
  chicken in spiced coconut
  sauce, 55
  coconut cream pie, 56
  coconut ice, 57
  coconut meringue case, 56
  coconut milk, 54
  coconut pudding, 57
  coconut rice, 56
  cosmetics, 54
  cultivation, 242
  fish and coconut curry, 55
  freezing, 54
  growing regions, 54, 242
  lemon coconut creams, 57
  macaroons, 57
  nutritional value, 211
  papaya milkshake, 126
  pineapple ambrosia, 146

preparation, 54
sauce, 57
uses, 54
cod: baked fish with lemon
  sour cream sauce, 91
  fish and coconut curry, 55
  salt cod with akee, 187
Cornelian cherry, 192
cosmetics: almond, 10
  apple, 14
  apricot, 22
  avocado, 26
  banana, 30
  coconut, 54
  cranberry, 58
  grape, 74
  grapefruit, 82
  hazelnut, 84
  kumquat, 88
  lemon, 90
  lime, 96
  melon, 104
  olive oil, 112
  orange, 116
  papaya, 126
  peach, 128
  peanut oil, 132
  pear, 135
  pine nut, 148
  pineapple, 144
  pomegranate, 158
  quince, 160
  rhubarb, 169
  strawberry, 174
  tangerine, 180
  walnut, 182
crab apple, 193, 230
cranberry, 58–61, 189
  apple cranberry sauce, 61
  candy, 61
  cranberry almond sauce, 61
  cranberry and turkey pie, 58
  cranberry fluff, 59
  cranberry grapefruit
  compote, 83
  cranberry layer dessert, 60
  cranberry orange compote,
  59
  cranberry orange sauce, 61
  cultivation, 216
  dip, 59
  frosting, 59
  growing regions, 58, 216
  jam, 198
  nutritional value, 211
  parfait, 60
  party punch, 61
  relish, 59
  sherbert, 60
  simple sauce, 60
  storage, 216
  stuffing, 59
  tart, 60
  uses, 58
cream, fruit: basic recipe, 204
  see also individual fruits
cream cheese: banana
  cheese, 32
  cheese and olive pâté, 113
  cherry cheesecake, 50
  cranberry dip, 59
  dressing for avocado, 27
  fig appetizer, 66
  lemon cheesecake, 93
  olive cheese balls, 112
  orange cheese bread, 122
  see also cheese
crème de cassis, 36, 39
croûtons, 205
cucumber: Balkan tarator
  soup, 182

melon and cucumber salad,
  105
cultivation, 214–42
  greenhouse, 243–6
  indoor, 246–7
cumquat, see kumquat
currants, 74
  fruit vinegars, 202
  see also fruit, dried
curry: curried pears, 136
  fish and coconut, 55
custard: lemon, 205
  orange, 205
  rich custard sauce, 205
  thick custard sauce, 205
custard apple, 187, 192
custard banana, 192

damson, 152, 228
  damson cheese, 155
  jam, 198
  pickled, 155
date, 62–5
  apple chutney, 20
  Chinese crêpes, 64
  chocolate date cake, 64
  chocolate dates, 64
  with cream, 63
  cultivation, 234
  date and walnut spread, 62
  date bread, 64
  date squares, 64
  date "sugar", 65
  date sweetener, 65
  dried, 62, 202
  growing regions, 62, 234
  Korean rice with, 63
  marzipan dates, 64
  Moroccan salad, 62
  Moroccan stuffed dates, 65
  nutritional value, 211
  orange and date salad, 119
  rum dates, 65
  steamed pudding, 63
  uses, 62
dates, red, 62
dewberry, 188, 218
diet: children, 209
  high-fiber, 208
  low blood sugar, 209
  rapid-action, 207
  single-fruit, 208
  vegetarian, 209
drying fruit, 202
duck: braised with olives, 114
  with Brazil nuts and
  bananas in orange sauce, 45
  with cherries, 49
  duckling Véronique, 75
  duckling with orange, 117

eggs: Avgolemono, 91
  with avocado sauce, 28
  savory walnut omelette, 184
  sweet walnut and apricot
  omelette, 185
  elderberry, 193
eggplant: Chinese in peanut
  sauce, 133

feijoya, 193, 247
fennel: olive and fennel salad,
  115
fig, 66–9
  appetizer, 66
  bonbons, 69
  in brandy, 68
  canning, 201
  cultivation, 234–5, 243, 244
  dried, 66, 202
  dulce de higos (candied), 69

fig and apple crispy bake, 68
fig and orange compote, 67
figgy pudding, 67
figs and peaches in cream, 68
freezing, 66
Grandmother's fig and walnut preserve, 69
growing regions, 66, 234
with ice cream, 68
Italian figs with salami, 67
jam, 68, 198
khoshaf (fruit salad), 67
nutritional value, 211
poultice, 66
preparation, 66
prosciutto with, 105
spiced preserve, 69
storage, 235
uses, 66
filbert, see hazelnut
flounder with almond sauce, 11
fools: basic recipe, 204
see also individual fruits
freezing, 203
see also individual fruits
fruit, dried: Dundee cake, 81
Gertie's Christmas pudding, 79
Irish fruit cake, 80
Irish spiced fruit loaf, 80
mazurek cygański, 79
nutritional value, 211
Selkirk bannock, 80
fruit butters: basic recipe, 200
fruit cheeses: basic recipe, 200

gallia melon, 104
garlic olives, 112
gelatin (table): basic recipe, 205
gin, orange, 125
ginger: gingered orange rice, 120
mango and ginger ice cream tart, 101
rhubarb and ginger preserve, 173
golden naranjilla, 193
gooseberry, 70–3
Charlotte, 71
chutney, 73
compote with ice cream, 72
cultivation, 214, 215–16
Eliza Acton's sauce, 70
English gooseberry fool, 71
freezing, 70
gooseberry orange fool, 71
gooseberry raspberry jam, 72
growing regions, 70, 214
jam, 72, 198
Mrs Marsden's grand recipe for gooseberry wine, 73
nutritional value, 211
pie, 71
Polish preserve, 73
soufflé, 72
spiced gooseberry orange preserve, 73
storage, 216
stuffing, 70
uses, 70
grape, 74–81
Austrian tart, 76
canning, 201
chicken and grape salad, 76
citrus grape conserve, 77
cosmetics, 74
cultivation, 219–20, 243, 244–5

diet, 208
drying, 202
duckling Véronique, 75
growing regions, 74, 219
jam-making, 198
juice, 77
nutritional value, 211
quail with, 75
red grape wine, 77
roast pheasant with grape stuffing, 75
in sour cream, 77
storage, 74, 220
Swedish grape gelatin, 76
uses, 74
in vinegar, 77
white grape wine, 78
see also fruit, dried
grapefruit, 82–3
broiled, 82
cranberry grapefruit compote, 83
cultivation, 229
diet, 208
flower water, 82
freezing, 82
grapefruit and carrot salad, 82
grilled, 82
growing regions, 82
minted grapefruit sherbert, 83
mixed fruit marmalade, 83
nutritional value, 211
preparation, 82
greengage, 152
candied, 156
greenhouse cultivation, 243–6
grenadine, 159
ground cherry, 191
ground nut, see peanut
guava, 193
bastida goiaba, 193
canning, 201
nutritional value, 211

haddock: baked fish with lemon sour cream sauce, 91
ham: ham and mango mayonnaise, 101
prosciutto with melon, 105
veal rolls with avocado and, 28
harvesting, 214–41
hazelnut, 84–5
cookies, 85
in caramel, 85
cosmetics, 84
cultivation, 239, 240–1
growing regions, 84, 240
hazelnut and cherry salad, 84
Nusstorte, 85
nutritional value, 211
preparation, 84
remedies, 84
soufflé, 85
storage, 84, 241
herbs: jellies, 21
lemon herb butter, 92
herring: Polish herring and apple appetizer salad, 15
hickory nut, 193, 239, 240
hoisin sauce: chicken with cashew nuts in, 47
honey: honeyed strawberries, 175
nut and seed drink, 46
red currant and honey fool, 166
honeyberry, 188

honeydew melon, 104
huckleberry, 40, 189
husk tomato, see Cape gooseberry

ice cream: basic recipe, 204
see also individual fruits
Indian fig, see prickly pear
Indian nut, see pine nut
indoor cultivation, 246–7

jackfruit, 194
jam: basic recipe, 198–9
see also individual fruits
Japanese medlar, see loquat
japonica, 160, 238
jam, 161
jelly (jam): basic recipe, 199
see also individual fruits
jelly (table): basic recipe, 205
see also individual fruits
jujube, 62, 194
juneberry, 189

Kirsch, 48
easy cake, 51
tropical fruit salad, 99
kiwi fruit, 86–7
Auckland steak, 86
chutney, 87
cultivation, 221, 245
freezing, 86
fritters, 87
Grace's Pavlova, 87
growing regions, 86
ice cream, 87
kiwi chicken salad, 86
pickles and chutneys, 200
preparation, 86
kumquat, 88–9
in brandy, 88
candied, 89
cosmetics, 88
cultivation, 229, 244
freezing, 88
growing regions, 88
marmalade, 89
melon and kumquat salad, 88
preparation, 88
spiced, 89
in syrup, 89

lamb: Caucasian, 53
Caucasian pilau with raisins, 78
Caucasian stuffed quinces, 161
cherry lamb mayonnaise, 49
lamb and apricot polo, 23
Lebanese ragoût with pine nuts, 148
Moroccan spiced lamb with orange, 117
with rhubarb sauce, 169
lavan melon, 104
leek and prune appetizer, 156
lemon, 90–5, 192
Avgolemono, 91
baked fish with lemon sour cream sauce, 91
baked lemon pudding, 92
cheesecake, 93
citrus grape conserve, 77
coconut creams, 57
cosmetics, 90
crêpes, 92
cultivation, 229, 244
custard, 205
freezing, 90
fresh lemon gelatin, 94

growing regions, 90, 229
ice cream, 94
lemon and artichoke salad, 92
lemon curd, 95
lemon herb butter, 92
lemon meringue pie, 93
lemonade, 95
marmalade, 95
mayonnaise, 205
Mazurck cytrynowy, 95
mixed fruit marmalade, 83
nutritional value, 211
remedies, 90
seviche, 96
soufflé, 94
steamed blueberry pudding, 41
Sussex pond pudding, 93
syllabub, 94
uses, 90
veal in lemon parsley sauce, 91
lime, 96–7
avocado lime cream, 29
broiled chicken with lime marinade, 97
candied, 97
citrus grape conserve, 77
cosmetics, 96
cultivation, 229, 244
freezing, 96
growing regions, 96–7, 229
lime curd, 97
papaya milkshake, 126
seviche, 96
sherbert, 97
strawberries in lime cream sauce, 175
uses, 96
liqueurs: basic recipe, 207
see also individual fruits
litchi, 98–9
canning, 201
cultivation, 236
drying, 202
freezing, 98
growing regions, 98, 236
litchi and almond chicken, 98
litchi and pineapple pork, 99
litchi pork, 98
melon and kumquat salad, 88
nutritional value, 211
preparation, 98
in syrup, 99
tropical fruit salad, 99
liver in pomegranate sauce, 158
loganberry, 189, 218
nutritional value, 211
summer pudding, 163
loquat, 194
cultivation, 235–6

macadamia, 194
mandarin orange, 180, 247
mango, 100–3
cultivation, 236–7, 245
dried mango chutney, 103
fresh mango chutney, 103
growing regions, 100, 236
ham and mango mayonnaise, 101
mango and ginger ice cream tart, 101
mango and pork salad, 100
mango cream, 102
mango fool Créole, 102
mango tea, 103
mangoade, 103

mousse, 101
nutritional value, 211
pickles and chutneys, 200
preparation, 100
relish, 102
remedies, 100
sauce, 102
sherbert, 101
in syrup, 102
tropical fruit salad, 99
mangosteen, 194
marmalade: basic recipe,
    198—9
see also individual fruits
Marsala: oranges in, 121
marzipan, 10, 13
marzipan dates, 64
mayonnaise: basic recipe, 205
    cherry lamb mayonnaise, 49
    ham and mango
        mayonnaise, 101
medlar, 194
    cultivation, 232
    nutritional value, 211
    storage, 232
melon, 104—8
    à la Scheherezade, 107
    avocado and melon
        cocktail, 105
    baked melon Alaska, 108
    baked spiced melon, 106
    with black currants, 107
    chilled melon soup, 104
    cosmetics, 104
    cultivation, 220, 243, 244,
        245
    freezing, 104
    growing regions, 104, 220
    Kang Kung (soup), 105
    melon and cucumber salad,
        105
    melon and kumquat salad,
        88
    nutritional value, 211
    with port, 107
    prosciutto with, 105
    with raspberries, 106
    remedies, 104
    storage, 220
    stuffed with fruits, 106
    uses, 104
    water ice, 107
    see also watermelon
meringue: apricot meringue
        cake, 24
    Austrian red currant tart, 167
    baked melon Alaska, 108
    coconut meringue case, 56
    Grace's Pavlova, 87
    lemon meringue pie, 93
    peach meringue pie, 129
    raspberry almond
        meringue, 164
    rhubarb meringue tart, 172
    strawberry meringued
        cream, 176
    walnut meringue bars, 185
milk: health shake (banana), 30
minerals, 210
mint: jelly, 21
    minted grapefruit sherbert,
        83
    red currant and mint sauce,
        168
monkey nut, *see* peanut
mulberry, 195, 234
    cultivation, 233
    nutritional value, 212
    sopa de amoras, 195
mullet, red: baked fish with
        cashew stuffing, 46

mushroom: avocado pilaf, 29
    cranberry and turkey pie, 58
musk melon, 220
mustard and red currant
        sauce, 168

naseberry, *see* sapodilla
Natal plum, 195, 201
nectarine, 110—11, 226
    baked, 111
    canning, 201
    chicken with, 110
    cultivation, 227—8, 243,
        244, 245—6
    dried, 110, 202
    flambéed, 111
    freezing, 110
    growing regions, 110
    liqueur, 111
    marmalade, 111
    nutritional value, 212
    sugared, 110
    uses, 110
noodles: with almonds, 11
    with tomatoes, cheese and
        olives, 115
nut trees: cultivation, 239—42

oats, rolled: breakfast crunch,
        34
    rhubarb with oat crumble, 172
ogen melon, 104
olive, 112—15
    beef and olive stew, 114
    braised duck with, 114
    cheese and olive pâté, 113
    cosmetics, 112
    cultivation, 237, 245
    freezing, 112
    garlic olives, 112
    growing regions, 112, 237
    Italian pepper and olive
        appetizer, 114
    noodles with tomato,
        cheese and, 115
    nutritional value, 212
    olive and fennel salad, 115
    olive and rabbit stew
        Niçoise, 114
    olive and salami salad, 113
    olive cheese balls, 112
    olive cheese pastries, 113
    storage, 112, 237
    stuffed, 112
    tapenade, 113
    tuna olive mayonnaise, 115
    uses, 112
olive oil, 112, 237
onion: bananas and onion, 31
    orange onion salad, 118
orange, 116—25
    baked pears with, 138
    beets in orange sauce, 119
    Bishop, 125
    bitter orange, 116
    blackberry orange mousse,
        35
    black currant yogurt ice
        cream, 38
    Boodle's orange fool, 120
    Buck's fizz, 125
    candied peel, 123
    citrus grape conserve, 77
    cosmetics, 116
    cranberry orange compote,
        59
    cranberry orange sauce, 61
    cranberry party punch, 61
    cranberry relish, 59
    crêpes Suzette, 121
    cultivation, 229

custard, 205
    diet, 208
    duck with Brazil nuts and
        bananas in orange sauce,
        45
    duckling with, 117
    fig and orange compote, 67
    freezing, 116
    fruit in a blanket, 145
    gingered orange rice, 120
    glazed cabbage à l'orange,
        119
    gooseberry orange fool, 71
    growing regions, 116
    health drink, 208
    marmalade, 124
    in Marsala, 121
    Mexican orange salad, 119
    mixed fruit marmalade, 83
    Moroccan date salad, 62
    Moroccan spiced lamb
        with, 117
    nutritional value, 212
    orange and almond cake,
        123
    orange and carrot salad, 118
    orange and date salad, 119
    orange cheese bread, 122
    orange gin, 125
    orange onion salad, 118
    orange passion pie, 127
    orange rice with almonds,
        120
    orange walnut cake, 122
    orangeade, 125
    petits pots de chocolat à
        l'orange, 121
    pomander, 116
    raspberry orange cream,
        163
    remedies, 116
    rhubarb orange jam, 173
    sauce Maltaise, 124
    shortbread, 123
    soufflé pudding, 120
    spiced gooseberry orange
        preserve, 73
    sweetmeats, 123
    syllabub, 94
    Thai orange and pork salad,
        118
    traditional marmalade, 124
    uses, 116
    watercress and Brazil nut
        salad with, 44
    wine, 125
    see also tangerine

Panama orange, 190
papaya, 126, 192
    cosmetics, 126
    cultivation, 225, 245
    Dulce de papaya verde, 126
    fried, 126
    growing regions, 126, 225
    milkshake, 126
    nutritional value, 212
    papaya strawberry
        appetizer, 126
    passion whip, 127
    pickles and chutneys, 200
    preparation, 126
parsley: veal in lemon parsley
        sauce, 91
passion fruit, 127
    cultivation, 221, 243
    freezing, 127
    growing regions, 127
    nutritional value, 212
    orange passion pie, 127
    passion curd, 127

passion whip, 127
    uses, 127
pastry: double crust pies, 204
    pre-baked pie shell, 203
    rich pie pastry, 203
    rough puff, 203
    basic pie pastry, 203
    sweet pie pastry, 203
    tarts, 204
paw paw, *see* papaya
peach, 128—31, 226
    broiled, 130
    in brandy, 131
    canning, 201
    chicken with, 110
    chilled summer peach
        soup, 128
    cosmetics, 128
    cultivation, 227—8, 243,
        244, 245—6
    drying, 202
    dumplings, 129
    figs and peaches in cream,
        68
    freezing, 128
    growing regions, 128
    Italian stuffed peaches, 130
    jam-making, 198
    melon à la Scheherezade, 107
    melon stuffed with fruits, 106
    nutritional value, 212
    parfait, 130
    peach and almond tart, 130
    peach and strawberry claret
        cup, 131
    peach drink, 128
    peach meringue pie, 129
    pickled, 131
    preparation, 128
    salad, 129
peanut, 132—4
    Chinese eggplant in peanut
        sauce, 133
    cosmetics, 132
    cultivation, 242
    gado-gado, 133
    Ghanaian chicken in peanut
        sauce, 133
    growing regions, 132, 242
    Indian chutney, 134
    macaroons, 134
    nutritional value, 212
    peanut brittle, 133
    peanut pork, 132
    peanut skillet biscuit, 134
    soup, 132
    uses, 132
pear, 135—9
    baked with orange, 138
    basic jelly recipe, 199
    bottled in cider, 139
    in brandy, 139
    in butterscotch sauce, 137
    canning, 201
    cheese broiled pears, 136
    in chocolate sauce, 137
    cosmetics, 135
    in cream, 136
    cultivation, 230—2, 244
    curried, 136
    drying, 202
    freezing, 135
    growing regions, 135
    marmalade, 138
    nutritional value, 212
    pear and apple preserve, 139
    pear and cheese salad, 136
    pears, beans and bacon, 136
    pickles and chutneys, 200
    preparation, 135
    preserved, 139

in red wine, 138
soup, 135
spiced pear pie, 137
storage, 232
pecan, 140–1
   cookies, 141
   creamy pecan nougat, 141
   cultivation, 239–40
   growing regions, 140, 239
   mango cream, 102
   meat loaf with pecan
      stuffing, 140
   nutritional value, 212
   old-fashioned American
      pecan pie, 140
   pecan balls, 141
   pecan cherry cake, 141
   savoury pecan rolls, 141
   uses, 140
pectin, 198, 200
peppers: baked fish with
      cashew stuffing, 46
   Chinese walnuts with, 184
   Italian pepper and olive
      appetizer, 114
persimmon, 142–3
   cultivation, 237–8
   drying, 202
   freezing, 142
   growing regions, 142, 237
   ice cream, 143
   nutritional value, 212
   persimmon fluff, 142
   persimmon pie, 143
   remedies, 142
   storage, 238
   Trader Vic's persimmons
      with rum, 143
   uses, 142
   water ice, 143
pests and diseases, 214–41,
   243
pheasant, roast with grape
   stuffing, 75
pickles: basic recipe, 200
   see also individual fruits
pies, double crust, 204
   see also individual fruits and
      nuts
pine nut, 148–9, 242
   cosmetics, 148
   growing regions, 148, 242
   Italian spinach with, 149
   Lebanese ragoût with, 148
   Mexican chicken with, 149
   pesto alla Genovese, 149
   soup, 148
   uses, 148
pineapple, 144–7
   ambrosia, 146
   canning, 201
   chicken with pineapple
      Chinese style, 145
   cosmetics, 144
   crystallized chunks 147
   cultivation, 225, 247
   diet, 208
   freezing, 144
   fruit in a blanket, 145
   gelatin, 146
   growing regions, 144, 225
   litchi and pineapple pork, 99
   melon à la Scheherezade, 107
   nutritional value, 212
   pina colada, 147
   pine and apple salad, 145
   pine–apricot jam, 147
   pineapple and banana
      breakfast drink, 144
   pineapple cream, 145
   preparation, 144

remedies, 144
roast, 145
storage, 225
tropical fruit salad, 99
upside-down cake, 146
pineapple guava, see feijoya
pistachio, 150–1
   baklava, 151
   cultivation, 242, 245
   growing regions, 150, 242
   ice cream, 151
   nutritional value, 212
   pistachio rice salad, 150
   pork and pistachio pâté, 150
   preparation, 150
   uses, 150
plantain, 30
   banana chips, 30
   cultivation, 224
   see also banana
plum, 152–5, 226
   apple and plum chutney, 20
   canning, 201
   chilled soup, 152
   chutney, 155
   compote with red wine
      syrup, 153
   in cream, 153
   cultivation, 228, 244
   drying, 202
   freezing, 152
   fresh plum compote, 153
   growing regions, 152
   jam-making, 198
   nutritional value, 212
   Pączki (doughnuts), 153
   pickled, 154
   plum brandy, 155
   Powidlaze śliwek, 154
   Rita's plum cake, 154
   storage, 228
   uses, 152
   varieties, 152
pomegranate, 158–9
   chicken with pomegranate
      syrup, 159
   cosmetics, 158
   cultivation, 238
   grenadine, 159
   growing regions, 158, 238
   juice, 158
   liver in pomegranate sauce,
      158
   nutritional value, 212
   preparation, 158
   remedies, 158
   syrup, 159
   uses, 158
   water ice, 159
pomelo, 229
pork: chops in apricot sauce, 23
   litchi and pineapple pork,
      99
   litchi pork, 98
   mango and pork salad, 100
   peanut pork, 132
   pork and pistachio pâté, 150
   with rhubarb sauce, 169
   roast pork with prunes, 157
   Thai orange and pork salad,
      118
port: Bishop, 125
   melon with, 107
potato salad with walnuts, 184
prawn: Amargoso salad, 109
preserving, 198–203
prickly pear, 195, 235
prune, 152, 228
   health drink, 152
   leek and prune appetizer,
      156

liqueur, 157
nutritional value, 212
prune and bacon skewers,
   156
roast pork with, 157
sauce, 157
steamed pudding, 157
pruning, 214–41

quail with grapes, 75
Queensland nut, see
   macadamia
quince, 160–1
   canning, 201
   Caucasian stuffed quinces,
      161
   chicken with quince
      stuffing, 160
   compote, 161
   cosmetics, 160
   cultivation, 238
   freezing, 160
   growing regions, 160, 238
   jam-making, 198
   jelly, 161
   nutritional value, 212
   preparation, 160
   ratafia, 161
   storage, 238
Quito orange, see golden
   naranjilla

rabbit and olive stew Niçoise,
   114
raisin, 74
   apple chutney, 20
   Caucasian lamb pilau with, 78
   chicken with raisin stuffing,
      78
   Fürstenbrot, 81
   wine, 81
   see also fruit, dried
rambutan, 196
raspberry, 162–5
   bananas with raspberry
      sauce, 32
   berry soup, 162
   cultivation, 217–18
   freezing, 162
   frozen raspberry cream, 163
   gooseberry raspberry jam, 72
   growing regions, 162, 217
   jam, 165
   juice, 36
   melon à la Scheherezade,
      107
   melon stuffed with fruits, 106
   melon with, 106
   mousse, 164
   nutritional value, 212
   parfait, 60
   raspberry acid, 165
   raspberry almond
      meringue, 164
   raspberry buckle, 42
   raspberry orange cream, 163
   raspberry red currant jam,
      165
   raspberry rhubarb jam, 165
   raspberry yogurt ice cream,
      164
   ratafia de framboise, 165
   remedies, 162
   rodgrod med flode, 167
   sauce, 165
   shrub, 162
   spiced pudding, 37
   strawberry and raspberry
      ice cream, 177
   summer pudding, 163
   tart with cream, 165

uses, 162
red currant, 166–8
   Austrian red currant tart, 167
   cultivation, 214, 215
   Cumberland sauce, 168
   Eliza Acton's jelly, 168
   glazed, 168
   growing regions, 166, 214
   jelly, 168, 199
   juice, 166
   melon stuffed with fruits, 106
   nutritional value, 212
   raspberry red currant jam, 165
   red currant and carrot salad,
      166
   red currant and honey fool,
      166
   red currant and mint sauce,
      168
   red currant and mustard
      sauce, 168
   rodgrod med flode, 167
   storage, 217
   strawberry and currant
      salad, 176
   strawberry and red currant
      ice cream, 177
   summer pudding, 163
   uses, 166
   water ice, 167
remedies: apple, 14
   blackberry, 34
   black currant, 36
   blueberry, 40
   cherry, 48
   chestnut, 52
   fig, 66
   hazelnut, 84
   lemon, 90
   mango, 100
   melon, 104
   orange, 116
   persimmon, 142
   pineapple, 144
   pomegranate, 158
   raspberry, 162
   strawberry, 174
   walnut, 182
   watermelon, 108
rhubarb, 169–73
   baked chicken with rhubarb
      sauce, 170
   Betty, 171
   blaeberry jam, 43
   compote, 172
   cosmetics, 169
   creamy rhubarb pie, 171
   cultivation, 223–4
   fool, 171
   freezing, 169
   growing regions, 169
   jam, 173, 198
   nutritional value, 212
   with oat crumble, 172
   Persian beef with rhubarb
      sauce, 169
   pie, 170
   preparation, 169
   raspberry rhubarb jam, 165
   rhubarb and ginger
      preserve, 173
   rhubarb burnt cream, 172
   rhubarb meringue tart, 172
   rhubarb orange jam, 173
   rhubarb pickle sauce, 173
   spring pudding, 171
   storage, 224
   uses, 169
rice: avocado pilaf, 29
   baked rice and apple
      pudding, 18

Caucasian lamb pilau with
    raisins, 78
coconut rice, 56
gingered orange rice, 120
Korean rice with dates, 63
orange rice with almonds,
    120
pistachio rice salad, 150
rose hip, 196
rosella, 196
rowan, 196
rum: banana daiquiri, 33
    Guyanan watermelon, 109
    oracabessa, 33
    pina colada, 147
    rum dates, 65
    solbaerrom, 39
    tangerines in rum and
        caramel sauce, 181
    Trader Vic's persimmons
        with, 143

sage jelly, 21
salami: Italian figs with, 67
    olive and salami salad, 113
sapodilla, 196, 212
sapote, 196
satsuma, 180, 229
    in syrup, 181
Seville orange, 116, 229
Sharon fruit, see persimmon
sloe, 197, 200
    wine, 197
sole: seviche, 96
Spanish lime, see honeyberry
spinach: Italian spinach with
    pine nuts, 149
stone fruits: cultivation, 226–8
    see also individual stone
        fruits
strawberry, 174–9
    berry soup, 162
    champagne cocktail, 179
    chocolate strawberry
        candies, 178
    colonial strawberry
        shortcake, 177
    cosmetics, 174
    in cream, 175
    cultivation, 222–3, 244, 246
    fragole dama bianca, 176
    freezing, 174
    French strawberry ice
        cream, 177
    honeyed strawberries, 175
    hot sauce, 177
    in lime cream sauce, 175
    melon à la Scheherezade, 107
    melon stuffed with fruits, 106
    nutritional value, 212
    papaya strawberry
        appetizer, 126
    parfait, 60
    peach and strawberry claret
        cup, 131
    preparation, 174
    preserve, 178
    remedies, 174
    sherried strawberries, 179
    Soyer's strawberry salad, 176
    strawberries jubilee, 176
    strawberry acid, 165
    strawberry and currant
        salad, 176
    strawberry and raspberry
        ice cream, 177
    strawberry and red currant
        ice cream, 177
    strawberry meringued
        cream, 176
    strawberry vinegar, 179

tart, 176
    uses, 174
    wild strawberry soup, 175
    wine, 179
sunflower seed: nut and seed
    drink, 46
sweet sop, 187, 192
syrups, fruit, 202

tamarind, 197
    nutritional value, 212
    tamarinade, 197
tangelo, 229
tangerine, 180–1
    cosmetics, 180
    cultivation, 229
    freezing, 180
    growing regions, 180
    nutritional value, 212
    preserve, 181
    in rum and caramel sauce,
        181
    salad, 181
    smoked tangerine chicken,
        180
    spiced, 89
    uses, 180
    see also orange
tart: basic recipe, 204
    see also individual fruits and
        nuts
tomarillo, see tree tomato
tomato: apple and green
        tomato chutney, 21
    Brazil nut bake, 44
    Lebanese ragoût with pine
        nuts, 148
    noodles with cheese, olives
        and, 115
tree melon, see papaya
tree tomato, 197
trout: with almonds, 11
    baked fish with cashew
        stuffing, 46
    with walnut sauce, 183
tuna olive mayonnaise, 115
turkey and cranberry pie, 58

uglifruit, 229

vanilla cream, 76
vanilla sugar, 205
veal: in lemon parsley sauce,
        91
    veal and cashew nut
        casserole, 47
    veal rolls with ham and
        avocado, 28
vinegars, fruit, 202
    see also individual fruits
vitamins, 210
vodka: nectarine liqueur, 111

walnut, 182–5
    Balkan tarator soup, 182
    banana Waldorf, 31
    beet and walnut relish, 184
    Çerkez tavuğu, 183
    Chinese walnuts and
        peppers, 184
    chocolate date cake, 64
    cosmetics, 182
    cultivation, 239–40
    date and walnut spread, 62
    Grandmother's fig and
        walnut preserve, 69
    growing regions, 182, 239
    Mexican soup, 182
    Moroccan date salad, 62
    nutritional value, 212
    orange walnut cake, 122

pickled, 185
    potato salad with, 184
    preparation, 182
    remedies, 182
    savory omelette, 184
    sherried apples with spiced
        nuts, 19
    storage, 239
    sugared, 185
    sweet walnut and apricot
        omelette, 185
    trout with walnut sauce, 183
    uses, 182
    Waldorf salad, 15
    walnut meringue bars, 185
walnut oil, 182, 239
watercress, Brazil nut and
    orange salad, 44
water ice: basic recipe, 204
watermelon, 108–9
    Amargoso salad, 109
    chilled soup, 109
    cultivation, 220
    diet, 208
    freezing, 108
    growing regions, 108
    Guyanan, 109
    nutritional value, 211
    pickles and chutneys, 109,
        200
    remedies, 108
    uses, 108
    see also melon
white currant, 166
    cultivation, 214, 215

storage, 217
strawberry and currant
    salad, 176
whiting: baked fish with
    cashew stuffing, 46
whortleberry, 40
wine, 74
    apricot, 25
    banana, 33
    basic recipe, 205–7
    blackberry, 35
    equipment, 205
    ingredients, 206
    Mrs Marsden's grand recipe
        for gooseberry wine, 73
    orange, 125
    peach and strawberry claret
        cup, 131
    pear soup, 135
    pears in red wine, 138
    plum compote with red
        wine syrup, 153
    raisin, 81
    red grape, 77
    white grape, 78
wineberry, 189, 218
worcesterberry, 189
    cultivation, 214, 216

yogurt: avocado dip, 27
    Balkan tarator soup, 182
    blackcurrant ice cream, 38
    raspberry ice cream, 164
youngberry, 189, 218
    with bananas, 189

Picture acknowledgments

Ardea 23, 27, 47, 182, 186, 191, 196; British Tourist Authority 19,
75, 79, 131, 139, 175, 219, 230; Stephanie Colasanti 55, 63, 122;
Mary Evans Picture Library 214, 215, 217, 220, 222, 223, 227,
234, 239, 241, 242; Fresh Fruit Information Bureau 31, 86, 167;
Brian Furner 11, 15, 35, 39, 46, 62, 66, 74, 83, 95, 103, 106, 107,
111, 127, 150, 154, 155, 158, 163, 170, 171, 179, 183, 188, 190, 191,
194, 197; Hawkley Studio Assocs. Ltd. 10, 26, 30, 34, 54, 58, 82,
94, 98, 110, 118, 127, 138, 151, 159; Ivory Coast Pineapple Bureau
146, 147; G. R. Roberts 38, 71, 87, 99, 115, 143, 187, 189, 194, 195;
SATOUR 22; Mallerman Summerfield 142; Syndication
International Library 198, 199; USDA 18, 43, 51, 59, 67, 90, 91,
102, 119, 126, 130, 134, 135, 174.